P9-DBQ-474

READINGS IN MANAGEMENT: LANDMARKS AND NEW FRONTIERS

BY THE SAME AUTHOR

Management: Theory and Practice, 1965, third edition 1973
The Impact of the Third Generation of Computers on Management, 1968
Organization, 1967
Modern Management Methods, 1966
The Decision-making Process in the Commercial Use of High-speed Computers, 1964
The Great Organizers, 1960
Staff in Organization, 1960
Planning and Developing the Company Organization Structure, 1952
Sources of Economic Information for Collective Bargaining, 1950
Greater Productivity through Labor-Management Cooperation, 1949
Economic Reconstruction of Italy, 1946
Preparation of Company Annual Reports, 1946
Annual Wages and Employment Stabilization Techniques, 1945
The Development of Foremen in Management, 1945
The Unionization of Foremen, 1945

McGRAW-HILL SERIES IN MANAGEMENT
Keith Davis, Consulting Editor

Allen Management and Organization
Allen The Management Profession
Argyris Management and Organizational Development: The Path from XA to YB
Beckett Management Dynamics: The New Synthesis
Benton Supervision and Management
Bergen and Haney Organizational Relations and Management Action
Blough International Business: Environment and Adaptation
Bowman Management: Organization and Planning
Brown Judgment in Administration
Campbell, Dunnette, Lawler, and Weick Managerial Behavior, Performance, and Effectiveness
Cleland and King Management: A Systems Approach
Cleland and King Systems Analysis and Project Management
Cleland and King Systems, Organizations, Analysis, Management: A Book of Readings
Dale Management: Theory and Practice
Dale Readings in Management: Landmarks and New Frontiers
Davis Human Behavior at Work: Human Relations and Organizational Behavior
Davis Organizational Behavior: A Book of Readings
Davis and Blomstrom Business and Society: Environment and Responsibility
DeGreene Systems Psychology
Dunn and Rachel Wage and Salary Administration: Total Compensation Systems
Dunn and Stephens Management of Personnel: Manpower Management and Organizational Behavior
Edmunds and Letey Environmental Administration

Fiedler A Theory of Leadership Effectiveness
Flippo Principles of Personnel Management
Glueck Business Policy: Strategy Formation and Management Action
Golembiewski Men, Management, and Morality
Hicks The Management of Organizations: A Systems and Human Resources Approach
Hicks and Gullett Modern Business Management: A Systems and Environmental Approach
Hicks and Gullett Organizations: Theory and Behavior
Johnson, Kast, and Rosenzweig The Theory and Management of Systems
Kast and Rosenzweig Organization and Management: A Systems Approach
Knudson, Woodworth, and Bell Management: An Experiential Approach
Koontz Toward a Unified Theory of Management
Koontz and O'Donnell Essentials of Management
Koontz and O'Donnell Management: A Book of Readings
Koontz and O'Donnell Principles of Management: An Analysis of Managerial Functions
Levin, McLaughlin, Lamone, and Kottas Production/Operations Management: Contemporary Policy for Managing Operating Systems
Luthans Contemporary Readings in Organizational Behavior
Luthans Organizational Behavior
McNichols Policy Making and Executive Action
Maier Problem-solving Discussions and Conferences: Leadership Methods and Skills
Margulies and Raia Organizational Development: Values, Process, and Technology
Mayer Production and Operations Management
Miles Theories of Management: Implications for Organizational Behavior and Development
Mundel A Conceptual Framework for the Management Sciences
Newstrom, Reif, and Monczka A Contingency Approach to Management: Readings
Petit The Moral Crisis in Management
Petrof, Carusone, and McDavid Small Business Management: Concepts and Techniques for Improving Decisions
Pigors and Pigors Case Method in Human Relations
Porter, Lawler, and Hackman Behavior in Organizations
Prasow and Peters Arbitration and Collective Bargaining: Conflict Resolution in Labor Relations
Ready The Administrator's Job
Reddin Managerial Effectiveness
Richman and Copen International Management and Economic Development
Sartain and Baker The Supervisor and His Job
Schrieber, Johnson, Meier, Fischer, and Newell Cases in Manufacturing Management
Shore Operations Management
Shull, Delbecq, and Cummings Organizational Decision Making
Steiner Managerial Long-Range Planning
Sutermeister People and Productivity
Tannenbaum, Weschler, and Massarik Leadership and Organization
Vance Industrial Administration

THIRD EDITION

READINGS IN MANAGEMENT: LANDMARKS AND NEW FRONTIERS

ERNEST DALE, Ph.D.

Wharton School
University of Pennsylvania
and Ernest Dale Associates

McGRAW-HILL BOOK COMPANY

New York St. Louis San Francisco Auckland Düsseldorf
Johannesburg Kuala Lumpur London Mexico
Montreal New Delhi Panama Paris São Paulo
Singapore Sydney Tokyo Toronto

Library of Congress Cataloging in Publication Data

Dale, Ernest, date comp.
Readings in management.

(McGraw-Hill series in management)
Includes bibliographical references.
1. Industrial management—Addresses, essays, lectures. I. Title.
HD31.D18 1975 658.4'008 74-23897
ISBN 0-07-015184-9
ISBN 0-07-015162-8 pbk.

READINGS IN MANAGEMENT:
LANDMARKS AND NEW FRONTIERS

1 2 3 4 5 6 7 8 9 0 V H V H 7 9 8 7 6 5 4

This book was set in Helvetica by Black Dot, Inc.
The editors were Thomas H. Kothman and Joseph F. Murphy;
the designer was Nicholas Krenitsky;
the production supervisor was Thomas J. LoPinto.
Von Hoffmann Press, Inc., was printer and binder.

To the memory of my father,
who taught me how to choose

CONTENTS

This is a collection of other men's flowers
for which I have merely provided the thread.
—Montaigne

Articles with asterisks did not appear in earlier editions of this book.

PREFACE

The plan of this book is the same as that of the third edition of my textbook, *Management: Theory and Practice,** and the same chapter headings have been used. However, it is designed not only as a supplement to that book but as an anthology of management writings that will provide informative and interesting reading for those who are unfamiliar with the textbook.

More than a fourth of the articles of this book did not appear in the earlier editions, and most of them were published after the second edition was issued. I have had to omit a number of valuable articles that were included in the second edition in order to make room for the new material, but I have tried to retain as many of the "landmarks" as possible. In selecting articles, I have been guided by the following criteria:

1. Which are the best discussions of the subjects covered in the textbook?
2. Which authors write English that is pleasurable to read?
3. Which authors should be introduced so as to stimulate further study?
4. What new developments have occurred in the field?

The newer developments include important changes in management's external environment stemming from government action and growing public concern over the quality of life, new approaches arrived at through behavioral science research, and developments on the international scene. In addition I have included new articles on the use of computers and the effects of computerization.

Since management is a subject that requires a multidisciplinary approach, I have used articles by economists, sociologists, psychologists, political scientists, and literary men. In addition, there are contributions by outstanding managers, many of which appeared in print for the first time in an earlier edition—for example, the reminiscences of W. C. Durant, the founder of General Motors.

Thus, this book is concerned with the manifold aspects of management: its nature, behavior, functions, techniques, internationalization, and prospects. The aim has

*McGraw-Hill Book Company, New York, 1973.

been to make it useful not only to students of management but to teachers, executives, and others interested in the field.

Insofar as possible in a field that touches on so many different aspects of human behavior and utilizes techniques drawn from so many different disciplines, I have tried to provide some interrelationship and continuity through introductions to each section, each chapter, and each article. But where the choice lay between omitting important subject matter and sacrificing interrelationship, I have decided in favor of inclusion of the subject matter.

I am grateful to the authors whose works are used and to the publishers who gave me permission to use the articles. Because many excellent articles are very long, it has been necessary to cut practically all those that appear in this book. Some of the authors have approved the cuts in their articles; but others have not seen the shortened versions, and if I have inadvertently distorted their meaning by omitting words, sentences, and paragraphs, I am deeply sorry.

I am indebted to Alice Smith for detailed and careful editing and for selection of a number of readings, and to Charles A. Meloy, Associate Professor, St. Peter's College, Jersey City, N.J., for technical assistance and contributions.

Ernest Dale

READINGS IN MANAGEMENT: LANDMARKS AND NEW FRONTIERS

PART 1 MANAGEMENT AND ITS ENVIRONMENT

To understand management—and the various theories and techniques the manager may employ in handling his work—it is necessary to understand what strictly managerial work is. The first chapter of this book, therefore, presents the views of several writers on the nature of the management job. But definitions broad enough to cover management work in all organizations and at all levels are necessarily rather abstract. For this reason, the second chapter presents articles dealing with the work as it shapes up in actual situations.

Then, although the word "management" implies authority, authority is never absolute. Both the organization within which the manager operates and the external environment impose constraints on him.

The internal constraints on the manager's actions vary widely, of course, since they depend on both his position within the organization and the nature and practices of the organization itself. However, for most business managers and for managers in many other fields there is one common denominator: the corporate form of organization, under which the chief executive is subject, in theory in all cases and in many cases in actuality, to the board of directors. Articles in Chapter 3 explain the theories of the corporation and the mechanics of its operation.

Constraints imposed by the external environment, which are often more restrictive than any imposed by the corporate framework, are considered in Chapter 4. These include the financial limitations, which are often imposed by other institutions (e.g., financial institutions), legal limitations, limitations imposed by labor, and technological limitations. In addition, there are the constraints imposed by public opinion, for if a company ignores public opinion, the changes the public proposes are likely to be incorporated in statutes, and in any case organized groups representing sizable sections of the public can affect a company's ability to sell its products.

1 What Is Management?

Attempts to describe the content of the management job have led to the identification of the function as an activity distinct from such technical functions as production, finance, and marketing. Economists, especially the great classical economist Alfred Marshall, therefore added management (or "organization," as Marshall called it) to the land, labor, and capital earlier specified as the factors necessary for business enterprise—or, for that matter, for any other type of enterprise of any size.

The systemization of this concept was left mostly to industrialists in Europe and the United States, where the work of H. M. Barksdale and his associates at the Du Pont Company was especially influential. Barksdale's name, it is true, is not widely known, but the concepts he developed influenced General Motors, in which Du Pont was a major stockholder for over forty years, and the concepts utilized at GM in turn influenced other companies. (In addition, some men in other companies worked along similar lines independently.)

A second economist who contributed to the idea of management as a distinct entity was Joseph A. Schumpeter, of Harvard, who developed the concept that the real driving force in business is innovation.

Then, in recent years, writers on management have begun to recognize that management is dealing with a number of variables that are dependent on each other. This approach is used in the excerpt from Prof. Harold J. Leavitt's book.

In addition to the attempts to define the management job by identifying its components, there have been many attempts to arrive at guidelines and techniques that could be used by any manager in any position anywhere. More recently, however, there has been a tendency to consider "contingency" management—which implies use of the theories and techniques that are most applicable to the situation, rather than the application of general guidelines to all situations. The last article in this chapter deals with a manager who practiced this type of management.

Alfred Marshall, who occupied the chair of economics at Cambridge University for many years, had a lifelong interest in business and management and was a great admirer of the captains of industry.

In his old age he put together in extensive book form his ideas on management, derived in part from his study of economics and in part from observations of business enterprises conducted over a number of years in many industrial countries. The result was *Industry and Trade*, which is an important combination of economic theory and reports of industrial practice.

Marshall had great understanding and knowledge of economic history, which led him to use the experience of the past to shed light on the present. He concluded that there were many similarities among the management jobs at different times and in different institutions. He observed that the heads of great business organizations (such as the Fugger family merchant banking enterprises in South Germany in the sixteenth century) performed many functions similar to those performed by the manager of a great landed estate or the master of his own college at Cambridge. He noted that the chief executives of these institutions might have different objectives—e.g., personal gratification, wealth, or scholarship—but that reaching the ends would always require management.

With good management, he showed, an organization could carry on for generations. Where good management disappeared, the organization itself might disappear too.

Management, a Long-practiced Skill

Alfred Marshall

Some of the modern problems of administration on a large scale were anticipated long ago by private and corporate owners of great estates: though they did not often need to balance their incomings against their outgoings closely.

Let us look at the business side of the functions of a great landed proprietor, and especially of one who has no easy access to the assistance of skilled professional business men equipped with the powerful appliances of modern times. Like a mediaeval baron or abbot, he is called upon to carry responsibilities as a capitalist undertaker and as an employer of labour, which may fairly be compared with those of the heads of very considerable businesses in the modern world. He must indeed look far ahead, estimate chances and balance risks when he decides whether to invest resources in (say) opening out a quarry, or setting up an additional mill: and, subject perhaps to some partial customary rights over persons on his estate, he will need to select those who are to superintend each new undertaking. If he is able, industrious, and alert, he will see that all men are put on work for which they are fit; and that each instrument of his resources is carried up to that margin or limit, at which any further employment of it would be inappropriate. On such an estate, everywhere and in all times, there will be found much delegation of authority, and a rough gradation of the difficulty and responsibility of each man's task: the lower rewards generally going to those whose physical toil is severe; and the higher to those who are called on to exercise discernment, judgment, tact, and a power of bearing responsibility, together perhaps with some modicum of initiative. On the estate, as in the modern business, the extent to which specialization, subordination, and the coordination of faculties and of tasks are carried has varied with the general conditions of the undertaking: but the principles will be always the same.

It is indeed true that the organization of a private estate is designed to afford gratification to its owner either directly; or through his friends and others to whose comfort, admiration, and perhaps envy, it contributes. If the arrangement of a stable is pleasing, it can be maintained, though the horses might be cared for equally well on a less expensive plan: if a tree is beautiful, it may be spared, although its trunk is not straight enough to make good timber: and so on. That is to say, although the organization of the private establishment gives scope for that scientific management, which attains a desired end by the least costly means; yet the means themselves are generally a considerable part of the desired end; and the end itself is not expressed in terms of money. It is not therefore

From *Industry and Trade: A Study of Industrial Technique and Business Organization and of Their Influences on the Conditions of Various Classes and Nations* (Macmillan & Co., Ltd., London, 1919), pp. 308–311.

under as rigorous a rule of arithmetical balance sheets, as is a modern business, which is closely run by competitors working for the same market with similar resources: but the differences between the two are not fundamental.

A somewhat similar freedom from the yoke of an exact balance sheet seems to have been enjoyed by those great merchants of early times, whose financial strength enabled them to gain increasing profits with ever increasing ease, so long as strength lasted and fortune favoured. The power of a Fugger, or even a de la Pole or a Canynge, controlled the fate of monarchs and of nations: and so vast, relatively to the aggregate movable wealth of Europe at the time, were the gains which resulted from their larger transactions, that they had little occasion to spend strength on petty economies. Although there was but little trustworthy information of distant affairs, beyond what could be obtained only at great cost and slow speed from private agents and correspondents, a few of them grasped the main threads of most of the chief business problems of Western Europe.

Even those features of large modern business, which are chiefly associated with joint stock ownership and control, were in some measure anticipated by the administration of powerful monasteries; and of other bodies in which the individual had no exclusive dominant rights.

The partial supersession of individual by joint stock enterprise has not changed the problems of business administration very greatly. But it has introduced a distinct new element into those problems.

Here it may be observed that the directors of a company are, strictly speaking, employees of it. Except in so far as they are themselves shareholders, they run no risks from its failure, beyond some loss of prestige; and a possible loss of employment, which they share with other employees. The shareholders bear the risks, but delegate nearly the whole of their functions, as owners of the business, to the directors and other employees. But in practice the directors, even though they own but a small part of the shares, are seldom displaced unless they have made grave errors: thus they may be regarded as "the head" of the company, in the sense in which decisions on large issues connected with a business belong to its "head"; though he may delegate decisions on minor issues to subordinates. Of course the directors of a company, like the partners in a private business, often share out among themselves the main control of particular groups of these issues, the collective meeting remaining the ultimate authority in large matters.

Even when management was recognized as a separate skill, the intricate task of analyzing it into its components was a lengthy and difficult process. Many managers have contributed to the development of the theory and practice of management. Perhaps one of the most outstanding of these was Hamilton MacFarland Barksdale, who served as general manager of the Du Pont Company around the turn of the century. The following is based on papers written by Barksdale and his associates, and includes excerpts from their writings. The papers were discovered by Ernest Dale with the help of John Lee Pratt (one of the last survivors of the group of young men Barksdale gathered about him) and Charles A. Meloy, a member of Ernest Dale Associates.

Hamilton MacFarland Barksdale and the Du Pont Contributions to Systematic Management

Ernest Dale and Charles A. Meloy

To be admitted to the small group of Olympians who contributed to the advancement of management requires both path-breaking ideas and the successful testing of those ideas in the market place. For ideas by themselves, however elegant and intellectually challenging they may be, must be evaluated by experience so that the chaff may be separated from the wheat, and the subjective clearly distinguished from the objective. The only real test in business management

From *The Business History Review*, Vol. XXXVI, No. 2, Summer, 1962, pp. 127–128, 132, 138, 145–146, 148, 150–151.

is the test of experience. Such a test of the validity of an idea or a good theory has been well put by the economist Milton Friedman of the University of Chicago:[1]

> A theory is "simpler" the less initial knowledge is needed to make a prediction within a given field of phenomena; it is more "fruitful" the more precise the resulting prediction, the wider the area within which the theory yields predictions, and the more additional lines for further research it suggests. . . . The only relevant test of the validity of a hypothesis is comparison of prediction with experience.

To qualify as a contributor to the body of management knowledge, therefore, a man should have added significantly to what may be considered to be "good theory" in the light of the above criteria.

Relatively few men qualify. The purpose of this paper is to advance for consideration as a management pioneer a man whose contribution is best known through the companies whose success symbolizes a fortunate combination of good ideas tested in the market place, namely, Du Pont and General Motors.

Barksdale's Work

This man is Hamilton MacFarland Barksdale, who probably was the single most original thinker on management among a number of outstanding thinkers in these two companies. He was, perhaps, the brightest of their rather remarkable stars. Yet because of his modesty and his belief that one's own happiness and success come through that achieved for others, he is hardly known to the outside world.

The principal step taken by Barksdale and his "young men" was the efficient integration of the many different concerns that had been acquired separately. Each had been run as an independent operating unit. Each had its own sales organization and branch offices. There had been no attempt to improve products, to introduce new ones, or to promote serious research (which, it was said, "could always be bought in Europe"). But all this changed under Barksdale.

The business-as-usual stereotype gave way to the formula of "low prices, large volume." Sales activities were coordinated through the appointment of a sales manager. Trade reports were instituted. These included an appraisal by the salesmen of both customers and prospects. Scientists and trained men were brought in and given freedom to pursue their specializations. Some were even given time off to continue their formal studies. An experimental laboratory was set up for product and methods research.

As a member of the Du Pont Executive Committee—one of the earliest general management committees in industry, and one of Barksdale's own innovations—Barksdale formulated objectives and policies, and initiated controls over the diverse operations.

The Executive Committee began by making general the policies, practices, and procedures developed at Repauno [one of the companies purchased by Du Pont] and established later by Barksdale and his associates through the H.E.O.D. (High Explosives Operating Department). Essentially these were put into effect by establishing central staffs, which developed the policies and controls that were enforced through the president and the Executive Committee.

Barksdale's principal contribution to management was his emphasis on the need for *systematization* in the solution of business problems. He wrote: "The history of innovations and inventions has been practically the same. The steam engine was scoffed at, the telegraph was laughed at and the telephone at first was hardly considered worthy of either derision or laughter, and System has been no exception to the rule. But System cannot be either thrown or laughed out of Court. A decision has been handed down in its favor in the Supreme Court of Business. It is alike the foundation upon which to build and the keystone in the arch of success."[2]

By "systematization," Barksdale meant the use of guide lines or criteria to govern business decisions and planned adaptation of them to

[1]Milton Friedman, "The Methodology of Positive Economics," in *Essays in Positive Economics* (The University of Chicago Press, Chicago, 1953), vol. 3, pp. 10 ff.

[2]High Explosives Operating Department [hereafter H.E.O.D.] meeting minutes, 1906.

specific problems. Criteria served as a series of rules or generalizations which would aid in the solution of specific problems, toward which a planned approach was required.

The generalizations were always made with reference to a basic goal or objective. This was principally the best possible long-run utilization of the capital invested by the owners in the business, i.e., the optimum rate of return on investment. As Barksdale put it: "The objects to be sought in any earnest effort at organization are *efficiency* (including thoroughness combined with promptness), *economy* (measured by ultimate results achieved), and *permanency* (the last being secured by the development of competent 'understudies' in every important position)." These were perfectly proper objectives in the light of the philosophy and mores prevailing in the business society of that day. Hence Barksdale put major emphasis on making his enterprises "second to none" in product quality and price. Starting from that basis, most other requirements of the business would be met.

Contributions to Theory

The method that Barksdale principally pursued in making his contributions to theory of any kind was *comparative analysis*. When he anticipated or was made aware of a problem, he first looked around to see whether there was an experience or a series of experiences on which he could draw for a solution (he frequently compared the experience of the different plants). Usually this would be an historical experience or the experiences of one or more executives. Barksdale would study these experiences, examine them for relevance, cull from them what appeared to him to be comparable, and then make the necessary adaptation for the solution of the current problem. From a number of such experiences and adaptations he, or one of his subordinates, would then prepare a paper with conclusions that would serve as guideposts or criteria in solving other similar problems in the future. These papers would be written and read in advance of the biannual meetings of H.E.O.D., and would then be discussed and questioned at the meetings. From the papers and discussions Barksdale would often draw generalizations or "policies" (guide lines) representing the sense of the meetings, and they would become precisely that in the conduct of the business. Usually they were developed by integrating experience with what appeared to be best in theory for the business. Barksdale was forever testing his policies to see how they worked out and was forever ready to modify his conclusions in the light of valid experience. In stating a policy, he always emphasized the need to leave room for individual effort, initiative, and thought.[3]

And the test for him was in rate of return on investment, which it was his aim to maximize within that framework of ethical, human, and legal bounds which had been set up for him by society. In this respect he was always working on what he considered to be the dimensions of leadership:

Innovation: through original and applied research, underpinning of technology wherever possible, and a development department devoted to discovering new uses for old products as well as new acquisitions. Barksdale liked to quote Governor Bates' observation that "in any field of endeavor the man who considers his education finished, or who thinks he has learned all there is to know in his trade, profession or business, will soon see the rearmost light of the procession pass by."[4]

Representation: principal stress on the relation of the company to its owners, with appropriate relations to employees and the local community. Thus, in regard to salary increases of employees, Barksdale took a position that might well redirect the thinking of some company managers today who often consider the stockholder the lowest entity on the corporate totem pole: "You must consider the plain business side of such propositions. It is all right and proper for you to be anxious to see your men get along, but you should not allow this feeling to blind you to the fact that we have, all of us, got to show at the end of the year a reasonable interest upon the money invested in these businesses or be compelled to acknowledge that we have made a failure."[5]

[3]H.E.O.D. meeting minutes, 1905.
[4]*Ibid.*
[5]Barksdale letter dated Aug. 17, 1894, to E. C. McCune.

Interpretation: Continuous emphasis on teaching and understanding as well as on correction to facilitate understanding of managerial goals.

Administration: Most important of all—continuous development of administrative skills.

In this development, Barksdale always proceeded within the framework of forecasted possibilities (toward that end an economist was appointed) and related this to possible economic objectives. And then there had to be the appropriate organization to reach these goals. Initially Barksdale worked this out on the production level with the individual powder mill as a unit of organization. He sketched out the various stages of growth of a powder mill, setting out the additional functions necessitated by larger size and the coordinate positions, thereby setting up assistant superintendents as well as assistants to superintendents. He took delegation of operating responsibilities as a matter of course, partly in order to make growth possible, largely also to train younger men and to offer them better opportunities. But as the size of the enterprises grew, especially by acquisitions, Barksdale's thinking turned increasingly to group management as the only practical means to ensure long-run continuity.

And from group management as an organization, Barksdale was led to consider its operating bases through the formulation of [organization] criteria, which he tested by experience at Du Pont.

And [the management] skills were continuously held together by the skill of communication on which Barksdale laid first stress, as can be seen from one of his few lengthy reflections on this subject:[6]

> Before we part I want to talk to you a little while upon a side of our work which affects me personally. It isn't possible in so large an undertaking as we are carrying on for the individual upon whom rests the responsibility for directing the work to do anything more than direct in a general way. To go into details is impossible. He performs his duty best when he succeeds in working out an organization—a scheme of organization—and then placing in each position to be filled the best available man and then endeavoring to see that in a general way the objects sought for by the organization and by the personnel are achieved. . . I know of no point at which there is failure, except to appreciate the full importance of cooperation, and unless that cooperation is achieved—the organization as a whole can't reach a full measure of success, and I, consequently, as an individual (will) fail. . . . To appreciate that importance (of cooperation) it is necessary for us to appreciate the magnitude of the operation ($1¼ to $1½ mill. per month cash expenditure). That expenditure takes place at a large number of points scattered from the Atlantic to the Pacific and from the Great Lakes practically to the Gulf. . . . I readily understand that men placed as superintendents must of necessity find it more difficult to get the broad point of view. I have been similarly placed.—I have been in charge of important works far distant from headquarters. I have gone through all the sensations you gentlemen have. I have dubbed many things as red tape which I would not have considered as such if I had taken the broad view. I was performing my duties as well as I knew how. I was at them every working hour my strength would permit. I was being called upon for information and data that seemed to me quite unnecessary. . . .
>
> Now it may be that these reports are unnecessary. A year ago we felt this might be the case and a committee was appointed to go into this and everything was eliminated that could be. I can readily understand that these reports cannot always be gotten off as the Main office wants them to, but I don't understand why, when a man finds that he cannot do that, he doesn't come forward and say so and give the reasons, and not let the man who is 1,000 or 2,000 miles away, and trying his best to help in the work of successful operation of the plants, remain in total ignorance.
>
> Personally, I am entirely satisfied that each superintendent who so departed from standard practice had a good reason for doing so. The mere fact that he had a good reason for doing it made it important from the standpoint of the welfare of all of us that this reason be stated. We have accomplished what we have only by a combination of all our brains . . . combined experience and combined observations. It isn't possible to continue an organization as large as ours if the individuals are going to, without advice, without any explanation, depart from standard methods adopted. The whole object of the organization is to get cooperation, to get for each individual the benefit of all the knowledge and all the experience of all individuals. If it isn't accomplished, the organization is a failure, and that is where this thing hurts me. . . . I am going to make a personal plea to you gentlemen to make it a point to take the broad view, not to look upon your own

[6] H.E.O.D meeting minutes, Oct. 11, 1909.

plant as the only thing to which you can render assistance, but to place yourself more in the position of one of several who are working for a common end. If you will bear those points in mind . . . I certainly would appreciate it because I certainly don't want to make a failure.

The "entrepreneur," as the economist Joseph A. Schumpeter analyzed the term, is the true manager as defined in this book; that is, he is an innovator as well as an administrator. He is not necessarily an "entrepreneur" in the original sense of the term, the man who undertakes the financial risks of a business, or the founder (although he often is); he is instead the man who introduces new ways of doing things.

Only entrepreneurs, Schumpeter believed, can be said to produce true profits. Because of their innovations their costs are lower than those of others in the same industries; yet they can charge the same going price and thus achieve a net gain greater than that customary in their fields. This does not mean that companies which continue to do things in the same old way cannot make a "profit" in the ordinary sense of the term, only that Schumpeter considered these profits more in the nature of quasi-rent or interest than true profits.

Schumpeter, like Marshall, was a great admirer of the innovator-manager, partly because of his knowledge of economic history and its heroes, partly because of his own practical involvement in the world of finance and enterprise in his younger days. Through the second quarter of this century, he was a major influence on economic thought.

The Entrepreneur as an Innovator

Joseph A. Schumpeter

For actions which consist in carrying out innovations we reserve the term Enterprise; the individuals who carry them out we call Entrepreneurs. This terminological decision is based on a historical fact and a theoretical proposition, namely, that carrying out innovations is the only function which is fundamental in history and essential in theory to the type usually designated by that term. The distinction between the entrepreneur and the mere head or manager of a firm who runs it on established lines or, as both functions will understandably often coincide in one and the same person, between the entrepreneurial and the managerial function, is no more difficult than the distinction between a workman and a landowner, who may also happen to form a composite economic personality called (in America) a farmer. And surely it is but common sense to recognize that the economic function of deciding how much wool to buy for one's process of production and the function of introducing a new process of production do not stand on the same footing, either in practice or in logic.

We will briefly note the points that are most important for our purpose.

1 It is not always easy to tell who the entrepreneur is in a given case. This is not, however, due to any lack of precision in our definition of the entrepreneurial function, but simply to the difficulty of finding out what person actually fills it. Nobody ever is an entrepreneur all the time, and nobody can ever be only an entrepreneur. A man who carried out a "new combination" will have to perform current nonentrepreneurial work in the course of doing so, and successful enterprise in our sense will normally lead to an industrial position which thenceforth involves no other functions than those of managing an old firm. Nevertheless, we have little difficulty in identifying entrepreneurship in the times of competitive capitalism. The entrepreneur will there be found among the heads of firms, mostly among the owners. Generally, he will be the founder of a firm and of an industrial family as well. The leading man may, but need not, hold or acquire the position that is officially the leading one. He may be the manager or some other salaried employee. Sometimes, he is the owner of a controlling parcel of shares without appearing on the list of responsible executives at all. Although company promoters are not as a

From *Business Cycles: A Theoretical, Historical, and Statistical Analysis of the Capitalist Process*, Vol. I (McGraw-Hill Book Company, New York, 1939), pp. 102–109.

rule entrepreneurs, a promoter may fill that function occasionally and then come near to presenting the only instance there is of a type which is entrepreneur by profession and nothing else.

2 But is should be easy to distinguish our function from those others which, though often found in combination with it, are yet not essential to it. The entrepreneur may, but need not, be the "inventor" of the good or process he introduces. Also, the entrepreneur may, but need not, be the person who furnishes the capital. This is a very important point. In the institutional pattern of capitalism there is machinery which makes it possible for people to function as entrepreneurs without having previously acquired the necessary means. It is leadership rather than ownership that matters. The failure to see this and, as a consequence, to visualize clearly entrepreneurial activity as a distinct function *sui generis*, is the common fault of both the economic and the sociological analysis of the classics and of Karl Marx. It is partly explained by the fact that previous ownership of the requisite producers' goods or of assets that may serve as collateral, or of money, makes it easier to become an entrepreneur, and the additional fact, alluded to above, that successful entrepreneurship leads to a capitalist position for the entrepreneur and, normally, his descendants, so that we do, as a matter of fact, find successful entrepreneurs very soon in possession of a plant and the other paraphernalia of a going concern. Two consequences follow, one of which is of an economic, the other of a sociological nature.

First, risk bearing is no part of the entrepreneurial function.[1] It is the capitalist who bears the risk. The entrepreneur does so only to the extent to which, besides being an entrepreneur, he is also a capitalist, but qua entrepreneur he loses other people's money. Second, entrepreneurs as such do not form a social class. Although, in case of success, they or their descendants rise into the capitalist class, they do not from the outset belong to it or to any other definite class. As a matter of historical fact, entrepreneurs come from all classes.

The above implies what it may nevertheless not be superfluous to state explicitly, that although entrepreneurs may be or become stockholders in their firms, mere holding of stock does not, any more than would mere ownership, make an entrepreneur. The only realistic definition of stockholders is that they are creditors (capitalists) who forego part of the legal protection usually extended to creditors, in exchange for the right to participate in profits. To the economist, the legal construction of an equity in this case is but a lawyer's fiction.

3 Let us visualize an entrepreneur who, in a perfectly competitive society, carries out an innovation which consists in producing a commodity already in common use at a total cost per unit lower than that of any existing firm. In this case, he will buy the producers' goods he needs at the prevailing prices which are adjusted to the conditions under which "old" firms work, and he will sell his product at the prevailing price adjusted to the costs of those "old" firms. It follows that his receipts will exceed his costs. The difference we shall call Entrepreneurs' Profit, or simply Profit. It is the premium put upon successful innovation in capitalist society and is temporary by nature: it will vanish in the subsequent process of competition and adaptation. There is no tendency toward equalization of these temporary premia. Although we have thus deduced profit only for one particular case of innovation and only for conditions of perfect competition, the argument can readily be extended to cover all other cases and conditions. In any case, it is evident that, though temporary, profit is a net gain, *i.e.*, that it is not absorbed by the value of any cost factor through a process of Imputation. It should be observed, however, that for profits to emerge it is essential that the "suicidal stimulus of profits" should not act instantaneously. As a rule, it does not. But cases are thinkable, occasionally occur, and may in the future be expected to occur more frequently. We then get innovation without profit, or almost without it, and thus realize the possibility of what we may term Profitless Prosperities.

Of course, in a stationary economy, even if disturbed by action of external factors, both the

[1]Risk, nevertheless, enters into the pattern in which entrepreneurs work. But it does so indirectly and at one remove: riskiness—and every new thing is risky in a sense in which no routine action is—makes it more difficult to obtain the necessary capital and thus forms one of the obstacles entrepreneurs have to overcome and one of the instances of resistance of the environment which explain why innovations are not carried out smoothly and as a matter of course.

entrepreneurial function and the entrepreneurial profit would be absent, and so would the bulk of what is in common parlance described as profits. For, although there would be rents and quasi-rents of factors owned by firms, also, in the case of a manager-proprietor, his "earnings of management" or wages, to which we may for the sake of argument add various interest items, and although there may be monopoly gains and (if we admit external disturbances) also windfalls and possibly speculative gains, it will be readily seen that all these items would, in the conditions of a stationary or even of a growing economy, sum up to much smaller totals than they do in reality. Innovation is not only the most important immediate source of gains, but also indirectly produces, through the process it sets going, most of those situations from which windfall gains and losses arise and in which speculative operations acquire significant scope.

It follows that the bulk of private fortunes is, in capitalist society, directly or indirectly the result of the process of which innovation is the "prime mover." Speculative maneuvers which are responsible for some, are evidently incidents to the process of economic evolution in our sense, and so are largely the unearned increments reaped by owners of natural resources—urban land, for instance—which account for others. Saving, consistently carried on through generations, could not have been nearly so successful as it was if there had not been surpluses, due to innovation, from which to save. But the position of the typical industrial or commercial or financial family directly originates in some act, or some series of acts, of innovation. When their period of entrepreneurship is past, those families live, it is true, on quasi-rents, often supported by monopoloid situations, or, if they entirely sever their connection with business, on interest. But a new production function practically always emerges if we follow up those quasi-rents or monopoloid gains or monetary capitals to their sources.

4 Profit, in our sense, is a functional return—its peculiarities and especially its temporary character constitute a justifiable reason for hesitating to call it an income—but it would not always be safe to locate the entrepreneurial function according to the criterion of accrual. Whether it accrues to entrepreneurs or not is a matter of institutional pattern. It does so most completely in that form of organization which is characterized by the prevalence of the family firm. In corporate industry profits accrue to the firm as such, and their distribution ceases to be automatic and becomes a matter of policy—shareholders, executives (whether entrepreneurs or not), and employees receiving, in the most varied forms (bonuses, tantièmes,[2] and so on) indeterminate shares in it or contractual equivalents for shares in it. Attempts by entrepreneurs to recover elements of profits to which there is no legal claim, account in part for a number of familiar practices *praeter legem* or *contra legem*.

Such struggles for a share in profits that have been made are, however, less important for our subject than the struggles to conserve the stream of profit itself. Secrecy regarding processes, patents,[3] judicious differentiation of products, advertising, and the like, occasionally also aggression directed against actual and would-be competitors, are instances of a familiar strategy, which in the public, as well as in the professional, mind have done much to veil the source and nature of profits in our sense, especially because that strategy may be resorted to in other cases as well. We realize at once that these devices are the same as those which play a role in cases of monopolistic competition and that the fact that they are met with in our case is precisely due to the other fact that an enterprise in our sense almost necessarily finds itself in an "imperfect" situation, even if the system be otherwise a perfectly competitive one. This is one of the reasons why we so persistently stress the relation between evolution and imperfection of competition. It follows that profits might, as far as this goes, be also included in the category

[2]*Editor's Note*: i.e., expense accounts and other perquisites.

[3]Patent legislation is one of the few instances of legal recognition of the social functions of profit in capitalist society. Patents may, of course, keep profits alive longer than would be required for those functions to be fulfilled and then become similar in nature to less approved practices. We intend neither social criticism nor social apologetics but it may be useful to state that these practices are responsible for a view frequently met in popular arguments for social reform, according to which profit is necessarily the outcome of antisocial activities and there is necessarily antagonism between receivers of profits and, say, consumers' or workmen's interests. In such propositions, the meaning of which greatly varies profits is in general used in a sense different from ours. But the above shows that there is a range of phenomena, within which profits in our sense are all but indistinguishable from surpluses, to which such indictments do apply.

of monopoloid gains. This, however, would blur the specific character of our case: not every generalization is profitable to the analyst—any more than every innovation is to the innovator. Moreover, profits change their character in the course of such struggles.

Not only is practically every enterprise threatened and put on the defensive as soon as it comes into existence, but it also threatens the existing structure of its industry or sector almost as unavoidably as it creates unemployment somewhere or other. An innovation sometimes may do so by its mere possibility and even before it is embodied in an enterprise. That structure, being a living organism and not merely the congeries of rational billiard balls that theory represents it to be, resents the threat and perceives possibilities of defense other than adaptation by a competitive struggle.

Situations ensue which produce the paradox that industry sometimes tries to sabotage that "progress" which it inexorably evolves by virtue of the very law of its own life. There is no contradiction in this. It is submitted, however, that our general schema derives some support from the fact that it resolves that paradox so easily and shows us how and why industrial "progress" comes to the majority of firms existing at a given time as an attack from outside.[4] Taking industry as a whole, there is always an innovating sphere warring with an "old" sphere, which sometimes tries to secure prohibition of the new ways of doing things—as the artisans' congresses did in Europe as late as the eighties of the nineteenth century—or to discredit them—the "machine-made product," for instance—or to buy them off—which is sometimes the real rationale of cartelization—or to penalize them, by fiscal legislation or in other ways, including public "planning."

[4]Sociologically, the case is, of course, not different from the case of a new scientific principle—or, for that matter, of a new way of seeing nature in the case of painting—which also comes as a hostile shock both to existing habits of scientific thinking—or of painting—and to those who expound or practice them.

5 It has been stated above that our assumption about New Firms carrying the new things into effect against resisting strata of old firms, which was to embody the characteristically different behavior in the face of new possibilities, may occasionally fail us. For the past it is obviously very realistic. Even in the present the writer is not aware of important instances which would prove it to be contrary to fact. But several minor ones he has observed. It is interesting to note that such absence of friction does not always make the path of progress smoother. In the country *X*, for example, all firms existing in the industry *Y* took at exactly the same time, about 15 years ago, to producing the article *Z* according to a new and much cheaper method. A deadlock ensued, very quickly remedied by an agreement which deprived that innovation of any effect beyond a surplus, unemployment, and some excess capacity. There is some reason to expect that such cases will increase in importance: on the one hand, technological research becomes increasingly mechanized and organized; on the other hand, resistance to new ways weakens. Any technological improvement which is becoming "objectively possible," tends to be carried into effect as a matter of course. This must affect the importance of the social function, and in consequence the economic and social position, of that stratum of capitalist society which exists by entrepreneurial achievement.

Already, the volitional aptitudes that made the successful entrepreneur of old are much less necessary and have much less scope than they used to have. However, it would be as great a mistake to overrate the length to which the process has as yet gone as it would be to ignore it. For our theme, it will be seen not to have proceeded far enough to matter for general contours.

As an economist, Schumpeter was interested in the impact of the manager on the economy as a whole, but much recent work has been focused on the complex interrelationships within a company. Emphasis on this is likely to grow, for as companies become larger and their organizations become more complex, it is more and more difficult to trace the probable side effects of a change in the handling of any one area of management responsibility. Here

Harold J. Leavitt, professor at Stanford University and one of the foremost writers on the psychological aspects of business, points out the importance of this fact by reference to technology, organization structure, and human relations.

The Volatile Organization

Harold J. Leavitt

We have one group that wants to solve the problem of unit X by working on *structure*, by changing the organization chart and the locations of authority and responsibility. We have another group that's going to solve the same problems *technologically*, by improving the analytic quality of decisions and applying new techniques for controlling and processing information. And we have a third group that's going to solve the very same problems humanly, by working on persons and interpersonal relations. But there is one more important point that needs to be made here, before you decide which one of these to use. They aren't mutually exclusive. No one of these actions will affect the way the task of division X gets done without also involving each of the other [factors]. *Structure* and *technology* and *people* are not separable phenomena in organizations. If we decentralize the unit, or if we change the present allocation of responsibilities, it will not only affect the problem but will also affect (perhaps adversely) people's attitudes and interpersonal relations. If you tighten controls, for example, some people may get angry or uncomfortable. If you switch from a functional to a product organization form, there will be new problems of interpersonal relations.

And if we play with the organization structure we will also get some effects on *technology*. The kinds of techniques that are now appropriate in a highly decentralized scheme—the accounting techniques for example—may have to be very different than those appropriate for highly centralized organizations.

And similarly, if we hire the technically oriented consulting firm, and go on to introduce the computer and new information flows, then we can darn well expect effects not only on the way the job gets done but also on structure and on people. If we can centralize information in locations where we couldn't centralize before, we will find decisions being made and responsibilities being taken in different places than they were being taken before. And while we may be talking about *de*centralization, that new information system may be pushing us toward centralization. We may also find that the kinds and numbers of people we need in our new, technically sophisticated organization may be quite different from the kind and number of members we needed before. Moreover some things that were done judgmentally and thoughtfully are now pretty well programmed, so that essentially they can be done by the machine—with some consequent effects on the attitudes and feelings of persons.

Finally, if we move in on the people side, hiring the human relations firm, we will encourage people to be more open and more valid in their communication, encourage people to take more responsibility, and encourage people to interact more with other members of the organization. If we do these things, let us not for a moment think that we can do them without exerting great pressure on our existing organizational structure. The authority system will change and so will the status system. And we will exert pressure on technology too. The newly freed-up people may want new tools or the abolition of old ones that have been technically useful but are psychologically frustrating.

Everything feeds back on everything else, so that although we started out to worry only about the relationship between structure and task, or technology and task, or people and task, we must end up worrying about the effects of changes in any one on all of the others. Some of those changes may be very helpful, but some may be negative. And the manager has

Reprinted from *Managerial Psychology*, 2d ed. (by permission of The University of Chicago Press, Chicago, 1964), pp. 321–325.

to somehow diagnose the secondary and tertiary effects of action in any one of these areas.

For organizations do not stand still. If we inject something into one part of the system bells begin to ring and lights begin to go on all over the system, often in places we hadn't counted on and at times we hadn't expected.

This is not to say that the complexity of the organization is so great that we can never tell what will happen when we do something. It is only to say that an organization is complex enough to make any simple structural or technical or human model inadequate. But we have made a lot of progress in understanding the complexities in the last few decades. We now know a good deal more about ways of acting on structure or people or technology; and we know somewhat more about how they are wired to one another. There is real progress in the organizational world. The three classes of consulting firms in our example should not be taken as an indication that things have gone to pot. On the contrary they are an indication of how much we have learned about organizations. And about how much we now know of ways to change or modify them.

The practitioner in each of these three realms may be oversold on his own product. He may be overly enthusiastic about all that can be done by changing structure, or technology, or people. Each may be partially and understandably blind to the perspectives of the others. But the manager need not be blind. He has lots more to work from than he did in the days when we so naïvely believed that the simple line drawing on the organization chart actually did capture the essence of our live, volatile organization.

The terms "management" and "administration" are often used interchangeably, but it is important to differentiate between them, for a man may be considered a "good administrator" merely because he follows established procedures and keeps things running smoothly (for a time, at least). A true manager, on the other hand, is always seeking improvement, and if he is a good manager the improvement is achieved. However, as the author of this article cautions, it should not be concluded that systems of planning, organizing, control, and so on, are valueless, merely that they should be adapted to the circumstances. Before his promotion, the good manager described here did carry out the management functions, but he relied on his personal contacts to ensure control and to determine when his plans should be changed. When he became plant manager, he was flexible enough to use more formal measures.

Management Means Action—Not Reaction

George S. Odiorne

In a metal working plant in the East two department managers were in competition for a plant manager's vacancy. The first was admittedly a good administrator. His knowledge of the affairs of his department was thorough and systematic. He worried over reports and controls which came to his desk daily, telling him how production, quality, safety, costs and spoilage were for the day or the week before. He established procedures and systems to feed back suggestions for improvement and better organization to the shop supervisors. He held regular meetings of his foremen and staff people to get their ideas. Yet he didn't get the job because his *results* weren't good enough.

The successful candidate received few formal written reports. He held conferences less than once a week, and then only when it couldn't be avoided. He had no charts on his walls showing him the level of various key indices. Most of his time was spent out in the plant talking with people, sticking his nose into offices of foremen and offering help when it was advisable. He always had time to look at any new gadget which one of the mechanics had put on a machine. He knew the union stewards and officers well, and chatted briefly with many of them daily. He was well acquainted with all of the employees, and was available for informal chats.

The decision to pick the second man for promotion didn't have anything to do directly with his practices and systems, or lack of them. He was chosen over the other solely because he made things happen. For him the department ran at peak efficiency. His people didn't let minutes slip away from them. If a line or a machine broke down the crew moved quickly to another one and kept working without delay, while the mechanics pitched in to get the first one back in operation. His output per hourly wage dollar spent was more than fifteen percent higher than that of his colleague. His spoilage was lower, his department had fewer accidents, and the number of union grievances filed with the personnel department was zero. Tireless, good-humored, optimistic and knowledgeable, he made things roll along with apparent ease.

Now, what was the difference between the two?

The important variation wasn't the methods they used, and we shouldn't induce from this example that good administration and procedures are foolish. In fact, once the new plant manager took over his job he used them well. The only point here is that there is a difference between *management* and *administration*. This big difference is that the manager makes things happen by whatever means are required, while the administrator follows certain procedures mechanically.

The administrator follows a stereotype pattern whether it applies in his situation or not. The manager sizes up the situation as it exists and decides to do those things which will make things happen whether they fit into the text or not. It's perfectly true that these administrative techniques may be just the ticket in some situations. In such circumstances the manager follows them, *as long as they continue to produce results*. When they cease doing that the manager does something different until he finds the techniques that produce the desired results.

Management Is Not a Passive Art

One of the major complaints of the experts in management development is that too many executives are looking for "a gimmick."

The enchantment of the gimmick or formula, whether it's psychological tests, work simplification, or a five step plan for selecting workers, is intriguing. The big attraction of such a formula is that it reduces management to something which is passive or mechanical. Simply learn how to use the formula, wait for people to bring the problems to you, apply the formula and the answer becomes obvious.

This would be a wonderful labor-saving device, but unfortunately there isn't one such formula worth mentioning. Underlying every successful organization is a corps of hard working people in management and staff positions who are actively seeking out flaws and defects which need remedying, and who also fix them up. But there's more to it even than that.

A manager is more than a problem solver. He'a a goal setter. Without waiting for others to ask him, he envisions things that should happen, and thinks through some possible paths by which the goal can be reached. At this stage he has few, if any, people who would agree with him that the goal is possible. Because he's active in deed as well as thought, however, he converts them into action in his plan, and enlists their talents toward reaching the goal which he dreamed up. Before long he has a full scale movement afoot and people become ego-involved in his goal just as if they themselves had thought of it. During the struggle to accomplish it, the battle to overcome competition, costs, and other problems in the way, he's there to help. He keeps them pointed toward the objective, and suggests and sets examples of how it can be reached.

Now he may do this by good administrative methods it's true. Being a good manager *doesn't preclude* being a good administrator. It merely implies that he's not a passive administrator who's more concerned with a "clean desk" or proper decor for his office because he's been told that is how administrators should look. Nor is he overly obsessed with procedures for control and review. The dominant trait of the manager who makes things happen is that he's *goal oriented*. It means further that he's actively and intelligently seeking that goal. He's doing more than presiding over a group of people, he's leading them somewhere. Furthermore, while he's doing that the chances are that he's hatching up even more ambitious objectives beyond that one.

Making Growth a Company Goal

Studies by the Stanford Research Institute of several hundred companies with records of growth show that there are several traits which are common to most of them. For one thing they are oriented to growth industries. Not only are the managements of these companies alert to where opportunities lie, they are not averse to dropping lines which are shrinking in market importance and future opportunity. Growth, and management action to accomplish it, are less likely to be found in the hay and grain business, or horseshoe manufacturing than in electronics, missiles, atomic energy, pharmaceuticals or chemicals. Far too many companies fail to grow, the Stanford studies show, because the managements have a sentimental attachment to products or processes which were once growing and profitable, but which time has now proven outmoded.

Take the case of the large food companies which still concentrate much of their top management time and energy into the flour business. Milling capacity is now far greater than is needed for the production of all the baking flour needed in this country, yet these firms allow the dead hand of the past to rule the future, and as a result channel energies in pursuit of a fading market.

Another food company, less tied to the past, has cast its lot with the newer growth lines—plus bold advertising—and is surpassing its competitors in growth of sales and profits. Needless to say, the latter also has about it the magic to attract the more talented and able young men who seek personal growth through identification with the company's goals of corporate growth.

Stanford's studies also showed that companies which have growth patterns have been led by management of great moral courage in making decisions in favor of growth and sticking with them to make the growth occur.

The Forces of Inertia

More often than competitors or actual opposition from those who have different objectives, the manager who makes things happen finds himself fighting a force called organizational inertia. This inertia takes many forms.

The first is the natural tendency of inertia within the manager himself. The tendency to coast along, or to look back "and see how far I've come" overtakes some managers and they turn into administrators. The truly action-oriented manager seldom spends much time walking around his accomplishments admiring what he's done in the past. He's too often engrossed in getting things moving toward the next higher goal.

Even when he hasn't this inward desire to taper off his efforts, the action getter finds that he has the heavy responsibility for spurring others to overcome their own inertia. This demands that he have several important capacities. He's got to be able to move projects and people off dead center and get them rolling toward his goals. He's got to generate enthusiasm for these goals so that people adopt them as their own, with the result that they generate enthusiasm on their own part for getting there. He must further instill a desire to excel and do the job fully and without mistakes or faltering. To do this demands several traits in the action-getting manager which he must assiduously cultivate at the risk of failure.

1 He's going to have to maintain optimism if he's going to overcome inertia. Most managers who make things happen have ego drives that push them on personally, and unbounded optimism and confidence that others will ultimately see his vision of what's to be accomplished despite repeated defeats and failures.
2 He needs a sound knowledge of people to impel them to produce and create. He needs to know what incentives are required to get action from others, and to have some artistry in using them.
3 He needs a certain callousness in demanding

high standards of performance from others who are helping him.

One of the greatest wellsprings of inertia in an organization is its *size*. The big organization develops built-in inertias, simply because it's so big.

A number of things occur when an organization grows in size. The first effect is that communications between the top and bottom, and between the various members, becomes difficult. This means that the left hand sometimes does things that duplicate or conflict with what the right hand is doing.

Another effect of bigness is that the personal touch between the owners and the employees is lost; or in the case of a publicly owned organization between the management and its staff and employees. Since it's this personal touch which is often at the heart of getting action in an organization, the top man finds he is limited greatly when he has a great organization to run, and must accordingly organize to overcome the effects of too much bigness,

Because the organization is big it requires more rule of law (called procedures and policies) in order to govern it. These are perfectly sound things to install, but they are part of that body of knowledge called *administration*, and at the same time they make it possible for managers to function at all, they aren't by any manner of means a guarantee of movement and growth. That happens when the manager in favor of action makes his personal impact on the organization.

Profit Requires Action

Being a successful manager in a commercial and industrial enterprise means a profit-minded one. Conversely, it's the profit-minded manager at any level who stands the best chance of moving upward. This is more than simple avarice, or single minded love of money for itself. It's largely because profit is a universal standard for measurement that is easily grasped by managers and quite clearly understood by those who judge his performance.

It's entirely possible that someday a more commonly held standard will come along, for example—service; but it must always meet the standard which profit has become—immediate, easy to calculate, universally accepted. Profit, for all the criticisms leveled against it, is the best available instrument and standard of managerial success and organizational performance. With adaptations it applies to any organization, even in Soviet Russia.

We hear a great deal of pious foolishness written and said about profit. At the annual congress of industry of the NAM each winter, solemn and quite pompous words are uttered in defense of this mysterious lubricant which causes the wheels of industry to turn. To some it becomes a divinely inspired instrument which it becomes sacrilegious to damn. This of course is not the point here.

There's still another error which is perpetrated by accountants when we think of profit. It's widely held fiction that profit is something exact and precise which comes without deviation of man-made influence out of the impersonal exactitude known as "the books" of the company. This of course is nearly as fallacious as the assumption of its divine nature. All of the ingredients which come out at the end of the year under the over-all label of "profit" are quite flexible and under the control of individual decisions of managers or administrators.

Such things as expenditures for research, training, public relations, personnel management, and so on are all drains on the immediate profit in the current accounting period. You'll note that all of these are the results of the decision of management to spend money out of current income in order to assure the future growth and stability of the company.

Profit, then, is more than an accounting term. It's a positive creation and standard of measuring effectiveness of management action and decision making.

Let's illustrate this. A large company begins by having some kind of trade advantage—either a patent right to exclusive manufacture of a product, or a dominant position in a market due to aggressive salesmanship. Theoretically each company has such a special advantage which keeps it alive in the face of competition.

Yet companies go bankrupt. One study of the 100 largest firms in the United States in 1927 shows that only 50 per cent of them still exist. In its early days the National Cash Register Company used to maintain an exhibit of machines produced by companies which had attempted to enter the adding machine business and had gone broke in the process. Oswald Knauth, former treasurer of Macy's store, once said that "almost all trade advantages can be duplicated." Except for certain patent arrangements or exclusive access to raw materials there are few advantages which a company can acquire that will preclude the necessity of managers who continue to discover and build up advantages for their own firms through personal leadership. These include actions which will build up its internal and external position, and the development of people, trade connections and experience which results in profit.

The world which Adam Smith depicted of automatic competition, with the functioning of "natural laws" arranging the levels of profits of the respective firms, was never really a picture of life. Profit is the result almost wholly of the *actions of managers* who exercise initiative and leadership of a dynamic nature, and of the people who respond to this leadership to carry through toward the goals of the organization.

There is probably no company in business today which couldn't be out of business through lack of profit inside of ten years if its management attempted to conduct its affairs simply through mechanical application of administrative practice, at the expense of the more vital, personal, and human application of individual leadership.

The Manager and the World Outside of Business

This individual leadership which produces action and results isn't limited to the four walls or administrative boundaries of the firm. Profit, survival, and growth of the firm today—and in the future—will demand that managers be able to make things happen in circumstances in which a lot of the important variables won't be under their jurisdiction. Let's look at a few of them:

- The company which isn't attuned to public opinion is taking undue risks with its future.
- Government actions have a vital part in business policy.
- What's happening abroad is sufficiently close to business decisions today that they must be part of the action-getting manager's calculations.

Clarence Randall, for many years chief executive of Inland Steel, points to the two major areas confronting American management in the future.

The first of these is added acceptance of the responsibility of business management for carrying out its share of social responsibility in the community in which it works. In this regard Mr. Randall feels that business management has come a long way.

Beyond this Mr. Randall feels that equally responsible behavior by managers must be forthcoming to discharge its responsibilities and apply equal resourcefulness in the face of world problems. He said:

> If we are willing to face outward as well as inward, American free enterprise can become a powerful force for good in the world, and can at the same time assure its own survival.

Good management then means action—and not reaction—to both internal conduct of its affairs, but also action for greater social responsibility in the narrow community in which it operates—and in the world beyond.

2
How Managers Carry Out Their Functions

The different concepts of management outlined in Chapter 1 are, of course, designed to be applicable to real situations, even though much of the material is couched in fairly abstract terms. But managers manage on many different levels, and the extent to which they can carry out entrepreneurial functions, such as innovation, may be limited. They may also be limited by their own natures if they have no taste for innovation.

Below are two pieces describing managers in action, managers who are worlds apart in their situations and in their natures. The Durant story is fact—or at least fact as it appeared to the manager himself—since it is taken from Durant's own autobiography, which he never finished and which, therefore, was never published. The story of the foreman, Buster, is fiction, but it is nevertheless "true" in that it describes a situation very similar to those that confront many first-line supervisors from time to time. It may, in fact, be a fictionalized account of an actual day in an automobile foreman's life, illuminated by the author's insight into situations and people.

William C. Durant (1861–1947) was the founder of General Motors and the genius who put together the automobile companies that formed the nucleus of today's enormous and very profitable corporation.

Durant was a true innovator. Originally he was a highly successful carriage maker, with a business that he built up on the basis of an innovation (in the springs and suspension). Although he did not invent this type of cart, he saw its possibilities and was the driving force that turned the idea into a going business.

But at the peak of his success, Durant became convinced that automobiles were bound to have an almost unlimited future and he turned to car making, creating and twice losing one of the most successful companies. And even while in the automobile business, he discovered Frigidaire, and almost managed to add oil wells in Mexico to his holdings. (He would have succeeded in the latter venture if the President of Mexico had not been assassinated before the ratification of the contract.)

Durant possessed great ability to spot and develop talent and assembled a galaxy of managers that included some of the ablest du Ponts and their executives (e.g., John Lee Pratt); also Walter P. Chrysler, Louis Chevrolet, Albert Champion, Alfred P. Sloan, Jr., "Boss Kettering," and many others. His one big shortcoming was his lack of system. After he was ousted from GM in 1920, he might have retired with several million; instead, he started another automobile company, which failed; then he pioneered in food chains and bowling alleys, but died having lost almost everything.

The following is the real "inside story," as recorded by Durant himself, of the founding of GM. It shows how Ford was almost added to the combination, and would have been but for the overcaution of a banker. It should be noted that many of the usual management problems that are still of concern arose in the discussions: unity of command, objectives, rate of return, share of the market, and so on.

The Briscoe mentioned here was with Maxwell-Briscoe, one of the early automobile companies.

The True Story of General Motors

William C. Durant

The place—Flint, Michigan, the "Home of the Buick."

The time—Six o'clock, evening, May 15, 1908.

I was dining with my daughter, Mrs. E. R. Campbell, when I was called to the phone. Chicago on the wire—Briscoe calling.

Briscoe: Hello, Billy, I have a most important matter to discuss with you, and want you to take the first train to Chicago.

Durant: What's the big idea, Ben?

Briscoe: Don't ask me to explain; it's the biggest thing in the country; there're millions in it; can you come?

Durant: Impossible; too busy; sorry. But I can see you here. Why don't you take the ten o'clock Grand Trunk arriving at seven o'clock tomorrow morning? I will meet you at the station and we will have breakfast together.

Briscoe: All right, I will be with you.

I met him at the depot, a hurried breakfast at the hotel, then to my office. Comfortably seated, Briscoe presented the following:

One of the partners of J. P. Morgan & Co. had made a small investment in the Maxwell-Briscoe Co. when it was first organized. Pleased with the progress the company was making and recognizing the possibilities he asked me if a sufficient number of motor car concerns could be brought together to control the industry. How would the leading companies regard a consolidation?

Would Briscoe canvass the situation and report? (At that time trusts and combinations were the order of the day—promotions of all kinds encouraged by the big banking interests.) Briscoe had no well-considered plan but wanted to get my ideas. He suggested calling a meeting of about twenty of the leading concerns, meaning Packard, Peerless, Pierce Arrow, Stoddard Dayton, Thomas, etc. What did I think of it?

I told him frankly that I did not believe the plan was workable. The proposition in my opinion was too big, too many concerns involved, too many conflicting interests to be reconciled.

"Why not modify your ideas, Ben, and see if you can get together a few concerns committed to volume production in the medium priced

From Durant's unfinished autobiography. I am grateful to Mrs. W. C. Durant and Aristo Scrobogna for their kind help in making the following excerpts available and for permission to reprint them.

class, all having a common objective, all heading for a highly competitive field?" I named as my choice Ford, Reo, Maxwell-Briscoe and Buick. I suggested that he first see Henry Ford, who was in the limelight, liked publicity and unless he could lead the procession, would not play. "Get Ford if possible, then take the matter up with R. E. Olds. When and if everything is arranged to your satisfaction, advise me of the time and place and I will attend your meeting."

Briscoe agreed. I then took him through the factory, showed him what we were doing, which quite surprised him, and put him on the Père Marquette train for Detroit, feeling quite pleased with his visit.

About two weeks later I received word to meet him and the others in Detroit. The place appointed for the meeting was the office of James Danaher in the Penobscot Building. In the public reception room were gathered the principals, their close associates and advisers. The room was small, no place to discuss business. I sensed, unless we ran to cover, plenty of undesirable publicity in the offing. As I had commodious quarters in the Pontchartrain Hotel and as the luncheon hour was approaching, I suggested that we separate (in order not to attract attention) and meet in my room as soon as convenient, giving the number of the room and how to locate it without going to the office.

When we were once more together Mr. Briscoe made his little speech, saying that he had paved the way for the nucleus of a gigantic combination and it was up to those present to work out and submit a plan that might appeal to J. P. Morgan and Co.

Then came what might be called a "painful pause." Mr. Briscoe had no definite plan and the matter had not been seriously considered by the others. To relieve the embarrassment, I submitted the following hypothetical question to Mr. Ford: If we were all agreed that a consolidation was a proper and wise procedure, and the Ford Motor Co.'s properties were appraised at $10,000,000, would he consider $6,000,000 a reasonable figure for the Reo Motor Car Co.? To which question Mr. Ford promptly replied that he had not the slightest idea of the value of the earning capacity of the Reo Motor Car Co. My next question, addressed jointly to Ford and Olds: With Ford at $10,000,000 and Reo at $6,000,000, would $5,000,000 for Maxwell-Briscoe appear unreasonable? This question, evidently out of politeness, was not answered.

Mr. Briscoe, the prime mover of the project, having very different ideas, seemed slightly displeased and asked me what about Buick. To which I replied that the report of the appraisers and auditors and the conditions and terms of the agreement would be my answer to his question.

This opened the way for a general discussion: How was the company to be managed? Who was to be the "boss"? How were the different companies to be represented? Could anyone suggest a plan? Briscoe took the position that the purchasing and engineering departments should be consolidated, that the advertising and sales departments should be combined, and that a central committee should pass on all operating policies.

I took the position that this would only lead to confusion; that there should be no change or interference in the manner of operating, that the different companies should continue exactly as they were. In other words, I had in mind a *holding company*. Briscoe came back jokingly with "Ho! Ho! Durant is for States' rights; I am for a Union." From that time and all through the luncheon, everybody except Henry Ford talked. Business conditions and the future of the industry were forecast, the hazards and uncertainties were gone into thoroughly, the desirability of a controlling organization agreed upon, the meeting breaking up with the best of feeling with a statement from Mr. Briscoe that he would see his people and report, and that, in all probability, we would be invited to meet in New York in the near future.

In due time, the call came and the manufacturers met with the representatives of the House of Morgan at the law offices of Ward, Hayden and Satterlee, New York City (Mr. Herbert Satterlee being a son-in-law of J. Pierpont Morgan).

Following the introductions, the usual questions were asked:

What percentage of the industry did the four companies represent? Would it not be desirable to increase the number? Could anything be gained by a consolidation of the four companies? How much capital was employed by the four companies, and could additional capital be used to advantage? When and by whom were the companies organized? How were they capitalized and by whom controlled? Would a consolidation attract or discourage competition? What were the objections, if any, to a motor car combination?

The only reply to the last question was by Mr. Ford. He thought the tendency of consolidation and control was to increase prices which he believed would be a serious mistake. He was in favor of keeping prices down to the lowest possible point, giving to the multitude the benefit of cheap transportation.

What would the consolidated company, if organized, be called?

Mr. Satterlee suggested the name "International Motor Car Company" and asked if there were any objections. He said that Mr. George W. Perkins, the active member of the Morgan firm, was very partial to that name, and was very much interested at that moment in the International Harvester Company and the International Mercantile Marine. There was no objection to the name. Incidentally, it was agreed that the firms would defray the expenses of the appraisals and audits; before adjourning, it was understood that the meeting called at the suggestion of Mr. Briscoe was purely informal; that there was to be no publicity, and no commitment on the part of anyone present.

I was satisfied that a consolidation was in the making, and began to put myself in position to act promptly when the time came. I went over the whole matter with my personal attorney, and friend, Mr. John J. Carton, and suggested that he draw up an agreement to be signed by the stockholders of the Buick Company authorizing me to act for them in an exchange of stock (Buick stock for stock of the International Motor Car Company to be organized), the exchange to be on exactly the same terms and under the same conditions as my own. The stock to be endorsed in blank and deposited in the First National Bank of Flint, Michigan, Mr. Bruce MacDonald, vice-president and cashier acting as trustee. (Ruled upon later as quite unusual, *every share* of the stock of Buick Company was endorsed and deposited under the agreement.)

While the bankers were investigating in their own way, and the appraisals and audits were being completed, frequent meetings were held in New York and it appeared that real progress was being made. While I was busy night and day with my regular work, I kept in close touch with Mr. Satterlee's office, and made many trips to New York during the hot summer of 1908.

During one of my visits to New York, Mr. George W. Perkins expressed a desire to see me and it was arranged for me to meet him at the train (he was leaving for Chicago to attend a meeting of the International Harvester Company) and ride with him as far as Albany. In his drawing room we had the opportunity of getting acquainted. I told him of my twenty years' experience in the carriage business and in reply to his questions gave him my views as to how the combination should be handled, and I think I sold him the "*holding company idea*." Mr. Perkins asked me what I thought of the proposed name, to which I replied that I considered it most appropriate. He then said, "I think we should protect it, and if you wish to join me, I will, upon my return from Chicago, file an application for a New York charter." This I agreed to and the matter was handled for joint account as proposed. Returning to New York, I went to Mr. Satterlee's office where I met Mr. Curtis R. Hathaway, a member of the firm of Ward, Hayden and Satterlee, who told me that the "Corner" (the office of J. P. Morgan & Co., so called) was very anxious to have me get in touch with Mr. Frederick Lynde Stetson, Morgan & Company's very able attorney. Mr. Hathaway took me over to the bank where we were escorted to the private elevator and directed to Mr. Stetson's office. Mr. Stetson was very cordial, said he had heard some very nice things about Buick, and understood that I was in complete control with authority to execute the agreement. I told him that the stock was deposited in the First National Bank of Flint with the understanding that if the merger was completed the exchange of the securities would be made, if the terms were satisfactory to me. Mr. Stetson asked if the depositors had knowledge of the new securities or any of the details regarding the new company, the size of the capitalization, etc., etc. I told him the stockholders had confidence in me and that the matter was entirely in my hands. Mr. Stetson said he doubted if a title of that kind would be sufficient and said he thought it might be necessary to have the Buick stockholders execute a new set of papers. I questioned the wisdom of changing or even suggesting a change in the agreement. Mr. Stetson insisted that he must have a better title and could not approve the exchange on the terms and under the conditions of the deposit agreement. I told him I was acting on the advice of my attorney and that I would get in touch with him immediately.

Up to that time I was what you might say "quite warm" for the merger, but after my interview with Mr. Stetson, I am frank to say that I cooled off "slightly."

Shortly after, the bankers notified the group that they would like to see us in New York and again we met in Mr. Satterlee's office. At that meeting were present several representatives of the Morgan bank, Messrs. Ford, Olds, Thomas, Briscoe, Maxwell, Hathaway, Satterlee, his son-in-law Mr. Hamilton, and myself. The bankers reported that they had made a complete study of the situation; that they favored a preferred and common stock issue; had agreed upon the capitalization (the preferred stock to be sold to obtain the money with a bonus of common).

We were told that generous subscriptions on the part of the manufacturers would have a favorable effect upon the public acceptance of the issue and Mr. Ford was asked how much of the preferred stock he would subscribe for. He replied that when he was first approached by Mr. Briscoe, he told Mr. Briscoe that he would sell his company for cash, but would not be interested in, or take stock in, any merger or consolidation. This was a great surprise and the bankers who were expecting a large subscription from Mr. Ford were quite disappointed. Mr. Satterlee requested me to step into the adjoining room and after shutting the door asked me what it was all about. I told him it was news to me; that the matter had never been hinted at or mentioned and suggested that Mr. Briscoe be called in. Briscoe said that Mr. Ford had correctly stated the case, but that he had shown such an interest as the matter progressed that Briscoe, whether rightly or wrongly, inferred that Mr. Ford had changed his mind and that he would go along with the others. Mr. Satterlee was quite put out and after giving the matter a few moments' thought went back into the other room and very diplomatically stated that there had been a misunderstanding, but that the matter of finance was entirely up to the bankers and when they had perfected their plans another meeting would be called.

Then, everyone, except myself, left the "sinking ship."

After we were alone and had partially recovered from the shock, Mr. Satterlee asked me what I intended doing. I told him I had come to New York several months earlier, and had been led to believe that the consolidation sponsored by the Morgan firm was being seriously considered and had so informed my people; that the Buick stock had been deposited and if released could never again be collected in the same form, nor would I have the courage, or care to make another attempt. I must have a consolidation.

Mr. Satterlee said, "Mr. Durant, you only have the Buick, how can you have a consolidation?" I replied that I would have no difficulty in securing another company, as a matter of fact I had one in mind at that moment—the Olds Motor Works of Lansing, Michigan. The company—one of the oldest in the business—was controlled by Mr. S. L. Smith of Detroit, and was being operated by his sons, Fred and Angus Smith, whom I knew intimately. While that company was not a financial success, I believed it had possibilities. Mr. Henry Russell, vice-president of the Michigan Central Railroad, a great friend of Mr. Smith, was president of the Olds Motor Works. I was acquainted with Mr. Russell and said that I would wire him immediately asking if he would meet me in Lansing the following Saturday, mentioning the fact that I would like to discuss a possible merger of Olds and Buick, which I did.

Satterlee asked about the capitalization and how the common stock was to be issued. I told him I had in the Buick organization a competent engineer, by name of Walter Marr, with whom I had worked closely for several years and I was quite sure he would set aside for my use a sufficient number of patents and applications against which the common stock could be issued.

Satterlee then asked what I intended to call the company. I told him that in view of the collapse of "the consolidation" I assumed Mr. Perkins would have no use for the name "International Motor Car Co." (owned jointly by us) and believed I would have no difficulty in arranging with him to take over his interest. Mr. Satterlee was not so sure that Mr. Perkins would care to surrender his interest and I suggested that he go over to the bank and talk the matter over with him. In about half an hour he returned and stated that Mr. Perkins preferred to reserve the name "International Motor Car Co." for possible use at a later date.

We then looked over the list of names which we had previously prepared when we were seeking a name for the consolidation and when we came to General Motors I selected that name and *as of that moment the General Motors Co. came into being* (1908).

[Durant succeeded in purchasing Olds with GM preferred stock. And since there was no market for the GM shares at that time, he agreed to buy back $2 million worth for $1.8 million in a year's time from one of the principal owners, who was also a creditor of the Olds Company, if the latter wanted to sell.

Then Durant approached Cadillac, whose owners wanted cash, not stock, for the property. Durant was planning to raise the money by issuing GM obligations when he was reminded of $1.8 million he owed to the former owner of Olds. ("This small matter I had entirely overlooked," he wrote.) But he wired Cadillac that he was withdrawing his proposition. A few months later, he paid the $1.8 million, and approached Cadillac again. The price had gone up, but he was able to finance the purchase through an issue of notes secured by the entire stock of Cadillac. In fourteen months, Cadillac's net earnings had equaled the final purchase price: $4.75 million.

GM now consisted of Buick, Olds, and Cadillac. So Durant felt it was time to approach Ford again. He tells what happened below:]

When the International Motor Car Consolidation—the Briscoe-Morgan plan—failed to materialize, it was generally understood that the Ford Motor Company could be purchased, but the price during the many conferences held in New York and Detroit had never been disclosed.

I had reason to believe that if we were successful, General Motors would not require any more motor car companies. Our time and energy from that time on should be devoted to building up or acquiring manufacturing plants to supply General Motors with the important items it would require in ever-increasing numbers, such as forgeries [i.e., forgings], bodies, castings, wheels, tires, axles, transmissions, steering gears, ignition systems, and small parts of all kinds.

Controlling this enormous volume would make it possible for these accessory plants to materially reduce costs because of the volume of business from General Motors which they could depend upon if motor cars and motor trucks, as I was firmly convinced, were to become important factors in the industrial life of America.

My twenty years' experience in the carriage business taught me a lesson. We started out as assemblers with no advantage over our competitors. We paid about the same prices for everything we purchased. We realized that we were making no progress and would not unless and until we manufactured practically every important part that we needed.

We made a study of the methods employed by the concerns supplying us, the saving that could be effected by operating the plants at capacity without interruption, and with practically no selling or advertising expense. We proceeded to purchase plants and the control of plants, which made it possible for us to build up from the standpoint of volume the largest carriage company in the United States.

On the day appointed it so happened that Mr. Ford had eaten something on the train the evening before that did not agree with him, and he could not leave the hotel, but authorized Mr. Couzens[1] to submit his proposition which he did: "Mr. Ford will sell the Ford Motor Company for $8,000,000 giving me the privilege of purchasing 25 per cent of the Company's stock as part compensation for service rendered, which I am prepared to take over. The balance of the purchase price, the remaining three-quarters interest, at $6,000,000 to be paid for as follows: $2,000,000 cash at the time of sale, the remaining $4,000,000 at 5 per cent interest due on or before three years.

"Mr. Ford to have his proportion of the annual profits on the stock which he carries until paid

[1] *Editor's Note:* James Couzens, one of Ford's top executives and later a U. S. Senator.

for and delivered. The profits last year were $3,200,000."

I asked Mr. Couzens if the sale carried with it the name Ford in connection with all automotive interests and if he would agree not to become interested in any other automobile company for a period of ten years.

He replied that Mr. Ford wished to retain the right to engage in motorizing farm implements (farm trucks not included); otherwise all the other conditions which I had stated would be included in the contract.

Mr. Couzens having delivered the message. I told him to say to Mr. Ford that I was in hopes that a deal could be worked out as suggested by him and that he would hear from me within ten days, that I regretted he was indisposed and hoped for him a speedy recovery.

[Durant attempted to raise the initial $2 million by a loan from the National City Bank, but was turned down. "It must be remembered," he wrote, "that the banks, as a rule, were not at that time in favor of the automobile industry, as a matter of fact, they were extremely antagonistic." So he made no further attempt to raise the money for the Ford purchase and notified Ford that it could not be financed at that time. Two years later, Durant met Couzens on a train, and the latter informed him that Ford earnings the previous year had been $35 million. Durant wrote: "By the way, Mr. Vanderlip (the bank president) never forgave himself for not obtaining the $2 million for me, and it was a standing joke for years whenever we happened to meet."]

In contrast to Durant, a top-level manager, the hero of the following short story is a manager on the lowest level, the foreman in charge of a group of rank-and-file workers.

The excerpt, cut down somewhat from the original, is from a volume of short stories all dealing with life in automobile plants. The author, Harvey Swados, novelist and short story writer, was an important observer of the labor scene and had himself worked in automobile plants.

Just One of the Boys
Harvey Swados

Buster had stuck it out on the auto assembly line as a spot welder for sixteen years, through the depression and most of the war; and when he put away his staff sergeant's uniform and came home from Louisiana, he claimed his seniority, no longer with any great expectations but feeling that it was only prudent, especially with rising expenses and a daughter starting school. Within a year he became a foreman; from time to time he was shifted from one line to another, but always it was made clear that his good qualities were appreciated, and there were even hints of better things to come.

Buster was willing to recognize that the little things that went with being a boss gave him as much pleasure as his improved status gave his wife. After nine years of it, he still liked coming to work in a dirty place with clean clothes on and knowing that he was not going to get them dirty. And everything that went with clean clothes. Not having to punch a time clock, but dropping in early instead to the body shop office to sign in and sit around on a desk edge talking over production problems. Not having to eat out of a lunch box on the floor, or in the huge, prisonlike cafeteria with its long tables sprayed with spat-out grape pits, tipped-over sugar bowls, wet bread crusts expanding in pools of coffee, and cigarette butts put out in Jello, but at one of the quiet, clean tables in the supervisors' wing of the cafeteria. Not having to change into overalls in the vaulted locker rooms smelling of tired men and tired feet, but hanging his hat and sport jacket in the foremen's private locker room.

From *On the Line* (Little, Brown and Company, Boston, 1957). Also available in paperback (Bantam Books, Inc., New York), pp. 98-114.

And of course the money.

Naturally you paid a penalty. You were constantly nagged by every boss who stood above you; there was no recourse if they chose to knife you, and if you wanted the job bad enough you held still and let them stick it into you. But to Buster this was the way life was.

But then the company built an enormous new plant out in the sticks, and Buster found that his problems were not only multiplied but infinitely more complicated than he had ever thought possible. In the old factory they had been building cars for over a quarter of a century. Everyone knew where everything was; everybody knew everybody else—almost, anyway.

The basic trouble, as Buster was not alone in seeing, was that there was no longer a solid core of men who were used to building cars, knew what was involved in sweat and labor, and wanted the jobs bad enough to turn up in fair weather or foul, on time and ready to work a full day plus as much overtime as would be needed to hit the production quota. Absenteeism was fantastic—you were sure of having enough men to keep the line rolling only on payday—and the turnover was something unbelievable unless you stood there and watched the faces come and go, come and go, in such numbers that you had to give up trying to learn their names because most of them wouldn't stay long enough to make it worth while bothering.

"As soon as you try to get them to see just beyond their noses," he complained to his wife, "they take the attitude you're a company man. I pick up pieces of lead six and eight inches long that my solder flowers have thrown away because they can't be bothered flowing with a short stick, and I tell them the price of a hundred pounds of lead and they laugh at me. I keep the sandpaper locked up according to instructions, and hand the boys out one piece at a time. They ask me why I'm so stingy, they ask me if I'm paying for it, and when I tell them that every single abrasive disc—the ones they toss around like kids with flying saucers—costs fifty cents, you know what they say?" He took a gulp of coffee. "They say, So what. You can't even get them to see that their jobs depend on keeping costs down. Even if you could, I don't think they'd care."

Buster smiled grimly to himself on the way to work the next morning.

When his men started coming in, he gave them each a hello as they ambled up from the time clock, opened their toolboxes and put on their aprons. It was always his policy to say hello and good-by to his men no matter how grumpy he or they felt. He wanted them to like him and respect him, not to fear or mistrust him. There were a few who understood, he was sure.

"Here," he would say to a new man standing around with his file dangling from his hand, trying to look interested, "let me show you how to use that. Guide it with your left hand. Keep your thumb and forefinger spread across the back of the file, and then just let it glide back and forth, like this. Don't rub, don't grip too hard. You know why?" he would smile at the awkward, nervous man. "Because this file can wear you down quicker than it can wear down the metal. Take it slow, easy and steady, remember to guide it, not force it, and you'll do fine."

It seemed to him that the men on the line, even those who came and went like ghosts, must know that he was doing his best both to pull production and to cover for them, even when he screamed at them at the top of his lungs.

"Buster is the best boss in the shop." He had heard it with his own ears; he knew the word got around, and he knew that it was true.

He had constantly to be teaching these new men to metal-finish, and as soon as one was well broken in, he would quit. That made no difference to the production men, who expected you to turn out forty units an hour if you had to do it single-handed. And to top it off the job-study engineers began to make tests on his line. They tried having his metal finishers do every fourth job instead of every third, but do the entire side instead of only the rear quarterpanel. This freed the metal finishers who had been specializing in front doors for other work, but it left Buster holding a bagful of complaints from men who didn't like to work in the first place and now felt that they had been tricked and overburdened.

Then the engineers decided to shake up yet another operation. Two men put the castiron hooks and chains on the cars on Buster's line: one hooked up the front ends, the other the back, so that each car could be swung into the air at the end of the line and floated into the bonderizing booth to be rust-proofed. These two men also fitted on the lighter hooks on which the doors were hung for both station wagons and panel trucks. Since their work was heavy (the hooks and chains weighed about twenty pounds apiece) but so unskilled that it would be learned in two minutes by anyone with two hands and a strong back, there was a tremendous turnover on the job.

Now, however, the experts decided that the smaller hooks could be installed at the very beginning of the line by the man who gunned the door plates and had been clocked as having time to spare. This left only the big chains and hooks to be attached. It was the engineers' opinion that this could be done by one man instead of two if he would pick up one hook with each hand and mount the line between two jobs, doing first the back of one car, then the front of the car directly behind it on the line.

They explained it to Buster before the day's siren blew, hitching up their belts beneath their white shirts and surrounding him aggressively, as if to shut off his complaints.

He said formally, "Those hooks get heavy."

"We've weighed them. They're well within the—"

"The point is that they get heavier as the day goes along. Especially if you ask a man to climb up and down with one in each hand. They're used to resting them against the stomach. You can't do that if you have to pick up two at a time."

"Let's try it," the little time-and-motion man said with finality. He raised his voice as the starting siren went off. "Where's your hook man?"

"I haven't got any yet. They took them both off to work in the duck pond yesterday. Horton is going to bring me a couple replacements from the employment office in a little while. Any minute."

They glanced at their stop watches. "We'll be back."

Then Horton, the production man, five years younger than Buster but five notches higher because he had an engineering degree and also, Buster was convinced, because he was a Mason like all the big wheels, came hustling up on his wiry bowlegs, towing along two new men, one old, one young. They stood at one side, new toolboxes in their hands, trying to look unconcerned as Horton spoke to Buster.

"Here's your men. You're only supposed to have one on the hooks."

"I know."

"Use the young kid for it. He's stronger."

Buster suppressed his anger. What kind of moron did Horton take him for?

"Besides," Horton finished, "the old boy's experienced. You won't hardly have to break him in." He lifted his hand abruptly in farewell and took off, humming as he bummed a ride on a passing engineer's bike.

Buster wheeled to examine the two men and discovered that the old boy, puffy and paunchy in his turned-up new dungarees, was staring at him with his head cocked to one side. He looked familiar.

"Say," Buster said tentatively, "don't I—"

"It's Frank, Buster. Frank's the name. I used to metal-finish when you were spot-welding, remember? It's been twenty years."

"Well, I'll be damned."

They shook hands. Clasping the older man's soft, tired hand, Buster found himself wondering why a man his age had to come back to work here after all these years. A little embarrassed, he said, "Welcome back."

"Thanks. I see a lot of faces—"

"Excuse me. The line's starting up, and I've got to get this other fellow going on the hooks. Start filing on the doors with that guy in the railroad cap, will you?" Buster turned to the glum youngster, who looked as though his mother had sent him off to work against his will. "Okay, put your gloves on, fellow, and I'll show you what I want of you."

He was a tall, doughy-faced Italian, with glittering black hair that he wore very long, completely covering the tops of his ears and meeting in back in what Buster had heard described as a duck's-ass haircut. His complexion was very white and bloodless, and the back of his neck above his shirt collar was pitted with deep, black-centered acne scars. Buster was a good Catholic and believed devoutly in not judging his fellow man by background or nationality, but he could not help thinking that this one looked like those neighborhood gang-warriors that you read about in the magazines; it wouldn't be surprising if he carried a six-inch switchblade knife.

The boy observed Buster coldly saying nothing, only muttering and nodding his head when Buster asked if he understood the work. After a few minutes the boy seemed to have caught on and Buster left him.

The next time he had a chance to look over the line and see how things were going—it must have been an hour later—he saw the Italian boy all the way up the line near the platform, twenty feet past where he should have been working. He was running sweat, and his oiled hair was falling over his ears. As Buster approached, he jerked his head angrily.

"How's it going?" Buster asked.

"I ain't Superman, Mac," the boy snarled, as he flung an iron chain into the rear of a station wagon with a crash.

"You can call me Buster. I'll help you get caught up." Buster half-trotted back to the head-high stack of hooks and chains that sat on a dolly at the middle of the line. Grabbing two, he hastened back to where he had been and hopped up onto the line. Crisscrossing each other, he and the boy had soon worked their way back to the center of the line.

"There you go," Buster said. He glanced down at the figured cotton sport shirt that Agnes had given him for his birthday—it was scored with red primer and dotted at the chest with droplets of sweat that had soaked through his undershirt. "Let's try to keep caught up, okay?"

"Christ," the boy said, and unloosed a torrent of obscene abuse on the factory and the entire auto industry. "I come in here to make a living, not to kill myself."

If the boy had looked and talked a bit differently, Buster would not only have sympathized with him, but would have tried to do something to lighten his load. As it was, he felt that the boy was swearing at him but didn't have the courage to do it directly. In the circumstances it was impossible to explain to the boy that he was being used as a guinea pig.

"Do the best you can," he said coldly. "You're entitled to twelve minutes' rest period before lunch. I'll check with the relief man to make sure you get your break."

"If I live that long," the boy replied.

Buster turned his back on him and sought out the relief man, who was doing Orrin's work.

"When Orrin comes back," he said, "get the new kid that's on the hooks. I don't want him griping that he didn't get his relief."

"When! When! How do I know when?" cried the relief man angrily. "Orrin cut his hand, he went to the hospital. He may be gone an hour. You want me to walk off his job here to make that kid happy?"

"Don't talk foolish. Stick with it, I'll see what I can do."

"You better not worry about the kid," the relief man warned as he bent to his work. "Better worry about all the guys that'll be on your neck for their relief if Orrin doesn't get back soon."

What the line needed, of course, was a utility man in addition to a relief man for just such situations, a good all-around man who could be slipped into any vacant slot in case of emergency. But the wheels wouldn't authorize the extra name on the payroll; they insisted that it was part of Buster's job to train up his men to cut down on accidents and minimize emergency situations.

Buster would just as soon have pitched in and given his men their relief himself, but it was against the union contract for a boss to touch a tool.

His men were not only working at a hard, steady pace themselves, but whenever they had a chance they lent a hand to the new man, handing him hooks and chains from the pile, sometimes doing a job themselves.

The boy was sweating furiously, trotting, lifting, cursing steadily. One of the tails of his gaudy shirt had worked up in back and hung free over his trousers, which were, Buster now noticed, an old pair of dress pants cut in zoot style, billowing at the thigh and so tight at the cuff that his ankles seemed bound with bicycle clips. For some reason these draggy pants, which would have been at home in a candy store or a cheap saloon, not here where men were busy working hard, infuriated Buster. Still, he knew that he was being unfair, and he stepped back out into the aisle to see if he could spot the two engineers. Once they saw that they had miscalculated, he would be able to ask for another man.

But they were nowhere in sight. Naturally. He swore to himself and hurried back to the boy, who raised his head and yelled, "This isn't work, it's slavery!"

Two of the men on the line looked up and laughed. There was no question about whose side they were on, and it made Buster feel as though in some subtle, indefinable way they were betraying him by siding with such a punk.

Nevertheless, he grasped one of the elephant-tusk hooks and was preparing to help the boy to catch up once again when he heard his name being called. He looked up and saw Hawks standing fifty feet ahead, one hand hooked in the fancy woven belt which he claimed a lady friend had given him, the other hand waving imperiously for Buster to hurry. Above his brilliant tie of stars, planets, and asteroids whirling dizzily against the white universe of his shirt, his mournful hangdog face was set for unpleasantness.

"Let's tighten up a little, what do you say," he said. "See if you can get your boys to understand that we've got to meet competition. Jobs like this one here can't go through."

It was true. There was an unchalked dent down low, below the taillight; but since it had slipped by Pop the inspector it was understandable that it should have been missed. Buster looked at the front of the job: it bore Orrin's initials. He put two fingers to his mouth and whistled up the relief man who was doing Orrin's work.

With deliberate slowness the relief man straightened up from his job and slouched forward to meet him. "Listen, Buster," he said flatly, ignoring the supervisor, who did not move but simply turned his back on them, "they're coming fast, and I got a lot of work. Can't your pick-up men take care of the little things we miss?"

"This isn't little." Buster pointed to the dent with his cigar. "You ought to know better than to let a job like this go by. You're getting a dime an hour extra for being a relief man. You want to keep on getting that dime, you better do the work right. Come on, clean it up and get back to your place."

The relief man flashed him a look of pure hatred. But he said nothing, instead dropped to one knee, inserted his arm with the file inside the taillight hole, and began to rap rhythmically at the dent. Buster stood watching him for a moment. He could think of nothing to say that would take the sting out of what he had just said, and so at last he turned to Hawks.

"I'm shorthanded today," he said to the supervisor, "and they're trying to make the hooks a one-man job, and—"

"Shorthanded? Didn't they give you two new men? I saw the schedule sheet myself."

"Yes, but one is going to metal-finish. He's too old for the hooks anyway, and the other one is breaking his hump. He just can't keep up."

"I know you like to stick up for your men." Hawks pulled a pendulous earlobe and stared at him sadly. "That's fine. Now try sticking up for me a little. I've got to turn out three hundred and fifty units before the night shift comes on. Think about that. Next time you see Horton, give him your complaint."

Thus dismissed, Buster returned to the line, grabbed a hook, and hopped up to give the new boy a hand.

The boy was a mess. He had not put on an apron, and his front was splotched with red primer dust. His face was blotched with red, and with hatred and self-pity, and he muttered to himself unceasingly as he strove.

"Tell you something," [Buster] said to the boy as they stood back to back on the moving line, working together. "I know what it is to work. Don't think I don't sympathize with you. I used to work. I worked for sixteen years before they made me a boss. And I had plenty of rough days like you're having now. It's all part of the game."

"Sixteen *years*," the boy sneered incredulously. "You must have been some quick thinker."

Buster clamped his jaws shut tight. He jumped off the line and lifted up another hook. Panting a little now, he said, "Jobs weren't as easy to come by in those days as they are now. If you made a living you were grateful, and you hung on."

"Times have changed."

"They sure have," Buster said. "But I haven't. I started working when I was fourteen, and I worked too long and too hard to forget what it's like. That's why I feel I'm still just one of the boys in spite of the fact that I've been a boss for nine years."

"Who did you get to know after those sixteen

years?" the boy asked insolently. "Or did you just wait for somebody to die off?"

Buster bit hard on his cigar. "You want to get anyplace in this world," he said coldly, "you better learn to smarten up."

The boy laughed as he flung back his long black hair. "I was *born* smarter," he replied, "than some of the characters around this dump."

When the siren blew for lunch, Buster had no appetite. He bought a bowl of stew and a cup of coffee and sat down at his customary place with a foreman from the grinding booth and Halstein, boss inspector.

The grinding booth foreman looked at him sympathetically. "Tough day today, Buster?" he demanded between gulps of soup.

Buster opened his mouth to tell them and then thought better of it. He crumbled a cracker into the stew and shrugged. "The usual."

Then Halstein, who Buster suspected stood in well with the Masonic clique, started to talk about a three-dimensional kite his boy had built, and Buster hardly listened. His eyes were searching for the little time-study man, who slipped in and out of the cafeteria like a ghost. At last Buster spotted him, two minutes before they had to return. He hastened over to him.

"You fellows changed that operation into a one-man deal on my line," he said quickly, "but you never came around to check on it."

"Tied up," the little engineer said tersely.

"Now look, it's just too much for one man. I'm short-handed as it is. I told you before—"

"We'll get to you this afternoon. Keep your shirt on."

How could anyone on the outside know how it was to be caught in the middle between zoot-suiters and college hot shots? Sometimes, he thought, the advantages didn't outweigh the headaches, not at all; and he could understand the men who had turned down chances to be made foremen, or who had given up foremen's jobs and returned to production, where they were covered by the unions and had no such worries, or had transferred into plant protection, where all they had to do was wear uniforms and look important. At his desk he lit a fresh cigar and, as the line started to roll once again, busied himself with the attendance sheets that had to be cleaned up. He had been at it for perhaps ten minutes and was just about finished when something, some instinctive feeling that all was not right, made him swivel about and stare.

For a moment everything looked normal. The line was going at a fairly fast clip and his men, their stomachs full, were working hard and steady. Then he realized what was wrong. None of the cars, not one of them, had any hooks on it—and the new boy was nowhere in sight.

His heart hammering, Buster leaped forward and took the nearest man by the arm.

"Where's that hook man? The new one?"

The metal finisher had an odd glint in his eye. "I haven't seen him since lunch."

"Why didn't you tell me?" Then seeing the man's face stiffen, "Never mind. Run down there and tell the relief man to come up here."

Without waiting, Buster grabbed two hooks and hurled them onto the station wagons before which he had been standing. If he did not get caught up within a very few minutes, the cars reaching the head of the line without hooks would not be able to swing off; they would pile up, and the entire line would have to be stopped. And it was on his neck.

Blindly, cursing the missing boy, Buster flung himself at the hooks and fastened them to the cars, bending over double in his haste. The blood rushed to his head and the vein in his left temple began to pound. He finished two jobs and ran headlong back to the stack of hooks for two more, his key ring falling from his pocket as he ran.

Buster did not dare to stop to hunt for help. As he passed another of his men kneeling with his file, he cried out, "Where's the new guy?"

And this man, too, grinned, "I hear he didn't even punch out. Just hit the road."

Trying to keep from growing panicky, Buster clambered stiffly onto the line with the two hooks and tried to consider how he could get word to supervision that he needed help quickly. A glance up and down showed no one in sight. His own men looked as though they could hardly keep their faces straight.

"I wouldn't mind," he said to the man kneeling below him, "if he'd only told me." He tried to keep his voice casual. "It's a free country. Nobody can make you work if you don't want to. But to sneak out without letting anybody know."

"It just shows you," the crouching man yelled up at him. "Even a crummy job like that, a job nobody wants and any dope can do, you got to treat a man right to do it right or you can't build cars."

"You're not telling me anything I don't know," Buster cried angrily, as he straightened his back and scrambled off the line. "All I ask is my men play square with me like I try to play square with—"

At that instant a booming crash rang out over all the other noises of the body shop. Everyone looked up at once, bewildered. The crash was followed by a horrible sound of rending metal. Then Buster knew what had happened. He was petrified inside with the positive knowledge that more was to follow; his tongue was frozen into silence; but his body continued to move automatically. Yes, it came again, another crash like the first, followed by more rhythmic thuds, until everyone on the line realized what was happening.

The Italian boy had taken his vengeance before running away. He had attached the hooks and chains of his last few jobs lopsidedly, in some cases only fastening one side, so that now, an hour after he had escaped, the cars tilted as they entered the narrow bonderizing booth, and, hanging off balance, crashed back and forth, back and forth, against the sides of the booth, metal smashing against metal as the cars were systematically pounded out of shape.

When the third car had begun to rocket back and forth in the booth, Buster, the sweat streaming down his cheeks, saw Hawks and Horton and two other white-shirted executives from quality control running down the aisle and clambering up the catwalk to the little metal door in the center of the bonderizing booth. Then a battery-powered scooter rolled up and the assistant plant superintendent hopped off, followed by three overalled maintenance men. Now that it was too late, the reinforcements had arrived.

Up and down the line his men, looking like strangers, were openly grinning. With every booming thud, every tearing sound, their grins grew wider. They didn't care that hundreds of dollars in time and labor were going down the drain; it amused them. They didn't care that the smashed hulks would have to be hauled out of the booth and dragged to a corner; they were already calculating the overtime they would earn repairing these wrecks. They didn't care that he was still hanging hooks, with the weight of them starting to stab in his groin, unable to summon help from the bosses, who now had something more important to keep them occupied. They thought he had it coming, and Buster, his heart wrenched in his chest, stared at their grinning faces and wondered how it could be that people who worked together could have so little human feeling. Don't they know I couldn't help it? he asked himself.

"Hey, Buster!" one of them called out. "Some symphony, eh?"

"Laugh," he replied grimly, "We may all get laid off for this."

"Say, Buster—how does it feel to work like a dog? Does it take you back to the old days? The good old days?"

Tossing a heavy hook contemptuously into the rear of a station wagon, he faced them out and said coolly, around his cigar, "I've worked harder, in my time. I never asked one man, never in my life, to do a job I wouldn't do."

The cigar tasted rancid in his gummy mouth, but it was a visible proof that he had not capitulated, that he was simply handling a passing crisis; so he refused to throw it away, or even to take it out of his mouth while he worked. But he could not prevent the sweat from pouring down his body, from forming huge, dark, telltale moons under the armpits of his sport shirt, from plastering the front of the shirt to his chest, from soaking through his slacks at the base of his spine, from dripping down his forehead onto the rims of his glasses, smudging and steaming the lenses.

He hated to do it, but half-blinded by his own sweat, he had to take off the glasses and stuff them into his shirt pocket. In a way it was worse than giving up the cigar would have been. Without the glasses he felt naked and exposed, and he knew that his face took on a stupid, blinking expression when his nearsighted eyes tried to adjust themselves to an uncorrected world.

On one of the passing panel trucks someone had scrawled in huge letters, no doubt with the chalk that he himself had handed out, *Too Many Chiefs, Not Enough Indians!*

Oh, they'd have something to talk about all the way home, and even after they got home—how the boss had been humiliated and made to work like a dog.

I'm through, he said to himself; I'll turn in my time and ask for a transfer; I can make my living without having to take this. Glancing down at the red primer dust which covered him, he could already hear his wife's voice added to all the rest.

"Kind of rough, hey, Buster?" It was Orrin, the only man on the line with a perfect attendance record; the only one who really liked hard work and hard pressure. "They won't hold you responsible. It wasn't your fault that young jerk ducked out."

Buster mumbled a reply. He was unsure whether these first words of sympathy he'd had all day were sincere or whether Orrin, having gotten wind of his possible promotion, was starting to suck around.

At that moment Horton and the quality-control man came over from the bonderizing booth. They seemed to think the scene was pretty funny, too, and they stood there, grinning, watching him sweat.

"You certainly must have browbeat that kid to make him walk out after four hours," Horton said. "Man, what a slave driver."

"I understand Accounting is going to bill you for the prorated extra labor cost on those four banged-up jobs," the quality-control man said.

"Very funny," Buster snarled. "Are you going to get me a man for this job or not?"

The quality-control man turned to Horton. "Didn't you hear them say Buster was going to have to work it off until he'd made up for his sins?"

"All right, all right," Horton said, smiling at his Masonic buddy, then turning to Buster, "Come on down off that line, they're getting you a replacement. You look like hell if I may say so, like Before in the Before and After ads."

It was true. Buster stared at himself in the washroom mirror when he had gone in to clean up for a minute, after they'd provided him with another man to finish out the day. He looked like Before, but he felt like After, long After. And what would you do if you threw it over? Who could you tell to go to hell? Yourself? That nameless herd who came and went like stockyard cattle? That clique of Masons who boosted each other and each other's relatives into all the key jobs, and would maybe one day make him an assistant supervisor, or a foreman over the body shop foremen, just to satisfy the Michigan crowd that they were bringing up men from the ranks?

When the day was over at last, he sat down for a while in the body shop office and went over with Hawks and several others the series of events that had been so costly to him and to production, but wouldn't even rate a footnote in the history of the corporation. They gave him to understand that it was a closed issue, dead and forgotten, if he would see to it in the future that such things wouldn't happen again.

3 The Corporate Framework

Since most companies and a great many other types of organizations are corporations, understanding of the corporate form is important in understanding the environment within which management must operate.

The first article in this chapter discusses the theoretical bases of the corporate form, and the next four deal with the mechanics of its operation.

At the top of the corporation is, of course, the board of directors, which is elected by the owners, the stockholders, but in practice is generally a self-perpetuating body since the directors currently serving nominate the new board members and the nominations are usually tantamount to election. The GM–Du Pont correspondence indicates some of the considerations that may be taken into account in the nominations.

Theoretically, of course, the directors are supposed to manage the corporation, even though they may delegate much of the actual management work to the president and the other corporate officers. In the past it was often customary for the board to do no managing at all, merely meet to rubber-stamp the recommendations of the chief executive. This situation is changing, however, as the next article explains. Further, this article points out, there are some who believe that the board's traditional role as representative of the stockholders—and only of the stockholders—may be undergoing a rather important change.

In any case, the stockholders have little or no power to oust directors, although the proxy fights publicized in the newspapers might make it appear that they do. The next article, which deals with proxy contests, explains why this is so. And some observers believe that the distance of the common stockholder from the seats of power is becoming ever greater. This viewpoint is expounded in the extract from Adolf A. Berle's book *Power Without Property.*

Finally, although the board of directors has great theoretical power and sometimes chooses to use it, the real power in the corporation is generally exercised by the chief executive, who is usually the president, although he may be the chairman of the board in some cases. The last article in this section deals with the job of the chief executive.

The development of theories of the corporation is more than an intellectual exercise, for the way a corporation is defined in part determines the powers that may be granted to it. For example, once the corporation was accepted as a "person" (even though a fictitious one), it was easy for courts to grant it many of the privileges normally attaching to individual citizens.

Charles C. Abbott, former dean of the Graduate School of Business of the University of Virginia, outlined the main theories of the corporation while a member of the economics department of Harvard University. The extract is drawn from a monograph that he prepared for his students.

Theories of the Corporation

Charles C. Abbott

Since the time of Aristotle it has been observed that man is a gregarious animal, and that his instinct for group activity leads him to many and varied forms of association. But few if any of the ways in which he organizes his enterprises are more widespread, possess a greater range of purpose or boast a longer lineage than that known as the "corporation." The ancient world contained numerous institutions of this character.

The history of the Middle Ages is [also] filled with the activities of corporate bodies. The convents and monasteries, the cathedral chapters, the various religious orders and many of the hospitals and universities were all organized and looked upon by the law as ecclesiastical corporations. In the secular field the boroughs and towns and the guilds of merchants and artisans existed as "bodies corporate." The great trading companies which arose at the end of the Middle Ages and around which centered so much of the economic history of the sixteenth and seventeenth centuries also took this form.

In the modern world churches, schools, colleges, hospitals, asylums, clubs, business enterprises and subordinate political bodies are all organized as corporations. The range of their objects is almost co-extensive with that of human interests, and almost every activity of any individual man is influenced in some degree by the corporations with which, one way or another, he is connected.

Moreover, in contemporary society the importance which corporations have for the sovereign power seems to be nearly as great as that which they have for the individual citizen. Directly or indirectly much of the revenue of the state is drawn from business corporations. Many governmental functions are carried on by municipalities and other types of public corporations, and the sinews of war, like the peaceful needs of the citizens, are mainly furnished by private commercial and financial enterprises of this type.

What, then, is meant by the word "corporation"?

Perhaps the primary feature of a corporation is that it exists to further certain purposes, particularly purposes which those persons who have associated themselves with it—usually voluntarily—would find it difficult or impossible to achieve merely as individuals. In the case of that legal curiosity, the "corporation sole," which contains only one member, the interest and purpose is that which the member has by virtue of his position or office, rather than as an individual.

In any case, whether the corporation is composed of one or many persons, its members possess as members a position in society at large and a relationship to the sovereign power which they would not have if the corporation did not exist. Hence, as has often been noted, it follows that a corporation has a personality of its own distinct from the personalities which compose it, a "group personality" different from and greater than its constituent individualities in the sense that the whole is greater than the sum of the parts. Since the group, as a group, can continue irrespective of a change in its membership, and since the interests which called the corporation into being are not dependent upon the continued membership of any particular individual, a corporation achieves a certain immortality separate from the mortality of its constituent parts. This fact is recognized in the legal

From *The Rise of the Business Corporation* (Edwards Brothers, Inc., Ann Arbor, Mich., 1936).

doctrine that a corporation "never dies." Finally, it may be noted that since the members of a corporation act in their corporate capacity as a unit—that is, like a single, natural person—legal problems have always arisen regarding the relationship of this unit with other members of society and with the sovereign power. In short, there has been the difficulty of reconciling the fact that this group or joint person performs many of the same acts and establishes many of the same legal connections that a single, natural person does. These problems have been handled differently at different times, and various powers and degrees of "legal competency" have been bestowed upon corporations by particular theories. But however these matters have been treated, it has never been possible to ignore them. For it has always been characteristic of corporations to possess and represent group interests, to have an existence independent of their individual members, and to act in many ways like single, natural persons. The essence of the corporate concept is contained in these features, and they indicate why this form of organization has been perpetually useful in the conduct of human activities.

When Blackstone wrote in the eighteenth century he stated that the inseparable incidents and powers of all "corporations aggregate," that is, corporations with more than one member, were: to have perpetual succession; to sue and be sued and to grant and receive by the corporate name; to have a common seal; and to make by-laws. The characteristics of the typical corporation have changed somewhat since Blackstone's time, and the business corporation with its special problems is largely a modern development, but the principles which he set forth to a large extent still hold.

The Corporate Charter

It is now generally agreed that corporations are created by the state, either by special enactment or through the medium of a general incorporating statute—that is, a statute which permits a group of men to incorporate themselves by compliance with its provisions—and that the charter granted by the sovereign authority is legal evidence of its incorporation. The charter states the name and purpose of the corporation, gives it a place of residence and enumerates the powers granted to it. One of the main privileges bestowed is the power to "take in succession," the ability to continue in existence in spite of a withdrawal of members or a change in membership.

The body of privileges, taken as a whole, affords the corporation a "legal personality," that is, an ability to enter legal relationships. The chief of these privileges are those which permit a corporation to purchase and hold land and chattels, to make contracts, to sue and be sued, and to have and act under a common seal, though the use of a common seal has largely fallen into disuse since evidence of corporate unity is now established in other ways. The liability of corporations for torts and crimes of their agents is usually not specified in the charters, although it is recognized in the courts.

In addition to these general provisions, the typical charter of the modern business corporation describes the position and responsibilities of the various participants. The stockholders' liability for debts of the corporation is usually limited to the amount of their original investment, and they are permitted to transfer their shares freely, so long as the corporation is notified and a record of the transfers kept in its books. The way in which the corporation is to be managed is defined. Not only is the corporation given the power to pass by-laws which are binding on its members, but the manner in which directors are to be elected and officers appointed is set forth and the various matters which the officers, directors and stockholders are to control are determined. Very often the issue of different classes of securities is authorized, and the rights and privileges attaching to each are established. Although all these matters and numerous others are often treated specifically in the charter, in many cases they are left to the decision of the directors.

When all these qualities are considered in their entirety it is obvious that the corporation is a particularly favored form of enterprise, and that the social implications of the powers which it possesses extend very far. It has, in fact, very much the same freedom of purpose that pertains to an individual person. Moreover, the "legal personality" with which the law invests it enables it to pursue these purposes with nearly the same liberty of action as that of the individual man. Previous to the passage of the general incorporating statutes the state scrutinized with considerable care the charters which it granted, but the passage of such acts has permitted the formation of corporate bodies by mere compliance with certain legal formalities, so that a corporation can be erected with almost the facility with which an individual proprietorship can be undertaken. But if a corporation has virtually the same freedom and legal competency as an individual man, it can, because of its power to "take in succession" and particularly because of its ability to raise very large amounts of capital, engage in undertakings impossible for a single person. It can embark upon ventures of a magnitude that would overwhelm a solitary entrepreneur, and it can form plans and initiate policies for a period in the future much longer than that practicable for any single business man.

The business corporation is, in one sense, merely a particular kind of business unit, yet it has a further economic significance. Admirably adapted to aid the exploitation of technological improvements and the development of large-scale production and management, it has, in the course of the Industrial Revolution, become the legal form, the social foundation upon which rests the great industrial structure of the modern world. In reaching this position it has acquired wealth and power greater than any one man can, in actuality, understand or control. At the same time it has become singularly independent both of the sovereign power which created it and of the men who compose it, curiously free of control from either direction. Intermediate between the citizen and the state, business corporations are today great immortal and autonomous entities in the economic structure, impersonal and independent.

The "Fiction" Theory

In Anglo-American law the "fiction" or the "fiction-concession" theory has been the dominant doctrine. This theory is not so much a single immutable dogma as it is a body of closely related ideas [and] the steadily increasing complexity of the corporate form has brought elaborations and varied applications of the fiction theory.

The fiction appears to be in the fact that the law treats a group of persons, organized as a corporation, as if it were a natural person. But although this group is not a natural person, the rights and duties which the law bestows upon it are equally bestowed by the law upon natural persons.

Whether the legal personality accorded corporations should or should not be considered "fictitious" would seem to depend upon whether such groups are judged proper legal subjects and capable of legal relationships without the permission of the state. The presumption in the fiction theory has been that they are not, and that this legal personality is a "concession" from the sovereign power.

It has, at times, been alleged that the fiction and concession theories, although merged in Anglo-American law, are of different origin. [But] if the state, through its handmaiden the law, chooses to regard certain groups of persons in a particular way, as a single, so-called "fictitious person," and consequently accords them privileges in conformance with this view, to all intents and purposes the state has designated this group as one to which special powers have been granted. It makes no difference whether this group is called a figment of the judicial imagination or the recipient of special favors from a munificent sovereign.

The "Real" and Contract Theories

The Anglo-American theory of the corporation has not gone unchallenged. Within the last fifty years at least two theories have been brought forward as alternatives—the "real" or "organic" theory, and the "individualistic" or "contract" theory.

The real theory has been expounded in considerable detail by various political theorists, of whom Otto von Gierke, often considered its originator, is perhaps the best known. He found in two concepts of old German law—the "Genossenschaft" or fellowship, and the "Gesammt Hand" or group hand—the basis of his theory of corporations. The fellowship is to be defined as a group of persons with a will independent and separate from that of its members; the group hand constitutes a group of persons with mutual rights and duties who are bound together by a legal tie. Combining these elements Gierke evolved his organic theory.

This theory develops a juristic formula for the interpretation of human association in which the "group person" is substituted for the "fictitious person." In this doctrine associations or "group persons" are conceived as real, as true "social facts," not as imaginary or fictitious entities created by the state. They are thought of as possessing personalities and wills entirely distinct from those of their members, and as being competent of themselves to hold property or to take legal actions. They are the result of "historical or social action," and are produced by the conscious acts of will of individual persons who bind themselves together by some sort of contractual relationship. As it has been succinctly put, corporations for Gierke are "living organisms, not legal mechanisms."

Since the state does not, and cannot in this theory, create such groups, they are believed to be proper legal subjects in their own right which the law must recognize.

Gierke believed that he had entirely abandoned the fiction theory, but it has seemed to critics of his doctrines that when the relations of the state and the corporation which he predicates are carefully studied his legal "recognition" is closely akin to the "concession" embodied in the fiction theory. Although according to his real theory the state is forced to recognize corporations, in performing this function it can, and indeed must, determine which are and which are not legal associations, it must limit the field of corporate activity and it must formulate the rights and duties of the participating members. Since in Gierke's doctrine there is no way whereby the state can be forced to give this recognition or to grant it in conformance with any set standards, his critics have thought that "recognition" is, in substance, merely a grant of privileges.

The "individualistic" or "contract" theory has as its background the individualistic treatment of corporate bodies by the Roman law, and for its immediate support the attempts of modern lawyers and political theorists to deal with the situation created by the recent great development of business corporations. Like Gierke's doctrine its purpose is to treat corporate problems in a more realistic fashion than does the fiction theory. Although this approach has been mainly expounded by lawyers, its exposition has been much influenced by sociological considerations.

This theory regards a corporation essentially as a business unit, not as a mystic entity. It looks upon a corporation as an association of human beings, bound together by a contract, with attributes—such as their relative voting strength within the corporation, their wealth, their knowledge or lack of knowledge of commercial affairs and their connections with other business firms—which affect their actions within the corporate body, and consequently the activities of the corporation itself. The corporation is not conceived as possessing a personality or a will of its own separate from those of its members; and the rights and duties of the participants in the enterprise are considered as having been granted to them as a group of individuals rather than as having been bestowed upon an independent entity to which they belong. The position of the corporation, in short, is reduced to that of a mere business arrangement, a technical device of the law.

Following are extracts from the corporate charter or certificate of incorporation filed by International Business Machines Corporation with the N.Y. Department of State in 1958, as amended through May 9, 1968. IBM was, of course, incorporated long before 1958, but corporations often find it necessary to file new certificates because changing conditions require new provisions.

The certificate includes eighteen articles, only some of which are reprinted here. The first merely states the name of the corporation, and the second defines the scope of its activities, which—as in the case of most corporations nowadays—is very broad. The extract starts with the third article.

But, like the constitution of a nation or a state, the charter lays down general principles only. Hence, it is supplemented by a set of bylaws, which may list the duties or powers of the board and its committees and those of the corporate officers and specify such things as the dates of the annual meetings.

The Corporate Charter

Third: The aggregate number of shares which the Corporation shall have authority to issue is one hundred twenty million (120,000,000) shares of capital stock of the par value of Five Dollars ($5.00) per share.

Fourth: The shares of the Corporation are not to be classified.

Subject to the provisions of the By-laws, as from time to time amended, with respect to the closing of the transfer books and the fixing of a record date, each share of the capital stock of the Corporation shall be entitled to one vote on all matters requiring a vote of the stockholders, and shall be entitled to receive such dividends, in cash, securities or property, as may from time to time be declared by the Board of Directors after provision for any reserves as working capital or for any other lawful purpose.

Fifth: The town and county within the State in which the office of the Corporation is to be located is the Town of North Castle, County of Westchester.

Sixth: The duration of the Corporation is to be perpetual.

Seventh: The number of directors of the Corporation shall be as provided in its By-laws, but not less than 9 nor more than 21.

[The eighth article lists the names and addresses of the directors for the first year, and the ninth gives the names and addresses of the subscribers to the certificate and the number of shares of stock each has agreed to take.]

Tenth: The Board of Directors may designate from their number an executive committee and one or more other committees, each of which shall consist of three or more directors, which committees shall, in the intervals between meetings of the Board of Directors and to the extent provided in the By-laws or the resolution of the Board of Directors establishing such a committee, have all the authority and may exercise all the powers of the Board of Directors in the management of the business and affairs of the Corporation to the extent lawful under the Business Corporation Law of the State of New York.

The Board of Directors shall from time to time decide whether and to what extent and at what times and under what conditions and requirements the accounts and books of the Corporation, or any of them, except the stock book, shall be open to the inspection of the stockholders, and no stockholder shall have any right to inspect any books or documents of the Corporation except as conferred by statute of the State of New York or authorized by the Board of Directors.

The Board of Directors may from time to time fix, determine and vary the amount of the working capital of the Corporation; may determine what part, if any, of surplus shall be declared in dividends and paid to the stockholders; may determine the time or times for the declaration and payment of dividends, the amount thereof and whether they are to be in cash, securities or property; may direct and determine the use and disposition of any surplus or net profits over and above the capital, and in its discretion may use or apply any such a surplus or accumulated profits in the purchase or acquisition of bonds or other pecuniary obligations of the Corporation to such extent, and in such manner and upon such terms as the Board of Directors may deem expedient.

Directors shall be stockholders, subject to the power of the Board of Directors from time to time to prescribe a reasonable time after qualification within which newly elected directors must become stockholders.

Each director, in consideration of his serving as such, shall be entitled to receive from the Corporation such amount per annum or such fees for attendance at meetings of the stockholders or of the Board of Directors or of committees of the Board of Directors, or both, as the Board of Directors shall from time to time determine, together with reimbursement for the reasonable expenses incurred by him in connection with the performance of his duties. Nothing herein contained shall preclude any director from serving the Corporation or its subsidiaries in any other capacity and receiving compensation therefor.

Eleventh: In the absence of fraud, any director of the Corporation individually, or any firm or association of which he is a member, or any corporation of which he is an officer, director, stockholder or employee or in which he is pecuniarily or otherwise interested, may be a party to, or may be pecuniarily or otherwise interested in, any contract, transaction or act of the Corporation, and

1 Such contract, transaction or act shall not be in any way invalidated or otherwise affected by that fact,
2 Any such director of the Corporation may be counted in determining the existence of a quorum at any meeting of the Board of Directors or of any committee thereof which shall authorize any such contract, transaction or act, but may not vote thereon, and
3 No director of the Corporation shall be liable to account to the Corporation for any profit realized by him from or through any such contract, transaction or act;

provided, however, that if any such director of the Corporation is so interested either individually or as a member of a firm or association or as the holder of a majority of the stock of any class of a corporation, the contract, transaction or act shall be duly authorized or ratified by a majority of the Board of Directors who are not so interested and who know of such director's interest therein.

To the extent permitted by law, any contract, transaction or act of the Corporation or of the Board of Directors or of any committee thereof which shall be ratified, whether before or after judgment rendered in a suit with respect to such contract, transaction or act, by the holders of a majority of the capital stock of the Corporation having voting power at any annual meeting or at any special meeting called for such purpose shall be as valid and as binding as though ratified by every stockholder of the Corporation and shall constitute a complete bar to any such suit or to any claim of execution in respect of any such judgment; provided, however, that any failure of the stockholders to approve or ratify such contract, transaction or act, when and if submitted, shall not be deemed in any way to invalidate the same or to deprive the Corporation, its directors, officers or employees of its or their right to proceed with such contract, transaction or act.

Twelfth: The Corporation may indemnify any person made, or threatened to be made, a party to any action, suit or proceeding by reason of the fact that he, his testator or intestate, is or was a director or officer of the Corporation, or of any other corporation which he served as such at the request of the Corporation, against the reasonable expenses, including attorneys' fees, actually and necessarily incurred by him in connection with the defense of such action, suit or proceeding, or in connection with any appeal therein, and including the cost of court approved settlements, to the extent and in the manner prescribed by the Business Corporation Law of the State of New York. Such right of indemnification shall not be deemed exclusive of any other rights to which such director or officer may be entitled apart from the foregoing provisions.

The Board of Directors in its discretion shall have power on behalf of the Corporation to indemnify any person, other than a director or officer, made a party to any action, suit or proceeding by reason of the fact that he, his testator or intestate, is or was an employee of the Corporation.

Thirteenth: The Secretary of State of the State of New York is designated as the agent of the Corporation upon whom process in any action or proceeding against it may be served, and the address within the State to which the Secretary of State shall mail a copy of process in any action or proceeding against the Corporation which may be served upon him is Armonk, New York 10504.

Stockholders select directors at the annual meeting, and the instrument used is the proxy card, commonly called "a proxy," although the actual proxy is the person or persons whom the stockholder appoints to vote his shares for him. In most cases, the persons who are appointed proxies may use their own judgment in voting the shares on matters that come before the annual meeting, although the slate of directors is always presented for a direct vote, and the bylaws of the corporation may require that the stockholders vote directly on certain other matters.

The proxy card shown contains a special proposition on which the stockholders were asked to vote directly: the 1969 Key Employees' Stock Option Plan. This is discussed in the proxy statement which follows. (A proxy card is always accompanied by a notice of the annual meeting and a proxy statement.)

Sometimes the special proposals submitted to the stockholders are made by the directors. In other cases, they may be made by individual stockholders. In the latter instance, they must by law be included in the proxy statement even though the directors disapprove of them.

The Proxy Card

SUN CHEMICAL CORPORATION—STOCKHOLDER'S PROXY

The undersigned hereby appoints *Norman E. Alexander*, *Stuart Z. Krinsly* and *Ralph S. Stillman*, or any one of them, proxies for the undersigned, with power of substitution, hereby revoking any proxy heretofore given, to vote all the stock of Sun Chemical Corporation which the undersigned is entitled to vote at the Annual Meeting of Stockholders to be held at the office of the Company at 750 Third Avenue, New York, New York, on April 17, 1969 at 11 A.M. and any adjournment thereof, with all the powers the undersigned would possess if then and there personally present and the undersigned authorizes and instructs said proxies to vote as follows:

(A) In the election of directors unless a checkmark is made in this box ☐;

(B) IN FAVOR OF ☐ AGAINST ☐ the proposal to adopt the 1969 Key Employees' Stock Option Plan set forth in Appendix A to the accompanying proxy statement; and

(C) In their discretion, upon any other matters properly coming before the meeting.

IF NO INSTRUCTION TO THE CONTRARY IS INDICATED, THE SHARES REPRESENTED HEREBY WILL BE VOTED IN THE ELECTION OF DIRECTORS AND IN FAVOR OF PROPOSAL (B).

(*continued, and to be signed on other side*)

Dated: . . . ., 1969

. . . .

Please date and sign as name or names appear hereon. Executors, administrators, trustees, etc. should so indicate when signing. A corporation should sign by duly authorized officer.

Important: This Proxy is solicited by the Management. Please sign and return in the enclosed envelope.

Reverse side.

Below is a part of the proxy statement that accompanied the card shown. Following the first two paragraphs, there is information on the nominees for directors (not reprinted here). This includes their positions, the number of shares of common stock each holds, and their remuneration. The proposition regarding the key employees' stock option plan, on which the stockholders have been asked to vote, is then explained, as can be seen. (A more detailed explanation is given in an appendix, not reprinted here.)

The Proxy Statement

SUN CHEMICAL CORPORATION

Proxy Statement

This statement is furnished in connection with the solicitation of proxies by the management of Sun Chemical Corporation to be voted at the annual meeting of stockholders of the Company referred to in the foregoing Notice. All proxies received pursuant to this solicitation will be voted and, where a choice is specified with respect to the proposal to adopt the 1969 Key Employees' Stock Option Plan, it will be voted in accordance therewith. Stockholders who execute proxies may revoke them at any time before they are voted.

The Company has outstanding 8,338 shares of $4.50 Preferred Stock, Series A, 4,147 shares of 5% Second Preferred Stock and 1,718,599 shares of Common Stock which are entitled to vote at the meeting, each share being entitled to one vote. Only stockholders of record at the close of business on March 3, 1969 will be entitled to vote at the meeting.

Adoption of 1969 Key Employees' Stock Option Plan

The Company's existing Key Employees' Stock Option Plan (the "1958 Plan"), which was adopted by the stockholders in 1958 and amended in 1960, provides for the granting of options to purchase up to 60,000 shares of Common Stock. To date, options to purchase 56,428 shares have been granted under the 1958 Plan, leaving only 3,572 shares available thereunder. In addition, options granted under the 1958 Plan after January 27, 1970 would not be "qualified stock options" as defined in Section 422 of the Internal Revenue Code and, accordingly, recipients of such options could not receive the favorable tax treatment accorded qualified stock options.

The Board of Directors has concluded that it would be in the best interests of the Company to provide a new stock option plan for the granting of options to key employees who are and will be responsible for the future growth and development of the Company. Such a plan would assist the Company in attracting and retaining competent personnel. Although the Executive Stock Purchase Plan is intended for the same general purpose, the Board believes that the intense competition for qualified executives makes it desirable for the Company to have available an additional incentive. The Board, therefore, recommends that the stockholders approve the 1969 Key Employees' Stock Option Plan set forth in Appendix A (the "1969 Plan").

General

The management does not know of any matters other than the foregoing that will be presented for consideration at the meeting. However, if other matters properly come before the meeting, it is intended that the persons named in the accompanying proxy will vote in accordance with their best judgment in such matters.

The entire cost of soliciting management proxies will be borne by the Company. Proxies will be solicited principally through the use of the mails, but directors, officers and regular employees of the Company, without additional compensation, may use their personal efforts by telephone or otherwise to obtain proxies.

Some stockholders do not bother to vote on the propositions presented to them; others vote by mailing in their proxy cards. All are, however, entitled to attend the annual meeting, where they have a chance to put questions directly to the company's management.

Some companies have millions of stockholders, and if all of them were to attend an annual meeting, there would be no auditorium big enough to hold them. However, only a handful, comparatively speaking, do attend; so this problem does not arise. Many are unable to come because the meeting is held at great distance from their homes or because they cannot spare the time from their regular occupations. Many others, for one reason or another, are not interested in taking part.

Because the attendance is so small, a number of companies now send each stockholder a report of the meeting, including a summary of the comments and questions from the floor. The piece that follows is an extract from the report of the Ford Motor Company's 1969 annual meeting.

The first part of the report presented here covers the discussion that followed presentation of the slate of directors; the second part, the discussion of a proposal routinely presented to the stockholders—the appointment of a named firm of public accountants as the company's independent auditors. Following this there is discussion of three proposals presented by individual stockholders, which were included in the proxy statement sent out in advance of the meeting. The last part of the report is devoted to general discussion and questions from the floor.

The Mr. Ford mentioned is, of course, Henry Ford II, chairman of the company's board of directors. Mr. Knudsen was president of the company at the time.

In the proxy count, the slate of directors and the independent auditors were approved by more than 99 per cent of the stockholders. The three proposals by individual stockholders were defeated by majorities of more than 95 per cent.

The Annual Meeting

Following the president's report, the 15 persons named in the proxy statement were nominated as directors and the four proposals contained in the proxy statement were presented. The questions and discussion on these matters are summarized here.

Nomination of Directors

How many directors' meetings are held, how long do they last and what fees are paid?

Mr. Ford said the Board holds 10 regular meetings a year, the average meeting lasts between two and three hours, and that each outside director is paid a fee of $10,000 a year plus $250 for each meeting attended.

Will there be any resignations from the Board in view of the agreement with the U.S. Department of Justice about eliminating certain interlocking directorships?

Mr. Ford said that the Company would have no other resignations by reason of the agreement with the Justice Department and explained that the reason Mr. Cabot did not stand for re-election was that he had reached the Board's normal retirement age.

As Mr. Murphy is chairman of Times Mirror Company, which publishes the Los Angeles Times, *as well as a Ford director, shouldn't the proxy statement say how much advertising revenue that newspaper received from Ford?*

Wright Tisdale, vice president—General Counsel, replied that everything considered material had been reported in the proxy statement. When another stockholder said he thought the amount of advertising placed in the newspaper of a company of which a Ford director is an officer was material, Mr. Ford indicated the question would be reviewed.

Proposal I—Ratification of Selection of Independent Public Accountants

Do the Company's auditors check for consistency between the financial statements contained in the Annual Report and figures contained elsewhere in the report?

Norman Bolz, a partner of Lybrand, Ross Bros. & Montgomery, replied that such a comparison is a regular part of the audit, and that the figures in the financial statements are entirely consistent with figures elsewhere in the report.

Does any firm, other than Lybrand, Ross Bros. & Montgomery or one of its associates, do any of the Company's auditing?

Mr. Bolz stated that Lybrand assumes responsibility for auditing the Company's operations worldwide and that most of Ford's foreign subsidiaries are audited by Lybrand's international firm, Coopers and Lybrand. With respect to Ford of Canada and a very few subsidiaries in other parts of the world where this is not the case, Lybrand does have supervision over the work performed by other auditing firms and regularly reviews such audits.

How long has Ford used its present independent public accountants, and is it time for a change?

Mr. Ford replied that the Company has used Lybrand since 1946, and that there is a regular rotation of the auditing staff that works on the Ford account. Because this allows for continuity, the Company believes this system is preferable to changing auditing firms.

How much were audit fees?

Vice Chairman of the Board Arjay Miller replied that Ford U.S. audit fees in 1968 totaled $610,000.

Proposal 2—Relating to Limiting Charitable, Educational and Similar Contributions by the Company

Mrs. Evelyn Y. Davis, a stockholder, introduced her proposal as presented in the proxy statement, and commented on it.

In response to her question, Mr. Ford said the Company's contributions in 1968 totaled $11.4 million, of which $10 million was contributed to Ford Motor Company Fund. Another stockholder said he opposed her proposal. He stated that contributions served the interest of the shareholder and the Company and $11 million in contributions in 1968 should be weighed against the $262 million in dividends paid to the Company's stockholders during that year.

Mr. Ford noted that a vote against the proposal was recommended by the Board of Directors for reasons given in the proxy statement.

Proposal 3—Relating to Cumulative Voting

Lewis D. Gilbert, a stockholder, introduced his proposal as presented in the proxy statement. He said cumulative voting would help to equalize the voting power of the various classes of Ford stock. He stated there was a growing recognition of the importance of cumulative voting, and said that several companies had recently adopted cumulative voting for the first time.

Mr. Ford said the Board recommended a vote against the proposal for reasons given in the proxy statement.

Proposal 4—Relating to Providing Transcripts of the Annual Meeting

Mr. Gilbert, who was also the proponent of this proposal, introduced it as presented in the proxy statement. He said editorial opinions may differ on what should be in the post-meeting report, and that by payment of a reasonable fee, a stockholder should be entitled to obtain a transcript and find out exactly what went on at the meeting.

Mr. Ford said that following the meeting, all stockholders are sent a summary report of the meeting, and that a more complete report is available on request. He said the Board recommended a vote against the proposal for the reasons given in the proxy statement.

General Discussion

While ballots were being tabulated, Mr. Ford opened the meeting to general discussion. Following is a summary of questions asked by stockholders that are believed to be of general interest, and of management's answers.

What percentage is required to call a special meeting of the shareholders?

Mr. Ford answered that 30% of the Common Stock or 30% of the Class B Stock is required.

What effect do thefts at Company locations have on profits?

Mr. Ford replied that the Company has a number of safeguards to protect against such losses, and that auditors constantly look into the matter. He said losses due to thefts last year were extremely small.

What would happen to the resale value of the Maverick if Ford were to introduce another small car next year?

Mr. Ford said the Company expects the Maverick's resale value to be high. And as to whether Ford planned to introduce another small car, he said the Company does not comment on future product plans.

In connection with reports of a dealer receiving cars with defects, is quality control adequate at Ford?

Mr. Knudsen replied that "as long as we have as many people putting automobiles together as we do today, certainly we are going to have some problems as far as quality is concerned. I personally do not believe that the quality of our products today is any worse—as a matter of fact, I believe our products are better than some time ago."

How effective is the skid-control braking system and what is its cost?

Mr. Knudsen said the system is excellent and is available on the Thunderbird and the Continental Mark III as a $197 option. He said about 1,500 such systems had been installed since first being offered on the Mark III last fall and on the Thunderbird in January.

Is there any truth to a rumor that Ford will have a relationship with a large bank, or from a bank holding company, to run a new credit card plan?

Mr. Ford replied that there is no truth to the rumor. He said the Company is running a test on a credit card system which enables customers to charge service or parts at dealerships.

How much Ford Motor Company stock is owned by The Ford Foundation?

Mr. Ford said the Ford Foundation owns about 25.8% of the total number of shares of Ford stock outstanding and that the amount is being reduced each year because the Company buys shares from the Foundation on a regular basis for corporate purposes, and the Savings and Stock Investment Plan trustee buys shares for its purposes. He said the stock held by The Ford Foundation generally cannot be voted.

What were the costs of recent labor disruptions at the Mahwah, New Jersey, plant and at facilities of Ford of Britain?

Mr. Ford said the New Jersey plant lost a second shift for a period of less than a week.

Mr. Knudsen said the disruptions at Ford of Britain had resulted in the manufacturing loss of about 73,000 units, or about $100 million in gross revenue.

Why has the Wixom, Michigan, plant experienced closings?

Mr. Knudsen said that since the beginning of the model year the Company had down time in its plants equivalent to 51 days, and that about half of that had been at Wixom since the beginning of the calendar year. He said this was not unusual, since the Wixom plant produces the Lincoln Continental, the Continental Mark III and Thunderbird luxury cars, which normally achieve their greatest sales levels in the early part of the model year.

How many recall campaigns has the Company conducted this year?

Mr. Knudsen said thus far this model year, the Company has had 12 recall campaigns involving about 214,000 units.

How is supplemental compensation determined?

Mr. Ford replied that the Compensation Committee of the Board of Directors sets the amount of supplemental compensation for each Company officer. No member of the Compensation Committee may be an officer or employe of the Company or be eligible for a supplemental compensation award.

How much did the Company spend on advertising during 1968?

Mr. Ford replied that total worldwide advertising expenditures for the Company and its subsidiaries totaled $205 million, or about 1.5% of sales.

How is Philco-Ford doing?

Mr. Ford said Philco-Ford was in the black in a good many areas, but that overall it was in the red during 1968. He said it was too early to tell how 1969 would turn out, but that the Company hoped Philco-Ford would do better than in the previous year.

What is the status of the Federal anti-trust suit which seeks to divest the Company of certain assets purchased from the Electric Autolite Company in 1961?

Mr. Tisdale replied that the Federal district court's ruling last June was partially in favor of the Government and partially in favor of the Company. He said the Company was now holding talks with the Government in an effort to see if a decree acceptable to both parties could be worked out.

How much would per share earnings be diluted by the conversion of all the convertible debentures and the exercise of outstanding stock options?

Mr. Ford said the dilution would be about 4 cents a share. He added, however, that we are buying shares for these purposes from The Ford Foundation to prevent any dilution.

What was the average cost of the stock acquired from The Ford Foundation?

Mr. Ford said about $51 per share last year.

When will Ford have a black dealer in Detroit?

Mr. Ford said that the Company hopes to have a black dealer in Detroit in the near future.

The stockholder is generally presented with a single slate of proxies, rather than with a choice. The same is true of the directors. They are nominated by the directors currently serving and, in the proxy statement, the names appear as a single slate.

Often, too, the real decisions are made outside the regular board meetings, in private conversations and correspondence. What goes on behind the scenes is important in judging how the power in corporations is exercised and the reasons for decisions on appointments to the board. But usually few records are kept of the preliminary debate, and when they do exist they are usually not available to the student of management. It is fortunate, therefore, that some of the informal discussions of one of the most important corporate boards in the history of management were made public in the Du Pont–General Motors antitrust trial of 1953. Through governmental subpoenas, some of the correspondence between directors became part of the record.

Du Pont had purchased a large block of General Motors stock in 1917 and because of its substantial ownership was represented on the GM board. The writers of the following letters were all board members of General Motors and included Alfred P. Sloan, Jr., who was also chief executive of GM, Lammot du Pont, board chairman of Du Pont, and Walter S. Carpenter, Jr., who was then president of Du Pont.

The letters show the high standards of ethics and trusteeship of all those involved and throw light on considerations taken into account in selecting new board members.

How Directors Choose Their Successors

[*Letter dated September 23, 1943:* From Alfred P. Sloan, Jr., then president of General Motors, to Walter S. Carpenter, Jr., then president of E. I. du Pont de Nemours & Company. In this letter Sloan outlines some general principles that he believes should govern selection of new directors. The principles are largely negative ones (no bankers, no suppliers, and so on) except for the second one, in which he mentions the need for consideration of geographical location. The "George Whitney" mentioned was the late president of J. P. Morgan and Company.]

Mr. Walter S. Carpenter, Jr.
President
E. I. du Pont de Nemours & Company
Wilmington, Delaware

Re: General Motors Organization—Board of Directors—Membership

My dear Walter:

I have your letter of September 22nd, referring to the above matter and also to our discussion at your Finance Committee meeting in Wilmington, last Monday.

I certainly owe you an apology for the lack of attention to your letter of April 8th. If you had asked me whether you had ever submitted a list of proposed directors, I certainly would have bet ten to one that you had never done so, but on referring to the file I see you did. Apparently what I did was to ask Mr. Smith to have the stockholders' list examined to see whether there

From correspondence among Du Pont and General Motors directors that formed a part of the record at the Du Pont–GM antitrust action in 1953.

were any available candidates that we would not ordinarily think of. He never submitted the list until today. I think what I intended to do was to deal with it all at once and his delay in sending the list to me prevented me from doing so. I am sorry that you had to raise the question again.

Now, taking everything that has happened in the past, together with the discussion at Wilmington, and in order to make progress, I think what I will do will be to submit to you, within a few days, a list of not to exceed ten names—probably there will be eight—out of which we ought to pick four, as that was the number we discussed in the Wilmington meeting, as being desirable.

I will use the following formula, and for the following reasons:

First: Frankly, I am opposed, and others are likewise, to further representation on the Board, of Bankers. We are all very happy with George Whitney, but if we add additional Bankers, especially now, I don't think the reaction will be favorable. I am against Bankers on Boards of industrial companies because they are accused (wrongly of course) of dominating the financial policies. Frankly, I would rather have no Bankers on the Board, for that reason. To move in that direction would, I think, be unfortunate.

Second: I think we should give some consideration to geographical location, and your list of April 8th, which I have referred to above, is set up on that basis.

Third: I think we must be careful to exclude those who represent interests that have relationship with General Motors, particularly in the buying and selling area.

Fourth: I will eliminate representatives of du Pont and du Pont affiliated companies, because I believe that you should determine what representation you want on the General Motors Board.

Fifth: I shall avoid making more than one recommendation from the same line of industry.

Sixth: I will ignore the holdings of General Motors stock, as an essential qualification.

You will hear from me shortly, with the list.

Very truly yours,
/s/ Alfred P. Sloan, Jr.

APSJr./K

c/c Messrs. Lammot du Pont
Donaldson Brown

[*Letter dated February 11, 1944*: Also from Sloan to Carpenter. Here Sloan discusses some of the reasons why he is not in favor of adding more bankers to the board—evidently Carpenter had proposed a few in a letter written the day before. However, Sloan notes that he might reconsider the idea if the bankers proved to be the best possible choice. As a matter of fact, two of the men mentioned, Henry C. Alexander (of J. P. Morgan and Company) and R. K. Mellon (of the Mellon Bank and Gulf Oil) later were elected to the General Motors board, the latter partly, perhaps, because of shareholdings in GM. The "J. T." referred to in this letter is John Thomas Smith, formerly general counsel of GM.]

Mr. Walter S. Carpenter, Jr.
President
E. I. du Pont de Nemours & Company
Wilmington, Delaware

Re: General Motors Organization—Board of Directors—Membership

My dear Walter:

I have your letter of February 10th, contents of which I have carefully noted. Thanks for the selection. As soon as I receive replies from others, which I have not as yet, I will analyze them all and then make a report and we can see what should be the next step.

You mention in your letter, you recall, certain individuals which were listed by you and which did not appear on the list of candidates selected by me. Here is the answer so far as that is concerned—perhaps it is right and perhaps it is wrong—I don't know.

Almost everybody here feels that it would be unwise for General Motors to add to its Board of Directors, important executives in large banks. We have, of course, George Whitney. He is an outstanding citizen and makes an outstanding contribution to the Policy Committee and to the Board, and I am not so sure that if we were certain that we could get another individual who would do as much, that, from what I am saying, would be made secondary to the fact that, after all, we want results. Anyway, Leon Frazer, Alexander, Stanley, Mellon and others, were eliminated on principle and not for any other reason. Please give me your reaction on this.

I might say further on the point, that I do not feel as strongly against an important bank outside of New York as I do inside New York, but I think to have three or four of the big banks represented on the General Motors Board of Directors, needs some consideration. So far as R. K. Mellon is concerned, of course I know him very well. Here again you raise the point of having on our Board, the du Pont group; J. P. Morgan, the Mellon interests, etc. Again, I would be willing to forget all this if we got the results that you have in mind.

In commenting as I have above, I do not want you to think I have accepted the philosophy that the public relations is determining the policies of General Motors. As a matter of fact, I am fighting that policy all the time because there is too much of it already, but I do think, as a practical point, we do not want to furnish too much ammunition for those who think that nothing can be done in General Motors except we consult J. P. Morgan & Company. I don't know whether you ever heard J.T. say or not, but during the bonus suit, Judge Leibell was heard to say that I, as President of General Motors Corporation, could not adopt any policy without it was approved by Mr. Morgan. You can just see how far reaching that type of thing goes.

While we are talking about the objective which you have in mind, I am wondering whether it would not be wise to add one more to our Policy Committee if we could get the right person, particularly having in mind what you say in next to the last full paragraph on Page 1 of your letter. I had in mind raising the question with Lammot, yourself and others, at the proper time, but it does seem to me that just having in mind the second point you make, that some one might well be picked out by the du Pont group to serve on our Policy Committee so that over a period of years they would learn to understand the business, just the same as Lammot and yourself do, at the moment.

Again dealing with your second point and having reference to the preceding paragraph of this letter, I feel that we are all apt to exaggerate what a Director can contribute to any Corporation. I am speaking, of course, of any large Corporation. Take your own Company, as a case study. I am not talking about what they might contribute as operating people. The smaller the Company and the smaller the Board, the less of course this applies because they can get closer to the business. I do not know but what the same applies in general to our own Board here, and we must recognize that on your Board and ours here we have many Directors who have grown up through the organization and who know a great deal about the background of the business, the personnel, the problems, and all that sort of thing. When we pass from such a set-up to dealing with people who have none of these qualifications, you not only have the time element, which you point out, but you also might ask yourself the very realistic question as to whether they have an opportunity to do what we too often think ought to be done.

Expressed otherwise, what I am trying to say is, that the real opportunity to serve in the way you and I are thinking about—at least academically—is on the Policy Committee rather than on the Board of Directors. Perhaps you may say that the latter leads to the former.

Very truly yours,
/s/ Alfred P. Sloan, Jr.
Chairman

APSJr./K

[*Letter dated July 12, 1944*: From Carpenter to Lammot du Pont, who had been chief executive of both Du Pont and GM but was then in his seventies. In this letter, Carpenter suggests names of Du Pont executives who might be considered for the GM board. (The "Brown" mentioned in the second paragraph is Donaldson Brown, who was originally with Du Pont but later became a GM executive in charge of finance and a member of GM's board.) The letter also includes some discussion of possible candidates for committee membership.]

[To] Mr. Lammot du Pont
Building

I submit the following thoughts to serve merely as a basis for more thought and discussion on the subject of du Pont's position on the General Motors Board.

I suggested that the following changes might

be made in du Pont's representation on the Board. I have not considered Mr. Brown in these lists, and certainly would suggest no change in his status in this respect.

Present List	*Prospective List*
Lammot du Pont	Lammot du Pont
H. B. du Pont	H. B. du Pont
J. J. Raskob	J. J. Raskob
W. S. Carpenter, Jr.	W. S. Carpenter, Jr.
P. S. du Pont	A. B. Echols
H. F. du Pont	Lammot Copeland or Emile du Pont

With respect to the du Pont members on the Policy Committee, I suggest for the present that that remain as at present, namely, Lammot du Pont and W. S. Carpenter, Jr.

With respect to the Bonus Committee, I suggest my withdrawal to be replaced by H. B. du Pont. Belin is our advisor on salaries here and, therefore, has occasion to interest himself actively in this general subject of compensation. In addition this will afford him an excellent opportunity of better familiarizing himself with the personnel in General Motors. As a matter of fact, he can, because of his position there carry his inquiry with respect to important personnel as far as he may wish to. This will afford a constructive background with respect to the selection of future important personnel in General Motors.

My present thought would be, also, that he would succeed to the first vacancy in du Pont representation on the Policy Committee. In order to better equip him for this it might be wise for him at the present time to review the Operating reports which come to the Policy Committee and offer any suggestions he may wish, through you or through me, to the Policy Committee meetings.

I suggest that H. B. du Pont retire from the Audit Committee, and that his place be taken by Mr. A. B. Echols. Mr. Echols is eminently qualified to serve as Chairman of the Audit Committee, and in that position will be able to review the performance of General Motors, not only from a purely auditor's standpoint, but that will serve him also as an excellent opportunity to keep in touch with the general financial position of the Company.

As Mr. H. F. du Pont has now retired from the Finance Committee of the du Pont I suggest that his place be taken by some member of the present or prospective Finance Committee. In this connection, I suggest the name of Lammot Copeland or possibly Emile du Pont, if it is probable that he will eventually become a member of the Finance Committee.

In addition to these changes, it seems to me that we should urge the selection of additional Directors to the Board as we have already so many times discussed in the Policy Committee.

/s/ W. S. Carpenter, Jr.
President

WSC:R

[*Note.* "Received Jul 12, 1944 Lammot du Pont" stamped at top of first page. In fourth paragraph the words "I suggest my" are underlined. Next to this the following note has been written: "All O.K. but does not meet the main requirement except in my minor degree as noted here."]

[*Letter dated May 3, 1945*: From Sloan to Carpenter. Here Sloan makes a distinction between Du Pont directors, who serve by virtue of Du Pont's large (but not majority) stockholdings in GM, and other "outside directors." He raises the question whether what he considers true outside directors could contribute very much since they would have so many other interests. (He excepts George Whitney because of his long service on the GM board.) The "Douglas" mentioned was Lewis W. Douglas, chief executive of Mutual Life at the time, a former Representative from Arizona and Ambassador to the Court of St. James's in London.]

Mr. Walter S. Carpenter, Jr.
President
E. I. du Pont de Nemours & Company
Wilmington, Delaware

Re: General Motors Corporation—Board of Directors—Membership

My dear Walter:

I have your letter of May 1st regarding the above subject and would like to pursue the matter a little further, if I may, at the moment.

I have a letter from Lammot and he is entirely satisfied with the suggested candidates providing that neither of them are on the operating side of the business which, as I said in my first letter supplemented by my second, is not contemplated. In other words, I agree on this.

However, I don't see completely eye to eye with Lammot about outside directors. He looks upon the "du Pont directors" as outside directors. They are, of course, technically. But, as I have said to him, the "du Pont directors" on our Board, like the operating people on our Board, believe in concentrating about all they have in the business of du Pont and General Motors whereas directors of the Whitney and Douglas type operate in quite a different atmosphere. That is probably a part of the banking business. Whether it is a part of the insurance business, I don't know.

George Whitney belongs to the Board of Directors of quite a number of industrial organizations. He gets around a lot because he lives in New York where many contacts are easily and continuously made.

Mr. Douglas is, in a way, quite a public character. He seems to spend a great deal of time in other things. How he gets along in the insurance business, I don't know.

It seems to me, therefore, that such people do bring into our councils a broader atmosphere than is contributed by the "du Pont directors" and the General Motors directors.

Knowing that you have been interested in expanding our Board and that others agree, whereas perhaps some others do not feel so strong about it, do you think that with these two candidates referred to in my letter as joining with us at the proper time, that we should seek other candidates more from the outside? This really raises the question as to whether you think an outside director can contribute much? Certainly George Whitney contributes a very great deal. He has been with us for a long time. He sits in at Policy Committee meetings and he is quite familiar with our business. A director not on the Policy Committee does not have that opportunity.

Very truly yours,
/s/ Alfred P. Sloan, Jr.
Chairman

APSJr./K

[*Letter dated December 10, 1945*: From Sloan to Carpenter. "John Pratt" is John Lee Pratt, for many years the virtual second-in-command at GM, who had retired in the 1930s and was a member of the board and a major stockholder. General Marshall had a reputation for moving younger men ahead in the Army, and Pratt apparently felt that his viewpoint would be of value on the board of directors of GM, also that his appointment might have public relations value. Sloan does not find the first point a valid one, for reasons he gives in the letter, but concedes that the second might be well taken.]

Mr. Walter S. Carpenter, Jr.
President
E. I. du Pont de Nemours & Company
Wilmington 98, Delaware

Re: General Motors Corporation—Board of Directors—Membership—General Marshall

My dear Walter:

John Pratt has been urging upon me the consideration of General Marshall as a member of our Board of Directors, and altho for various reasons I am not very sympathetic to the idea, I think that others ought to know about it because my point of view may be wrong.

First: John has been impressed with what General Marshall has done in organizing the Army for war. He is impressed with the fact that the General has selected younger men and has promoted them over older men. In other words, in some cases he has taken associates of his at West Point—men whom he has grown up with—and given younger men preference, in one way or another. John seems to think that if he is a member of our Board of Directors he may present a point of view on that that will be helpful.

My point of view is that where the Army has been expanded 100% it is both easy and essential that the younger men be given higher places because there are not enough to go around. Personally, I don't think, on the record, that our position is at all unfavorable with regard to the promotion of younger men. John makes the point that he is not concerned with the job. What he is concerned with is the increasing age of the lower levels of administration. But he is talking about broad generalities without specific knowledge. I do not think the actual facts make that particularly important. I also make the point against the proposal that a director, as such, can do very little except make a comment once or twice about a point that he has in mind. The only way to make the point effective, if it is sound and desirable, is to hammer at it continuously day in and day out and maybe after four or five years you begin to get somewhere. A director is not in a position to do that. What I am trying to say is, that the philosophy has got to be accepted by the administration as a part of their operating technique and I feel quite certain as it stands now, the administration recognizes the point that John is trying to make. Therefore, from that point of view I think very little would be accomplished.

Second: General Marshall is 65 years old. And while he undoubtedly is very active, intelligent, experienced and all that sort of thing, the question arises as to whether we should take on, as a new director, any one in that age area. John agrees with that, in part and has technically withdrawn his recommendation on that count. But I still think that others ought to know about it because other considerations might overbalance that point.

Third: I said to John that I thought General Marshall might do us some good, when he retires, following his present assignment—assuming he continues to live in Washington; recognizing the position that he holds in the community and among the governmental people and the acquaintance he has—and he became familiar with our thinking and what we were trying to do, it might offset the general criticism as to the general negative attitude toward big business, of which we are a symbol and a profitable business, as well. It seems to me that might be some reason, and in that event the matter of age would not be particularly consequential.

I should like to have your point of view.

Very truly yours,
/s/ Alfred P. Sloan, Jr.
Chairman

APSJr./K

[*Letter dated December 13, 1945:* Lammot du Pont's view of the preceding.]

Mr. Alfred P. Sloan, Chairman,
General Motors Corporation,
Broadway at 57th Street,
New York 19, New York.

Dear Alfred:

Your letter of December 10th, in regard to General Marshall as a member of the Board, was duly received.

In general, my thinking is the same as you have indicated yourself. Put briefly, I would not favor his election to the Board, although I have a great admiration for him in his military work, and have met him in that connection two or three times, and always received a favorable impression.

My reasons for not favoring his membership on the Board are: First, his age, second, his lack of stockholdings; and third, his lack of experience in industrial business affairs.

Yours sincerely,
[Lammot du Pont]
CHAIRMAN OF THE BOARD.

LduP/MD

[*Letter dated May 22, 1946*: From Carpenter to Donaldson Brown, who was planning to retire from the active management of GM. Carpenter urges him to retain his board membership at least, particularly since Lammot du Pont is planning to resign from the GM board.]

Personal & Confidential
Mr. Donaldson Brown, Vice Chairman
General Motors Corporation
New York 19, N.Y.

Dear Don:

At the present time there are five men on the General Motors' Board (L. du Pont, A. B. Echols, H. B. du Pont, L. Copeland and W. S. Carpenter, Jr.) who are members of the du Pont Board and who are not officers of General Motors. In addition there are, of course, you and Mr. Sloan, who are members of the du Pont Board and also officers of General Motors.

You will recall that at the last Finance Committee meeting here Lammot indicated his disposition to resign from that Board at its next meeting, which will be on June 3rd. There was also some discussion regarding a successor to Lammot, in order that our representation there might continue in the future substantially as it is at present.

Later in the day you, Lammot and I discussed the question of your own withdrawal as an active officer in General Motors. While I regretted that very much at the time, and still do, I gathered that you had pretty well made up your mind to do so. While I am still not hopeless in this connection, I do presume that it is appropriate to consider what alternatives might hang upon your decision to go through with your present plans and it is in that connection, and only in that connection, that I bring up the following.

Specifically, my inquiry is this—If you should decide to resign as an officer of General Motors, may we assume for the present that you would be willing to continue at least as a member of the du Pont Board and Finance Committee and also that you would continue to remain as a member of the General Motors' Board, and, in that way, serve as a replacement of Lammot on that Board as a representative of du Pont's interest on that Board?

I can think of many reasons why this would be a desirable arrangement.

It goes without saying that your knowledge and background of experience of the General Motors' situation equips you eminently well to serve in this capacity, with benefits both to du Pont and General Motors.

I think that your continuance as a member of the General Motors' Board would tend to soften somewhat the shock at this time of the withdrawal of both you and Lammot at the same time.

I feel that by your continuing this interest in General Motors, it tends to dissipate any unhappy feeling upon the part of the General Motors' official family that your withdrawal from active service there might otherwise create.

You will recall that at our last Finance Committee meeting here it was suggested that we have a meeting on Wednesday, the 29th, to consider a replacement for Lammot. I have not discussed this question with any members of the Finance Committee since our last meeting, so that, in that respect, I am not in any position to suggest this as a definite plan, but offhand I cannot feel that there would be anything but an enthusiastic acceptance of this arrangement if agreeable to you.

Will be very glad to hear from you at the earliest date you feel you care to reply.

Yours sincerely,

[Walter S. Carpenter]

WSC/ivt

[*Letter dated September 30, 1947*: From Sloan to Carpenter. Here Sloan suggests criteria and individuals for membership on the finance committee and the board of directors. C. F. Kettering was an executive of GM and an inventor. Apparently Sloan felt that he would be likely to lead the meetings into technical discussions that would be interesting but would distract the members from the main business.]

Mr. Walter S. Carpenter
President
E. I. du Pont de Nemours & Company
Wilmington 98, Delaware

Re: General Motors Organization—Board of Directors

My dear Walter:

Our loss in the death of John Thomas Smith creates, of course, a vacancy on our Board of Directors, also on our Financial Policy Committee. The purpose of this letter is to deal with those facts.

I wrote you some time ago suggesting that Nick Dreystadt be elected to the Board of Directors. Almost since the beginning, the chief executive in charge of Chevrolet has been on the Board. Nick Dreystadt qualifies in every way plus, and I think that he is entitled to the recognition. I am sure you do too except for the fact that it drives us more into an increase in the membership among those who are in the operating organization. However, time will take care of this, up to a point. I am inclined to think that irrespective of the point, which I appreciate, we ought to go ahead and elect Nick at the October meeting.

With regard to the Financial Policy Committee, it was my thought in dealing with the membership of first Policy Committee, that we should have some operating people and some people completely detached—preferably large stockholder interests and also others who were familiar with the operating organization, who would concern themselves only with the policy phase of the business. With the separation of the Policy Committee into two parts, I think that the same rule applies and that we should give consideration in the membership of this Committee again to large stockholder interests and, again, those who know something about the operations of the business itself. This latter group would naturally include executives who had retired and who would still be effective from the policy point of view—at least for a certain number of years. I feel quite strongly that we should not increase the membership of the Financial Policy Committee by bringing in executives who are still active in the administration end of the business. They belong in the Operations Policy Committee, according to my point of view.

If this is correct thinking, then E. F. Johnson would be eligible; likewise Ed Fisher. There are no retirements pending that would make other candidates available within the formula I have suggested, within the next three years. O. E. Hunt would be the next eligible candidate on the basis of that formula, but before that time other changes will certainly develop. The question also arises whether you feel that there should be another representative of the du Pont Company on this Committee. Technically, you already have two members—Don and yourself, but Don is not active in the du Pont organization and perhaps you might think you would rather have somebody who was more active. For instance, Echols or perhaps Henry du Pont. Either of these would add weight to the Committee, I am sure, particularly Echols because of the financial and other problems that arise. Such candidates also would be within the formula which I have already mentioned.

C. F. Kettering would also be eligible under the rule; likewise C. S. Mott. I don't think C. S. would fit into the picture very well, for a good many reasons and I do not think he would be enthusiastically received by the administration end. So far as Ket is concerned, I do not think he would contribute much to the particular problems that come before the Financial Policy Committee and I think he would perhaps be likely to reduce the efficiency of our meetings by leading us into most interesting subjects but not in any sense related to the purposes of this particular activity.

There is no reason why we should take action on these matters at the October meeting unless we are ready to do so.

Very truly yours,
/s/ Alfred P. Sloan, Jr.
Chairman

APSJr./K

[*Letter dated September 15, 1948*: Sloan raises the question whether a man should invariably be disqualified for membership on the board solely on the grounds that he is a supplier.]

Mr. Walter S. Carpenter, Jr.
Chairman—Board of Directors
E. I. du Pont de Nemours & Company
Wilmington 98. Delaware

Re: General Motors—Board of Directors—Membership

My Dear Walter:

I am rather disappointed that I shall be unable to be in Wilmington on Monday at the time of the next Board of Directors meeting because, of necessity, I am leaving that day for Murray Bay—a fact which you of course fully appreciate. I am inclined to think perhaps I will ask for an appointment in Wilmington within a week or two because I would like to get some further action on the above subject. In the meantime I would like to ask for what I might call a ruling, or point of view on your part, as to one specific phase of the matter.

I have in mind two or three industrialists who would add prestige and bring experience into our Board of Directors. They are people who I am sure would be helpful in the years to come. In one case the individual is head of a corporation which is a supplier to General Motors to the extent of 20%; the other is Chairman of the Board representing a stockholder interest having very little to do with operations of a corporation which also has about 20% of General Motors business.

I realize the importance of having not only men of experience and ability, but I would like to have industrial experience in a financial line rather than pure banking experience which, unless it is supported by a good deal of contact with industrial problems, is, from my point of view, more or less academic. In trying to pick out candidates of this type, with our ramifications so broad, we usually find some relationship such as I have mentioned above.

Now I realize that it would be better to have members on our Board having no relationship whatsoever with a corporation of a business character; at the same time should we accept this as a definite rule? If we should say that an individual is not a candidate if he was connected with a corporation which was supplying us material to the extent of not to exceed 20% of our needs, should that be a barrier and prevent us from considering men in that position?

I have just written a letter to Henry Hogan asking for opinion from the Corporation's point of view. As a matter of fact, I am inclined to think that my question perhaps has more bearing on the men who accept the appointment than it would as to General Motors.

What I am really asking, therefore, is:—Would you be prepared to accept as eligible for our Board of Directors, men whom you would be glad to have, from every point of view except that they might have relationships as a supplier to the extent of 20% of General Motors needs.

Very truly yours,
/s/ Alfred P. Sloan, Jr.
Chairman

APSJr./K

[*Memo dated September 16, 1948*: Carpenter's reply to the preceding. He notes that Du Pont itself is a supplier, but points out that its representatives on the board are there because it is also a large stockholder.]

To: Lammot du Pont
From: W. S. Carpenter, Jr.

I would like to talk to you about this sometime.

I am wondering whether an objection to the inclusion of a director solely on the ground that he may be a supplier comes with good grace from us, in view of our own position.

It is true that because of our stockholdings we are surely entitled to representation on the G. M. Board but in spite of this we cannot urge too strongly that a supplier is, irrespective of other merits, to be disqualified.

Although, as the preceding article shows, some directors have always taken an intense interest in the affairs of their companies, in the past there were many who were content to regard a directorship as a sinecure. They attended meetings—and collected their fees—but did not inquire too closely into what the managers were doing. This may still be the case in some companies, but the situation is changing quite quickly—both because directors may be sued for neglect as well as for malfeasance and because various influential groups of citizens are demanding change. The article below explains the changes that are occurring and the reasons for them.

Change Invades the Boardroom

Peter Vanderwicken

Gone—or at least going—are the days when being a corporate director was much like being a member of a relaxed and exclusive gentlemen's club. The very nature of the job is being re-examined and has become a subject of controversy. And directors themselves are feeling pressure to take on increased responsibility. A well-thumbed copy of *The Wreck of the Penn Central* is visible on many a director's desk, and most will admit that the famous fiasco has frightened them into re-examining their own performance as fiduciaries for the stockholders.

Perhaps more than anything else, a rising tide of lawsuits by disgruntled stockholders claiming to have been misled about a company's true condition has forced directors to be more careful and thorough. For the last several years the number of liability suits has been steadily rising.

Reprinted from the May, 1972, issue of *Fortune* magazine, pp. 156–159, 282, 285, and 290, by special permission.

Now a corporation need hardly breathe bad news before its directors find themselves hit. Barely a fortnight after Ampex Corp. announced that it expected to write off at least $40 million in losses for last year, the company and its directors (including one who had been dead for some months) were sued.

What's more, the courts and Congress are gradually extending the liabilities of directors. Under the consumer-product safety bill now before Congress, a director might be liable for civil penalties of up to $10,000 if he *should have known* of a forbidden act or misrepresentation by the corporation. As the standards become tougher, directors' liability insurance becomes costlier and harder to get. (Lloyd's of London recently stopped insuring directors against potential liabilities for polluting the environment.)

Boards of directors have also been feeling some heat from the SEC, which has been getting at them via broadened disclosure requirements for "insider" stock transactions and steadily more rigorous interpretations of the securities acts, particularly their provisions against conflicts of interest.

A Window with Two Views

All these pressures are aimed at making directors more diligent in performing their traditional (and legal) role as representatives of the stockholders. But according to a new concept that is gaining ground both within and outside the corporate community, directors should have a broader role: they should become answerable to the public at large, or to various segments of it. Employees, consumers, women, blacks, environmentalists, and young people are demanding that the corporation pay more attention to their views and interests. One way in which some corporations have responded is to add members of some of these groups to the board of directors.

There are two conflicting concepts of the role of such atypical directors, who clearly are not being added to boards to represent the stockholders. One view is expressed by John Bunting, chairman of the First Pennsylvania Banking & Trust Co., who recently added a black businessman, a black lawyer, a female television producer, and a college student to his board. His new directors, he says, do not represent blacks or television viewers or students; their function is to broaden the perspective of management, to be management's "window to the world." A quite different view is held by Philip Sorensen, a Washington lawyer who is chairman of the Project on Corporate Responsibility. He sees the new, atypical directors as monitors for the public at large, as the public's "window into the corporation."

As a result of all this, board meetings in many companies are becoming a lot more serious (and a lot more interesting) than they were even five years ago. The chairman of a major metal company recalls that "at my first board meeting in this company five years ago, one director fell asleep in his chair." That never—or hardly ever—happens today. Forced to accept responsibility for what the corporation does, directors are working harder to be sure they know what it's doing—and to influence its policies.

The varied and mounting pressures on directors are bringing about a basic rethinking of just what a corporate director's duties are. Directors tend to be surprisingly vague about that. Ask a dozen of them what their duties are, and you'll hear nearly a dozen different replies. The law still says the directors' job is to manage the company, but they really haven't done that for a long time. Many executives believe that the board's most useful function is simply to advise management—when asked. There are some matters a chief executive cannot discuss with his subordinates, and a director can often provide experienced, informed, and responsible advice that the chief executive otherwise could not get. Robert P. Gwinn, chairman of Sunbeam Corp., says of directors: "I think the great thing is to be able to talk to them, to use them as a sounding board." But the board also imposes a discipline on management just by existing. Says Justin Dart, chairman of Dart Industries: "You're like a student in class, reporting on your stewardship."

There is a common agreement that, whatever else its duties are, the board has one basic function: it must select and evaluate the company's chief executive. It is hard to see how many boards can appraise or replace management, however, since even today most directors are the managers wearing different hats. In small companies still run by their founders, the board generally is dominated by insiders—i.e., executives of the company. In large companies, too, the management still tends to dominate the board of directors. A recent FORTUNE survey shows that insiders hold half or more of the seats on the boards of twenty-one of the fifty largest industrial corporations. But the insider dominance has been slipping a bit. In the last five years the top fifty industrials together have reduced their number of inside directors by thirty-four, to 324, and added fifteen outsiders, bringing the outsider total to 444.

The problem with inside directors is their lack of independence, and this troubles many executives. Inside directors are subordinates of the chief executive, dependent upon him for their careers; it is difficult for them to challenge or oppose the chairman.

A Friendly Avoidance of Questions

But if inside directors are not independent enough to represent the stockholders or the public effectively, outsiders often lack the necessary knowledge. There is a growing recognition that no board of a dozen or so outsiders, most of them busy men with large managerial responsibilities of their own, can know enough about another large, complex corporation to provide an effective check on its management. "Let's be honest," says Dr. John Rettaliata, president of the Illinois Institute of Technology and a director of fourteen companies. "You really don't know what's going on. If management really wants to put something over on a director, it can." Moreover, it's usually not considered cricket for outside directors to question the chief executive's decisions. The boardroom is still something like a clubroom, and a strict etiquette prevails. Discord and embarrassment are unwelcome.

As a result of these constraints, boards often find it difficult to evaluate management effectively or to ensure adequate succession. The Penn Central board appeared to desire harmony above all else. The Pan Am board seemed slow to face up the need for a drastic management change, though it finally did replace Chairman Najeeb Halaby. Some boards that have brought about changes in management have been unable to acquire a stable management team. White Motor had a rapid succession of short-term chief executives. International Paper has seen a confusing stir of top-management comings and goings in the last decade.

While directors generally are still counselors rather than overseers of management, the heightened pressures on them have brought some notable changes in their working habits. The traditional 2:00 P.M. meeting, preceded by a pleasant lunch, has almost invariably been replaced by a morning meeting, often followed by a liquorless lunch with a presentation by a division manager, say, or a pension-fund trustee. More and more meetings stretch into two days.

Meetings have become more frequent, as well as longer. The relaxed quarterly meeting is, in most companies, a thing of the past; the boards of thirty-seven of the fifty largest industrial companies meet at least ten times a year. Some directors contend that if a board meets four times a year or less, that is a sign of a badly managed company.

Boards increasingly are working through committees. The smaller, specialized groups can delve more deeply into particular operations of the company, and their greater knowledge enables them to question management's premises more closely. The most popular new committee is audit; nine of the top fifty industrials have added an audit committee in the last five years (though nineteen still do not have one). It usually consists of two or three outside directors, and meets semi-annually with the company's independent auditors, without company officers present, to review the adequacy of the accounting procedures.

Executive committees, which act for the full board between meetings, are now standard; forty-four of the top fifty have them. All but four of the fifty have executive-compensation or stock-option committees (many have both). The most committee-oriented among the largest companies is Firestone Tire, which has no less than thirteen. The fifty largest industrials together have 206 board committees, an average of about four each.

"It's Their Fault, Not Mine"

Despite the pressures on directors to become better informed, 23 percent of the 1,500 large companies and banks surveyed last year by Heidrick & Struggles, a Chicago management-consulting firm, still send their directors no information at all before board meetings. And 21 percent even limit their directors' access to company data. But the trend is definitely toward providing directors with much more information. Most companies send their directors detailed financial data in advance of each meeting. Many send them copies of the company's press releases and new-product announcements. More chairmen are sending their directors copies of news stories and stock analysts' reports on the company and its competitors, and comparative operating figures for competitors. Some chief executives write biweekly or monthly letters to their directors, outlining management's most important current problems.

A few companies—generally the largest—provide detailed staff work for their directors, mailing them before each meeting an analysis of every issue to be discussed, the possible alternative decisions, the pros and cons of each, and the management's recommendation. New directors of Green Giant Co. receive a looseleaf "Policy Book," which describes the company's goals and policies in each segment of the business. It also describes the company's organization and the duties of the board and its committees, and includes the texts of the articles and bylaws. Robert Gwinn says: "I send my directors a tremendous amount of material, and if they don't know what's going on in Sunbeam, it's their fault, not mine."

Still, it is not so easy to devise a workable means of keeping outside directors adequately informed. Even pounds of reports from the chief executive may reflect only the management line, and may hide or minimize serious problems that a director could later find himself responsible for not having known about.

An interesting experiment in informing directors—and using their knowledge—is under way at Texas Instruments. Three directors are designated "officers of the board" and spend at least thirty days a year on T.I. business. They are expected to study the company's operations in depth and relate them to the changing economic, social, and political environments. One of the three is a former senior vice president of T.I.; the other two are outsiders.

The officers of the board concentrate on long-range goals and planning, but they may look into any aspect of the company's operations and talk with any employee. Their special knowledge of the company gives T.I.'s insider-dominated board the benefit of fully informed outside advice in policy making, capital-appropriations decisions, and the setting of corporate priorities.

On Golf Courses in the Low Sixties

The future will almost certainly see an expanding role for the professional director. Usually a retired executive, the professional director serves on the boards of a half dozen or more companies. He has more time to become informed about a company than a board member who has an executive job of his own. The professional director's involvement on several boards, moreover, can give him a broad perspective. But while a number of men have cast themselves as professional directors, the practice has not yet gained wide acceptance.

Indicative of some of the problems a would-be professional director encounters is the story of Thomas R. Wilcox, who resigned last year as vice chairman of First National City Bank. Wilcox considered becoming a professional director (he was already on five boards), but he gave up the idea. He found that a director still needs an institutional affiliation to provide him with status, research assistance, and credibility as a competent executive. He also found that a director's compensation, even multiplied by a half dozen companies, did not provide an adequate income. Directors are typically paid a fee of around $200 for each meeting they attend, although more and more companies are paying annual retainers of $2,500 to $5,000 as well. Finally, Wilcox concluded, a professional director would be haunted by "the constant specter of conflict of interest." So Wilcox decided to accept an offer to become vice chairman of

Eastman Dillon, Union Securities & Co., and continue serving on boards (currently seven) as a sideline.

At least one of the difficulties Wilcox encountered—the view that an executive's retirement reduces his value as a director—appears to be receding. A growing number of chief executives are looking for men around sixty-two to serve as directors from their retirement until around seventy. These chief executives dispute the contention of some others that retired executives quickly lose touch with changing business conditions and that the value of their counsel therefore declines. "Those who argue retirees are out of touch are wrong," says James Beré [chairman] of Borg-Warner. "Times are changing. We're seeing managers become heads of companies relatively young. I'm forty-nine. I believe a chief executive should not serve too long. That means we're going to have some real experienced guys in their low sixties who should not be on golf courses."

What may force increasing acceptance of retired executives as directors is the mounting concern about the potential conflicts of interest facing the director who holds an executive post in another company. Contacts that in the past would have been considered normal business relationships are now perceived as being fraught with actual or potential conflicts. Speaking of professional directors, Signal's Forrest Shumway says: "I don't think they're a good idea particularly, but I think we're coming to it because of the absurd pressures by the government to prevent conflict of interest."

The Missing Institutions

Concern about conflicts of interest has kept one large class of shareholders from being represented on corporate boards of directors. Institutional investors now own shares representing 28 percent of the value of all stocks listed on the New York Stock Exchange, but only a few institutions, or their shareholders or beneficiaries, are represented on boards. If any one institution is represented, the access to inside information might give it an advantage over others in buying or selling the company's stock.

Two thoughtful businessmen have independently proposed a way to resolve this problem. They are Richard H. Jenrette, president of Donaldson, Lufkin & Jenrette, a brokerage firm that specializes in trading for institutions, and James Robison, the just retired chairman of Indian Head, Inc., a diversified manufacturer of glass, textiles, and auto parts. Jenrette and Robison suggest establishment of a non-profit association or foundation that would provide directors to represent institutions and their shareholders. This organization, financed by the institutions, would employ—and itself pay, perhaps $100,000 a year each—a number of highly competent professional directors. Each would serve on several boards, representing all institutions and their shareholders.

More difficult to solve are the puzzles presented by those new directors—blacks, women, defenders of the environment, and so forth—who are not even thought of as representatives of stockholders. What *is* their responsibility to stockholders? Do these newcomers represent particular interest groups or the public at large? If they are representatives, should the constituencies represented have some say in choosing them? Such questions will be nagging at businessmen and others in the society for years to come, but the drift toward more and more representation of nonstockholder groups is already evident. "When I came in as president of this company," says Pillsbury's Chairman Robert Keith, "I was pretty much told that the constituency was the stockholders, the employees, and the customers. Now I don't think that at all. It's broadened tremendously. Now our constituents include youth, the environment, and the public health."

So far, however, few boards of directors have set up formal machinery to handle the concerns of these new constituents. Only one of the fifty largest manufacturing companies, for example, has a board committee clearly concerned with the public interest: this is G.M.'s "public-policy committee," which monitors the corporation's performance in a wide range of public matters, including minority employment and pollution control. A few smaller companies have created similar committees. Pillsbury, for example, has a "public-responsibility committee" with one officer and four outside directors; it has been assessing the company's work in the areas of public health and nutrition. Boards of some other companies are beginning to check on such concerns by less formal means.

A Reminder Even if Silent

The new kinds of directors gradually appearing in boardrooms have already begun to influence the thinking of management. General Motors executives believe that the presence on their board of Leon Sullivan, a black minister and vocational-training administrator, keeps them a little more alert to the problems of G.M.'s black employees than they might otherwise be. The presence of Frank Thomas in the boardroom of First National City Bank makes the management more sensitive to the consideration that its prosperity depends heavily on the health of New York City, and Citibank has been more generous in financing housing for low-income city dwellers than it might otherwise have been. John Bunting of First Pennsylvania says that his diverse new directors "influence me by their mere presence. The fact that I have a woman on my board reminds me of things that I should be paying attention to, even if she doesn't say a word. The same thing for blacks."

But there are those who envision—some with hope and some, no doubt, with fear—a very different kind of role for the new, atypical directors, a role that includes a measure of power, not merely influence. Building up in the society are a variety of pressures for intrusion of public interests or group interests into the decision making of corporations. Questions arise about how far such tendencies can go without fundamentally altering the nature of the corporation and of the business system in which it functions. Unless countervailing tendencies set in to offset the increasing pressures for outside control, the present currents of change in corporate boardrooms will prove to be only harbingers of much greater changes to come.

Even though many, perhaps most, directors and managements are doing a good, conscientious job, it might be desirable to provide some way in which the owners could meter their performance. However, about the only way in which the entrenched management of a large company can be ousted is often the proxy contest, and as the following article shows, this is far from an ideal method. A good management may be ousted simply because another group is anxious to gain control, and the common stockholders may lose in the process. The following is based on a study prepared for the Bureau of Business and Economic Research, School of Business Administration of the Georgia State College of Business Administration.

Blueprint for a Proxy Contest

Leland Carling Whetten

Well-planned proxy contests usually begin with a quiet buying of stock in the name of brokers or nominees. As the beneficial owner is unknown, a corporate management is placed in a very awkward position. However, unexpected strength in stock plus a sharp increase in shares held in a broker's name usually signifies that a contest is in the making. Moreover, a well-organized opposition group tends to use the same broker or group of brokers in successive contests. Hence, an analysis of the broker making the stock acquisitions affords a clue to the possible opposition.

The second warning that an opposition group is being organized usually comes in the form of letters from shareholders unknown to company officers. These letters demand certain detailed financial information. After some days or weeks of this, the opponent (or a front man) usually requests an appointment to meet the company's

From *The Atlanta Economic Review*, August, 1960, pp. 13–16, an article abridged from the author's monograph, *Recent Proxy Contests: A Study in Management-Stockholder Relations*, Bureau of Business and Economic Research, School of Business Administration of the Georgia State College of Business Administration, Bulletin No. 6.

chief executives in person. At this meeting the announcement is made that he represents a large quantity of stock. Certain major reforms are demanded, which may border on the preposterous.

Rumors: The First Stage

During the early preparatory stages of a contest, the company is the subject of a whispering campaign. Rumors persist that a spin-off, merger, or liquidation is imminent. These rumors are harmful to management in many ways. In the first place, [they are] demoralizing both to existing shareholders and to employees. Each group envisions its future economic position with the company as becoming insecure. In the second place, speculators are attracted to the company as the public hastens to take advantage of various "tips." When the rumored spin-off or other action does not materialize, management is blamed for not having fulfilled the buyer's expectations. The entrapped shareholders tend to ally themselves with the opposition.

Ground Rules

Good ground rules assure an orderly stockholders' meeting. They also simplify the inspection and tabulation of proxies. Since voting tends to be high at the time of a contest, the number and kinds of defective proxies are multiplied; hence, all points capable of being reduced to mutual understanding are all to the good.

Between 400,000 and 500,000 shares were challenged in the Montgomery Ward contest. Several shareholders, for example, signed everything sent them by both sides but failed to date many proxies. In situations of this nature, postmarks must be examined accurately unless the ground rules specify differently. One holder sent in a proxy to the opposition, and later the same day sent one in to management. The envelopes were postmarked one hour apart. The proxy had this message scribbled on it: "Dear Mr. Wolfson [the most prominent member of the opposition group]: please go and lie down; you must be very tired." Another proxy for one hundred shares was sent in to management. The words, "Provided Avery [then chief executive] retires," were written thereon. This proxy was challenged on grounds of whether it was conditional and was held in abeyance to await a ruling by the inspectors. Some days later a Ward attorney walked into the room where the proxies were being tabulated and said: "I would like to have that proxy delivered up." When the proxy was handed to him, he said: "I offer this as a good proxy. Mr. Avery resigned this morning."

Costs

The corporation will pay all out-of-pocket expenses incurred by management as they accrue. In addition, opposition will seek reimbursement in the event its slate is victorious.[1] The following expenses are indicative of others that will arise if insurgents win:

a A new public accountant will (as a general rule) be appointed, and time will be required to train him.
b Positions must be provided for those who helped the opposition; many will be newly created.
c A new general and legal counsel will be appointed.
d A new insurance agent will be appointed. To the extent that existing contracts are canceled, the company is penalized for having acquired protection on a short-term basis.
e Any contracts in progress relative to loan of funds, merger, and so forth are upset.

Except where management has been remiss, the damage to public and investor confidence in a company is great. Moreover, the operating schedules of management are interrupted to organize a contest in self-defense.[2] These intangible costs are not capable of exact measurement.

[1]Steinberg v. Adams held that a stockholder could be reimbursed for a successful proxy contest. See Steinberg v. Adams, 90 F. Supp. 604 (1950).

[2]At times the executive is the company's chief salesman, visiting customers in person and signing up some of the biggest orders. Mr. Robert R. Morse, Jr., president of Fairbanks-Morse, was tied to his desk for a two-year period in 1956–1957 by the marathon battle with Penn-Texas. "What the fight cost the company just in terms of Bob's time can never be determined," sighed one associate. See *The Wall Street Journal*, April 30, 1958, p. 18.

Results

Any attempt to summarize the results of a given contest is presumptuous. Reforms advanced by opposition may have been gained although opposition was defeated. Moreover, even when opposition won, improved market price of stock, earnings, dividends, and so forth may have been more the result of economic forces within the business cycle than anything associated with the contest. In several cases, however, there seem to be general tendencies.

Where cumulative voting was used and opposition sought only representation, the harmonious functions of the board varied. Some were smooth, with the minority making real contributions. Other boards were in constant turmoil. Regardless of which side was in control, representation on the executive committee was generally denied the minority; and often legal actions of one sort or another ensued.

If the opposition slate was victorious, partial or complete liquidation followed. "Assets are turned around," as the saying goes. This statement implies that both custom and tradition are expendable and drastic measures are often forced through to make the company show a profit. Some measures were constructive, but others were not.

Waging the Contest

The fact that opposition forces often enter the contest at a slight disadvantage is partially offset by the negligence of a larger segment of satisfied stockholders who do not bother to send in proxies. Generally this group is favorable to incumbents. In contradistinction, shareholder lethargy is not great among the "protest vote." This group will support opposition by mailing in proxies. For this reason, meticulous arrangements are made by each side to assure maximum support. In the opinion of many, a strong political organization is necessary.

Often proxy material uttered in a contest resembles that of a low-grade political campaign. Each side declares that it is the sworn friend of the stockholder, and the opposition declares that its motive for seeking office is to enhance or protect the interest of other owners. Proxy material of the opposition tends to rely heavily on exaggerated statements of intent.

As proxies are received, comparison is made with the stockholder list to ascertain those outstanding. Usually, a personal solicitor will visit this group as the campaign draws to an end. If the stockholder has already sent in a proxy for the opposition, an attempt will be made to bring about a change of mind.

The political organization not only is responsible for delivering a large vote but must also take those precautionary measures to assure that the holder does not inadvertently vote the wrong way. In order to avoid a misunderstanding, different-colored proxies are used by opposing sides. In this way the stockholder is expected to identify his preference according to the proxy color.

Management and the Proxy Contest

Certain companies became large and successful, partly because of the close team organization among top management. Are there tests which can be used to measure the quality of that group? Inadequate plant maintenance and depletion of inventory reserves are but two expediencies available to shortsighted executives who desire to inflate profits temporarily. Likewise, work developed over a period of years and policies adopted by long-visioned management may be about to bear fruit to a company having experienced low earnings. Profits alone are not a reliable criterion.

In general, people buy stock to make money, not to enjoy the blandishments of management, dutiful or otherwise. Some are primarily speculators who hope to benefit from circumstances not necessarily related to the skill of management. By contrast, others are investors who desire to profit from the skillful management of a growing business. A management, however, cannot hope to remain in office just because it is competent and successful.[3] The stockholders must, in the preponderance, consist of a well-informed investment-minded group who tend to

[3]In several cases studied, the opposition won although management had been reasonably successful. After his company made the largest profit of a single year the president of R. Hoe & Company was dismissed by an opposition. Management of the Minneapolis & St. Louis Railway Company had also been successful, but experienced similar results.

discount short-term gyrations. Such an electorate tends to give management greater freedom in making long-range plans. It is immaterial that the stock is actively traded. What counts is the motive in buying.

When an opposition group wins a proxy contest, replacements among board members and chief executives tend to follow. Past loyalties and traditions are expendable when they do not fit into the new plan. For this reason, once a dissident group is formed, a chief executive may experience a conflict between company loyalty and personal goals. His resistance to the insurgents' demands means that his employment will be abruptly terminated if the opposition slate is victorious. Moreover, during the contest his competence may be severely questioned and his reputation put in jeopardy. This economic plight is felt keenly by those who have devoted a lifetime to the service of one company and whose future earning power is associated with that firm. Hence, when continued future control is doubtful, the temptation to seek the best possible compromise tends to be strong. Obviously, this particular motivation has prevented a great many contests. However, tendencies by top management to compromise an impending contest for personal considerations serve to weaken the force and effect of professional management.

Probably the major reason for the difficulty of winning proxy fights lies in the divorce between ownership and control. Prof. Adolf A. Berle, Jr., of the Columbia University Law School and its political science faculty, was among the first, if not the first, to analyze this. His first book on the subject, *The Modern Corporation and Private Property* (of which Dr. G. C. Means was co-author), appeared in 1933.

In 1959 he carried the analysis further, and distinguished a new stage in the shift of power from the owners. In this extract he explains both what he terms the first three stages in the "fission of property" and this newer fourth stage.

The Fission of Property

Adolf A. Berle, Jr.

Present norms of capital accumulation have already occasioned changes in the power relation between individuals and productive enterprise. Their continuance will make these changes more profound.

The rise of the corporate system, with attendant separation of ownership from management was the first great twentieth-century change. In three decades it led to rise of autonomous corporation management. The second tendency, pooling of savings, voluntary or forced, in fiduciary institutions now is steadily separating the owner (if the stockholder can properly be called an "owner") from his residual ultimate power—that of voting for management. In effect this is gradually removing power of selecting boards of directors and managements from these managements themselves as self-perpetuating oligarchies, to a different and rising group of interests—pension trustees, mutual fund managers and (less importantly) insurance company managements.

These emerging groups are themselves self-perpetuating. Though allied to corporate managements, they are on the margin of that world, closer to the world of bankers than to the world of production and sales executives.

Something even more significant is happening than a shift in power relations. Property (not to speak of ownership) is undergoing a profound reorganization. Its effects we can only dimly apprehend.

Economic Initiative

Property is in essence relationship between an individual (or perhaps a group of individuals) and a tangible or intangible thing. (The Roman Law called it a "*Res*"; the common law still does.) We have to interpret the word "thing" rather broadly. There are incorporeal as well as physical "things." Bodies of knowledge, written and unwritten, in the technical laboratories of many corporations have little physical substance, but they are so real that they can be bought and sold. Their money-worth often exceeds the worth of many items in a corporation's plant and property account, despite the accounting tradition that "conservatism" requires "patents and processes" to be carried at nominal valuation. In speaking of property, we here include incorporeal as well as corporeal items.

Changing Location of Power

Our former owner-possessor began by ceding his direct legal relationship to the *Res* when he turned it over to the corporation and took instead a piece of paper called a "stock certificate." But he, perhaps with his family, retained absolute stockholder control. His stock certificates represented a right to receive dividends when his board of directors declared them and a share in assets if the corporation should be liquidated (this rarely occurs in the case of any great corporation). The stock certificates also included the right to vote—which if one had more than a majority in practice meant the right to nominate and to express a choice for or against the men who are to be directors. In fact, though not in technical law, it meant power to give them orders. As long as our original owner had in his own possession enough shares of stock to dominate the annual meeting, because he had a majority of votes, or so long as with three or four friends, he could accumulate a majority, he had what the financial districts call "control." Control is, quite simply, capacity to make or unmake a board of directors.

Control is a great deal, but by no means everything. Directors when he had elected them were not, and in law are not now, his "agents." They are at liberty to defy his instructions. Their judgment, not his, must govern until he replaces them. Discharge of directors appears simpler than it actually is. Stockholders who discharge directors save for weighty and adequate cause are apt to find it difficult to secure the services of other able men in their place. The banks with which the corporation deals grow nervous; banks are easily upset. As in the case of a President who wishes to throw out a Cabinet Member without damaging himself, the reasons must be cogent and the record well documented. The management responsibility, for the moment, is thrown back on controlling stockholders who may or may not have or be able to attract the requisite combination of energy, character, and talent to deal with the situation. In violent changes of management, the enterprise is apt to suffer.

Stockholder "control" in a large enterprise does not ordinarily continue for any long space of time. Normally, a generation is its span. The really great enterprises now are commonly not "stockholder controlled," though there are a few striking exceptions.

The second stage below absolute stockholder control is called in financial markets "working control." It exists where an individual or group has less than a majority of the stock, but has sufficient affinity with or influence over the board of directors of the corporation so that existing directors will use their power to name a management slate to send out proxies to the stockholders along lines suggested by the holders of "working control." But again we have introduced an essentially political element. A substantial percentage of stockholders with small holdings practically always can be counted on to follow the lead of the management through sheer inertia. In practice this means that they will sign and return any proxy sent them by the management. Another proportion of stockholders can be counted on to do nothing. If the votes of the group that invariably follows management are added to those of the large (though nonmajority) stockholder, the result is "working control." To maintain "working control" in this situation, the large stockholder must therefore have and hold close relationship with the management. The size of holdings needed to maintain "working control" varies inversely with the breadth of distribution, that is, the greater the number of small stockholdings of the stock of the company in question, the less stock is needed to maintain (in alliance with management) "working control."

At this stage, the "owner," if a stockholder or stockholding group can be thus described, must maintain a variety of political relationships with the management. The power is shared. The management position is quite possibly as strong as the stockholding position.

The decade of great expansion, the years of the First World War, and the fantastic, expansive, and catastrophic speculative years which continued until 1929 ended the existence of absolute stockholder control as a norm. It was succeeded by the "working control" stage; but by then many of the great corporations had already passed into the third phase—"management control."

"Management control" is a phrase meaning merely that no large concentrated stockholding exists which maintains a close working relationship with the management or is capable of challenging it, so that the board of directors may regularly expect a majority, composed of small and scattered holdings, to follow their lead. Thus they need not consult with anyone when making up their slates of directors, and may simply request their stockholders to sign and send in a ceremonial proxy. They select their own successors. Theoretically it is possible for someone outside management to mobilize the army of small stockholders, aggregate their votes, and displace the existing directors. But the task is huge, the expense great, and the results problematic.

This is the locus of power over and the norm of control of the bulk of American industry now. Nominal power still resides in the stockholders; actual power in the board of directors. Probably the largest holders of stocks could still exercise a powerful force if they worked together—which they do not and probably cannot. Included in this top stratum are surviving individual holders of "working control" of which (as noted) there remain a good many; most of this second-stage group are also apparently outward bound for elimination.

Essentially these stockholders, though still politely called "owners," are passive. They have the right to receive only. The condition of their being is that they do not interfere in management. Neither in law nor, as a rule, in fact do they have that capacity.

Now appears the fourth stage. In this situation emerge the newer mechanisms, the fiduciary institutions, by which these dispersed stockholdings are once more becoming concentrated. True, the number of individuals expecting to receive benefits from the stock through the medium of these institutions is vastly increasing. But as distribution of income increases, voting power becomes increasingly concentrated.

So we discern the latest and apparently inescapable future norm in our chassé of property and power. Economic benefits by way of dividend or other distributions accruing to shares of stock are received by these impersonal institutions to be redistributed to their policyholders or to their pension beneficiaries—but wholly without direct relationship between the recipients and the stock, let alone the corporation. A pensionnaire or policyholder may conceivably have in the shadowy beyond (especially in a mutual company or cooperative) some astronomically distant and purely theoretical possibility of sharing in the assets of the insurance company or trust. But for all practical purposes he has a contract right to a stated sum of money only. His pension trust or his insurance company may have working, or even absolute, control of the Union Pacific Railroad or the United States Steel Corporation—but he has no part whatever in that. His right is to receive money only, and it depends on a status position of some kind based on his having fulfilled a stated set of conditions. He would not know—and it would be immaterial if he did know—what voting power his insurance company or his pension trust held with respect to the management of Union Pacific or United States Steel. He could not influence the situation in any case. He is, if possible, more passive-receptive than ever. His relation to the "things" that make up American industry has simply ceased.

Even though some boards of directors are taking a greater interest in managing the affairs of their companies, the chief executive still has great power and will probably continue to have greater influence than anyone else in the corporation. This article on his job is based on both analysis and personal experience, for the late Charles R. Hook, Jr., served as president of the Kudner Advertising Agency and as a vice-president of the Chesapeake & Ohio Railway, and was the son of a former president of Armco Steel Company.

The Functions of the Chief Executive

Charles R. Hook, Jr.

First let me emphasize the obvious: the chief executive is not only a personality; he is *by far* the most powerful and the most influential personality in the business. Not only his official pronouncements and his business decisions, but also his most casual remarks are carried by the grapevine, industry's best communication system, throughout the length and breadth of the organization. They are analyzed and reanalyzed, interpreted and misinterpreted, and scrutinized for hidden meanings and indications of how the wind blows. *And no straw is too insignificant to escape notice—if it is propelled by this particular wind.*

The reason for this is not obscure. It lies in the fact that the chief executive, more than any other person, has the power to affect not only the security of the members of his organization—but even more important their *ambitions* and their hopes for the future.

Man is basically an emotional and not a logical animal and such things as fear and hope play a more dominant part in everyday business decisions than intellectual or logical determinations. The *power* of these emotions carries the influence of a chief executive like a tidal wave through the organization.

The significant thing is not that the chief executive is so powerful but that, strangely enough, he himself is the last one to realize it or at least to realize the extent of the fact.

Why does he underestimate his influence? Is it because of modesty? Is it because he cannot see himself or his job from the perspective of the people under him—because he is on the wrong end of the grapevine?

I don't think it is either of these. I think it is due to something entirely different. The great power of the chief executive derives not alone from his own native ability, which may be very great and usually is, but primarily from the office that he holds—the office of chief executive. He may personally give to the office new meaning and integrity. He may make it a fine and wonderful thing. But whether he is an unsuccessful haberdasher or a genius, the top office, and thus much of the power, is his, regardless.

What does the average human being do when he finds himself in this important position? I would guess he looks in the mirror and sees the same face that was there the morning before. He doesn't realize that when he gets to work it is no longer the same face to anybody but himself. He undervalues his power and responsibility because he underestimates himself and because he underestimates the power inherent in the position.

He undervalues both himself and the job because he thinks of both in terms of his own past. He thinks, not of where he is, but of how he got to where he is.

He may be a financial genius, or outstandingly successful in marketing, production, or finance. On the other hand, he may be a seniority compromise, or have married the boss's daughter. Whatever the reason for his being there, it's sufficient. The important fact is that he is there.

Many men modestly view their ascendancy with real wonder. But humility isn't enough. Genuine acceptance of the fact—acceptance of responsibility, not resignation—is what is called for. When Margaret Fuller said, "I accept the universe," Carlyle retorted, "Gad, she'd better." So for the boss.

Once he has accepted the reality of his new position in high office, he has to face up immediately to one stubborn fact. As chief executive he is still only one manpower. As an individual he can be the source of great

From a talk given to a top management group, April, 1952.

organization accomplishment and inspiration, or he can, in effect, qualify for the clerks' union by burying himself in paper work. The result will depend on how he uses his one manpower.

A complicating factor, and one generally greatly underestimated by subordinates, is the special demands upon the boss's time and person. These inevitably increase with the size of the business: for example, his relationship with his directors, his relationship with major ownership and stockholders, with big customers, with industry committees, his leadership in major financing, his responsibility for key governmental contacts, and special community obligations.

Most of these groups—and they can have great impact on the business—*demand* that they see only the boss and not a subordinate. As a result, the top executive necessarily *spends a large part of his time away from his office* and another significant chunk of it writing letters, answering the telephone, and seeing people from outside the company.

These external responsibilities are important. Most of them can't be delegated, but they can be reduced if they are put in realistic perspective, viewed objectively, and studied seriously.

But, important and time-consuming as they are, these external responsibilities are of secondary importance. The chief executive's main responsibility is to his organization, if he is to maximize his one manpower.

Fortunately, in view of all the external demands on his time, it is the quality of his company relationships and the quality of his decisions that determine his success as an officer. *His basic responsibility—basic—is to create an atmosphere in which his organization will work harmoniously,* intelligently, imaginatively, and happily. He will create some kind of a spirit, some kind of a way of life for the organization because he can't help it. Whether he is aware of it or not, or whether he tries to or not, he creates it because of his position and power.

His job, of course, is to set a tone that will release the full capacities of the top management group and through them the capacities and heart and imagination of all subordinate officers. Whether he is going to be able to do this will depend to a significant extent on one factor. It will depend on their belief in their chief executive, their faith in him as an individual, and in his purposes and character.

Faith is a two-way street. It has to be given before it can be received. People in business soon learn whether it is safe to differ with the chief executive when circumstances demand it. One of the first things they find out is whether the boss really wants to know what their problems are and what they see the chief difficulties of the company to be. Faith will not be forthcoming from men who have learned from experience that it is best to agree with the ancient Chinese philosopher who said, "He who thinks differently than the King washes his hands in his own blood."

But just the give and take of personal faith and understanding are not enough. The members of top management and their subordinate officers want more than that from their chief executive. These men want to be proud of their boss's decisions on important matters. They want to believe that his decisions are based on high purpose and integrity. *Their evaluation of the kind of decisions they can expect—and what the chief executive stands for—creates what we call morale, the capacity of a group of people to work together with maximum effectiveness.*

So whatever the boss is will be reflected inevitably throughout the entire organization and will go a long way towards molding the character—the business character—of every man in it. *And it certainly will decide whether the company receives the full contribution of its executive manpower.*

I come then to this conclusion: the great, the inescapable responsibility of the chief executive is not only to perform functions well—but to make himself big enough for the shoes he has to fill, strong enough for the power that is his.

Whatever the reason for his being in the top position, he has to bring to it more than competence in any one field, more even than administrative skill or individual brilliance. He has to bring to it above all a realization of the meaning of his position and of his power, a realization that he, in the last analysis, is the company. Therein he differs from all other officers.

For no matter how great his abilities in any one area, no matter how great his accomplishments as a businessman, as an organizer, the job will always demand more of him. He must work for purposes beyond himself, bigger than himself. He has the duty to see to it that his responsibility matches his power and authority. Let me summarize briefly:

1. *The chief executive is the most important individual in the business*, yet only too often he underestimates his influence.
2. *His importance lies mainly in his office*, which is endowed with unique power regardless of his personal capacity, simply because it is the office of the chief executive.
3. *It is he who creates the spirit of the organization*, its *way of life*, its *integrity*, its *ability to function as a unit*, its *policy*, its *hope*.
4. *How the individual and the office mesh is the single most important factor in the success of the chief executive and of the company.*

What the chief executive *does* is certainly important. But what he *is*, what he stands for, is more important still. *For he will determine whether the business receives the full creative potential* of its people.

In conclusion let me quote a few words a thousand years old. They are as true today as then:

"The efficiency of the army consists partly in the order and partly in the General, but chiefly in the latter, because he does not depend upon the order, but the order depends upon him."

4 The External Framework

Although—as the article by Charles R. Hook, Jr., in the preceding chapter pointed out—the chief executive has enormous power and influence within his organization, there are serious limitations on his power imposed by the external environment, which includes a number of other agencies that may, and generally do, restrict his power.

The constraints due to the external environment are of many kinds, from those imposed by financial institutions to those developed by organized groups among the general public. And, of course, in recent years governments—Federal, state, and local—have tended to enact more and more regulations that a company cannot disregard without incurring penalties.

The first article in this chapter discusses the ways in which a company may be hampered in its efforts to expand by its inability to raise capital from outside sources, and the second considers some of the restraints imposed by the Federal government. The third deals with labor unions, and the next two discuss the constraints imposed by the general public, organized and unorganized.

Finally, there are the technological limitations, which always exist and which affect practically all companies. Two articles deal with these.

As this article explains, financial needs have a major influence on company structure. A few investors can seldom provide enough capital for major expansions; hence a company cannot usually grow very much without tapping other sources of capital by issuing stocks or bonds to the general public. And the larger a company grows, the easier it often is to obtain new money at favorable rates.

Prof. E. A. G. Robinson, of Cambridge University, is one of England's outstanding industrial economists.

Financing and Growth

E. A. G. Robinson

The cost of production of a firm and its size will depend not only upon the technique of manufacture, and upon the efficiency of management and sales, but also upon the ability of the firm to borrow the capital necessary for its activities. If opportunities for borrowing depend in any sense upon size, the problems of finance will influence the optimum scale of production. In practice, we find that the task of raising capital exerts important influences both upon the size and upon the structure of firms. It does this in two ways; firstly through the rates at which firms can borrow, secondly through the amounts that firms of different types of organisation can borrow at any given rate. A firm in one set of circumstances may be able to borrow small amounts at a comparatively favourable rate, another firm in another set of circumstances may be able to borrow small amounts at a less favourable rate, but larger amounts at a more favourable rate than the first firm. The policy and structure of the firm may be determined by its choice between these two alternatives.

Where a large capital is necessary, the joint stock company with limited liability has become common. The company form of organisation enables the promoters or controllers of business to pass on to the general public any part of the task of financing a business which they do not themselves wish to undertake. The shareholders of a company perform two separate functions. They provide the capital and they run the risks, the risks either of losing their money or achieving wealth. The promoters of the company may hand over the performance of both these functions to the general public, themselves becoming no more than leading shareholders or even withdrawing entirely, or they may retain in their own hands most of the risks and opportunities, and apply to the public only for the provision of capital at fixed, or virtually fixed, rates of interest.

The ordinary investor is content as a rule to provide capital more cheaply than those who are in a position to promote and control businesses. The latter expect a higher return for their activities of enterprise and the bearing of the initial risks than will be secured by a shareholder in a mature and stable undertaking. The passing on to the general public of the task of providing capital makes possible also the employment of large amounts of saving which might otherwise be wasted. Stocks and shares are issued, which may be quickly realised by sales on the Stock Exchange. This possibility will enable those who have savings available for a comparatively short period to put them at the disposal of industry. These many short strands of savings may be spun together into a continuous thread of constantly available resources.

So long as the firm is owned and run by a single individual, he may regard the protection of limited liability as unnecessary. For it serves only to protect any property which he possesses outside his business,and if this property is small, he may regard the costs of turning his firm into a company as unjustified. If, however, he wishes to expand faster than his savings permit, and to give the undertaking an existence independent of the lives of its owners, he must turn it into a [corporation].

There are many leaders of business to-day, particularly in those industries where initiative and a willingness to take risks are important, who hold the view that the public company type of organization, which makes them responsible

From *The Structure of Competitive Industry*, rev. ed. (James Nisbet & Co., Ltd., London, Cambridge University Press, London, and The University of Chicago Press, Chicago, 1958), pp. 50–51, 53–54, 56–57.

in part at least to others, is a cramping influence upon their enterprise, that checks and safeguards are necessary which, apart from shareholders, they would have regarded as superfluous, that pressure will be put upon them to do things which in the long run they do not consider wise, that the autocracy which is the foundation of their efficiency will be confined and limited. If this view is justified, then in certain cases a firm must choose between greater immediate efficiency and a higher rate of growth.

This conflict between freedom and capital is not universal. There are many men who are unaffected by a responsibility to shareholders, who can command and mould a firm, whatever its theoretical organisation, into the forms which fit their own genius. There are others who regard any dependence upon money power with abhorrence. Complete independence is, however, seldom possible. It is a proper function of the banking system to provide a part of the working capital of industry.

In general, the large firm possesses, of course, an advantage. Its name is better known to the investing public, its standing can be more easily ascertained. A large firm may be able to borrow more than its present circumstances warrant, while a small firm of better real standing may go short. The greater ease with which firms can borrow money may be one factor leading to the vertical integration of large undertakings, or the absence of vertical disintegration where we should have expected it. The large firm may be able to borrow so much more easily and cheaply the funds required to exploit a new source of raw materials, or to take advantage of new processes of manufacture of some subsidiary product, that though it may be technically less well fitted to control these further processes, there may be economies to be secured by it doing so.

The advantage which a large firm possesses in this way, combined with the growing size of efficient units in many industries, is making the task of growing up to the optimum scale more and more difficult. Its financial structure has given the joint stock company a continuity of life greater than that of the individuals who control it. In the nineteenth century, firms grew, matured, and declined. The firms in an industry, in Marshall's famous simile, resembled the trees of the forest. Some were at their full height, others growing towards it, others were decaying. In this century the firm's cycle of life is far less pronounced. A firm is built up, usually as a private company, it reaches maturity, it declines, but it does not die. It is reorganised, new blood is brought in, and the firm may quickly return to the strength of its maturity. In some industries, mostly the younger industries, new firms spring up frequently. A number survive the diseases of childhood, and grow to the size of the largest. But in the older industries the new firms are rare. Growth is impossible or too slow, and capital can be better applied to the re-equipment of existing undertakings. In such industries, since the risks of a new enterprise must be great, the influences of finance lie on the side of the large firm, and on the side of stability rather than of change.

Laws designed to ensure that companies doing business with the Federal government promote socially desirable objectives are not new, but their influence is becoming more and more widespread. This is because the number of companies holding or seeking government contracts has become very large and because new laws have been passed imposing new restrictions. This might seem to be all to the good, but as this article points out, there may be losses as well as gains. Murray L. Weidenbaum is Mallinckrodt Distinguished University Professor at Washington University in St. Louis and formerly served as Assistant Secretary of the Treasury.

Social Responsibility Is Closer than You Think

Murray L. Weidenbaum

While businessmen and academicians continue to debate the desirability of companies becoming more "socially responsible" (however they choose to define the term), many seem to have overlooked the fact that the debate may be largely over for an important sector of the American economy. In the case of the many companies that do business with the Federal Government, the very act of signing the procurement contract forces them to agree to performing a wide variety of "socially responsible" actions. These requirements range from favoring a wide variety of disadvantaged groups to a concern with the quality of life and the environment.

The magnitude of the government's procurement outlays, and particularly their importance to government-oriented firms, create opportunities for implementing a host and variety of governmental economic and social aims through the contract mechanism. The Federal Government thus can and does require that firms doing business with it maintain "fair" employment practices, provide "safe" and "healthful" working conditions, pay "prevailing" wages, refrain from polluting the air and water, give preference to American products in their purchases, and promote the rehabilitation of prisoners and severely handicapped. Table 1 contains a representative listing of such ancillary duties which are required of government contractors.

Historical Development

One of the earliest attempts to bring about social change through the government procurement process was the enactment of the Eight Hour Laws, a series of statutes setting standards for hours of work. In 1892, the notion of an eight-hour day was first extended to workers employed by contractors and subcontractors engaged in federal projects.[1]

The use of the government contract as a means for promoting social and economic objectives became widespread during the depression of the 1930's. In the face of high unemployment and depressed wages, Congress enacted the Buy American Act and most of the current labor standards legislation governing public contracts, including the Davis-Bacon Act and the Walsh-Healey Public Contracts Act.

The economic mobilization during World War II gave further impetus to this use of the government purchasing process. Executive orders requiring nondiscrimination in employment by government contractors were justified by the need to encourage maximum use of the nation's scarce manpower and other resources. A similar concern during the Korean War led to provision encouraging the placement of government contracts and subcontracts in areas of substantial labor surplus.

Rarely have these social provisions been eliminated or even scaled down, even when the original depression or wartime conditions justifying them were no longer present. Rather, the trend has been to extend their application. In 1964, for example, an amendment to the Davis-Bacon Act broadened the prevailing wage concept to include certain fringe benefits as well as actual wages.[2] The Service Contract Act of 1965 extended to service employees of contractors the wage and labor standard policies established by the Davis-Bacon Act and the Walsh-Healey Public Contracts Act. In 1969, the Contract Hours Standard Act was amended to give the Secretary of Labor authority to promulgate safety and health standards for workers on government construction contracts.

More recently, the federal procurement process has been utilized as the leading edge of the effort to reduce barriers to the employment of minority groups. In 1970, the hiring of apprentices and trainees was required on federal construction projects. In 1971, all government contractors and subcontractors were required to list

[1]These statutes have been superseded by the Work Hours Act of 1962, 76 Stat. 357.

[2]Public Law 88–349, 78 Stat. 238.

Reprinted by permission from the July, 1973, issue of the *Michigan Business Review*, pp. 32–35, published by the Graduate School of Business Administration, The University of Michigan.

Table I Special Social and Economic Restrictions on Government Contractors

Program	Authority	Purpose
Improve Working Conditions		
Walsh-Healey Act	41 U.S. Code 35–45	Prescribes minimum wages, hours, age, and work conditions for supply contracts
Davis-Bacon Act	40 U.S. Code 2761a–1–5	Prescribes minimum wages, benefits, and work conditions on construction contracts, over $2,000
Service Contract Act of 1968	41 U.S. Code 351–357	Extends the Walsh-Healey and Davis-Bacon Acts to service contracts
Convict Labor Act	Executive Order 325A	Prohibits employment on government contracts of persons imprisoned at hard labor
Favor Disadvantaged Groups		
Equal Employment Opportunity	Executive Orders 11246 and 11375	Prohibits discrimination in government contracting
Employment Openings for Veterans	Executive Order 11598	Requires contractors to list suitable employment openings with State employment systems to assist veterans in obtaining jobs
Prison-Made Supplies	18 U.S. Code 4124	Requires mandatory purchase of specific supplies from Federal Prison Industries, Inc.
Blind-Made Products	41 U.S. Code 46–48	Requires mandatory purchase of products made by blind and other handicapped persons
Small Business Act	15 U.S. Code 631–647	Requires "fair" portion of subcontracts to be placed with small business concerns
Labor Surplus Area Concerns	32A Code of Federal Regulations 33	Requires preference to subcontractors in areas of concentrated unemployment or underemployment
Favor American Companies		
Buy American Act	41 U.S. Code 10a–10d	Provides preference for domestic materials over foreign materials
Preference to U.S. Vessels	10 U.S. Code 2631; 46 U.S. Code 1241	Requires shipment of all military goods and at least half of other government goods in U.S. vessels
Protect the Environment and Quality of Life		
Clean Air Act of 1970	42 U.S. Code 1857h–4	Prohibits contracts to a company convicted of criminal violation of air pollution standards
Care of Laboratory Animals	ASPR 7-303.44	Requires humane treatment by defense contractors in use of experimental or laboratory animals
Humane Slaughter Act	7 U.S. Code 1901–1906	Limits government purchases of meat to suppliers who conform to humane slaughter standards

Table I (Continued)

	Promote Other Government Objectives	
Embargo in Ships Engaged in Cuban and North Vietnam Trade	ASPR 1–1410 (Armed Services Procurement Regulation)	Prohibits defense contractors from shipping any supplies on foreign flag vessels that have called on Cuban or North Vietnamese ports
Use of Government Facilities	ASPR 7–104.37	Requires defense contractors to purchase jewel bearings from government facility
Use of Government Stockpile	ASPR 1–327	Requires defense contractors to purchase aluminum from national stockpile

Source: Commission on Government Procurement.

job openings with State employment service offices.[3] This was especially intended to help Vietnam veterans reenter civilian labor markets.

Disadvantages and Shortcomings

The benefits of using government contracts to promote basic social policies are quite clear. Important national objectives may be fostered without the need for additional, direct appropriations from the Treasury. To a congressman, this may seem a painless and simple approach. Because restrictive procurement provisions seem to be costless, the government has been making increasing use of them.[4] Any disadvantages, being more indirect, receive less attention.

Yet, upon reflection, these special provisions are all burdens on the governmental procurement process. They cannot but increase overhead expenses of private contractors and federal procurement offices alike. Many of the provisions also exert an upward pressure on the direct costs incurred by the government. Supposedly, the basic concern of governmental buyers is to meet public needs at lowest cost. Yet, special provisions such as the Davis-Bacon Act have tended to increase the cost of public construction projects through government promulgation of wage rates higher than would have resulted if the market were allowed to operate without impediment.[5]

Many of these provisions reflect the notions of an earlier age. The prohibition against convict labor was enacted because of the concern over "chain gang" workers which was a live public issue several decades ago. Changing attitudes on rehabilitation since then have cast doubt on the validity of the negative approach. In fact, under another and more recent statute, federal prisoners may work for pay in local communities under work release programs.

The greatest shortcoming of the use of government contracts to foster unrelated economic and social aims is the cumulative impact that they have on the companies themselves. Forced to take on so many of the concerns and attitudes of government agencies, it should not be too surprising that the more government-oriented corporations have come to show many of the negative characteristics of government bureaus and arsenals. The advantages of innovation, risk-bearing, and efficiency may be lost to the public and private sectors alike. That is a high price to pay for legislating social responsibility.

[3]Weekly Compilation of Presidential Documents, 376 (1970), article III, section B4; Executive Order 11598, 3 CFR 161 (Supp. 1971).

[4]See *Report of the Commission on Government Procurement*, Washington, Government Printing Office, 1972, Vol. 1, pp. 110–124.

[5]John P. Gould, *Davis-Bacon Act*, Washington, American Enterprise Institute for Public Policy research, 1971.

Although the basic attitudes of management and union officials may differ widely from each other, many contracts are signed without resort to a test of strength in the form of a strike. This is possible because a balance of power exists and neither side wants a strike unless it is fairly sure of winning quite a lot more than it could get through a peaceful settlement. Here Edward Peters, drawing on one of his many experiences as a government conciliator, describes what actually happens in a collective bargaining session.

Reaching an Agreement between Labor and Management

Edward Peters

The amiable chatting around the conference table subsided into a lull as the negotiators waited expectantly for the conciliator to make the appropriate remarks which would open the bargaining session. The conciliator who had joined in the good-natured bantering a moment before, brushed his hand across his eyes, then straightened up and assumed an almost exaggerated air of serious formality. He pulled a piece of scratch paper to him and, with pencil poised, said, "My information on the issues between you, which I derived from the telephone conversations leading to this meeting, is really very sketchy. I would greatly appreciate it if one or both of you could give me a more detailed picture."

Lloyd Turner, the president of the corporation and controlling stockholder, looked up from a sheaf of papers he had been shuffling nervously, and cast an aggrieved look at Bert Frazier, the union business agent. "Bert," he said, "why don't you lead off and give him your version of the situation? We'll add to it with anything that you leave out."

Frazier nodded and proceeded with an account of the union's position. As he was talking, the conciliator looked around him and, almost without articulating to himself, began to make his own estimate of the routine aspects of the situation.

Frazier explained that the union had been mandated by the membership to ask for a 30¢-an-hour increase, because of the rising cost of living and the inadequacy of the present wage scale, which was hardly enough to provide a living wage for the employees. The employees had been determined at the union meeting, and had expressed themselves to the negotiations committee, "Don't come back with less!" However, the committee was more cognizant than the membership of the employer's problem of competitive prices in the face of rising production costs. It was well aware of the fact that the employees could not expect to get all they wanted. Therefore, during the past several weeks of negotiations the committee had, on a number of occasions, gone to bat with the membership. It had persuaded them to come down, first to 25¢ an hour, then to 20¢ an hour, and finally, in an effort to break the impasse, the committee itself had come down to 15¢ an hour. This was done without the sanction of a union meeting and was much below anything they had hoped the membership could be prevailed upon to accept.

Turner presented the position of the management. He appreciated how the employees felt. Of course, they are not making enough money, but who is? If it were within his power, he would give them twice what they are asking for. But what purpose would it serve, if, by so doing, the company is put out of business and nobody has jobs? The company has to stay in line with its competitors. It is already way out of line with the stamp and die market; it is paying from 10¢ to 30¢ an hour more, in comparable classifications, than its fifteen leading competitors on the Pacific Coast, let alone the competition it is getting in Knoxville, Tennessee, and Birmingham, Alabama, where they are able to turn out castings and plates at an amazingly low price. He doesn't see how the union can expect the company, when it is so far out of line with its competitors, to be pushed even further out of line. The whole thing just doesn't make sense to him. If the negotiations were handled solely on the basis of economics, he should be asking for a wage reduction to bring him in line with his

From *Conciliation in Action: Principles and Techniques* (National Foreman's Institute, Inc., New London, Conn., 1952), pp. 3–18.

competition so that more work could be provided for everybody. But he recognizes that the union would have a problem in that connection and, therefore, he hasn't raised the question. However, he feels that if the problem were presented properly to the employees, they would appreciate the company's difficulties and go along with a 4¢ offer, which, under the circumstances, is exceedingly generous and way beyond anything contemplated in the first instance.

Meanwhile, the conciliator was weighing the surface aspects of the situation in his own mind. Last year, the General Motors settlement of 12½¢ an hour had established a reference point for the negotiations in many industries. While 12½¢ could not be said to have emerged as a clear-cut pattern, it was an undoubted psychological reference point for negotiations in many industries of this type. Many of the more powerful unions were able to get a 12½¢ settlement or even better. Many other settlements had been below this figure. This year the range of wage settlements in many leading industries in the area, and in the nation, was from 6¢ to 10¢ an hour.

The conciliator reasoned to himself, "Last year when the larger unions were settling for 12½¢ an hour, although some went below it, this union accepted 10¢ an hour. The same unions who negotiated 12¢ an hour last year are not able to get more than 10¢ an hour this year, and many are settling for less. It follows that this union cannot expect to get more than 10¢ an hour. On the other hand, the management may well have high hopes that it can go below 10¢ an hour just as it went below the reference point the year before, and, therefore, it is probably shooting for 6¢ to 8¢ an hour. The hard bargaining will be in the area of between 6¢ and 10¢ an hour."

At a certain point in the discussion the conciliator said, "There are some questions I have in mind, and some possibilities have occurred to me which I think would be more appropriately pursued in separate session where no one's collective bargaining position can be prejudiced. I would like to meet with the union first."

In the separate meeting with the union committee, the conciliator nodded sympathetically as the various members impressed upon him further how determined they were, how difficult their situation was, and how adamant the membership was against making any further concessions.

Then he said, "I don't know what the outcome of the situation will be, but it seems fairly obvious that management is dead-set against a 15¢ settlement. If that is your rock-bottom position, I'm no medicine man. I can't do the impossible. I think that my job would be much easier if you were able to consider something under 15¢ an hour."

The committee hastened to reaffirm its position—how they would like to cooperate with the conciliator, but how, unfortunately, they had made the mistake of hitting rock-bottom before he had entered the picture.

In the separate talk with the management committee, the conciliator continued sympathetically to nod his head as Turner and his group elaborated on the impossibility of meeting the union's position and how far the elastic had been stretched in making the offer of 4¢ an hour.

Turner said, "Personally, I think they would be glad to take 6¢, but I don't see how we can do it."

The conciliator said, "Possibly you're right. It's a little too early to say. It's a sure thing that they won't close on 4¢. It is conceivable they might take 6¢ as the breaking point, but I would be misleading you if I indicated that figure with any degree of optimism. However, I'll explore the situation further with them."

The conciliator returned to the union group and said, "I'm afraid you fellows are still very far apart. I haven't any new offer from the management for your consideration, but there are indications that there could be 6¢ in the cards. Maybe there is more, but I certainly didn't get any indication of it in my discussion with them."

The committee members snorted at the very thought that such a ridiculously low figure as 6¢ could be considered at all.

The conciliator went on, "It is still a little too early for me to have a definite opinion, but my guess is that 6¢ is not too far away from their closing position. In any case, unless you fellows give me something more to work with, I haven't any way of getting them to change their offer, and start them moving up. I am convinced that if you stay frozen on 15¢, they are going to remain frozen on 4¢."

Frazier asked for a caucus with his committee. The conciliator waited outside for about ten minutes and then was called back in.

Frazier said very solemnly, "I've had quite a job convincing this committee that we ought to stick our necks out with the membership a little more, and it's going to be tough, but we think that we can sell 13¢ to the people."

The conciliator said, "Well, at least you've given me something to work with, although I still think you may be too far above the management's closing position."

The conciliator returned to the management group and said. "I have definite indications from them of 13¢, which probably means that they are shooting for a closing figure of 10¢. No one can be certain but 10¢ might well be their breaking-off point. I have the feeling that at this stage they would not have indicated 13¢ to me unless they were ready to close at 10¢."

Turner said, "Even if you are right, 10¢ is too far off. We would, if we thought it would close the situation, improve our 4¢ offer a little even though it is very much against our better judgment, but the present competitive situation in the industry, etc., etc., would make 10¢ out of the question. Those fellows must be smoking opium."

"Well," said the conciliator, "how about letting me indicate definitely that there is 6¢ in the cards? They've indicated a change in their position, and I don't think it would prejudice your position drastically if you let me indicate a reciprocal change in your offer. Otherwise, you'll have no chance at all of an agreement." The management acquiesced.

The conciliator returned to the union committee and said, "The indications I had of 6¢ have now been definitely confirmed by the management. But, that's as far as they'll go with me. Offhand, I think they're shooting for a closing figure of 8¢, which may well be the breaking-off point."

Frazier threw his hands up and said, "No soap. If a strike is what they want, that's what they'll get."

With the resumption of joint negotiations it became apparent that no further progress could be made. It was suggested that the negotiations be recessed for a five-day period.

Five days later the negotiations opened very acrimoniously. In the interim, a mass meeting of the union had been called and a vote taken to strike if an agreement was not reached. The deadline was now two days away. The union made official its proposal of 13¢ and the management made official its counterproposal of 6¢. The conciliator asked for another separate conference between the parties.

He said to the union, "I think it's evident that if 13¢ is your rock-bottom position, you're headed for a strike. It is not for me to determine what your best interests are; I can only suggest to you what I think are the possibilities."

The committee members began to assure the conciliator that 13¢ was definitely their final position when Frazier cut in, "Look fellows, I've worked with the conciliator before; he's a good guy. I think we ought to take him into our confidence and let him know where we are really headed. Pete, frankly, and for heaven's sake don't spill this to the management yet; it is entirely for your information—11¢ is what we will accept."

The conciliator went into a session with the management and said, "I am more than ever convinced that 10¢ is their final position, only this time it is not a matter of speculation. If I am wrong, I am definitely not wrong by more than 1¢. You gentlemen will have to determine your own interests in this situation. I think it would be presumptuous of me to try to spend your money. All I can indicate is what I honestly think is the minimum concession from you that will avert a strike."

The management looked very serious and said, "We realize that what you say is true, and frankly we are trying to make up our minds whether to take a strike."

The conciliator asked, "What have your relations with the union been in the past?"

"Oh, they tend to drive a pretty hard bargain, but on the whole we have no complaint."

"How is your situation during the life of a contract? Do you have a lot of headaches with the men; screwball grievances, etc.?"

"No, as a matter of fact, once I sign the contract," said Turner, "I can throw it in the bottom drawer of my desk and probably not have to pull it out more than a few times in the course of the year."

"Well," said the conciliator, "it seems as

though you would have very little to gain by accepting the cost of a strike. Which is your lesser evil, to meet the increased cost of their minimum demand, or underwrite the cost of what may be a long and drawn-out economic contest?"

Turner asked for a caucus with his committee. They were in a huddle for half an hour. When the conciliator resumed discussions with them, Turner told him, "Pete, we'll go 8¢ and they may as well face the fact that that's the end of the line. If they push us any further than that, we'll take anything they want to throw at us."

The conciliator returned to the union group and told them, "I'm convinced that if you are determined to hold out for more than 8¢, then get ready to pull the pin. This looks like *it*."

Frazier said, "Well, I may be out of line with my committee in saying this, but if you get them to offer us a dime, it will be a hell of a job, but we'll sell it."

The management committee was adamant. They stayed firm on 8¢. The union committee remained equally adamant on 10¢. The conciliator said to both groups, "All I can suggest is, let's have a resumption of joint discussion; let management make its offer of 8¢ with the definite understanding that the union will counter with a 10¢. Somewhere along the line one of you might convince the other to back off."

They agreed, and across-the-table discussions were resumed. The discussions went on for hours. Rehashes were rehashed again. The conference took on the hue of a filibuster. Everyone doodled on scraps of paper. Finally, the conciliator took a calculated risk.

"Gentlemen, I would like to throw something out across the open table for your mutual consideration. I want you to understand that I am not a judge as to what's best for people, but a strike is such a serious thing, and the differences between you, in comparison to the distance you have already gone, should not be insurmountable. I would like to ask both of you to consider a closing figure of 9¢."

Frazier and Turner looked each other in the eye. Somewhere a communication established itself without a word between them. The question in each other's eye was, "If I move to 9¢, will you move to 9¢?"

Frazier said, "Well, we are willing to give it some consideration for the sake of averting a strike."

Turner nodded his acquiescence. The tension was gone as he buzzed his secretary to come in and take down a memorandum of agreement. The good-natured bantering was resumed over who would buy the drinks.

When a stagecoach passenger sued the manufacturer of the coach because he was injured in the breakdown of the vehicle, the case was thrown out of court on the ground that there was no contract between the manufacturer and the passenger. This defense (known as "privity") has long since been unavailable to manufacturers, and as this article shows, other defenses have been crumbling as well. Thus the possibility of consumer suits now constitutes one of the major restrictions on business imposed by the external environment.

They No Longer Say, "I Got a Lemon"—Nowadays, They Say, "I'll Sue"

As recently as 1960, there were fewer than 50,000 product-liability cases in the courts. In 1963 the number jumped to 250,000; in 1970, to 500,000. It's expected to pass the million mark by 1975. It's getting to be a gold mine for lawyers and a terrific headache for businessmen.

Says H. D. Hulme, a Westinghouse quality-control manager: "Today, a poorly made product is not passed off with the remark, "I got a lemon." More likely the words are, "I'll sue.' "

From *Forbes*, Apr. 15, 1972, pp. 55–57. Reprinted by permission of FORBES Magazine.

The suits—and sometimes the judgments—can be for staggering amounts. Only the other day a California lawyer, David L. Caplan, filed a class-action suit on behalf of a man named Vernon H. Kendricks and 3,000 John Does against three supermarket chains for more than $40 million. He charged them with selling ordinary food as organic food. Another California lawyer, George A. Peters, author of *Product Liability and Safety*, recalls an award of $21.8 million for an accident caused by the absence of a baffle in the wing fuel tank of a small aircraft.

Of course, there is often a wide gap between the amounts asked and the amounts awarded—and especially the amounts actually paid after the case has been appealed. Still, the cost to a company can be substantial. In one case, Meinert *vs.* Searle, a woman who developed a blood clot in her intestines after taking The Pill collected $250,000. Searle was covered by product-liability insurance. Alfred S. Julien of the law firm of Julien, Glaser, Blitz & Schlesinger, who handled the case, now has about 50 similar ones in the courts. Searle's losses could run into the millions. Earnings would not be directly affected, but the cost of the insurance the company must carry does, of course, cut earnings down.

In Cole *vs.* Pfizer, a cook at a Veterans Administration hospital in upstate New York, who came down with polio after taking Sabin polio vaccine, collected $550,000.

In Sheedy *vs.* Warco, the widow of a driver who was killed when his brakes failed collected $250,000.

Company Bankrupted

The threat of such suits has been a major factor in persuading companies to recall products. The cost of recalling or recapturing a product can run to millions. Abbott Laboratories estimates that recalling 6 million intravenous-feeding bottles, destroying them and closing the facility that produced them cost $8.5 million. When a banker, Samuel Cochran Jr., died of botulism poisoning after eating a can of Bon Vivant vichyssoise, the cost of recalling all its products drove the company into bankruptcy. Says Bon Vivant president Andrew Paretti: "There isn't a good packer in the country, even the biggest, who could withstand a total recall without going broke." It cost Campbell Soup $5 million just to recall two kinds of soup processed in one plant.

Strangely, only a handful of insurance companies write product recall insurance—Fireman's Fund, Lloyds of London, the Insurance Co. of North America, Employers Insurance Co. of Wausau and the CNA Insurance Group—and only about 200 U.S. companies have signed up for it, roughly half of them with Fireman's Fund.

Giant manufacturers like du Pont and General Motors insure themselves against product-liability suits. GM, for example, absorbed the costs of suits based on alleged defects in the Corvair; how much that came to nobody knows except GM. Other manufacturers take out policies which, says an underwriter, "may range from $300,000 for a company that makes stapling machines to $100 million for a drug company." A drug company's $100 million might cost it several million a year; premiums, the underwriter adds, are negotiated. "We have to judge each risk separately.

"Say you're a supplier for a Detroit auto manufacturer, with sales of $500,000. If you're making a simple part, which can go wrong but won't cause the car to crash, you might have to pay between one-fourth of 1% and one-half of 1% of sales. On the other hand, if you're making a part for the brakes, you might have to pay 1½%. The longevity of a product is a factor, too. If you're making toys, well, they don't last very long. But if you're making electric toasters, they're likely to last for ten years. You sell 1 million of them a year, and in ten years you're going to have 10 million of them around. Lord knows how many people they may electrocute."

From Profit to Loss

Once a profitable little sideline, product-liability insurance is fast becoming a headache for the insurance companies. Says Victor T. Ehre, president of the Utica Mutual Insurance Co.: "Product-liability coverage from a profits standpoint has been deteriorating by leaps and bounds.

. . . We recently concluded a case in which we won a suit after a three-month trial; the attorney's fee was $17,000, not including previous costs for pre-trial preparations. We can hardly afford such Pyrrhic victories."

According to Ehre, general liability insurance, which covers product liability, was once "consistently one of the most profitable classes of insurance. . . . For the 15 years leading up to 1966, underwriting profits on general liability, bodily injury and property damage averaged about 15%. In 1966 the profit dropped to about 6%. In 1967 profit disappeared entirely and the class produced a loss of about 2%. In 1968 the loss rose to 5%."

The sudden jump in the number of product-liability suits is not entirely the result of "consumerism." Ralph Nader did encourage it with his attacks on the Corvair and his book *Unsafe at Any Speed*, but the basic reason is a series of court decisions, starting in 1960, that completely revolutionized the law of product liability. Where the rule once was *caveat emptor*, let the buyer beware, it's now *caveat venditor*, let the seller beware.

The result, says Bernard Kaapcke of the Insurance Information Institute, is that, "In any package, product or part sold in the U.S. today, there may be hidden a ticking time bomb." Under the court decisions of the past decade, he points out, a manufacturer can be held "strictly liable for damages to consumers even though there is no contract or other direct relationship, and no showing of negligence."

In fact, he can be held liable even if the consumer misuses his product. Robert C. Battle, vice president of Alexander & Alexander, insurance brokers, recalls the case of a woman, bothered by bugs, who bought a can of a nationally marketed insecticide. She sprayed herself with it and had a violent allergic reaction. She sued—and collected.

How It Started

For years, manufacturers were protected from product-liability suits by a rule of law known as privity. This meant that, if a product was defective, the buyer could sue only the man he bought if from, not the company that made it. The dealer, in turn, could sue the wholesaler, who could sue the company. This was such a long and costly process that hardly anyone ever brought suit. In 1916 the rule of privity began to crumble, but manufacturers still were protected from product-liability suits because the consumer had to prove negligence.

In 1960 the wall protecting manufacturers broke with the case of Henningsen *vs.* Bloomfield Motors.

Claus Henningsen bought a Plymouth from the authorized Chrysler dealer in Bloomfield, N.J. Several days later, while his wife Helen was driving it, the steering wheel came off. The car ran into a brick wall and was totally demolished. Mrs. Henningsen sustained painful injuries.

Was Chrysler guilty of negligence in the manufacture of the Plymouth? The experts said the car was too badly damaged for them to determine what had gone wrong. One could only say that "something down there had to drop off or break loose." Henningsen could not prove negligence, and previous courts had ruled that there could be no damages without proof of negligence. This time the court ruled that the victim does *not* have to prove negligence.

Chrysler appealed, but the New Jersey Supreme Court upheld the lower court. In effect, the Supreme Court ruled that Henningsen had an implied warranty that the car would operate reasonably well, that the steering wheel would not come off in his wife's hands.

After that came a swift series of court rulings that further opened manufacturers to product-liability suits. As things stand now in most of the states of the Union, anyone injured by a defective product can sue everyone connected with the product—the manufacturer, his suppliers, his distributors, the retailers. He can bring class actions on behalf of everyone who bought the product. All he need prove is that for some reason, the product doesn't work the way a reasonable man—and perhaps even an unreasonable one—has a right to expect.

Professor David L. Rados of Columbia University's Graduate School of Business wrote in the

Harvard Business Review: "So far no advertising agency has been held negligent in the preparation of copy, but such action can reasonably be expected. Even industry associations and testing laboratories, which are organizations remote from the injured consumer, may soon have to face actions."

According to Robert B. Johnson, vice president of Continental Insurance Co., insurance companies have already been sued for product liability after their inspectors gave a manufacturer advice on how to make his product safer. The suits have been "based upon the alleged negligence of the insurance company in not making certain that the insured corrected the unsafe condition."

Cashing In

Naturally, the legal profession has been quick to cash in on the changed situation. Says a Midwest insurance association executive: "As the idea of no-fault auto insurance spreads, we find more and more lawyers turning to product-liability suits. It's now the big thing."

Product suits still have a way to go before they become the lawyers' bonanza that auto accident suits are. Complains one specialist on product liability: "In auto-liability suits, the insurance companies settle more often than not, but in product-liability cases they can't settle except with the consent of the company, and companies are loath to give consent because they want to uphold the integrity of their products. So you have to fight, and that can be costly to a lawyer. These product-liability suits are among the most difficult of all pieces of litigation."

An insurance company executive answers: "Well, yes and no. What happens is, they don't bother with small claims except to bring a class action. They concentrate on the whoppers. If they collect, say, $350,000 for a client, that's $100,000 for them, minus costs. Get one real sour product; get 50 cases; and you've made yourself a million."

To the Rescue

The paradox is that manufacturers, wholesalers, retailers and insurance companies may get some relief from, of all things, the consumer movement. This has led several congressmen to introduce bills to set up a government agency with the power to establish and enforce product standards. One such bill has already been reported out by the Senate Commerce Committee by a vote of 17 to 1.

Normally, businessmen grumble about new burdens of regulation. In this case, the National Association of Manufacturers came out in favor of regulation. Testifying for the NAM before the Commerce Committee, AMF Vice President Stanley Groner said: "As far as we can determine, manufacturers overwhelmingly recognize the legitimate interest of the Federal Government in the safety of products in national markets."

Any way you slice it, though, it's getting to be a tougher world for businessmen—and a happier world for lawyers.

In theory, competition—especially price competition—is supposed to act as a check on the power of large corporations in a free enterprise economy. But in cases where new companies will find it practically impossible to enter the industry in competition with established giants, the restraints imposed by competition may be minimal. However, there are other sources of countervailing power in the external environment—government, labor unions, farmers' organizations, and so on. This article discusses two of the newer sources of countervailing power: consumerism and environmentalism, both of which are receiving support from government. (The environmentalists, in particular, have succeeded in having many of their goals enacted into law.) Charles G. Leathers is associate professor of economics at the University of Alabama.

New Dimensions of Countervailing Power: Consumerism and Environmentalism

Charles G. Leathers

Two rather militant protest movements, consumerism and environmentalism, recently have become quite active in the American economy. Both advocate goals that inevitably tend to place greater constraints on the practices of private enterprise, particularly of large corporations.

Born of frustration, the militancies of both movements tend to be democratic and nonviolent, and as yet largely nonpolitical. Goals of both appeal to members of most socioeconomic groups. Active participants include business executives (especially in the case of environmentalism), professional people, housewives, and factory workers, as well as "radical" college students. The major point of interest is that both consumerism and environmentalism are at the brink of acquiring social power.

The exercise of power in a pluralistic system of political economy has long been the cause of concern and some anxiety for economists and policy makers. In a very important way consumerism and environmentalism directly relate to the exercise of *countervailing power*, a concept of social control of giant corporations conceived by John K. Galbraith several decades ago.[1]

In this article, consumerism and environmentalism serve to demonstrate that countervailing power tends to have an immature and a mature phase, with these two movements exemplifying the latter. Immature countervailing power tends to be inadequate and easily destroyed. In contrast, the mature variety promises a more durable regulatory device capable of producing a stable balance of socioeconomic power in a modern economy of giant power concentrates.

[1]*American Capitalism: The Concept of Countervailing Power* (Houghton Mifflin Company, Boston, 1952). Subsequent comments will refer to the revised Sentry edition, 1956, Chapters 9 and 10.

The Principle of Countervailing Power

Countervailing power was described by Galbraith as a natural phenomenon that tended to emerge in response to, and to ultimately neutralize, uncurtailed market power acquired by large firms.

Where price competition as a social protector had greatly diminished, there was no cause for alarm or lament. For, insofar as "original" power positions are achieved by large firms, such as power on one side of the market, there exists a natural tendency for large organizations to virtually automatically appear in juxtaposition to established oligopolies. These large organizations would use their power to neutralize the original power of the oligopolies. Thus new restraints on the opposite side of the market appeared to replace competition. The lack of competition creates the other, with the consequences that private economic power is held in check by those who are subject to it. Competition continues to play its important role, but in markets where competition is weak, the presence of countervailing power provides the restraint.

There were, to be sure, admitted limitations upon the effectiveness of countervailing power. It was not certain to develop in sufficient strength in all markets. Where it failed to develop adequately, it became the appropriate function of government to sponsor its development by especially disadvantaged groups, such as labor and farmers. Moreover, a major limitation of countervailing power was its tendency to lose effectiveness during inflationary conditions. Thus, a new type of public policy, in contrast to commission regulation or legal prosecution under antitrust legislation, was added—the deliberate use of governmental powers to encourage and assist the development of countervaillance and to shore up defenses against infla-

From *MSU Business Topics* (published by the Graduate School of Business Administration, Michigan State University, East Lansing, Mich.), Winter, 1972, pp. 64–72. Condensation reprinted by permission of the publisher, Division of Research, Graduate School of Business Administration, Michigan State University.

tion. As one consequence, a more positive role was assigned to the activities of pressure groups as a means of generating public support of countervailing power.

Countervailing Power of Consumerism

One of Galbraith's more intriguing examples of the social benefits of that power was the protection provided consumers by the market advantages possessed by large retail chains.[2] As large oligopsonistic buyers, chains were able to command lower prices from similarly large oligopolistic producers. Part of the gains were then passed along to the consumers in the form of lower retail prices. It was, according to Galbraith, in the best interest of the chains to maintain low prices for volume operations. Consequently, they used their own power to resist higher prices originating from the producing corporations.

In light of subsequent developments, either Galbraith was wrong about countervailing power in general, or the example of chain stores protecting the interests of consumers was exaggerated. Potential countervailing power of chains has increased as they have increased their share of the retail market. Competition evidently also has increased with the advent of the discount department stores. In some instances, competition and countervailing power possibilities have been consolidated as chains of discount stores have emerged. Yet, in his later book, *The New Industrial State*, Galbraith conspicuously omitted mentioning an increase in either regulatory force in consumer markets. Rather, consumers are visualized as more or less willing dupes of the "revised sequence," although they can contract out, that is, ignore the persuasive appeals of advertisements.[3]

The consumerism movement, with the supermarket boycotts by housewives, the emergence of Ralph Nader as a folk hero, and the numerous attempts by consumer groups to secure national and state consumer protection legislation in the form of truth-in-packaging and truth-in-lending statutes, vividly proclaims that if protective power has been provided by retailers, it has been inadequate. Why have retail chains and discount stores been unable or unwilling to exert effective countervaillance? Several conjectures can be offered in way of explanation that both preserve and enhance the concept of countervailing power.

First, resistance to higher prices has been circumvented by producers through deliberate deterioration in the quality of the product. Since changes in quality are often very difficult to substantiate, the chains could provide little protection against such practices. Consequently, concern with quality has become a driving force of consumerism.

A second factor that has aggravated consumers to the point of organized resistance has been frustration over the manipulation of consumer demand via advertising. The public appears to be increasingly hostile to the tepid concern with honesty in advertisements, in no small part due to such social critics and exposers as Nader and Galbraith. In connection with the growing alliance between retailers and producers in consumer manipulation, Galbraith once noted in response to critics of his thesis that as demand functions become generally inelastic (the prime objective of persuasive advertising) greater opportunity emerges for coalitions between interests that are otherwise opposed in bargaining.[4] Against advertising and its possible objectionable features, the retailers naturally would not provide countervailing power for the simple reason that stronger (less elastic) demand for the producers' products means stronger demand for those products when handled by the retailers. Hence, the interest of the retailers and the producers coincides.

In addition, two factors cited by Galbraith as detrimental to the effectiveness of countervailing power have been active in the American economy. Countervailing power could be avoided or eliminated through vertical integration. The effect would be to remove the conflict between two groups by uniting them under the same organization. The extent to which integra-

[2] *Ibid.*, pp. 118–122.

[3] *The New Industrial State* (Houghton Mifflin Company, Boston, 1967), Sentry edition, pp. 212–215.

[4] "Countervailing Power" in *Papers and Proceedings of the 66th Annual Meetings of the American Economic Association*, 64, No. 2 (May, 1954), pp. 4–5.

tion has weakened the power of retail chains is debatable, but it undoubtedly has occurred. Even more powerful has been the force of the severe inflation that has plagued the economy since 1966.

One point in the logic of countervailing power escaped Galbraith, which explains his overemphasis on retail chains as protectors of consumer interest. Part of its imperfection lies in its inability to be truly effective when private enterprise is expected to countervail the power of private enterprise. It is much more effective when the groups opposed have different social goals, such as labor unions and farmers; special efforts are necessary to produce really workable countervailing power. It is more a function of society than a function of the market, but assuming society recognizes its legitimacy and induces its development, it can become a viable force.

Hence, as certain groups in the private sector do become dominant, special attention is required from government in fostering the development of effective countervailing power. During the previous decades, the needs of labor and farmers have preoccupied the government's attention. In seeking to alter the distribution of income, little concern was extended to the ability of the consumer to maximize his use of that income. The logical sequence of the principle of countervailing power would be to expand the balance by increasing the power of consumers. Thus the consumerism movement represents the natural tendency for organizations to arise in cases of social power vacuums to act as countervailing forces. The responsiveness of government action (or simply the threat of such action) provides the movement with the thrust of real power that it needs to succeed. In brief, government recently has found itself in a position of political expediency to lend a sympathetic ear to the mounting organized complaints of consumers, if for no other reason than the vulgar strategy of seeking voter identification for electoral support.

Evidence of the growing power of consumerism can be easily detected within the behavior of the business community and government agencies. For example, the recently displayed tendencies of a number of corporations to respond in a more positive and concerned manner to consumer complaints can be directly related to consumerism. Such features as hot lines to corporate headquarters so consumers can vent frustrations at the top level, the establishment of consumer service departments, the encouragement of letter writing by customers dissatisfied with the company's products or services, more rigorous quality controls such as more specific estimates of the product's life span, and greater clarity in warranties have not as yet produced great major changes.[5] They do, nevertheless, explicitly connote an increased concern on the part of producers and sellers with customer satisfaction. Logically that concern stems from a recognition of the latter's power.

The actual power of consumerism is largely sponsored by the federal government. Evidence that the government is beginning to take action in a new and suggestive manner is available. For example, the Federal Trade Commission recently issued special orders to the four major domestic automobile producers and three foreign producers to substantiate specific claims made for their products in advertisements. These special orders constituted a landmark as the first to be issued by the FTC under a resolution adopted in response to a petition filed by Ralph Nader requiring all advertisers to furnish the commission on demand with documentation for advertised claims made for a product's safety, performance, quality, or comparative price. The FTC plans to make public any data the companies produce, except for trade secrets, in an effort to help consumers judge the validity of advertised claims.[6]

As yet, the impact of these orders upon consumer welfare and the producers' behavior is unknown. The importance of the move by the FTC lies in indicating a possible major shift in public attitude toward the rights of business to conduct marketing operations under the traditional assumption that buyers possess sufficient intelligence to protect themselves against possible false claims by producers. Consumerism as a countervailing power may have sufficient appeal to acquire real effectiveness as an organized force backed by appropriate legal as-

[5] "Seller Beware," *The Wall Street Journal*, June 21, 1971 and July 1, 1971.

[6] "Car Makers Ordered to Prove Ad Claims as FTC Opens Drive," *The Wall Street Journal*, July 14, 1971.

sistance. Much depends upon the reactions of the firms involved and the FTC. If the latter takes a strong stand, and follows it up with similar orders to other industries, the consequences could be of major proportions.

Ecological Movements

Like consumerism, environmentalism has been recognized by the business world as a force not to be taken lightly. Indeed, it has special appeal even to business leaders. In the modern American economy, private industry reacts to factors other than the traditional profit motive. Whether or not corporations have developed a social conscience or sense of social responsibility, the day is long past when large private enterprise could afford to ignore hostile public opinion.

Moreover, the environmental problem transcends the traditional bounds of social problems in the sense that as a health problem it tends to affect everyone to some degree, the rich as well as the poor, although obviously not in equal portions. Consequently, it is hardly surprising that the personal reaction of corporate officials to the pollution problem is essentially the same as for other people.

Unfortunately, it is virtually impossible to ascertain what actual effect the voluntary endeavors by private enterprise have had toward eliminating pollution. While corporate officials may voice approval of and endorse the environmental cause, the ultimate response of the corporation involved may be distinctly less enthusiastic. If forced to substantially reduce pollution, industry stands to have its revenue-cost flows severely altered. Despite the general acceptance of the modern corporation as a non-maximizer of profits, significant adverse impact on the corporation's profit stream is a serious matter. Although willing to bear a share of the total costs of cleaning up the environment, perhaps largely due to the personal concern of corporate management, industry's reaction is understandably negative toward policies that threaten to increase production costs.

Historically, society has subsidized industry by allowing it to pollute. Industry stands ready to defend its historical privilege to escape the full costs of production as a necessary and just condition for satisfying the tremendous demand from society for ever expanding levels of output. The environmentalist movement represents an alteration of that traditional singular demand to deliver the goods. Now industry is faced with a dual demand function with almost dialectic components. It not only is expected to deliver the goods, but also to accept responsibiltiy for the high social cost that accompanies production of many products. While a portion of these costs, and hence the responsibility, possibly could be shifted to the consumers by way of higher prices, industry has no guarantee that consumers will accept that burden except on a very gradual basis.

As a result of the dual demands upon industry, a feeling of uncertainty has been noted among businessmen: "Businessmen simply do not believe that, in a showdown, consumers would accept a 'lower standard of living.' They believe that given a choice between having autos with pollution and banning autos to rid pollution, the American consumer will stick with his wheels."[7] Partly due to this so-called credibility gap, industry has not become totally committed to ending pollution. As one corporate official noted, "Industry will do whatever people ask us to do and what they will pay us for doing."[8] In a basically free enterprise economy, industry still remains more responsive to inducements of pay than requests, unless those requests are prefaced by force. Environmentalist movements are clearly providing that force.

Assuming that the above has proved that consumerism and environmentalism do have power, and the source of that power has been isolated, it is possible to generalize about the development of countervailing power.

Immature countervailing power tends to be largely a market phenomenon with private enterprise countervailing the power held by other private enterprises.

Mature countervailing power, in contrast, does not directly emanate from the private market, but originates more from broader social agitation which in the beginning may be characterized as undifferentiated frustration. As with consumerism and environmentalism, it is usually difficult to ascertain with certainty the location

[7]"The Trade-offs for a Better Environment," *Business Week*, Nov. 4, 1970, p. 63.
[8]*Ibid.*

of the power creating the frustration. Who, for example, is primarily responsible for consumer woes and pollution? Frequently, it appears to be the "system" rather than any specific group at fault. Once some part of the system has been identified (if only vaguely) as the culprit, countervailing forces tend to acquire momentum as the counterorganization (consumerism or environmentalism, for example) develops specific purpose and form. An essential distinction is that the key to the development of effective mature power is public sponsorship, not private market sponsorship, largely because of the vagueness of the position of original power and the absence of a pecuniary surplus.

Galbraith emphasized that the opportunity to obtain a share of the pecuniary surplus enjoyed by those holding original power is a prime motivator of countervailing forces. Such a surmise unfortunately overemphasizes the development of immature countervailing power, with its responsiveness to the market system of pecuniary motives. Consumerism and environmentalism both serve to demonstrate the narrowness of that original proposition and the greater fruitfulness of nonmarket sponsorship of mature power. While farmers and labor were able to obtain a share of the pecuniary surplus enjoyed by others, consumerism can benefit only indirectly through improved quality of goods and services and greater knowledge in transactions. Thus, a possible increase in real income replaces the prospect of an increase in pecuniary income. For the environmentalists, the benefits are even more indirect, consisting largely of a reduction of real costs being borne for goods not necessarily received.

The abstractness of the surplus involved may be integral to the belated appearance of organized groups representing consumer and environmental interests. In fact, a generalized modification of the Galbraithian surplus motivation may be ventured. Countervailing power tends to appear more quickly in its immature form when direct pecuniary inducements exist. The more abstract the surplus the more delay probably will be involved in the generation of effective power. Yet, the immature power tends to be impermanent and largely ineffective in the long run, falling victim to vertical integration and inflation. Mature power is less susceptible to such disadvantages. There is less likelihood that the opposing parties will become united.

Immature elements of power are not necessarily absent from mature power. The marginal contribution of private countervailing power may be of more than minor importance. It would seem, for example, that the interests of corporations producing antipollution devices may produce an extra stimulus to the enthusiasm of the total movement and could provide a strong nucleus of support from the private sector.

Countervailing power satisfies the goal of social peace and tranquility, and should be judged accordingly. Wider social movements with interests that are not derived as a direct consequence of jockeying for market positions are more easily assimilated into such goal frameworks. In a troubled pluralistic society, that behavioral situation becomes all the more important. Goals of both groups, especially those of environmentalism, relate more closely to alleviation of social tensions than to traditional competitive goals of market models with direct pecuniary drives. The accomplishment of these goals through countervailing power will soothe and reduce some rather dangerous social tensions existing in our society.

Maturity in countervailing power has yet another dimension. In the case of environmentalism, the consumer might ultimately be forced to bear the cost of cleaning up the environment. On the other hand, a strong consumerism position could reduce the amount of the costs otherwise passed on to the purchaser. If the power of both develops, then the power of business will be countervailed on two sides (or even three if a union exists). In mature structures of countervailing power, such a multibalance of power is to be expected.

Conclusions

It should be emphasized that the power of either movement is, at this moment, no more than embryonic. This article has dealt with trends, rather than actual power positions. What both movements seem to lack are strong coherent organizations and a full commitment from government to supply the requisite muscle. There is definitely a lack of a social or economic class coherency among the members of either movement, which tends to increase the difficulty of realizing a successful power position. In the end, however, the disadvantages may turn into advantages. The broad appeal of the issues and goals may attract a sufficiently broad political base that no political party or candidate can afford to ignore it.

As a final comment we return to Galbraith's plea that countervailing power be recognized and nurtured as a public policy. Its benefits are worthy of closer scrutiny by economists and policy makers. It is directly derived from the pluralistic notion of checks and balances that has made American society sufficiently flexible to avoid major breakdowns. Viability in policy has not been realized through traditional regulatory legislation. Countervailing power appears to be a realistic substitute and complement to traditional policy. Whether the potential countervailors are consumerists, environmentalists, or another aggrieved group, it behooves national public action to sponsor the development of the requisite power.

For some large and prosperous companies, financing does not present too great a problem. Some small companies are not too much hampered by legal limitations. Some companies are not unionized. But virtually every company that produces a tangible product and many that provide only services are hampered by technological limitations. These limitations are analyzed by Prof. P. Sargant Florence, formerly dean and professor of commerce at the University of Birmingham, England, who has devoted a lifetime to the study of the corporation, with special reference to technology and size.

Some Technological Factors

P. Sargant Florence

The activities of different industries and orders of industry differ in certain physical, technological and distributive characteristics, which can be shown to influence deeply the different ways these industries are organized. *Physical* characters of greatest influence are the durability through time, and transportability through space, of materials and products; though their gradability and divisibility are also important. But more basic still is the distinction between industries producing physical goods, to which durability and transportability can apply, and industries providing services.

Weight of materials, weight of product, and power of machines, all vary widely between industries. This wide range of the physical characters of various industries may be expected to cause, and does, in fact, cause, a wide range of differences in their location, organization and methods of government.

Before materials become usable products, they normally pass through several technical processes, like cotton through carding, spinning, weaving, dyeing, dressmaking before it becomes clothes. Some of these consecutive processes may rank as separate industries so that one industry may be grouped as an early stage (e.g. textile) and another as a late-stage (e.g. clothing) industry. A further important grouping often, though not always, identical with 'early' and 'late' is *process* industry and *assembly* industry. Spinning 'processes' the raw cotton, dressmaking assembles cloth into various shapes. [The accompanying table] places the more important (and some other) manufacturing industries according to their position in the whole course of production.

Lines drawn in [the table], for instance, indicate that buildings are assembled from the products of sawmilling, brickmaking and the iron and

From *The Logic of British and American Industry: A Realistic Analysis of Economic Structure and Government* (The University of North Carolina Press, Chapel Hill, N.C., 1953), pp. 7–12.

THE TECHNICAL FRAMEWORK OF PRODUCTIVE AND DISTRIBUTIVE RELATIONS

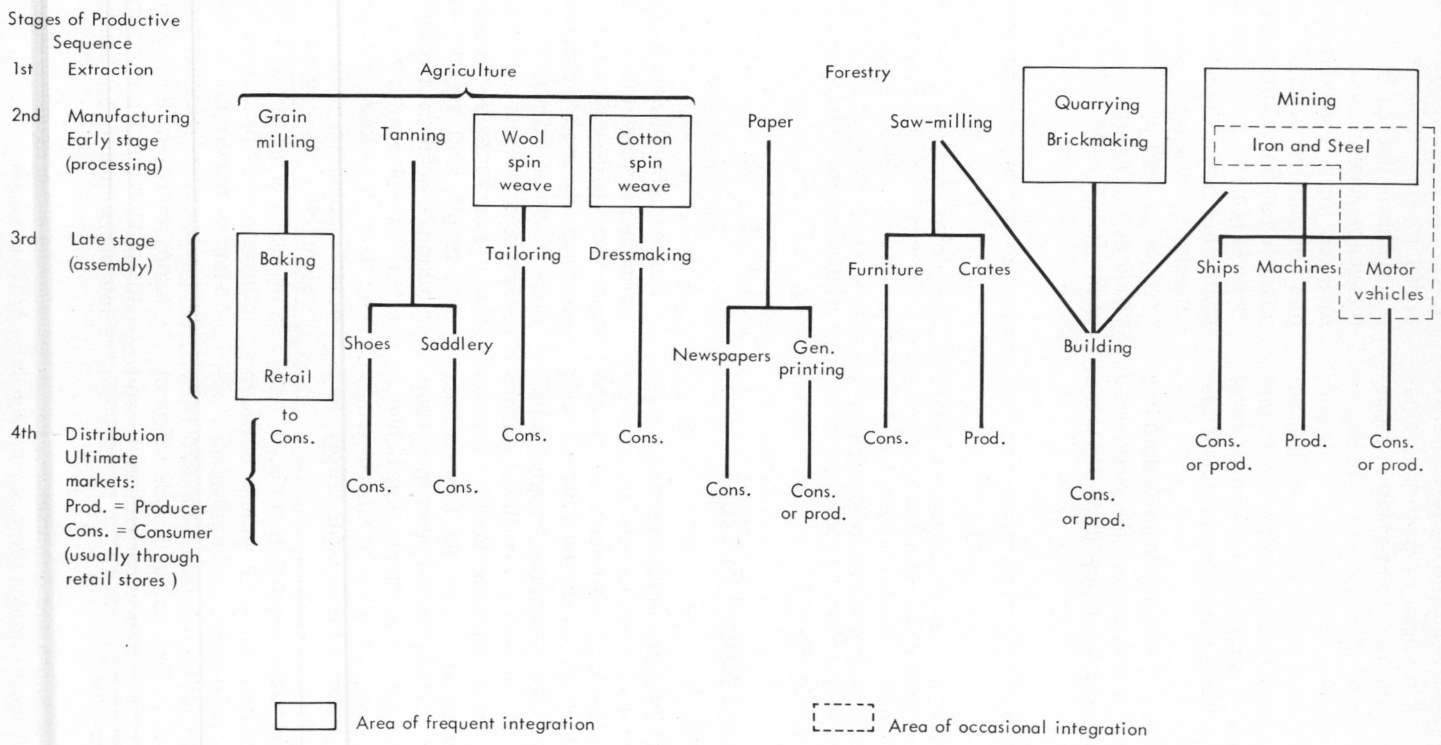

Stages of Productive Sequence
1st Extraction
2nd Manufacturing
Early stage (processing)
3rd Late stage (assembly)
4th Distribution
Ultimate markets:
Prod. = Producer
Cons. = Consumer (usually through retail stores)

Agriculture
Grain milling
Baking
Retail
to Cons.
Tanning
Shoes
Saddlery
Cons.
Cons.
Wool spin weave
Tailoring
Cons.
Cotton spin weave
Dressmaking
Cons.

Forestry
Paper
Newspapers
Gen. printing
Cons.
Cons. or prod.
Saw-milling
Furniture
Crates
Cons.
Prod.

Quarrying
Brickmaking
Building
Cons. or prod.

Mining
Iron and Steel
Ships
Machines
Motor vehicles
Cons. or prod.
Prod.
Cons. or prod.

Area of frequent integration

Area of occasional integration

steel industry. And though the lines are, to save confusion, not indicated in the table, the saddlery industry assembles together iron and steel (and brass) as well as leather products. Not all manufacturers fall, however, into these early and late divisions. Outstanding exceptions are the pottery and glass industries, where both early processing and later finishing are usually performed in one plant, starting with the clay and sand, and ending up with ware for the consumer's house. The rubber and the hosiery industries, though they start somewhat further from the raw material, also process *and* assemble into tyres, tennis balls and stockings ready for the consumer.

Most manufactures, as [the table] sets forth, split into early- and late-stage industries. The early-stage manufactures proceed from raw materials which they process or 'refine' into more homogeneous materials which the late-stage manufactures may assemble. It is indeed the very fact that this refinement so often occurs in the technological course of production which permits the early and late stages to be performed by different plants in different industries. The refined, homogeneous and usually compact product (steel billets, cloth, flour, leather, paper) can be transported cheaply over long distances from the refining plant to the next stage, usually assembly.

Early-stage manufacturing does not usually engage in assembly work and they usually change heavy material into light transportable products; but the converse is less true. Some late-stage manufactures, especially in food and chemicals, go on processing. But even in these industries the modern trend toward packaging or canning of foods, soaps and drugs for the delectation of the consumer is making the last stages an assembly technique.

Distribution (including storing and transport) to the customers can be taken as part of the technical process of supplying wants. To the early-stage manufacturer, the customer is by definition another manufacturer, but to the late-stage manufacturer the customer may be another manufacturer or the final consumer. [The table] gives examples of late-stage industries making for either. The question for which of these two markets a product is destined will be found to exercise a strong influence on the manufacturer's organization. The outstanding type of late-stage manufacturing for another manufacturer is machine-making. It is this industry which is the chief manufacturing contributor to capital formation, so important to the economist.

To complete a technical framework of reference that claims to be realistic and comprehensive, certain industries must be added that do not fit into the *vertical* stages. The public utilities supplying electrical power, gas and water serve 'diagonally' all stages of manufacture as well as the consumer; and there is a further market situation where things are taken for collection (e.g. scrap merchants, insurance agents, banks) or repair. This 'property service' tends to follow the organization pattern of personal service, rather than of manufacturing.

Apart from machine-making the bulk of manufactures fall into two technical types each with a complex or 'syndrome' of at least four characters in common: the late-stage, assembly, for-consumer, from light-material type; and the early-stage, processing, for-producer, from heavy-material type. Most writers of the popular sort have seized on the light or heavy characteristic as symptomatic of the whole complex, though it may not be the weight of material that really matters.

The degree to which an industry makes use of machines—its mechanization or investment generally—will be found another technological determinant of forms of industrial structure and organization. The degree of mechanization is itself determined by the physical nature of materials (e.g. greater where materials are uniform and gradable) and by the nature of the work (i.e. processing, assembly or distribution). Mechanical, piped or wired distribution or collection is achieved in the so-called octopoid industries, like gas, water, electrical supply or sewage disposal, where tentacles stretch into each home or factory. But, historically, machines were first applied to the processing manufacturers, cotton and wool textiles, rather than clothing; iron and steel, rather than engineering; and the horsepower per man is generally at a different level in the early heavy-material, processing manufactures than in the later stage, and usually lighter material, assembly manufactures.

A high degree of mechanization which is indicated fairly directly by a high horsepower per man, is reflected indirectly by the high financial ratios of capital to wages per year and by high fixed assets in company balance sheets relative to total assets or to capitalization and, more broadly, by high capitalization compared to output of workers employed.

In the following, one specific aspect of the limitations imposed by technology is discussed: the effect of technology on size. It is generally considered that there is an optimum size, different for different industries, optimum in that it results in the lowest unit costs. Technology tends, however, to set merely a lower limit on size, as this article explains.

The Optimum Firm

E. A. G. Robinson

In any industry there is usually to be found sometimes one, sometimes more than one size to which a firm has apparently tended to grow. This size, which Alfred Marshall taught us to call the 'representative' firm, may not be the optimum at the moment; circumstances may have so changed that some size, perhaps slightly different, perhaps, as is not improbably the case in the cotton industry to-day, wholly different from the older one, is now to be preferred. The representative firm of to-day probably represents the scale of production which, having regard to the circumstances of the industry, was looked upon as the best scale of production sometime in the recent past.

By the optimum firm, we must mean a firm operating at that scale at which in existing conditions of technique and organising ability it has the lowest average cost of production per unit, when all those costs which must be covered in the long run are included. I am not for the moment concerned with questions of maximum profitability. When an element of monopoly is present, the price need not coincide with average cost, and maximum profit may be made by charging a price at which the firm does not sell enough to exhaust the full economies of scale. I am here concerned only with costs and the relation of costs to size. The establishment of this optimum firm will be in part the result of conscious decision by business men who are considering how they most profitably can invest their resources; in part it will be the product of the forces of competition, which tend, as a rule, to eliminate the inefficient and to encourage the efficient. Both these elements play their part because competition only indirectly gives an advantage to the firm with the lowest average long period cost of production. Short period competition tends as a rule to select the firm whose short period cost of production is lowest.

The optimum firm is likely to result from the ordinary play of economic forces where the market is perfect and sufficient to maintain a large number of firms of optimum size. It will not necessarily emerge where the market is limited and imperfect. If a firm, to secure additional sales, must attract customers, either from rival products or from greater distances, by accepting a lower price, that firm may actually decrease and not increase its profits by expanding to the optimum size. In these circumstances, it will be likely to remain at that smaller size at which its additional receipts from selling more are equal to its additional costs in producing more.

The forces which determine the best size of the business unit, assuming that the market is sufficient to absorb the whole production of at least one firm of optimum size, may be divided into five main categories: technical forces, making for a technical optimum size; managerial

From *The Structure of Competitive Industry*, rev. ed. (James Nisbet & Co., Ltd., London, Cambridge University Press, London, and The University of Chicago Press, Chicago, 1958), pp. 10–11, 12–14, 17–22, 24–25, 31–32.

forces, making for an optimum managerial unit; financial forces, making for an optimum financial unit; the influences of marketing, making for an optimum sales unit; and the forces of risk and fluctuation, making for a unit possessing the greatest power of survival in the face of industrial vicissitudes. These five forces may, in certain cases, lead to an approximately similar optimum size. In other cases, the benefits of growth on the technical side may balance losses from growth through the building up of an industrial unit too large to be managed with the highest degree of efficiency and flexibility. The advantage of a large unit for selling may in yet other cases be balanced by the disadvantage of large productive units in time of depression. Conflicts between the best technical scale and the best managerial scale can be resolved by different devices and forms of organization.

The Division of Labour

In his famous first chapter of *The Wealth of Nations*, Adam Smith has described the various advantages to be secured by the Division of Labour. He takes his example from a very trifling manufacture; but one in which the division of labour has been very often taken notice of, the trade of the pin-maker. Since Adam Smith's day, mechanical and industrial progress has led us to more and more minute division of labour. A pair of shoes is made now by groups of men and women working at some 240 different operations. The manufacture of watches, typewriters, motor cars, is broken up into many tiny parts. Even the old model T Ford was, according to its designer, the product of 7,882 different jobs. More simple products are incapable of such fine subdivision.

The principle of the division of labour requires a firm sufficiently large to obtain the maximum profitable division of labour. The size necessary to obtain this will be different in different industries; it will be different even in different departments of the same manufacture. In some instances, a further division of labour is by the very nature of the process impossible. In cotton spinning, the sequence of processes has long been divided into the greatest number technically possible. In weaving, a further subdivision of the operations of the loom is unthinkable. The large spinning or weaving firm differs hardly at all in equipment from its small competitor, but a firm of less than 20,000 spindles would probably be unable to keep running at full capacity certain of the larger units of its machinery. In other instances, the maximum subdivision of processes is achieved in some departments while the scale of production is comparatively small, while other departments continue to secure further subdivision of labour as the scale of production increases.

If two engineering firms, for instance, be compared, the one large, the other on modern standards comparatively small, the division of labour in the machine shops may be found to extend little further in the large firm than in the small. It happens only seldom that a single worker or a single machine handles the whole output of one component. In most instances, several workers will be simultaneously doing the same work on a series of similar machines. In the large shop there will be more, in the small fewer such machines; the division of labour will not be greater in the one than in the other, and, were it possible, division of labour could be secured as readily in the smaller as in the larger firm. But at other points such division of labour is possible. If one compares two motor firms, one large and one small, the large firm possesses an elaborate assembly line; here one worker or group of workers perform for the whole output of the firm that particular job for which they are responsible. The smaller firm has a more rudimentary assembly line. Each worker performs several tasks, which in a larger firm are divided between several men. In this case, then, there is a gain from a larger scale of production, but the gain is limited to those processes where further subdivision is possible only if the firm grows bigger. If the subdivision could be achieved by replacing two men both simultaneously doing the whole job by two men each doing a different portion of the job, it is unnecessary for the firm to grow to secure the division. It is only necessary to increase the scale of production in order to obtain further division of labour if the whole output is already handled by a single man or a single machine, and the necessary division of labour cannot be obtained by a mere rearrangement of their tasks.

Integration of Processes

We must then search for other technical gains from large scale production. The first that we discover has not yet, so far as I know, been christened. I am going to call it the Integration of Processes. The large firm often differs from the small firm in having fewer rather than more processes of manufacture. The process of the division of labour is being reversed; one large machine can be designed to take over what has hitherto been done by a series of manual, or less completely mechanical operations.

It is only the large firm that can afford to keep the very expensive machinery of this type running to its full capacity, and the large firm therefore enjoys advantages which are beyond the reach of the self-contained small firm.

The small firm has a means of escape from the difficulty, an escape very confusing to our attempt to analyse the structure of an industry. Where some given process requires a scale of production considerably greater than the smaller firms in an industry can achieve, this process tends to be separated from the main industry, and all the smaller firms get this particular process performed for them by an outside specialist firm. Thus the industry becomes broken up into two or more industries, and each is enabled to work at its most convenient scale of production. The specialist firm, working for a number of the smaller firms, is on a larger scale than any of the individual firms could have achieved for that particular process or product.

This method of escaping the limitations of particular processes by breaking the continuity of production from first to last within a single firm, I am going to call Vertical Disintegration, to distinguish it from the similar but opposite expedient of Vertical Integration, which consists in the combination of one stage of production with other previously separated stages of production, under the control of a single firm. Its importance lies in its power to eliminate the advantages of very large scale production, where those advantages are limited to one or two processes of manufacture. But it is not a practicable method of escape where the advantages are too many, or where the processes cannot by their nature be separated and given to an outside firm, as in the case of motor chassis assembly work. In these instances, the advantages of the Integration of Processes must, other things being equal, form a factor favourable to further growth of the firm.

The Large Machine

The gain from the Integration of Processes arose from the unification of a number of processes hitherto performed in series, so that they might be performed simultaneously. A somewhat similar economy will arise also where, when output has sufficiently increased, one process which has hitherto been performed by a number of parallel workers may be taken over by a single machine. Once a machine has been developed to perform some duty, an economy lies with those who can afford to employ it. Some machines are cheap, and can be supplied as tools to every worker, since the saving of time when he needs them will pay for their cost. Others are expensive, and no firm can afford them unless it can operate them continuously.

We must consider for a moment what are the factors that determine the gain from using machines more fully. The greater is the fixed cost per day of possessing a given machine, the greater will be the economy from spreading that cost over a larger output. The fixed cost per day will depend first upon the price of the machine, second on the rate of interest and depreciation which must be paid. If something happens to reduce the cost of the machine, or to lower the rate of interest, the penalty for working it below its full capacity is reduced, and the advantage to the large firm which can so employ it is less. Moreover, for some machines the depreciation is mainly the result of wear and tear, for others it is the result of obsolescence. Where wear and tear is the only factor, the smaller firm, using its machine over a longer period, must pay higher interest charges, but not a higher proportion of the initial cost of the machine, for each unit of product. Where obsolescence is important, the small firm working its equipment below the full capacity of the machinery must pay both a higher interest charge and a higher proportion of the initial cost. We can see then that the optimum firm is not an absolute and unchanging thing.

The economies to be secured from the integration of processes, and from the spreading of the overhead costs of large machines, give us a hint to another factor which helps to determine the technical optimum. We have so far been considering plant whose minimum size is capable of dealing with a large output. But in other cases, we can see that while a smaller mechanical unit is technically possible, a larger one may be more efficient.

So far, we have discussed only the technical efficiency of the large unit as compared with that of the small. We are concerned also with the cost of the large unit as compared with the cost of the small. If the large unit, though technically more efficient, were more expensive to construct per unit of its future output of service, this gain might disappear; but in practice the larger unit is nearly always relatively cheaper to construct than the smaller. If we compare the capital cost of two electrical generating stations, one of the largest efficient size, the other of small size, each representing about the same technical development, we find that the smaller station costs almost twice as much, for each kilowatt of capacity, as the larger station.

It is clear that, in many cases, the large mechanical unit is both more efficient in operation and cheaper to construct than the smaller. It has a second advantage; it is cheaper also, in many cases, to operate, for many machines require an individual or a team to work them, whatever their size may be.

The Balance of Processes

It will be seen, then, that in very many cases an increase in the size of the mechanical unit gives an increase of efficiency, and that if the greatest technical efficiency is to be achieved, the size of the firm must be sufficient to use the largest mechanical unit necessary to its full capacity. But here again a complication arises. Mechanical units do not arrange themselves easily into groups such that they give their best results with an output, one of one hundred units a day, another of two hundred, a third of four hundred, so that they can be fitted neatly into the industrial jigsaw. There will be several different mechanical bottle-necks in the firm, each requiring to be used, for greatest efficiency, up to its fullest capacity, but each requiring a different daily output in order that it may be so used. The escape from this difficulty may be a compromise, one machine being over-driven, so that it produces slightly more than it can with optimum efficiency, another producing slightly less. Where the difference between the optimum outputs is small, this will very likely be the solution adopted, but where the optimum outputs are considerably different for the two mechanical units, the best solution may be a kind of L.C.M. of all the various outputs, in which three units of one machine, four of another, five of a third, give a balance in which all the units can conveniently be used approximately to their full capacity.

Effect on Size of Firm

The size of the optimum technical unit will depend upon how far these economies continue. They will not continue indefinitely. A large furnace is more economical than a small furnace, but a point comes beyond which further growth is uneconomical. A large ship is faster and more economical than a small ship, but a point is reached beyond which an increase of size is an impediment rather than an advantage. Docks and canals are limited in capacity. The depth of water available may be insufficient for the safe operation of very large vessels. In other instances, further economies of the division of labour or of the integration of processes cease to arise, for the greatest possible advantage of existing technique has been secured. Another invention might perhaps necessitate a larger unit, perhaps even a unit vastly different, but for the time being there is no technical advantage in further growth.

Optimum technical units are large in two wholly different types of industry: in those in which the product or the productive machinery is physically very large, as in steel making, the rolling of steel plates and sections, or ship building: and in those in which the final product is highly complex in that it is built up of a great number of small parts, which are conveniently produced under a single roof, as in the case of the manufacture of typewriters, watches, cash registers, or motor cars. Optimum technical units are small where the product is both small and simple, as in the case of the manufacture of cutlery, the weaving of standard cloths, or the making of shoes. Thus we can predict, to some extent and within a given stage of technical development, the probable upper limit of the optimum technical unit in an industry. But we cannot be dogmatic concerning the limit to the growth of efficiency with size. The integration of processes is essentially discontinuous. There comes a point where, as output grows, a revolution of method becomes possible, and economies, which had for a period apparently ceased, again begin to arise with further growth.

But even where economies of larger scale cease completely, it is unlikely that countervailing diseconomies will begin to arise on the purely technical side. Thus the technical costs of production are likely to fall as more is produced up to a certain limit, and thereafter to remain constant.

PART 2 THE BEGINNINGS OF MODERN MANAGEMENT

Definition of the manager's job and understanding of the environment within which managers operate make up a foundation on which to build further knowledge of management: specifically, knowledge of the difference between good and bad management, and of the theories and techniques managers can use to good advantage.

While many thinkers and practitioners have contributed to our knowledge of these matters, the three men whose work is presented in this section typify the three main schools of thought on what constitutes good management. Most later writers belong, consciously or unconsciously, to one of these three schools. First, there is the view that management can be regarded primarily as a matter of measurement and mathematics. Second, there is the school which holds that the manager succeeds or fails largely according to his ability to understand and utilize the findings of sociology and psychology. Finally, there are those who hold that there is a separate and identifiable science of administration.

The first of these schools may be said to have originated with Frederick W. Taylor, the second with Elton Mayo and his fellow-researchers, and the third with Henri Fayol. But this does not mean that later thinkers who belong to the same schools of thought necessarily agree with these men in all particulars, or even very much with their general ideas. The approach is a matter of viewpoint rather than one of acceptance of previous ideas.

Thus the modern descendants of the Taylor school are the management scientists (whose work is discussed in Part 5 of this book), and they follow Taylor only in their reliance on measurement and mathematics; they do not necessarily agree with any of his views on ways to increase productivity or promote good industrial relations.

Again, the writers and practitioners who have been examining the management job from the psychological and sociological viewpoints may not agree with Mayo's views; in fact, as they have looked more closely, they have found that situations within factories and offices are much more complicated than he realized, and that his prescriptions were perhaps oversimplified.

Finally, the followers of Fayol, while they seldom, if ever, disagree with the principles he enunciated, have expanded and added to them.

5 The Scientific Management Movement

Many of the techniques used by managers today have their roots in the scientific management movement that aroused enormous enthusiasm among managers in the first two decades of the twentieth century.

Frederick W. Taylor, the founder of the movement, who is often called the "Father of Modern Management," developed what was essentially the science of industrial engineering and applied the term "scientific management" to his system.

In brief, the Taylor system embodied the following: (1) a differential piecework plan under which the worker would receive a higher piece rate if he met a standard and the high rate would apply to all the pieces produced, not just to the number above standard; (2) development of the standard by timing each separate motion necessary to perform a task; and (3) careful planning to ensure that the most efficient motions and the best tools and machines were used.

There were other features, but Taylor himself considered that the value of his system lay in the fact that it would produce a "mental revolution" on the part of both management and labor. Employees, he reasoned, would be quite willing to work harder if they could earn a great deal more by doing so, and management would profit so much by the increased productivity that it would be willing to pay them more. Since the amount of work to be done in a day and the payment for it would be "scientifically" determined, there would be no reason for management and labor to quarrel.

The mental revolution that Taylor predicted did not occur, but his system did produce a revolution in management thinking that led to higher productivity. Managers were induced to plan work more carefully than they had before, and, more important, they began to realize that improvements in methods need not depend on chance inspiration but can be discovered by systematic study.

Some systematic study of the kind Taylor advocated had been undertaken long before Taylor was born, as the first article in this chapter shows. But it was Taylor and his associates who made the study of work processes a normal feature of industrial management. In the second article presented here, Peter Drucker places Taylor's contribution in its proper perspective.

The next two articles, by Taylor himself, reveal his ideas on employee relations, and the following two deal with the work of two other writers prominently identified with the scientific management movement: Frank B. Gilbreth, who carried motion study further than Taylor ever did, and Harrington Emerson, who extended the sphere of scientific management from the shop floor to the councils of higher management. Finally, an article critical of the movement is included.

Charles Babbage (1792–1871) is about the only one of the early (pre-Taylor) students of management in industry whose work is fairly well known today. Because he was the inventor of a forerunner of the computer, there has been great interest in him in recent years.

Babbage also wrote a good deal about the management of production, and in some ways anticipated Taylor. However, Babbage himself was only one of many early students of management who did so, as the following article shows. (Footnote references have been omitted here, although they are, of course, given in the original, because the books and articles mentioned would probably be difficult for the average reader to obtain.)

Prof. John Hardie Hoagland, from whose Ph.D. dissertation the following excerpt is taken, is now associated with the School of Business, Michigan State University.

Some Early Management Studies

John Hardie Hoagland

Babbage's works have been characterized as far in advance of their time and [he has been called] the first to study industrial organization from the scientific standpoint. The classical intrepretation of management history has taught that very little study was made of industrial management problems before the end of the nineteenth century and consequently practically none prior to Babbage.

Actually, a great many significant studies of industrial management problems were made prior to Babbage and some of these definitely influenced Babbage's work. Plenty of earlier material is available if the researcher will dig for it. There is enough industrial management information prior to Babbage to fill many dissertations. So many unrecognized, important earlier developments in management literature were uncovered in this research that it became necessary to limit the presentation to only some of the earlier industrial management developments and to only some of the factors which influenced Babbage. The result is that this is only a sampling of developments.

The concept of a fair day's work was selected for review because: (1) it was one to which Babbage referred, both directly and indirectly, (2) it was one which received a great deal of attention in later industrial management writings, (3) it indicated the type of work done prior to Babbage, and (4) it provided information about allied subjects.

As an example of earlier work in this area of a fair day's work note that in the latter half of the seventeenth century the Académie des Sciences invited scholars to study the operations done by the worker in his workshop, in order to help him do a better job. Probably as a result of this, De la Hire presented his paper, "Examen de la Force de l'Homme" before the Académie in 1699. This study was largely of men lifting, carrying, and pulling weights and an analysis of why the force exerted depended upon the method of using human strength.

The most famous early experiments and observations on the amount of work men could do in a day were made by M. Charles Augustus Coulomb, the same French doctor who proved Coulomb's laws of electricity. The observations of Coulomb were first published in 1781 and then republished in 1809 and 1821. Unfortunately for the history of industrial management concepts, this work is not known to have been translated into English. If it had been, the famous pig iron and shoveling experiments of F. W. Taylor might not have received the undue recognition they have and Taylor's claim to great originality might have been unmasked long ago.

The length of Coulomb's article precludes full translation here but the following are translated excerpts indicating some of his ideas.

> There are two things to be distinguished in the work of men and animals—the effect which their energy can produce when applied to a machine and the fatigue which they undergo in producing this effect. To obtain the most from a man's energy it is necessary to increase the effect without increasing the fatigue; that is to say, supposing that we have a formula which represents the effect and another the fatigue, to obtain the greatest advantage of animal

From *Charles Babbage: His Life and Works in the Historical Evolution of Management Concepts*, Ph.D. dissertation (Ohio State University, Columbus, Ohio, 1954).

energy it is necessary that the effect divided by the fatigue is at a maximum.

Thus the whole question reduces itself to a search for a way to combine the different degrees of force, of speed, and of time, so that a man, with equal fatigue, may furnish the greatest quantity of action.

Bernoulli, who discussed this question . . . evaluates the daily work of men, in all types of work, at a weight of 1,728,000 pounds raised to one foot. . . .

(Taking fatigue into consideration, Coulomb calculated from various experiments and observations the amount of daily work a man performed in climbing stairs, with a load and without one. From these he developed a formula to determine the maximum useful effect of a man climbing a stairway with a weight. He concluded that for maximum results a man should carry 53 kilograms per load. Comparing this with the load they sometimes carry Coulomb showed that workers cannot themselves properly conclude as to what is the proper amount to carry.)

Other chapter headings were as follows:

Comparison of the quantity of action men can furnish when they are traveling on a horizontal plane or without a load.

Concerning the quantity of action which men can furnish in their daily work when they transport loads in wheelbarrows.

Concerning the quantity of action which men can furnish in pile-driving, a movement which is executed when they raise the ramshead to strike and drive in the piles.

Concerning men acting on levers.

Concerning the quantity of action which men consume in their daily work when they work the earth with a spade.

M. Schulze, in 1773, made studies of twenty men of different size and weight. He wanted to know what force men could be expected to exert in industrial applications and to test the formulae and conclusions of earlier writers.

On this same subject of a fair day's work M. Christian in his *Traité de Mécanique Industrielle* wrote the following comments. (Translated from the French)

[When] a large portion of the muscles of a man's body are used . . . it is necessary to give frequent intervals of rest and to reduce the effective work of one day to two or three hours at the best. The muscles of the man are not all equally suited. . . .

Francis Gerstner in discussing general rules for the application of animal power [in 1831] made statements such as the following:

Muscular strength, frequent practice, age, sex, and even the will to exert power, have a great influence on the effort of man, and therefore it is plain, that *the absolute extent* or value *of this power* cannot here be fixed with certainty.

It is well-known, that every man can exert a greater strength or carry a heavy burden, when the work is of no long duration, or if the burden has not far to be carried, or can soon be laid down.

Gerstner arrived at various formulae and considered such things as "How is the work to be arranged, that the *expense of carrying* at a fixed price for daily work *may be the least*? Or if the price for carrying a Cwt. *be given*, how is the workman to manage his work, so as *to earn the highest possible daily wages*?" He concluded, "The expense of transport for a hundredweight per mile is therefore smallest, where the men work with their mean velocity through the ordinary working time."

The preceding excerpts in this chapter show conclusively that there certainly were studies of how much work a man could do in a day long before the time of Babbage. There is no doubt that not only did Babbage know of many of these earlier works but many persons knew of them. These ideas and studies were not buried and forgotten but were written about in popular industrial books and magazines and taught to men of industry.

Subjects similar to those previously discussed led to even more specific studies of applications to industry. For example, studies were made as to how much force a person could exert for a short period of time using tools such as the following: draw-knife, auger, screw-driver (one hand), bench vise handle, chisel and awl (vertical pressure), pinchers and pliers, hand plane, hand or thumb vise, hand saw, stock bit, and small screw-drivers (twisting by the thumb and forefinger only).

Later management writers have tended to be critical of Taylor, on the ground that he paid insufficient attention to human relations. In this article, Peter F. Drucker, distinguished lecturer at New York University and a well-known management consultant, points out that Taylor's work was a necessary prerequisite to any important efforts to improve the lot of the workingman. The Society for the Advancement of Management, to whom this discussion was originally addressed, is an amalgamation of two earlier societies that grew out of the scientific management movement: the Taylor Society and the Society of Industrial Engineers.

Frederick W. Taylor: The Professional Management Pioneer

Peter F. Drucker

It is only natural for adolescent sons to rebel against their sires. And so we should not be surprised that there has been a rebellion against Frederick W. Taylor in the evolving discipline of management during the last twenty or thirty years. Now, however, I believe that management has matured sufficiently for this rebellion to be quite purposeless. After all, it is an old observation that the father gains in wisdom and stature at an incredible rate, while the son grows from 20 to 27 or so.

Indeed, I believe that we are about to rediscover what Taylor really did and what he really means. And high time, too. The popular game of belittling Taylor makes not much more sense than a belittling of Newton because all he did was to create the science of physics without, 300 years ago, being able to anticipate quantum mechanics. Indeed, just as we can only have quantum mechanics because a Newton gave us classical physics, we can only have today all the new, shiny tools and concepts of modern management theory because a Taylor founded the study of work and the study of organization 75 years ago.

It is easy enough to criticize Taylor because he was not much concerned with distribution or with (so the critics say) "social problems" or with "human relations." But we only can afford to be concerned with these important things because Taylor solved, in essence, the problem of production. As long as we cannot produce, we need not spend time or thought on distribution, let alone on human relations.

The ability to fill the belly comes first—and that, in terms of an industrial system, we owe to Taylor whose work multiplied the productivity of production to the point where we now know, as no one could even imagine before, that we can produce.

The Discipline of Management

Equally important, Taylor made possible the discipline of management. He did not take work for granted, but looked at it, studied it, and made it capable of being quantified. Without this, no systematic, let alone any "scientific," concern with Man in production and distribution, and also with Man working in human teams, could even be dreamed of.

Before Taylor, the one thing everybody knew was that the only way to get more product was to sweat harder. Taylor showed us that the key to productivity is not harder work, but smarter work; that is, an understanding and a systematic analysis of work (including, let me remind you, the relationship in work between different people to which Taylor gave a great deal more thought than his detractors ever realized).

We would not be able to concern ourselves with any of the things, neglect of which his critics now charge to Taylor: the human factor, the social values and goals, the management process itself, but for the fact that Taylor relieved us of the perpetual worry over the sheer ability to produce, which had haunted mankind for untold ages until Taylor made productivity the result of systematic thinking and analysis and, therefore, of an organized, purposeful discipline.

All of the vaunted "Management Sciences" of today—Operations Research, Systems Analysis and, indeed, Human Relations—are part of the

From the speech given by Mr. Drucker at the annual awards dinner of the Society for the Advancement of Management, June 12, 1967, when he received the Taylor Key, the society's highest award. Reprinted from the *Advanced Management Journal* (which is published by the society), October, 1967, pp. 8–11.

Taylor heritage. This is particularly true of Human Relations, for Taylor was one of the first to conceive of the satisfaction of the worker as a central goal of industrial endeavor.

Today, we hear a great deal about the "third way," the way that transcends both Capitalism and Communism. But in their traditional meaning—and, otherwise, they have very little meaning—Taylor transcended them. Both take for granted that there is a God-given natural limit to what can be produced—a limit that has remained completely unchanged and unchangeable at least since the first agricultural settlement 7,000 years ago. Taylor showed that there is no such limit, and he showed that the basic problem is not *who* should get the immutable pie, but how to make the pie larger. He made obsolete both "isms" of the 19th Century. In fact, he solved what the 19th Century considered *the* social question.

I do not think it extravagant to consider Frederick Taylor the one relevant social philosopher of this, our industrial civilization. To be sure, he could only apply the tools that were available at his time—just as Newton could not have used the cyclotron. To be sure, he concerned himself with the burning issues of his day—and by solving them, made it possible for us to concern ourselves with other issues. But these issues of his day had to be solved first before we could even perceive the issues we now see. He wrote and talked in the language of his time rather than in our language.

But what he was saying in this language that seems so archaic to us today is very modern and very up-to-date and is, indeed, the foundation for all those bold ventures of ours that aim at creating social and economic development throughout the world. It is only because of Taylor that we can even dream of such a goal—for its pre-condition everywhere is the freeing of man from the age-old thralldom to unproductivity and, even worse, to totally unsystematic, unscientific, essentially thoughtless, animal drudgery.

What Management Is

But while I believe strongly that we are about to re-discover how bright, how far ahead, how wise the father of our discipline has become as we, ourselves, grew older and somewhat more mature; while I am convinced that we no longer have to stress our differences with Taylor to emphasize our own independence but increasingly can proclaim with pride our debt to him and our origin in him; I also believe that there is one great lesson he taught us which we have not yet re-discovered—and a lesson which may be as important as any of the substantive knowledge and insight we owe him.

Taylor not only created management as a discipline and as a field of study; he not only made a contribution which no one, so far, has matched in impact and importance, let alone exceeded; he also showed us in his personal example what management is and what the student of management has to be.

Taylor started out as a successful manager himself—his title, in modern terminology, would probably be "Senior Vice President" or its equivalent. He was a theorist, a student, a scholar of management. And he was the first management consultant. In other words, he combined theory and practice, thought and experiment, doing and teaching, in one person and in one life.

This no longer seems to be fashionable today. Indeed, there is a strong trend, especially in the academic fraternity professing management, to divorce theory from practice, study from experiment, teaching from doing. There is a strong tendency to deny Taylor's insight that management is a clinical field, that is, a field in which practice without theory is just as useless as theory without practice, a field in which effective work requires that a man be equally at home in his study with his books and at the bedside of the patient, equally at home in conceptual theory and in actual effective application. In a clinical field, however, to try to be "pure," whether pure theorist or pure practitioner, is self-condemnation to total sterility.

A Discipline and a Profession

Frederick Taylor stands at the beginning of our work and discipline as students and practitioners of management, both in respect to what we know about the field and in respect to what we know, or ought to know, about the kind of person it takes to work in the field. He established both management as a discipline and management as a profession. And it is high time that we re-discovered him in both capacities.

Taylor was not, in fact, indifferent to the welfare of rank-and-file employees, although, as this article shows, he would have agreed with Drucker's view that higher productivity was necessary if any real improvement in their lot was to be possible.

The article that follows is an extract from one of a series of talks Taylor once gave to the students at Harvard Business School and is taken from the typescript now in the archives of the Baker Library at Harvard. The italics are Taylor's, and so is the notation to mention a particular case at the end of the extract.

This talk shows clearly that far from being indifferent to the feelings of the workers or regarding them as little more than machines, Taylor had a basic respect for them and, indeed, believed that they were no different fundamentally from the young gentlemen at Harvard Business School and other members of "our class," as he phrased it. If his view of motivation appears a little oversimplified in that he believed that man at work was essentially an "economic man" who would work harder only to the extent that he could gain monetarily by doing so, he did not believe that working men were any different from managers in this respect.

Much of the advice he gave to the future managers at Harvard Business School is still good today—especially his warning to avoid airs of superiority on the one hand and an effort to appear "one of the boys" by dressing sloppily or deliberately using bad grammar on the other.

The Working Man

Frederick W. Taylor

Now, I assume that most of you gentlemen are not the sons of working men, and that you have not yourselves worked during any long period of time, at least, with working men, and on the same level with them. If you had had this experience it would be superfluous on my part to call your attention to the one most important fact to be borne in mind in the study of working men. This fact is, that in all essential matters, they are just the same as you and I are. The working man and the college professor have fundamentally the same feelings, the same motives, the same ambitions, the same failings, the same virtues.

The working classes of the United States are, in the main, sensible men. Not all of them, of course, but they are just as sensible as we are. There are some fools among them; so there are among us. They are, in many respects, misguided men. So are we. They require a great deal of information that they have not got. So do we. They are narrow, particularly narrow in their knowledge of men who are not workmen. So are we narrow, most of us particularly narrow in our knowledge of workmen. Those of us whose acquaintance with workmen consists chiefly in seeing them slouching along the street on their way back from work with dirty clothes, chewing tobacco, in many cases hardly looking up as they pass one by, stolid and indifferent-looking, almost inevitably come to the conclusion (not usually in words, but none the less definite) that these men are a different kind of animal from you and from me. On the other hand, the workman who sees in men of our class merely the outward signs of prosperity—good clothes, and the possession of carriages and automobiles,—the careless holiday look, accompanied by short working hours,—the workman who sees these outward signs is apt to conclude that men of our class are a different kind of animal from the working man. The narrowness of the workman, then, in judging us, is no greater than our narrowness in judging him.

While both classes of men are essentially the same, the effect of the surroundings of each is to temporarily accentuate and intensify certain qualities; so that, under these special influences, there are actual differences between the two classes. And in dealing with working

From a series of lectures given at the Harvard Graduate School of Business Administration, Boston, 1909–1914.

men the prejudices occasioned by this difference in viewpoint should be understood and allowed for.

We must not forget that workmen have spent their lives in obeying other people's orders; that is, they occupy the position of apparent inferiority to us. Do not imagine, however, [that] they are one whit less self-respecting than you and I are. They look upon themselves as just as good and just as important as you and I. Since, however, men of their class constantly receive orders, while they see men of our class frequently in our capacity of giving orders, it is inevitable that they should conclude that many of us, at least, look upon them as our inferiors. Suspicion, when in contact with men of our class, should be recognized as one of the workman's prominent characteristics. They are always on the lookout for some sign that we think ourselves their superior, or that we look down upon them. Now, the personal loyalty of his men is still of the greatest importance to a manager, and it is necessary for the employer who wants the kindly regard and the respect of his workmen not only not to be a snob, but to carefully avoid the slightest semblance of snobbery. He should carefully avoid putting on lugs or style of any kind, and he should wear clothes that are inconspicuous. He should cultivate the simplest and most unassuming manner, and use plain, everyday words when possible, without letting the men see that he is making an effort to do so. They are as keen to detect the slightest condescension or effort to "work" them or toady to them as they are to resent any airs of superiority.

Shortly after serving my apprenticeship, I worked in a shop under the superintendence of a college graduate. His natural carriage led him to hold his head rather high in the air, and he had an imperturbable, rather wooden face, and looked at one with an expressionless eye. Every day he would walk through the shop, hardly saying anything to any of the workmen. In addition to this, he had the habit of using a silk handkerchief with perfume on it. This man was not only disliked but cordially hated by all the men. They could stand the silk handkerchief and the perfume, but the corner of the handkerchief which he always left sticking out of the breast pocket of his coat was too much for them, and I must say that I personally cordially shared their hatred. Years afterward I discovered he was rather a kindly, nice sort of man.

If one hopes to get into close and friendly touch with workmen, it is above all desirable that they should be talked to on their own level, by those who are over them. Each employer should, as far as possible, learn the names of his workmen. A good memory for names and faces is almost as valuable an asset for a superintendent as for a politician. Even in the largest establishment he should make it a point to know by name a considerable number of his men in each section of the works, and as he walks through each department he should either speak to them by name, give them a nod and a word or two, or at least a friendly recognition of the eye. To do this, however, without any real interest back of it, is worse than not doing it at all.

In giving an order, except of course in time of great emergency, invariably use the word "*Please*." In doing this it is not necessary to leave the slightest doubt on the mind of the workman that he is to do exactly as he is told. *Suaviter in modo, fortiter in re*, applies with equal force to all men.

Regardless of the method of doing it, however, men would far rather even be blamed by their bosses, especially if the "tearing out" has a touch of human nature and feeling in it, than be passed by day after day without a word, and with no more notice than if they were a part of the machinery. When superintendents and foremen are in the habit of encouraging their men to talk freely with them, the opportunity which each man has of airing his mind freely and having it out with his employers, is a safety valve, and if the superintendents are reasonable men and willing to treat with respect what their workmen have to say, there is absolutely no reason for labor unions and strikes.

It is not the paternal schemes that mess into their private affairs, nor the large charities, however generous they may be, that are needed or appreciated by workmen, so much as small acts of personal kindness and sympathy, which establish a bond of friendly feeling between them and their employers, and convince workmen that those over them are exactly the same kind of men as they are, and that they do not look down upon them. To succeed in this, however, it is far from being necessary, as many people think, for an educated man to talk ungrammatically with his men, to ostentatiously wear slouchy and dirty clothes, to leave off collar and cravat, or to have a dirty face and hands. These, as well as all other forms of affectation, will be promptly recognized and despised by the men. The cultivation of friendly personal relations with workmen which was absolutely essential for success with the old type of management, and which is one of the prime necessities of the management of the present day, will also continue to be important in the management of the future, though perhaps not as indispensable as it has been.

When a change or improvement in the management of the workmen of an establishment is contemplated, the fact must be recognized that it is impossible, even with ample funds, to carry on many reforms or make many changes at the same time. Reforms, much needed reforms, take a great deal of time, and while being made are aggravating both to employers and their men. And many changes so upset both sides as to make economical work impossible. If you try too many changes at the same time you will lose your workmen on the one hand, and tire your managers to death on the other. It is therefore of the greatest importance to make those changes and reforms first which shall count for the most.

For success, it becomes absolutely necessary, then, to know what *it is that workmen want most*, because, viewed from the standpoint of the selfish man, even, if you are able to give the workman what he is most anxious for, it will be more nearly possible for you to obtain in return what you want most from him; namely, *good work done fast, and therefore cheaply*.

Let me remind you that the wants of workmen are essentially the same as yours and mine. Now, the two things that the average man in our class wants more than anything else are a high salary and the chance for advancement. We will accept all kinds of philanthropic gifts, such as houses built on the company's grounds, fine offices and office furniture, short hours, long vacations, free libraries, free courses of public lectures, fine parks, etc. But all of these things will count for less with us than a large salary and the opportunity for advancement. We prefer a large salary to spend just as we see fit, to receiving a smaller salary and having our employer spend the rest of it in giving us the kind of improving things and the luxuries which he thinks we ought to have.

Now, the workman wants just what we want; high wages and the chance for advancement. He would also like lots of other things, such as comfortable lavatories, free lectures, night schools, athletic grounds, village improvement societies, and mutual benefit associations. But in most cases, if the management is busy trying to give him these things, they will neither have the time nor the spare money to spend in preparing to give him high wages.

Do not understand me as saying that welfare work and all such secondary aids to workmen should not be undertaken. They should all come along in their proper time, but I wish to emphasize the fact that they should not be allowed to interfere with doing those things which are necessary in order to give workmen what they want most, namely, *high wages*. I am obliged to dwell longer, perhaps, than seems necessary on this fact, since so many men are now running around the country stating just the opposite, namely, that you should take up the welfare work and the philanthropic schemes first.

(Mention here the series of strikes and financial disturbances that have occurred in the National Cash Register Co., the model welfare establishment of the whole world.)

Taylor always insisted that he was in no way anti-union, but most unions did not agree with him. This extract makes it easy to see why. For if pay and hours were outside the jurisdiction of the unions, a good part of their reason for being would disappear. Some unions would agree with Taylor's denunciation of forced slowdowns, but none could accept the idea that pay and hours can be "scientifically determined."

Apparently Taylor thought that unions were necessary only in companies that had not yet introduced scientific management.

Labor Unions

Frederick W. Taylor

I am firmly convinced that the best interests of workmen and their employers are the same; so that in my criticism of labor unions I feel that I am advocating the interests of both sides.

I am far from taking the view held by many manufacturers that labor unions are an almost unmitigated detriment to those who join them, as well as to employers and the general public.

The labor unions—particularly the trades unions of England—have rendered a great service in the past, not only to their members, but to the world, in shortening the hours of labor and in modifying the hardships and improving the conditions of wage-workers.

In my judgment the system of treating with labor unions would seem to occupy a middle position among the various methods of adjusting the relations between employers and men.

When employers herd their men together in classes, pay all of each class the same wages, and offer none of them any inducements to work harder or do better than the average, the only remedy for the men lies in combination; and frequently the only possible answer to encroachments on the part of their employers is a strike.

This state of affairs is far from satisfactory to either employers or men, and I believe the system of regulating the wages and conditions of employment of whole classes of men by conference and agreement between the leaders of unions and manufacturers to be vastly inferior, both in its moral effect on the men and on the material interests of both parties, to the plan of stimulating each workman's ambition by paying him according to his individual worth, and without limiting him to the rate of work or pay of the average of his class.

The amount of work which a man should do in a day, what constitutes proper pay for this work, and the maximum number of hours per day which a man should work together form the most important elements which are discussed between workmen and their employers. I have attempted to show that these matters can be much better determined by the expert time student than by either the union or a board of directors, and I firmly believe that in the future scientific time study will establish standards which will be accepted as fair by both sides.

There is no reason why labor unions should not be so constituted as to be a great help both to employers and men. Unfortunately, as they now exist they are in many, if not most, cases a hindrance to the prosperity of both.

The most serious of the delusions and fallacies under which workmen, and particularly those in many of the unions, are suffering is that it is for their interest to limit the amount of work which a man should do in a day.

Forbidding their members to do more than a given amount of work in a day has been the greatest mistake made by the English trades unions. The whole of that country is suffering more or less from this error now. Their workmen are for this reason receiving less wages than they might get, and in many cases the men, under the influence of this idea, have grown so slow that they would find it difficult to do a good day's work even if public opinion encouraged them to do it.

In forcing their members to work slowly they use certain cant phrases which sound most plausible until their real meaning is analyzed. They continually use the expression, "Workmen should not be asked to do more than a fair day's

From a series of lectures given at the Harvard Graduate School of Business Administration, Boston, 1909–1914. The manuscript was never published and is now in the archives of the Baker Library.

work," which sounds right and just until we come to see how it is applied. The absurdity of its usual application would be apparent if we were to apply it to animals. Suppose a contractor had in his stable a miscellaneous collection of draft animals, including small donkeys, ponies, light horses, carriage horses and fine dray horses, and a law were to be made that no animal in the stable should be allowed to do more than "a fair day's work" for a donkey.

Promotion, high wages, and, in some cases, shorter hours of work are the legitimate ambitions of a workman, but any scheme which curtails the output should be recognized as a device for lowering wages in the long run.

Any limit to the *maximum* wages which men are allowed to earn in a trade is equally injurious to their best interests.

The "minimum wage" is the least harmful of the rules which are generally adopted by trades unions, though it frequently works an injustice to the better workmen. For example, I have been used to having my machinists earn all the way from $1.50 to seven and eight dollars per day, according to the individual worth of the men. Supposing a rule were made that no machinist should be paid less than $2.50 per day. It is evident that if an employer were forced to pay $2.50 per day to men who were only worth $1.50 or $1.75, in order to compete he would be obliged to lower the wages of those who in the past were getting more than $2.50, thus pulling down the better workers in order to raise up the poorer men. Men are not born equal, and any attempt to make them so is contrary to nature's laws and will fail.

Union labor is sacred just so long as its acts are fair and good, and it is damnable just as soon as its acts are bad. Its rights are precisely those of non-union labor, neither greater nor less. The boycott, the use of force or intimidation, and the oppression of non-union workmen by labor unions are damnable; these acts of tyranny are thoroughly un-American and will not be tolerated by the American people.

Taylor did some work on motion study, but the most careful and detailed work in that field was done by one of his contemporaries, Frank B. Gilbreth. In the extract that follows, Gilbreth discusses the motions used in bricklaying and some of the factors making for the one best way of doing the job.

It should be noted that the aspects of motion covered in these pages are only a few of those he discussed in his book on motion study. He also considered such other variables as acceleration and its effect, the extent to which a motion was automatic, the combination with other motions and the sequence, and the cost of a motion (e.g., the cost of the time a bricklayer would spend picking up dropped mortar versus the cost of the mortar itself).

Variables of Motion

Frank B. Gilbreth

A general rule of motion economy is to make the shortest motions possible.

Eliminating unnecessary distances that workers' hands and arms must travel will eliminate miles of motions per man in a working day as compared with usual practice.

Example.—Put the wheelbarrow body as close as possible to the pile that is to be put into it, so that the distance the packets are carried from the pile to the barrow, or the sand from the pile to the barrow, will be the shortest distance possible.

Of the necessary distance to be walked or reached, have as much of it as possible done by the low-priced man, and have as little of it as possible done by the high-priced man.

Example.—With bricks, have the tender put the pack of brick as near the final resting place of the brick as conditions will permit, so that when

From *Motion Study* (D. Van Nostrand Company, Inc., New York, 1911), chap. 4. Reprinted in William R. Spriegel and Clark E. Myers (eds.), *The Writings of the Gilbreths* (Richard D. Irwin, Inc., Homewood, Ill., 1953), pp. 191–194.

the high-priced man picks up a pack of, say, eighteen bricks, he requires a short motion only.

Necessity

The necessity of the motion is such an important variable that an investigator is tempted at first glance to divide all motions into necessary and unnecessary, and to eliminate with one stroke those that appear to him unnecessary. A more thorough investigation will be apt to prove that no such summary elimination is advisable.

A motion may be unnecessary motion in a necessary sequence, or it may be a necessary motion in a certain sequence, but the whole sequence may be unnecessary or inadvisable.

Example.—In opening a paper bag of cement the average untrained laborer usually cuts the bag in two and removes the paper in several pieces and with many motions. The correct way is to cut the bottom with a shovel and pull the bag upward in one piece by grasping the bag just above the string.

This example shows both how motions may be unnecessary in themselves and how they may belong to a sequence that is unnecessary.

The only final solution as to the necessity of a motion will come when the trades are completely standardized. It is impossible to determine whether or not a motion is absolutely necessary until the method of doing the work in which it is used is standard.

Examples—1 Motions which were relatively proved necessary in laying brick by the "pick-and-dip" method or "stringing-mortar" method, the brick being lifted from the stock platform, became absolutely unnecessary when the "packet-on-the-wall" method of handling brick was adopted.

2 The same thing is true of motions eliminated by handling mortar in a fountain trowel.

Path

The determination of the path which will result in the greatest economy of motion and the greatest increase of output is a subject for the closest investigation and the most scientific determination. Not until data are accumulated by trained observers can standard paths be adopted. The laws underlying physics, physiology, and psychology must be considered and followed. In the meantime, merely applying the results of observation will reduce motions and costs and increase output to an amazing degree.

The path most desirable is usually that which permits gravitation to assist in carrying the material to place.

Example.—We have found that the most economical height for laying brick is twenty-four inches above where the bricklayer stands, while it is most economical to pick the brick from a height about three feet above where the bricklayer stands; that is, about one foot higher than the top of the wall where the brick is to be laid.

Playing for Position

Each motion should be made so as to be most economically combined with the next motion, like the billiard player who plays for position.

The direction in which a motion is made may affect the time required for a subsequent motion.

Example.—In laying brick the motion of placing the mortar for the end joint can be done the quickest if it is done in the direction of the next motion, such, for example, as the next motion that puts the trowel in the position to cut off the hanging mortar.

The sequence of motions in bricklaying, that determines when the particular motion is to be made that puts the mortar in the end joint, depends upon whether the "pick-and-dip" or the "stringing-mortar" method is used.

When the motions are made in the correct sequence, many of them can be combined so that two, and in some cases three, motions can be made as one motion, in but little more time than is required for one motion.

Example.—Cutting off mortar, buttering the end of the laid brick, and reaching for more mortar all as one motion, in the "pick-and-dip" method.

Speed

Usually, the faster the motions, the more output. There are other advantages to speed of motions besides the fact that they require less time.

Speed increases momentum, and this momentum may be utilized to do work.

Example.—The momentum of the brick helps to shove the mortar better into the joint.

Again, high outputs are generally the result of the habit of speed in motions. Habits of speed are hard to form, and they are hard to break.

Next to fewest motions, speed of motions is the most important factor of high record of outputs.

The list of variables here given makes no claim to being complete. The field of study is so immense that it is impossible as yet to give a complete and detailed method of attack.

It will be noted in reading the discussion of the variables that it has been found extremely difficult to handle each one separately. It is needless to tell the student, the investigator, the cost-reducing manager, that, difficult as the task is, for the best results each variable must be studied alone. The effects of all variables but one must be eliminated, or, better perhaps, all variables but one must be maintained constant.

Quicker results may often be obtained by studying several variables simultaneously, and for short jobs this may be advisable. But for long jobs of repetitive work there is no way so accurate and satisfactory as studying one variable at a time.

Close to the Taylor group but not of it was Harrington Emerson (1853–1931). Whereas the interest of Taylor and Gilbreth was focused largely on the physical work done in industry by rank-and-file employees, Emerson approached scientific management from the viewpoint of the company as a whole. Thus in his book *Twelve Principles of Efficiency*[1] he concentrated on such things as overall objectives, cost accounting, and the functions of staff departments.

His single most important contribution to the scientific management movement, however, may have been his testimony in the Eastern Rate Case before the Interstate Commerce Commission in 1910–1911, when he opposed the railroads' application for a rise in rates. Called as a witness by Louis D. Brandeis (later Supreme Court Justice), who represented the shippers, Emerson stated that the railroads could save "a million dollars a day" by improving their efficiency. This made the headlines and popularized the idea of scientific management.

Saving a Million Dollars a Day

Harrington Emerson

Mr. Brandeis. You have been quoted, Mr. Emerson, as stating that in your opinion, by the introduction of proper efficiency system or scientific management, the railroads of the United States could effect an economy of perhaps $300,000,000 a year, or not less than $1,000,000 a day.

Mr. Emerson. That is correct—that is, I have been quoted as having stated that.

Mr. Brandeis. Is it your opinion that that is the fact?

Mr. Emerson. At least that.

Mr. Brandeis. And in which of the departments of the railroad operation is it that large economies can be effected, in your opinion?

Mr. Emerson. In all the departments except traffic. The efficiency of the traffic by my standards is very high; that is, the efficiency of expense in the traffic departments.

Commissioner Prouty. Just what do you mean by the traffic departments?

Mr. Emerson. That is one of the classifications, one of the five classifications, is it not?

Commissioner Prouty. You mean the traffic

[1](The Engineering Magazine [publisher], New York, 1911).

From *Scientific Management and the Railroads: Being Part of a Brief Submitted to the Interstate Commerce Commission by Louis D. Brandeis* (The Engineering Magazine [publisher], New York, 1911), pp. 83–88; evidence given in 1910.

department as classified by the Interstate Commerce Commission?

Mr. Emerson. Yes.

Mr. Brandeis. Would you state to the Commission on what you have based your estimate that so large an economy in operation is possible?

Mr. Emerson. There were four different ways of attacking the problem. The final conclusion is a composite from the results obtained by the four different methods.

First, the long experience I have had in investigating intimately American shops all over the country had led me to realize that certain inefficiencies existed in different classes of labor, inefficiencies due to the absence of proper standard methods. These inefficiencies averaged fairly well over the whole country. They averaged fairly well in all businesses. Taking those inefficiencies as my judgment determined them and applying them to the bills for labor and for material in the railroads, I arrived at a certain result, which aggregated in excess of $300,000,000. That was one way of getting at it.

Another way of getting at it was to take—

Commissioner Prouty *(interposing).* Let us see if we understand that. Did you take the amount of the payroll in those departments and say that there was ten per cent actual inefficiency in this labor and subtract ten per cent from the amount of the payroll?

Mr. Emerson. No, I took the report, for instance of 1908—

Commissioner Prouty *(interposing).* I do not mean that ten per cent was the figure you used, of course.

Mr. Emerson. I understand. The total labor bill for 1908 was $1,035,000,000. That covered all of what I classify as personal services as distinguished from materials and capital charges. Those are the three elements of expense. These are classified as to different lines of operation. I put an efficiency opposite each one of these classes, based on my general knowledge, that would have applied to other business as well as to the railroad business, and, as you state, multiplied it and arrived in that way at an estimate of the inefficiency of labor.

Commissioner Prouty. And that was over $300,000,000?

Mr. Emerson. Oh, no, not for the labor alone.

Commissioner Prouty. Do you remember how much it was for labor alone?

Mr. Emerson. In the neighborhood of $240,000,000, I think it was, for labor alone.

The next plan was to take the divisions as provided for by the Interstate Commerce Commission, and using such knowledge as I had in my experience, to check up the different operations like locomotive repairs, car repairs, shop machinery and tools, and track work, and to take each item of the total bill for all the railroads—$1,667,000,000, I think, for that year—and place opposite those items the inefficiency subdivided as to material and labor, and arrive at another estimate.

Commissioner Prouty. What do you mean by "inefficiency of material"?

Mr. Emerson. Engineers know very well and have determined how much horsepower you ought to get, or how much water you ought to evaporate from a pound of coal. If you are using a great deal more coal than that, there is an inefficiency. There is an ideal result which you ought to get which would be a horsepower from one-fifth of a pound of coal. The highest attainment they ever get is a horsepower from a pound. That is a very high ideal. If you find people are using either eight or nine or ten pounds of coal per horsepower, it measures a certain amount of inefficiency compared to the practically attainable. That is an illustration. The fuel is the largest single item of expense, so a large amount of this saving might be from the fuel. That is the second way of determining this waste. The third was the comparative method. All railroads are efficient in certain directions. They are tremendously efficient in certain directions. Each railroad has some particular spot in which it is more fortunate perhaps than other railroads. Taking the different railroads of the country and visiting them and investigating them, and finding out that one had an efficient way as to maintenance of locomotives, another as to maintenance of cars, that a third had an efficient way as to maintenance of shop machinery and tools and the fourth had an efficiency as to maintenance of track; and taking all these different bright spots that the railroads had evolved through the special genius of the men connected with or interested in those particular departments, you got a third standard—a standard, for instance, let us say, of six cents a mile as being an adequate amount on the average to maintain locomotives, or a standard of $35 as being an adequate standard to maintain cars.

Mr. Brandeis. Freight cars?

Mr. Emerson. Freight cars. Some months ago, when I was addressing the Railway Club in Pittsburgh, I stated this standard of $35 per car. Mr. Turner of the P. & L. E. was the spokesman of the opposition. He said they had been long waiting to get a chance at me, and the chance had now come; that they were tired of assertions of this kind being made, that they were from Missouri and the time had come for a show down. He said: "Mr. Emerson stated $35 a car. I want to know where he gets his facts and what right he has to get up any standard of that kind." I told them about a number of roads that had attained that, and the next day I went around to see Mr. Turner. I said, "Turner, what does it cost you to maintain your freight cars?"

He said, "I do not know. I never figured it out that way. I have always figured it by the mile and not by the freight car." I said, "Can you find out very easily what it is?" He said, "Yes." So in the course of half an hour his chief clerk brought in the figures, showing their cost of maintenance per car was $31.01. *(Laughter.)* I very much regretted that I had not known that fact at the time they had me on the stand before the Club.

In the same way as to maintenance of locomotives. I think the records of the Pittsburgh and Lake Erie are probably among the model records of the United States. In checking them up I found Mr. Turner had accomplished the maintenance of his locomotives, that are heavy power, for somewhere between $1200 and $1500, one of the lowest records I know of in the United States.

That is the third way of ascertaining standards. That means you can apply haphazard that standard to any road. It means it gives you a general average on which you can base a conclusion. That method checked up with the other two methods in revealing losses aggregating not less than $300,000,000.

The fourth method was in particular. In connection with the work of the Santa Fe we made an investigation or scientific investigation, of which you have heard from the other gentlemen on the same system. I took the costs as they were. I finally found out why those costs were, what losses were occurring, and what could be done by the management to eliminate those losses. We set up as a standard of measurement, because you have to have some unit of measurement, what has since been called the road unit. If you take the locomotive alone, it may stand in the roundhouse for a whole year and would have no repairs. If you take the mileage alone, it might be a light locomotive running a number of miles, and that would not be a fair measurement; but when you combine the mileage the locomotive makes in the course of a year with its weight, you have a unit that at least in some respects is better than the unit of either the single locomotive or the locomotive miles.

Using that unit, we found in the fiscal year ending 1904 the cost of locomotives had been $101 per road unit as an average on the whole system. By investigating the matter and inducing the management to put in various scientific studies, that was reduced in the next year to $78, and in the third year to $74. At that time I presented to Mr. Kendrick an exhaustive study of locomotive operation, covering eighteen hundred locomotives and all their records for five years, as to all the different divisions and the different causes and the different items of expense. It was probably one of the most complete statements of locomotive operation that was ever made. I did not make it myself. It was made for me by one of my assistants, and with the assistance particularly of the statistical department. He could not have done anything if he had not had access to the vast accumulation of statistics that had been collected for use by that department.

Mr. Brandeis. You mean the statistical department of the Santa Fe?

Mr. Emerson. Yes, the statistical department of the Santa Fe. I stated at that time, in final report, that I saw no reason why the Santa Fe should not be able to maintain its locomotives for fifty dollars per road unit. That was thirty-three per cent lower than they had attained at that time. I am still of that opinion.

That was the fourth method. The same system was applied to other items of locomotive work. Taking up those four methods, they all of them gave me substantially the same result, within $30,000,000 or $40,000,000 of each other.

Mr. Brandeis. Then your estimate as to the absence of efficiency and of the possible saving is based upon the assumption and belief and deduction that in the very large part of the service this high efficiency attained in the Chicago-New York trains is absent?

Mr. Emerson. That is correct. I have studied the comparative records of the leading railroads of the United States and tested them by the unit standard cost. I have been in the shops of a great number of different railroads, my assistants have been in the shops of nearly all of the important railroads of the United States, either visiting them or working in them, so I have a very fair knowledge as to the extent in the past. At the present moment I do not know, but up to the last year I know what the condition was in the various railroad shops of the country.

If I find that the unit cost of performance is high on a railroad, I conclude that one of two things is true: either that they do not have the methods of scientific management, or that there is an undue number of dependent sequences.

In his books Harrington Emerson drew largely on his experience in reorganizing the Santa Fe railroad, a job he did in his capacity as consulting "efficiency expert," a term he himself coined. This singling out of an industry for criticism, and still more his testimony in the Eastern Rate Case, aroused the opposition of many railroad managers. Here a writer for their trade paper, the *Railway Age Gazette*, serves as spokesman for them.

The bitterness felt by some railway men is shown not only by the serious criticisms but by the ridicule of Emerson's writing style. This latter criticism was not entirely unjustified, for he did tend to draw on analogies rather far afield from the matter in hand.

The Mistakes of Efficiency Men

A number of years ago one of the now leading efficiency engineers was engaged in a large industrial plant to introduce a piece work system. Stop watch in hand, he timed the various operations and tabulated the results. His attitude toward the workmen was impersonal. He was a scientist(?) in his laboratory. He was a man apart. The men around him recognized him as such. Lacking their confidence, coöperation was impossible. But from the standpoint of the efficiency engineer this was unnecessary; his faith was in his theories and principles. Consequently, when he appeared in the shop and began his observations, machines would often be slowed down with loss of output or speeded up with damage to tools. Every device known to the various trades was resorted to, to block him at each turn. The result was that after two years of effort the establishment of a satisfactory piece work system was as far from realization as it had been when the task was started. Then a practical man was called in. He acquainted himself with the machines and their capacity. He mingled with the men and gained their confidence. He explained that the object in view was two-fold, to increase the output at a reduced cost per unit to the company, and at the same time to enable the men to earn more. Within six months he had accomplished results that the efficiency man had spent two years in an effort to secure. Why? because he appreciated the importance of the man element.

Yet they tell us that practical men follow the rule-of-thumb, that they have not had the time and do not possess the ability to analyze closely the successive steps in the almost myriad opera-

From one of a series of articles that appeared in *Railway Age Gazette*, Jan. 6–May 5, 1911. The magazine also published an editorial and several letters from readers on the subject.

tions of a large shop, that because of a lack of scientific knowledge they are not competent to determine proper methods of work or secure the best results from operation. It is undoubtedly true that many practical men lack the peculiar qualities required by the efficiency engineer. But are the efficiency men assisting them in this direction? Rather, are they not practically ignoring the experience of practical men in their endeavors to establish the efficiency system, or to clarify the atmosphere surrounding it? Do they not give too little credit to the capacity of such men—inherent in some, acquired by many—to handle men, to convince them of their mistakes, to gain their sympathy and to establish that *esprit de corps* without which no organization is efficient? Under these conditions, efficiency engineers should not be surprised that practical men view with distrust their efforts in fields in which they have had no actual training.

An understanding of the psychology of the crowd as represented by a shop filled with workmen, possessed in large measure by most successful factory and railway managers, master mechanics, roundhouse and shop foremen, cannot be replaced by a theory of management nor ignored with impunity in introducing efficiency methods. Of two men entering a shop apparently equally equipped, one was found to be analytical and critical both in respect to the details of his work and his fellow workmen, but lacking the magnetism that makes for leadership. The other, with less analytical ability and often wrong in his theories, possessed a personality that gave him an influence over the men around him. Which, naturally, became the leader, afterwards the foreman, then the superintendent? Such men, by the law of selection, represent the great majority of those who manage our railways and superintend our industrial and railway shops. Whatever their failings, they are to be reckoned with.

While many a shop foreman, superintendent or master mechanic may have no proper appreciation of the beauties of the philosophy of efficiency, may be unable to follow the line of reasoning of the efficiency men, may be mistaken in his belief that his men are more efficient than the "assays" have shown, and may have much to learn, he has usually reached his position because of certain qualifications possessed in greater measure by him than by the other men with whom he has been associated. And in introducing efficiency methods in his department it is a fatal mistake to omit the first essential, his good will, because almost invariably except through him the good will of the men cannot be secured.

Unscientific

Is it scientific to use as evidence cases of low efficiency and consequent high costs and unsatisfactory service, or of improvements that have followed the introduction of efficiency methods, without an equally fair statement of all the conditions that surround the operations? Or to search through the records for an especially poor performance to set alongside an especially good one, irrespective of the causes and the general tendency in either case? All thoughtful accountants appreciate how misleading statistical data may be unless all the concurrent factors are taken into consideration and proper allowances made for them. Whatever the unit of measurement, it is unsafe and improper to draw definite conclusions from too narrow a range of data.

A good record of one month may really be a poor one when all the facts are known. For example, in an industry where the different operations that precede the completion of a certain unit are scattered over a period of several months, the output during a particular month may, and usually does, bear no direct relation to the cost of operations during the month in question. In a shop building steam engines, machine tools, passenger cars, or similar equipment, requiring perhaps two months or more to assemble complete, it is the height of folly to assume that the cost of the operations in a given month divided by the output represents the cost per unit, and indicates whether the results are satisfactory or otherwise.

Impatience for Results

Perhaps next to the failure of the efficiency men to appreciate the importance of the human element, the most certainly fatal mistake they have made is their impatience for results.

Instead of establishing the system in one department, and proving its worth so unequivocally that it is demanded in other departments, certain efficiency men have urged its speedy extension to other departments, for the reason that unless it is introduced into all and recognized as the established system, there is danger that it will fail in the department in which it was initially instituted. One of the most unfortunate results of the impatience is the opportunity that is given to labor to organize and present a solid front of opposition to their establishment. It is both unnecessary and unscientific to demand or expect permanently satisfactory results in introducing scientific management without giving it time to grow in favor. If the efficiency men have profited by this mistake, which has been the direct cause of many of their failures, they have gained much.

Neglect of Common Sense

Another factor all too frequently overlooked is the opportunity for increasing efficiency and reducing costs through simple expedients. Many a successful superintendent has accomplished by the exercise of ingenuity and common sense what efficiency engineers, after exhaustive investigations and the introduction of theoretical schemes of doubtful value, have failed to bring about. Instead of following the line of least resistance they seem to prefer indirect and devious ways. Successful practical men know of better methods. If, for example, the cost of a certain class of locomotive repairs is running at, say, 12 cents a mile, the superintendent may reach the conclusion that it is too high. It is not necessary that he should make an extended investigation in order to determine exactly how excessive his costs have been. Comparative figures interpreted by common sense and good judgment will tell him closely enough for his present purpose, and he may conclude that the cost should average not over nine cents. He has thus arrived, through the expedient of a simple determination of the possibilities, at a standard which may be termed a practicable ideal cost as distinguished from a theoretical ideal cost. Then by another simple calculation of charges and credits, and through comparative records by divisions, roundhouses and shops, the percentage of inefficiency may be determined and localized. If traceable to defective organization this can be corrected; if due to some inherent weakness in the design of any particular part of the locomotive, the part can be strengthened. This, of course, is not the "scientific" method, for it does not attempt to determine for every separate operation included in the cost of repairs the actual cost and efficiency. It is enough for all practicable purposes at this stage to know that the costs are computed on the same basis as formerly and that the figures for different periods are properly comparable, so that if costs are reduced from 12 to 9 cents a mile he is assured that it is not in the bookkeeping but that a reduction of 25 per cent has actually been made.

It is a fair statement that if in a certain instance locomotive or car repairs are excessive by, say, 30 per cent, it will cost less than half as much to save the first 20 per cent as to save the last 10 per cent. In fact, it is not unlikely that it would be practically impossible to secure the last 10 per cent, however elaborate a system might be installed. When the cost of a system is equivalent to the possible savings, it is, of course, only a useless burden. Proof that a high efficiency can be reached without recourse to a highly specialized system is found in the fact that it is recognized even by the scientific engineers that on many of the representative railways and in scores of industrial shops, low costs of operation accompanied by a high standard of service have been maintained for years. The possible economies through somewhat unscientific but effective calculations, comparisons and allowances, are enormous.

Incompetent Counsel

When the efficiency men are charged with the mistake of giving incompetent counsel when their advice is sought, they are taken to task for ignoring one of the principles upon which their structure of shop management is built; for among the principles enumerated by Mr. Emerson in the series of articles current in the *Engineering Magazine*, not the least prominence is given to "competent counsel."

It has been correctly stated in the *Railway Age Gazette* on various occasions that the interest in efficiency methods and scientific management has been increasing rapidly. It is a question, however, whether this is not in spite of, rather than because of, their exposition by certain efficiency men who are recognized as the leaders of the new philosophical school. Railway and industrial managers have been asking for bread and they have been given a stone. In the April number of the *Engineering Magazine* is published the eleventh of the series of articles on "The Twelve Principles of Efficiency," entitled "The Ninth Principle—Standardized Conditions." Recognizing the importance of having conditions standardized and the economic loss due to the absence of standards, one naturally looks for valuable suggestions regarding this feature of scientific management. If there are any such suggestions in the article in question, a second and a third reading have failed to disclose them. As a philosophical dissertation, it may have a place, but as a contribution to the cause of scientific management it is sorely deficient. It opens with an interesting chapter from the life of the grub, followed by a comparison of the standards of the spider and the firefly with those of man, much to the detriment of the latter. Egypt and her pyramids have a place, then consideration is given to the evolution of the aeroplane. Efficiency principles are compared to the framework of a dome. The eight-hour train between New York and Chicago, and the three-day schedule for general repairs to a locomotive are prophesied, but no hint is given of the methods that will bring them into being. A large publishing house (which, if we read correctly between the lines, paid dearly for the introduction into its plant of a certain system of shop management) is put on the rack with other business men, who do not progress because of "imaginary specters that terrorize the soul." The article closes with an appeal for standardizing conditions in "our lives, our shops and our nation." To what extent competent counsel is given to those who are interested in standardizing conditions can be judged from the above summary.

It is not unusual for certain efficiency men to refer the failure of their plans to a lack of coöperation on the part of those in authority. Is it not rather that the counselor has failed to give sound advice, and that consequently results have not squared with the promises? His attitude is too often that of one who never needs but always gives counsel. That prejudice sometimes exists is no doubt true, but this is perhaps no more marked than that of many of the efficiency men toward the organization common to nearly all railway and industrial shops.

Conclusion

The nature of these observations has precluded the possibility of a recognition of the good that has been accomplished by the efficiency men, either directly or as a result of the publicity that has followed their utterances. The fact that we have charged them with many and serious errors has not blinded us to those features of their systems which have merit. It is not our province to refer to them here in detail; it would be unfair, however, and might lead to a misconception of the purpose of these studies to close them without a word of commendation for those among the efficiency men who have urged the principles of a common sense management in the face of almost insurmountable obstacles. It has been largely a campaign of education, and a call has gone out to operating men of all classes to seek a more intimate knowledge of the details of their business. The charge of gross inefficiency that has become a popular slogan, while much exaggerated, has led to systematic plans to reduce waste, and economies have already resulted, which had not been considered within the realm of possibility. From whatever point of view this science of management may be considered, and in all the heat of argument, it should be remembered that the law of the survival of the fittest holds in the economic as in the animal realm, and that because the principles of scientific management are vital to our industrial life, they have come to stay.

6
Elton Mayo and the Human Relations School

Like Taylor and most of the other members of the scientific management movement, (George) Elton Mayo (1880–1949) was primarily interested in management as it affected the rank and file in industry, and, again like Taylor, he was interested in increasing productivity. But his viewpoint was entirely different. He believed that the economic motive to produce on which Taylor laid so much stress was unimportant compared with emotional and nonlogical attitudes and sentiments.

Mayo was a psychologist by profession. As professor of industrial research at the Graduate School of Business, Harvard University, he had a great influence on the development of the social sciences and on practicing managers as well. Much of his writing was based on the well-known Hawthorne experiments, with which he was associated for a time and which are briefly (and unsympathetically) outlined in the piece by Daniel Bell, which follows the two articles taken from Mayo's own writings.

Most of the criticism of the Hawthorne studies, in fact, has been somewhat on the grounds Bell cites. The next article, by Alex Carey, presents a different type of criticism, for it questions the validity of the studies themselves. Following it is a reply by Dr. Jon Shepard.

The final article in this chapter takes issue with the views of both Taylor and Mayo.

During and immediately after World War I, Mayo became greatly concerned with the antipathy between management and labor in his native Australia, where he was affiliated with Queensland University. In 1919, when he was lecturing on philosophy there, he published a little-known essay in which he foreshadowed some of the conclusions he later drew from the Hawthorne studies.

Social Growth and Social Disintegration

Elton Mayo

Individualism failed to see that man, socially speaking, holds his past and future in his present. And individualism consequently, though it gave us an economics and a politics, failed to give us a science of society and government.

In its practical applications it has worked out in a fashion quite contrary to the intentions of its authors. By opposing society, described as a mere formless anarchy of persons, to the unity of the State, democracy made it seem that social unity can only come by way of State activity.

John Stuart Mill believed that a sound democratic autonomy cannot be based otherwise than upon a wide area of sane and logical public discussion.

This last condition modern democracies, and especially Australia, have failed to realize. Logical persuasion cannot be made to operate easily and quickly over wide areas of relatively ignorant people.

Nemesis is already overtaking our leaders in that with all the will in the world to unite the community in the face of threatened disaster (i.e. the class struggle), they cannot do so.

Viewed from the standpoint of social science, society is composed of individuals organized in individual groups, each group fulfilling some function for the society. Taking this fact into account, psychology—the science of human nature and human consciousness—is able to make at least one general assertion as to the form a given society must take if it is to persist as a society. It must be possible for the individual as he works [to see] that his work is socially necessary; he must be able to see beyond his group to the society. Failure in this respect will make disintegration inevitable.

The average worker of the present sees industries not as social functions but as the scene of a "class war."

The workman is still conceived [by the employers] as a mere item in the cost of production rather than as a citizen fulfilling a social function. No increase in wages or improvement of working conditions can atone for the loss of real autonomy and of all sense of social function.

The social function of the more important occupations having been obscured, an attempt has been made to solve the resulting problem by political means. State control in the form of industrial arbitration tends to stereotype and make permanent the social fissure between the employing class and the majority of those employed. Political organization tends to widen the breach and to make differences irreconcilable. This is the situation in Australia; the democracies of Britain and America would seem to be developing speedily in the same direction. Revolution or civil war is the only logical outcome of the present irreconcilable attitude of Australian political parties. The methods of "democracy," far from providing a means of solving the industrial problem, have proved entirely inadequate to the task.

Union leadership, it may at least be said, is no longer in the hands of the most highly skilled trade representatives; facile eloquence and a partisan hostility to all employers have become the appropriate qualifications.

The social regime which the "practical man" or the "capable manager" would introduce, if he had his way, would be at least as dependent upon regulation as socialism and far more dully mechanical. One consequence of this foolish amateur philosophizing is that too many already regard their work merely as a form of payment for such pleasure as they are able to find in their "spare" time.

The most perfect business mechanisms have been elaborated, only to find that the "intract-

From *Democracy and Freedom. An Essay in Social Logic* (Macmillan & Co., Ltd., Melbourne, Australia, 1919, Workers Educational Series No. I), pp. 5, 16, 30, 37, 40–44, 51–53, 60, 63.

able" working class refused to adopt them. "Taylorism" is the latest of these achievements, and its mere name was enough to provoke the greatest industrial disturbance ever known in Sydney. As a system, Taylorism effects much in the way of economy of labour; its chief defect is that workmen are not asked to collaborate in effecting such economies; a method is devised without their knowledge and then imposed on them. What wonder if workers are suspicious of such innovations. So long as commerce specializes in business methods which take no account of human nature and social motives, so long may we expect strikes and sabotage to be the ordinary accompaniment of industry. Sabotage is essentially a protest of the human spirit against dull mechanism. And the emphasis which democracy places upon political methods tends to transform mere sporadic acts of sabotage into an organized conspiracy against society. But for this sinister feature of modern industrial life our commercial leaders cannot be held blameless.

No social system can be considered satisfactory which deprives the great majority of mankind of every vestige of autonomy. No society is civilized in which the many [work] in the interest of the few. When "work" signifies intelligent collaboration in the achievement of a social purpose, "industrial unrest" will cease to be.

Man is civilized only when he functions in a social scheme or system which endures through successive generations and is continuously developed toward the better expression of human capacities of thought and will.

Mayo's ideal was a society (in the plant and in the world at large) in which there was an absence of conflict and a feeling of security—both mental and economic—among its members, and he felt that the mental security, at least, had been achieved in an earlier day when everyone knew his place. While he realized that any return to the exact practices of the past was both impossible and undesirable, he thought that the spirit of belonging formerly enjoyed could be recreated if managers would acquire and exercise the proper social skills. The following extract from one of his books presents this viewpoint.

The Seamy Side of Progress

Elton Mayo

Frédéric Le Play was a French engineer whose professional work, early in the nineteenth century, took him widely through the length and breadth of Europe. As early as the year 1829, he had come to doubt whether rapid technical and industrial development was altogether beneficial to the various European communities in which he worked. For twenty-five years, with this in mind, he made careful observations of the living conditions of the many diverse groups of workers with whom he was associated.

His general finding is that in simpler communities, where the chief occupation is agriculture or fishing or some primary activity, there is a stability of the social order that has ceased to characterize highly developed industrial centers. In these simpler communities every individual understands the various economic activities and social functions, and, in greater or less degree, participates in them. The bonds of family and kinship (real or fictitious) operate to relate every person to every social occasion; the ability to cooperate effectively is at a high level. The situation is not simply that the society exercises a powerful compulsion on the individual; on the contrary, the social code and the desires of the individual are, for all practical purposes, identical. Every member of the group participates in social activities because it is his chief desire to do so.

Le Play's finding with respect to the modern and characteristically industrial community is

From *The Social Problems of an Industrial Civilization* (Division of Research, Harvard Graduate School of Business Administration, Boston, 1945), pp. 5–15.

entirely contrary. He finds in such communities extensive social disorganization: the authority of the social code is ignored, the ties of kinship are no longer binding, the capacity for peace and stability has definitely waned. In these communities, he says, individuals are unhappy; the desire for change—"novelty"—has become almost passionate, and this of itself leads to further disorganization.

Remarkably similar observations were made toward the end of the nineteenth century in France by Emile Durkheim, founder of the French school of sociology. He says that the difference between a modern and technically developed center and the simple, ordered community is that in the small community the interests of the individual are subordinated, by his own eager desire, to the interests of the group. The individual member of this primitive society can clearly anticipate during infancy and adolescence the function that he will fulfill for the group when adult. This anticipation regulates his activity and thinking in the adolescent period and culminates in a communal function and a sense of satisfaction when he is fully grown. He knows that his activities are wanted by his society, and are necessary to its continued life. He is throughout his life solidaire with the group.

During the nineteenth century, the rapid development of science and industry put an end to the individual's feeling of identification with his group, of satisfaction in his work. Durkheim develops this in some detail.

In extreme instances, we may find individuals who have lost all sense of social relationship or obligation—the melancholic, the suicide, the "lone wolf," or the criminal. Even in those instances where the quest for group relationship finally succeeds—fortunately still a majority, although diminishing—the individual is not equipped by experience immediately to understand the nature of social relationship. And his group consequently represents a lower level of unity and obligation to the common purpose than the primitive.

In a modern industrial society we consequently find two symptoms of social disruption.

First, the number of unhappy individuals increases. Forced back upon himself, with no immediate or real social duties, the individual becomes a prey to unhappy and obsessive personal preoccupations.

Second, various groups when formed are not eager to cooperate wholeheartedly with other groups. On the contrary, their attitude is usually that of wariness or hostility. It is by this road that a society sinks into a condition of *stasis*—a confused struggle of pressure groups, power blocs, which, Casson claims, heralds the approach of disaster.[1]

Earlier studies tend naturally enough to look back at the life of simpler communities with regret; they tend inevitably to the conclusion that spontaneity of cooperation cannot be recovered except by reversion to the traditional. This, however, is a road we cannot travel in these days; for us there can be no easy return to simplicity.

But the implication of such opinion does not detract from the value of Le Play's or Durkheim's observations. The real importance of these studies is the clear demonstration that *collaboration in an industrial society cannot be left to chance*—neither in a political nor in an industrial unit can such neglect lead to anything but disruption and catastrophe. Historically and traditionally our fathers worked for social cooperation—and achieved it. But we for at least a century of the most amazing scientific and material progress have abandoned the effort—by inadvertence, it is true—and we are now reaping the consequences.

Every social group, at whatever level of culture, must face and clearly state two perpetual and recurrent problems of administration. It must secure for its individual and group membership:

1 The satisfaction of material and economic needs.
2 The maintenance of spontaneous cooperation throughout the organization.

Our administrative methods are all pointed at the materially effective; none, at the maintenance of cooperation. The amazing technical successes show that we—our engineers—do know how to organize for material efficiency. But problems of absenteeism, labor turnover,

[1]Stanley Casson, *Progress and Catastrophe* (Harper & Row, Publishers, Incorporated, New York, 1937).

"wildcat" strikes, show that we do not know how to ensure spontaneity of cooperation; that is, teamwork.

The problem of cooperation is far more difficult of solution with us than in a simple or primitive community. In a simple society, the extent of change from year to year, or even from century to century, is relatively small. Traditional methods are therefore brought to a high degree of perfection; almost from birth disciplined collaboration is drilled into the individual. But any study of such simple societies, whether by anthropologists or sociologists, possesses small relevance to the problems that so sorely beset us now. In these days of rapid and continuous change, the whole conception of social organization and social discipline must be radically revised. And, in this, the so-called "radicals" are of small aid, being not radical but reactionary: they would require us to return to a form of social organization that has been made obsolete by technical advance.

There is an unrealized difference between two principles of social organization—the one, that of an *established* society; the other, that of an *adaptive* society. The advantages of an established society are many; and the majority of liberal, or even revolutionary, movements of our time take origin in a strong desire to return from present uncertainty to established certainty—a desire that is in fact reactionary and opposed to the spirit of the age. In the small town of sixty years ago, the choice of occupation offered a young man was small; he might follow his father's trade of blacksmith or carpenter or he might try to advance a step—bank clerk, teacher, or clergyman. His choice was usually made, or made for him, before he entered his teens, and thereafter his way of life was determined by what he was to be.

Even those who entered factory or business—both small scale, as measured by the present, but both rapidly coming to maturity in the nineteenth century—did so under these conditions. The boy was thus apprenticed in some fashion to his life work and his trade, and began to acquire simultaneously technical capacity and the art of communication with his fellows. In the usual case this group changed but little during his apprenticeship. Thus through practice at his trade with the same group of persons, he learned to manipulate the objects with which he worked and to understand the attitudes and ideas of his companions. Both of these are of immense importance to successful living. Dr. Pierre Janet, in fifty years of patient, pedestrian, clinical research, has shown that sanity is an achievement and that the achievement implies a balanced relation between technical and social skills.

Little of the old establishment survives in modern industry: the emphasis is upon change and adaptability; the rate of change mounts to an increasing tempo. *We have in fact passed beyond that stage of human organization in which effective communication and collaboration were secured by established routines of relationship.*

Put in ordinary language, the apprentice learned to be a good workman, and he also learned to "get on with" his fellows and associates. This second acquisition was clearly understood to be an essential part of his training; many colloquial phrases existed to describe it, such as, for example, "getting the edges rubbed off," "learning to take the fences," and so on—homely similes that recognized the value for society of such experience. Unfortunately this important social discipline was never clearly specified as a necessary part of the individual's education, and consequently, when the tempo of technical change was accelerated, no one posed a question as to the consequence for individuals and society of a failure to maintain and develop social skill. In the universities, we have explicit and excellent instruction in the physicochemical sciences and engineering: but we have provided no instruction or experience to replace or develop the social aspect of the apprenticeship system. It is no longer true that every individual will have a continuity of daily association with others that will allow him slowly to acquire a skill of communication and of working with them. It is more than probable that, in any part of the modern industrial scheme, an individual's personal associates will constantly change. We live in a constant flux of personal associations, as of technical procedures.

But the remedy cannot be a return to simple apprenticeship and the primitive establishment.

It is certain that the passage from an established to an adaptive society is one we have to make; we have put our hands to the plough and cannot turn back. We have undertaken to transform an economy of scarcity into an economy of abundance, and the technicians are showing us the way. We are committed to the development of a high human adaptability that has not characterized any known human society in the past, and it is our present failure in this respect that finds reflection in the social chaos which is destroying civilized society. Can this present failure be translated into future success? The way forward is not clear, but certain starting points can be discerned: we are in need of social skills, skills that will be effective in specific situations. When a man has developed a skill, it means that the adjustment of his whole organism, acting as a unit and governed by his thinking and nervous system, is adequate to a particular point in the situation which he is handling. No verbal statements however accurate can act as substitute.

Like the scientific management movement, Mayo's ideas have met with severe criticism from both managers and sociologists. To those of an individualistic cast of mind, the idea that a "sense of belonging" is all-important is naturally repugnant. Others see the social skills Mayo advocated as merely a means of manipulating employees so that managers may continue to devote their efforts to the old ends of money and power. One of the most outspoken critics is Daniel Bell, who was formerly labor editor of *Fortune* magazine and is now a professor of sociology at Harvard University. It is interesting to note, however, that since this piece was written, a number of theorists have become greatly concerned about ways in which the work process itself can be made less dehumanizing, and that some managers have attempted to act on their theories. Some of the things that are being done in this respect are described in later chapters.

Drops within the Social River

Daniel Bell

By and large the sociologist, like the engineer, has written off any effort to readjust the work process; the worker, like the mythical figure of Ixion, is chained forever to the endlessly revolving wheel. But the spectacle has its unnerving aspect, and the sense of dehumanization is oppressive. Industry has been told, therefore, that production may suffer when only the mechanical aspects of production are considered. Hence the vogue in recent years of "human relations." Its rationale is stated by Cornell sociologist William F. Whyte. The "satisfactions of craftsmanship are gone, and we can never call them back," he writes. "If these were the only satisfactions men could get out of their immediate work, their work would certainly be a barren experience. There are other important satisfactions today: the satisfactions of human association and the satisfactions of solving technical and human problems of work."

The statement summarizes the dominant school of thought which has grown out of the work of the late Elton Mayo of the Harvard Business School and his followers. For Mayo, following the French sociologist Emile Durkheim, the characteristic fact about the modern scene is the presence of constant, disruptive change. The family, the primal group of social cohesion, breaks up as a work and educational unit; neighborhood roots are torn up, and social solidarity, the key to human satisfactions, gives way to *anomie*. If solidarity is to be reestablished, it will have to be done within the corporation and factory. "The manager," writes Fritz Roethlisberger, Mayo's chief disciple at the Harvard Business School, "is neither managing men nor managing work; . . . he is administering a social system."

In this, as in many instances, social engineering imitates art. Twenty years ago the first "solidarity hymn" was penned by Aldous Huxley, in his *Brave New World*, and the refrain voiced

From *Work and Its Discontents* (Beacon Press, Boston, 1956), pp. 23–29.

by the Alphas and Betas could be the school song for industrial sociology:

> Ford, we are twelve; oh make us one
> Like drops within the social river.
> Oh, make us now together run
> As swiftly as thy shining flivver.

This is not the place to recapitulate the many criticisms that have been made of the Mayo school. The fundamental point, as it affects the worker in his own work environment, is that the ends of production are taken as "given" and the worker is to be "adjusted" to his job so that the human equation matches the industrial equation. As one management consultant, Burleigh Gardner, succinctly phrased it: "The more satisfied [the worker] is, the greater will be his self-esteem, the more content he will be, and therefore, the more efficient in what he is doing." A fitting description not of human, but of cow, sociology.

The source of this interest in "human relations" was the famous experiment during the thirties at the Hawthorne works of the Western Electric Company in Chicago, perhaps the single most painstaking experiment in the history of the social sciences. The question that first interested the researchers was of the relationship of fatigue to output. A group of five girls were subjected to exhaustive study; the methods were the most meticulous in regard to scientific procedure and control. A series of possible "variables" affecting production were listed, e.g. amount of heat, degree of light, variations in menstruation cycles of the workers; and for a period of thirteen weeks at a time, one factor was changed or studied and all others were kept constant. "A skilled statistician," Roethlisberger reports, "spent several years trying to relate variations in the physical circumstances of these five operators. For example, he correlated the hours that each girl spent in bed the night before with variations in output the following day. Inasmuch as some people said the effect of being out late one night was not felt the following day but the day after that, he correlated variations in output with the amount of rest the operators had had two nights before. . . . The attempt to relate changes in physical circumstances to variations in output resulted in not a single correlation of enough statistical significance to be recognized by any competent statistician as having any meaning."

Then came the great *éclaircissement*. In period XII of the experiment, the girls were returned to a bread-and-water diet, so to speak—a 48-hour week without rest breaks, without lunches, the same illumination as when the experiment began. Yet output kept rising. It then became clear that the workers were responding, not to any of the physiological or physical variables, but to the interest and attention centered on them. The experiment itself, not any outside factor, was the missing link, the unknown determinant.

This led to the second phase of the Hawthorne experiment: the introduction of ambulatory confessors, or walking counselors, ready at any moment to stop and listen to a harassed worker air his woes. Counseling for Mayo was meant to be "a new method of human control." But of this, as of all such objectives, one can ask: Control of whom for what purposes? The answer has been given by Roethlisberger: in counseling, one seeks to shift "the frame of reference," so that the worker sees his grievance in a new light. As one Hawthorne counselor described this process: "In the case of the down-graded employee . . . her focus of attention shifts from alleged inequities, transfer and down-grading grievances, etc. . . . to her unhappy home life; then, when she returns to her original grievance, things do not look so bad."[1]

While "human relations," as a result of the tremendous publicity given to the Hawthorne findings and of Mayo's further work, became a great vogue, personnel counseling in the broader sense did not spread widely for a while, even within the Bell Telephone System where it originated. The reason, in large measure, was that management itself did not fully understand its function. There seemed to be no tangible "payoff" in diminished cost or increased production that management could point to; moreover, it seemed to some to represent too much

[1]The explanation recalls an old folk tale: A peasant complains to his priest that his little hut is horribly overcrowded. The priest advises him to move his cow into the house, the next week to take in his sheep and the next week his horse. The peasant now complains even more bitterly about his lot. Then the priest advises him to let out the cow, the next week the sheep, and the next week the horse. At the end the peasant gratefully thanks the priest for lightening his burdensome life.

"coddling." Since the Second World War, and largely because of the continuing influx of women into the work force, counseling has become more and more an adjunct of a company's medical service to its employees. Some large companies, like Du Pont and Eastman Kodak, maintain staff psychiatrists. Many, like Hughes Aircraft and Raytheon, have full-time social workers who advise employees on a multitude of problems.

It was the psychologist in this instance, however, who taxed the manager for not appreciating the benefits of what Huxley called "advanced emotional engineering." And it was the growing prestige of the management consultant that led management to accept these psychological gimmicks.

While counseling lagged, "communication and participation" quickly became great management fads. In theory, "communication" is supposed to open a two-way street whereby those down the line can talk back to those above and thus "participate" in the enterprise. In few instances have such systems become operative. In most cases communication consists simply of employee newsletters or "chain-of-command" conferences in which vice-presidents meet with managers, managers with supervisors, supervisors with foremen, and so on down the line. In some cases, the system operates with a characteristic advertising-agency twist. At Westinghouse, for example, statements of company policy were recorded on tape, and by dialing on the inter-plant telephone system one could listen to the messages given to the hundreds of top supervisors. The dial number ostensibly was a secret, confined to 1,200 supervisory employees. In practice, it was a secret in name only, since supervisors were instructed to "leak" the number "confidentially" to various employees, and these men, gleeful at knowing a secret, quickly spread the information to others. The result was that thousands of workers eagerly rushed to listen to hortatory talks which at other times might have been received with utter indifference.

There are two points to be noted about the vogue of "human relations." One is that, in the evident concern with understanding, communication and participation, we find a change in the outlook of management, parallel to that which is occurring in the culture as a whole, from authority to manipulation as a means of exercising dominion. The ends of the enterprise remain, but the methods have shifted, and the older modes of overt coercion are now replaced by psychological persuasion. The tough brutal foreman, raucously giving orders, gives way to the mellowed voice of the "human-relations oriented" supervisor. The worker doubtless regards this change as an improvement, and his sense of constraint is correspondingly assuaged. In industrial relations, accommodation of a sort has replaced conflict. The second point is that these human-relations approaches become a substitute for thinking about the work process itself. All satisfactions are to be obtained in extracurricular areas: in the group, in leisure pursuits. Thus the problems of work are projected outward and swathed in psychological batting.

This tyranny of psychology has led management into a curious discounting of the "economic man." We are told that what the worker really wants is security, recognition, rewarding personal relations, and that he is more concerned with these than with other "larger, out-of-plant, off-the-job issues." "Labor disputes," writes a Harvard Business School authority, "are often stated in terms of wages, hours of work and physical conditions. Is it not possible that these demands are disguising, or in part are symptomatic expression of, much more deeply rooted human situations which we have not learned to recognize?"

Such a statement suggests more about Harvard Business School than about the workers; it suggests that the academic doesn't know how to talk to a man in the shop. To say, in fact, that the American worker is not really or primarily interested in money contradicts, in a deep sense, the very motive power of the economic system. Why else would people submit themselves to such a work environment?

Much of the current belief (on the part of both academicians and managers) in the importance of nonfinancial incentives stems from the findings of the Hawthorne studies, for they were the first in this area to be widely publicized. This article questions the very foundations of those studies, holding that the findings were actually "surprisingly consistent with a rather old-world view about the value of monetary incentives, driving leadership, and discipline." It should be noted that not only is the article somewhat condensed from the original but also most of the footnotes have been omitted. In the original piece, all statements are fully documented, generally by references to the account prepared by the original researchers (*Management and the Worker* by Fritz J. Roethlisberger and William Dickson).

The views of the author, who is with the University of New South Wales, have not, of course, gone unchallenged. One rebuttal appears as the next article.

The Hawthorne Studies: A Radical Criticism

Alex Carey

There can be few scientific disciplines or fields of research in which a single set of studies or a single researcher and writer has exercised so great an influence as was exercised for a quarter of a century by Mayo and the Hawthorne studies. Although this influence has declined in the last ten years as a result of the widespread failure of later studies to reveal any reliable relation between the social satisfactions of industrial workers and their work performance, reputable textbooks still refer almost reverentially to the Hawthorne studies as a classic in the history of social science in industry.

One might have expected therefore that the Hawthorne studies would have been subjected to the most searching and skeptical scrutiny; that before the remarkable claims of these studies, especially about the relative unimportance of financial rewards compared with purely social rewards, became so widely influential, the quality of the evidence produced and the validity of the inferences from it would have been meticulously examined and assessed. There have been broad criticisms of Mayo's approach and assumptions, many of them cogent. They include charges of pro-management bias, clinical bias, and scientific naiveté. But no one has applied systematically and in detail the method of critical doubt to the claim that there is scientific worth in the original reports of the Hawthorne investigators.

Background

The Hawthorne studies[1] comprise a long series of investigations into the importance for work behavior and attitudes of a variety of physical, economic, and social variables. The principal investigations were carried out between 1927 and 1932, whereafter economic depression caused their suspension. The component studies may be distinguished as five stages:

Stage I: The Relay Assembly Test Room Study. (New incentive system and new supervision).

Stage II: The Second Relay Assembly Group Study. (New incentive system only).

Stage III: The Mica Splitting Test Room Study. (New supervision only).

Stage IV: The Interviewing Program.

Stage V: The Bank-Wiring Observation Room Study.

Stages II and III were "designed to check on" (and were taken to supplement and confirm) the Stage I conclusion "that the observed production increase was a result of a change in the *social situation* . . . (and) not primarily because of wage incentives, reduced fatigue or similar factors."[2] *Stage IV* was an interviewing program

[1]The most detailed account of these studies is contained in Fritz J. Roethlisberger and W. J. Dickson, *Management and the Worker* (Harvard University Press, Cambridge, Mass. 1939).

[2]Morris S. Viteles, *Motivation and Morale in Industry* (Staples, London, 1954), p. 185.

From The *American Sociological Review* (published by the American Sociological Association), June, 1967, pp. 403–416. Reprinted with permission of the Association and the author.

undertaken to explore worker attitudes. *Stage V* was a study of informal group organization in the work situation.

The two later studies (IV and V) resulted directly from conclusions based on Stages I–III about the superior influence of social needs. Observations made in both were interpreted in the light of such prior conclusions. Hence it is clear that Stage I was the key study, with Stages II and III adding more or less substantial support to it. The present paper will therefore be limited to a consideration of the evidence produced in Stages I–III for the famous Hawthorne conclusions about the superior importance for work behavior of social needs and satisfactions.

The Preferred Incentive System and Output

Stage I: Relay Assembly Test Room (new incentive and new supervision). In Stage I of the Hawthorne studies, five girls who were employed assembling telephone relays were transferred from the factory floor to a special test room. Here their output of relays was recorded for over two years during which a large number of alterations were made in their working conditions. These alterations included a much less variable assembly task, shorter hours, rest pauses, freer and more friendly supervision, and a preferred incentive system. These changes were introduced cumulatively and no control group was established. Nonetheless, it was originally expected that the study would yield information about the influence of one or another physical condition of work.

At the end of two years, the girls' output had increased by about 30 percent. By this time, the investigators were confident that the physical changes in work conditions had been of little importance, and that the observed increase was due primarily to a change in "mental attitude" of the employees resulting from changed methods of supervision. This change in mental attitude was chiefly characterized by a more relaxed "relationship of confidence and friendliness . . . such . . . that practically no supervision is required."[3]

However, the standard report of the study recognizes that any of several changes introduced concurrently could, hypothetically, have caused both the observed change in mental outlook and the associated increase in output.

First hypothesis: changes in work task and physical context. The investigators allow that "the fact that most of the girls in the test room had to assemble fewer types of relays could not be entirely ignored. Operator 5's performance offered a convincing example. Of all the girls in the room she had had more different types of relays to assemble and of all the girls her output rate had shown the least improvement." Whitehead reports that "later (1930–31) her (Operator 5's) working conditions were in line with the rest of the group and her comparative standing in the group definitely improved."[4]

However, it was subsequently found that statistical analysis of the relevant data (i.e., the varying output of five girls who were subjected to numerous cumulatively introduced experimental changes) did not show "any *conclusive* evidence in favor of the first hypothesis." On this ground the investigators "concluded that the change from one type of relay to another familiar type did not sufficiently slow up output to explain the increased output of the relay test room assemblers as compared with the assemblers in the regular department." This conclusion leads the investigators to dismiss from further consideration the possibility that changes in task and conditions played any part at all in the observed increase in output.[5]

Second hypothesis: reduced fatigue due to rest pauses and shorter hours. The investigators recognized that "the rest pauses and shorter hours (may have) provided a relief from cumulative fatigue" resulting in higher output. They acknowledge that the fact that the rate of output of all but the slowest worker declined once the girls were returned to standard hours is "rather

[3]George A. Pennock, "Industrial Research at Hawthorne," *Personnel Journal*, February, 1930, p. 309.

[4]T. North Whitehead, *The Industrial Worker* (Oxford University Press, London, 1938), Vol. I., p. 65.

[5]The scientifically illiterate procedure of dismissing non-preferred explanations on the grounds that (i) the experimenters had found no *conclusive* evidence in favor of them and/or (ii) there was no evidence that any *one* of these explanations, considered by itself, accounted for *all* the effect observed, recurs throughout Roethlisberger and Dickson's report of the Hawthorne studies. This procedure is never applied to preferred hypotheses, which are assumed to be well-founded provided only that the evidence *against* them is less than conclusive. See, e.g., Roethlisberger and Dickson, *op. cit.*, p. 160 and pp. 96, 108, 127.

convincing evidence in favor of this argument." Yet the investigators eventually dismiss these factors on the grounds that under the new conditions of work neither work curves nor medical examinations provided evidence that fatigue effects were present. Viteles has commented bluntly in this connection: "It is interesting to note that (these grounds) are exactly the same used by other investigators in illustrating the effectiveness of rest pauses *by reason of reduced fatigue.*"[6]

By these arguments, the investigators eliminated the first two of the four hypotheses originally proposed as alternative explanations of the 30 percent increase in output observed in Stage I. This left two contending "explanations," the new incentive system, and the new kind of supervision and related social factors. The problem of choosing between these explanations led directly to the next two major experiments.

Stage II: Second Relay Assembly Group (new incentive system only). "The aim of (this experiment) was to reproduce the test-room situation (i.e., Stage I) only in respect to the one factor of method of payment, using another group of operators. Since method of payment was to be the only alteration from the usual situation, it was thought that any marked changes in output could be reasonably related to this factor."

Five girls who were employed on the same sort of task as the girls in Stage I under normal conditions on the factory floor were given the preferred incentive system which had been used throughout Stage I. Under this system, the earnings of each girl were based on the average output of the five. Under the regular payment system, the earnings of each girl were based on the average output of the whole department (i.e., about 100 girls).

Almost at once the Stage II girls' output increased by 12.6 percent. But the experiment caused so much discontent among the rest of the girls in the department, who wanted the same payment conditions, that it was discontinued after only nine weeks. The output of the five girls promptly dropped by 16 percent.

The change in payment system alone (Stage II) produced as much increase in output in nine weeks (possibly five weeks) as was produced in about nine months by change in payment system together with a change to genial supervision (Stage I). Yet this comparison appears not to have made any impression on the investigators' confidence about the superior importance of social factors.

Stage III: Mica Splitting Test Room (new supervision but no change in payment system). In *Stage I*, numerous changes had been introduced, resulting in a 30 percent increase in output. In *Stage II*, only one of these changes (the preferred incentive system) was introduced and a rapid 12 percent increase in output resulted. In *Stage III*, "the test-room situation was to be duplicated in all respects except for the change in pay incentive. If . . . output showed a trend similar to that noted in (Stage I), it would suggest that the wage incentive was not the dominant factor in the situation." Stage III, then, sought to test the combined effect on output of change to a separate room, change in hours, and the introduction of rest pauses and friendly supervision. Again a selected group of five girls was closely studied and an increase in output was recorded—15.6 percent in fourteen months or, if one follows Pennock, 20 percent in twelve months.

Assuming with Roethlisberger and Dickson that Stage I and Stage III have some minimum comparability, it is important to examine precisely how the investigators dealt with the evidence from these stages for the purpose of the comparison.

Comparison Between Results in Stages I, II, and III. (i) Stage III produced a claimed 15 percent increase in rate of output over fourteen months. Thereafter the group's average rate of output declined for twelve months before the study was terminated due to the depression and lay-offs. The investigators attribute this decline *entirely* to anxieties induced by the depression,[7] ignoring the possibility that the preceding increase might also have been influenced by changing general economic and employment

[6]Morris S. Viteles, *Industrial Psychology*, (Norton, New York, 1932), p. 475. Italics in original.

[7]Viteles comments on this period of declining output: "Both 'the investigators and the operators were of the opinion that the rates on the new piece parts were not high enough in comparison with the old.' Nevertheless scant consideration is given to the possibility that . . . a reduced appeal to economic motives could readily account in large part for the very severe drop in output observed during this final phase of the *Mica Splitting Room experiment.*" Viteles, *Motivation . . . , op. cit.*, p. 191.

conditions. They do this despite evidence that output among a group of 5,500 Hawthorne workers rose by 7 percent in the two years preceding the experiment.

(ii) In Stage III, the output rate for each girl shows continuous and marked fluctuations over the whole two years of the study. To obtain the percentage increase to be attributed to each girl the investigators chose, for each girl, a "peak" output period within the study period and measured her increase as the difference between this peak and her output rate at the outset of the study. These peaks occur at different dates for different girls. To secure the 15 percent increase that is claimed, the study is, in effect, terminated at different conveniently selected dates for different girls. There is *no one period* over which the group achieved the 15 percent average increase claimed.

(iii) In Stage I, two measures of the workers' performance are used: total output per week, and hourly rate of output by weeks. It is not clear from Roethlisberger and Dickson's report of Stage I whether the increase is in *total output* or *rate of output*. It is described only as "increase in output," and "output rose . . . roughly 30%," which would ordinarily be taken to mean an increase in *total output*. But the investigators make it clear in passing that throughout the studies they used rate of output per hour as "the most common arrangement of output data" by which to "portray the general trend in efficiency of each operator and of the group." Whitehead, who produced a two-volume statistical study of Stage I as companion volumes to Roethlisberger and Dickson's standard report, is very clear on this point: "All output will be expressed in the form of a *rate* . . . as so many relays per hour."

However, Whitehead employs throughout his study the description "*weekly rate of output*" when he means *rate of output per hour by weeks*. This practice, coupled with his habit of not labelling the ordinates of his charts dealing with changes in output, and added to by Roethlisberger and Dickson's use of phrases such as "increase in output" to mean both *increase in rate of output per hour* and *increase in total output*, has led to widespread misinterpretation of the Hawthorne results, and textbook accounts which are seriously in error.

Several points are of present importance. For Stage I, it is not clear whether the 30 percent increase in output claimed refers to *rate of output* or *total output*. It does not matter which measure is used to calculate percent increase in output in Stage I since the total hours worked per week at the end of the study period is only 4.7 percent less than at the beginning. Thus, an increase of the order of 30 percent would result from either method of calculation. In Stage III, however, it makes a great deal of difference which method is used, and hourly rate of output is the only measure used. Thus, the 15 percent "increase in output" claimed for Stage III is an increase in *rate of output per hour worked*, not in *total output*. Indeed, it is only by this measure that any increase *at all* in output can be shown.

If *total output per week* is used to measure performance in Stage III, the 15 percent increase claimed for Stage III reduces to less than zero because although output per hour increased by 15 percent, the weekly hours decreased by 17 percent, from 55½ to 46⅙.

From Evidence to Conclusions. By subtracting the 15 percent increase in Stage III (which is an increase in *rate* of output) from the 30 percent increase in output in Stage I (which is all, or nearly all, an increase in *total* output), the investigators conclude that 15 percent remains as "the maximum amount (of increase in output) to be attributed to the change in wage incentive" introduced in Stage I. The investigators acknowledge the wholly speculative nature of this calculation, yet go on to assert in a summary of events to date that the conclusion "seemed to be warranted from the test room studies so far . . . that it was impossible to consider (a wage incentive system) as a thing in itself having an independent effect on the individual."

It is important to appreciate just how invalid are the inferences made. In Stage I, friendly supervision and a change to a preferred incentive system led to an increase in total output of about 30 percent. In Stage III, friendly supervision without a change in payment system led to no increase in total output, but to a less than compensating increase in output per hour over a period during which working hours were reduced from 55½ to 46⅙. This could be interpreted to mean that when working hours exceed about 48 per week such extra working-time may bring little or no increase in total output—a finding which had been well-established many years before.[8] This interpretation would have left the way clear to attribute the 30 percent increase in Stage I entirely to the preferred incentive system. Instead, by the rather special method of analysis and argument that has been outlined, the investigators reached the conclusion that the effect of a wage incentive system is so greatly influenced by social considerations that it is impossible to consider it capable of independent effect.

A similar situation holds with regard to Stage II. As Stage II was planned, the "method of payment was to be the only alteration from the usual situation" with the express intention that "any marked changes in output" could then be "related to this factor." There *was* a marked change in output—an immediate 12 percent increase. There *was* an immediate change in behavior—the other girls in the department demanded the same conditions. This would seem to require a conclusion in favor of the importance of a preferred incentive system, but no such conclusion was reached.

In the interpretation of the Stage II results, Roethlisberger and Dickson noticed, *post hoc*, that somewhere in the "daily history record" of the Stage I group was a reference to a comment by one member of that group that a "lively interest" was being taken in their output by members of the new Stage II group. Twenty-four pages later we are told that "although output had risen an average of 12% in (Stage II) it was *quite apparent* that factors other than the change in wage incentive contributed to that increase . . . *There was some evidence* to indicate that the operators in (Stage II) had seized upon this test as an opportunity to prove to everyone that they could do as well as the (Stage I) operators. They were out to equal the latters' record. In view of this, even the most liberal estimate would put the increase in output due to the change in payment alone at somewhat less than 12%." (Italics added). Since no additional evidence had been produced, this judgment lacks any serious foundation.

Stage II was "designed to test the effect of a (change in) wage incentive" on output. The preferred incentive system was introduced and output immediately rose 12 percent. It was withdrawn and output immediately dropped 17 percent. Not encouraging results for anyone who believed that wage incentives were relatively unimportant and incapable of "independent effects." Yet these awkward results were not only explained away but converted to positive support for just such conclusions, all on the basis of a single hearsay comment by one girl.

The investigators carry the day for the hypothesis that "social factors were the major circumstances limiting output." They conclude that "none of the results (in Stages I, II and III) gave the slightest substantiation to the theory that the worker is primarily motivated by economic interest. The evidence indicated that the efficacy of a wage incentive is so dependent on its relation to other factors that it is impossible to separate it out as a thing in itself having an independent effect."

It remains to consider more closely the complementary Hawthorne claim that it was friendly supervision and social factors which were the principal influences leading to the large rise in output in Stage I.

A Closer Look at Friendly Supervision in Action

The *whole* of the Hawthorne claim that friendly supervision and resulting work-group social relations and satisfactions are overwhelmingly important for work behavior rests on whatever evidence can be extracted from Stage I, since that is the only study in the series which exhibits even a surface association between the introduction of such factors and increased output.

Stage I began with five girls specially selected for being both "thoroughly experienced" and "willing and cooperative," so there was reason to expect this group to be more than ordinarily cooperative and competent. Yet from very early in the study "the amount of talking indulged in by all the operators" had constituted a "problem," because it "involved a lack of attention to work and a preference for conversing together for considerable periods of time." The first indication in the report that this might be a serious matter occurs on August 2nd, 1927, twelve

[8]Horace M. Vernon, *Industrial Fatigue and Efficiency* (Dutton, London, 1921).

weeks after the girls' installation in the test-room, when four of the five operators were brought before the foreman and reprimanded for talking too much. Until November, however, "no attempt had been made to do away with this privilege, although several attempts had been made by the foreman to diminish what seemed to him an excessive amount of talking." But Operators 1A and 2A in particular continued to fail to display "that 'wholehearted cooperation' desired by the investigators." "Any effort to reprimand them would bring the reply 'We thought you wanted us to work as we feel'", since that was what the supervisors had told them at the beginning of the study.

By November 17th, 1927, the situation had not improved and disciplinary rules were resorted to. All of the operators were required to call out whenever they made mistakes in assembly, and they were prevented from talking. By December, "the lack of cooperation on the part of some of the operators was seriously alarming a few of the executives concerned." Supervisors were asked to give the girls a "hint" by telling them that they were not doing as well as expected of them and that if they didn't improve they would lose their free lunches.

From now on the girls, but especially 1A and 2A, were "threatened with disciplinary action" and subjected to "continual reprimands." "Almost daily" 2A was "reproved" for her "low output and behavior" (sic). The investigators decided 1A and 2A did not have "the 'right' mental attitude." 2A was called up before the test-room authorities "and told of her offenses of being moody and inattentive and not cooperative." She was called up again before the superintendent. Throughout this period output for all five girls remained static or falling. After eleven weeks of serious but ineffective disciplinary measures and eight months after the beginning of the study, 1A and 2A were dismissed from the test room for "gross insubordination" and declining or static output.

1A and 2A were replaced by two girls chosen by the foreman "who were experienced relay assemblers and desirous of participating in the test." These two girls (designated Operators 1 and 2) were transferred to the test room on January 25th, 1928. They *both* immediately produced an output much greater (in total and in rate per hour) than that achieved by *any* of the original five girls on their transfer to the test room and much above the performance *at any time* of the two girls they replaced.

Operators 1 and 2 had been friends in the main shop. Operator 2 was the only Italian in the group; she was young (twenty-one) and her mother died shortly after she joined the test room; after this "Operator 2 earned the larger part of the family income." "(F)rom now on the history of the test room revolves around the personality of Operator 2." Operator 2 rapidly (i.e., without any delay during which she might have been affected by the new supervision) adopted and maintained a strong and effective disciplinary role with respect to the rest of the group, and led the way in increased output in *every* period from her arrival till the end of the study. In this she was closely followed by the other new girl, Operator 1.

At the time that Operators 1 and 2 were brought into the test room, daily hours of work were shortened by half an hour but it was decided to *pay the operators the day rate for the half hour of working time lost*. A little later, the working day was reduced by a further half hour, and again the girls were paid for the time (one hour per day) they didn't work. Later still, the girls were given Saturday mornings off and again they were paid for the time not worked.

Summing up experience in the test room up to *exactly* the time when the two operators were dismissed, the investigators claim that "it is clear" that over this period there was "a gradual change in social interrelations among the operators themselves, which displayed itself in the form of new group loyalties and solidarities . . . (and) . . . a change in the relations between the operators and their supervisors. The test room authorities had taken steps to obtain the girls' cooperation and loyalty and to relieve them of anxieties and apprehensions. From this . . . arose . . . a change in human relations which came to be of great significance in the next stage of the experiment, when it became necessary to seek a new hypothesis to explain certain unexpected results of the inquiry." In view of the evidence reviewed here this would seem to be a somewhat sanguine assessment of developments in the test room up to this point.

It is already clear that whatever part satisfying

social relations at work—resulting from free and friendly supervision—may have played in producing the increase in output, there were other influences likely to have been important, e.g., a period of fairly stern discipline, the dismissal of two workers, and their replacement by people of rather special personality and motivation. In order to assess these various influences on output it is necessary to consider how work performance varied during the periods when these changes were introduced. This is difficult because none of the reports of the Hawthorne studies provides actual figures covering the way in which output changed throughout Stage I. Consequently, one must work with such estimates as can be derived from the various graphs and charts of output-change that are supplied, and supplemented by occasional statements in the texts which give additional quantitative information.

An Examination of the Evidence: Variations in Supervisory Practice and Variations in Output

For present purposes, Stage I may be divided into three phases: Phase I: the first three and a half months in the test room during which supervision seems to have been fairly consistently friendly, casual, and at low pressure; Phase II: a further interval of about seven months during which supervision became increasingly stern and close. This phase culminates in the dismissal of two of the five operators and their replacement by workers of rather special character and motivation. Phase III: a final long period during which output rose rapidly and there was a return to free and friendly supervision.

Supervision during Phase I. "Besides the girls who composed the group under study there was a person in the experimental room who was immediately in charge of the test." This was the test-room observer whose two-fold function was "to keep accurate records . . . and to create and maintain a friendly atmosphere in the test room." He "assume(d) responsibility for most of the day to day supervision" while in other matters such as accounting, rate revision, and promotion, responsibility rested with the foreman.

It is quite clear from Roethlisberger and Dickson's account that during Phase I the supervisors did everything in their power to promote a free, cooperative, and noncoercive relationship. At the outset of the study the girls "were asked to work along at a comfortable pace" and were assured "that no attempt would be made to force up production." They were led to expect changes in working conditions which might be "beneficial and desirable from the employees' point of view," and were told that there was no reason why "any (such) change resulting in greater satisfaction of employees" should not be maintained, and this "regardless of any change in production rate." "The test room observer was chiefly concerned with creating a friendly relation with the operators which would ensure their cooperation. Some weeks after the study began, there was a friendly talk with the doctor about the physical examinations and ice cream was provided and a party planned. Also, the girls were "invited to the office of the superintendent who had talked to them, and in various other ways they had been made the object of considerable attention."

Output during Phase I. There was "no appreciable change in output" on transfer to the test room, but there was a "downward tendency" during the first five weeks thereafter, despite facilities which "made the work slightly easier."

At the end of five weeks, the new wage incentive system was introduced and output increased. From the output chart this increase may be estimated at 4 or 5 percent. However, this increase must be accepted with some caution, for the investigators report that the "change in method of payment necessitated a change in piece-rates." It was apparently judged that under the new conditions of work (which did not include all of the types of relay assembled on the shop floor, and where there was one layout operator to five assemblers instead of one to six or seven as on the shop floor), new rates were necessary. We are told that "the chief consideration in setting the new piece-rates was to determine a rate for each relay type which would pay the operators the same amount of money they had received in the regular department for an equivalent amount of work." But it is well-established that the unreliability of time-study ratings can be expected to yield errors of at least 5 percent between different ratings of similar tasks. So no great reliance can be placed on the observed 4 or 5 percent increase in output following the introduction of the new incentive system and the associated new piece-rates. Indeed, there is perhaps some recognition of this in Roethlisberger and Dickson's introductory comment that early in the study "a change in wage payment was introduced, a necessary step before the *experiment proper* could begin. Phase I ends after fifteen weeks of friendly supervision with a somewhat doubtful increase of 5 percent which occurred with the introduction of a preferred incentive system.

Supervision during Phase II. "The second phase . . . covering an interval of approximately seven months was concerned with the effects of various kinds of rest pauses." The investigators emphasize that by the *beginning* of this phase not only was supervision friendly, but the relation between workers and supervisors was "free and easy." Their account of actual supervisory behavior during succeeding months supports these claims. (i) On each of the four occasions when rest pauses were varied, the girls were consulted in advance, and on all but one occasion their expressed preferences were accepted. (ii) The investigators decided to pay the girls their bonuses monthly instead of weekly, but when the girls were told about this decision they objected and the plan was dropped. That the girls "felt free to express their attitudes" and that the investigators altered their plans out of regard for these attitudes is said to be "typical of the supervisory technique employed" which "proved to be a factor of utmost importance in interpreting the results of the study." (iii) Later the girls were given free lunches and were consulted about what should be served.

However, the problem of excessive talking among the girls worsened. No attempt had been made to prohibit talking, although four of the girls had been "given a talk regarding their behavior." Now this "lack of attention to work and preference for conversing together for considerable periods" was judged to be reaching such proportions that the "experiment was being jeopardized and something had to be done." A variety of disciplinary procedures of increasing severity were applied, but with little effect. Finally, the leaders in talking (operators 1A and 2A) were dismissed from the test room "for lack of cooperation which would have otherwise necessitated greatly increased disciplinary measures."

Output during Phase II. There was no change in weekly output during this six-month period. "Total weekly output does not decline when rest pauses are introduced, but remains practically the same during all the rest period experiments."

Supervision during Phase III. At the beginning of Phase III, the two dismissed girls were replaced by two girls chosen by the foreman. Something has already been said about the way in which these girls at once took and maintained the lead in output and about how one of them, who had a special need for more money, took over the general leadership and discipline of the rest of the group.

From then on supervision again became increasingly friendly and relaxed. This friendliness of supervision often had a very tangible character. From the arrival of the new workers in the test room, the observer "granted them (all) more and more privileges." The preferred incentive system, the rest pauses, the free lunches, and the "parties" following the regular physical examinations all continued. In addition, within the next eight months the girls were first paid for half an hour per day not worked, and then for an hour a day not worked, and finally for Saturday mornings not worked. Approximately eight months after the arrival of the new girls, all these privileges except the preferred incentive system and the parties were withdrawn. The girls were warned in advance about this withdrawal of privileges and were assured that the new and heartily disliked conditions "would terminate after approximately three months." Despite this promise, the girls' work deteriorated immediately: they wasted time in various ways such as reading newspapers, eating candy, and going for drinks and the observer shortly "discovered that the girls were attempting to keep the output rate low . . . so as to make sure that rest pauses would be reinstated." The observer "again tried to stop the excessive talking" by "reprimand and threat." He told the girls that "unless excessive talking ceased it might become necessary to continue the experiment without rest pauses for a longer period."

At this point, the girls had been in the test

room eighteen months and had achieved nearly all the eventual 30 percent increase in output. Yet it would seem that Operator 2, the incentive system, and the other privileges, as well as "reprimand and threat" played a significant part in determining the work behavior and output of the group. It is also clear from Roethlisberger and Dickson's account that for a great part of the time following the arrival of Operators 1 and 2, the girls worked very well and happily and that while they did so, supervision was relaxed and friendly and relations continued to be satisfactory. But there would seem to be good grounds for supposing that supervision became more friendly and relaxed because output increased rather than vice versa.

Output during Phase III. Output for the whole group rose markedly during the several months after the dismissal of 1A and 2A, owing chiefly to the contributions from the new operators. Thereafter, the group's total output rose more slowly for a further year (with a temporary drop when the Saturday morning shift was discontinued for a time).

Summary of Evidence about Supervision and Output

(i) Apart from a doubtful 4–5 percent increase following the introduction of a preferred incentive system, there was no increase in weekly output during the first nine months in the test room, despite a great deal of preoccupation on the part of the supervisors with friendliness towards the workers, with consultation, and the provision of a variety of privileges not enjoyed on the factory floor.

(ii) From the beginning of what Roethlisberger and Dickson describe as the "experiment proper," that is, after the period in which the new incentive system was introduced, there was no increase in weekly output during the next six months. When it became apparent that free and friendly supervision was not getting results, discipline was tightened, culminating in the dismissal of two of the five girls.

(iii) The dismissed girls were replaced by two girls of a special motivation and character who *immediately* led the rest in a sustained acceleration of output. One of these girls who had a special need for extra money rapidly adopted and maintained a strong disciplinary role with respect to the rest of the group. The two new girls led the way in increased output from their arrival till the end of the study.

(iv) Total output per week showed a significant and sustained increase only after the two girls who had the lowest output were dismissed and replaced by selected output leaders who account for the major part of the groups' increase, both in output rate and in total output, over the next seventeen months of the study.

(v) After the arrival of the new girls and the associated increase in output, *official* supervision became friendly and relaxed once more. The investigators, however, provide no evidence that output increased because supervision became more friendly rather than vice versa. In any case, friendly supervision took a very tangible turn; by paying the girls for time not worked the piece-rate was in effect increased.

Discussion and Conclusions

The critical examination attempted here by no means exhausts the gross error and the incompetence in the understanding and use of the scientific method which permeate the Hawthorne studies from beginning to end. Three further studies were conducted: the Bank Wiring Observation Room Study; the Interviewing Program; and the Counselling Program. These studies cannot be discussed here, but I believe them to be nearly as worthless scientifically as the studies which have been discussed.[9] This should not be surprising, for they arose out of "evidence" found and conclusions reached in the earlier studies and were guided by and interpreted in the light of the strongest preconceptions based on the conclusions of the earlier studies.

There are major deficiencies in Stages I, II and III which have hardly been touched on: (i) There

[9]For substantiation of this judgment with respect to the Bank Wiring Observation Room Study see A. J. Sykes, "Economic Interest and the Hawthorne Researches: A Comment," *Human Relations*, 18 (August, 1965), pp. 253–263.

was no attempt to establish sample groups representative of any larger population than the groups themselves. Therefore, no generalization is legitimate. (ii) There was no attempt to employ control data from the output records of the girls who were *not* put under special experimental conditions. (iii) Even if both of these points had been met, the experiments would still have been of only minor scientific value since a group of five subjects is too small to yield statistically reliable results. Waiving all these points, it is clear that the objective evidence obtained from Stages I, II, and III does not support any of the conclusions derived by the Hawthorne investigators. The results of these studies, far from supporting the various components of the "human relations approach," are surprisingly consistent with a rather old-world view about the value of monetary incentives, driving leadership, and discipline. It is only by massive and relentless reinterpretation that the evidence is made to yield contrary conclusions. To make these points is not to claim that the Hawthorne studies can provide serious support for any such old-world view. The limitations of the Hawthorne studies clearly render them incapable of yielding serious support for any sort of generalization whatever.

If the assessment of the Hawthorne studies offered here is cogent, it raises some questions of importance for university teachers, especially for teachers concerned with courses on industrial organization and management. How is it that nearly all authors of textbooks who have drawn material from the Hawthorne studies have failed to recognize the vast discrepancy between evidence and conclusions in those studies, have frequently misdescribed the actual observations and occurrences in a way that brings the evidence into line with the conclusions, and have done this even when such authors based their whole outlook and orientation on the conclusions reached by the Hawthorne investigators? Exploration of these questions would provide salutary insight into aspects of the sociology of social scientists.

The criticism of the Hawthorne studies in the preceding article is persuasive, but there are arguments against the point of view it expresses, and Dr. Shepard, who is a professor of sociology at the University of Kentucky, has marshalled some compelling ones. The reader can best make up his or her own mind on the validity of the studies by examining the account in the major source book on the subject, *Management and the Worker* by Fritz J. Roethlisberger and William J. Dickson. Other sources of interest are *Hawthorne Revisited* by Henry J. Landsberger (Cornell University, Ithaca, N.Y., 1958) and *Counseling in an Organization: A Sequel to the Hawthorne Researches* by Dickson and Roethlisberger (Division of Research, Graduate School of Business Administration, Harvard University, Boston, 1966).

On Alex Carey's Radical Criticism of the Hawthorne Studies

Jon M. Shepard

The Hawthorne research has never lacked critics. Two relatively recent articles[1] have raised some issues anew. Both Sykes and Carey criticize the Hawthorne researchers for minimizing the motivational impact of economic incentive on worker behavior. It is Carey's criticism, radical by his own admission, that prompts the following comments. Is it possible that Carey's criticism of the Hawthorne studies could be elevated beyond an acceptable contribution as a critique to a questionable position of authority? The writing of this note was prompted by the possibility that such a danger exists. It is felt that new generations of teachers and students deserve an exposure to Carey's errors in inter-

[1]The preceding article and A. J. M. Sykes, "Economic Interest and the Hawthorne Researchers," *Human Relations*, Vol. XVIII (1965), pp. 253–263.

From the *Academy of Management Journal*, March, 1971, pp. 23–31.

pretation and logic, and that the Hawthorne studies, in the original, should continue to provide a necessary reference.

Carey argues that without any substantial evidence the Hawthorne researchers disregarded financial incentives in the explanation of work behavior and raised supervision and resulting interpersonal satisfaction to primacy. Within the research reports, Carey contends, there is evidence supporting the primary impact of financial incentive on productivity. The Hawthorne researchers, in Carey's view, groundlessly rejected this evidence. Some of the evidence he marshals does open the results to the interpretation that financial rewards significantly influence morale and behavior at work. Yet, Carey himself presents evidence from the original Hawthorne research supporting the position that the effects of wages are, as these investigators contended, interrelated with various social factors. Granting that some of the original evidence supports the efficacy of money in increasing productivity, this note is intended to balance the self-admitted radical critique offered by Carey. If, as Carey argues, the Hawthorne researchers overstated their case, he is vulnerable to the same charge. Pointing out the shortcomings of the Hawthorne research is a service, but categorizing this research as "worthless scientifically" is not.

General Perspective: The Role of Financial Incentives in the Hawthorne Research

Carey attributes to the Hawthorne researchers the claim of the "relative unimportance of financial rewards compared with purely social rewards." But in the writings of the original Hawthorne researchers, reference is not made to any one factor or, more particularly, to "purely social rewards." An examination of the writings of Mayo, Whitehead, and Roethlisberger and Dickson reveals that each took a balanced position. For example, this statement from *Management and the Worker*[2] indicates a more holistic approach than Carey is willing to credit them with:

> Throughout the course of the experiments matters, vitally important to management, such as hours of work, wage incentives, and methods of supervision, had been examined. The mere fact that carefully conducted experiments failed to provide conclusive findings on these subjects was in itself very illuminating. Hitherto management had tended to make many assumptions as to what would happen if a change were made in, for example, hours of work or a wage incentive. They now began to question these assumptions and saw that many of them were *oversimplified* (emphasis supplied). They began to see that such factors as hours of work and wage incentives were not things in themselves having an independent effect upon employee efficiency; rather, these factors were no more than parts of a total situation, and their effects could not be predicted *apart from the total situation* [p. 185] (emphasis supplied).

This same point is made in another segment of *Management and the Worker*:

> At least two conclusions seemed to be warranted from the test room experiments so far: (1) there was absolutely no evidence in favor of the hypothesis that the continuous increase in output in the Relay Assembly Test Room during the first 2 years could be attributed to the wage incentive factor *alone* (emphasis supplied); (2) the efficacy of a wage incentive was so dependent on its relation to other factors that it was impossible to consider it as a thing in itself having an independent effect on the individual. Only in connection with the interpersonal relations at work and the personal situations outside of work, to mention two important variables, could its effect on output be determined [p. 160].

Carey quotes from this last passage, but in the process of editing gives a significantly different slant to its meaning: "the conclusion seemed to be warranted from the test room studies . . . that so far it was impossible to consider (a wage incentive) as a thing in itself having an independent effect on the individual." By failing to note that the Hawthorne researchers saw wages as potentially important, but only as part of the mix, Carey is later able to attribute to the Hawthorne researchers the belief "that wage incentives were relatively unimportant and incapable of independent effects." The Hawthorne researchers did state that it was impossible to consider wages as a thing in itself exerting an

[2]F. J. Roethlisberger and William J. Dickson, *Management and the Workers* (John Wiley and Sons, Inc., New York, 1939).

independent effect on the individual, but they did not conclude, as Carey states, that wages were "relatively unimportant." If the above quote had not been edited, it would have shown the multiple causation approach of the Hawthorne researchers. But instead, Carey chose to make his central point without qualification.

Carey attributes to the Hawthorne researchers the "claim that friendly supervision and the resulting work group social relations and satisfactions are overwhelmingly important for work behavior." In fact, a reading of Carey leaves the impression that supervision was considered by the Hawthorne researchers to be the cure-all for industrial relations. Over one-half of his article is devoted to the relationship between supervision and productivity. Yet, Roethlisberger and Dickson are unmistakably clear in their interpretation that satisfactions and dissatisfactions at work are the product of a myriad of social influences, both inside and outside the work organization. The Hawthorne researchers did not attribute the level of employee satisfaction to any single factor, and certainly did not isolate style of supervision as the explanatory variable. Roethlisberger and Dickson merely assume a basic sociological perspective: ". . . it is not possible to treat . . . material goods, physical events, wages, and hours of work as things in themselves, subject to their own laws. Instead, they must be interpreted as carriers of social value. For the employee in industry, the whole working environment must be looked upon as being permeated with social significance. Apart from the social values inherent in his environment, the meaning to the employee of certain objects or events cannot be understood." [p. 374]

Carey translates the Hawthorne researchers' generic reference to the "social situation" to mean personal satisfactions growing out of "friendly supervision." That this translation is too limited is also reflected in this passage from Whitehead:

> Thus each member of the Test Room Group began to build up a more or less vivid *attitude* with regard to her working situation which was compounded of a number of things: day-by-day experiences (including sentiments arising out of these); logical or pseudological concepts (with their corresponding sentiments); attitudes toward their own skills as an essential ingredient in the activities; sentiments with respect to increasing output rate; altered relations both in the plant and at home resulting from their unusual situation and earnings (with sentiments); sentiments and concepts with regard to their *supervision* (emphasis supplied); sentiments and concepts with regard to their future as it was affected by the experiment; and so forth. All these strands of experience, beliefs, concepts, and sentiments built up together into a stable combination or aggregate which may be referred to as the operator's attitude toward her work situation.[3]

Carey, then, has resurrected an old line of attack, namely, that the Hawthorne researchers elevated work supervision to primacy. Following his writeup of the interviewing program, Mayo himself makes a statement contradicting this charge: "The interviewing program showed that the major difficulty was no mere simple error of supervision, no easily alterable set of working conditions; it was something more intimately human, more remote. 'Supervision,' indeed, had shown itself to be another word which meant so many things that it meant nothing. In every department there was a human situation, these situations were never identical—and in every different situation the supervisor played a different part."[4]

Evidence: The Role of Financial Incentives in the Hawthorne Research

The basic position of the Hawthorne researchers was that financial, environmental, and physiological factors could not be considered alone, i.e., outside of a social context. Carey himself cites evidence that the financial incentive, taken alone, is not enough. In the third phase of the Hawthorne research, Carey notes that the new incentive system did not produce any increase in weekly output for the first 6 months. It was only after the dismissal of the two poorest performers and their replacement with two other girls with a special motivation for money that output rose. The rise in productivity is attributed to one of the new girls whose special desire for money stemmed from her status as primary supporter of her family and the fact that her father had just

[3]T. N. Whitehead, *The Industrial Worker* (Harvard University Press, Cambridge, Mass., 1938), p. 248.

[4]Elton Mayo, *Human Problems of an Industrial Society* (The Viking Press, New York, 1962), p. 94.

become temporarily unemployed. Carey offers a quote from *Management and the Worker* which may be cited as evidence for the Hawthorne multivariate approach: "On the whole, from January to November 1928, the Relay Test group showed no very marked developments apart from a growing tendency for the discipline to pass from the hands of the supervisor to those of the group itself, largely as represented in the person of operator 2." One perfectly tenable interpretation of this passage is that output increased not because of the incentive system—indeed 6 months had passed without it exerting any effect—but rather because one of the girls assumed leadership of the *group* and influenced her fellow workers to increase their output.

Moreover, Carey, referring to these same workers, cites the following passage which indicates that financial incentive alone did not appear to be a sufficient motivator: "Approximately 8 months after the arrival of the new girls, all these privileges except the *preferred incentive system* (emphasis supplied) and the parties were withdrawn. The girls were warned in advance about this withdrawal of privileges and were assured that the new and heartily disliked conditions 'would terminate after approximately 3 months.' Despite this promise, the girls' work deteriorated immediately: they wasted time in various ways such as reading newspapers, eating candy, and going for drinks, and the observer shortly 'discovered that the girls were attempting to keep the output rate low . . . so as to make sure that rest pauses would be reinstated.'"

Finally, on the matter of evidence presented by Carey, he quotes Roethlisberger and Dickson: "Although output had risen an average of 12 percent in Stage II, it was *quite apparent* that factors other than the change in wage incentive contributed to that increase. . . . *There was some evidence* to indicate that the operators in Stage II had seized upon this test as an opportunity to prove to everyone that they could do as well as the Stage I operators. They were out to equal the latters' record. In view of this, even the most liberal estimate would put the increase in output due to the change in payment alone at somewhat less than 12 percent." (Italics added by Carey.) Carey dismisses this statement by writing that "since no additional evidence had been produced, this judgment lacks any serious foundation." He implies, in effect, that knowledge of the social context, which cannot be entered in a statistical table, is inadmissible evidence. Carey chose the strictly quantitative approach to social research. This would seem to rule out some of the most creditable sociological research.

Carey excludes from consideration the latter stages of the Hawthorne research, the interviewing stage, and the Bank Wiring Observation Room Study, which in Carey's view are scientifically worthless because ". . . they arose out of 'evidence' found and conclusions reached in the earlier studies and were guided by and interpreted in the light of the strongest preconceptions based on the conclusions of the earlier studies." Pronouncements on the validity of a piece of research should rest on an examination of that research, not on a judgment regarding the origin of the hypotheses which the research purports to test. Moreover, evidence from the latter research stages runs counter to Carey's thesis. In particular, omission of the Bank Wiring Observation Room experiment deprives us of information crucial to judging the Hawthorne studies—some of the strongest support for the argument that wage incentives are filtered through social factors.

Workers in the Bank Wiring Observation Room were on a group financial incentive plan. The thinking underlying financial incentive plans is that if one is paid more he will produce more; financial incentive plans are partially intended to get around the problem of restriction of output. However, in the Bank Wiring Observation Room there was a very clear informal norm of productivity set by the group at a point below the level of production which individuals could have actually produced. In fact, workers stopped early, loafed, and used various other means in order not to exceed the informal production maximum. Social sanctions were applied to workers who produced more than or less than what the group had apparently settled on informally as the amount of production constituting a "day's work."

The fear was expressed by workers that if they produced to capacity the production standard would be raised and they would have to work harder for the same pay, or some workers would be laid off. This could be interpreted as an effort on the part of the workers to maximize their long-term income and to protect their jobs. Be that as it may, the fact remains that the production level was maintained by group pressure. Workers who did not share the fear of a raised standard nevertheless restricted production as a result of social pressures. Ample documentation of evidence to buttress the Hawthorne researchers' thesis that wage incentives are socially conditioned is contained in *Management and the Worker*.

Sykes convincingly demonstrates the effort by Roethlisberger and Dickson to explain away the possible contribution of worker pursuit of economic interest to production restriction in the Bank Wiring Observation Room. This tack by Roethlisberger and Dickson was as unnecessary as it was unfortunate—unfortunate because it made them vulnerable to justified criticism; unnecessary because there is sufficient evidence in their findings as well as from subsequent research to buttress their position that financial incentives are conditioned by social and psychological factors which lead to behavior quite different than would be expected on the assumption that workers individually respond in the direction of maximizing income. If, instead of trying to suppress the influence of economic incentives as they did in their conclusions on the Bank Wiring Observation Room, Roethlisberger and Dickson [pp. 531–535] had interpreted the findings from this final research stage in terms of their earlier overview, they would have been on quite solid ground. Their failure to do so does not mean that their work should be ignored, but that it should be viewed in its totality.

It is enlightening to know that the Hawthorne researchers chose to see money as simply part of the mix without definitive evidence. What is unfortunate is Carey's implication that the Hawthorne research findings should therefore not be taught in classrooms or printed in textbooks. By arriving at such a devastating conclusion, Carey discards the baby with the bath. The Hawthorne evidence on the role of financial incentives in motivation was not conclusive. But as stated above, research subsequent to the Hawthorne studies tends to support their position that financial incentives are filtered through social and psychological variables. For example, the conclusions of Locke, Bryan, and Kendall in a recent study are very much in agreement with the basic position of Roethlisberger and Dickson: "The results of the five studies reported here are consistent with the hypothesis that goals and intentions are important determinants of behavior, and with the hypothesis that they are the mechanism by which monetary incentives influence behavior. All five studies showed significant relationships between goals or intentions and behavior within and/or between different monetary incentive conditions. Further, in each of the five studies it was demonstrated that if goal or intention level was controlled or partialed out, there was no effect of amount of incentive on behavior."[5] More generally, after an extensive review of the literature, Opsahl and Dunnette write, "much remains to be learned before we will understand very well what meaning money has for different people, how it affects their job behaviors, which motives it serves, and how its effectiveness may come about. It is probably doubtful that there will ever be a 'theory of money' in the sense that money will be given a unique or special status as a psychological variable. It is true that money functions in many ways, depending upon the setting, the antecedent conditions, and the particular person involved."[6] In sum, Opsahl and Dunnette conclude that while we know little about the role of financial incentives under specified conditions, it seems clear from the evidence that money is not an independent variable of itself. A major contribution of the Hawthorne research remains its early and influential exposure of the "economic man" for the myth it has since been proven to be.

Conclusion

Carey's article is unfortunate because it is misleading. A reading of Carey without familiarity with the original Hawthorne research reports would leave one with the impression that these researchers summarily dismissed financial in-

[5]Edwin A. Locke, Judith F. Bryan, and Lorne M. Kendall, "Goals and Intentions as Mediators of the Effects of Monetary Incentives on Behavior," *Journal of Applied Psychology*, LII (1968), p. 119.

[6]Robert L. Opsahl and Marvin D. Dunnette, "The Role of Financial Compensation in Industrial Motivation," *Psychological Bulletin*, LXVI (1966), p. 97.

centives in favor of a particular style of supervision. But this alleged exclusive emphasis on supervision was not theirs; it was developed later by others. Granted that the Hawthorne researchers are in some measure open to the criticisms leveled by Carey and Sykes the dichotomy between supervision and financial incentives advanced by Carey should not be perpetuated. A primary contribution of the Hawthorne researchers remains their attempt to place financial incentives in a social context. Evidence Carey himself used as well as evidence from the Bank Wiring Observation Room shows that reason enough existed for the Hawthorne researchers' rejection of financial incentive as a variable exerting an independent effect entirely of itself.

Taylor's researches were originally sparked by his experience with what he called "soldiering" on the job—that is, with the restrictions on output imposed by the immediate work group. Mayo and his associates in the Hawthorne researches were also concerned with this phenomenon. And both the proponents of scientific management and the members of the Mayo school felt that the solution lay in changing conditions within the company. Here, however, is an article that suggests that the problem must be considered in a wider context. The author, who is a professor at Manchester University in England, conducted his research by actually working in a shop.

'Systematic Soldiering' in Industry

T. Lupton

In his pioneer writings on scientific management, Frederick Winslow Taylor often used the term 'systematic soldiering' to describe the behaviour of workers who set and maintain standards of output below the expectations of management.

Taylor thought restriction of output was due to archaic methods of industrial administration. He held it barbarous to believe that a 'fair day's work' is a matter of argument, and claimed that it could be scientifically assessed. Given the standard, then the proper task of management is to see that the work-place is properly laid out, the proper tools provided as and when required, and so on. Then, given the right incentives, individual workers would strive to reach and maintain the standard; always provided that workers were properly selected and trained for the tasks they were assigned.

Underlying Taylor's argument are ideas about industrial society and individual human motivation. He believed that there exists a strong bond of common interest which links employers, managers, and workers, and links all these into the wider society. The existence of this bond becomes obscured, so the argument goes, by the difficulties and disagreements which arise when these groups come together in a productive process, which is organized on traditional rule-of-thumb lines. It is these disagreements which are often fastened upon and exploited by special interests, such as trade unions. However, if the productive process were to be rationally organized, the underlying community of interest would become more apparent. People would see that the rewards they received were commensurate with their contribution to a common purpose. Taylor's main idea about human motivation was that individuals would respond to the offer of more money for more effort, overcoming their natural laziness, and co-operating willingly.

These ideas and solutions have been sharply criticized. It has been argued that society is not merely an agglomeration of materialistic individuals, upon whom patterns of organization can be stamped. Neither the offer of more cash, nor the use of techno-administrative systems, however ingeniously devised, will of themselves enlist the full co-operation of workers, or of anyone else. To achieve heightened co-operation, so the argument goes, management must learn social skills; must give good leadership; listen, consult, inform, and so on.

From *The Listener*, Mar. 31, 1960, pp. 563–565. Publication of the British Broadcasting Corporation.

The theory on which this argument rests regards the group, rather than the individual, as the significant unit. Men form groups, and groups set standards of behaviour for their members. Therefore it is management's task to see that small groups within the organization are somehow imbued with enthusiasm for the aims of the whole.

These two points of view about restriction of output and wider problems of industrial co-operation together form a basis for most modern management practice and teaching. For the most part they rest on theories generalized from management experience, or, at second hand, from the findings of social scientific research. They seek their explanations of human social behaviour and develop techniques to modify it, within the factory context. There are other ways of looking at the problem, and other modes of analysis, which might be more fruitful.

'Allowed Times' and Bonus Earnings

In carrying out my research I worked as a labourer in an engineering workshop. There were a score or so semi-skilled, male assembly workers in the shop. Mostly, these were young married men, and, typically, they had worked at two or three other jobs before coming to the firm. All of them were of the working class, not only in the sense that they were wage-earning manual workers but in the sense that they came from families of wage-earning manual workers and mostly lived in rented houses in densely populated urban areas with others of their kind.

The men worked mostly in stable pairs of 'mates.' Over and above their basic rates of pay they were paid bonus, as individuals, according to the time they saved on the times allowed to complete each assembly job. These allowed times were established after stop-watch studies carried out by rate-fixers, and usually after a good deal of bargaining about the rate-fixer's initial offer.

Most of the assembly work coming into the shop carried an allowed time, and the possibility of bonus earnings. It came in great variety, in small batches or single orders. The allocation of work to the men was carried out by the foremen. There was no mass-production sequence. Each assembly job was started and completed by one pair of mates, or sometimes by one person. All the men endorsed the general view that the firm was a good one to work for but they were critical in detail about management planning as it affected them.

When I worked there the workers had evolved a form of adjustment to their situation which took the shape of a fairly tight control by the whole group over the bonus earnings of individuals. There was a ceiling on earnings, and, since earnings were related to output through the bonus scheme, it would seem that this was a clear-cut case of what has been described as restriction of output. Before jumping to this conclusion, it would be as well to look more closely at the kind of controls which the workers exercised over output, at what they said about them, and at the attitude of managers to their behaviour.

The chief instrument of control was the cross-booking procedure. Some tasks yielded little bonus for much effort, some much bonus for little effort—the so-called tight and loose times. To have declared the exact time saved on loose times, as they were formally required to do, would, as the men believed, have been an invitation to management to tighten them up. And this would have meant loss of bonus, or giving more effort for the same bonus. So when booking time men were careful to observe the rule not to book over the 'ceiling'. So some surplus hours were kept 'up the cuff', or in the 'bank'. These could be used either to offset the effect of tight times, or as a safeguard against situations when, owing to programming difficulties, work became short, and time had to be booked at the 'lower' time rate. I have heard this practice described as 'squirrelling' in other industries. And I have heard of numerous examples of this 'cross-booking' technique from other workshops. The total effect of the 'fiddle', as it was called in the shop, was to introduce stability into earnings by ironing out potential fluctuations due to factors outside the control of the workers.

The 'fiddle' also gave workers some leeway to hold the pace of work at a level which they considered reasonable. And they were quite specific about what this pace was. Too great a deviation from this pace by individuals, either up or down, in all but exceptional cases, invited adverse comment, which was usually effective.

Collective Action

Clearly these workers shared certain ideas about the proper pace of work and the proper level of earnings for them as semi-skilled workers, and they acted collectively upon them. They also valued stability in earnings. It is not easy to trace the source of these ideas, nor the process by which they come to be expressed in certain kinds of action. My hunch is that the general ideas are the result of experience of working-class boys in the home and the community, which become particularized as the result of industrial experience. Newcomers to the group in which I worked found little difficulty in accepting the norms and practices of the group. The social process by which the group preserved the norms by using sanctions of sarcasm, ridicule, and hard argument was plain to see and to understand.

It was my impression that the managers did not regard the 'fiddle' as restriction of output; and I myself thought that, given the circumstances, the complete abolition of cross-booking would have had little effect on levels of output. It would seem that the problem is partly one arising from the shape of our social structure generally; which gives rise to differential sets of expectations of different social strata, rather than a problem wholly arising within the factory, and susceptible to administrative solutions.

This idea of the extra-factory origin of notions of work-pace and earnings level, and even attitudes to work and to managerial authority, seems to be borne out by studies of women workers carried out at Manchester. In general, we have found a lack of interest amongst women workers in collective pace setting or bonus manipulation. Women workers also seem to be ready to sanction behaviour which in general conforms to the demands and expectations of management. It is true that in factories where women work the productive process usually lends itself to tighter management control and to a fairly precise definition of management expectations, where the tasks are repetitive and of short duration and where standardized components are used. But it is also clear that factory work is of secondary importance to women, when compared to the business of being a wife and mother, or a prospective wife and mother. Values appropriate to another career are, as it were, carried temporarily into the workshop and may help to explain women's different behaviour at work.

If what I have said makes any sense it is obvious that limits are set by the whole social structural context of factory work to the effectiveness of purely administrative or 'human relations' solutions to the problem of management-worker co-operation.

Some of the reasons for differences in behaviour and values between managers and workers may be sought in their position in the social structure, but since social strata or classes are partly defined by occupation these two things are to some extent mutually dependent. The extent of the social and cultural gulf between managers and workers may be affected in particular cases by economic and technological factors, by size of enterprise, by local tradition, and so on. There is some evidence to show, for example, that the smooth industrial relations of the steel industry are encouraged by the team organization characteristic of steel technology; by the promotion opportunities this offers to semi-skilled workers; and by the low labour component in costs, which eases the downward pressure on wages. Steelworks often dominate a local community, so that traditions of family association with the industry develop. In mining, however, where there are similar community traditions, it is the economics and technology of mining which seem to emphasize management-worker antagonism.

As one looks at each industry or factory, in its social-structural and community setting, one begins to discern characteristic patterns of connected influences, which are associated with characteristic modes of workshop behaviour and management-worker relationships. It does not follow that such behaviour and relationships cannot be changed but it is clear that there are limits to the effectiveness of technical and administrative expedients.

Social scientists will see that I am pleading for more research of the kind which examines factory social behavior within its social-structural and economic context, and less research on 'bits' of behaviour out of context—labour turnover, communications, and the like. They may disagree with my conclusions, but would think the point was worth making. But managers and trade unionists, who are showing increasing interest in the work of social scientists in industry, are less interested in theoretical questions of research design and the formulation of research problems than in the immediate implications of research findings for industrial policy.

The findings of recent research on workshop behaviour do lead to *some* conclusions which may be generalized. The evidence I have mentioned supports a view that the concept of a 'fair day's work' is a social concept, as well as a technical and physiological one. If this is so then it follows that there will be arguments about it, however refined the techniques of time study and rating may become; and I would take this to be an argument for more workshop on-the-spot bargaining about the relationship between effort and reward, involving workers and their representatives. Many firms have introduced such procedures, but too often they seem to rest on a basis of paternalism, rather than on recognition of discrepant but equally valid claims and ideas. To develop such procedures fully might involve some hard re-thinking about trade-union structure and policy, particularly about the role and status of workshop representatives, as well as about the basis of authority in industry.

One further conclusion is suggested, and this refers to the training of managers. Miss Joan Woodward, in her work on the relation between technology and management structure, has cast doubt on the value of teaching so-called general principles of administration. Research on workshop behaviour confirms this view. But I would go further and say that a manager should know, in addition to his professional skills and techniques, a good deal about the relationship of industry and society, and about the methods of the social sciences.

Although there are few who would quarrel with this as an idea, so strong is the demand for technological skills that this kind of teaching, if it is attempted at all, is frequently regarded as rather marginal activity. I believe that it should be given a prominent place in the training of managers and technologists.

7
Fayol the Universalist

Neither Taylor nor Mayo was much concerned with top management problems except to the extent that top management policies affected the work on the lowest level. Although they approached the matter from different viewpoints, both were mainly interested in increasing the productivity of the rank and file. Even Harrington Emerson, who was concerned with top management decisions, did not attempt to develop a science of management; instead, he concentrated on techniques (e.g., cost accounting) that are helpful to management but are not management itself.

In contrast, Henri Fayol (1841–1925) attempted to develop a science of administration, and the principles he developed are widely used today in planning and developing company organization structure. Among the most widely used are "unity of direction" (one head and one plan for each activity) and "unity of command" (each person should have only one boss). Another often utilized is the principle that responsibility should be equal to authority—now generally stated as "Authority should be commensurate with responsibility"; in other words, the incumbent of each position should be given enough authority to carry out all the responsibilities assigned to him. Fayol also attempted to identify the strictly managerial functions, which he listed as planning, organization, command, coordination, and control.

Fayol was careful to state that his principles should not be considered rigid rules. In the book in which he described his system, he wrote: "There is nothing . . . absolute in management affairs. Seldom do we have to apply the same principle twice in identical conditions; allowance must be made for different changing circumstances."[1] Yet he believed that there was a universal science of management applicable alike to "commerce, industry, politics, religion, war, or philanthropy."[2]

However, Fayol probably would not have accepted the view, held by many who have adopted his principles, that there is such a thing as a universal manager who can manage any type of organization with equal success. While he said that the need for technical knowledge decreases with a rise in the management hierarchy, he felt that even top managers could not depend on administrative skills alone. In fact, in discussing the qualities needed by top management, he gave administrative ability a weight of only 50 per cent in the case of a manager of a very large firm, and only 25 per cent in the case of the small-firm top executive.

Fayol was a Frenchmen, and in his attempt to develop logical fundamental principles was no doubt influenced by the habits of thought inculcated by Cartesian philosophy. He was probably influenced also by the writings of the classical economist, Adam

[1] *General and Industrial Management* (Sir Isaac Pitman & Sons, Ltd., London, 1949), p. 19. Trans. by Constance Storrs. (The material in this book was first published in 1916 in the bulletin of a French trade association.)
[2] *Ibid.*, p. 41.

Smith—his discussion of specialization in *General and Industrial Management* duplicates those of Smith and J. B. Say, the French equivalent of Smith.

But more than anything else he drew on his experience as a top manager in industry—some thirty years as managing director of a great French mining and engineering combine.

The following excerpt is taken from one of Henri Fayol's essays. Although he did not claim that administrative ability was the only skill needed by a manager, he did believe, as this paper shows, that, *other things being equal*, methods of administration could make the difference between success and failure. Here he tells how a change in administration, which he instituted when he became managing director of the Commentry, Fourchambault, and Décazeville combine, reversed a trend toward failure, and lists some of the practical procedures he used.

The Importance of the Administrative Factor

Henri Fayol

Among the many factors that determine the prosperity—or ruin—of an industrial enterprise there are external causes: changes in the competitive situation, inventions and discoveries, tariff changes, wars, cataclysms, etc., and internal causes: changes in raw material resources or the finances of the enterprise or in the ability of its personnel at all levels of the hierarchy.

The administrative ability of the personnel is one of the elements in the prosperity of the enterprise, but there are so many others that vary simultaneously that it would be a gross error to conclude that success is always a sign of good administration; the contrary is often seen: prodigies of administration may be accomplished in the liquidation of some unhappy business; the constituents of prosperity are so numerous and so diverse that it is generally difficult to disentangle the effects of administrative action therefrom.

Here, however, is an industrial experience in which the effect of the administrative factor is clearly evident.

Under the influence of different causes, a great mining and metallurgical enterprise, the firm of Commentry, Fourchambault and Décazeville, was declining and on the road to bankruptcy, when a change occurred, in 1888, in the way in which the administrative function was carried out; and, without modification of anything else, without improvement in any of the adverse factors, the business began to prosper and has not stopped growing since. With the same mines and factories, with the same financial resources, the same markets, the same board of directors and the same personnel, solely because of a new method of administration the company experienced a rise comparable to its earlier fall.

The dividend curve in the figure shows the financial development of the enterprise.

Having become, in spite of myself, the managing director of that company in 1888, I immediately extended to the whole enterprise the method that I had worked out and tested during my twenty years as a manager of Commentry.

The practical procedures of this method are known:

A program of action prepared by means of annual and ten-year forecasts.

An organization chart to guarantee order and assure each man a definite place; careful recruiting and technical, intellectual, moral, administrative training of the personnel in all ranks in order to find the right man for each place.

Observation of the necessary principles in the execution of *command* [i.e., direction].

Meetings of the departmental heads of every division; conferences of the division heads presided over by the managing director to insure *coordination*.

Universal *control*, based on clear accounting data rapidly made available.

The application of positive administration is, in my opinion, the sole cause of the change which occurred, beginning in 1888, in the development of the firm of Commentry, Fourchambault and Décazeville. Certainly it cannot be attributed to an improvement in business conditions because competition in the north and east became more formidable; nor to the situation of the Commentry mine, which worsened daily. Nor can it be attributed to the metallurgical ability of the new managing director, which was zero. This incompetence put in sharp relief the importance of administrative capacity under the circumstances.

I have been told that a disturbed and dissatisfied shareholder said, not without reason: "A metallurgist was needed, and they've chosen a miner!" Actually, the public does not clearly

From *L'Eveil de l'Esprit Public* (Dunod, Paris, 1927), pp. 269–274. Translated by Ernest Dale.

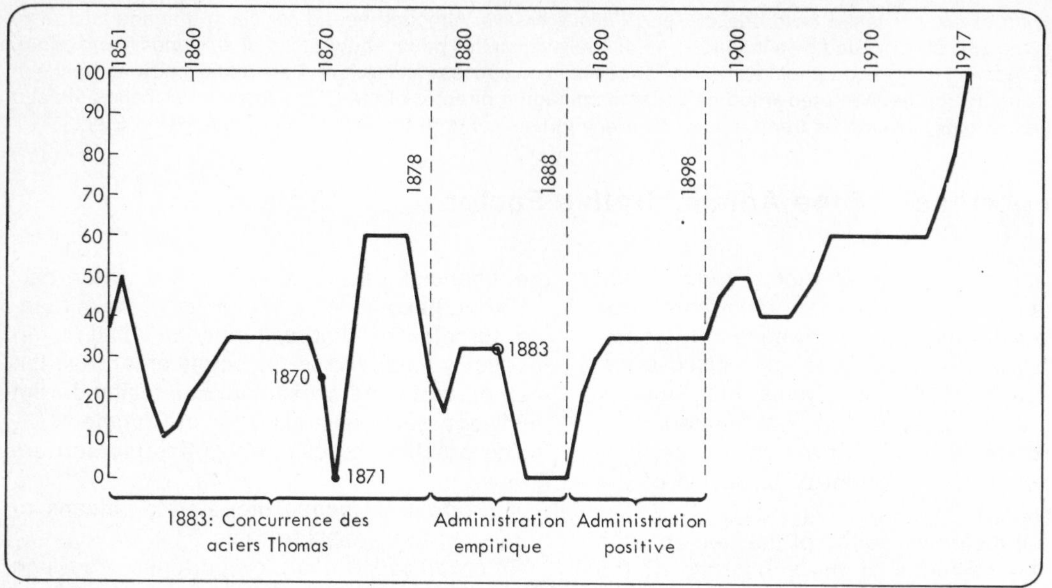

Graph showing the dividends distributed by the Commentry, Fourchambault and Décazeville Company from the time it was founded until 1917. From 1878 until 1888, administration was haphazard. Under Fayol's direction the dividends rose sharply, and the advance continued even after he had left the company.

recognize management as a separate entity; it judges competence solely by technical ability. From this point of view, the company needed a managing director competent at once in mining, metallurgy and civil engineering since these were the main divisions. If such a man existed and could have been discovered, it is doubtful that a company whose future was not assured could have succeeded in getting him.

There, in broad outlines, is the most striking experience that made me understand the importance of administration in business. I have had many others, both before and after this one, but never have I encountered a situation in which such a combination of circumstances—if not permanent—had persisted for so long a time and the only factor that changed was management.

This shows, in my opinion, the influence that administrative ability has on the prosperity of an enterprise and justifies the place I claim for administrative function in the attention of the chief executives.

At the same time, this is an encouraging point: years of laborious effort are necessary to improve the technical knowledge of *all* personnel; to improve administrative competence, to introduce and make general among subordinates the use of sound methods [of administration] requires only months.

In the lower ranks, professional competence is most important; in the higher, administrative competence is dominant, the more so the larger the organization. If the workmen, the foremen, the engineers lack technical competence, the technical capacity of the whole business is weakened; on the other hand, it is not essential that these agents be perfect administrators. But if the managing director and the other top executives lack administrative capacity, the administrative capacity of the whole enterprise is reduced, little by little, to zero.

It is, then, in the top echelon and in the neighborhood of the summit that the administrative capacity of the whole organization is concentrated and can percolate downward to the immediate subordinates of the top men and those below that level, for the example of the top man is the living law. The executive who is capable and willing to take the trouble can transform the exercise of the administrative function in his business in a matter of months.

PART 3 THE MANAGEMENT FUNCTIONS

Although management is an integrated activity, it is easier to comprehend its scope if it is broken down into its component parts. These parts—the functions the manager performs—may be listed as organization, planning, staffing, direction, control, innovation, and representation.

Some managers, of course, handle tasks that fall under none of these headings, for many of them do work that is not strictly management. In fact, most of them do so, except those at the very top. But in handling the management part of their work they are always performing one or more of the functions listed above.

This section deals with each of the seven functions in turn and with the various theories concerning the way each can best be handled, and it may be noted that each of the theorists tends to follow one of the three main schools of thought identified in the last section. Then, since techniques are necessary in acting on any theory, some of the articles touch on the techniques to be used in handling the management functions.

Finally, since the manager must constantly make decisions in the course of performing each of these functions, the last chapter deals with the theory and practice of decision making.

8 Theories of Organization

There are a number of schools of thought on organization theory, but the two principal ones are the classical school and the behaviorist school, the former stemming largely from Henri Fayol and the latter to some extent from Elton Mayo. While members of the same school do not always agree with one another, in the main they take the same approach to the subject.

Fortunately for the student and practitioner of organization, the theories and practices advocated by the two schools are not mutually exclusive. It is possible to draw on both in organizing a company or a department. To achieve the best results, therefore, it is well to be aware of the contributions each may make.

The first excerpt reprinted in this chapter contrasts the two schools and offers some criticism of both. Next, there are articles dealing with classical theory (called "the management process school of thought" by one of the authors); then there are excerpts from the writings of those who take the behaviorist approach. The final article sums up all the theories of organization developed to date, including some of the most recent.

Prof. W. J. M. Mackenzie of the University of Manchester (England) is a political scientist, and since both political science and administrative science deal with human beings, scientists in the two fields encounter many of the same difficulties. Here he examines the shortcomings of two schools of thought on administration and makes some suggestions for improvement. He also points out that the differences between the conclusions promulgated by the two schools are due in part to a difference in viewpoint about the ends the organizer should be seeking.

Science in the Study of Administration

W. J. M. Mackenzie

Time and motion study has advanced beyond Taylor and Gilbreth, but the principles of administration are much where Fayol left them. This is partly because much later writing is so careless as to be disreputable, but there are also inherent difficulties in this approach, quite similar to those which dishearten the economic theorists. For one thing it must have postulates, and postulates are either tautologies or the axioms of common-sense. These points are discouraging but not fatal. The crucial difficulty is in the transition from deduction to experiment. This is a procedure of great difficulty, even in natural science; in administrative science it has not even been tried. It is a tautology to say "efficiency declines if the correct span of control is exceeded": if one combines this with another tautology, for instance that "efficiency declines if the chain of command is too long," one can arrive by a fairly strict process of reasoning at other propositions, some of which will sound interesting. But if they are fairly stated they will indicate which courses of action are mutually exclusive, not which course of action is right. This will be a service to anyone who finds himself in a situation to which the alternatives are relevant; but it is not what we expect from natural science. We expect to be told that "in certain circumstances the way to get *A* is to do *B*"; not that there are six alternative ways, any of which might in unknown circumstances be the right one.

Much has been written, but the authors seem to have muddled it. One is reminded of the conclusion of Kipling's "Brugglesmith": "Though his feet were not within six inches of the ground, they paddled swiftly, and I saw that in his magnificent mind he was running—furiously running."

This unfortunately has often been the point at which political scientists first meet scientific administration, and what they see of it shocks them.

Elton Mayo and Later Behaviorists

They are less likely to be repelled by the school which may be associated [with] the name of Elton Mayo. His work was mainly on the sociology of industry, at the level of the factory worker; its application to the manager is new and tentative, and it is not certain how it will work out. But enough has been done to show that the attempt is a continuation of traditions long familiar in political science. One of these is the search for an all-embracing science of society, in which political scientists have always been involved.

There are two problems at the outset. Literature about the science of administration is addressed primarily to administrators; there is a proper element of idle curiosity in it, but its excuse for existing is that it will help the administrator to do his job better. Unfortunately the deductive school and the sociological school do not agree about what his job is. This is concealed by their definitions of administration, which look very similar.

Both schools of thought regard administration as combination to effect a purpose. For the deductive[1] school that purpose is solely the purpose of the manager, though of course he may have received it as "policy" from a higher

[1] *Editor's Note*: i.e., the classical.

From a lecture given at the London School of Economics on November 5, 1951; reprinted in *The Manchester School of Economic and Social Studies*, Vol. XX, No. 1, January, 1952, pp. 7–22. Reprinted here by permission of Kraus Reprint Corporation, New York.

level of decision. The "data" are a purpose and a number of men; the manager's job is to organize the men so as to attain the purpose. The manager makes the organization, but he is himself outside it; he acts upon it, and he may learn from it, but he is not changed by it. In relation to it, he is God. This view of purpose does not flow from the nature of the deductive method, but from the climate of thought in which it was developed and the readers for whom it was designed; it was written for those who lived still in an atmosphere of individualism, and it paid a tribute of respect to the legal fiction that shareholders govern directors, directors govern managers, managers give orders to workmen. There is a chain of command; something called "command" flows through channels which can be marked by little arrows on a chart.

Sociology by its terms of reference proceeds on other assumptions; its axiom is that social relations exist and can be known. Human beings in so far as they affect one another are in relationship, and their relationships can be studied. The object of the science is to produce rules about the behaviour of human beings in combination, as the object of chemistry is to produce rules about atoms in combination. These rules may claim only a low degree of probability, but within the limits set they will enable us to predict what combinations human beings will form in particular social circumstances. There are difficulties about this; the only one relevant here is that of the position of the administrator in relation to the group. If he affects the group he is (for the sociologist) in relationship with it; the more he affects it the more intimately he is a part of it, and the more necessary it is to study him in relation to the group as well as the group in relation to him. These are one social fact, not two. The sociological student of administration sets out to teach managers how to run their businesses better; he is apt to come back with a set of rules which say how managers are likely to behave, in relation to the various groups to which they belong. The perfect set of rules would say how managers *must* behave—meaning that if they did not behave thus they would in our society cease to be managers very soon.

The second issue is closely related to this point. It seems impossible in ordinary usage to talk about administration except in terms of purpose. We administer to get something done; if there is no purpose, it is not administration. Yet purpose is particularly hard for the sociologist to handle, a difficulty common to sociology and psychology. Purpose is not a thing which we can directly observe in others. We know—at least we are convinced that we know—our own purposes, and we know what symptoms in our own actions belong to purpose. Other people's purposes we deduce from their actions, and the evidence is often difficult. Our own symptoms may not be typical; the others may deliberately or by accident mislead us; and in any case man's actions are never wholly rational. The word "rational" is natural in this context; the idea of purpose is closely related to that of reason, and the concepts of reason and unreason, conscious, subconscious and unconscious, are a fruitful score of puzzles for philosophy and psychology. These difficulties are still present if we look away from the purpose of the manager, and put purpose into the group. The sociological study of administration, as distinct from other sociological studies, would be the study of the organisation of a group in relation to its common purpose.

As political theorists we have been here before. "Purpose" in ordinary speech means the purpose of some person; whose purpose is the common purpose of a group? If there is such a thing as common purpose, the group is to that extent a person; if the group is a person, what then are the persons who compose it? If the General Will really is a Will, what becomes of you and me? Perhaps, as it is fashionable to say, it is all a matter of using the wrong language: perhaps the word "purpose" has meaning in regard to the individual, but is merely a source of confusion and false analogy when applied to the group.

The first difficulty, that of the leader who in one sense governs the group, in another sense is governed by it, is a paradox which we meet every day and get over well enough in practice. The second is a much more serious barrier to the sociological study of administration, and the difficulty is not eased by the determined efforts which have been made to outflank it. One successful school of sociology—that associated with Durkheim and with the British tradition in social anthropology—has set up its science on the assumption that the study of society can dispense with the concept of purpose. It has tried to use the language of physiology, not that of introspection. Sociology is treated as rejected in sociological explanation, as teleology had been rejected by the nineteenth century in biological explanation. For the idea of "purpose," are substituted the ideas of "structure" and "function."

This is an attitude which it is difficult to sustain consistently, and few writers succeed in following their own rules. But the distinction is a real one. "Purpose" implies a relation of means to end. It is a "straignt line" relationship; straight lines can be linked, but in such a chain each link is directly related only to its neighbours. "Function" implies a balance of parts interacting within a complex whole which tends towards equilibrium—an interlocking or circular relationship. The classic exposition is that in which Durkheim discusses at length the Division of Labour: the *purpose* of specialisation is to increase the specialist's income, the *social function* of specialisation is to maintain social solidarity. Individuals, as we know, introduce specialisation for their individual purposes: but if our point of interest is not the individual but society, for us the relevant thing about specialisation is not its relation to individual purposes, but its relation to other social facts.

This need not mean that we forget individual purpose or subordinate individual purpose to social function. One can study the individual or study society without implying that the individual and society are eternally separate and contrasted.

All this is "scientific" in principle; and (so far as a layman can judge) it has had real success in practice. It is true that Elton Mayo's story of the Hawthorne experiment has been told so often that it has become a sort of parable, more apt in sermons than in textbooks; and probably there is not a large field in which changes in group relations can be measured by reference to a simple and uniform variable such as industrial output. But these doubts are not fatal to the claim of this sociology to be a science; at most, they suggest that it is moving away from the concept of science as natural science, and back to the wider sense, the "Baconian" sense, in which science includes an orderly empirical study of the natural world.

The new method ought in principle to be applicable to any group in any country; to a jungle village, or a factory, or a government office. Hence the latest theme in the science of administration is the application of this sociological method to administrative groups. That is why we are being made familiar with the distinction between formal and informal organisation, and are taught to regard informal organisation as logically prior and practically more important.

Formal organisation is to be found in the organisation chart and in the distribution of duties list, it is imposed by the manager as sovereign, or agent of the sovereign, to serve the purpose of the sovereign. Informal organisation is the structure of the group, and within the group is the manager, the titular sovereign himself; the group has its status system, its laws of solidarity and expansion, its parts are functionally related, and to its law the manager conforms. If the formal organisation does not fit the law of the social situation, so much the worse for the formal organisation; it is waste paper.

This is a very summary view of a theme which permits many interesting variations. A good many of them invite detailed discussion; in the present context it is possible only to consider a few issues which are more general and perhaps less interesting.

Some Difficulties

There are, to begin with, three difficulties which are in theory not insuperable. In the *first* place, exponents of this new approach do not always play fair. They set out to seek conclusions about social life; they finish with conclusions about the good life. The good life, they teach, is that of the group; integration is happiness, extrusion from the group is unhappiness; unhappiness is the supreme evil, and it is our duty to eliminate it. A line of connection leads from Figgis and other pluralists, through the guild socialists and Miss Follet, to Elton Mayo and to much sociology which claims to be science and not philosophy. The science of groups can probably be disengaged from the ethics of groups; but no one has done it yet, and till it has been done this school of thought will repel many whose ethical presuppositions differ from theirs.

Is it the duty of miners to be happy or to produce coal? Of soldiers to be happy or to win wars? Of civil servants to be happy or to govern well? It is well enough to say that some integrated groups find happiness in efficiency; unfortunately other groups are equally happy, their morale is first-rate, and their contribution to the larger community is zero. Perhaps in time we may learn how to make the miserable happy and how to make the happy both industrious and good; but at present our repertoire of tricks is limited. In fact, it is not easy to find in modern society any group which is effectively self-contained: most men and women belong to many groups, and relations cutting across group boundaries are often more important than those within them.

Secondly, it is not derogatory to the important work which has been done on the sociology of industry to say that it is not the sociology of industrial administration; it is related to industrial administration only as social anthropology is related to colonial administration. So far the social anthropologists, though they have thought a lot, have said little about the sociology of white administrators in primitive countries; industrial sociologists and social psychologists have been equally shy in investigating the business man and the entrepreneur. There has been much talk but few experiments.

But the science of administration cannot grow out of the practice of administration unless empirical research is possible, and there are a good many practical difficulties about that. The managing director is likely to be a more elusive and recalcitrant guinea pig than the factory operative. After all, what is *he* to get out of it? Even the fact of investigation may damage prestige, which is one of the administrator's main assets in dealing with his staff, his public and his superiors. As has been said so often, the social investigator is a factor in the situation which he investigates, and the investigator of higher administration will not get far unless his presence adds to the prestige of higher administration.

The *third* practical difficulty is that of recording experience in an impersonal way. Most situations in public administration, and even in business administration, are extremely complicated, and different observers see different things in them; it would be possible for two honest and accurate historians to write quite different stories of the action taken by a government department in one day at a crisis of its history. Notionally, there are two ways of overcoming this, which can be used singly or in combination. One is to train all researchers in a single school of thought, so that their interests are alike; they look for the same things and use the same language to describe them. The other is to abandon the study of big administration, and to look for very simple instances of administrative situations; even perhaps to create them artificially. The second trick is difficult to arrange; the first is all too easy. Schools of sociology tend to harden into cliques which are mutually hostile and unintelligible. What is more, they slip back easily into reliance on deduction as against observation; they are back in the "spectral woof of impalpable abstractions," the "unearthly ballet of bloodless categories,"[2] from which they had hoped by science to break free.

These difficulties are quite serious. But supposing them to be overcome, will the sociology of administration be the science of administration which we set out to find? The methods of sociology have been very successful in describing the work of offices and factories in terms of status, communications, and group solidarity; they have not been at all successful in dealing with the process of planning or with the place of the public in relation to the administrative group. Perhaps this is not accidental, but a necessary consequence of the procedure adopted by the science of sociology. The idea of administration, like the idea of government, cannot be separated from that of purpose; this form of sociology has made progress only by substituting for purpose the concept of function. Our trouble, as students of administration, is that we want to hold on to both. If we lose hold of purpose we cannot understand the administrator, because his role is to organise other men for a purpose which is not theirs; he is the government, the purpose is his purpose, even if he pursues it in the interests of the governed and

[2]F. H. Bradley, *Principles of Logic* (2nd ed.), Vol. II, p. 591.

under their influence. But if we lose hold of function we are back in the old view of men as atoms, which is both false and ethically repugnant.

In this the student of administration is no worse off than other students of politics. Politics is primarily concerned with the giving of direction to human affairs. But politics must reckon also with the facts of the situation; the politician who ignores the laws of social equilibrium will come unstuck—so will the administrator. Is it then right to say that the study of administration is [a] part of political science?

This is too large an issue to pursue here. But it is safe to say that political scientists have perplexed themselves for centuries by attempting to hold together in one view two conceptions of the nature of politics, and that administrative scientists now find themselves in the same dilemma. If the analogy holds good, we cannot expect to find a science of administration based on the analogy of natural science, nor even one based on the wider eighteenth century conception of scientific method. We can find science *for* administrators, and it is to be hoped that we shall; but the only science *of* administration will be science in the oldest sense of the word. It will be an organised body of knowledge which can be taught, but it will not claim that it conforms closely to the model of natural science, that it is in all its parts verifiable, or that it is infinitely progressive. Administrative science, in fact, will be political science, and the political scientist is in his profession condemned to live forever upon the frontier between two worlds, the world of philosophy and the world of natural knowledge. This is a position of discomfort and responsibility: but that (after all) is politics.

Professor Mackenzie discussed the theories in general. The following is a more specific example, which presents the classical or traditional theory at its most classical. In the book from which these paragraphs are taken, Alvin Brown listed no less than ninety-six principles of this nature, although only twenty-three are reprinted here.

Brown, once a vice-president of the Johns-Manville Corporation, wrote a number of well-known books on organization. In the book from which this excerpt is taken, later chapters explain the principles and illustrate their application to the industrial enterprise.

The Principles of Organization

Alvin Brown

Purpose

1 Organization is a means to more effective concerted endeavor.

Scope

2 Organization deals exclusively with individuals and their relations.
3 Organized endeavor is no more than the sum of individual endeavors.

Precedence

4 Organization precedes endeavor.
5 Organization precedes the selection of members of enterprise and determines the requirement thereof.
6 Organization should determine the selection of personnel rather than personnel determine the nature of organization.
7 The larger the enterprise, the less occasion is there for organization to be influenced by personnel.

Responsibility

8 Responsibility inheres exclusively in individuals.

9 Responsibility cannot be shared with another.

10 The nature of a responsibility is not altered by change of the person who performs it.

Delegation of responsibility

11 Each responsibility is created by delegation from one having that responsibility.

12 Each responsibility is created by delegation from one having a greater responsibility.

13 No member can delegate responsibility to another who already holds any part of that responsibility.

14 A member does not, by delegation, divest himself of responsibility.

15 Two members should not delegate responsibility to the same member.

16 The inherent relationships of obligation and authority arise automatically from delegation of responsibility.

Obligation

17 The acceptance of a responsibility creates an equivalent obligation for its performance.

18 Obligation for the performance of a responsibility runs to the delegant of that responsibility and to no one else.

19 The obligation for performance of a responsibility can be discharged only by the obligor.

20 No member can divest himself of any part of the obligation for performance of his responsibility.

21 The obligation for performance of a responsibility is not impaired by change in the definition of responsibility.

22 A responsibility must be performed exactly as it is conceived by the delegant.

23 If a deputy be unwilling, for whatever reason, to perform his obligation as conceived by his delegant, his only alternative is dissociation from his responsibility.

The danger of observing any set of principles too exactly is that some of those in the organization may come to regard organization as an end in itself, rather than as a means to an end. This attitude, which is satirized in the verse below, sometimes develops in large organizations, although most classicists are inclined to be fairly flexible in their observance of the principles. Fayol himself emphasized that his principles were to be regarded as guidelines, rather than immutable laws.

The Bureaucrat's Prayer

Oh Thou, who seest all things below,
Grant that Thy servants may go slow;
That we may study to comply
With regulations till we die.

Teach us, O Lord, to reverence
Committees more than common-sense;
Impress our minds to make no plan
And pass the baby when we can.

And when the Tempter seems to give
Us feelings of initiative,
Or when, alone, we go too far
Recall us with a circular.

Mid fire and tumult, war and storms,
Sustain us, Blessed Lord, with forms,
Thus may Thy servants ever be
A flock of perfect sheep for Thee.

—Anon.

A persuasive presentation of the classical viewpoint is found in this short piece by Harold Koontz of the Graduate School of Business Administration at the University of California, Los Angeles. It will be noted that he does not consider the findings of the various behavioral sciences unimportant. He does believe, however, that the principles provided by Fayol and his successors cover a field well worth study in its own right.

The Management Process School of Thought

Harold Koontz

The management process approach to management theory perceives management as a process of getting things done by people who operate in organized groups. By analyzing the process, establishing a conceptual framework for it, and identifying the principles underlying the process, this approach builds a theory of management. It regards management as a process that is essentially the same whether in business, government, or any other enterprise, and which involves the same *process*, whether at the level of president or foreman in a given enterprise. It does, however, recognize that the environment of management differs widely between enterprises and levels. According to this school, management theory is seen as a way of summarizing and organizing experience so that practice can be improved.

Often referred to (especially by its critics) as the "traditional" or "universalist" school, this school was actually fathered by Henri Fayol. However, many of his offspring did not know of their parent, since Fayol's work was eclipsed by the brighter light of his contemporary, Frederick W. Taylor, and since the first widely available English translation of Fayol was not made until 1949. Other than Fayol, most of the early contributors to this school dealt only with the organization portion of the management process, largely because of their greater experience with this facet of management and the simple fact that planning and control, as well as the function of staffing, were given little attention by managers before 1940.

This school bases its approach to management theory on several fundamental beliefs. Specifically:

1 Managing is a process which can best be dissected intellectually by analyzing the manager's functions.
2 Long experience with management in a variety of enterprise situations can be grounds for the distillation of certain fundamental truths or generalizations—usually referred to as principles—that have a clarifying and predictive value in the understanding and improvement of managing.
3 These fundamental beliefs can become focal points for useful research both to ascertain their validity and to improve their meaning and applicability in practice.
4 Such beliefs can furnish elements, at least until disproved, of a useful theory of management.
5 Managing is an art, but, like medicine or engineering, one which can be improved by reliance on sound underlying principles.
6 Principles in management, like principles in the biological and physical sciences, are true even if exceptions or compromises of the "rules" prove effective in a given situation.
7 While there are, of course, many factors which affect the manager's environment, management theory need not encompass *all* knowledge in order for it to serve as a scientific or theoretical foundation for management practice.

The basic approach this school takes, then, is to look first at the functions of managers—planning, organizing, staffing, directing, and controlling—and to distill from these functions certain fundamental principles that hold true in the complicated practice of management.

Also, purely to make the area of management theory intellectually manageable, those who subscribe to this school do not usually attempt to include in the theory the entire areas of sociology, economics, biology, psychology, physics, chemistry, and so on. This is done not because these other areas of knowledge are unimportant and have no bearing on management, but merely because no real progress has ever been made in science or art without significant partitioning of knowledge. Yet anyone would be foolish not to realize that a function which deals with people in their various activities of producing and marketing anything from money to religion and education is completely independent of the physical, biological, and cultural universe in which we live.

From "Making Sense of Management Theory," in Harold Koontz (ed.), *Toward a Unified Theory of Management* (McGraw-Hill Book Company, New York, 1964), pp. 3–5; a report of a symposium held at the Graduate School of Business Administration, University of California, Los Angeles, Nov. 8, 9, 1962.

Although members of the classical school tend to hold that the general principles of organization are applicable to all organizations of all types, they have always recognized that one cannot organize a company or any type of human effort merely by mechanical observance of the principles. And perceptive managers have always been aware that just as the organization structure affects the members of the organization, they as individuals affect the structure itself. This viewpoint is presented here in an excerpt from the writings of Henry S. Dennison (1877–1952), who was for many years president of a (Framingham, Mass.) company bearing his name. He was a pioneer in the application of much of the new thinking on management, including the ideas put forth by psychologists, and in what later became known as executive development. His little book *Organization Engineering* was a classic in its day, and the following excerpt from it shows how he anticipated some of the ideas of later writers.

Organization Engineering

Henry S. Dennison

To understand fully the nature of the men and women in a working group, and to relate them to each other and to the organization as a whole in such ways that quite literally they "work with a will," is a task demanding powers of analysis, sympathy, and imagination. Attention must focus upon causes and effects in the field of human behavior. Effective action must be founded in an inclusive and sympathetic but, nevertheless, accurate, detached, and scientific appreciation of human nature. Hence it is here regarded as a task requiring the training and technique of an engineer.

As in electrical engineering we organize a field of electrical forces and resistances by arranging them into a structure of maximum usefulness, so in organization engineering we must seek to arrange a field of human forces and resistances—human motives, purposes, feelings, knowledges, and abilities—so that they interwork for maximum usefulness.

The primary data of any project in organization engineering are the special characteristics of just those human beings by whom it is to be manned. Proposals for representative forms of government, for liberty of credal interpretation, for measures of military discipline, or for functionalized factory management cannot be judged in abstraction. Their discussion is significant only as applied to men and women of known characteristics.

The members of an organization vary widely among themselves in physical powers, in mental development, and in their responses to emotional stimuli. Organization engineering has first to discover within any given group the prevailing conditions and develop its forms of organization and general operating measures so as to accommodate itself to them. It will also, where it is possible by selection and training, make closer adaptation of its members to the purposes of the organization and to each other.

The ultimate in organization would require that the incentives, regulations, and personal contacts of each member should be such as to allow him to develop and put to most valuable use all of his powers. Since no two members are exactly alike there would be, theoretically, separate provisions for each. But all members, though different, are compounded of quite similar elements; their differences are in large part differences in the proportions in which these elements are represented. Hence, some reasonably uniform general measures can usually be devised. An important practical task of the organization engineer lies in so grouping the personnel and devising the general rules that the largest possible number are effectively provided for; at the same time he must be ready to deal with individual cases wherever the unsuitability of general rules causes losses which outweigh their gains in convenience and cost of administration.

The structural form of an organization affects and alters the spirit which works through it. The spirit alters and re-creates the structure. The running of an organization and the building of it depend upon each other—affect and are affected by each other.

The importance of right structure of organization is sometimes undervalued, because with the right men almost any kind of organization can run well. This is true, but is by no means the whole truth. With the finest of personnel, an illogical organization structure makes waste through internal friction and lost motion; it fails

From *Organization Engineering* (McGraw-Hill Book Company, New York, 1931), pp. 2–9.

to retain and develop good men and to invite into its membership new men of high quality. Ability, tact, and good purpose cannot be established by law—they can, however, by law be made possible or virtually impossible.

The specific purposes which organizations are created to serve influence both their structures and their operating plans, and, in so far as they are known, they affect their members directly in all degrees of intensity from low neutrality to high self-devotion or severe revulsion.

There are, then, within an organization four principal systems of interacting forces: the members, the operating measures, the structural relationships, and the purposes. The immediacy and intimacy with which interaction takes place among them increases as a group advances from a loose aggregation of people towards full organic unity. When so far along that one would call the group organized, few material changes can be made anywhere in it which do not affect it everywhere.

Outside the organization there is also its environment affecting it and affected by it. As national culture and the church react upon each other, so do community and factory. Working hours determine the ways in which leisure hours are utilized as truly as the uses of leisure hours affect the hours of work. The trade within which a company finds itself has its "practices" which limit that company's freedom of behavior in its markets; but that company's behavior is, nevertheless, one of the forces which determine the character of these trade practices. Sometimes external influences are slight and can be disregarded; sometimes, again, they are of crucial importance.

A pervasive element in the calculations of organization engineering is Time. Many of the best results of social changes are of slow maturity. Hence, close upon the heels of any decision of what to do must come the decision of when and how fast to do it. In organization engineering the expectation or promise of quick permanent results is often the mark of the tyro or charlatan.

The strain and discouragement of frankly facing the complex tangle of motives at work in most human situations tempt everyone into the errors of oversimplification. Too impatient to follow the tangled skein through, everyone at one time or another—to a greater or a less extent—finds rest and comfort in making believe that things are not so mixed up as in reality they are, and in deducing some embracing theory from a starched and ironed cosmos.

Many consider that the first great departure from the classical theory was embodied in the book *The Functions of the Executive*[1] by Chester I. Barnard. Barnard was for many years an executive of the New Jersey Bell Telephone Company and ultimately served as its president; later he was president of the United Services Organization (the USO) and of the Rockefeller Foundation. In *The Functions of the Executive*, he stressed the idea of the corporation as a cooperative system that included not only the executives and employees, but the investors, the suppliers, and the customers. In the following essay, he summarizes and updates his ideas.

Concepts of Organization

Chester I. Barnard

The conception of organization at which I arrived in writing *The Functions of the Executive* was that of an integrated aggregate of actions and interactions having a continuity in time. Thus I rejected the concept of organization as comprising a rather definite group of people whose behavior is coordinated with reference to some explicit goal or goals. On the contrary, I included in organization the actions of investors, suppliers, and customers or clients.

When the acts of two or more individuals are

[1](Harvard University Press, Cambridge, Mass., 1938.)

From *Organization and Management* (Harvard University Press, Cambridge, Mass., 1948), pp. 112–116, 119–121, 124, 132–133.

cooperative, that is, systematically coordinated, the acts by my definition constitute an organization. Every such act is a component simultaneously of two or more systems as determined by its functions. Thus every act of organization is also an act of some individual and is his contribution to the organization. When two or more organizations cooperate, the cooperative acts are simultaneously (1) of individuals, and either (2) of the organization contributing the act and (3) of the second organization participating, or (4) of a new complex organization embracing the two original organizations cooperating, or of all four. This simultaneous functioning of the cooperative act of an individual in two or more organization systems provides the interconnection which results in complex organizations.

This will seem to many, no doubt, a strange, artificial, unrealistic kind of thing chiefly because they will not realize that this is precisely the kind of thing they are working with in their minds in a rough-and-ready way all the time.

You could not completely understand a specific act of a human being without knowing all the organizations in which the *act* functioned as a part. If this sounds "abstract" and "unrealistic," let me put it this way: you cannot deal effectively with people unless you can get their "point of view," which means knowing what "influences" govern their behavior. This is easily said but really almost impossible to *comprehend* without a *conception* which treats it as simpler than it is. This is the great function of a good conceptual scheme. It makes it possible to deal consciously and effectively with infinite complexity.

In a community all acts of individuals and organizations are directly or indirectly interconnected and interdependent. Analogously all elements of the physical universe are said to be interconnected and interdependent. For convenience obviously necessary in some degree, we disregard the interconnections which we consider minor or trivial and distinguish those that are direct and that constitute stable systems or organizations, just as we do in the case of physical systems. Usually the organizations which are stable are those which are named or can be readily named. When two stable organizations cooperate, it is convenient to regard the cooperative acts as common to both organizations only, and not as creating a new and enlarged organization. The exception to this is where this interorganization cooperation is itself a stable system constituting a complex organization.

Among the simplest of organizations is the exchange of goods between two men, A and B. Perhaps we often fail to think of an exchange as cooperative, because emphasis is so much placed upon conflict of interest or bargaining in a hostile sense, conditions that may precede exchange; but a moment's reflection is sufficient to see that an exchange is based upon *agreement* to effect a *transaction*, a coordination of acts of the two parties, the acts being mutually dependent and interconnected.

Establishing the Cooperative Relationship

It needs little exposition to show that whether the services of employees or of customers are in question, it is necessary to bring either into cooperative relationship before they can or will cooperate. In both cases the techniques of advertising and salesmanship are employed, with persuasion as a major characteristic. "Salesmanship" is not a word used with respect to active efforts to secure employees, "personnel work," "employment work," "recruiting," being the words used; but salesmanship is what it is. This is especially evident today when trying to secure skilled mechanics. It is an important aspect of recruiting "college material." It is the business of getting people to look at what you have to offer as inducements and incentives for cooperation and of persuading them to accept the offer. A confusion as to the nature of the functions may be due to the fact that we predominantly think of employees as seeking jobs, rather than employers as seeking employees, just as we predominantly think of sellers seeking customers. In many, perhaps most, instances the buyers of goods may be said to seek the seller, not the seller the buyer, especially if we disregard the effect of advertising.

When once the cooperative relationship has been established, the exchange that constitutes organization is to be elicited. The exchange in one case (that of the employee) is services for money, in the other (that of the customer) money for services (the act of transferring goods or services). It hardly needs discussion that it is one thing to get the employee on the pay roll, and another to get the services. Similarly, it is one thing to get the customer in the store, another to make the sale.

The maintenance of morale among employees depends upon attitudes, "fair treatment," working conditions, inducements, and incentives. So does also the maintenance of morale—the desire and willingness to cooperate, that is, to purchase—on the part of customers. If it is attained, it is called "goodwill." How much a part of the conditions of organization it is, is indicated by the fact that goodwill is often a (salable) asset of the business enterprise. The techniques in both cases are identical or similar, the chief variations being due to time, place, and degree of continuity of cooperation. Thus customers are influenced by incentives (values, prices), by manner of treatment, by kinds of persons with whom they must associate to cooperate (quality of salespeople), the working conditions—location, cleanliness, light, air, crowding, etc.—of merchandising. One needs to know little of business to see how important this is in business "policy."

I have not extended the argument to wholesalers, investors of various kinds, distributors, to whom it equally applies, because the reader can readily do this for himself, if sufficiently acquainted with business to find the above analysis intelligible.

The conceptual scheme of the theory of formal organization on which *The Functions of the Executive* was constructed follows:

Principal Structural Concepts

1 *The Individual*. As a preparation for important work with human beings as salesman, politician, teacher, personnel man, or executive this concept is important; for I believe all men tend to regard others in two extremes: (1) either as they would like to regard themselves—completely exercising free will, and independent; or (2) as completely nonindividual, "dumb," responsive nonentities. Appropriate personal behavior is acquired by intuition, social experience, hard knocks; but beyond the range of strictly personal behavior some kind of intellectual comprehension seems advisable if not necessary. But the doctrine is difficult, labored, abstract, abstruse.
2 *The Cooperative System.*
3 *The Formal Organization.*
4 *The Complex Formal Organization.*
5 *The Informal Organization.*

Principal Dynamic Concepts

1 *Free Will.*
2 *Cooperation*. Defective in the omission of cases of simple economic exchange as a type of cooperation.
3 *Communication.*
4 *Authority.*
5 *The Decisive Process*. It is called in the book "The Theory of Opportunism." So far as I know, this concept, like that of the formal organization, may be original. I believe it to be for sociological purposes by far the most important suggestion. It is not sufficiently developed in the book to make this apparent, and would probably need a book to make it so. The requirements of decisive behavior (as contrasted with responsive behavior) are such as to be a chief determinant of ideas, norms, conventions, institutions, and social habits (including business routines and devices), and of organization itself as necessary equipment for the exercise of the propensity to make conscious decisions.
6 *Dynamic Equilibrium*. This concept I believe is very close to that which Professor Copeland called "adaptation to changing conditions."
7 (Executive) *Responsibility*.

Roughly, Parts I and II are the "anatomy" or structure of cooperation; Parts III and IV are its physiology or economy.

Many behaviorists have questioned whether the hierarchical form of organization, which produces a structure shaped roughly in the form of a pyramid, is the most efficacious. As a possible alternative, some have suggested the "matrix organization," which is described in this article. Dr. Argyris, formerly chairman of the department of administrative sciences at Yale and now on the Harvard faculty, believes that the matrix organization is appropriate in some circumstances, whereas the pyramidal organization works better in others.

This article is based on some of the findings of a long-range study of top management problems, a project headed by the author.

The Matrix Organization

Chris Argyris

Writing in *Industrial Management Review*, Jay W. Forrester suggests that the organization of the future may eliminate superior-subordinate relationships and substitute for them the individual self-discipline arising from self-interest created by a competitive market mechanism within the system. The individual would negotiate continuously changing relationships. Each individual would be a profit center whose objective would be to produce the most value for the least activity; who would have the freedom to terminate as well as to create new activity, who would have access to all the necessary information. The organization of the future would be rid of internal monopolies which is the usual status of most traditional departments.

The movement toward what Forrester is predicting may be seen in the increasing use of the project team and the matrix organization.

The Matrix Organization

A matrix organization is designed less around power and more around who has the relevant information. A project team is created to solve a particular problem. It is composed of people representing all the relevant managerial functions (e.g., marketing, manufacturing, engineering and finance). Each member is given equal responsibility and power to solve the problem. The members are expected to work as a cohesive unit. Once the problem is solved, the team is given a new assignment or disbanded. If the problem is a recurring one, the team remains active. In many cases, especially in defense programs, the project manager is given full authority and responsibility for the completion of the project, including rewarding and penalizing team members. An organization may have many teams. This results in an organization that looks like a matrix:

Representatives of:	**Project 1**	**Project 2**	**Project 3**
Manufacturing			
Engineering			
Marketing			
Finance			
	Team 1	**Team 2**	**Team 3**

Although I would agree with Forrester, I believe that the organizations of the future will be a combination of both the old and new forms of organization. The old pyramidal forms will be more effective for the routine, non-innovative activity that requires little, if any, internal commitment by the participants. However, as the decisions become less routine, more innovative, and as they require more commitment, the newer forms such as the matrix organizations will be more effective.

The future executive, then, must have two interrelated skills: He must be able to differentiate clearly between the old and new forms; he must know the conditions under which he will use the different organizational forms. Moreover, he will need to become skillful in several different kinds of leadership styles, each consistent with a particular form. For example, an authoritarian leadership style is more consistent with the traditional structure. A participative style, on the other hand, with the link-pin organization defined by Rensis Likert, is one that develops risk-taking for the matrix organization.

If recent research is valid, then the majority of executive leadership styles tend to conform to the traditional pyramidal style. This is not surprising, since leadership styles and organizational design would naturally go together. The findings that did surprise us were:(1) the degree to which the executives believed in leadership styles that were consonant with the matrix organization, and (2) the degree to which they were unaware that they were *not* behaving according to their ideals.

Another important requirement for future executives therefore is an awareness of their actual leadership style. Unless they develop such awareness, they are not going to be able to unfreeze their old styles, develop new ones, and switch from one style to another as the administration situations and organization structure are changed. Unless the style-switching can be clearly identified by the person and the receivers, confusion will result.

Executives in the matrix organization will also need to learn, if I may be permitted to oversimplify, that there are two kinds of tension—unproductive and productive. A person can experience unproductive or crippling tension but cannot control it. The reason he cannot may be external (pressure from his superior) or internal (inability to control his own demands on himself, plus the accompanying feelings of impatience and guilt aimed at himself).

Productive tension is the kind that the individual can control, and which comes from accepting new challenges, taking risks, expanding one's competencies, etc. These are the very qualities that are central to the matrix organization. Thus the executive of the future will have to learn how to define internal environments that challenge people, stretch their aspirations realistically, and help them face interpersonal reality. Some examples are financial controls that reward people for risk-taking, incentive systems that reward excellence (not average performance), work that is designed to use people's complex abilities. To put this another way, we need to develop competence in manipulating the environment, but not the people. (They should have the freedom to choose whether or not they will enter the new environment.)

Intergroup Conflict

The matrix organization will be made up of teams drawn from representatives of the traditional line functions. This will lead to much intergroup conflict within the team as well as between teams. Instead of trying to stamp out intergroup conflict as bad and disloyal, the executives must learn how to manage it so that the constructive aspects are emphasized and the destructive aspects de-emphasized. This means that the organization needs to put on the table for diagnosis of interdepartmental fires, the incidents of throwing the dead cat over into the other department's yard, the polarized competitive warfare in which success is defined by the participants in terms of which side won rather than the contribution to the whole.

The executives will have to learn how to bring the groups together so that: (1) each discusses and seeks, in private, to agree on its views and attitudes toward the other and toward self, after which (2) the representatives of both groups talk together in the presence of the other group members, followed by (3) private discussion to establish the way they are perceived by others in order to (4) develop (through representatives) an understanding of the discrepancy between their and others' views.

Most organizations send their executives to university executive programs or to internal executive programs usually designed following the concept of the university. I do not want to get into philosophical discussions about the nature of university education at this point. I would like to point out, however, that there may be a discrepancy between the characteristics of university education and the needs of the matrix organization.

The university has typically assumed that learning: (1) is for the individual, (2) occurs when it is given, (3) is tested by contrived examinations of the knowledge acquired, (4) need not be relevant to any immediate problem and (5) should be designed and controlled by the educator; it is the task of the educator to define the problems, develop ways to solve them and define the criteria to decide who passes and who does not.

The matrix organizations require that learning: (1) focus on individuals in team systems, (2) occur where the problem is located, (3) be accomplished by the use of actual problems, (4) be tested by the effectiveness of the actual results, and (5) be controlled by those participating in the problem (aided by the educator as a consultant).

Executive education in the matrix organization will focus on system effectiveness. This means that the central educational department will now become an organizational development activity. It will have systems as its clients. A small team of consultants will enter the system and develop a diagnosis of its human and technical effectiveness. These data will then be fed back to representatives at all levels of the system in order to generate, at the grass-roots level, action recommendations. A steering committee composed of representatives of the client system and the organizational development will then prepare a long-range educational program designed to increase the immediate as well as the long-range effectiveness of the system.

Classes may then be held at the plant location or at a central facility, depending upon: resources needed, time available, availability of the "students" as well as the faculty. Teams and not disconnected individuals will study together for the majority of technical and management subjects. These will be actual working teams. This will pressure the faculty to develop learning that is valid for the real problems of the team.

To put this another way, education will be for organizational and system diagnosis, renewal and effectiveness. It will be held with groups, subject material and faculty that are organic to the organization's problem. One of the dangers of this education is the possibility that it will focus on the trivial, short-range problems. The quality control in this area will depend partially on the diagnostic competence of the faculty. In defining the problem they can help the organization to get to the underlying and basic causes. The students can also help by being alert to the validity of the education being offered.

Some critics wonder if teams of people working together can be pulled away from work. The answer, in my experience, is affirmative. The fear, for example, that the company will be in trouble if the top team leaves for a week, has been quietly exploded in several cases. The explosions have been quiet lest, as one president put it, "it be learned how well things ran while the top management was away."

Tuning the Motor

This new type of education is central to the work of the system. Thus, the team is not being pulled away from work. Indeed, in many cases it is pulled away *in order to work*. Systems, like cars, need to have their organizational hoods opened and the motor checked and tuned.

Finally the concern of being away physically from the location should be matched with the concern about the number of hours being consumed needlessly while at work. In studies, I have found that as many as half the meetings and as much as three quarters of the time spent at meetings are not productive and worse than unnecessary.

At one time, not too long ago, it appeared that the advocates of "human relations" theories of organization clearly represented the forces of light, in contrast to the devotees of the older classical theories of organization. Now researchers are not so sure, for studies have shown that the problem of organization is much more complicated than was originally supposed, and that there are no simple solutions that are applicable to every company, or even to all sections of the same company. This article outlines and appraises the changing theories of organization as they have developed over the past few years, and points out that some gains have been achieved, even though no hard-and-fast principles have been developed. Charles Perrow is a sociologist, now with the State University of New York at Stony Brook, and the author of a number of books and articles. The article below is an adaptation of the discussion in his book *Complex Organizations: A Critical Essay* (published by Scott, Foresman & Co., Glenville, Ill.). Notes have been omitted here.

The Short and Glorious History of Organizational Theory

Charles Perrow

From the beginning, the forces of light and the forces of darkness have polarized the field of organizational analysis, and the struggle has been protracted and inconclusive. The forces of darkness have been represented by the mechanical school of organizational theory—those who treat the organization as a machine. This school characterizes organizations in terms of such things as:

- Centralized authority
- Clear lines of authority
- Specialization and expertise
- Marked division of labor
- Rules and regulations
- Clear separation of staff and line

The forces of light, which by mid-twentieth century came to be characterized as the human relations school, emphasize people rather than machines, accommodations rather than machine-like precision, and draw inspiration from biological systems rather than engineering systems. This school has emphasized such things as:

- Delegation of authority
- Employee autonomy
- Trust and openness
- Concerns with the "whole person"
- Interpersonal dynamics

Scientific Management

The forces of darkness formulated their position first, starting in the early part of this century. They have been characterized as the scientific management or classical management school. This school started by parading simple-minded injunctions to plan ahead, keep records, write down policies, specialize, be decisive, and keep your span of control to about six people. These injunctions were needed as firms grew in size and complexity, since there were few models around beyond the railroads, the military, and the Catholic Church. And their injunctions worked. Executives began to delegate, reduce their span of control, keep records, and specialize. Planning ahead still is difficult, it seems, and the modern equivalent is Management by Objectives.

But many things intruded to make these simple-minded injunctions less relevant:

1 Labor became a more critical factor in the firm. As the technology increased in sophistication it took longer to train people, and more varied and specialized skills were needed. Thus, labor turnover cost more and recruitment became more selective. As a consequence, labor's power increased. Unions and strikes appeared. Management adjusted by beginning to speak of a cooperative system of capital, management, and labor. The machine model began to lose its relevancy.

2 The increasing complexity of markets, variability of products, increasing number of branch plants, and changes in technology all required more adaptive organization. The scientific management school was ill-equipped to deal with rapid change. It had presumed that once the proper structure was achieved the firm could run forever without much tampering. By the late 1930s, people began writing about adaptation and change in industry from an organizational point of view and had to abandon some of the principles of scientific management.

3 Political, social, and cultural changes meant new expectations regarding the proper way to treat people. The dark, satanic mills needed at the least a white-washing. Child labor and the brutality of supervision in many enterprises became no longer permissible. Even managers could not be expected to accept the authoritarian patterns of leadership that prevailed in the small firm run by the founding father.

4 As mergers and growth proceeded apace and the firm could no longer be viewed as the shadow of one man (the founding entrepreneur), a search for methods of select-

Reprinted by permission of the publisher from *Organizational Dynamics*, Summer, 1973, pp. 3–14.

ing good leadership became a preoccupation. A good, clear, mechanical structure would no longer suffice. Instead, firms had to search for the qualities of leadership that could fill the large footsteps of the entrepreneur. The search for leadership traits implied that leaders were made, not just born, that the matter was complex, and that several skills were involved.

Enter Human Relations

From the beginning, individual voices were raised against the implications of the scientific management school. But no effective counterforce developed until 1938, when a business executive with academic talents named Chester Barnard proposed the first new theory of organizations: Organizations are cooperative systems, not the products of mechanical engineering. He stressed natural groups within the organization, upward communication, authority from below rather than from above, and leaders who functioned as a cohesive force.

The year following the publication of his *Functions of the Executive* (1938) saw the publication of F. J. Roethlisberger and William Dickson's *Management and the Worker*, reporting on the first large-scale empirical investigation of productivity and social relations. The research highlighted the role of informal groups, work restriction norms, the value of decent, humane leadership, and the role of psychological manipulation of employees through the counseling system. World War II intervened, but after the war the human relations movement, building on the insights of Barnard and the Hawthorne studies, came into its own.

The first step was a search for the traits of good leadership. It went on furiously at university centers but at first failed to produce more than a list of Boy Scout maxims: A good leader was kind, courteous, loyal, courageous, etc. We suspected as much. However, the studies did turn up a distinction between "consideration," or employee-centered aspects of leadership, and job-centered, technical aspects labled "initiating structure." Both were important, but the former received most of the attention and the latter went undeveloped. The former led directly to an examination of group processes, an investigation that has culminated in T-group programs and is moving forward still with encounter groups. Meanwhile, in England, the Tavistock Institute sensed the importance of the influence of the kind of task a group had to perform on the social relations within the group. The first important study, conducted among coal miners, showed that job simplification and specialization did not work under conditions of uncertainty and nonroutine tasks.

As this work flourished and spread, more adventurous theorists began to extend it beyond work groups to organizations as a whole. We now knew that there were a number of things that were bad for the morale and loyalty of groups—routine tasks, submission to authority, specialization of task, segregation of task sequence, ignorance of the goals of the firm, centralized decision making, and so on. If these were bad for groups, they were likely to be bad for groups of groups—i.e., for organizations. So people like Warren Bennis began talking about innovative, rapidly changing organizations that were made up of temporary groups, temporary authority systems, temporary leadership and role assignments, and democratic access to the goals of the firm. If rapidly changing technologies and unstable, turbulent environments were to characterize industry, then the structure of firms should be temporary and decentralized. The forces of light, of freedom, autonomy, change, humanity, creativity, and democracy were winning.

Bureaucracy's Comeback

Meanwhile, in another part of the management forest, the mechanistic school was gathering its forces and preparing to outflank the forces of light. First came the numbers men—the linear programmers, the budget experts, and the financial analysts—with their PERT systems and cost-benefit analyses. From another world, unburdened by most of the scientific management ideology and untouched by the human relations school, they began to parcel things out and give some meaning to those truisms, "plan ahead" and "keep records." Armed with emerging systems concepts, they carried the "mechanistic" analogy to its fullest—and it was very productive. Their work still goes on, largely untroubled by organizational theory; the theory, it seems clear, will have to adjust to them, rather than the other way around.

Then the works of Max Weber began to find their way into social science thought. At first, with his celebration of the efficiency of bureaucracy, he was received with only reluctant respect, and even with hostility. All writers were against bureaucracy. But it turned out, surprisingly, that managers were not. When asked, they acknowledged that they preferred clear lines of communication, clear specifications of authority and responsibility, and clear knowledge of whom they were responsible to. Gradually, studies began to show that bureaucratic organizations could change faster than nonbureaucratic ones, and that morale could be higher where there was clear evidence of bureaucracy.

What was this thing, then? Weber had showed us, for example, that bureaucracy was the most effective way of ridding organizations of favoritism, arbitrary authority, discrimination, payola and kick-backs, and yes, even incompetence. His model stressed expertise, and the favorite or the boss' nephew or the guy who burned up resources to make his performance look good was *not* the one with expertise. Rules could be changed; they could be dropped in exceptional circumstances; job security promoted more innovation. The sins of bureaucracy began to look like the sins of failing to follow its principles.

Enter Power, Conflict, and Decisions

But another discipline began to intrude upon the confident work and increasingly elaborate models of the human relations theorists (largely social psychologists) and the uneasy toying with bureaucracy of the "structionalists" (largely sociologists). Both tended to study economic organizations. A few, like Philip Selznick, were noting conflict and differences in goals, but most ignored conflict or treated it as a pathological manifestation of breakdowns in communication or the ego trips of unreconstructed managers.

But in the world of political parties, pressure groups, and legislative bodies, conflict was not only rampant, but to be expected—it was even functional. This was the domain of the political scientists. They kept talking about power, making it a legitimate concern for analysis. There was an open acknowledgement of "manipulation." These were political scientists who were "behaviorally" inclined—studying and recording behavior rather than constitutions and formal systems of government—and they came to a much more complex view of organized activity. It spilled over into the area of economic organizations, with the help of some economists like R. A. Gordon and some sociologists who were studying conflicting goals of treatment and custody in prisons and mental hospitals.

The presence of legitimately conflicting goals and techniques of preserving and using power did not, of course, sit well with a cooperative systems view of organizations. But it also puzzled the bureaucratic school (and what was left of the old scientific management school), for the impressive Weberian principles were designed to settle questions of power through organizational design and to keep conflict out through reliance on rational-legal authority and systems of careers, expertise, and hierarchy. But power was being overtly contested and exercised in covert ways, and conflict was bursting out all over, and even being creative.

Gradually, in the second half of the 1950s, and in the next decade, the political science view infiltrated both schools. Conflict could be healthy, even in a cooperative system, said the human relationists; it was the mode of resolution that counted, rather than prevention. Power became reconceptualized as "influence," and the distribution was less important, said Arnold Tannenbaum, than the total amount. For the bureaucratic school—never a clearly defined group of people, and largely without any clear ideology—it was easier to just absorb the new data and theories as something else to be thrown into the pot. That is to say, they floundered, writing books that went from topic to topic, without a clear view of organizations, or better yet, producing "readers" and leaving students to sort it all out.

Buried in the political science viewpoint was a sleeper that only gradually began to undermine the dominant views. This was the idea, largely found in the work of Herbert Simon and James March, that because man was so limited—in intelligence, reasoning powers, information at his disposal, time available, and means of ordering his preferences clearly—he generally seized on the first acceptable alternative when deciding, rather than looking for the best; that he rarely changed things unless they really got bad, and even then he continued to try what had worked before; that he limited his search for solutions to well-worn paths and traditional sources of information and established ideas; that he was wont to remain preoccupied with routine, thus preventing innovation. They called these characteristics "cognitive limits on rationality" and spoke of "satisficing" rather than maximizing or optimizing. This is now called the "decision making" school, and is concerned with the basic question of how people make decisions.

This view had some rather unusual implications. It suggested that if managers were so limited, then they could be easily controlled. What was necessary was not to give direct orders (on the assumption that subordinates were idiots without expertise) or to leave them to their own devices (on the assumption that they were supermen who would somehow know what was best for the organization, how to coordinate with all the other supermen, how to anticipate market changes, etc.). It was necessary to control only the *premises* of their decisions. Left to themselves, with those premises set, they could be predicted to rely on precedent, keep things stable and smooth, and respond to signals that reinforce the behavior desired of them.

To control the premises of decision making, March and Simon outline a variety of devices. For example, organizations develop vocabularies, and this means that certain kinds of information are highlighted, and others are screened out—just as Eskimos (and skiers) distinguish many varieties of snow, while Londoners see only one. This is a form of attention directing. Another is the reward system. Change the bonus for salesmen and you can shift them from volume selling to steady-account selling, or to selling quality products or new products. If you want to channel good people into a different function (because, for example, sales should no longer be the critical function as the market changes, but engineering applications should), you may have to promote mediocre people in the unrewarded function in order to signal to the good people in the rewarded one that the game has changed. You cannot expect most people to make such decision on their own because of the cognitive limits on their rationality, nor will you succeed by giving direct orders, because you yourself probably do not know whom to order where. You presume that once the signals are clear and the new sets of alternatives are manifest, they have enough ability to make the decision but you have had to change the premises for their decisions about their career lines.

It would take too long to go through the dozen or so devices, covering a range of decision areas, but I think the message is clear.

It was becoming clear to the human relations school, and to the bureaucratic school. The human relationists had begun to speak of changing stimuli rather than changing personality. They had begun to see that the rewards that can change behavior can well be prestige, money, comfort, etc., rather than trust, openness, self-insight, and so on. The alternative to supportive relations need not be punishment, since behavior can best be changed by rewarding approved behavior rather than by punishing disapproved behavior. They were finding that although leadership may be centralized, it can function best through indirect and unobtrusive means such as changing the premises on which decisions are made, thus giving the impression that the subordinate is actually making a decision when he has only been switched to a different set of alternatives. The implications of this work were also beginning to filter into the human relations school through an emphasis on behavioral psychology (the modern version of the much maligned stimulus-response school) that was supplanting personality theory (Freudian in its roots, and drawing heavily, in the human relations school, on Maslow).

For the bureaucratic school, this new line of thought reduced the heavy weight placed upon the bony structure of bureaucracy by highlighting the muscle and flesh that make these bones move. A single chain of command, precise division of labor, and clear lines of communication are simply not enough in themselves. Control can be achieved by using alternative communication channels, depending on the situation; by increasing or decreasing the static or "noise" in the system; by creating organizational myths and organizational vocabularies that allow only selective bits of information to enter the system; and through monitoring performance through indirect means rather than direct surveillance. Weber was all right for a starter, but organizations had changed vastly, and the leaders needed many more means of control and more subtle means of manipulation than they did at the turn of the century.

The Technological Qualification

By now the forces of darkness and forces of light had moved respectively from midnight and noon to about 4 A.M. and 8 A.M. But any convergence or resolution would have to be on yet new terms, for soon after the political science tradition had begun to infiltrate the established schools, another blow struck both of the major positions. Working quite independently of the Tavistock Group, with its emphasis on sociotechnical systems, and before the work of Burns and Stalker on mechanistic and organic firms, Joan Woodward was trying to see whether the classical scientific principles of organization made any sense in her survey of 100 firms in South Essex. She tripped and stumbled over a piece of gold in the process. She picked up the gold, labeled it "technology," and made sense out of her otherwise hopeless data. Job-shop firms, mass-production firms, and continuous-process firms all had quite different structures because the type of tasks, or the "technology," was different. Somewhat later, researchers in America were coming to very similar conclusions. Bureaucracy appeared to be the best form of organization for routine operations; temporary work groups, decentralization, and emphasis on interpersonal processes appeared to work best for nonroutine operations. A raft of studies appeared and are still appearing, all trying to show how the nature of the task affects the structure of the organization.

This severely complicated things for the human relations school, since it suggested that openness and trust, while good things in themselves, did not have much impact, or perhaps were not even possible in some kinds of work situations. What might work for nonroutine, high-status, interesting, and challenging jobs performed by highly educated people might not be relevant or even beneficial for the vast majority of jobs and people.

It also forced the upholders of the revised bureaucratic theory to qualify their recommendations, since research and development units should obviously be run differently from mass-production units, and the difference between both of these and highly programmed and highly sophisticated continuous-process firms was obscure in terms of bureaucratic theory. But the bureaucratic school perhaps came out on top, because the forces of evil—authority, structure, division of labor, etc.—no longer looked evil, even if they were not applicable to a minority of industrial units.

The emphasis on technology raised other questions, however. A can company might be quite routine, and a plastics division nonroutine, but there were both routine and nonroutine units within each. How should they be integrated if the prescription were followed that, say, production should be bureaucratized and R&D not? James Thompson began spelling out different forms of interdependence among units in organizations, and Paul Lawrence and Jay Lorsch looked closely at the nature of integrating mechanisms. Lawrence and Lorsch found that firms performed best when the differences between units were *maximized* (in contrast to both the human relations and the bureaucratic school), as long as the integrating mechanisms stood half-way between the two—being neither strongly bureaucratic nor nonroutine. They also noted that attempts at participative management in routine situations were counterproductive, that the environments of some kinds of organizations were far from turbulent and customers did not want innovations and changes, that cost reduction, price, and efficiency were trivial considerations in some firms, and so on. The technological insight was demolishing our comfortable truths right and left. They were also being questioned from another quarter.

Goals, Environments, and Systems

The final seam was being mined by the sociologists while all this went on. This was the concern with organizational goals and the environment.

Borrowing from the political scientists to some extent, but pushing ahead on their own, this "institutional school" came to see that goals were not fixed; conflicting goals could be pursued simultaneously, if there were enough slack resources, or sequentially (growth for the next four years, then cost-cutting and profit-taking for the next four); that goals were up for grabs in organizations, and units fought over them. Goals were, of course, not what they seemed to be, the important ones were quite unofficial; history played a big role; and assuming profit as the pre-eminent goal explained almost nothing about a firm's behavior.

They also did case studies that linked the organization to the web of influence of the environment; that showed how unique organizations were in many respects (so that, once again, there was no one best way to do things for all organizations); how organizations were embedded in their own history, making change difficult. Most striking of all, perhaps, the case studies revealed that the stated goals usually were not the real ones; the official leaders usually were not the powerful ones; claims of effectiveness and efficiency were deceptive or even untrue; the public interest was not being served; political influences were pervasive; favoritism, discrimination, and sheer corruption were commonplace. The accumulation of these studies presented quite a pill for either the forces of light or darkness to swallow, since it was hard to see how training sessions or interpersonal skills were relevant to these problems, and it was also clear that the vaunted efficiency of bureaucracy was hardly in evidence. What could they make of this wad of case studies?

We are still sorting it out. In one sense, the Weberian model is upheld because organizations are not, *by nature*, cooperative systems; top managers must exercise a great deal of effort to control them. But if organizations are tools in the hands of leaders, they may be very recalcitrant ones. Like the broom in the story of the sorcerer's apprentice, they occasionally get out of hand. If conflicting goals, bargaining, and unofficial leadership exist, where is the structure of Weberian bones and Simonian muscle? To what extent are organizations tools, and to what extent are they products of the varied interests and group strivings of their members? Does it vary by organization, in terms of some typological alchemy we have not discovered? We don't know. But at any rate, the bureaucratic model suffers again; it simply has not reckoned on the role of the environment. There are enormous sources of variations that the neat, though by now quite complex, neo-Weberian model could not account for.

The human relations model has also been badly shaken by the findings of the institutional school, for it was wont to assume that goals were given and unproblematical, and that anything that promoted harmony and efficiency for an organization also was good for society. Human relationists assumed that the problems created by organizations were largely limited to the psychological consequences of poor interpersonal relations within them, rather than their impact on the environment. Could the organization really promote the psychological health of its members when by necessity it had to define psychological health in terms of the goals of the organization itself? The neo-Weberian model at least called manipulation "manipulation" and was skeptical of claims about autonomy and self-realization.

But on one thing all the varied schools of organizational analysis now seemed to be agreed: organizations are systems—indeed, they are open systems. As the growth of the field has forced ever more variables into our consciousness, flat claims of predictive power are beginning to decrease and research has become bewilderingly complex.

The systems view is intuitively simple. Everything is related to everything else, though in uneven degrees of tension and reciprocity. Every unit, organization, department, or work group takes in resources, transforms them, and sends them out, and thus interacts with the larger system. The psychological, sociological, and cultural aspects of units interact. The systems view was explicit in the institutional work, since they tried to study whole organizations; it became explicit in the human relations school, because they were so concerned with the interactions of people. The political science and technology viewpoints also had to come to this realization, since they dealt with parts affecting each other (sales affecting production; technology affecting structure).

But as intuitively simple as it is, the systems view has been difficult to put into practical use. We still find ourselves ignoring the tenets of the open systems view, possibly because of the cognitive limits on our rationality. General systems theory itself has not lived up to its heady predictions; it remains rather nebulous. But at least there is a model for calling us to account and for stretching our minds, our research tools, and our troubled nostrums.

Some Conclusions

Where does all this leave us? We might summarize the prescriptions and proscriptions for management very roughly as follows:

1 A great deal of the "variance" in a firm's behavior depends on the environment. We have become more realistic about the limited range of change that can be induced through internal efforts. The goals of organizations, including those of profit and efficiency, vary greatly among industries and vary systematically by industries. This suggests that the impact of better management by itself will be limited, since so much will depend on market forces, competition, legislation, nature of the work force, available technologies and innovations, and so on. Another source of variation is, obviously, the history of the firm and its industry and its traditions.

2 A fair amount of variation in both firms and industries is due to the type of work done in the organization—the technology. We are now fairly confident in recommending that if work is predictable and routine, the necessary arrangement for getting the work done can be highly structured, and one can use a good deal of bureaucratic theory in accomplishing this. If it is not predictable, if it is nonroutine and there is a good deal of uncertainty as to how to do a job, then one had better utilize the theories that emphasize autonomy, temporary groups, multiple lines of authority and communications, and so on. We also know that this distinction is important when organizing different parts of an organization.

We are also getting a grasp on the question of what is the most critical function in different types of organizations. For some organizations it is production; for others, marketing; for still others, development. Furthermore, firms go through phases whereby the initial development of a market or a product or manufacturing process or accounting scheme may require a non-bureaucratic structure, but once it comes on stream, the structure should change to reflect the changed character of the work.

3 In keeping with this, management should be advised that the attempt to produce change in an organization through managerial grids, sensitivity training, and even job enrichment and job enlargement is likely to be fairly ineffective for all but a few organizations. The critical reviews of research in all these fields show that there is no scientific evidence to support the claims of the proponents of these various methods; that research has told us a great deal about social psychology, but little about how to apply the highly complex findings to actual situations. The key word is *selectivity*: We have no broad-spectrum antibiotics for interpersonal relations. Of course, managers should be sensitive, decent, kind, courteous, and courageous, but we have known that for some time now, and beyond a minimal threshold level, the payoff is hard to measure. The various attempts to make work and interpersonal relations more humane and stimulating should be applauded, but we should not confuse this with solving problems of structure, or as the equivalent of decentralization or participatory democracy.

4 The burning cry in all organizations is for "good leadership," but we have learned that beyond a threshold level of adequacy it is extremely difficult to know what good leadership is. The hundreds of scientific studies of this phenomenon come to one general conclusion: Leadership is highly variable or "contingent" upon a large variety of important variables such as nature of task, size of the group, length of time the group has existed, type of personnel within the group and their relationships with each other, and amount of pressure the group is under. It does not seem likely that we'll be able to devise a way to select the best leader for a particular situation. Even if we could, that situation would probably change in a short time and

thus would require a somewhat different type of leader.

Furthermore, we are beginning to realize that leadership involves more than smoothing the paths of human interaction. What has rarely been studied in this area is the wisdom or even the technical adequacy of a leader's decision. A leader does more than lead people; he also makes decisions about the allocation of resources, type of technology to be used, the nature of the market, and so on. This aspect of leadership remains very obscure, but it is obviously crucial.

5 If we cannot solve our problems through good human relations or through good leadership, what are we then left with? The literature suggests that changing the structures of organizations might be the most effective and certainly the quickest and cheapest method. However, we are now sophisticated enough to know that changing the formal structure by itself is not likely to produce the desired changes. In addition, one must be aware of a large range of subtle, unobtrusive, and even covert processes and change devices that exist. If inspection procedures are not working, we are now unlikely to rush in with sensitivity training, nor would we send down authoritative communications telling people to do a better job. We are more likely to find out where the authority really lies, whether the degree of specialization is adequate, what the rules and regulations are, and so on, but even this very likely will not be enough.

According to the neo-Weberian bureaucratic model, as it has been influenced by work on decision making and behavioral psychology, we should find out how to manipulate the reward structure, change the premises of the decision-makers through finer controls on the information received and the expectations generated, search for interdepartmental conflicts that prevent better inspection procedures from being followed, and after manipulating these variables, sit back and wait for two or three months for them to take hold. This is complicated and hardly as dramatic as many of the solutions currently being peddled, but I think the weight of organizational theory is in its favor.

We have probably learned more, over several decades of research and theory, about the things that do *not* work (even though some of them obviously *should* have worked), than we have about things that do work. On balance, this is an important gain and should not discourage us. Organizations are extremely complicated. To have as much knowledge as we do have in a fledgling discipline that has had to borrow from the diverse tools and concepts of psychology, sociology, economics, engineering, biology, history, and even anthropology is not really so bad.

9 The Development of Staff

Line executives are those in charge of functions that contribute directly to the main objectives of the business; staff executives are those who provide counsel and special services to the line. For reasons that are outlined in the first article in this chapter, the trend in recent years has been to add more and more specialized staff departments.

There are those who believe that the distinction between line and staff is obsolete and should be abolished. Few, if any, large companies have gone along with this viewpoint to date, however, even though conflicts between line and staff executives have long constituted a problem for higher management. Some of the reasons why these conflicts arise are explained in two articles in this chapter.

Then, since staff functions contribute only indirectly to the success of the business, it is often hard for top managers to gauge their value or for the staff men themselves to prove the importance of their work. The last article in this chapter suggests a method by which the performance of the staff may be appraised.

The book from which this article is taken was based in part on an in-depth study of the organization practices in 166 large and medium-sized companies. This study revealed that staff departments are increasing both in size and in number in most companies. Also, about two-thirds of the group studied believed that the powers, or at least the influence, of the staff groups was increasing. In contrast, only four of the hundred large companies and four of the sixty-six medium-sized companies believed that staffs were becoming more subordinate to the line.

The Growth of Specialized Staff

Ernest Dale

In general, the larger the company, the more numerous the specialized staff groups are likely to be. In a small company, there may be no staff people at all apart from personal staff represented by the owner-manager's private secretary. This does not mean that all the staff functions found in the larger company are not performed in the small company; it means merely that they are considered part of the line jobs. Thus the owner-manager may plan production himself, interview all candidates for positions, handle the purchasing, and so on. And in the case of functions that require special training—accounting, for example—he may purchase the services of outside experts.

Once the company starts growing, however, it will probably acquire an accountant of its own because it will have enough work to keep him busy full time; or, if it does not, it will at least need a small office force and may find it economical to appoint an office manager who is also an accountant.

Other staff functions may be delegated to line department heads. Thus the production manager may purchase the production materials, plan and control the production, and select his own subordinates. The sales manager may select and train the salesmen.

But, as soon as the company's employees begin to number in the hundreds, it may become both necessary and economical to segregate many of the staff functions from the line jobs. Thus the company may acquire a purchasing agent, a personnel man, a production planner, and so on. In hiring specialists of this type, the company may be conscious also of a need for better and more detailed work in many of the specialized areas. A busy sales manager, for example, can do little market research; probably the best he can do is discuss conditions with his salesmen and with some of the customers and perhaps read up on conditions in the trade press. However, with the help of a special market researcher, he can get much more detailed information on markets, consumer preferences, and so on.

At first, a new staff department may consist of one man and a secretary. But, as the company grows, the staff departments tend to become very large and to be split into subdepartments, each under the supervision of a manager. For example, in a large company, the accounting department may include sections for each of these: budgeting, taxes, cost accounting, credit management, internal auditing, and general accounting. Each of these is a specialty in itself and will often be better performed if it becomes the responsibility of a specialist in that one phase of the work.

In addition to the need for more staff functions that arise merely because of company growth, there are developments in the outside world that increase the need for new and different specialties. The scientific management movement, with its emphasis on the possibility of great increases in productivity through systematic study of methods and time study, gave rise to industrial engineering. Widespread unionization has made collective bargaining a specialized field; advances in technology have resulted in quicker product obsolescence and the need for product research.

Rapid technological developments are also responsible for the elevation of such functions as "reliability" to full departmental status in some companies. In a company that is producing, say, single parts or ordinary machines, even fairly complex ones, ordinary quality control procedures may suffice. But in a rocket system there are tens of thousands of interrelated parts,

From *Organization* (American Management Association, New York, 1967), pp. 62–64.

and if there are 50,000 of them, each with a reliability of more than 99 per cent, there may be only one chance in three that the rocket will ever get off the ground.[1]

Again, the growth of worldwide markets has induced many companies that formerly confined their efforts to domestic sales to "go international" and has spurred others that have always exported their products to manufacture abroad or license foreign manufacturers to produce their products. Hence some of the companies covered in the AMA survey had created such staff departments as "international product planning" and "licensing."

The close interest government has displayed in the conduct of companies in recent years also has given rise to new staff departments—called by such names as "civic and governmental relations" and "public affairs." The heads of such departments may have vice-presidential status, and their responsibilities are much broader than those of the ordinary public relations department. Thus in one such company the vice president for public affairs is in charge of both governmental contacts—as conducted by the Washington representative—and a public relations department.

Other staff departments have been organized as management has come to take a longer-range view of its responsibilities; such groups as long-range planning and business or corporate development exist in quite a few of the companies covered in the AMA survey.

[1]J. C. Jessen, "Plant Engineering Responsibility in Plant Start-Up," *Techniques of Plant Maintenance and Engineering*, Clapp & Poliak, Inc., New York, 1961, p. 268.

One of the best analyses of the way in which differences between line and staff executives arise was written by Prof. Melville Dalton of the University of California. This was based on first-hand investigations undertaken some years ago in a number of companies. His is a very perceptive and illuminating insight into the nature of the conflicts and the methods employed by staff specialists to achieve their ends in situations in which the line resents their activities.

Staff-Line Conflicts

Melville Dalton

[The] theoretically satisfying industrial structure of speciallzed experts advising busy administrators has in a number of significant cases failed to function as expected. The assumptions that (a) the staff specialists would be reasonably content to function without a measure of formal authority over production, and that (b) their suggestions regarding improvement of processes and techniques for control over personnel and production would be welcomed by line officers, require closer examination. In practice there is often much conflict between industrial staff and line organizations and in varying degrees the members of these organizations oppose each other.

The aim of this paper is, therefore, to present and analyze data dealing with staff-line tensions.

Data were drawn from three industrial plants[1] in which the writer had been either a participating member of one or both of the groups or was intimate with reliable informants among the officers who were.

Approached sociologically, relations among members of management in the plants could be viewed as a general conflict system caused and perpetuated chiefly by (1) power struggles stemming in the main from competition among departments to maintain low operating costs; (2) drives by numerous members to increase their status in the hierarchy; (3) conflict betwen union

[1]These plants were in related industires and ranged in size from 4,500 to 20,000 employees, with the managerial groups numbering from 200 to nearly 1,000. Details concerning the plants and their location are confidential.

From "Conflicts between Staff and Line Managerial Officers," *American Sociological Review*, Vol. XV, No. 3, June, 1950, pp. 342–350.

and management; and (4) the staff-line friction which is the subject of this paper. This milieu of tensions was not only unaccounted for by the blueprint organizations of the plants, but was often contradictory to, and even destructive of, the organizations' formal aims. All members of management, especially in the middle and lower ranks,[2] were caught up in this conflict system. Even though they might wish to escape, the obligation of at least appearing to carry out formal functions compelled individuals to take sides in order to protect themselves against the aggressions of others. And the intensity of the conflict was aggravated by the fact that it was formally unacceptable and had to be hidden.

Mobile Behavior of Staff Personnel

As a group, staff personnel in the three plants were markedly ambitious, restless, and individualistic. There was much concern to win rapid promotion, to make the "right impressions," and to receive individual recognition. Data showed that the desire among staff members for personal distinctions often over-rode their sentiments of group consciousness and caused intra-staff tensions.

The relatively high turnover of staff personnel quite possibly reflected the dissatisfactions and frustrations of members over inability to achieve the distinction and status they hoped for. Several factors appeared to be of importance in this restlessness of staff personnel. Among these were age and social differences between line and staff officers, structural differences in the hierarchy of the two groups, and the staff group's lack of authority over production.

The staff officers were significantly younger than line officers. This would account to some extent for their restlessness. Being presumably less well-established in life while having greater expectations and more energy as well as more life ahead in which to make new starts elsewhere if necessary, the staff groups were understandably more dynamic and driving.

Age-conflict was also significant in staff-line antagonisms. The older line officers disliked receiving what they regarded as instruction from men so much younger than themselves, and staff personnel clearly were conscious of this attitude.

Explaining the relatively few cases in which his staff had succeeded in "selling ideas" to the line, an assistant staff head remarked: "We're always in hot water with these old guys on the line. You can't tell them a damn thing. They're bull-headed as hell! Most of the time we offer a suggestion it's either laughed at or not considered at all. The same idea in the mouth of some old codger on the line'd get a round of applause. They treat us like kids."

The unsophisticated staff officer's initial contacts with the shifting, covert, expedient arrangements between members of staff and line usually gave him a severe shock. He had entered industry prepared to engage in logical, well-formulated relations with members of the managerial hierarchy, and to carry out precise, methodical functions for which his training had equipped him. Now he learned that (1) his freedom to function was snared in a web of informal commitments; (2) his academic specialty (on which he leaned for support in his new position) was often not relevant for carrying out his formal assignments; and that (3) the important thing to do was to learn who the informally powerful line officers were and what ideas they would welcome which at the same time would be acceptable to his superiors.

Usually the staff officer's reaction to these conditions is to look elsewhere for a job or make an accommodation in the direction of protecting himself and finding a niche where he can make his existence in the plant tolerable and safe. If he chooses the latter course, he is likely to be less concerned with creative effort for his employer than with attempts to develop reliable social relations that will aid his personal advancement.

The formal structure, or hierarchy of statuses, of the two larger plants from which data were drawn, offered a frustration to the ambitious staff officer. That is, in these plants the strata, or levels of authority, in the staff organizations ranged from three to five as against from five to

[2]From bottom to top, the line hierarchy consisted of the following strata of officers: (1) first-line foremen, who were directly in charge of production workmen; (2) general foremen; (3) departmental superintendents; (4) divisional superintendents; (5) assistant plant manager; (6) plant manager.

In the staff organizations the order from bottom to top was: (1) supervisor (equivalent to the first-line foreman); (2) general supervisor (equivalent to the general foreman); (3) staff head—sometimes "superintendent" (equivalent to departmental superintendent in the line organization). Occasionally there were strata of assistant supervisors and assistant staff heads.

ten in the line organization. Consequently there were fewer possible positions for exercise of authority into which staff personnel could move. Unable to move vertically to the degree possible in the line organization, the ambitious staff officer could enlarge his area of authority in a given position only by lateral expansion—by increasing his personnel. Whether or not aspiring staff incumbents revolted against the relatively low hierarchy through which they could move, the fact remains that (1) they appeared eager to increase the number of personnel under their authority, (2) the personnel of staff groups *did* increase disproportionately to those of the line, and (3) there was a trend of personnel movement from staff to line, rather than the reverse, presumably (reflecting the drive and ambition of staff members) because there were more positions of authority, as well as more authority to be exercised, more prestige, and usually more income in the line.

Behavior in the plants indicated that line and staff personnel belonged to different social status groups and that line and staff antipathies were at least in part related to these social distinctions. For example, with respect to the item of formal education, the staff group stood on a higher level than members of the line.

Staff members were also much concerned about their dress, a daily shave, and a weekly hair-cut. On the other hand line officers, especially below the level of departmental superintendent, were relatively indifferent to such matters. Usually they were in such intimate contact with production processes that dirt and grime prevented the concern with meticulous dress shown by staff members. The latter also used better English in speaking and in writing reports, and were more suave and poised in social intercourse. These factors, and the recreational preferences of staff officers for night clubs and "hot parties," assisted in raising a barrier between them and most line officers.

The social antipathies of the two groups and the status concern of staff officers were indicated by the behavior of each toward the established practice of dining together in the cafeterias reserved for management in the two larger plants. Theoretically, all managerial officers upward from the level of general foremen in the line, and general supervisors in the staff, were eligible to eat in these cafeterias. However, in practice the mere taking of one of these offices did not automatically assure the incumbent the privilege of eating in the cafeteria. One had first to be invited to "join the association." Staff officers were very eager to "get in" and did considerable fantasying on the impressions, with respect to dress and behavior, that were believed essential for an invitation. One such staff officer, a cost supervisor, dropped the following remarks:

> There seems to be a committee that passes on you. I've had my application in for three years, but no soap. Harry [his superior] had his in for over three years before he made it. You have to have something, because if a man who's in moves up to another position the man who replaces him doesn't get it because of the position—and he might not get it at all. I think I'm about due.

Many line officers who were officially members of the association avoided the cafeteria, however, and had to be *ordered* by the assistant plant manager to attend. One of these officers made the following statement, which expressed more pointedly the many similar spontaneous utterances of resentment and dislike made by other line officers:

> There's a lot of good discussion in the cafeteria. I'd like to get in on more of it but I don't like to go there—sometimes I have to go. Most of the white collar people [staff officers] that eat there are stuck-up. I've been introduced three times to Svendsen [engineer], yet when I meet him he pretends to not even know me. When he meets me on the street he always manages to be looking someplace else. G—d— such people as that! They don't go in the cafeteria to eat and relax while they talk over their problems. They go in there to look around and see how somebody is dressed or to talk over the hot party they had last night. Well, that kind of damn stuff don't go with me. I haven't any time to put on airs and make out I'm something that I'm not.

Staff Need to Prove Its Worth

To the thinking of many line officers, the staff functioned as an agent on trial rather than as a managerial division that might be of equal importance with the line organization in achieving production goals. Staff members were very conscious of this sentiment toward them and of their need to prove themselves. They strained to develop new techniques and to get them accepted by the line. But in doing this they frequently became impatient, and gave already suspicious line officers the impression of reaching for authority over production.

Since the line officer regards his authority over production as something sacred, and resents the implication that after many years in the line he needs the guidance of a newcomer who lacks such experience, an obstacle to staff-line cooperation develops the moment this sore spot is touched. On the other hand, the staff officer's ideology of his function leads him to precipitate a power struggle with the line organization. By and large he considers himself as an agent of top management. He feels bound to contribute something significant in the form of research or ideas helpful to management. By virtue of his greater education and intimacy with the latest theories of production, he regards himself as a managerial consultant and an expert, and feels that he must be, or appear to be, almost infallible once he has committed himself to top management on some point. With this orientation, he is usually disposed to approach middle and lower line with an attitude of condescension that often reveals itself in the heat of discussion. Consequently, many staff officers involve themselves in trouble and report their failures as due to "ignorance" and "bull-headedness" among these line officers.

On this point, relations between staff and line in all three of the plants were further irritated by a rift inside the line organization. First-line foremen were inclined to feel that top management had brought in the production planning, industrial relations, and industrial engineering staffs as clubs with which to control the lower line. Hence they frequently regarded the projects of staff personnel as manipulative devices, and reacted by cooperating with production workers and/or general foremen (whichever course was the more expedient) in order to defeat insistent and uncompromising members of the staff. Also, on occasion (see below), the lower line could cooperate evasively with lower staff personnel who were in trouble with staff superiors.

Line Authority over Staff Promotion

Every member of the staff knew that if he aspired to higher office he must make a record for himself, a good part of which would be a reputation among upper line officers of ability to "understand" their informal problems without being told. This knowledge worked in varying degrees to pervert the theory of staff-line relations. Ideally the two organizations cooperate to improve existing methods of output, to introduce new methods, to plan the work, and to solve problems of production and the scheduling of orders that might arise. But when the line offers resistance to the findings and recommendations of the staff, the latter is reduced to evasive practices of getting some degree of acceptance of its programs, and at the same time of convincing top management that "good relations" exist with officers down the line. This necessity becomes even more acute when the staff officer aspires to move over to the line organization, for then he must convince powerful line officers that he is worthy. He may compromise with line demands and bring charges from his staff colleagues that he is "selling out," so that after moving into the line organization he will then have to live with enemies he made in the staff. In any case, the need among staff incumbents of pleasing line officers in order to perfect their careers called for accommodation in three major areas: (1) the observance of staff rules, (2) the introduction of new techniques, and (3) the use of appropriations for staff research and experiment.

Staff personnel, particularly in the middle and lower levels, carried on expedient relations with the line that daily evaded formal rules. The usual practice was to tolerate minor breaking of staff rules by line personnel, or even to cooperate with the line in evading rules, and in exchange lay a claim on the line for cooperation on critical issues. In some cases line aid was enlisted to conceal lower staff blunders from the upper staff and the upper line.

While the staff organizations gave much time to developing new techniques, they were simultaneously thinking about how their plans would be received by the line. They knew from experience that middle and lower line officers could always give a "black eye" to staff contributions by deliberate mal-practices. Repeatedly top management had approved, and incorporated, staff proposals that had been verbally accepted down the line. Often the latter officers had privately opposed the changes, but had feared that saying so would incur the resentment of powerful superiors who could informally hurt them. Later they would seek to discredit the change by deliberate mal-practice and hope to bring a return to the former arrangement. For this reason there was a tendency for staff members to withhold improved production schemes or other plans when they knew that an attempt to introduce them might fail or even bring personal disrepute.

Line officers fear staff innovations for a number of reasons. In view of their longer experience, presumably intimate knowledge of the work, and their greater remuneration, they fear being "shown up" before their line superiors for not having thought of the refinements themselves. They fear that changes in methods may bring personnel changes which will threaten the break-up of cliques and existing informal arrangements and quite possibly reduce their area of authority. Finally, changes in techniques may expose forbidden practices and departmental inefficiency. In some cases these fears have stimulated line officers to compromise staff men to the point where the latter will agree to postpone the initiation of new practices for specific periods.

In one such case an assistant staff head agreed with a line superintendent to delay the application of a bonus plan for nearly three months so that the superintendent could live up to the expedient agreement he had made earlier with his grievance committeeman to avoid a "wildcat" strike by a group of production workmen. The lower engineers who had devised the plan were suspicious of the formal reasons given to them for withholding it, so the assistant staff head prevented them (by means of "busy work") from attending staff-line meetings lest they inadvertently reveal to top management that the plan was ready.

The third area of staff-line accommodations revolved around staff use of funds granted it by top management. Middle and lower line charged that staff research and experimentation was little more than "money wasted on blunders," and that various departments of the line could have "accomplished much more with less money." According to staff officers, those of their plans that failed usually did so because line personnel "sabotaged" them and refused to "cooperate." Specific costs of "crack-pot experimentation" in certain staff groups were pointed to by line officers. Whatever the truth of the charges and counter-charges, evidence indicated (confidants in both groups supported this) that pressures from the line organization (below the top level) forced some of the staff groups to "kick over" parts of the funds appropriated for staff use by top management. These compromises were of course hidden from top management, but the relations described were carried on to such an extent that by means of them—and line pressures for manipulation of accounts in the presumably impersonal auditing departments—certain line officers were able to show impressively low operating costs and thus win favor with top management. In their turn the staff officers involved would receive more "cooperation" from the line and/or recommendation for transfer to the line. The data indicated that in a few such cases men from accounting and auditing staffs were given general foremanships (without previous line experience) as a reward for their understanding behavior.

The author of the following article, a professor at Columbia University, is an outstanding sociologist, and hence greatly concerned with the social effects of organization. Here he points out that the proliferation of staff and the subdivisions provided by the formal organization have enabled many staff men to disregard the social consequences of the systems they promote.

The Limited Perspective of Staff Specialists

Robert K. Merton

New applications of science to production by the engineer do not merely affect the methods of production. They are inescapably social decisions affecting the routines and satisfactions of men at work on the machine and, in their larger reaches, shaping the very organization of the economy and society.

The central role of engineers as the General Staff of our productive systems only underscores the great importance of their social and political orientations; the social strata with which they identify themselves; the texture of group loyalties woven by their economic position and their occupational careers; the groups to whom they look for direction; the types of social effects of their work which they take into account—in short, only by exploring the entire range of their allegiances, perspectives, and concerns can engineers achieve that self-clarification of their social role which makes for fully responsible participation in society.

But to say that this poses sociological problems for "the" engineer is to make a reference so inclusive and vague as to mean little at all. The large and multifarious family of men called engineers have a far-flung kinship, but they also have much that marks sub-groups off, each from the others. There are military, civil, mechanical, chemical, electrical, and metallurgical engineers, and so on down through the hundreds of titles found among the members of national engineering societies. But whatever their specialty, so long as they are concerned with the design, construction, or operation of the equipments and processes of production, they are confronted with social and political implications of their position in society.

A nascent trend toward full recognition of these implications is curbed by several obstacles, chief among which, it would seem, are (1) marked specialization and division of scientific labor, (2) the applications of professional codes governing the social outlook of engineers, and (3) the incorporation of engineers into industrial bureaucracies.

Specialization

The intensified division of labor has become a splendid device for escaping social responsibilities. As professions subdivide, each group of specialists finds it increasingly possible to "pass the buck," for the social consequences of their work, on the assumption, it would seem, that in this complex transfer of responsibility there will be no hindmost for the devil to take. When appalled by resulting social dislocations, each specialist, secure in the knowledge that he has performed his task to the best of his ability, can readily disclaim responsibility for them. And, of course, no one group of specialists, the engineer any more than the others, alone initiates these consequences. Rather, within our economic and social structure each technological contribution meshes into a cumulative pattern of effects, some of which none has desired and all have brought about.

The Professional Ethic

Deriving in part from the specialization of functions, engineers, not unlike scientists, come to be indoctrinated with an ethical sense of limited responsibilities. The scientist, busy on his distinctive task of carving out new knowledge from the realm of ignorance, has long disclaimed responsibility for attending to the ways in which this knowledge was applied. (History creates its own symbols. It required an atomic bomb to shake many scientists loose from this tenaciously held doctrine.)

So, in many quarters, it has been held absurd that the engineer should be thought accountable for the social and psychological effects of technology, since it is perfectly clear that these do not come within his special province. After all, it is the engineer's "job"—note how effec-

From "The Machine, the Worker and the Engineer," *Science*, Vol. 105, Jan. 24, 1947, pp. 79–81.

tively this defines the limits of one's role and, thereby, one's social responsibility—to improve processes of production, and it is "not his concern" to consider their ramified social effects. The occupational code focuses the attention of engineers upon the first links in the chain of consequences of technological innovation and diverts their attention, both as specialists and as citizens, from succeeding links in the chain as, for example, the consequences for wage levels and employment opportunities.

Bureaucratic Status

The employment of large numbers of engineers and technologists in industrial bureaucracies further shapes their social perspectives. Knit into a bureaucratic apparatus, many engineers take their place as experts in a subaltern role with fixed spheres of competence and authority and with a severely delimited orientation toward the larger social system. In this status, they are rewarded for viewing themselves as technical auxiliaries. As such, it is not their function to consider the human and social consequences of introducing their efficient equipments and processes or to decide when and how they are to be introduced. These are matters for administrative and managerial concern.

Max Weber and Thorstein Veblen, among others, have pointed to the danger that this occupational perspective, involving the rationalized abdication of social responsibility in favor of the administrator, may be transferred by engineers beyond the immediate economic enterprise. From this transference of outlook and the resulting trained incapacity for dealing with human affairs there develops a passive and dependent role for engineers and technologists in the realm of political organization, economic institutions, and social policy. The citizen-self threatens to become submerged in the occupational-self.

As technical specialists thus attend to "their own" limited tasks, the over-all impact of technology upon the social structure becomes nobody's business through default.

Management by objectives is a system under which a manager draws up a list of his objectives for a given period of time, then discusses them with his superior. When the superior accepts them (with or without modifications), the objectives become the yardstick against which the manager's performance is measured. As this article notes, objectives for line managers are fairly easy to arrive at, but the job of the staff man is different. Yet, the author points out, staff objectives can be made definite, and progress toward them can be measured if they are set properly. Prof. McConkey is with the department of business and management at the University of Wisconsin and also heads his own consulting firm. He has held several executive positions with large companies.

Staff Objectives Are Different

Dale D. McConkey

The dramatic growth of the Management by Objectives (or Management by Results as it is often termed) system has raised the importance of objectives to a new high. It is a rare occurrence today to read through a publication on management without encountering material on some aspect of objectives or the objective setting process. The abundance of literature notwithstanding, there is a definite dearth as it concerns the differences between writing staff objectives [and writing] objectives for line managers. Most writers devote little time or attention to these distinctions and appear to proceed on the erroneous basis that if differences do exist they are so slight and exert such a small impact that they need not be considered.

Although objectives, if properly structured and applied, are as applicable and beneficial to staff managers as they are to their line associates, there are a number of basic differ-

From *Personnel Journal*, July, 1972, pp. 477–483 and 537.

ences. Certain of these differences apply during the preparatory work leading up to writing the objective, while others concern the method and form of actually structuring the objective. The final result sought for both line and staff managers must be realistic, measurable, and profit oriented objectives.

Management by Objectives provides the staff manager with the vehicle and opportunity by which to gain acceptance of his function and recognition of his contributions. MBO provides the opportunity only. The degree to which the manager capitalizes on this opportunity depends in large part on how adept he becomes in structuring measurable objectives.

Number of Objectives

It is frequently necessary for the staff man to have a greater number of objectives than the line manager. For example, one can secure a fairly accurate measurement of a sales manager (line) by reviewing his performance on two objectives: the dollar revenue which he generated and the amount which he spent to reach the revenue figure. A measure of equal validity can be realized by reviewing a production manager (line) in light of the volume he produces and the unit cost at which the volume was produced. These rather easy measurements are possible because in both instances, the primary accountability can be expressed in one or two objectives even though both of these line managers will usually have other objectives of a secondary nature.

This is decidedly not so with the average staff manager. Take, for example, the job of the typical financial manager who may well be responsible for major functions which include: accounting, budgeting, data processing, treasury and financial analysis. An evaluation of how well he accomplished his data processing objective would give no hint as to how well he accomplished his treasury objective. Similarly, outstanding achievement of the budgeting objective would provide no clue, by itself, to what results were realized on the accounting objective. The same is true for the lawyer who may be a hotshot at settling claims but who falls down on his objective of providing labor law counsel to his fellow managers.

Length of Objectives

Just as the staff manager requires a greater number of objectives to adequately measure his performance, his objectives usually require more detail and are therefore more lengthy.

The staff training and development responsibility of a personnel manager will illustrate this point. He cannot merely state in his objective that it is "to conduct a development program." This would not be specific and could not be measured. His objective likely will read along the following lines:

> My training and development objective will have been accomplished when:
>
> A 20 clerk-typist trainees have successfully completed the beginner's typing course and are qualified for assignment.
>
> B 5 computer programmers have completed Course B and have passed the practical and written examinations.
>
> C A program has been formulated and recommended in final form to the president providing for the training of a qualified replacement for each manager above Salary Level 14.

Timing

Line managers enter and participate in the annual objective setting process from the very first day; staff managers must necessarily wait until some future time. As much of the staff manager's objectives will depend upon the line objectives and what is required of the staff manager to support the line, the staff manager must receive initial guidance from the line. This does not mean the staff manager should be forced to wait until all line objectives have been discussed and given final approval. He can and should be permitted to begin his deliberations as early as possible. This can be accomplished by having all line managers give the staff managers a copy of the very first draft of their objectives and a copy of each additional draft. As objectives usually progress through two or three drafts prior to approval, this permits the staff manager to participate in the objective setting process at each step of the way. It is infinitely better than waiting until much later in the year, when all line objectives have been given final approval, and then suddenly springing the line objectives on the staff manager at the last minute when time is running out.

Up to this point the discussion has concerned those objectives which the staff manager must structure to support line objectives. There is another broad and important subject area for staff objectives in which the staff manager can clearly take the initiative without waiting for any cue from the line. This category includes those objectives which the staff manager should structure to improve his effectiveness within his own department—objectives which have little, if anything, to do with line operations in terms of the need for coordination. Examples of this type of objective are the treasurer who recommends an objective to increase the yield from 5% to 6% on funds available for investing and the industrial engineer with an objective of reducing his manpower costs by 5% on certain recurrent projects.

Project Oriented

As contrasted to many line objectives which tend to be broad and all encompassing, e.g. a profit objective which requires the manager to coordinate and bring together all of the components which contribute to profits, the objectives for staff managers frequently are project oriented, i.e., they deal with a narrower, specific action. This has been found to be especially true with research and engineering managers and with other technically oriented staff jobs.

This project orientation leads to another difference; the target periods for accomplishing the objectives are shorter than for line objectives. The experience of Scully-Jones and Co., manufacturers of tool holders, is a good example. This company approves a schedule of proposed starting and completion dates for each of its design and engineering managers. Research and development performance has been redefined in terms of personalized short-term goals. This company reports the change has brought about improved work quality and completion dates of projects have become more realistic.[1] Similar experience has been echoed by research, design, engineering, and development managers in roughly fifty companies with whom the subject has been discussed.

Examples of these project oriented objectives with short target periods are:

A Determine appropriate procedures for measuring chemical changes to fiber surfaces, by October 1, 1972.

B Complete bill of material for major project "A" on July 1 and then release to production.

C Complete physical reorganization of laboratory by August 15

D Maneuver project "D" to a make or break decision by October 1.

E Reduce frozen assets to $100,000 by June 15.

F Reduce tardiness rate to 3% by April 1.

Structuring

In addition to the differences relating to the length and project nature of staff objectives, there is another one which should be observed—namely; the structuring of the objective in terms [that] permit evaluation of the total performance of the staff manager.

To illustrate this point let's select the job of a purchasing manager whose major responsibilities include: procurement, value analysis, warehousing, vendor relations, sales of surplus, direction of purchasing department, and others. One of the principles for writing objectives is that they should address themselves only to priority matters, not routine ones. In this particular case it is assumed the purchasing director, based on an analysis of priorities, recommended and secured approval for four major objectives which covered his responsibilities for procurement, warehousing, sales of surplus, and value analysis. Because of the existing priorities, he did not recommend objectives relating to direction of his department and vendor relations, both of which are important functions. As these latter two functions do not appear on his list of objectives, he probably won't be measured on them either on an interim basis during the year or on a final basis at the end of the year unless some major problem develops which will bring the situation to the attention of his superiors. How, then, can the manager's performance be

[1] *The Manager's Letter*, May 20, 1967, American Management Association, New York.

measured with respect to functions for which no objective has been written?

One obvious answer is to require the manager to have at least one objective for each major function for which he is accountable. This alternative has definite disadvantages. First, [it] results in a set of objectives in which the priorities range from very high to none. If practiced by all managers in an organization, the result is a long, hodgepodge collection of objectives which may detract from the lesser number of real high priority, make or break, gut type objectives. Secondly, the longer the list of objectives, the more will be the detail, time, and administrative routine required to police and administer them. While there is nothing magical about any given number of objectives, it is evident that the lesser the number, the better.

The second alternative is to follow the principle of writing objectives only for priority matters and adopt some other simple technique for keeping track of functions not covered by an objective. This is the practice followed by the preponderance of companies known to the author. These companies handle the matter by setting up a secondary list of measuring indices which are easily monitored and administered. Alternatively, these are labeled "standards of performance" or "performance indicators." First, the manager writes objectives covering the priority matters which he must accomplish during the target period. Those segments of his responsibility not covered by the objectives are considered standards of performance. For example, it may be company policy that a purchasing director place all orders within three days after receiving a purchase requisition and this would become a standard of performance—not an objective—for him.

Interim Reviews

Almost all well run MBO programs include a provision for interim reviews, at least quarterly, of the manager's progress. Most of the major objectives of line managers, e.g. revenue figures, production volume, unit costs, sales costs, etc., are broken down in the budget by months and quarters as a matter of routine. Thus, when the time arrives for a quarterly review, these breakdowns clearly show where the line manager should stand at that point. Such is not true of staff managers. Usually there are no natural breaking points and so these must be provided for by the staff manager by the way he structures his objectives. Assume, for example, the instance of an industrial engineer whose objective for the year requires him to lay out a complete plant. The annual objective of this manager should be divided into segments as follows:

Layout of Department A
—Complete by April 1

Layout of Department B
—Complete by July 1

Layout of Department C
—Complete by October 1

Layout of Department D
—Complete by November 1

Layout of Department E
—Complete by December 31

Two Bosses

All enlightened management personnel would frown on a man having more than one superior, yet the staff manager often approaches the situation in which he must serve two masters. One of his bosses is the person to whom he reports—his immediate superior; the other is the manager to whom he must provide service, or advice and counsel. A good example of this is the research manager in charge of both basic and applied research. He is responsible almost solely to his immediate superior for the basic research part of his job. However, he may be servicing several other managers with respect to the applied part of his accountability. He must demonstrate his contributions to all of the other managers, plus his boss, for applied research. Thus, when structuring his applied research objectives, he must handle them in such fashion that [he] can secure the concurrence of his fellow managers and his immediate superior—a not inconsiderable task, especially if his immediate boss is not in sympathy with or knowledgeable of the applied research needs of the other managers. The line manager's job in this regard is usually much less trying as he must please one boss and usually on a narrower range of possible subject matter.

Communications

It is almost an axiom that line managers must be kept informed in view of their direct relationship to the primary functions of the company and its mission. For example, it would be a rare occurrence if the marketing department were not informed of some production problem bearing on production's ability to fill orders or for production not to be quickly apprised of a cutback in planned sales and orders. Unfortunately, the same cannot always be said when it comes to staff departments. Often they are not informed of these major changes or, if informed, often much later. This does violence to the MBO approach, requiring as it does that the efforts (objectives) of all managers—both line and staff—be closely aligned and meshed to achieve the over-all corporate objectives. A concerted effort is required by all managers in the organization to insure that staff managers are continually informed on all matters about which they need to know. When communications weaknesses do occur, the staff manager should take the initiative in bringing them to light.

Changing Objectives

One of the more important criteria for writing effective objectives is that they should change from one target period to the next, not necessarily in subject matter, but in the degree or form of the task. This criterion helps insure that objectives change in keeping with the changing priorities of the company and its departments, and that various programs are not perpetuated once the need for them has been satisfied. It is especially applicable to staff objectives because the need for changes in line objectives is much more obvious than is the case with staff. For example, when a company changes its profit target from one million dollars in 1971 to one and a half million dollars in 1972, it is rather apparent that line objectives such as those dealing with sales revenue and production volume and costs must change to meet the changing company objective. This need for change is not so apparent for many staff objectives dealing with subjects like training, safety, community relations, and vendor relations. Often, there is a tendency to continue these programs in a rather routine manner without examining them for possible changes precipitated by the change in the profit objective. In all cases where the staff manager recommends the same objective from one target period to the next, he should clearly indicate it is the same objective and the reasons why it continues to be applicable.

Deliberation Required

Perhaps the greatest difference in writing staff objectives is the extent of the deliberation required on the part of staff to zero in on meaningful objectives, especially the subject matter of the objectives. Much of the deliberation required is concerned with the staff man trying to determine the real reason why he and his job exist in the first place. For example, a financial manager isn't there merely to keep books; he's there to make a certain contribution to profit or other form of progress such as accomplishing an objective to reduce the amount of time required to place feedback reports in the hands of other managers to aid them in making better and faster decisions. Likewise, a purchasing manager isn't retained merely to buy the materials required to run the business; he's there to make a profit contribution like getting the best quality materials and the best vendor service at the lowest possible price. An industrial engineer shouldn't be accountable for conducting efficiency studies; he should be strictly accountable for certain cost reductions or effecting other tangible results. It is this mental wrestling which is necessary on the part of the staff manager to determine his real mission and then translate it into specific objectives which requires the added deliberation. Contrast this with the more self-explanatory and easily discernible mission of the usual line manager. It is rather obvious that the sales manager is there to sell and the production manager is there to produce. Thus, while the job title itself will usually suggest the subject matter of objectives for line managers, such is decidedly not true for the staff manager. He first must probe, discuss with other managers, and then decide the subject matter.

Authority to Act

To a much greater degree than the line manager, the staff manager is often plagued by a lack of knowledge [of] what authority he may have to carry out an objective. This can be especially troublesome to the staff manager in light of the "two bosses" situation discussed previously. It is suggested most strongly that if there is any confusion whatever in the staff manager's mind about his authority concerning an objective, he endeavor to resolve it before the objective is approved or, at the very minimum, include as an adjunct to the objective a statement of the authority he believes he has or will require to accomplish the objective. It is a truism of writing attainable objectives that the person responsible have the proper authority and control over the objective. Otherwise he may well fail to attain it because of matters outside his control.

Conclusion

Objectives and the whole Management by Objectives system are as applicable to the staff manager as they are to the line manager. Staff managers can and should be included in the objective setting process both for the benefit and progress of the individual manager and [for] his company as a whole. The staff manager who would make his maximum contribution with objectives should:

1 First appreciate and understand the differences required to structure staff objectives.
2 Determine the subject area of his objectives for the particular target period.
3 Secure confirmation of his accountability and authority.
4 Structure realistic, measurable, and attainable objectives.

10 The Mechanics of Organization

Whereas a great many companies have been impressed by the findings of behavioral science research, most are still organized along largely classical lines—although some of the behavioral findings may be utilized in structuring some departments and/or subsections.

This chapter contains articles dealing with the ways in which an organizer may divide the work and provide means of coordination, which, no matter what theory he subscribes to, is the practical problem he faces. The first article discusses the division of work as a classicist approaches it, and the second a means of coordination that is becoming fairly popular as the number of staff departments increases and the burden on the top man becomes greater. The third article treats of another means that may be used to decrease the burden on the chief executive, although it usually does not eliminate the pyramidal form of organizations that is the result of following the classical principles.

Following this is an article dealing with a method of organizing production that is, in part at least, in accord with the teachings of the behaviorists since it places more responsibilities on groups of rank-and-file employees. It was developed, however, as a means to greater efficiency rather than as a way of motivating the production workers.

The last three articles deal with decentralization through divisionalization, a form of organization adopted by many large companies with a view to eliminating some of the disadvantages that an over-large bureaucratic organization is likely to encounter.

The work of the organization department of the Standard Oil Company of California has extended over thirty years and has had an important influence on other companies. One outcome of that work was the pioneering volume *Top-management Organization and Control*, by Paul Holden, Lounsbury Fish, and H. L. Smith[1]; another was *The Management Guide*,[2] published by the company itself and widely distributed to other companies.

Here Lounsbury Fish, organization counsel for Standard Oil of California, and later with the Standard Oil Company (New Jersey), summarizes some definite guides for the organizer.

Organization: Foundation of Management

Lounsbury Fish

Most organizations have just evolved. Additions and changes in the general plan have been made, from time to time, to meet specific needs on the basis of expediency with little regard for overall design or rationality. The difficulties of managing, under these conditions, may be likened to living in a house, built one room at a time, over the years, by different tenants, without benefit of architecture. While, in many cases, considerable effort has been devoted to putting individual rooms in the old house in some kind of order in the interests of greater efficiency, the primary need is usually to redesign or modernize the house itself, to assure that it has just the number and type of rooms required to best meet present day needs, and that these are properly articulated to produce a well balanced whole.

The Elements of a Sound Plan

As an organization grows in size and complexity, it becomes increasingly necessary for Management to divide its load, delegate its responsibilities, decentralize its burdens and to provide adequate concentration and specialization of supervisory attention at focal points throughout the enterprise. The more widely the management task is divided up and distributed in response to these pressures, however, the greater the need and the difficulty of effecting proper coordination and control.

The basic organization problem, therefore, is twofold—to subdivide the total responsibility into logical, separable component responsibilities or "sub-contracts" for which others may assume the burden and so satisfy the needs of delegation, decentralization and specialization—and at the same time to assure that these components are properly integrated, related, balanced and tied together in a manner which will facilitate effective coordination and control. In great measure, the difficulties experienced in the administration of large operations result from the fact that the component responsibilities are illogical and ill-defined, a product of evolution rather than of coordinated design.

The component responsibilities. Whether component responsibilities represent departments, divisions, subsidiaries, branches, sections, committees, staff agencies or executive offices, they should measure up to the following general qualifications if the organization is to "click":

Each should comprise a logical, separable field of responsibility—a natural subdivision of the total task, whose scope and jurisdiction can be clearly defined. These may be relatively distinct sub-enterprises such as product or regional divisions or subsidiaries; functional divisions, like manufacturing, marketing, accounting; geographical outposts, such as regional, district or branch offices or plants; or staff aspects of the management job.

Each should represent a clear-cut "contract" for which a properly qualified executive, supervisor, or staff man can be held squarely responsible and accountable. Responsibility is a definite thing—"you either is or you ain't" responsible.

Each should have easy, workable relationships with other associated components, with a natural, definable basis of division between them. It should be clear where one responsibility "leaves off" and the next begins.

[1](McGraw-Hill Book Company, New York, 1951). First published in 1939.
[2]By George Lawrence Hall with the assistance of other members of the department on organization (Standard Oil Company, California, 1948); 2d ed., Franklin E. Drew and George Lawrence Hall (eds.), 1956.

From *Advanced Management* (quarterly journal of the Society for the Advancement of Management), Vol. XI, No. 2, June, 1946, pp. 52–55.

Each should represent a relatively homogeneous and cohesive field of responsibility, made up of elements which are compatible, related, having some common bond. The responsibility for any single undertaking should not be divided.

Each should contain all elements which are parts of a closely related group, which "belong" together, which comprise a complete entity. Conversely, it should not contain incompatible or "foreign" elements which are more properly parts of other assignments. Placing constituent responsibilities in the wrong packages is the surest road to discord and confusion, even among friends.

The primary or operating components. The first consideration in organizational design is the division of the total enterprise into its component "enterprises"—its operating departments, divisions, or subsidiaries and their subordinate operating elements and sub-elements. This primary breakdown establishes the basic pattern of organization, the levels of management, the basis for decentralization.

At the Company level, this basic subdivision may be on a functional, product division or regional basis, according to the nature of the business. At lower levels, these broad vertical divisions may be broken down into appropriate district, branch, area, plant and sub-plant proprietorships. This final resolution of the operating structure should normally proceed from the bottom up. For example, in a national marketing organization, the first step would be to select the branch offices from which the market could be most effectively and economically covered. The row of branch offices thus evolved would constitute the bottom level of sales management. The next step would be to consider the need for regional offices from which the branches could most advantageously be supervised, coordinated, and perhaps supplied. These elements would constitute another level of management. And finally, there would be the problem of tying the regional offices into the central sales office—at a still higher level.

Every effort should be made to keep the number of management levels at an absolute minimum in order to facilitate administration and avoid delay, multiple handling and red tape. The number of levels is dependent upon the number of primary components requiring executive coordination, and the number of these which it is feasible to group for such coordination at a higher level. Obviously, the minimum number of management levels will result where each proprietary executive (or supervisor), in ascending order, has a jurisdiction embracing "all he can *satisfactorily* manage." In this connection, there is a practical limitation on the number of subordinate components with which an executive can satisfactorily deal and still provide the necessary guidance, stimulation, coordination and control to make their combined efforts fully effective. Experience indicates that when this number exceeds five to seven or eight subordinate elements, depending upon their character, overburdening of the executive office and its attendant difficulties are likely to result. On the other hand, if a major unit is split into less than three or four subordinate responsibilities, the executive burden is hardly spread enough to justify the additional level created.

The executives or supervisors in charge of these operating components are focal points of proprietary responsibility. They constitute the line organization—they are the main links in the chain of command. Upon their shoulders rests the major burden of "getting out the wash." Each is the boss, the head man within his field, and should have a primary title in recognition thereof.

At the top level, the Chief Executive exercises the proprietary responsibility with respect to the enterprise as a whole. At the next level, the executives in charge of operating departments, divisions, and subsidiaries play a similar role with respect to their fields of jurisdiction. At lower levels, we find the executives in charge of regions, districts, branches and plants performing a corresponding function within the limits of their operating domains. Finally, at the base level, we have the foremen and supervisors, in immediate charge of operations, exercising the proprietary responsibility with respect to their smaller parts of the show.

All other component responsibilities are secondary, supporting elements which should be centered and oriented around these proprietary focal points. Considerable organizational confusion results from failure to recognize the important distinction between primary and secondary responsibilities.

The secondary or staff components. Wherever the administrative burden exceeds the personal capacity of the proprietary executive, he needs a staff. Through this means, he can secure the necessary assistance, specialized knowledge and concentration of attention upon the different aspects of his responsibilities which will permit him to do a fully effective management job. His staff members may assist him in conceiving needs, in formulating plans and programs, in handling special problems, and in different aspects of supervision, coordination and control. The staff is basically an elaboration of his office, not another level of management.

It is not enough, however, that each proprietary executive have a competent and well organized staff with whom he may share the burdens of his office. The similar staff elements in support of *all* proprietary executives at all levels of operation should be set up in parallel fashion. Each should receive close functional guidance and coordination from the top office in its field. This is a most important factor in coordinating and facilitating the administration of all activities throughout the Company in harmony with the views and policies of top management.

For many years, organization of the comptroller's functions has served as a model of staff effectiveness in many concerns. The general plan has been for the comptroller to place a "sub-comptroller," trained in the overall company system, in each department or subsidiary with the acquiescence of the local manager. The sub-comptroller is directly responsible to his manager for supplying necessary information and service in support of operations; at the same time, he is functionally responsible to the chief comptroller for compliance with the general company system and methods within his field. This well proved plan could be advantageously used as a model for the organization of other staff functions which find application throughout the enterprise, such as personnel relations, organization planning, and sometimes engineering, purchasing, etc.

Tests of a sound plan. In briefest terms, therefore, we may say there are four prime requisites of a sound organization plan:

1 *Division* of the overall operating "contract" into a logical, coordinated system of "sub-contracts" and "sub-sub-contracts."
2 *Delegation* to the responsible "contractor"—the executive (or supervisor) in charge of each such operating component—of the fullest measure of proprietary responsibility and authority which it is practicable to assume at his level.
3 Development of adequate *staff support* around these focal offices, as necessary to assist the "contractor" in assuring the full and effective discharge of the management obligations so delegated.
4 Clear-cut *functional coordination* of related staff activities at all levels throughout the enterprise.

As a final test of organizational adequacy in support of any executive office, let us visualize The Executive, sitting at his desk, faced with the many responsibilities and obligations of management. Let us, for a moment, consider that each of his problems or "worries" is reduced to writing and that these papers are stacked in an impressive pile upon his desk. The Executive's task is to divide up and delegate the bulk of these worries among the members of his staff (who, we will assume, are represented by baskets on his desk), reserving for himself those primary obligations which he as chief must personally assume.

If he is able to go through this pile and, without hesitation, sort and toss each of his delegable worries, neatly and clearly, into one of the staff baskets with confident expectation that it will be properly taken care of—then he has a good organization both as to plan and people.

A Well-designed Structure

Modernization and streamlining of a large organization to assure simplicity, strength, and clarity cannot be accomplished in a day—it is a long-range job. An effective approach is through the development of an ideal or optimum plan for the entire enterprise, to serve (a) as a basis of comparison in checking the adequacy of the existing plan, (b) as a guide in making immediate improvements which can be effected without dislocation, and (c) as a longer-range goal toward which to work as it becomes opportune to make needed changes of a more delicate or far reaching character, as in the partition, consolidation or reallocation of major responsibilities.

Such a plan should be laid out with complete objectivity, starting from scratch, with a large blank sheet of paper. Existing arrangements, personnel, precedents and traditions should be forgotten and attention concentrated upon working out a new plan—not as it *is* but as it *should be* if one were free to start anew. It is essentially a design job, an architectural procedure, and the architect should put himself in the Chief Executive's shoes and, in consultation with those who are best informed in regard to the different activities, devise an organizational mechanism through which the Chief Executive and his associates can most easily and effectively manage the business.

It is most important, both in its formulation and presentation, that the optimum plan thus evolved be considered as a long-range guide and objective, to be approached gradually, over a period of time, as it becomes opportune to make the necessary changes, rather than as a proposal for immediate wholesale reorganization. Modifications of the major character usually required to put a large organization in first class shape can seldom be put into effect at any one time without entailing unnecessary dislocation.

For obvious reasons such a plan would ordinarily be given only limited circulation, at the discretion of the Chief Executive. Its principal use would be as a master guide and stimulus toward the orderly development and recommendation of needed changes as they become timely.

A well designed master chart is only half of a good organization plan. The other half consists of "tickets" defining the basic obligations of each key position under the plan. In general, these tickets should cover the following aspects of the job in clear and concise language:

1 The primary obligation of the job—variously termed the basic responsibility, the "contract," the province and scope, the mission, task, or objective.
2 The principal component functions or responsibilities involved in achieving the main objective.
3 The relationships or mutual obligations between the organizational component or position concerned and other components or positions with which it must deal.
4 The extent of and limits upon the authority which the position is expected to exercise.

These tickets should be worked out in collaboration with the executives concerned. They should represent the basic charge from the principal executive—what the top office is holding this position responsible and accountable for. They should be approved by the principal executive.

Close collaboration of key personnel in the development of their own tickets is one of the most fruitful means of assuring understanding. This should be supplemented by further individual and conference discussion, as necessary.

In any event, discussion of the organization plan and the general executive and supervisory obligations thereunder, should play a major part in any executive or supervisory training program. Some companies distribute a generalized organization plan as a part of the orientation of all new employees.

As staff departments become more numerous, the mechanics of ensuring coordination become more difficult to arrange. One way of doing this is the appointment of a vice-president of administration to whom all or a number of the staff departments report. The following article describes the scope of this position.

Allen R. Janger is on the staff of the Conference Board and a well-known writer on organization.

The Vice-president, Administration: What and Why

Allen R. Janger

Of all the words in the business vocabulary, "administration" is one of the most broadly used. It approaches even "management" in vagueness and popularity. In some contexts, it conjures up small mountains of paper work, all neatly tied in red tape. In other possibly more modern contexts, administration and, more particularly, "administrative management" suggest some of the highly sophisticated concepts of company planning and control sometimes associated with the newer computer and data processing systems.

But for organization planners and other people for whom looking at company organization charts is something more than an idle pastime, the word "administration" often suggests one of the newcomers to the corporate level: the vice-president, administration. Of course, he doesn't always go by that name. A recent Conference Board inspection of corporate organization charts turned up such titles as "executive vice-president, administration and finance," or "vice-president, administrative services." Most often, however, the executive carries the title "vice-president, administration," and that, when organization planners gather, is usually what the position is called.

To bring this position into sharper focus, The Conference Board has attempted to analyze the VP, administration, in twenty companies. Initially positions that have just the title "administration," or some variation of this title, were included. Nine, for example, carry the title "vice-president, administration," or "vice-president, administrative services." Three are "directors of administration." One is a "senior vice-president, administration." And one is a "manager of administration."

Then six others were included with the composite title of "finance and administration," "manufacturing and administration," "administration and material." Such titles may represent something different from just "administration," but whatever these differences may be, they are not reflected in the responsibilities or in the reporting relationships of the incumbents.

It should perhaps be stressed that the position is not only found in large companies. The VP's, administration, come from companies of all sizes, the smallest having only a few hundred employees.

From the analysis of the organization charts, position guides and other explanatory materials supplied by the twenty companies, three points stand out as general characteristics of the VP, administration.

1 The creation of the job of vice-president, administration, is an organizational response to the chief executive's need to save time.
2 The vice-president, administration, is primarily a coordinator of traditionally separate major staff functions, such as finance [and] personnel.
3 The vice-president, administration, is both generalist and specialist, but his role as generalist often predominates.

Saving the Top Man's Time

Ask an executive why his company has a vice-president, administration, and somewhere in the conversation he is likely to note that the position "decreases the number of positions reporting directly to the chief executive." For many companies this is no doubt their basic if not their only reason for setting up the position.

As companies grow so does the extent of the chief executive's responsibilities, particularly in the areas of external relations, planning and policy formulation. This may leave the chief executive with inadequate time for supervision and coordination of major units reporting to him.

As companies grow, moreover, the degree of interaction between certain units and certain areas of responsibility may also grow. For example, a company's concern with control of its growing business may lead to increasing inter-

From the *Management Record* (Conference Board), July–August, 1962, pp. 28–32.

action between the personnel administration and finance units.

These increased demands on the chief executive's time and greater interaction of corporate-level staff units often lead companies to set up "general executives" to provide needed coordination of these units. Some general executives coordinate only staff units, others coordinate only operating units, and still others coordinate operating, staff and even other general executives. The VP, administration, is evidently one of the general executives with staff responsibilities. Of the general executives carrying "administration" titles, eighteen out of the twenty have only staff units reporting to them; the other two men coordinate both staff and operating executives.

Coordinating Major Staff Functions

As one company puts it, in carrying out his coordinative role the vice-president, administration, "makes decisions affecting more than one group, has various authorities formerly held by the president, and is able to relieve the president of many day-to-day functions in these areas [the areas reporting to him]."

This coordination may involve keeping closer watch over staff units, thus acting as an extra set of "eyes and ears" for the chief executive. Coordination may also involve representing the functions for which he is responsible on corporate councils, gaining "command support" for their undertakings. And it may involve integrating the work of his units into over-all company planning. The vice-president, administration, is not usually involved in the day-to-day routine of the units reporting to him. Such supervision is the responsibility of each unit head. The creation of the title of vice-president, administration, according to one firm, "does not necessarily diminish the responsibility of the executive reporting to this position."

In a few companies, vice-president, administration, is almost synonymous with "chief of staff." All, or almost all, the existing corporate staff reports to him. One company groups all corporate-level staff functions under the head of administration. As this company explains, the unit "provides staff services at the headquarters level to top management and to the operating divisions throughout the company as required."

Describing the circumstances in which its administration unit was formed, another company notes, "the line activities were generally grouped under a vice-president of operations and the staff under the vice-president, administration."

Still another company explains that it initially "created the position of vice-president, nontechnical operations . . . this title was useful internally to distinguish from vice-president, technical operations . . . however, neither of these titles was useful externally and they were later changed to the vice-president, administration, and to the vice-president, manufacturing, respectively."[1]

When all the units that report to the vice-president, administration, in the twenty companies are listed, it becomes apparent that almost all major staff functions are represented. (See the table.) Only marketing-sales is missing from the list.

When the companies are looked at individually, units appear to be assigned to the vice-president, administration, on a fairly random basis. On closer inspection, however, the work these units perform is interrelated—that, after all, is one of the reasons they require coordination.

Among the twenty vice-presidents, administration, four patterns seem dominant:

1 Operations-oriented administration units—Five companies have administration departments in which personnel administration is grouped with a purchasing and/or manufacturing unit. And in three out of these five, all three functions—personnel administration, purchasing-traffic and manufacturing—are coordinated by the vice-president, administration.
2 Finance- and legal-oriented administration units—Five companies have administration departments in which finance and legal-secretarial functions are commonly grouped, sometimes alone and sometimes with units from other functional areas.

[1]These distinctions between administrative and operating or technical management operate, of course, as broad rules of thumb. They are not strictly followed by either of the above companies in assigning responsibility for units. The "vice-president, nontechnical," for example, never included all nontechnical corporate staff functions and the second company's vice-president, administration, never had responsibility for all corporate staff functions.

UNITS REPORTING TO THE VP, ADMINISTRATION, IN TWENTY COMPANIES[1]

Unit Titles and Functional Areas	Companies		Unit Titles and Functional Areas	Companies	
Personnel administration	15		Purchasing-traffic	6	
Industrial relations; personnel administration		13	Purchasing		3
Organization planning		5	Traffic; traffic and transport		3
Management development		1	Materials		2
Management compensation		1	Manufacturing-engineering	5	
Industrial security		1	Facilities planning		4
Employee benefits		1	Operating services		1
Medical		1	Quality control		1
Finance	10		Policies and practices		1
Controller		6	Product programming		1
Treasurer		5	Management methods		1
Finance		2	Public relations	5	
Secretary-treasurer		1	Public relations		3
Budget		1	Corporate relations services		2
Financial control and budgets		1	Governmental services		1
Insurance		2	Community relations		1
Legal-secretarial	7		Operating executives	2	
General counsel		3	Manufacturing		1
Secretary		3	Sales		1
Real estate		2	Research	1	
Administrative services	7		Long-range planning	1	
Administrative services		4	Corporate development	1	
Management engineering		1	Purchasing and administrative services	1	
Records management		1	Radio facilities and operations	1	
Administrative planning		1	Military contracts	1	

[1]Since companies often have more than one unit in a functional area, the number of unit titles exceeds the number of companies working in the area.

3 Relations-oriented administration units—Five companies have administration departments in which personnel administration is grouped with public relations and/or administrative services functions. In one of these companies a vice-president, administration, is described as being responsible for coordinating "various aspects which affect our employees, the public and our stockholders."

4 General administration units—Five departments combine under "administration" a broad range of functional activities having to do with men, money and the company as a legal and public entity. In all of these companies finance and personnel administration are included under administration, and in three of the five, finance and personnel are joined by legal-secretarial functions.

It might be noted that all the units include personnel administration, finance or both. This is by no means a coincidence, but reflects the fact that many vice-presidents, administration, are finance or personnel administration executives whose positions have been enlarged by the addition of other functional responsibilities. It also suggests that group titles such as "finance and administration," "manufacturing and administration," and the like are indications of the background of the incumbent and of the orientation of his work.

More Generalist than Specialist

Like all corporate-level executives, the vice-president, administration, plays two roles. He is a "generalist" participating heavily in over-all company planning and control, and he is a "specialist" fulfilling a staff role that emerges from the functions he coordinates.

Some of the twenty companies describe this specialist role in terms of work unique to the vice-president, administration; that is, in terms of an "administrative function."

One vice-president, administration, for example, has the function of "planning and general direction of . . . administrative management activities; *i.e.*, developing improvements in general . . . management practices; stimulating the adoption and practice of improved management by all departments; and providing leadership and general guidance of the activities of the [departments that report to him]." Another company speaks of "administration's" role as providing "staff services in the field of general management . . . which is concerned with problems pertaining to the planning, control, and coordination of the traditional major functional subdivisions of management responsibility."

There is often a hum of data-processing equipment in the background when companies speak of administration. In one company, administration involves "integrated top management control." This firm makes its vice-president responsible for "a completely integrated planning and monitoring unit." Still another company, also thinking in terms of integrated forms and procedures, data processing, and statistical control units, conceives of the administration function as dealing with over-all control of company operations.

Then, there is the vice-president, administration, whose first responsibility is "to work toward creating a feeling of understanding between the company and its employees and developing plans and practices for this end."

Obviously, each company's concept of the "administrative function" carried out by the VP, administration, is more or less custom tailored to fit its needs. As a specialist, therefore, the VP's job varies from one company to another.

However, of possibly greater significance is his role as "generalist." And here, as might be expected, the consensus is easier to discern. Some companies describe the vice-president, administration, as "the president's deputy," as "an extension of the president's office in a good many ways" that deals with matters of "a direct concern to the president." Such matters usually are more closely related to company rather than to division or department objectives, or involve interdivisional problems. They may be so critical as to affect the survival and growth of the company. These are for the most part matters on which the chief executive has authority for making final decisions or which he must refer to the board of directors for final approval.

In a sense this makes the vice-president, administration, a member of what might be called a leadership or top-management group composed of other general executives and major staff executives. Much of his time may be spent in reviewing and preparing written reports and recommendations for the chief executive and in attending *ad hoc* meetings called to discuss a given problem of company-wide significance. In some companies he participates in the work of a formally designated council of top company executives, or serves as a member of one or more formally designated management committees.

These formal "councils of executives," called the "president's office" or "the chief executive office," are appearing with greater frequency on company organization charts and suggest that there is a growing consciousness of the leadership role of top management. The existence of these formal and informal leadership groups does not in any way destroy or limit the chief executive's responsibility and authority to make decisions. But these groups do influence the decision-making process.

At the top of many organization charts is a box labeled "office of the president." Since a number of names appear in this box, it might appear that the companies are being run by a committee all members of which have equal power. But this is seldom, if ever, the case, as this article explains.

Second Thoughts on the "Office of the President"

An organization chart, with its precisely drawn lines connecting tidy rows of boxes, makes a corporation's top management structure seem sleek and orderly. But it rarely, if ever, has been. And harried chief executive officers, symbolized by the box at the top where all the lines eventually lead, are constantly reminded of that reality.

Pressures on the chief executive officer have taken a quantum jump in the last 20 years, and they are bound to increase. The pace of business, as it diversifies its activities, demands fast reaction time. The thrust for international business adds to the complexity, and keeping pace with new technology creates another pressure point.

Traditionally, the chief executive has not shared the burden. Instead, he has rigidly followed the dogma that the single chief executive can handle the task if he is competent. He has used the techniques acceptable to his peers: decentralization, profit centers, staff specialization. The pattern prevails in most U.S. corporations today.

The Group Must Speak as One Voice

But a number of companies have found the single chief executive officer concept wanting. So they have taken a page from European business and created a multiple chief executive function. Using labels ranging from "office of the president" to "corporate executive office," their objective is to help the chief executive at the highest level.

The companies that have taken the step range across the industrial scene. Caterpillar Tractor Co. made the plunge in the mid-1950s, long before other companies that later switched had even considered the idea. Two or three years ago, the roster expanded rapidly. Among the companies that adopted variations of the technique: General Electric, Borden, Scott Paper, Singer, Ampex, and Continental Can.

The growing list prompted some organizational specialists to predict that the traditional concept of a single chief executive officer was becoming obsolete. But such predictions were obviously premature, since additional converts are arriving very slowly.

Establishing a president's office is not a move to be taken without thorough deliberation, cautions Peter F. Drucker, professor of management at the Graduate School of Business of New York University and a consultant on top management organizations. Drucker, a vocal critic of the single chief executive in American business, is not much more optimistic about a group, although he concedes it has potential. "The president's office has a chance, provided the people involved know the rules, and very few do."

Drucker has some rules of his own. First each member has to know his position clearly in respect to the other members and must work constantly to keep them informed. The entire organization must be convinced that there is no appeal from any one member of the group, "even though there always should be one man at the head of the table, and this requires a great deal of self-discipline."

In addition, the company must avoid putting men into the group "who fortify each other's blind spots," Drucker says. "This makes for the worst kind of situation and is the reason to carefully think why you bring a man into the president's office." The selection has to be impersonal and never should be used to kick an executive upstairs.

Even if his rules are followed, Drucker remains pessimistic. "It may be a necessity but it isn't the solution to managing complexity. So far, I haven't seen many cases where it has worked."

Harrison F. Dunning, chairman and chief executive officer of Scott Paper, differs sharply. Dunning feels that the task of managing a company's internal growth plus the growing social and civic demands on the man at the top make the office of chief executive much more manageable when it is occupied by three men.

The other two members of the office are Vice-chairman Paul C. Baldwin, in charge of staff departments, and President Charles D. Dickey,

From *Business Week*, Oct. 3, 1970, pp. 42–43.

Jr., who is responsible for all operating departments. Says Dunning: "The other two have made decisions in my absence I wouldn't have made. And I've probably made some they wouldn't make. But it hasn't happened many times. When it does, I back them."

It would be naive to assume that any major decision is made in the absence of the *primus inter pares* of any office of the president. But the strategy of Dunning, certainly first among equals at Scott, is crucial if the top group is to gain acceptance. The boss must back his associates or else the device becomes a diffuse and nebulous mass. Depending on where it is poked by the line managers, it produces an inconsistent—and unpredictable—response.

Equally hazardous is the impression by subordinates that creating a president's office means that the company is being run by committee. Attempting to dispel such notions, a member of one company's president's office, describing the process, says, "We never vote, but if we did, the voting power would doubtless be six votes for the chairman and chief executive, three for the president, and one for each of the executive vice-presidents."

Borden President and Chief Executive Officer Augustine R. Marusi, who installed a president's office shortly after he was named to the job in 1967, insists that the device is not "a Tinkers-to-Evers-to-Chance routine." He adds: "There is only one chief executive officer and that's me. But in a big diversified company, you need the input of a lot of ideas. It allows me to communicate with my associates in a way that transcends the inhibitions existing in a traditional line organization."

Marusi began with a three-man office, consisting of himself and two executive vice-presidents. Each of the executive vice-presidents was assigned responsibility for specific operating divisions and subsidiaries. "We've switched around the responsibilities to get a new management overview and it has worked well," he says. "Horizontal moves shake out different points of view and I wouldn't hesitate to switch their responsibilities around again."

Recently, the Borden financial vice-president was added to the group. "He had talent in finance that we didn't have and the group needed him," explains Marusi, adding that the structure allows him to fulfill his idea of the chief executive's function as "being visible both inside and outside the company."

A Concept with Many Variations

Other chief executives have different notions, depending on their own style of leadership. Consequently, the shape of the president's office lacks any sense of solid consistency as a management concept. Not surprisingly, it is tailored to what the chief executive in power wants it to be.

At Singer, for example, Chairman and President Donald P. Kircher maintains responsibility for major operational and organizational matters in his three-man group. Donald W. Smith, chairman of the executive committee, supervises new product development, manufacturing, inventory control, and physical distribution as well as the "transfer and utilization of technology throughout Singer." Andrew J. Reinhart, who used to be Singer's controller, joined in January and concentrates on "current operations, particularly with units that are off their budgets."

At the time Kircher created the president's office two years ago, the company had just developed an operating group structure and was digesting its acquisition of General Precision Equipment Corp., which Smith had headed. Kircher wanted a device that would lighten his load in running a company that had more than doubled in size in 10 years. But, says Reinhart, "He did not want the President's Office to get too far away from operations."

Reinhart contends that the structure has allowed Kircher to spend more time in long-range planning and evaluating the organization, as well as in dealing with the public as Singer's chief executive officer. And Singer product group executives, he says, have more direct contact with Kircher.

General Electric Chairman and Chief Executive Officer Fred J. Borch designed the multiple chief executive function when the company reorganized in 1968. When the dust had settled from the realignment, Borch had 10 groups reporting to him. There are limits on any job, he says, and "I realized I couldn't get my arms around 10 groups."

As a result, the president's office was created, consisting of Borch, the late GE chairman Gerald L. Phillippe, and three former group vice-presidents who were elevated to executive vice-presidents and into the new structure. Unlike Borden's Marusi, Borch did not want members to have direct accountability. Assigning accountability means advocacy, says Borch, "and this five-man group was charged with the responsibility for running the entire company. We wanted a review and challenge approach."

In place of direct responsibility for any particular segment of GE, the members have what Borch calls "primary cognizance responsibilities," or the assignment to review and challenge operations in their areas.

When Phillippe died less than a year after the new group was created, GE abandoned the title of president. Borch assumed the title of chairman, the three executive vice-presidents were named vice-chairmen, and the name of the group was changed to the corporate executive office.

The latest evolution of the concept occurred this summer, when Borch added the corporate executive staff, composed of four senior vice-presidents, and the corporate administrative staff, headed by a senior vice-president. Borch says that the corporate executive staff adds another dimension to GE's planning effort and aids the corporate executive office in determining where GE should be heading.

The corporate administrative staff is charged with coordinating functions ranging from employee relations and accounting to legal and public relations—the staff functions that previously kept the headquarters staff too busy to lay any strategic plans.

Grooming Men for the Job at the Top

GE's model, by far the most elaborate around, has drawn criticism as a prime example of overorganization and a mechanism that insulates top management from operating realities. Borch insists the structure is the best approach to managing a giant enterprise in its current operations, and insures that top ranking officers will engage in long range planning. By broadening responsibilities, he adds, more people get a look at the whole company and the new senior vice-presidents "are all excellent candidates for the chief executive office."

Grooming successors to the top corporate job is an obvious attraction of the concept of the president's office. But this assumes the new structure becomes permanent, and that has not always happened. Union Carbide set up a president's office in 1964, when the company was pushing overseas. Chairman Birny Mason, Jr., and three other senior officers divided the responsibilities. Last year when one of the members, President Kenneth Rush, was named as ambassador to West Germany, Mason abandoned the concept.

"It was set up for a specific reason and purpose and it worked well," says Mason. But the expansion of Union Carbide internationally had been launched and it "became unnecessary to have that additional layer. We have always tried to have the simplest form of organization, so in order to have a clean organizational structure, I eliminated it." However, Mason adds, "We would not preclude the possibility of doing it again if we felt it was needed."

Management theorists who back the group approach to the chief executive's job concede that they are in a minority now. But, they contend that the team at the top may be the escape valve for the pressure bearing down on the chief executive.

Group technology is a way of organizing the production process that, its proponents believe, not only reduces manufacturing costs but facilitates sales by reducing the lead time in filling orders. Although many companies may have been following a similar system for some time, as this article points out, a new technique is more likely to win widespread acceptance if it is "packaged" under a new name.

What Is Group Technology?

"Group technology" is a direct translation from the original Russian. Like linear programming, it is something the communists can teach the capitalists about running a business. It is intended to do two things:

- To cut the massive quantity of resources tied up as stocks and work-in-progress in the typical industrialised economy, a quantity that is disproportionately high in Russia, and which has had Russian planners worried for a long time.
- To cut delay between ordering and getting components.

Britain appears to fall down badly on just these two points. Britain's record on stock control is poor compared with Germany and Japan. In 1969 British manufacturers' stocks totalled a staggering £7,295 mn, which was well over half the gross national product contributed by the manufacturing sector. For work-in-progress the total was £2,713 mn. Similarly, poor delivery dates are a common reason why engineering components and finished manufactured goods are bought abroad in preference to the same goods available in Britain at the same prices.

Batch production is the section of manufacturing industry in which excessive build-ups of stocks and work-in-progress tend to occur. When the batches are small, materials and semi-finished components travel amazing distances between the various processes and machines. Aeons elapse between the time the raw material is fed in and a marketable product emerges.

The problem is multiplied several times where the manufacturer has to cope with rapid changes in the pattern of orders. In the motor industry, for instance, a sudden shift in emphasis from one model to another is a common event; but it produces an immediate call for quick delivery of the necessary parts from the supplier.

So Simple?

The principle of group technology sounds deceptively simple, even platitudinous. The manufacturer lists the whole range of batch-made parts, often running into hundreds or thousands. He then looks for common factors and groups them into families. (Even in supposedly well-organised companies, many very similar types of components will be being made in small batches, quite independently of each other, probably having been designed at different times for different purposes, with nobody noticing how very similar they were.) The parts are then grouped into families: short fat ones, long thin ones, etc. The groups are then classified by a code, like a postal zip code, so that the code number itself indicates the characteristics of each.

Stated simply, it sounds too obvious for words. "Why give it a special name? We've been doing this sort of thing for years," engineers might say. But the figures show how much room for improvement there is. Many management techniques (eg, management-by-objectives) really are nothing but the most elementary common sense. Yet experience suggests that the best way of getting common-sense techniques across to busy and preoccupied managers is to package them up, give them an exciting new name, and sell them as something new. And because group technology has implications both for salesmen (better, more competitive delivery) and finance directors (less capital locked in work-in-progress), marketing men, finance men and managing directors should not kid themselves into thinking it is some technical gimmick that can be left with the production manager and forgotten. The implications are wider then this. And group technology in practice tends to produce increased job satisfaction (in the factory) and hence lower labour turnover; and it allows wages to be linked more closely with performance.

Thus at **Rank Taylor Hobson** (the instrument manufacturer in the Rank group) the 12,000 parts machined there were analysed by shape, size, length and material and given a 36-digit code. There proved to be 430 very simple parts all shaped very like a washer. Among them were 30 that were identical in diameter and length. They had been designed separately for different purposes and nobody had noticed that they

From *The Economist*, London, Mar. 6, 1971, pp. 68–69.

were identical. Small batches of each had continued to be made separately, with much (expensive) resetting of machinery and shunting of small batches of each from one part of the factory to another.

Walker Crossweller makes a wide range of taps and shower parts. It found that 15% of the types accounted for 75% of the finished product value; and a further 15% for another 15%. It applied group technology to this 30% of parts. This reduced, from 600 feet to 90 feet, the average distance travelled by materials during the manufacturing process; output rose from 6 parts an hour to 14, with equipment and workforce unchanged.

GEC-Elliott has used group technology to streamline the manufacture of control valve bodies. Less than half its plant is on group technology, and only a simple coding system has been used. Even so, overall manufacturing time has been cut from 63 days to 18. Work-in-progress has been cut by 45%.

International Computers' management information system at Castlereagh, Belfast, uses group technology as its starting point. Work-in-progress and stocks have been cut by £l.4 mn.

Ferodo illustrates the most comprehensive application of group technology in Britain so far. Ferodo makes brake linings and is a subsidiary of Turner & Newall. Ferodo initially was worried about the level, the cost and the sheer volume of its work-in-progress. More serious, as a supplier to the motor industry, it was unable to meet orders quickly enough. It was even contemplating building a special factory just to deal with sudden urgent orders. Instead, group technology was used, and used with such success that it is now being applied to the whole brake-lining production process: from mixing of the raw material (asbestos and resins) to a brand new process for making the basic curved shape; out of this curved shape a curved section is cut, which is then machined down to the size of lining required.

Ferodo had:

- 25 different mixes of raw material.
- 150 different radii of lining. From these
- 3,500 basic shapes were cut, leading to,
- 17,000 catalogued sizes.

The top diagram [on page 196] shows the route travelled by a typical one of those 17,000 brake linings through the factory (in fact there were two adjoining factories, separated by a road); the diagram also explains the routes followed by five other linings chosen at random.

The bulk of the floor space of these two factories was taken up by work-in-progress, queuing up for one machine or another. The layout of the machines was not quite as ludicrous as it looks. They were laid out by type: all the drilling machines together, all the grinding machines together, the milling machines together, etc, But, having grouped all its types of final products into families, with code numbers, and analysed all the operations entering into the making of each, Ferodo was then in a position to reorganise the machine layout. The machines were put into groups of 14. Each of the machines does one of the jobs involved in making a lining, and all are linked by roller conveyors. The batch comes in and is passed from machine to machine as each operation is finished. Each group is subdivided into "cells" of six men; they move from one machine to another as required, having now been trained to use all of them. Each team sees its own workload through. At the end of most shifts, they can look at the batch of marketable products they have made. Work-in-progress has been cut by seven-eighths. Orders are dealt with in one-eighth of the time. Because speed of delivery was crucial, the direct labour force was not cut. But fewer "progress chasers" and clerks were required.

Having solved its major problem, Ferodo went on to apply group technology to the rest of its manufacturing operations:

- It found that, of the 25 mixes in use, five represented 46% of total factory output. Technically it was essential that the mixing of asbestos and resins be carried out in small batches of 125 lb. But in fact all the initial weighing, preparation and subsequent processing could be carried out on a much larger scale. In turn this allowed the whole mixing process to be automated. As a result the workforce engaged in batch mixing was cut down from 20 to four including the supervisor.

PLANT LAYOUT—BEFORE GROUP TECHNOLOGY INTRODUCED

FACTORY 1

Each block represents a bank of machines doing the same operation

Work in progress

Flow line for a typical component A

Materials in

Doors

1

Doors

FACTORY 2

Out

Examples of other components: -
B: 1,2,5,4 → out
C: 1,2,3,2,4 →
D: 1,2,5,1,2,4 →
E: 3,2,1,2,5,1,2,4 →
F: 3,2,4→
etc, etc, etc

2

3

4

5

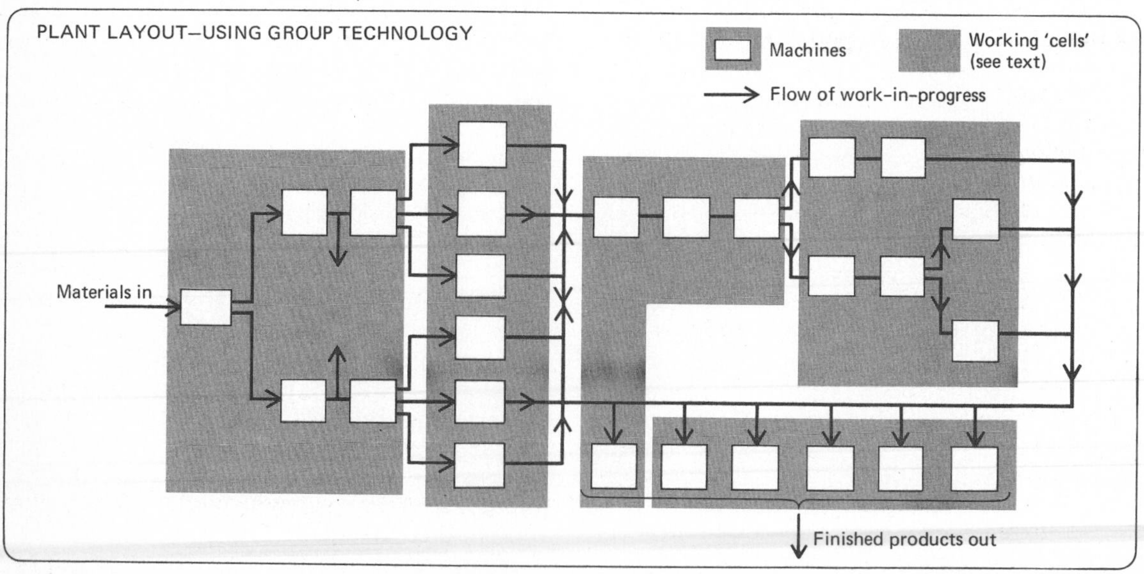

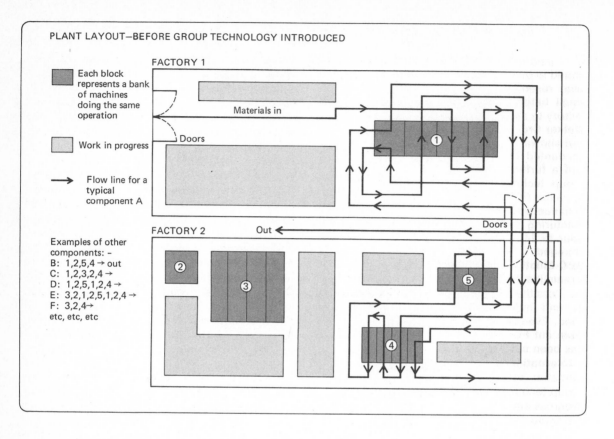

This diagram shows one small area of the factory in the top diagram.

- Traditionally each mix was then baked into semifinished asbestos in a mould of the radius required. But again it was found that the same handful of radii was used in the bulk of the batches. So a special machine was bought that could produce the stuff in semi-continuous lengths, which could then be chopped off in the widths required.

Investment

Wherever possible existing machines are used. But some considerable capital investment in new machines was required, meaning that over the 18 months in which the system was put in, capital investment in new machinery was one-third more than would otherwise have occurred. But this investment was covered more than twice over by the resulting disinvestment in work-in-progress.

Inevitably, labour problems cropped up. When an initial pilot line on the new basis was put in, people were taken on specially to man it. Different wage rates and bonuses developed among these and among existing staff. So Ferodo held a series of meetings and sold the idea to the men through the shop stewards. Once convinced that neither jobs nor earnings were threatened, the men co-operated.

Group technology has now been shown in practice to produce dramatic improvements in stocks/work-in-progress levels and in delivery times in widely differing types of batch manufacturing operation, and not just in engineering. Provided other manufacturers overcome their delusion that they already use something like it, it ought to become used increasingly widely in the coming years.

In 1920, General Motors consisted of a number of almost autonomous companies, all operating with little control from headquarters. William C. Durant (see Chapter 2), who had put the company together, had not devoted much time or thought to coordination. (John Lee Pratt, one of his associates, once recalled that no one knew how much money had been appropriated all together.)

In the early days, however, the company was growing so rapidly that the need for change did not become evident until a recession occurred after World War I. At that time Alfred P. Sloan, Jr., then a vice-president and later chief executive, proposed the following plan of reorganization, which was designed to preserve the advantages of decentralized operations but add a measure of coordinated control.

The plan was later adopted by GM and was copied, with some adaptations, by a number of other companies. It was based in part on similar plans used by the Du Pont Company, then a large stockholder in GM, and on discussions with Du Pont executives, among them Hamilton Barksdale (see Chapter 1), who was a director of Chevrolet at the time.

General Motors Corporation Study of Organization

Alfred P. Sloan, Jr.

This study is founded upon two principles:

1 The responsibility attached to the chief executive of each operation shall in no way be limited. Each such organization headed by its chief executive shall be complete in every necessary function and enabled to exercise its full initiative and logical development.

2 Certain central organization functions are absolutely essential to the logical development and proper control of the Corporation's activities.

Major Control

The term "Major Control" is specified as all authority down to but not including the President of the Corporation. The "Major Control" in the line of authority is specified as follows:

1 Stockholders
2 Directors
3 (*a*) Finance Committee
   (*b*) Executive Committee

[The functions of the stockholders and the directors were those usually specified in corporation charters and bylaws. The finance committee, which was to report directly to the board, was to be headed by a vice president in charge of finance, who was to formulate financial policy for the whole corporation, subject to the approval of the board and of the stockholders, where necessary, as when capital stock issues were to be authorized. The executive committee, which was headed by the president, also reported to the board, and was made up of the heads of operations—one representative from each of the larger operations and one from each *group* of smaller operations.]

Executive Control

The President of the Corporation has the entire responsibility of properly interpreting the policies formulated by Major Control and distributing them through the organization in such manner as he may elect.

[Next the staff assistance to be provided for the president was listed. This included an operations staff, a finance and accounting staff, a general advisory staff, and a personal staff.]

Each unit under the jurisdiction of the Corporation constitutes an operation and is a part of the operations staff. Such operations as are of major importance are represented by an executive officer who has no duties to perform other than that particular operation. Other operations of less importance may be and should be grouped together. Such grouping has the advantage of limiting the number of executives reporting directly to the president. Manifestly operations which have certain common characteristics should be placed together. In the groupings recommended consideration has been given to three factors.

1 Operations having both commercial [i.e., sales] and manufacturing problems and that distribute part of their products outside the corporation itself.
2 Operations which from a manufacturing standpoint present similar problems and have no outside commercial relations.
3 Operations which might be more effectively grouped geographically.

The responsibility of the head of each unit is absolute and he is looked upon to exercise his full initiative in developing his operation to the fullest possible extent and to assume the full responsibility of success or failure. Where units are grouped, each group is subject to executive control as a group, usually by a Vice President of the Corporation. All questions of policies which the General Manager of the individual operations desire[s] advice concerning, or support on, are taken up with the executive in charge of that particular group, thus further relieving the President of the Corporation.

[The memorandum suggested four broad groupings: (1) Motor Car Group; (2) Accessory Group; (3) Parts Group; and (4) a Miscellaneous Group.

The car operations were grouped according to the first criterion listed above. They were engaged in both manufacturing and commercial operations, and their products were sold to the general public, only incidentally within the corporation.

The accessories group was formed on somewhat the same basis since less than half of its production was sold within the corporation, and the sales activities had many problems in common.

The parts manufacturing operations, on the other hand, sold their production entirely to other divisions of the corporation, and such questions as prices to be charged were to remain a matter of general policy outlined by major control and subject to the jurisdiction of the president. These operations were divided into three groups on a geographical basis, each headed by a general manager.

In the miscellaneous group were operations in process of development and those not logically falling into any of the other groups.]

Financial and Accounting Staff

The General Financial and Accounting Staff constitutes the central organization of accounting and is under the direction of a Vice President of the Corporation who is also Chairman of the Finance Committee. It is recommended that the accounting within each individual unit be subject to the complete control of the Chief Executive of that unit.

The necessary coordination between the Vice President in charge of this executive staff and the accounting within each unit is through the President, to the chief executive of such unit or group of units. All finances and accounting pertaining to the Corporation as a whole, such as the designation of banks of deposit; handling of surplus funds, payment of dividends, matters pertaining to stock records and transfers; payment of taxes against the Corporation as a whole and all such general financial and accounting functions are within the province of the general financial and accounting staff.

[In recognition of] the desirability of proper coordination between the various executive staffs, a General Accounting and Finance Advisory Committee is recommended. This Committee to consist of the Vice President in charge of the General Financial and Accounting Staff as Chairman, with the President of the Corporation ex-officio and with such other members, preferably two, as the President may designate, preferably two Vice Presidents of the Operations Staff best qualified to consider financial matters pertaining to operations as well as financial control. The object of this advisory committee is to coordinate the needs of the central financial and accounting organization with the individual operations in order to develop a policy which will work to the best interest of the Corporation as a whole, also to interpret to the financial and accounting staff the needs and viewpoint of the operations staff.

General Advisory Staff

The General Advisory Staff is to constitute in reality a group of organizations or departments, large in some cases, small in others [depending] upon the necessity of each line of work. The purpose of this staff is to advise the chief executives of the Operations Staff concerning problems of technical and commercial nature which are themselves so broad and require so much study as to be outside of the scope of a single operation. The Advisory Staff is practically consultant to the Operations Staff and while it may develop and disseminate information and data to the Operations Staff and stands ready to be called upon for advice on such functions as it may be in a position to furnish, the Operations Staff is independent and may accept or reject the advice of the Advisory Staff subject to the general supervision of the President.

The General Advisory Staff is under a chief executive who is a Vice President of the Corporation.

[The advisory staff, it was recommended, should include the following groups:]

Purchasing section. To study sources of supply, tendencies in prices of materials in general use by the Corporation, especially those [that might form] the basis for general contracts. Also to coordinate the purchasing of the various purchasing departments with a view to getting the greatest benefit possible for the Corporation as a whole.

Engineering and research section. To act in an advisory way to the engineering departments of the units with a view to disseminating information of interest to all [and] to undertake research work that would be beyond the province of any individual operation. To examine and report upon new inventions submitted to the Corporation. To undertake the development of new devices required by one or more operating divisions. To develop designs of new products which the Corporation may wish to undertake. In no sense shall the engineering and research section supersede the functions of the engineering departments of any individual operation.

Plant engineering section. To undertake the design of all building structures, also the construction.

Manufacturing and plant layout section. To advise on the proper layout of new manufacturing units and the development of additions to existing units. To investigate the merits of new devices and methods for manufacturing and to disseminate information pertaining to such developments through the various operations. To develop statistical data pertaining to methods and devices used in a general way by various operating divisions to the end that the most effective methods may be developed and used by all operations. To become acquainted with the manufacturing methods of all divisions to the end that the best method in use may be recommended to all divisions so that such methods may be standardized throughout all

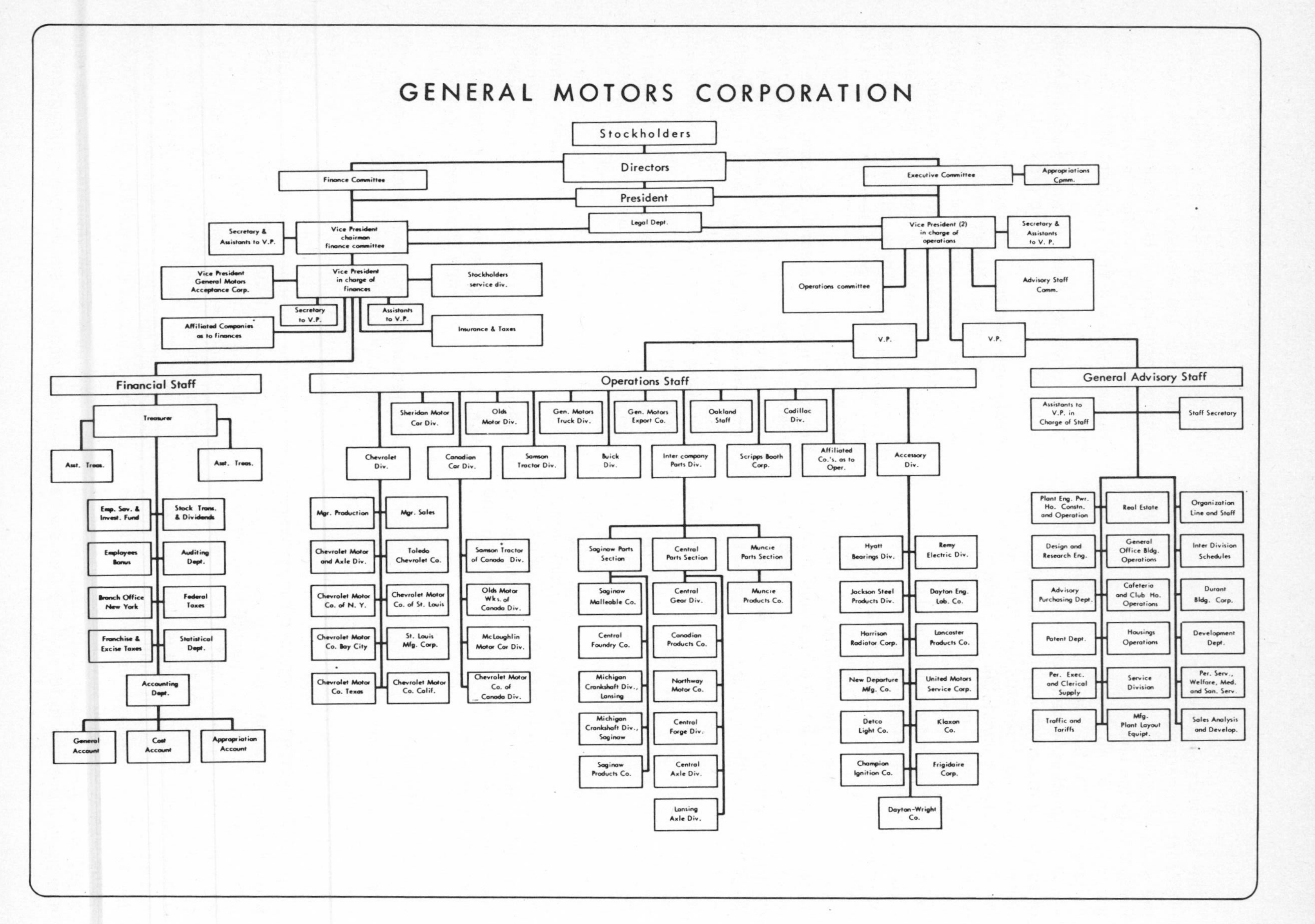
GENERAL MOTORS CORPORATION
Stockholders
Directors
Finance Committee
Executive Committee
Appropriations Comm.
President
Legal Dept.
Secretary & Assistants to V.P.
Vice President chairman finance committee
Vice President (2) in charge of operations
Secretary & Assistants to V. P.
Vice President General Motors Acceptance Corp.
Vice President in charge of finances
Stockholders service div.
Operations committee
Advisory Staff Comm.
Secretary to V.P.
Assistants to V.P.
Affiliated Companies as to finances
Insurance & Taxes
V.P.
V.P.
Financial Staff
Operations Staff
General Advisory Staff
Treasurer
Asst. Treas.
Asst. Treas.
Emp. Sav. & Invest. Fund
Stock Trans. & Dividends
Employees Bonus
Auditing Dept.
Branch Office New York
Federal Taxes
Franchise & Excise Taxes
Statistical Dept.
Accounting Dept.
General Account
Cost Account
Appropriation Account
Sheridan Motor Car Div.
Olds Motor Div.
Gen. Motors Truck Div.
Gen. Motors Export Co.
Oakland Staff
Cadillac Div.
Chevrolet Div.
Canadian Car Div.
Samson Tractor Div.
Buick Div.
Inter company Parts Div.
Scripps Booth Corp.
Affiliated Co.'s. as to Oper.
Accessory Div.
Mgr. Production
Mgr. Sales
Chevrolet Motor and Axle Div.
Toledo Chevrolet Co.
Chevrolet Motor Co. of N. Y.
Chevrolet Motor Co. of St. Louis
Chevrolet Motor Co. Bay City
St. Louis Mfg. Corp.
Chevrolet Motor Co. Texas
Chevrolet Motor Co. Calif.
Samson Tractor of Canada Div.
Olds Motor Wks. of Canada Div.
McLoughlin Motor Car Div.
Chevrolet Motor Co. of Canada Div.
Saginaw Parts Section
Central Parts Section
Muncie Parts Section
Saginaw Malleable Co.
Central Foundry Co.
Michigan Crankshaft Div., Lansing
Michigan Crankshaft Div., Saginaw
Saginaw Products Co.
Central Gear Div.
Canadian Products Co.
Northway Motor Co.
Central Forge Div.
Central Axle Div.
Lansing Axle Div.
Muncie Products Co.
Hyatt Bearings Div.
Remy Electric Div.
Jackson Steel Products Div.
Dayton Eng. Lab. Co.
Harrison Radiator Corp.
Lancaster Products Co.
New Departure Mfg. Co.
United Motors Service Corp.
Delco Light Co.
Klaxon Co.
Champion Ignition Co.
Frigidaire Corp.
Dayton-Wright Co.
Assistants to V.P. in Charge of Staff
Staff Secretary
Plant Eng. Pwr. Ho. Constn. and Operation
Real Estate
Organization Line and Staff
Design and Research Eng.
General Office Bldg. Operations
Inter Division Schedules
Advisory Purchasing Dept.
Cafeteria and Club Ho. Operations
Durant Bldg. Corp.
Patent Dept.
Housings Operations
Development Dept.
Per. Exec. and Clerical Supply
Service Division
Per. Serv., Welfare, Med. and San. Serv.
Traffic and Tariffs
Mfg. Plant Layout Equipt.
Sales Analysis and Develop.

divisions with the resulting economy and efficiency. To design and develop special machinery resulting in economical production of parts in general use by the Corporation.

[Other sections in the General Advisory Staff would be the patent counsel, the legal section, an insurance section, a real estate section, a general office section (to manage office buildings, not the offices), a housing operations section, a cafeteria and clubhouse section, an organization section (to keep charts and records of organization and to advise on organization), a tax section—also those listed below.]

Development section. To study questions pertaining to the development of the Corporation's activities not at present represented on its Operations Staff with a view to increasing its profits by the manufacture of parts previously purchased or supplementing of its present operations by entering entirely new lines of development. To undertake the investigation of properties that would be desirable for the Corporation to acquire, through purchase or otherwise.

Traffic and tariff. To advise the Operations Staff regarding all matters relating to traffic. To study, and to represent the Corporation before transportation authorities. To prosecute cases before the Interstate Commerce Commission.

Inter-division schedule. To develop with the cooperation of individual operations information pertaining to the proposed production schedule to the end that all operations are properly advised as to their responsibilities and to properly distribute the production of the Parts and Accessories Groups to the end that proper provision may be made for all demands and the most effective results thereby obtained.

Personnel section. To advise with the Operations Staff as well as the Advisory Staff pertaining to executive and clerical supply of personnel. To investigate and supply a record of applicants desiring connections with the Corporation and to keep in touch with applicants that will tend to strengthen the various staffs of the Corporation.

Personal section. To handle all questions pertaining to welfare work, have jurisdiction over the medical and sanitary service of the various operations in any advisory way and to advise with the various operations as to all matters of such character.

Sales and advertising section. To study in a general way all matters pertaining to sales policy, advertising, etc. To develop statistics that will guide the Operations Staff in their sales and advertising work on such matters as would be beyond the scope or the capacity of an individual operation. To advise the sales department of the Operations Staff as to proper advertising medium, best style of copy and all other matters of similar character.

President's Personal Staff

The President's personal staff is divided into two general divisions:

1 Personal assistants to the President
2 Appropriations Committee.

Personal assistants to the President. One or more assistants will be designated by the President for such duties as the President may elect to attach to such appointment.

Appropriations Committee. This Committee is to investigate, on behalf of the President, the propriety of extensions to the Corporation's units represented by betterments to existing properties or additions through the acquisition of new properties as may be recommended by the executive in charge of any operating division or group of operations or by the Vice President in charge of the General Advisory Staff. The Appropriations Committee has the privilege of drawing on the General Advisory Staff for such technical information and assistance as in its judgment may be desirable.

The organization principles on which Sloan based his plan are listed below. Even today, more than fifty years later, General Motors' organization structure is based on these principles. Richness of content combined with brevity should be noted.

Mr. Sloan's Organization Principles

I Establishment by the Board of Directors and its committees, of uniform policies and procedures to govern the over-all operation of all divisions in any area in which such consistency is judged to be necessary for the best interests of the corporation as a whole.

These assure coordination and direction of division management toward the accomplishment of corporate objectives and permit review of results.

II Delegation of full authority, within this framework of uniform policy and procedures, with corresponding responsibility for the use of the authority so delegated.

This results in maximum initiative on every managerial level and at every point requiring administrative judgment, by the men closest to all the facts of the situation and with full responsibility for their decisions.

III A continuous flow of ideas and information upward and downward through the management organization, by means of executive visits, formal reports and frequent meetings of staff and line executives at all appropriate levels.

This results in education and understanding of the purposes of higher management and of the reasons for the establishment of or change in policy or procedure at all levels of management. At the same time it produces an upward flow of information to the executives of the diverse situations arising in operations, full knowledge of which is necessary if appropriate changes in policy or procedure are to be accomplished intelligently and promptly.

General Motors was divisionalized from its inception because it was formed by the amalgamation of a number of automobile companies, each of which remained largely autonomous. Thus Sloan's organization plan was designed to introduce better coordination and control rather than to decentralize decision making.

On the other hand, many companies that have grown rapidly already have coordinated control but do not have decentralized operations; and since most decisions of any importance must be referred all the way to the top, their operations become more and more inflexible as new layers of supervision are added and the decision makers become further and further removed from actual observation of events. To cope with this situation, many of them have divisionalized their operations—that is, they have divided their organizations into a number of semiautonomous units similar to those that existed (and still exist) in General Motors. In this article, Prof. Richard Heflebower, of the economics department of Northwestern University, discusses the advantages of this form of organization and some of the problems it may give rise to.

Observations on Decentralization in Large Enterprises

Richard B. Heflebower

The decentralization of decision-making in large to giant enterprises, which has grown apace in American business, introduces a concept of internal structure of the firm that has important implications for organization theory. In the extreme, an enterprise decentralized in this regard might be looked upon as a group of teams bound together by certain common objectives and the ultimate authority of the top command. Such an arrangement might affect both the efficiency of the large corporation, and its conduct in external markets and, for both reasons, have important economic implications.

This organizational plan, the decentralization of decision-making, is undertaken especially as the means of effective general direction and control once the corporation has acquired certain characteristics of which large size is the most frequent. Executives are impressed by the lengthening of lines of communication even before the enterprise reaches giant scale. By the same token, and in the absence of decentraliza-

From *The Journal of Industrial Economics* (Basil Blackwell, Oxford, November, 1960), pp. 7–22.

tion, the number of decisions that a handful of executives must make mounts at least proportionately. Furthermore, they make their choices at increasingly greater distances, in time and in the number of layers of transmittal, from the primary sources of information. No wonder they see creeping inefficiency in the wings.

Thus far the expression 'decentralization of decision-making' has been used without giving it precision; at the extreme, and in the organizational plan to be emphasized here, it amounts to setting up inside the corporation a series of 'quasi-firms.' The divisions (and subdivisions) are not made into firms, in the full sense, because they are not autonomous legal units that are free to choose their objectives. Instead the overhead authority, or the corporation's top management, provides decision criteria and may issue specific orders, and these together may prevent maximization of the division's profits. Yet, within the area of discretion prescribed, each major division is expected ordinarily to react to buying and selling markets (whether these are outside the corporation or involve intra-corporate transfers of commodities in various states of production and distribution), and to conduct its operations between those markets, in the fashion that will contribute the most to the overall profits of the corporation. In the short run, the test of whether it does so is often, but not necessarily, its own divisional profit and loss statement.

The concept of the quasi-firm indicates that a sufficient zone of discretion must be granted to the management of the division so that it will take an entrepreneurial, not a bureaucratic, view of its situation and at the same time can, with propriety, be held to account for performance.

Whatever the level in the company's hierarchy being studied, the issue is whether the decentralized unit has a scope of decision-making such that it can function as a quasi-firm and be expected to be responsible for its operating results. If one can visualize such a unit operating as a quasi-firm without price discretion in either buying or selling, then, in a sense, cost per unit of volume becomes the criterion of performance. But more generally, price discretion in line with a policy instruction would seem to be in order. The exceptions would be chiefly where similarity of price action among divisions, say those laid out on an area basis, is a dominating consideration. But the principle of the quasi-firm establishes a presumption in favor of the maximum discretion feasible for each division in its buying and selling activities.

Those encompass more than external transactions, for intra-corporate transfers are often one side or even both sides of a division's 'market' operations, a fact which gives rise to difficult questions about the 'prices.' Much of the quasi-firm concept becomes meaningless if these transfer prices do not reflect what amount to market transactions. Otherwise transfer prices, perhaps in level and certainly in timing and degree of variation, would be arbitrary and so would any profit and loss statement reflecting them. Any judgment of performance on the basis of such profit and loss statements might easily reward the wrong divisional management.

In a series of transfers among vertically related divisions, use of prices that accorded with a cost rule, such as specified margin over direct costs, would pass the full impact of favorable or unfavorable market conditions to the division that finally sells outside. The top management's ability to decide what should be done about that last price, or judge performance of various divisions other than on a unit conversion or distribution cost basis, would be handicapped.

One final method of obtaining such a price is to simulate a market by using best bids from outside. This could result in quite inaccurate prices [except] where the top management not only permits but also encourages outside purchases or sales when the terms are better.

That would not only help solve the intra-company transfer price problem but also have another fundamental 'market-disciplining' effect. The division that loses sales by that means would then have excess capacity and an unfavorable income statement because a 'customer' division bought outside. Such a policy, however, could have some unique effects if, in the industry as a whole, there were excess capacity in the particular processing operation. Profit margins generally would be low. If any outside firm were to shade prices, and the subdivided giant's division using the product were to buy outside at that price, and that saving be transmitted to subsequent division and finally to the outside sale at the last step, the whole price structure would soon collapse. Indeed, full use of the outside buying or selling alternative when prices there are more favorable, is inconsistent with a policy by the large firm of stability of final selling prices. But this is a phase of the economic effects of decentralization to be considered later.

Putting together the idea of a zone of responsibility for the division much narrower than that of an autonomous enterprise of the same size, and of a high degree of freedom of action in that zone, it is quite possible that decisions will be more 'rational' than in an autonomous corporation whose whole volume is similar to that of a division of the giant.

The final implication of a managerial sort to draw from the guasi-firm concept of the decentralized unit is the possibility of 'internal competition.' This takes a variety of forms. The managements of units at the same level, say geographic divisions, are rivals in the sense of trying to make the best showing. A standard way of doing so is to reduce costs. Vertically related units are rivals over transfer prices and even over product design. All units' heads are rivals for recognition and promotion. Indeed, it is possible that such striving for divisional efficiency, unless it does harm to the corporation as a whole, tends to cumulate. One might even conclude that it would take unusual incompetence in the top command to make the corporation as a whole inefficient where it set profit-maximizing criteria for divisions.

One reason why that view of the effect of decentralization might be too optimistic is the possibility that, simultaneously, there emerges a conflict between the longer-term ends of the corporation and the shorter-term zone of action and criteria of performance applied to the divisions. Because of the limited scope assigned to them, and the use of a short-period profit and loss statement as the chief test of performance, the division's decisions are likely to be biased toward short-term ends. Its own authority relates primarily, and often exclusively, to short-period operations. It has to ask upstream for capital; it cannot go to the capital market nor does it have the right even to use the internal funds generated by its own activities.

Turning to the economic issues the summary picture just sketched of the large, decentralized corporation leads logically to the issue of efficiency of corporations of large size and often with varied and complex operations. Until recently economic theory generally used the 'U-shaped' curve of the firm, a graphic exposition of the idea that after a minimum efficient size was reached, the firm's costs per unit tended to rise as it became larger. For some time it has been recognized that this conclusion rested, inherently, on the assumption that the method of management, or the organization for carrying it out, does not change materially with the size of company. But from Adam Smith on, it has been emphasized that the methods of production, particularly as to the amount and type of capital equipment used, ordinarily change with the scale of operations. Why not a similar development with respect to management? The lag in study of this possibility may stem from economists' lack of interest in actual managerial organization and procedures. Or it may have been a carry-over from the owner-entrepreneur concept and the corollary of the limited life or capacity of one man. When one looks at decentralized decision-making those human limitations can still be recognized but their consequences be denied. The key is the separation of those functions that must be exercised by the counterpart of the entrepreneur-owner, that is by the top management, from those than can be delegated to subordinates operating within an 'organization for decision-making.' That organization requires persons of different capacities in different parts of the organizational hierarchy. Obviously, it requires a different type of top executive, not the field commander to use a military analogy, but the strategist, the master of logistics and the skilled coordinator. Pursuing the analogy, the field commanders, in their roles as such, must have different qualifications; those of skill in making 'field' or operating decisions and in executing them. But will the field commanders, now with lesser responsibilities than an autonomous entrepreneur would have but with a substantial area of choice and opportunity, and egged on by more modest financial incentives but with the prospects of a higher rung on the hierarchical ladder, drive for efficiency of feel claustrophobia despite all the doors the decentralization plan provides?

No general or final answer can be given but clearly the size at which the specter of inefficiency arises has been pushed 'far to the right' on the scale. The often quoted data that show profit rates of the largest corporations to be lower than for firms somewhat smaller quite probably reflect the adverse effects on the former of their 'responsibilities' as price leaders but with little power to discipline non-followers. [Also] the assertion that firms that have grown beyond 'minimum efficient size' have not become less efficient is quite persuasive. 'Grown' should be emphasized, for there is evidence to the contrary where size was achieved by merger. But even for those that have expanded by building it should be underscored that they are the successful enterprises and their success may reflect unique skill of individuals in performing the managerial task, or favored factor price or technology, and not the advantages of the management plan as such. All that it is safe to conclude with respect to efficiency of large enterprises is that there is lack of evidence that costs per unit rise within the size range experienced thus far. On the other hand, neither is there convincing evidence of added efficiency with growth beyond a sizeable, but not a giant 'minimum efficient size.' On the basis of present evidence, it seems best to base economic analysis and policy proposals on the assumption that the long-run cost curve of the firm is horizontal beyond a sizeable but not a giant scale. [And] it seems probable that the major reason for that conclusion, in contrast to the earlier view of growing inefficiency with large size, is the favorable influence on efficiency of the decentralization of decision-making.

The second economic issue has to do with whether the quasi-firm established by decentralization of decision-making means that the divisions will be different performers in external markets than would be true if selling and purchasing were centrally directed by the corporation. An affirmative answer does not stem necessarily from the first of the economic consequences of decentralization, that is, its effects on the costs of performing what is done within the corporation, or between the level at which it purchases materials outside and makes the final sale to outside customers. To the extent that such efficiency is gained by decentralization, it is not necessarily translated into different performance in external markets. While one can grant that decentralization should expedite reactions to external market developments, there remains the basic question whether the guides to that action are different than they would be in the absence of decentralization of the making of the relevant decisions.

Presumably the part of the company's business that constitutes the appropriate product line for selling would be included within one division or quasi-firm. Consequently the corporation's share of the market for that product line will still be represented by one entity. There would follow the same concern about more or less price competition, about whether to attempt more of less product differentiation, and about other practices as seller (or buyer). It is not evident that the bases for choices among such alternatives will be different than were the parent and its top management in direct command. True, if one division has a product that is a close substitute for that of another division—plastic versus metal toys—or each has a brand of refrigerators such as the 'G.E.' and 'Hotpoint' brands of the respective divisions of the General Electric Company—rivalry might be quite unrestrained. Indeed, the top management would have to impose restraints on divisions to prevent such behavior. But such conduct in external sales is not general and even when it exists, it is by no means certain that the character of the market is affected as it would be were each division an autonomous corporation. What is particularly lacking is evidence that two such divisions would engage in price competition.

Finally, the managerial and the economic come together on one point that could easily be overlooked, that is, that the most clearly efficacious decentralization of a giant enterprise into quasi-firms rests heavily on the vigor of the rivalry in the external markets. At best this would mean that when purchases or sales are made in external markets active competition there would force each division to be aggressive in buying and selling outside. In addition, it would mean that the external market would provide valid guides to, or at least aid in determining, transfer prices within the corporation. If that is not done because there is no usable external price with which to compare those transfers, then the free opportunity, if possible, to do business with outside suppliers or customers is not a valuable guide unless there is an active market outside. In a very fundamental sense, therefore, the success of such decentralization turns on the maintenance of a competitive environment for the firm.

But where the success of decentralization so enhances the growth of those corporations which possess the marginal amount of the qualities necessary for growth that a radical reduction occurs in the number of firms and degree of rivalry so that external markets are not effectively competitive, then the potential advantage of decentralization would be lost by mere success of a few firms. While economists have not yet been able to come up with a definitive theory of the performance of markets where sellers are very few, they know that it is likely that, except possibly where technological progressiveness is a socially desirable outlet for individual action, competition will be less effective in its dual role of whip and rein where the rivals are very few rather than more numerous.

As to whether decentralization of a large corporation lessens its 'economic power', or the public's judgment of its power, the conclusion must be negative. Granted that this 'power' is a vague concept—those who use it most studiously avoid giving it precision—but it must refer to the firm's total impact on the political-economic life of a society and ordinarily transcends its influence on the market for a particular product. The corporation may not wield that power consciously or, if aware of its strength, may use it charily. But the mere fact that it agrees to or refuses a wage demand, that it invests more or less, or that it increases or decreases its rate of employement, means that a single corporate entity is responsible for a not insignificant impact on the economy. It becomes the synonym for power and wealth and is open to abuse by those who control and to the attack of the demagogue as well as to the analysis of the careful student. While the public relations surveys may show that there is wide preference for such giants' products, behind the mention of its name may lurk the fear of the size of the vast and impersonal organization. Indeed, the mere success of decentralization provides a basis for a serious question that is sometimes put as 'If subdivisions have that much autonomy, why General Motors?' The response is vigorous, of course, but by no means consists only of 'economic' as distinct from 'private' advantages. That question, even if successfully answered in terms of economic benefits, may not dispose of all of the quite proper concern on socio-political grounds.

Looking ahead, if realignment of functions between the central office and a succession of divisions and subdivisions removes the inefficiency restraint on growth, what, if anything, stops it? If the cost curve does not turn up at some point, will the more successful (in using this managerial arrangement) grow without limit? By definition—as the uniquely efficient—their growth should exceed that of the national output, so their share of economic activity conducted by them would increase. That could foretell an economic order of blocs and groups which, even if they functioned well in the sense of the coordinating of sectors of the economy, could still be inviting the hand of government. That hand would more likely be to regulate or to own than to re-form giant enterprises into smaller but not necessarily less efficient enterprises.

11 The Dynamics of Organization

As Henry S. Dennison pointed out (see Chapter 8), the people within the organization affect the structure just as the structure affects them. This has been recognized ever since formal organization charts and manuals were first introduced in business, and even those who believe most strongly in the classical rules of organization point out that the principles must be disregarded at times because of the personalities of those affected. Thus they recommend that the ideal organization, drawn up according to the principles, be considered a goal toward which the organizers should be working, rather than a plan to be introduced immediately.

Practical managers have always recognized this also. Thus when P. S. du Pont, as president of the Du Pont Company, submitted a formal organization chart to the board of directors, he recommended that it be modified in accordance with the needs of those who had to live within the organization.

It is also recognized that the formal charts and manuals can never provide more than an approximate picture of the organization, for side by side with the formal organization there exists an informal organization growing out of the needs of those within the structure. The Hawthorne studies brought this out; Chester I. Barnard emphasized it; and later writers have paid even more attention to the informal structure and its consequences.

The informal organization has many aspects. On the lowest level, it may show itself in an informal agreement to hold production down and keep standards from becoming too tight. In other cases, including many in management, a man may gain more authority than is formally granted to him because he has influence with higher management or because others have found that he can help them with their problems. Conversely, a man may relinquish some of his authority and some of his responsibilities because he is uninterested in certain parts of his job or because he cannot adequately handle all of it. In the later case, there are likely to be empire builders among the other managers who are only too eager to fill the vacuum he has created.

The first article in this chapter describes some of the aspects of the informal organization and some of the ways in which it may actually have value. The second cites observed instances of the functioning of the informal structure.

The effect of personalities and the informal organization are known as "the dynamics of organization," in contrast to the mechanics, which were covered in the last chapter.

Prominent among those calling attention to the informal organization were the Hawthorne researchers, and one of those who assisted with the experiments was Thomas North Whitehead, son of the great philosopher Alfred North Whitehead (who was himself sympathetic to the studies).

T. N. Whitehead is perhaps the most philosophical and articulate of the Hawthorne researchers, and he is among the most modest of scholars. He is deeply concerned with the problem of corporate and societal disorganization and with methods of minimizing it.

Here he points out that many of the activities of the informal organization are quite valuable in that they constitute a form of horizontal coordination often not provided for in the formal organization and that their value may frequently be enhanced by simple changes in formal procedures.

The Inevitability of the Informal Organization and Its Possible Value

T. N. Whitehead

The division of social activity into ordinary living on the one hand and business on the other was not the result of custom or of the direct needs of human intercourse; it depended on the chance evolution of technological procedures. The industrial organization is controlled without adequate regard for the social lives of those involved by a type of man highly skilled in the logical, reflective thinking suitable to the rapid evolution of technology. This does not imply that the modern executive is indifferent to the welfare of those beneath him, but it is true that this welfare has not been the primary force in moulding the industrial organization.

The modern executive is indeed in a peculiarly difficult situation. In the first place, an executive does not literally lead his human material, he organizes it. It is broadly true to say that he cannot compare with his employees in the performance of any one of their several tasks. The occupation of an executive is different, not only in detail but also in kind from that of his men; their respective sentiments and attitudes are based on radically different experiences. The modern 'leader' is no longer quite a member of his group, working by their side and sharing their daily lives.

Secondly, it follows from this that the social organization of the group is not oriented primarily towards their executive, but towards some informal leader of their own choosing—one of themselves. For every group has its leader, or an inner ring of leaders, a miniature aristocracy. Thus, whether he realizes the fact or not, the executive is in danger of directing a formed society from without; a society that will evolve defense mechanisms and sentiments of antagonism if its social living appears to be in danger of interruption.

Thirdly, the executive is himself a social being and his general attitudes are oriented by his society, but this society is not the group he is directing and his attitude is not moulded by them. The executive is a member of a highly competitive 'progressive' society anxious for its preservation and for its advancement, and his more general outlook necessarily conforms to this social pattern. I say 'necessarily conforms' because this society chose him for that very reason. Thus his activities are directed by his society's desire for 'economic progress' rather than by any needs of his employees. It is true that these latter are also members of the society outside, though they may well come from a different stratum, but as a working group they have little part in forming and sharing their executives' social sentiments.

Fourthly, the control which the executive exercises over his group has no explicit relation to their social life. Its purpose is simply to organize their activities with a single eye to their technological efficiency, and with the intention of elaborating and introducing improved procedures as quickly as may be.

It is a well-known fact amongst industrialists that the lines of authority in an organization are mainly vertical, from the worker to the president, but the lines of collaboration tend to run horizontally between officials of approximately level rank. This second line of collaboration has usu-

From *Leadership in a Free Society* (Harvard University Press, Cambridge, Mass., 1936), pp. 78–79, 114–118.

ally no recognition in the formal set-up of the company; it is an unofficial activity held in check by the formal organization built on more or less vertical lines. Now these two organizing principles correspond to a fundamental difference in the place at which initiative is exercised. Horizontal lines of collaboration, in so far as they are effective, result in daily adjustments elaborated at the level at which the problems arise. Thus initiative remains in the hands of those whose daily activities have shown the need. On the other hand, when the process of collaboration is forced up the lines of formal authority, integration and initiative take place above and are brought down to the relevant level in the form of orders.

The all-round foreman is an instance of horizontal collaboration; only, as in the case of certain foreign dictators, he happens to comprise all the collaborators in his own person—he collaborates with himself in his various capacities; there lies his weakness, and implicitly he seems to know it. For anyone with a first-hand experience of factory life will recognize the many unoffical ways in which a foreman creates a small group of collaborators officially denied to him. John, an elderly mechanic, shows some aptitude for training novices and he, unrecognized by the formal organization, is the de facto trainer for the shop. Tom is quick at figures and he looks after the foreman's paperwork. Someone else can fix the machines and keep them working; and so on. These men are the foreman's unofficial collaborators, and they represent him in his many capacities. Without such a shadow staff, the position of the foreman would be quite hopeless; but he very reluctantly admits to such assistance, for it is not recognized and is often not tolerated by the senior executives.

Thus the foreman, on his own initiative and in concert with his group, has elaborated a modification to meet a visible situation; visible, that is, to the working group. But management, so far from assisting this display of initiative at the relevant level, is usually blankly ignorant of it and tends to discourage what it sees. And yet a development on these lines is worthy of considerable thought, for it does make possible a modification within a group to meet the circumstances that arise there, and it simultaneously relieves the foreman of an impossible combination of tasks. The Western Electric Company is engaged in a careful survey of the extent to which such unofficial organizations have taken place, and its tentative findings are exceedingly interesting. They illustrate the continual tendency for adjustments to take place at the level at which the need becomes evident, and the degree to which a formal organization can easily act as a check on such natural growth. Thus, management unwittingly holds back its employees from effecting technical changes to meet needs visible to them. And this brings us to a generalization of wide application. *No society or organization is averse to change, provided the initiative for that change takes place at the relevant level—at that level where the daily activities have shown the need. Under those conditions, change will present itself not as an interruption, but as the natural flow of social living.*

Any group is apt to accept change in technical matters arising out of its own activities. It is not necessary for the average member to have explicitly seen the need or the advantage of the change in advance. What is required is that when the accepted leader points out the way, something in the follower's own experience and reflections shall make him believe in the fitness of the suggestion. A considerable portion of this sentiment of agreement arises from the follower's attitude of acceptance, or loyalty to his leader, and not from any direct understanding of the situation. This is a vitally important point, for it is impossible to suppose that all needed change in industrial groups will arise from circumstances with which the individuals are familiar.

Large questions of company policy do not usually disclose themselves in the daily activities of the workers. Such questions are visible only to the senior executives and, provided these are the accepted leaders, all ranks are willing to leave the initiative there. But most, not all, of the changes introduced by management into a working group do concern small matters which have arisen from within that group. The group are failing on delivery, have high operating costs, have neglected quality, or are careless of company property; circumstances like these give rise to most of the small detailed changes which are resisted so bitterly when initiated in the offices of the executives. And yet experiments and exceptional organizations here and there have shown that it would not be impossible to reorganize working groups so as to enable them to supply much of the integration and initiative needed to cure their own ills. To the extent to which this is accomplished, management would represent itself as a body assisting its groups in working out their own visible problems, rather than as disturbers of social living. Management would be called upon to effect an integration as between small groups.

This is not a scheme for employees' representation, though that has its place; it amounts to suggesting that initiative should not be too exclusively concentrated at the top but should be encouraged at every level in those matters relevant to that level. Moreover, the form of the encouragement should be that of evolving an organization which will enable each level to obtain a perspective of its own problems and then to handle them effectively.

Any large and enduring organization must possess a formal structure and forms of procedure. In the case of a nation, this comprises its constitution and its laws. A commericial company functions under the relevant laws supplemented by its own constitution and regulations. These latter require continual modification to meet changing conditions; but where the formal structure attempts to force new procedures at variance with the situation as seen by those affected—or worse, hampers attempts at natural growth, then poor integration is likely to result. An example in point is the habitual failure of the formal structure to accommodate itself to the existing horizontal collaboration. It should be the object of company regulation to give form and assistance to such a growth, and to ensure its orderly evolution.

Observation shows that every group will elaborate a social situation of some sort; the questions are whether or not this situation shall content the group in the first place, and incline it to accept the leadership of management in the second. No one has ever experienced a group from the inside which did not have its habitual ways of procedure, its common attitudes and sentiments. Where such social understandings are conspicuously few, the picture is inevitably one of wild confusion. The same general remarks apply to the development of horizontal collaboration. It is regarded as dangerous to have activities flowing along lines other than those of authority. But the fact is that such activity is the order of the day, and no complex community could survive for a moment under any other arrangement. Again, the question is whether this shall be recognized and persuaded to organize itself around the purposes of management by a recognition of its function, and by assisting that function to improve itself.

What is required is not so much a set of rules enforcing any particular collaboration, as an organization which will make it really effective. Thus, if some department is in fact habitually obtaining information from another by unofficial means, this rather suggests that the information is found useful, and a few procedures for obtaining it with less trouble might be devised. Where the need is experienced towards the top of the managerial ladder, the means are usually devised, but the same need is not so habitually recognized or favoured when it arises lower down.

These two suggestions are not intended to be exhaustive nor are they applicable to all cases. The central thesis is that management, to be successful in leading its groups through successive changes, must ensure that the changes are designed with reference to the actual social activities of those groups. To accomplish that, initiative should be placed so far as possible at the level at which the change is to take place, and where its need is visible in terms of daily activity. This does not imply statements to the effect that management's 'door is always open' to suggestions from below, but the evolution of an organization such that it will naturally fall to the relevant body of people to take the initiative. The simplest way to achieve this is really to know the human situation within the firm, and to be alert for evidence of attempted initiative. With an unsuitable organization, such evidence often takes the form of unofficial, or even officially discouraged action. If activity of this sort is regarded not merely as a breach of discipline, but as the (possibly unwise) expression of a need, then the rearrangement will often suggest itself.

Despite the tendency of people in industry to form informal organizations, the following excerpt shows that too loose a formal organization may trouble some people as much as a too tight structure troubles others.

Here two British sociologists report on two studies of the organization of research laboratories. The first was made in a group of Scottish firms, the second in a group of English companies, which were larger and more committed to research than those in the Scottish group. (In half the latter the laboratories were later disbanded or disrupted by resignations of their leaders; in others the laboratory forces were converted into new departments, such as test departments.)

Mechanistic and Organic Systems

Tom Burns and G. M. Stalker

There seemed to be two divergent systems of management practice. Neither was fully and consistently applied in any firm, although there was a clear division between those managements which adhered generally to the one, and those which followed the other. Neither system was openly and consciously employed as an instrument of policy, although many beliefs and empirical methods associated with one or the other were expressed. One system, to which we gave the name 'mechanistic', appeared to be appropriate to an enterprise operating under relatively stable conditions. The other, 'organic', appeared to be required for conditions of change. In terms of 'ideal types' their principal characteristics are briefly these:

In mechanistic systems the problems and tasks facing the concern as a whole are broken down into specialisms. Each individual pursues his task as something distinct from the real tasks of the concern as a whole, as if it were the subject of a sub-contract. 'Somebody at the top' is responsible for seeing to its relevance. The technical methods, duties, and powers attached to each functional role are precisely defined. Interaction within management tends to be vertical, i.e., between superior and subordinate. Operations and working behaviour are governed by instructions and decisions issued by superiors. This command hierarchy is maintained by the implicit assumption that all knowledge about the situation of the firm and its tasks is, or should be, available only to the head of the firm. Management, often visualized as the complex hierarchy familiar in organization charts, operates a simple control system, with information flowing up through a succession of filters, and decisions and instructions flowing downwards through a succession of amplifiers.

Organic systems are adapted to unstable conditions, when problems and requirements for action arise which cannot be broken down and distributed among specialist roles within a clearly defined hierarchy. Individuals have to perform their special tasks in the light of their knowledge of the tasks of the firm as a whole. Jobs lose much of their formal definition in terms of methods, duties, and powers, which have to be redefined continually by interaction with others participating in a task. Interaction runs laterally as much as vertically. Communication between people of different ranks tends to resemble lateral consultation rather than vertical command. Omniscience can no longer be imputed to the head of the concern.

Difficulty of Changing

The central problem of the Scottish study appeared to be why the working organization of a concern did not change its system from 'mechanistic' to 'organic' as its circumstances changed with entry into new commercial and technical fields. The answer which suggested itself was that every single person in a firm not only is (a) a member of a working organization, but also (b) a member of a group with sectional interests in conflict with those of other groups, and (c) one individual among many to whom the rank they occupy and the prestige attaching to them are matters of deep concern. Looked at in another way, any firm contains not only a working organization but a political system and a status structure. In the case of the firms we

From *The Management of Innovation* (Tavistock Publications, London, 1961, and Quadrangle Books, Inc., Chicago), pp. 5–7, 92–94.

studied, the existing political system and status structure were threatened by the advent of a new laboratory group. Especially, the technical information available to the newcomers, which was a valuable business resource, was used or regarded as an instrument for political control; and laboratory engineers claimed, or were regarded as claiming, elite status within the organization.

Neither political nor status preoccupations operated overtly, or even consciously; they gave rise to intricate manoeuvres and counter-moves, all of them expressed through decisions, or discussions about decisions, concerning the internal structure and the policies of the firm. Since political and status conflicts only came into the open in terms of the working organization, that organization became adjusted to serving the ends of the political and status system of the concern rather than its own.

The individual manager became absorbed in conflicts over power and status because they presented him with interests and problems more immediately important to him and more easily comprehended than those raised by the new organizational milieu and its unlimited liabilities. For increases in the rate of technical and commercial change meant more problems, more unfamiliar information, a wider range of work relationships, and heavier mental and emotional commitments. Many found it impossible to accept such conditions for their occupational lives. To keep their commitments limited meant either gaining more control over their personal situation or claiming exemption because of special conditions attached to their status. These purposes involved manoeuvres which persistently ran counter to the development of an organic system, and raised issues which could only be resolved by a reversion to a mechanistic system.

The Scottish study developed eventually into two complementary accounts of the ways in which the adaptation of management systems to conditions of change was impeded or thwarted. In one, the failure to adapt was attributed to the strength of former political and status structures. In other terms, the failure was seen as the consequence of an implicit resistance among individual members of concerns to the growth of commitments in their occupational existence at the expense of the rest of their lives.

The Organic System in Practice

In the electronics industry proper, one begins to meet concerns in which organization is thought of primarily in terms of the communication system; there is often a deliberate attempt to avoid specifying individual tasks, and to forbid any dependence on the management hierarchy as a structure of defined functions and authority. The head of one concern, at the beginning of the first interview, attacked the idea of the organization chart as inapplicable in his concern and as a dangerous method of thinking about the working of industrial management. The first requirement of a management, according to him, was that it should make the fullest use of the capacities of its members; any individual's job should be as little defined as possible, so that it will 'shape itself' to his special abilities and initiative.

In this concern insistence on the least possible specification for managerial positions was much more in evidence than any devices for ensuring adequate interaction within the system. This did occur, but as a consequence of a set of conditions rather than of prescription by top management. Some of these conditions were physical; a single-storeyed building housed the entire concern, two thousand strong, from laboratories to canteen. Access to anyone was, therefore, physically simple and direct; it was easier to walk across to the laboratories' door, the office door, or the factory door and look about for the person one wanted, than even to telephone. Written communication inside the factory was actively discouraged. Most important of all, however, was the need of each individual manager for interaction with others, in order to get his own tasks and functions defined, in the absence of specification from above. When the position of product engineer was created, for example, the first incumbents said they had to 'find out' what they had to do, and what authority and resources they could command to do it.

In fact, this process of 'finding-out' about one's job proved to be unending. Their roles were continually defined and redefined in connexion with specific tasks and as members of specific co-operative groups. This happened through a perpetual sequence of encounters with laboratory chiefs, with design engineers who had worked on the equipment the product engineers were responsible for getting made, with draughtsmen, with the works manager, with the foremen in charge of the production shops they had to use, with rate-fixers, buyers, and operatives. In every single case they, whose only commission was 'to see the job through', had to determine their part and that of the others through complex, though often brief, negotiations in which the relevant information and technical knowledge possessed by them would have to be declared, and that possessed by others ascertained.

The sheer difficulty of contriving the correct social stance and the effective social manner for use in different negotiations, the embarrassment of having so to contrive, and the personal affront attached to failure to achieve one's ends by these means, induced in managers a nervous preoccupation with the hazards of social navigation in the structure and with the relative validity of their own claims to authority, information, and technical expertise.

'Normally', said a departmental manager, 'management has a sort of family tree showing who is responsible for what, and what he is responsible for. It's a pity there's nothing like that here. It's rather difficult not knowing; there's a lot of trouble caused by this—you get an assistant to a manager who acts as though he were an assistant manager, a very different thing.' Another man, a product engineer, said 'One of the troubles here is that nobody is very clear about his title or status or even his function.' A foreman, explaining his relationship with senior managers, said of one, 'It's generally gathered, from seeing T. standing about looking at the room when something is being done to it and looking over machines, that he's in charge of plant and buildings.' The same foreman, discussing his own job, said that when he had first been promoted he had been told nothing of his duties and functions. 'Of course, nobody knows what his job is in here. When I was made foreman I was told to get on with the job—was just told 'You'll start in on Monday', so I came in and started in. That was really all that was said.'

The disruptive effects of this preoccupation were countered by a general awareness of the common purpose of the concern's attitudes. While this awareness was sporadic and partial for many members of the firm, it was an essential factor in, for example, the ability of the 'product engineers' to perform their tasks, dependent as they were on the co-operation of persons and groups who carried on the basic interpretative processes of the concern. Indeed, discussion of the common purposes of the organization featured largely in the conversation of cabals and extra-mural groups.

An even more important part was played by common beliefs and a sense of common purpose in the limiting case of rapidly changing conditions we encountered; a concern recently created to develop electronic equipment and components for the commercial market. While a hierarchy of management may certainly be said to have existed, positions in it were defined almost entirely in terms of technical qualifications. The conversion of this structure of technical expertise into a concern with commercial tasks required a continuous process of self education. There were two major aspects of this process. First, individual tasks in the concern were defined almost exclusively as a consequence of interaction with superiors, colleagues, and subordinates; there was no specification by the head of the concern. Secondly, this continuing definition—and redefinition—of structure depended for its success on effective communication. At the end of a discussion with senior members of staff, it was explicitly acknowledged that the organizational problems of the enterprise turned almost entirely on finding the right code of conduct which would make for effective communication—to avoid occasions, as one head of a laboratory put it, 'when I'm explaining a point to a chap and he says "Yes, yes" and I'm not at all sure whether he's caught on.'

12 How an Organization Grows

As an organization grows, its structure naturally becomes more complicated. Jobs that could once be handled by a single person are split and split again; new layers of supervision are inserted between the top man and the rank and file.

Sometimes a company continues to operate with the same organization structure for a long time after it has actually outgrown the plan. But there comes a point when it can no longer do so, and then it must institute a complete reorganization, realigning duties and responsibilities, and perhaps adding new coordinating positions.

There are many ways in which a company can grow, ranging from simply doing more of the same type of business to entering entirely new fields. The way chosen will depend on the strategy adopted by those in charge of the organization, which in turn will depend on their conception of the opportunities open to them. The first article in this chapter outlines various avenues of growth; the second discusses one particular way in which a company may grow.

Various methods by which a company may grow are described here by Sir Ronald Edwards, formerly of the London School of Economics and later connected with the management of public power, and H. Townsend, his associate at the school. Their discussion is based on many first-hand studies in industry (mainly British).

The Growth of Firms

R. S. Edwards and H. Townsend

Firms grow for many reasons. New products, improved methods of manufacture, economies of large-scale production, plentiful supplies of factors of production, changed channels of distribution or expanding markets may all contribute to the growth of firms; but growth may be attributed only partly to such impersonal forces. The personal forces, the energy and enterprise of the people in the firms, are just as important. Firms exist in an economic setting; but men and women determine what is made of that setting. We shall examine the impersonal forces that influence the activities of firms later. First, we wish to emphasise the importance of people.

Leadership

A man who drives a business to success might as easily drive it to bankruptcy in a different set of circumstances. One can only make assumptions about whether he would recognise the difference in the circumstances. We know of one businessman who was in fact driving his firm with great vigour down the road to ruin. Certain conditions, which he neither controlled nor understood, changed. [And] when a number of people have played a part it is not easy to distinguish their contributions and say who was mainly responsible for success, whether it was the man at the top or the men below him, the man with the personality or the men in the background.

Nearly everything that we might say about people must therefore be very tentative. We can, however, say with complete confidence that character and personality matter. If firms are brought to outstanding success it is usually due to a handful of people and sometimes to one exceptional person. Any firm that is reasonably well managed is likely to make some headway if the market conditions are favourable; but the firms that forge ahead are driven on by men who are more than administrators. We can also say with confidence that there is no one 'type' of successful businessman. Nevertheless, we believe that certain characteristics occur in successful businessmen more often than would be the case if they were a completely random sample of humanity.

First, there is strength and willingness to work hard, immensely hard in some cases; secondly, perseverance and determination amounting at times to fanatical single-mindedness; thirdly, a taste and flair for commerce, an understanding of the market place; fourthly, audacity—a willingness to take risks that are sometimes large gambles; fifthly, ability to inspire enthusiasm in those whose co-operation and assistance are essential; and finally, toughness amounting in some men to ruthlessness. In varying combinations and proportions these qualities seem to be found in the leadership of most businesses that have grown substantially.

It will be noticed that this list does not include either technical expertise or administrative skill. Many successful businesses have been built up in the past by men who did not themselves possess these qualities. Technicians and administrators could be and often were brought in at a level just below the leadership. In future this may be less easy. Industry is becoming an increasingly complex mixture of scientific, technological, economic and administrative problems, and, in consequence, it may well be that industrial leadership will call increasingly for a grasp of the technological issues involved.

The possession of inventive skill by itself or scientific knowledge by itself is not, and is not likely to become, a sufficient condition of success in business, even when backed by hard

From *Business Enterprise: Its Growth and Organization* (Macmillan & Co., Ltd., London, The Macmillan Co. of Canada, Limited, Toronto, and St. Martin's Press, Inc., New York, 1958), pp. 32–34, 38–40, 42, 44–45, 47, 49–51, 53–59. Reprinted by permission.

work, although there are cases where an inventor has also had the financial acumen and business skill to build a big business and maintain control of it.

There is one other general point we would make. The qualities possessed by the builders of firms are not necessarily those best suited to sustaining firms once they have grown. Sound administration and common prudence will often keep a business running smoothly, although they are only likely to be sufficient for building up a business in the most favourable circumstances. Indeed the kind of gamble that is frequently part and parcel of rapid growth would make a strange bed-fellow with tidy administration. More than one successful industrialist has queried this statement with us, usually on the ground that a business cannot afford to stand still and therefore needs the same qualities of leadership at all stages. Those who make this point are in most cases themselves the founders of their firms. In the sense that a business that settles down to a humdrum existence may easily slip back, the point has substance. On the other hand, the established concern, with strong reserves and well staffed with competent technologists, sales staff, administrators and financial men under good general management, will usually go steadily forward even though it lacks the single-minded devotion, daring and resilience usually required to build up a new business. This is a substantial difference.

Opportunity

Firms may be made to grow by business leaders; but leadership is not sufficient in itself to ensure expansion. Opportunity is also essential and opportunity cannot always be commanded. For example, it is quite likely that there were potential Morrises and Austins to be found in Britain in the late nineteenth century and, if there were any, they would have been effectively excluded from motor manufacturing by the notorious 'Red Flag' Act which remained unrepealed until 1896.[1]

To some extent the opportunities that come to a firm are contrived by it, to some extent a firm may take advantage of situations which are open to be exploited by others, and to some extent opportunity is a matter of luck. Chance plays a very important part indeed.

It may be argued that success is unlikely to be a matter of luck in the long run. If a firm consistently secures and exploits opportunities it cannot be merely lucky. But it is quite possible for a firm to be lucky in finding a major opportunity which sets it on its way and it is equally possible for it to be unlucky and not to find one. It is quite possible for a firm to seize an apparent opportunity and make a big investment which comes off, and it is equally possible for it to make a big investment which fails and from which it is unable to recover.

The over-riding factor in business life is that the future is hidden. The businessman can see no further into the future than the rest of us. He has to guess and back his guesses with hard cash. As we hear so little about the bad forecasts we may be apt to look on growth as a more automatic outcome of business ability than it in fact is. We hope that the examples will make it plain that chance plays a major role in industry.

Emphasis on the characteristics of business leaders and on the part played by opportunity may have given the impression that the growth of firms is an idiosyncratic phenomenon. There is always a strong individual element in the history of any firm; but a number of forms of growth may be distinguished. Firms often adopt different forms of growth at different times. This section is intended to put our early remarks into perspective and to illustrate once more the variety of industry.

Increasing Output of Existing Products

The most obvious, but by no means the most usual, way for a firm to grow is for it to do more of what it is doing already, i.e. to grow without diversification of processes or products.

Arthur Guinness Son and Company Ltd. is perhaps the most famous example of a firm which has grown by doing more of what it was doing already. The story of the development, told in the words of the Rt. Hon. Alan Lennox-

[1] *Editor's Note*: The Act provided that no powered vehicle could move on a highway unless preceded by a man, on foot or on horseback, carrying a red flag.

Boyd, M.P., formerly a director of Guinness, is as follows.

'The first Arthur Guinness took, on the 31st December, 1759, a 9000-year lease of an existing small brewery in Dublin. At that time, and for many years after, they brewed ale and stout or porter, as it was then called. I would say that the first milestone in the road that has led to our success was the decision to concentrate on one product. There is an entry in one of the old brewing books that reads as follows: "Today April 22nd 1799 was brewed the last ale brew." Since then we have brewed nothing but stout or porter. That is unique among brewers. The decision was taken when the founder was an old man and his son had already begun to take a large part in the business. Whoever made the decision, it was a stroke of genius.

'The second and similar vital decision is not so easy to pinpoint. It was probably never a single definite decision, but became the invariable policy. This was the restriction of the Guinness activities—or rather those of brewing branch—to brewing alone. In spite of many other activities of the first Arthur, the second Arthur and his son were only brewers. Moreover, nothing in the nature of either vertical or horizontal trustification was attempted.

'It is usual for breweries to own their own maltings. The Guinness policy on the other hand has been to malt only a small proportion of their requirements—just enough to give them a clear insight into all the problems of barley and malt.

'Guinness have never owned their retail outlets. This policy, while natural in the early days of their history, was later a decision reached, and over and over again confirmed, after the closest consideration. All this is part and parcel of that singling out of the objective which has throughout characterised the direction of this great business by successive members of the Guinness family, which I would add has in my experience been a characteristic of some of the most successful businessmen I have known. If then I were asked the chief reason, in so far as one can be dogmatic in such a matter, for the success of Guinness, I would say without hesitation that it has been due to the singleness of purpose.'

Adding Products Made by Similar Processes and Sold in Similar Markets

The commonest way for a firm to grow is probably by adding to the range of products already being sold other products of much the same type. The motor vehicle manufacturer who adds to his range of cars and the radio manufacturer who increases the number of models of his television receivers are examples. The same technological resources and knowledge are used and the products are sold in similar markets for similar purposes though perhaps to different income groups or to people with different tastes.

Mars Ltd., the confectionery makers, is a good example of a firm which has grown by increasing the range of its products. Mars was founded in 1932 and before the War only one product was made, the Mars Bar. Since the War, the company has introduced a number of new lines when openings have been seen for confectionery that can be sold in large quantities and therefore be produced on a very large scale with high speed, automatic machinery.

Exploiting Technological Knowledge in Different Markets

Very often firms make it their business to specialise in a particular field of knowledge and to go into whatever markets there are for the fruits of that knowledge. Thus a firm may specialise in knowing a particular material and in making things for which this material is suited.

The growth of the Morgan Crucible Company Ltd. illustrates such specialisation in knowledge and diversification in products. This company has developed in two distinct directions from the two original materials used for crucibles: plumbago, sometimes called graphite and little removed from what the layman knows as carbon, has been the basis of one side of the business, and clay the basis of the other. The products of the company now include carbon, graphite and metal graphite brushes for electrical machines, carbons for arc lamps, carbon products used in the electrical, mechanical, metallurgical and chemical trades, sintered metal products and also resistors for the radio and electronic industries. Furnaces are made for melting metals and a series of products have been introduced based on the refractory properties of clay. The company has gradually made use of more refined materials, such as alumina and silicon carbide, as scientists revealed the qualities of these materials.

Adding New Technologies to Meet the Same Demand

Sometimes a firm specialises in answering a particular type of problem and as new technologies are developed and become relevant to that problem they are incorporated into the firm's activities. A good example of this form of growth is W. & T. Avery Ltd., which started two hundred years ago as a blacksmith's shop where 'stilliards' were made for weighing. Over the years this firm developed the manufacture of scale beams, steelyards, money scales and cart weighing machines. Today scales are made for every weighing need from that of a human hair to a loaded goods train, and, as they have developed, optical, electrical, hydraulic and pneumatic methods of measuring or obtaining a state of equilibrium with loads placed upon the scale have each been harnessed. Early machines for testing the strength of metal transmitted the applied load through weighing levers and recorded it on a steelyard similar to those used in weighing machines, so Avery's entered the physical testing machine field, and now make static and dynamic testing machines of many types. The products of the business, whether scales for the grocer or equipment for the distribution of oil products, are concerned with a single type of problem—the measurement of weight or numbers or stresses or volumes—and all involve precision engineering in their manufacture.

Adding New Technologies to Meet New Demands

A go-ahead management is quite likely to take advantage of any new techniques within its ken, whether they are of use in improving existing products or methods of production or whether they involve expansion into new fields. Such has been the case with the Decca Record Company Ltd.

Decca was founded in 1929 and its early history was one of great difficulties culminating in a capital reconstruction in 1939. However, the board of the company had been joined by Mr. E. R. Lewis, a stockbroker, in 1931, and in Lewis Decca possessed a leader of courage, skill and energy. An important landmark was reached in 1932 when Decca bought Brunswick Ltd., an English subsidiary of Warner Brothers, which brought within Decca's orbit such artists as Bing Crosby and the Mills Brothers.

Decca's growth has been financed partly with borrowed capital and partly with profits from the record business which has itself undergone a series of revolutionary changes. [A] main change was the introduction of the long-playing [LP] record. Decca had been working on the problems of LP and had solved all the problems save one when the Columbia records appeared. The unsolved problem was that of producing the records with a commercially acceptable rate of rejection. Lewis determined to go ahead on the basis of work done by Lord Halsbury's team who had got to the point of producing experimental records subject to an 80 per cent rejection rate before Halsbury left to join the National Research Development Corporation. This rejection rate was subsequently brought down in the course of day-to-day production. Decca's first LP records were issued in the U.S.A. in 1949, about a year after Columbia but ahead of some other major companies in that country.

While these developments were in progress Decca entered the television field, and their large projection television screen marks the current phase of this line of development in the entertainment industry.

An opportunity firmly grasped took Decca into radio navigation, skilled and energetic staff took them into high fidelity recording and reproduction, and courage caused them to lead the way in Britain with long-playing records. Those responsible would not claim that their pioneering efforts were technically beyond their competitors. What this study shows is that vision, energy, enthusiasm, audacity and hard work will enable a firm with fairly modest resources to steal a march on powerful rivals.

Exploiting the Research Programme

It is important to note that what firms make in [science-based] industries is increasingly determined by what they achieve in their research. When something has been discovered or invented that looks as though it might be of economic value, the firm responsible will follow this potentially successful line. Du Pont are in the nylon business because the brilliant work of Carrothers on long-chain polymers led them there. I.C.I. discovered polyethylene as a result of fundamental research into chemical reactions at high pressures, and have developed their extensive manufacture of Polythene from this discovery.

Glaxo Laboratories Ltd. is another firm which has been led by research into strange fields. Glaxo food products were put on the market by Joseph Nathan and Company Ltd. as far back as 1908 and were well known for their advertisements 'Glaxo Builds Bonny Babies'. The first move towards the pharmaceutical industry was made through the fortification of food products with vitamins. In 1926 Ostelin, a Vitamin D2 product, was manufactured. Then Glaxo itself was fortified, first with Vitamin D to prevent rickets, and later with iron. Glucose was also fortified with Vitamin D and marketed under the name of Glucodin. This led on to wider work in the field of vitamins followed in 1939 by work on radiological contrast media. Early in the War the firm began to take an interest in penicillin, and in 1944 a deep culture plant was set up.

In 1935, the Glaxo Department of Joseph Nathan and Company was constituted a private company, a wholly-owned subsidiary of Nathan's. In 1947, this subsidiary was converted into a public company and took over the whole of the Nathan undertaking, the original parent company being liquidated. Glaxo Laboratories Ltd. now have four factories in this country employing about 4,000 people and also a number of overseas subsidiaries. The issued capital and reserves exceed £10 million.

The growth of the pharmaceutical side of the business was stimulated by a large investment in research. It was spurred on by the fact that the baby food business became increasingly unremunerative owing partly to the government subsidy to National Dried Milk which made it harder to sell branded products. The management, in consequence, sought outlets for the skill, vigour and resources of the company, outlets which might involve bigger difficulties and bigger risks but which held out altogether bigger prospects.

Firms which employ large expensive staffs of highly trained research workers are under constant pressure to keep developing, and one of the greatest problems they face is how to decide what not to develop. Some of the largest and most research-minded firms have discovered or invented many things outside the main lines of their business and have entered the new fields which these discoveries and inventions indicated. In some cases they have burnt their fingers and now take up new developments in unfamiliar fields less freely.

Products in Joint Supply or Joint Demand

Chemical processes are important forces leading firms to grow by diversifying their products. These processes usually yield by-products for which uses are being constantly sought. Sometimes it is possible to sell the by-product without further processing, but very often additional work is needed to bring it to a saleable state and the manufacturing firm may have to enter markets with which it has no prior acquaintance.

This is true of other industries making joint products. Thus the great meat-packing industry of Chicago is intensively engaged in trying to find uses for those parts of the animals which have hitherto been thrown away. Research of this kind led Armour and Company into the production of the hormone *acth* which is extracted from the pituitary glands of pigs.

Many firms have grown by taking advantage of complementary markets even though the products have required different technologies in their manufacture. The women's fashion industry provides interesting examples of firms growing by introducing complementary products. Every important Parisian couturier sells perfume, and some of the most important perfume names, such as Chanel, Molyneux, Lelong and Lanvin, are those of well-known dress-designers, although some of the names are now attached to houses which no longer create gowns. The cosmetic industry has also become closely allied to the fashion trade, particularly in the promotion of such things as lipstick colours.

The Dunlop Rubber Company Ltd. grew through complementarity of a different kind. The Dunlop business started with the first practical invention of a pneumatic tyre by J. B. Dunlop in 1888. One of the great problems was to secure the tyre to the wheel. This was solved by Welch and others with the beaded-edge tyre and the well-base rim. The close relationship between rim and tyre put Dunlop into the engineering business as well as the rubber business. What follows from this type of beginning is illustrated by the Dunlop Aviation Division. Having started with tyres they followed with wheels, later with brakes and hose, and later still with many purely engineering components such as brake controls, compressors, oxygen bottles and so on.

Making What Was Bought

When firms grow without increasing the number of stages of production they undertake, they are said to expand horizontally. Expansion backwards to earlier processes of production or forwards to later stages of marketing is termed, despite the mixture of metaphors, vertical growth. Vertical growth is seldom found in isolation as firms generally increase their output at the same time as they undertake additional processes of production or marketing. The distinction between horizontal and vertical forms of growth does, however, clarify the possibilities open to firms.

Thus Tube Investments Ltd. decided to make a substantial part of their own steel [by] purchase of the Round Oak Steel Works.

Since [then] Tube Investments have substantially increased their steel interests by a big expansion at Round Oak Works and by the purchase of the Park Gate Iron and Steel Co. Ltd., the Renishaw Iron Co. Ltd., and a half share in the Byfield Ironstone Co. Ltd. These three new acquisitions include blast furnaces and iron ore mines. Tube Investments are thus engaged in processes that take them right the way from their raw materials through tubular components to cycles and other finished products. In addition to producing tube steel T.I.'s steel companies produce many other types of steel which they continue to sell in the open market.

Reaching Forwards toward the Ultimate Customer

Industrial history is full of examples of firms which in the course of their growth have taken up later stages of processing or have undertaken part of the work formerly performed by independent distributors.

An interesting current example of expansion forwards toward the final consumers is the purchase of baking interests by Spillers Ltd., the flour-milling concern. In his statement covering the year 1954–55 the chairman said: 'During the year the board gave close consideration to the question of extending our financial interest in the baking industry (which has hitherto been quite minor) with the dual object of effecting some insulation against fluctuations in the flour trade deriving from circumstances outside our control and enabling us to have a closer connection with the consuming public. It was decided that in the prevailing circumstances it would be wise to do so. This decision was assisted by the fact that a substantial proportion of the baking industry is composed of family businesses, some of whom, by reason of the effect of taxation and in particular of estate duty, are anxious about the continuity of operations in their present form. We have therefore both before and since January 31, 1955, extended our investment in baking and the results will in due course be reflected in the overall earnings of the group. It is right to say that this in large measure represents a change in policy on our part, but I consider that it is in the best long-term interests of the company.'

Brewers are perhaps the most striking example of manufacturers who have moved forwards into retailing. The practice of brewers buying public houses is a very old one but it developed rapidly in the nineteenth century. It seems to have continued even during the period 1834–69 when licenses for public houses were freely available. It received a very big fillip during the 'eighties and 'nineties when the large brewers were fighting for control of licensed premises. Although the licensing restrictions are undoubtedly an important factor in this development, it also seems to be the case that brewers regarded public house property as a natural outlet for their surplus resources. In 1952, 33 brewery companies each owned over 500 houses and together owned nearly 50 per cent of the total number of houses.

Other examples of forward integration are to be found in the rubber tyre, petrol and shoe industries. One recent and interesting example is provided by the establishment of 'Wedgwood Rooms' in selected department stores: by agreement between Josiah Wedgwood and Sons Ltd. and the stores concerned, the Wedgwood firm takes responsibility for stocks, fittings and displays, and for the engagement and training of the saleswomen.

Growth in Many Directions

The forms of growth that have been described are not mutually exclusive. Firms may find opportunities for expansion first in one direction and then in another. The form of growth adopted at any one stage may be distinguished, but it is evident that many grown firms are the products of multiple lines of development.

Pilkington Brothers has been built up by vertical and horizontal expansion in a great number of directions. It has become the sole British source of sheet and plate glass; but it is also responsible for many other products. In the words of the chairman, Sir Harry Pilkington: 'There are several other kinds of glass that we now manufacture in England, either ourselves or through subsidiary companies, and in almost all we are either the sole producer or are very much the predominant one: for example, glass blocks for building purposes; high voltage insulators for power lines; fiberglass for a variety of important uses; opaque wall-lining glass; and wired glass for factory roofs. In none of these kinds of glass is there any obstruction to other people entering the trade as manufacturers, unless it be that our prices are too low to make it attractive. In all these kinds of glass that are susceptible to export we have developed a large export trade and are therefore fully exposed to the stimulus of competition and are not subject to the temptation of complacency that is usually supposed to be the lot of . . . firms who are in a dominant position. . . .

'In the course of our growth we have expanded both into other branches of the glass industry and into ancillary undertakings of one kind and another. . . . We acquired our own coal mine at St. Helens about seventy-five years ago and operated (sometimes at a loss) right up till nationalisation in 1947 so as to provide a reliable source of high quality coal that we needed to produce the gas with which the raw materials of glass are melted. We had, and still have, our own brick works at St. Helens, mainly to ensure a good supply of bricks for building the glass-making tanks and for works buildings and warehouses generally. We have, of course, our own machinery shops and in addition have arrangements with outside engineering factories for the manufacture of special machinery to our own design. We buy shiploads of timber in Sweden to make our own packing cases in our own timber yard—and so on.'

When a company grows by any of the methods described in the preceding article, it is, in effect, building on what it already has: by simply increasing production and sales of its products; by entering somewhat related fields; or by exploiting products developed in its own research laboratories. In the United States, however, a different road to growth has been quite popular recently—expansion into entirely unrelated fields by the purchase of other companies. This has produced what have come to be called "conglomerate companies," made up of subsidiaries or divisions that have little in common except unified financial management.

Although the formal organization structure of a conglomerate is not likely to be much (if any) different from the formal structure of any divisionalized company, some writers have made a distinction in that they have seen the conglomerates as "free form"—and thus more flexible—than the conventional divisionalized company. Some have stated that this free form, even though they define it as a matter of attitude rather than of structure, constitutes an entirely new type of organization that may be expected to make for outstanding success.

Whether or not this will prove true in the long run cannot be forecast with any certainty. However, as the following article shows, results have often fallen short of the optimistic forecasts.

The Multicompanies: The Most Spectacular Corporate Form of the 1960s

At the very moment when a large segment of U.S. industry appeared to have taken up the conglomerate idea, the idea itself was becoming increasingly suspect. Conservative observers had long questioned whether over the long term it was possible for a single company to cope with the complex problems of operating a half dozen or more different businesses, much less achieve the high earnings goals most conglomerate companies had set for themselves. But no one really knew. The whole idea was just too new.

There cannot be much doubt that the conglomerate idea has been oversold. Its proponents had hailed it as the corporate archetype of the next half century, "the quintessence of modern management," as Walter Kidde's president, Franc M. Ricciardi, called it. Change was the governing principle of contemporary life, and only the conglomerate corporation—free-form, multi-industry—could provide the flexibility to cope with it. Day-to-day operations were no longer the big thing. What mattered was the management of capital. Through an astute combination of mathematics and management a conglomerate was supposed to become more than the sum of its parts. "Shaped by change," orated Gulf & Western's president, David Judelson, the conglomerate "responds to change and will continue to meet its challenges. Today it is already the corporation of tomorrow."

In its simplest terms, the notion of bringing together a number of unrelated businesses within the same corporation was anything but new. There are close to a dozen apparently traditional U.S. corporations which possess a breadth of unrelated diversification at least as great as that of the so-called conglomerates. Most of them became so through internal growth rather than recent acquisitions, but the route is less important than the results, and in financial terms the results are rarely brilliant. The multicompany—conventional or conglomerate—is anything but a resounding success. There are, it is true, managerial triumphs like Textron. But they are the exceptions rather than the rule. The bulk of U.S. multicompanies score well below the median for U.S. industry at large in profitability, while their growth records are more modest than their aspirations would suggest. This is true of the older multicompanies as well as the newer conglomerate types.

From *Forbes*, Jan. 1, 1969, pp. 77–78, 80, 83–86.

The Pragmatists

That this should be so is hardly surprising. Many of the U.S. multicompanies are patchworks of diversity, formed as accident or opportunity permitted. They diversified—or most of them did—out of necessity rather than calculation, sometimes because their original businesses were dying or going nowhere, sometimes because they were threatened with takeovers themselves. The conglomerators like to talk as if the challenge of change was technological. But it rarely has been.

Even Textron, which popularized the conglomerate idea, diversified originally in the haphazard effort to escape the cycles in its textile business. This same expediency has dominated the newer companies that have moved into the multicompany ranks in recent years.

The Aggressive Agglomerators

There is yet another kind of multicompany, one that follows the pattern of diversification not in self-defense, not out of expediency, but to get big, really big. They are the aggressive agglomerates, those vaultingly ambitious companies that have made the art of acquisition-making one of the wonders of the age.

These companies diversified because their proprietors recognized that the flexibility of U.S. accounting practices offered opportunities for the acquisition-minded company. In a sense, the corporation was no longer primarily a vehicle for conducting a business; it had become a machine for compiling an earning record—whether through internal growth or acquisition didn't much matter. The result was that over the past five or six years a handful of clever and ambitious executives were able to transform a group of small and prosaic companies into what now ranks, on the basis of the raw figures, as the most dynamic group in all of U.S. industry.

For such companies, given their dominantly financial objectives, the question of fit, of balance, even of return on investment no longer much mattered. Significantly, the cornerstone of their long-range planning is the realization of a certain minimum annual increase in per-share earnings [ranging from 15 to 20 to 40 percent].

Growth of the magnitude envisioned by most of these companies does not exist in real life, or not for long or on any large scale. Thus, to meet such goals, companies may be forced to make further acquisitions just to keep the pace—for cash if they can, for stock if they must.

The price alone doesn't much matter under pooling-of-interest accounting. What matters is being able to increase earnings per share, and that's accomplished by being certain that net income increases more rapidly than the number of shares it has to be spread over. Companies with high P/E ratios—and most of the aggressive agglomerates have assiduously cultivated them— have little difficulty in doing so. And for those that don't have them, convertible securities used to do the trick, until the Securities & Exchange Commission discouraged that by insisting that convertibles be considered as part of common stock. Warrants now have become one increasingly popular alternative. Another is the acquisition of real estate, insurance companies and other financial institutions whose assets offer the opportunity to dress up the record by reporting capital gains as per-share earnings.

The conglomerate type of multicompany aims very high. But the problems of creating, much less managing, one are so difficult that it would be rash, particularly in a period of prolonged economic boom, to assume that any of these companies necessarily has the ability to sustain its long-term objectives.

The Might-Have-Beens

What happens if these companies should be forced to halt their acquisition programs and operate the businesses they already have? That basically is what happened to another large group of multicompanies a few years back. All of them launched major acquisition programs in the Fifties and early Sixties and have spent much of their efforts ever since trying to undo the damage.

For these companies there came a day of reckoning, a time when their momentum faltered: because a recession revealed how unprofitable some of their acquisitions had been. None of these companies really collapsed, and their records are not really bad, simply unimpressive. Management turned reluctantly to trying to manage what it had put together—to selling off the mistakes and upgrading what remained.

All of which clearly indicates that the last chapter on the multicompany-conglomerate phenomenon is yet to be written. When it is written, a happy ending is by no means assured for a good many of today's most publicized corporations.

13 Planning and Forecasting

Perhaps the most important way in which management can contribute to corporate growth is by systematically planning for it. This is done by forecasting the possibilities and developing programs to take advantage of them well before circumstances make it necessary to make revisions in company products or practices. And this in turn requires constant follow-up, what the economists have called the *ex ante* and *ex post* approach; that is, continual revision of the assumptions on which the plans were based as circumstances change, and development of new means of closing any gaps between planned and actual results.

Planning today is both short and long range. Short-range plans cover at least the next fiscal year; long-range plans extend at least five years into the future, and sometimes as far ahead as ten to twenty years.

Basic to planning is economic forecasting, ascertaining at least approximately the general level of the economy, since company sales revenues, on which all plans must be based, will depend in part on prosperity or recession. Economic forecasting is especially important in short-range planning since definite commitments for expenditures must be made in advance for the short range. In the first article in this chapter, some of the current means of short-term forecasting are presented and some suggestions on their use are offered. That article is followed by ironic comment in verse on one school of forecasters.

A business, of course, needs many types of plans—short-range plans for the company as a whole, marketing plans, production plans, and others. For top management, however, the job is strategic planning—the development of the strategy the business will employ to preserve and enlarge its place in the economy. This is discussed in the second article in this chapter.

Planning of strategy and the associated tactics enhances the chance of success in both new and current ventures, but it does not eliminate all risks, as the next two articles show. One deals with a very well-developed plan that because of a number of factors did not work out in practice, and the other with a case in which a company neglected to consider all the contingencies that might interfere with the smooth execution of its plan. The final article presents a technique—product life cycle planning—that will help to take some of the uncertainty out of the planning process.

There are many methods of forecasting economic conditions over the short range, but all have shortcomings. Here Prof. John P. Lewis, long on the staff of the School of Business of Indiana University and later a member of the President's Council of Economic Advisers, points out the contributions of the various methods and their shortcomings as well, and suggests that the several techniques be synthesized.

The NBER leading indicators he mentions are certain statistical series (e.g., building contracts, new orders for durable goods) which are likely to turn up or down in advance of a general upturn or downturn. "Econometric" forecasting is done through the construction of mathematical models or equations in which various factors in the economy are given mathematical values and their effect on each other ascertained through solution of the equations.

Short-Term General Business Conditions Forecasting

John P. Lewis

I propose to focus my discussion on five varieties of forecasting techniques that currently constitute the professional economic core of the activity—(1) leading indicators of the National Bureau of Economic Research (NBER) variety, (2) the leading monetary indicators that have been pioneered by Professor Milton Friedman and his associates, (3) use of those surveys of spenders' intentions and of other compilations of advance plans and commitments that, I believe, Martin Gainsbrugh was the first to label collectively as "foreshadowing indicators," (4) econometric model-building, and (5) that looser, less elegant, but more comprehensive variety of model-building that has been called many things, which I prefer to label "opportunistic."

We shall be passing over a rather mixed bag of forecasting practices that I have labeled elsewhere as the "agnostic techniques"—meaning by that those more or less self-evidently weak methods for probing the future.[1] [People] may, for example, adopt a no-change hypothesis, projecting the latest period's level to the coming period, or, if they want to be a bit more sophisticated, they may extrapolate the recent trend to future periods. In the very best contemporary forecasting, of course, there are a number of points at which practitioners still fall back on precisely this procedure. However, if no-change extrapolations were the craft's universal methodology, it would be professionally bankrupt.

General expectations surveys also belong in the "agnostic" category. I am referring now to surveys, not of respondents' spending intentions or even of their own sales expectations, but of their anticipations of general business conditions. Such general expectations surveys may provide the forecaster with some useful data of a psychological sort, but if they are viewed as producing self-contained forecasts in their own right, their use rests on the hypothesis that the blind can lead the blind—if they do it collectively, that is.

NBER Leading Indicators

The point has been rather widely made that the National Bureau of Economic Research type of leading indicator analysis constitutes a good bit less than a complete set of forecasting tools. This comes as no shock to the more responsible users and proponents of leads-and-lags analysis.

In the first place, the NBER leading indicators are inherently weak devices for detecting the *magnitude* of coming changes in business conditions. Their purpose is the detection of coming turning points, but they have little capacity for disclosing how sharp the turn will be or how high or deep the upswing or downswing will go.

In the second place, the leading indicators as a group are quite short-range devices. Even if there were no problem of garbled signals, they would, as a group, give us no more than six months' advance notice of a coming downturn in the economy—and far less than that in the case of upturns.

[1]J. P. Lewis, *Business Conditions Analysis* (McGraw-Hill Book Co., New York, 1959), chap xvi.

From *The Journal of Business* (Graduate School of Business, The University of Chicago), Vol. XXXV, No. 4, October, 1962, pp. 343–356.

In the third place, there *is* a problem of garbled signals. Looked at individually the leading indicators series run jagged courses. When any given wiggle occurs it usually takes two or three months to tell whether the leading indicator really has turned a significant corner or not, and by then, of course, much of its lead has been eaten up. Moreover, the leads of the particular indicators are not consistent from cycle to cycle, making it difficult to guess how soon a signaled change may occur. More important, the several leading indicators almost never all point in the same direction, especially in months just prior to general turns in business conditions. And while the "diffusion indexes" represent a natural and probably necessary attempt to cope with this last problem, they suppress most of the illuminating detail in the series that underlie them; typically they give no weight to the magnitudes of the expansions and contractions in the component series; they weight all of the components together as if they were of equal intrinsic importance; and, despite all of this, the diffusion indexes themselves are highly irregular in their movements.

Finally, as a self-sufficient technique, the leads-and-lags approach has this major limitation: it implicitly assumes a very high degree of structural rigidity in the economy. It has no adequate way of coping, for example, with major changes in the structure of demand. It is in such terms, I think, that one must explain the few past occasions—in 1951, 1956 and 1959—on which the leading indicators have given concerted and prolonged false signals.

The Leading Monetary Indicators

The rest of us are much indebted to Friedman and his colleagues for emphasizing in recent years the degree to which the rate of change in the money supply tends to lead changes in general business activity, and changes in monetary reserves lead the money supply, and changes in central bank policy lead monetary reserves.

But to accept the leading monetary indicators as *sufficient* tools for predicting general business conditions would seem to me a most bizarre procedure. It would rest on the hypothesis that, for predictive purposes, the economy could be treated as if central bank decision-making were the only significant independent variable in the system. For better or worse, things are more complicated than this. The capacity for influential autonomous decision-making is far more widely dispersed. Considerable quantities of it lodge also, for example, in the Congress, in the White House, in the Finance Committee of the United States Steel Corporation, in Detroit, in all the great industrial houses and major labor organizations in the country and, even, in fifty million households. The responsible general forecaster must, somehow or other, directly concern himself with all of this pivotal decision-making, not just with a particular slice of it.

The leading monetary indicators also have two more specific limitations.

First, the series on changes in monetary reserves and in the money supply, even after seasonal adjustment, are, like many of the NBER leading indicators, subject to rather violent gyrations. Thus it is much harder to detect, from the current data, a change of direction in the smoothed trends of these series than might first appear when one looked at the dramatic shifts in the ex post multi-month averages that the published charts of these series typically display.

Second, I would make the strange-sounding complaint that the average lead that the rate of change in the money supply is alleged to have over general cyclical downturns—namely, some twenty months since the mid-twenties, according to one of Sprinkel's recent papers[2]—is really *too long* to be very useful for forecasting purposes. Recent cyclical fluctuations in the American economy have appeared more or less to have followed a three-phase format. In a recession phase activity falls away from its long-term growth trend. In a second, recovery phase, it moves back up toward the long-term trend. But then, in a third, normal-growth or normal-prosperity phase, it moves *along* the trend. And this is the key point: most of us would say that it is impossible to predict at the time it starts how

[2]B. W. Sprinkel, "Relating Financial Factors to the Business Cycle" (address to the annual meeting of the National Association of Business Economists, Chicago, October 24, 1961 [Harris Trust and Savings Bank, Chicago, mimeographed]).

long this third, along-the-trend phase of the cycle is likely to be. The duration of the prosperity phase appears to depend upon the particular sequence of demands—first, in autos, for example, then in plant and equipment or national defense, and then perhaps in state and local government—that happens to emerge as a result of the particular combination of decision-making that occurs in a particular field.

Thus to tell me—as in effect the monetary change indicator does—that these prosperity, along-the-trend phases of cycles since the twenties have *averaged* about twenty months really does not help very much. It gives me no confidence at all that such will be the case this particular time. Especially it gives me no such confidence if I believe, as I do, that there is nothing inevitable or immutable about cyclical rhythms and that deliberate discretionary changes in federal fiscal and monetary policies often decisively affect the duration of prosperity periods.

Foreshadowing Data

If it is jousting with a straw man to disprove the self-sufficiency of the leading indicators as forecast devices, it would be still worse to belabor the point that foreshadowing data—the spenders' intention surveys, the federal budget, contract construction awards, new orders of durable goods manufacturers, and so on—do not in themselves constitute a full kit of forecasting tools. For I know of no serious developer or advocate of such data who has ever hinted that they can singlehandedly generate a forecast. However, because one still does occasionally encounter people who seem to think that if we could only finish the job of blanketing the GNP with intentions surveys, we would have the forecasting problem licked, let me venture just a few comments on the limitations of the foreshadowing series.

The coverage of the foreshadowing series is not yet all that it might be. There are some gaps—notably in the case of state and local government outlays—where spenders do indeed make advance plans, commitments, or conditional spending decisions (in the case of state and local governments they are a matter of public record) but where we simply have no agency yet that has assumed the task of systematically collecting or sampling and collating them.

But there are major segments of the GNP—notably in the area of consumer soft goods and services—that are destined, I should think, to remain effectively immune to intentions surveys for the simple reason that buyers in these fields do not do enough coherent advance planning so that they themselves can recognize and report it.

Finally, there is the familiar but important point that the existence of plans, even strongly intentioned plans, offers no assurance that they will be carried out. The forecaster must convert the finding of an intentions survey into a forecast at his own peril. In particular when he makes such a conversion he must assume that the general economic developments that the expenditure planner does *not* foresee are not going to thwart his spending intentions. Modigliani has supplied us with a very intriguing refinement of this point—namely, that if the survey can canvass a respondent's sales or income expectations at the same time it canvasses his spending intentions and if it can be shown that past discrepancies between intended and actual outlays have been related to the discrepancies between expected and actual sales or incomes, it may be possible systematically to "correct" the intentions figure for forecasting purposes—*if* the forecaster is in a position to second-guess respondents' reported sales or income expectations.[3] This approach seems to me to have considerable promise.

Econometric Models

Econometric model-building already has gone a long way toward overcoming limitations with which I would have charged it a few years ago. But it is still far short of having surmounted its basic problem of excessive rigidity—that is, in effect, excessive simplification. To attempt to cram the myriad complexity of the economy into even a thirty-two-equation model entails an her-

[3]Franco Modigliani and K. J. Cohen, *The Role of Anticipations and Plans in Economic Behavior and Their Use in Economic Analysis and Forecasting* (Bureau of Economics and Business Research, University of Illinois, Urbana, Ill., 1961).

oic abstraction. This is evident if one considers the model's lack of nimbleness in adjusting to the sort of temporary and significant but unusual development that is forever cropping up and of which the looser model-builder routinely takes account.

Indeed, I would urge sector-demand specialists who have not already done so to look carefully in [Daniel] Suits' March, 1962, article in the *American Economic Review* at the demand functions for their own particular sectors—at the equations, for example, for automobiles, for other consumer durables, and for housing starts. They are apt to find themselves a bit amazed that a forecasting technique that indulges in such gross oversimplifications with respect to the particular sectors in which they are expert can produce such generally good GNP forecasts as the model has done in recent years. That it can, of course, is dramatic testimony to the importance in general forecasting of that quality which is econometric model-building's particular strength—namely, the quality of internal consistency. Even when many of its sector legs rest on quite mushy foundations, a model of the economy whose income-distribution and receipts, expenditures, and savings relationships all are internally consistent, judged by past experience, has a pretty fair chance of hitting the aggregates. But this does not mean that mushy sector forecasting and an incapacity for encompassing the idiosyncrasies of a particular period are admirable qualities in their own right.

Opportunistic Model-building

It is almost a contradiction in terms to imagine the looser forms of model-building as being self-sufficient with respect to the other techniques. For the very essence of this approach—the reason I call it "opportunistic"—is its scavenging quality. Opportunistic model-building is a procedure for gathering data, information, and insights of just about any conceivably relevant kind and for assembling them, in some orderly manner, into a coherent and quantified statement of prospects.

Nevertheless, as a kind of horrible example, one can conjure up an imaginary forecaster who might take some pleasure in thinking of himself as a model-builder and would indeed express his outlook judgments in the form of a GNP breakdown. But his would be strictly a laundry-list style of forecasting. He would simply go down the sector list, making up forward estimates, one by one, by some intuitive process out of whatever mix of past data, current gossip, and recent comments in the business press he happened to have at hand. He would not even bother to avail himself of the foreshadowing data systematically. He would ignore the insights that the NBER leading indicators might give him into the timing of coming changes in general activity and the help that the leading monetary indicators could supply as to prospective money and credit conditions. He would simply put down his sector forecasts, tot them up, and call the sum his forecast. The entire theory of aggregate demand determination underlying his analysis would consist of the national-income accounting identity that the GNP equals the sum of its parts. His analysis would contemplate no intersectoral, no income-expenditure, and no asset-expenditures interactions. The only internal-consistency test to which it would submit would be one to make sure that the GNP components did, indeed, add up to the total. And his mathematical requirements would be limited, not just to arithmetic, but to addition and subtraction.

Although I have called the foregoing an imaginary horrible example, a good bit of the actual short-term forecasting being done today comes uncomfortably close to fitting this description. This serves only to prove that something fairly close to go-it-alone opportunistic model-building is, indeed, possible. But it also, it seems to me, is almost self-evidently foolish.

Joining the Techniques Together

By way of conclusion, let me indicate how the five forecasting techniques upon which we have been focusing can sensibly complement one another. Perhaps this can be conveyed most succinctly by describing what I would regard as an ideal short-term forecasting exercise.

In the first place, this would be a group exercise. Outlook analysis is an activity, I think, in which the group has an inherent advantage over the lone wolf, partly because it benefits from a division of labor, partly because it must be considerably judgmental and gains from an effort to achieve a consensus. Second, it would be a continuing exercise. I frankly would become bored as a member of a staff that gave its uninterrupted attention to the business outlook, and there are comparatively few organizations that could afford a fairly elaborate staff that had this single function. However, we are conjuring up an ideal, and there is no denying the expertise that comes with daily immersion in the outlook problem. Third, it would be a rather highly structured exercise. The free-wheeling virtuosity of gifted seat-of-the-pants analysts always is impressive, but it also is commonly overrated, and it has very little transferability. One quality of an ideal forecasting organization would be a considerable ability to maintain continuity despite changes in personnel. Well-defined tasks, procedures, and analytical doctrines would all contribute to this end.

I would place at the head of such a staff a seasoned opportunistic model-builder with a good measure of forecasting experience, theoretical sophistication, and executive ability. I would associate with him three deputy directors, each of whom would have cognizance of the whole operation. The balance of the staff would be composed mainly of specialists who were immersed in the lore and data of particular demand and/or industry sectors.

The format of my idealized exercise would be a simultaneous equation model and all members of the staff would require the limited command of mathematics necessary for translating their views into the terminology of such a model and for comprehending its manipulation. The point here would be for the exercise to avail itself of the maximum internal-consistency insurance, and its feasibility would depend upon ready access to adequate computer services.

The equations in the model, however, would be subject to constant tending. Variables (and, as necessary, equations) would be added or subtracted and parameters would be altered as fast as, and for whatever reason, the staff judged such changes appropriate. In fact, each equation would constitute a summary statement of the staff's presently operative forecasting doctrine for the particular demand sector or the particular income relationship involved. It would be the responsibility of each sector forecaster to keep his equation(s) in a continuing state of repair so that at any given moment the most accurate forecast of which the staff currently was collectively capable, with the help of a computer, could be cranked out of the model with minimum delay.

Foreshadowing data with built-in adjustments, where appropriate, would figure very prominently as inputs into the model. Monetary and credit variables would be more explicitly knit into the model than has been customary with econometric models to date, with the leading monetary indicators being incorporated as lead devices for signaling later changes in the money supply and credit availability. Moreover, despite the realistic complexity that would be built into the model, the forecasting staff would not consider its findings inexorably bound to the model results. In particular, the NBER leading indicators would be used as an independent aid for timing prospective changes of course in the economy, a feat at which opportunistic model-building is notoriously clumsy.

This, perhaps, is enough to convey the gist of what I have in mind. Few of us, probably, ever will work in circumstances that closely parallel the conditions just sketched. But at least we can strive for whatever intertechnique collaboration fits our particular scale of operations. We can recognize that not merely should the several respectable short-term forecasting techniques be able to coexist; they have far more to gain from outright alliance than they do from internecine bickering.

As the last article pointed out, even a thirty-two-equation mathematical model of the economy is likely to leave out many important factors, and it may also be excessively rigid. Thus many economists are wary of putting too much faith in the predictions that result. The following verses were written by Sir Dennis Robertson, the great Cambridge economist, who apparently was one of those who are not convinced equations alone can produce accurate forecasts of the coming state of the economy.

The Non-econometrician's Lament

Sir Dennis Robertson

As soon as I could safely toddle
My parents handed me a model.
My brisk and energetic pater
Provided the accelerator,
My mother, with her kindly gumption,
The function guiding my consumption;
And every week I had from her
A lovely new parameter,
With lots of little leads and lags
In pretty parabolic bags.

With optimistic expectations
I started on my explorations,
And swore to move without a swerve
Along my sinusoidal curve.
Alas! I knew how it would end;
I've mixed the cycle and the trend,
And fear that, growing daily skinnier,
I have at length become non-linear.
I wander glumly round the house
As though I were exogenous,
And hardly capable of feeling
The difference 'tween floor and ceiling.
I scarcely now, a pallid ghost,
Can tell *ex ante* from *ex post*;
My thoughts are sadly inelastic,
My acts incurably stochastic.

The purpose of forecasting is, of course, to facilitate planning, but a business needs not only tactical planning, for which the short-term indicators may be useful, but strategic planning as well. Here Dr. Ackoff, professor of statistics and operations research at the University of Pennsylvania, defines strategic planning, explains the content of a strategic plan, and presents pointers on ways in which such a plan can provide helpful guidelines for the operation of a business.

The Meaning of Strategic Planning

Russell L. Ackoff

The distinction between *strategic* and *tactical* planning is not usually well defined. As a consequence, these terms are frequently used ambiguously if not interchangeably. [But] it seems to me that there are at least three identifiable differences.

In general, we do not consider very short-range planning strategic. For example, a manager's plans for tomorrow's activity would normally be regarded as tactical, not strategic. But how long must the range of planning be in order to be considered to be strategic? There is no one answer, because in dealing with time we deal with a continuum. All we can say is the longer the range of planning, the more strategic it is. More specifically, however, I would suggest that planning for industrial organizations can be thought of as strategic only when the period involved is three years or longer, preferably five.

The second distinction between strategic and tactical planning is how much of an organization is being planned for. Planning becomes increasingly strategic as the portion of the organization encompassed by it approaches unity. Thus corporate planning is likely to be more strategic than is market planning or product planning.

The third differentiating characteristic of strategic planning lies in its emphasis on the establishment of goals. Tactical planning accepts a set of goals established by a "higher echelon" and seeks ways of obtaining them. Strategic planning tends to be more oriented to ends.

Plans cover a wide diversity of activities, and hence different people have specified the content of a plan in different ways. My own specification involves five essential parts.

These parts cannot, of course, be prepared

From the *McKinsey Quarterly*, Summer, 1966, pp. 49–60. Paper presented at the third annual Advanced Operations Research-Management Science Seminar held at the Wharton School, University of Pennsylvania.

independently; since planning deals with a system of decisions, each part of a plan is necessarily dependent on at least one another. All five parts should be developed simultaneously.

Objectives and Goals

The first part of a strategic plan is a statement of organizational objectives and goals. (Goals are objectives to which a desired time for attainment has been attached.)

Effective planning obviously requires that objectives and goals be operationally defined so that the degree of their attainment can be measured. For example, to assert that the company seeks to attain "leadership in its industry" or "good public relations" means nothing without ways of measuring the degree to which these corporate objectives are attained. A statement of goals should not read like a sermon, as is commonly the case. It should be a set of instructions that provides means for quantitative self-evaluation.

Among the least operationally defined goals and objectives are those involving the concept of *profit*. First, profit is a figment of the accountant's imagination. By changing one's accountant or accounting system one can easily create or destroy profits. Therefore, profit is not so much a matter of fact as it is a matter of policy. It is by *defining* profit, not merely proclaiming its sovereign importance, that a major corporate objective is set. To be "for profit" is no more meaningful that being "for virtue" without spelling out what virtue is.

If profit is not defined, moreover, the consequences can be serious. For example, one large corporation showed an annual operating loss over two decades. Once the shareholders became convinced that this was not a chance event they installed a new president. In his inaugural address he promised that the company would show a profit in his first year of office, and it did. For that year, no equipment was replaced no matter how bad it was; no maintenance was done except the minimum required to keep the equipment running; telephone calls, travel, and the use of supplies and outside services were cut to the bone. During his second year of office the president negotiated a merger in order to avoid bankruptcy.

Obviously, most of us would say the company's behavior was ridiculous; profits were not calculated correctly because future costs incurred in that year were not taken into account.

How *should* future costs that are currently incurred be taken into account—or, for that matter, future earnings? How should lost opportunities be accounted for? What is a rational discounting factor? How should the uncertainties of the future costs and income be taken into consideration? Unless questions like these about profit, or market share, or return on investment, are answered explicitly in operationally meaningful terms, such statements as "We want to increase our profit (or market share, or return on investment) by X percent a year" are not very helpful.

Once objectives and goals are operationally defined, it is necessary to provide some principle for aggregating them. I am reminded of a manager of marketing in a large corporation who was driven to a nervous breakdown by his inability to resolve conflicting demands imposed on him by corporate headquarters. He was told to increase both his profits and market share, but was provided with no indication of the relative importance of these two objectives. Unable to accomplish both, he was driven into a neurotic oscillation between them. The company was lucky because only the man had a breakdown: the company didn't. Other companies have not been so fortunate.

Corporate goals, it seems to me, ought to be formulated for each of the next five years, and sketched for the tenth year. These formulations should be reviewed annually. In addition, goals should be formulated for each major class of product or service.

Operating Policies

The second part of a plan should contain a statement of operating policies. In a strategic plan, operating policies need not be established for each sub-unit of the organization; these are better formulated in tactical plans prepared by the sub-units themselves. The strategic plan should be concerned only with policies that involve interactions between the largest components of the organization.

One major policy question relevant to every

organization is: What kind of business is the company in? Is it railroads or transportation? Petroleum or energy? Television or entertainment? Beverages or food? Again, what portion of the organization's future income is to come from products that exist now, and what portion from products yet to be developed or introduced?

In what geographic area should the company operate? Should it expand, nationally or internationally? If so, where and at what rate?

To what extent should the company automate not only its production but its data handling and decision making? How should the transition to automation be carried out, particularly as it affects people?

These are the kinds of general policy questions that should be considered in planning. To decide them properly, an explicit concept or model—however crude and qualitative—of the firm and its market is required. A model of the market is particularly important. If I had to identify any one reason for the failure of most planning, I would cite the inability of most companies to explain why their products are consumed.

Consider petroleum products for automobiles. I have been through planning sessions in petroleum companies in which discussion centered about octane ratings and additives for gasoline. Most consumers neither know nor care what octanes or additives are or do. Few if any can distinguish different brands of gasoline on the basis of performances. Yet they buy it rationally.

A number of studies have shown that consumers do not pick a brand of gasoline. Instead, they pick a service station—and they do this in such a way as to minimize the time required to make the purchase. If the producer understands the consumer's preoccupation with service time, he has a basis for effectively planning his distribution and sales, as well as his product.

Resources: Requirements and Provisions

The third part of a plan involves the generation and allocation of resources. There are four types of resources: men, machines and plant (i.e., equipment), materials, and money. Therefore financial planning—the only common type of resource planning—does not constitute comprehensive resource planning.

The questions to be answered in this part of the plan are: Given the objectives, goals, and operating policies, what resources of each type will be required, when, and by whom? How can these resources best be generated, developed, or acquired? If investigation shows that required resources are unavailable, then the goals or the policies will have to be revised until these parts of the plan balance. Thus there is a continuing interaction between setting goals, specifying operating policies, and planning resources.

In resource planning it is important to keep in mind the obvious fact that changing the amount of resources allocated to an activity by a certain percentage does not necessarily affect productivity by the same percentage. I have seen one R & D department that increased in size by a factor of ten and produced fewer new products per year than the smaller unit from which it grew. Nine pregnant women cannot produce a baby in one month. Doubling expenditures on advertising or salesmen may not double sales; conceivably, it might even have the effect of decreasing them.

Organizational Structure

The fourth part of a plan should provide working drawings and specifications for the organizational structure that is required to carry out the plan effectively. Very briefly, the plan of the organization's structure should contain the following essential parts: First, it should provide a classification of the types of decisions required to carry out the organization's task. Second, it should indicate who, or what position, is to have the authority for each type of decision. If more than one person is involved, the plan should specify how decisions are to be reached by the group—i.e., whether any given participant's approval or disapproval is necessary or sufficient (or both) for accepting or rejecting any proposal. Third, the plan should specify who is responsible for carrying out each decision. Fourth and last, it should contain the design of an information system that will enable these decisions to be made and implemented effectively.

Clearly, each decision cannot be considered

separately; therefore, it is necessary to classify them in some way. In a five-year plan prepared for the Lamp Division of General Electric, management decisions were classified as follows: (1) matters affecting the status and stature of managers; (2) matters affecting the organization and operations of an operating unit; (3) matters affecting the organization and operations of a coordinating unit; (4) matters affecting the interaction of operating and coordinating units; and (5) matters affecting products in such a way as to involve more than one function.

These decisions were further sub-classified by (a) the amount of money involved, (b) the number of organizational units affected, (c) the duration of the effect, and (d) the reversibility of the decision.

Controls

The most essential assumption in any planning process is that much of the plan will turn out to be wrong. Therefore, a plan should provide a procedure for determining where it is failing and why, and provision for correcting itself on the basis of this analysis. To accomplish this, a *control system* is required. Such a system in turn requires an organizational unit charged with the control responsibility and so placed in the organization's structure that it has access to the decision makers and the information required to carry out its function. Such a unit must be directly responsible to those managers who accept or reject the plan itself and who therefore have authority to modify it in operation.

A control system makes it possible not only to correct for errors but also to respond to unforeseeable changes in conditions such as technological breakthroughs, international conflicts, shifts in the economy, or modification of the laws under which the organization must operate. Lack of responsiveness to change is the best indicator I know of the need for planning in an organization.

Patterns of Planning

Most plans, of course, do not contain all five of the elements I have specified. There is a wide divergence between the principles and the practice of planning.

Satisficing. Most current planning is of this type. In it the planning process begins with the setting of goals which are believed (though seldom demonstrated) to be both feasible and desirable. Attribution of these properties to the goals is usually based on consensus among the planners. Once these goals are set—and they are usually set independently of other aspects of planning—operating policies are sought which will hopefully attain the goals and are acceptable both to management and to the people who must carry them out.

Feasibility in this context usually implies (1) no significant departure from current policies and practices, (2) at most, moderate increases in resource requirement, (3) no significant changes in the organization's structure (since this usually meets with opposition), and (4) little or no provision for possible errors or changes from expectations; hence, little concern with controls.

Such planning concentrates almost exclusively on obtaining a feasible set of operating policies. It seldom formulates, let alone considers, alternative sets of policies.

Satisficing is usually defended with the argument that it is better to produce a feasible plan that is not optimal than an optimal plan that is not feasible. This argument is only superficially compelling. Reflection reveals that it overlooks the possibility of obtaining the best feasible plan. Optimality can (and should) be defined so as to take feasibility into account, and the effort to do so forces us to examine criteria of feasibility that are seldom made explicit in the satisficing process. Furthermore, the approximate attainment of an optimal plan may be more desirable than the exact attainment of an inferior one.

Not surprisingly, this type of planning seldom produces a significant break with the past. It usually produces a comfortable continuation of most current policies, practices, and aspects of the organization's structure, correcting only obvious deficiencies. Satisficing, since it often appears to be more concerned with justifying or correcting the past than with affecting the future, appeals to organizations that place great emphasis on survival and little on growth and development. It also appeals to planners who are unwilling to stick their necks out.

Optimizing. In this second type of planning, the setting of goals and the selection of operating policies interact with one another; an effort is made not to do just well enough, but to do as well as possible. Resource requirements, and means of generating and allocating resources, are taken into account.

The optimizing approach to planning is largely a product of operations research. It calls for the development of mathematical models of the system being planned for—models that can be analyzed or simulated to determine the effect of different policies and resource allocations on organization performance.

We have not yet learned how to construct single unified models of the firm that are both convenient to manipulate and sufficiently detailed to yield optimal overall plans. Hence, multiple models, each representing a part of the system, are normally constructed and made to interact with one another so as to obtain approximately optimal solutions to planning problems.

Now let's look at the negative side of the optimization pattern of planning. First, organizational structure is seldom explicitly treated in such planning because models of this aspect of a firm have only begun to be developed. At present the best we can do is to optimize complex structures relative to very simple problems, or simple structures relative to complex problems; we cannot yet optimize complex structures relative to complex problems. But where quantitiative optimization techniques alone are inadequate to produce a plan, they can often be combined with enlightened judgment to produce an approximately optimal plan. In general, attempts to optimize structure currently require extensive use of qualitative judgments. Too many optimization-oriented researchers prefer to avoid such judgments and hence omit this essential aspect of planning.

Second, consider how optimization techniques are used to handle the problem of control. These techniques can take into account only those uncertainties concerning the future which can be identified beforehand. Through optimization, furthermore, we can develop a control unit or monitor to be *added to the system* to deal with these predictable uncertainties—but we cannot provide a control unit that is *built into the system*, leading to increased self-control of the units already in the system. This distinction and its significance it not easy to define or grasp. I will try to clarify it by considering a third approach to planning which attempts to correct this deficiency of the optimization approach to planning. This third approach to planning is not prevalent in current practice. It is an aspiration that is yet to be realized.

Adaptivizing. The need for control arises not only out of our inability to forecast the future without error, or even our inability to conceive of all possible future states; it arises also out of variations in the present. To plan only for the "average" (or any other single value) of a variable activity is to invite crises, breakdowns, and poor use of facilities: imagine the performance of a highway that is designed only to accommodate its average load. Therefore, it is desirable to plan organizations and operations which not only can *adapt* to major changes in the future but which can also *adjust* themselves to short-run fluctuations in the demands that are made on them. Consider what is necessary to take care of such variations.

First, we obviously require flexibility of plant and equipment. For example, the direction of traffic flow in the third Lincoln Tunnel connecting New Jersey and New York City can be reversed, depending on the change in demand from morning to evening. Such flexibility can be planned for, frequently with considerable economies to the organization. Three tunnels, one of which is reversible, can carry the same load as four, given the asymmetry of automobile traffic into New York from morning to night. Ideally, we would like to have facilities that expand or contract with use. This is possible to some extent. But since it is never completely possible, use itself should be subjected to some control.

There are two approaches to control. One attempts to stabilize demands made on a system over the long run, the other over the short run.

Consider the long-run orientation first. A major manufacturer of machine tools was subject to fluctuations in demand as great as three to one in successive years. This prevented effective use of facilities and personnel. The company looked for another highly cyclical product line, involving the same technology, whose variations in demand ran counter to those of machine tools. It found such a class of products in highway construction equipment and entered the business. By so doing it reduced the variations of annual production loads to only a fraction of what they had been previously.

Thus, one way to obtain control over the future is to reduce the variations one might expect in the behavior of essential parts of the system or its environment.

Consider another company, which produces a raw material for other processes in more than 3,000 different forms. Of these, only 10 per cent accounted for all of the profits and most of the volume of the business. Small orders for the remaining large number of small-volume, unprofitable items led to continuous disruptions of production schedules, which were geared for long, continuous production runs of the high-volume profitable items. Marketing management refused to drop the small-volume unprofitable items from the company's product line, or raise their prices even to cover costs, because—it argued—this would antagonize customers and cause them to take their orders for the profitable items to other suppliers who would satisfy their smaller needs.

To reduce the uncertainties of the small orders, as well as their unprofitability, an incentive scheme was developed for the sales force. It was profit rather than volume-oriented; it paid no commission on sales of unprofitable items, and higher commissions than before on the profitable ones. In the first year of its operation, sales of more than half of the unprofitable items in the product line dropped to zero—and sales of the profitable items increased!

The principle involved in this last type of control is one of the most important in adaptive planning because it provides an effective way of handling short-range, as well as long-range, variations in the system. It involves motivating participants in the system to act in a way that is compatible with the interests of the organization as a whole, and it does this by providing incentives which make individual and organizational interests more compatible.

Toward a Self-Planning System

If a completely adaptive system could be designed, it would require no planning. To the extent that adaptive planning succeeds, therefore, the need for planning is reduced. The ultimate ideal of the adaptive planner is a system for which planning is no longer necessary.

Strategic planning is not only desirable; it is also difficult, costly, and time-consuming. Indeed, the type of planning I have described requires the full-time commitment of an organization's *best* managerial and research personnel. But I know of no other activity in a company that can yield so large a return on the investment made in it.

The production of the Edsel car was one of the most carefully planned moves in business history, and the advance promotion of the new car was so great that its subsequent failure received an enormous amount of publicity. Here Dean Reynolds, of the School of Business Administration, Wayne State University, who was associated with the company at the time, describes how this failure occurred through a combination of mistakes in the execution of the plan and sheer bad luck.

The Edsel: Faulty Execution of a Sound Marketing Plan

William H. Reynolds

There have been more costly new product failures than the Edsel, failures that have been more disastrous from the standpoint of a firm's future, and failures stemming from more egregious mistakes. The Edsel, nevertheless, is one of the most conspicuous new product failures in business history. The events leading up to the tragedy (or down to the comedy) are examined in this account.

From *Business Horizons*, Fall, 1967, pp. 39–46.

The story begins in 1946, when young Henry

Ford had just taken over management of the company. The major problem facing him was a serious need for top level management personnel. This problem was met in two ways, by pirating General Motors and by capitalizing on the fortuitous appearance of the so-called "Whiz Kids." One of the executives pirated from General Motors was Lewis Crusoe, who is—depending on the point of view—either the hero or the villain of this article. The Whiz Kids were several young Air Force officers who had worked together on Air Force logistics and whom Ford hired as a group after World War II.

The Marketing Plan

By 1954, Ford had a young, ambitious, and reasonably experienced management team; new and modern facilities; a revitalized group of dealers; money in the bank; and a solid consumer franchise in the low price field. (Ford came very close to beating Chevrolet in sales in 1954.) This combination of circumstances led Ford to decide to expand its share of the market. The marketing plan that was developed took the form of a head-on assault upon the General Motors car lines. Ford intended to bring General Motors to its knees.

Crusoe, as much as anyone else, was responsible for Ford's plan of battle. [He] had gone from corporate finance to become vice-president and general manager of the Ford division (where he had scored notable successes), and from there to executive vice-president—car and truck divisions.

He was a man with enormous merchandising flair. The two-passenger Thunderbird was Crusoe's car; someone once commented that no one except him would have thought that a combination of the discomfort of a sports car and the performance of a family sedan would be irresistibly appealing.

Crusoe realized that tackling General Motors successfully would not be easy; consequently, his plan was many faceted. [It] envisaged a car-for-car attack, with the principal effort in the middle against the B-O-P's.[1] One is reminded of Pickett's charge at Gettysburg. Nevertheless, the rationale behind the plan was compelling—and remains compelling in retrospect.

First, Ford looked at trends in sales by car lines. It was clear in the middle fifties that the sales of medium price cars were increasing as a percentage of the total market while the sales of lower price cars were declining. The Mercury, Ford's only medium price entry, had never done particularly well. If the trend continued, Ford saw itself almost out of business in a few years. *Second*, the trend to higher price cars was confirmed by the fact that even low price cars were increasingly sold "loaded"; also, more expensive cars in lower price lines were selling better than those at the bottom of the line. *Third*, with incomes rising, the number of people in the income groups that bought low price cars was declining. In comparison, the number of people in the income groups that bought medium price cars was increasing. *Fourth*, people who bought Ford cars when they were young tended to trade them in on B-O-P's when they became more affluent. To retain these owners, strong entries in the medium price field were essential.

The reasoning was sound then, and is sound now. The decision to introduce the Edsel was wise. Its execution was faulty and plagued by bad luck.

Realistic appraisal of the magnitude of the task was the reason for almost everything done wrong by Ford in its assault on General Motors. For instance, Crusoe, and others, felt that the new entries would stand a better chance if handled by independent, divisional profit centers. It was believed that the Edsel should be merchandised by a separate Edsel division, aggressively concerned with its fate.

This marketing scheme led to the establishment of five car divisions—Ford, Mercury, Continental, Lincoln, and Edsel—in place of the original Ford and Lincoln-Mercury divisions. Suddenly, there were five divisional controllers instead of two, five divisional industrial relations managers instead of two, five marketing managers instead of two, and so forth. The divisions were expensive, and raised break-even points impossibly high, and Ford simply did not have the management personnel to staff them adequately. Talent was spread too thinly, with young

[1]Buicks, Oldsmobiles, and Pontiacs.

and eager but inexperienced managers handling important and and responsible jobs.[2]

A network of new dealerships was established for the Edsel. These new dealers tended to be underfinanced, and many of them were not skilled traders. The company had assumed that if a Ford dealer handling the Edsel encountered price resistance, he would steer the customer to a Ford. In retrospect, it seems probable that Ford or Mercury dealers could have done a better job than the hastily assembled Edsel dealers.

As part of the push behind the Edsel, the car was introduced in four series and a multitude of models, backed by enormous advertising. Such extensive promotion increased expenses, and it is possible that the advertising caused the public to expect too much of the car.

Another mistake from the same root source—realistic recognition of the size of the job—was a decision to try to get as many Edsels as possible on the road immediately after introduction. Ford wanted people to see the car, and to look upon it as an established make. A failure to adhere to quality standards was the result. Most of the "bugs" in the Edsel were ironed out fairly quickly, but not until after the damage had been done.

Finally, the styling of the Edsel turned out to be a grievous error. One cannot attach too much blame to Ford executives for this. For security and other reasons, no automobile manufacturer before the Edsel used consumer research to test the appeal of advanced models prior to introduction. Instead, designers and executives relied on judgment. The styling of the Edsel may have failed because the judgment of the designers and executives who approved it was too well-informed. For instance, the vertical grille on the Edsel was compared by some executives to the classic cars of the thirties, the LaSalle and the Pierce Arrow. Others were reminded of European sports cars with vertical grilles, the Alfa-Romeo and the Bugatti. At least one executive thought that the Edsel grille resembled the front end of the Navy Grumman fighter plane.

None of these associations was clear to the car-buying public. Few remembered the LaSalle and the Pierce Arrow; even fewer were familiar with the Alfa-Romeo and Bugatti. The grille was considered peculiar looking and became the subject of countless jokes. On the other hand, the people responsible for the design of the Edsel wanted the car to look distinctive and different. It is possible that they would have welcomed a research finding that the car did not look like other cars.

[2]I was involved in building a new office building and plant for the new Lincoln division. The building was depopulated when the Lincoln division was discontinued in 1957 and was still half-vacant in the early sixties. Some of my friends call it "Reynolds' folly." I was one of the inexperienced managers mentioned in the text.

Alleged Mistakes

Ford was primarily concerned about the market represented by the upward trend in trading from a Ford to one of the B-O-P's. This market could be identified with a high degree of precision; registration lists plus a screening procedure made it easy to single out for further interviewing persons who had left Ford for a GM middle price make. One could then investigate the customers' preferences in automobile design and write advertising themes accordingly. It was found that people in this market wanted their cars to be elegant and luxurious to communicate their rising status. At the same time, since they were still relatively young, they wanted cars sporty in appearance and high in performance. To reach this market, the stylists working on the Edsel tried to make its design reflect a combination of elegance and youthfulness. Advertising copy stressed the same two points.

The B-O-P's of the middle fifties were all somewhat stodgy cars. None was either elegant or particularly youthful. They appeared vulnerable to the approach taken with the Edsel.

As it turned out, the Edsel failed to accomplish the objectives established for it; nevertheless, the plan itself was probably sound. Less than three years after the introduction of the Edsel, Semon Knudsen set almost identical objectives for the Pontiac and was phenomenally successful.

Moreover, the research done by the Edsel division cannot be faulted. If one goes through the bound volumes of Edsel research reports in the Ford archives, one is struck—after a somewhat eerie feeling is overcome—by the sophistication of the techniques used and the perspicacity of the findings. No styling research was conducted, but, as noted at that time, no one in the industry was doing such research. Otherwise, the research was comprehensive.

Finally, the name "Edsel" was unquestionably bad, with few associations and those mostly unfavorable. But other brands with equally unfortunate names have been successful. "Buick" is perhaps the ugliest word in the language. The name of the Edsel certainly did not help, but it is unlikely that it had much to do with the failure of the car.

Bad Luck

In addition to mistakes, real and alleged, the Edsel encountered incredibly bad luck. Unfortunately, it was introduced at the beginning of the 1958 recession. Few cars sold well in 1958; few middle price cars sold; even fewer Edsels sold.

A less-known piece of bad luck was the agreement against racing and the advertising of power and performance signed by the members of the Automobile Manufacturers Association in 1957. The Edsel had been designed to be the "hottest" car on the American road. High performance was one of the central elements in the sporty, youthful image the car was to project. The 1957 agreement knocked the pins out from under this major selling point.

The third piece of bad luck is more nebulous. For some reason a rash of "Hate Detroit" articles and books began to flood the market at about the time the Edsel was introduced. John Keats published his *Insolent Chariots*, with drawings by Osborn, and the poet Robert Lowell wrote a line refering to our "tailfin culture." Young men customizing their cars began to remove chrome, take out grilles, take off wheel covers, and perform surgery on tail fin sheet metal. The flashy Edsel was utterly out of tune with this trend in taste.

It might be charged that Ford management should have anticipated this trend. To a certain extent, it did. As early as 1952 Ford began studies of a small domestic car similar to foreign imports. But no one really anticipated the radical change in taste that took place. It is hard to see how anyone could, given the kind of car market that existed in 1955 and 1956, when most of the crucial decisions were made.

The Failure

It was apparent a month or so after introduction that the Edsel was unlikely to achieve the share of market necessary for it to be successful. Ford management took steps immediately to cut losses. The Edsel division was discontinued and combined with Mercury in a new organization called the "M-E-L division," for Mercury-Edsel-Lincoln. (The Continental division had already been absorbed by Lincoln.) Many members of Ford middle-management were laid off or reduced in rank or pay. Higher ranks also suffered.

The damage to morale was devastating. Young Ford executives became convinced that their superiors regarded them more as expensive headcount than as members of the management team. Jim Nance, formerly of Studebaker and Hotpoint, was put in charge of the M-E-L division. One of his first acts was to issue a general letter saying that layoffs were pending but that every man's record would be carefully considered. One manager commented, "The letter says to feel good if you get fired, because it means that a better man got your job." "Gallows" humor became common in executive dining rooms.

The Edsel itself was kept alive by heroic measures through two model changes and was finally allowed to die early in the 1960 model year. In the meantime, it lost its vertical grille and adopted a grille resembling that of the Pontiac.

The real tragedy was suffered by the Edsel dealers, many of whom lost their life savings when the car went under. Most of the Ford executives and managers who were released went on to other, and in many cases, better jobs. Some were kept on until they found these jobs, and did not experience even the briefest unemployment. The Edsel dealers, as risk-taking entrepreneurs, lost real cash.

A failure, properly understood, can make a man—or a corporation—wiser, stronger, and more effective. It can also enfeeble man or a corporation. For a time, after the Edsel, it appeared that the latter was true of Ford. Ford cars became dull and undistinguished. Chevrolet and Pontiac captured the image of performance, high styling, and youthfulness that Ford had held since the advent of the V-8 in the early thirties. Ford market penetration declined year by year. Ford management wondered why, and initiated study after study.

In the meantime, the lessons of the Edsel were slowly and painfully being absorbed. One lesson was organizational. Ford has not tried to establish any new automotive divisions or dealership networks. The company learned that effective management organizations and dealership networks cannot be set up by fiat, and that distribution is a central consideration in new product introduction.

Second, Ford learned to use marketing research. In part, this was a consequence of fear. If a mistake were made, Ford managers wanted to be able to point to the research that had caused it. Ford researchers underwent the curious experience of a management that placed more confidence in research findings than the researchers did themselves. The result, however, was healthy. Ford management, partly because of the lack of confidence caused by the Edsel, is immunized against believing that their own preferences are identical to those of the public.

Third, the massive rigidities of brand shares came to be respected. One cannot destroy an established brand simply by offering what one conceives to be a better version of the same item. The strategy of indirection is imperative. One must look for unprotected flanks or undefended weak points. General Motors had no car like the four-passenger Thunderbird or the Mustang when these two highly successful cars were introduced.

Perhaps the principal lesson to be learned from the Edsel is that a company must be careful of youthful overconfidence and youthful inability to accept occasional failures as inevitable. The introduction of the Edsel was reasonably wise; the reluctance to accept its failure was not.

Most companies plan to grow, and often they plan for growth by acquisition of other companies. But in doing so, they must try to not to overlook any contingencies, for there are a number of possible pitfalls. This article outlines the growth history of a company that made a number of mistakes in its efforts to grow by acquiring other companies, but eventually was able to achieve most of its objectives. The author is an executive in the management services division of Ernst & Ernst, a well-known New York accounting firm, and the author of a book, *Cost Controls for Industry* (Prentice-Hall), and of a number of articles. He is also a consulting editor of the magazine in which this article appeared.

A Backward Look at Forward Planning

Thomas S. Dudick

Many companies in pursuit of the obvious advantages of size, both in operating economy and prestige, have pursued it while neglecting the most common warnings of good business sense. Penn Central Railroad, which achieved giant corporate size by merging two transportation companies with entirely different methods, operating philosophies, and even computer systems, is only the most prominent recent example. There are others, less publicized but equally disastrous.

Growth is good, yes, but only if it is a balanced growth. If it is just a reckless striving for size, without regard for other factors—compatibility, staff abilities, eventual goals—then it can become a disaster. Consider, for example, the Durard Company.

The Durard Plastics Company's products consist of plastic molding, metal stamping, and related hand assembly operations. The product line includes such items as push buttons for radios, plastic knobs for appliances, plastic bot-

Reprinted by permission of *Management Adviser*, January–February, 1972, pp. 15–19.

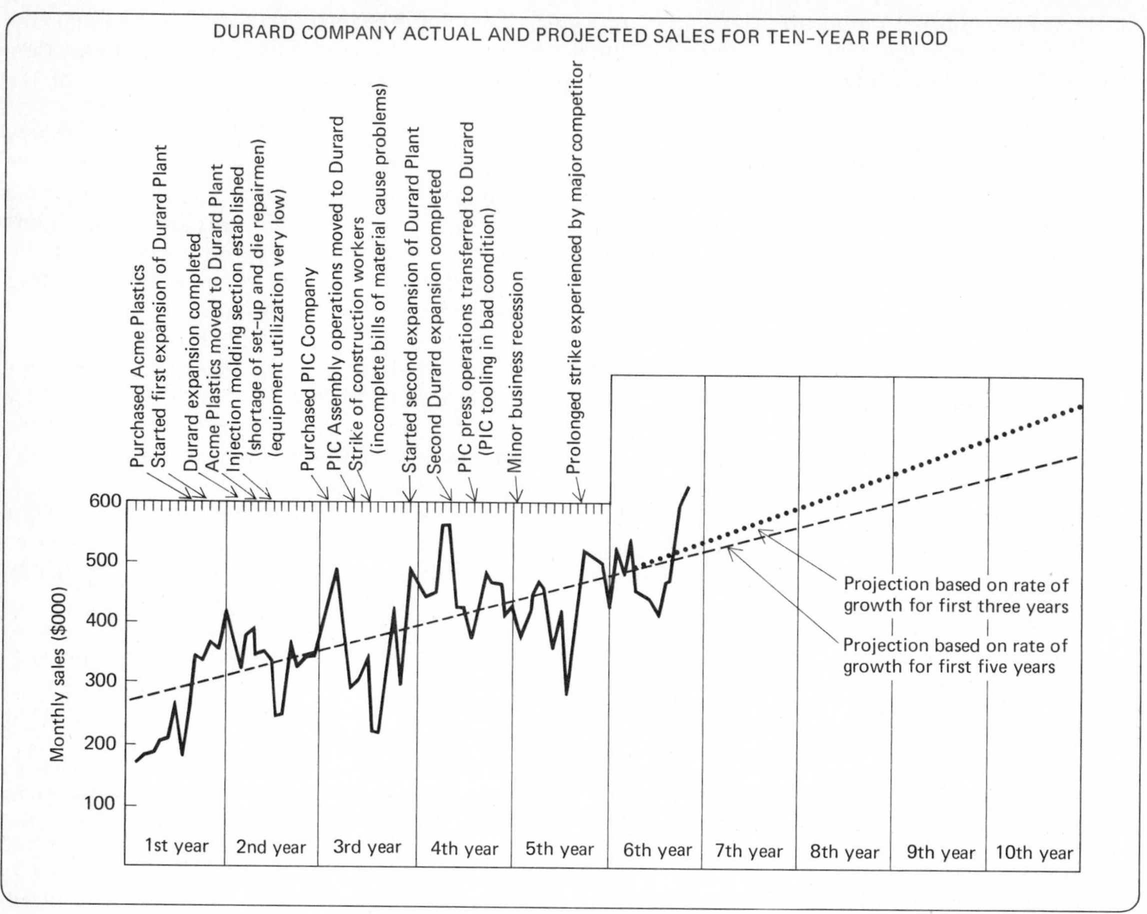

tles with caps, electric shaver parts, small radio cabinets, and a variety of metal parts used in the appliance industry.

The management of this company wanted to increase its share of the market. It planned to achieve this goal through the purchase of established companies as well as through internal expansion. As each acquisition was digested, the plan was to move the operations to the town of Durard, for which the parent company was named.

The management of the company was disappointed in its progress—and changed general managers three times during a six-year period. The chronology of events leading to management dissatisfaction was as follows:

Purchase of Acme Plastics and expansion from within. Acme Plastics became a part of Durard in August of the first year—as indicated in the pictorial diary represented by the chart above. This acquisition resulted in a substantial increase in sales volume, as well as profits. Since plans called for all Acme activities to be moved to Durard, a building expansion program was undertaken. This was completed in the spring of the second year, and the move was made. Concurrently with the completion of this move, 12 injection molding presses were purchased and set up in the expanded plant. The combination of the Acme move and the establishment of an injection molding department proved to be "too big a bite." Since only key supervisory personnel of the Acme Company were transferred, critically needed skills, such as setup men and die and mold repair men, were in short supply. Utilization of equipment, which had normally been running at 95 per cent, now dropped to an average of 45 to 50 per cent. The new injection molding presses ran less than 25 per cent of the time for several months following installation while "bugs" were being taken care of and operators and setup men trained.

Naturally, these problems reflected themselves in reduced sales volume as well as reduced profits. As a result, the second year ended with a loss.

Sales had slipped throughout the second year because of the company's inability to make shipments to customers. Some improvement was experienced during the third year. Utilization of the equipment transferred from Acme increased to 75 per cent—somewhat short of the desired 90 to 95 per cent. The newly purchased injection molding equipment still lagged at 65 per cent of production goals. The company believed it would take from six to nine months more before utilization of the equipment could attain optimum levels. The profit outlook still was not good but improvement seemed in sight. Because the Durard Company was in sound financial condition, it was able to weather the storm. Under similar conditions other companies would have failed.

Purchase of the PIC Company. The general manager, who had been with Durard two years, had been released and replaced by a new man. The new man was advised of the company's interest in growth and of the recent problems that had been encountered.

Shortly after taking over, the new general manager learned that the PIC Company, which was in financial straits and losing money, could be purchased at a bargain price. This purchase would permit Durard to immediately get into another related product line and pick up PIC's customers. With the Acme move out of the way, the decision was made to purchase PIC and to transfer the operations to Durard as soon as possible.

Within two months, the unprofitable hand assembly items were moved. It was felt that the high labor rates paid at PIC's former location made profits there out of the question. The substantially lower rates in the Durard area should help considerably. Although the rates were lower, management miscalculated on two other counts:

1 Purchasing and production scheduling personnel were unfamiliar with the new product line. Bills of material were incomplete because PIC personnel had carried this information "in their heads" rather than in documented records.
2 The Durard plant could not accommodate the PIC press operations. The trouble was not lack of space but the wrong type of floor construction. PIC's heavy presses required heavily reinforced floors.

PIC press operators and tool shop men were leaving as soon as they could find other employment—knowing that their tenure was limited. Downtime on presses, because of shortage of skilled personnel, increased astronomically. Plans for the second Durard expansion were hurriedly made, but actual work could not start because of an unexpected strike that closed down all construction in the area. Finally, with the settlement of the strike, construction began late in the year. Durard made a small profit that year, but its working capital was becoming strained.

The second expansion was completed late in the spring of the fourth year. Production schedules were firmed up and certain PIC items were now running at high volume. But then problems began to mount again. The tools used at PIC were of a poor quality—no longer meeting the tighter requirements of the industry, which had greatly increased the use of automated assembly equipment. As a result, many fabricated parts that did not meet the greater tolerances that were required had to be scrapped or reworked.

It was obvious that a substantial retooling program was required. In the meantime, productivity had dropped and production schedules had to be "juggled" frequently to satisfy specific customer demands. The tooling program would require from 15 to 18 months. In the meantime, production output continued to drop with a resultant slippage, of course, in sales and profits. To add to the problems, a business recession developed near the end of the fourth year during what was normally a high volume production period. Although the recession was relatively mild, productivity continued to slip while the company frantically tried to find competent tool makers to speed up the retooling program. At this point the general manager was relieved of his responsibilities and still another new man was brought in.

The new manager (let's call him Norm Bayard) was somewhat surprised to learn that his predecessors had had such a short tenure. He realized that if he mechanically picked up the reins, without some deeper investigation, he might fall victim to the same problems that had resulted in the release of his predecessors.

In his "get acquainted" interviews with the members of his staff, he decided that he would attempt to determine exactly what the problems were and how they might have been prevented—or, at least, greatly minimized. He sensed that some of the staff would, undoubtedly, in the role of "Monday morning quarterbacks," apply the 20/20 vision of hindsight to impress the new boss. To avoid being misled, Norm double-checked all statements that were made. If he was told that bad tools had been at fault, he asked such questions as:

- Were the tools poorly designed or were they merely worn out and in need of maintenance?
- Could better maintenance have prevented the problem?
- Was it possible that only some of the key high volume tools were the source of the problems? In that case, would the availability of a duplicate set of tools have allowed for the needed maintenance?

Without being obvious, Norm gradually accumulated a "bank" of information which was correlated with past sales. To this he added the data accumulated during his own tenure. The pictorial diary was then prepared. Since growth was being emphasized by the company, two projections were made for the balance of the ten-year period. These were based on:

- Rate of growth for the first three years.
- Rate of growth for the first five years.

The first three years would project the trend if the high rate of sales increase experienced in the first three years could be duplicated. The five-year period, on the other hand, was a more conservative estimate because it reflected the problems incident to the PIC move and the effect of a business recession. The favorable effect of a major competitor's strike, which occurred in the sixth year, was not included because this was considered to be a non-recurring windfall.

Corrective programs that had been instituted by Norm and his predecessor gradually began to take hold. Although production volume continued to slip, defective production was reduced materially. It was now only a matter of time before the problems of tooling and setup would be corrected. The Durard Company had profited immensely from the long strike of its competitor because it was able to take business on a more selective basis and set up certain equipment to run continuously, day-in and day-out. One-shift operations were expanded to two shifts and the work week was extended to 45 hours. Sales and profits soared—somewhat relieving a serious shortage of working capital.

Norm felt that the pictorial diary of problems experienced by the Durard Company, as depicted on page 240, could serve a two-fold purpose:

1 It would provide a history of past events and demonstrate their effect on operations.
2 The availability of this type of data would be helpful in management meetings to reinforce the need for solid planning.

It seemed that the two previous general managers had moved too quickly to fulfill the company's desire for growth—with the consequence that the company's working capital had been seriously impaired. As a result of this and the other observations made by Norm, the following *Ten Commandments for Expansion* were established:

1 Expand in your own field of expertise. Competition is tough enough without giving your competitors a built-in advantage.
2 Evaluate the market potential before expanding. Check the life cycle of your products to assure that you don't find yourself making a horse-and-buggy product in the automotive age.
3 Check possible monopoly restrictions. There's no point in expanding and then going through divestiture proceedings.

4 Evaluate your financial resources. Determine the potential effect on working capital if things don't go according to plan.
5 Check what your competitors are doing. If they have already embarked on a major expansion program, you may want to take a different course to avoid a large investment in excess facilities of that particular product.
6 Don't expand just for the sake of size. There's nothing to be gained by increasing sales at the sacrifice of profits.
7 Coordinate engineering and production activities. Make certain that bills of material and process specifications are documented rather than being kept in someone's head. This applies to nonmanufacturing activities with equal force.
8 If the design of a product is changed, modify the tooling immediately. Waiting until the order is processed can mean expensive delays and problems in scheduling.
9 Don't expand beyond the limits of available skills. Hold expansion within the limits of the skills that can be made available in the foreseeable future—otherwise efficiency and utilization of equipment will suffer.
10 Transfer the required skills—hourly as well as salaried. If some employees are reluctant to relocate, ask them to stay on for an additional six-month period to train employees at the new location. The extra travel and living expenses will be far cheaper in the long run.

As this article explains, many products have life cycles marked by growing sales volume as they win acceptance in new markets, then a "saturation point" followed by declining or stable sales as the market becomes merely a "replacement market." This concept is useful in planning sales efforts—and helps to explain the behavior of the markets for consumer durables. John E. Smallwood has been director of economic and marketing research for Whirlpool Corporation and has held other important positions in the marketing and financial fields with leading companies.

The Product Life Cycle: A Key to Marketing Strategy

John E. Smallwood

The product life cycle can be the key to successful and profitable product management, from the introduction of new products to profitable disposal of obsolescent products. The fundamental concept of the product life cycle (PLC) is illustrated in Figure 1.

In application, the vertical scale often is measured in saturation of the product (percentage of customer units using), while the horizontal scale is calibrated to represent the passage of time. The breakdown in the time scale is shown by stages in the maturity of product life. The saturation scale, however, is a guide only and must be used accordingly. When comparing one product with another, it is sometimes best treated by use of qualitative terms, not quantitative units. It is important to the user of the product life cycle concept that this limitation be recognized and conceptual provisions be made to handle it. For example, if the basic marketing unit chosen is "occupied U.S. households," one cannot expect a product such as room air conditioners to attain 100 percent saturation. This is because many households already have been fitted with central air conditioning; thus, the potential saturation attainment falls well short of 100 percent of the marketing measurement chosen.

To overcome this difficulty, marketing managers have two basic options. They can choose a more restrictive, specific marketing unit such as

From *MSU Business Topics* (published by the Graduate School of Business Administration, Michigan State University, East Lansing, Mich.), Winter, 1973, pp. 30–35. Condensation reprinted by permission of the publisher Division of Research, Graduate School of Business Administration, Michigan State University.

"all occupied U.S. households that do not have forced air heating"; homes without forced air heating are unlikely candidates for central air conditioning. It can be anticipated that room air conditioners will saturate not only *that* market, but portions of other markets as well. On the other hand, on the basis of informed judgment, management can determine the *potential* saturation of total households and convert the PLC growth scale to a measurement representing the degree of attainment of potential saturation in U.S. households. The author has found the latter approach to be the more useful one. By this device, automatic washers are considered to be at 100 percent saturation when they are at their full potential of an arbitrarily chosen 80 percent.

Consider Figure 1, where various products are shown positioned by life cycle stages: the potential saturations permit the grouping of products into like stages of life cycle, even when their actual saturation attainments are dissimilar. Automatic washers (which are estimated at 58 percent saturation) and room air conditioners (30 percent) are positioned in the same growth stage in Figure 1; freezers (29 percent) and refrigerators (99 percent), on the other hand, are in the maturity stage. This occurs because, *in our judgment*, freezers have a potential of only about one-third of "occupied households" and thus have attained almost 90 percent of that market. Automatic clothes washers, however, have a potential of about four-fifths of the occupied households and at about 70 percent of their potential still show some of the characteristics of the growth stage of the PLC. General characteristics of the products and their markets are summarized in Figure 2.

Figure 1 Life cycle stages of various products.

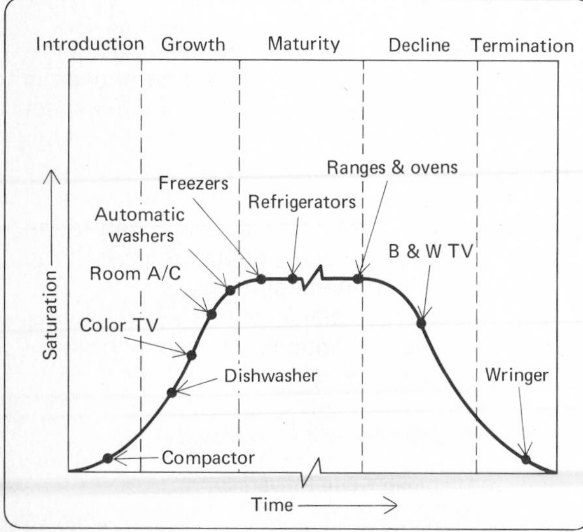

The product life cycle concept is illustrated as a convenient scheme of product classification. The PLC permits management to assign given products to the appropriate stages of acceptance by a given market: *introduction*, *growth*, *maturity*, *decline*, and *termination*. The actual classification of products by appropriate stages, however, is more art than science. The whole process is quite imprecise; but unsatisfactory as this may be, a useful classification can be achieved with management benefits that are clearly of value. This can be illustrated by examining the contribution of the PLC concept in the following marketing activities: sales forecasting, advertising, pricing, and marketing planning.

Applications to Sales Forecasting

One of the most dramatic uses of the PLC in sales forecasting was its application in explaining the violent decline in sales of color TV during the credit crunch recession of 1969–70. This occurred after the experience of the 1966–67 mini-recession which had almost no effect on color TV sales that could be discerned through the usual "noise" of the available product flow data. A similar apparent insensitivity was demonstrated in 1958, in 1961, and again in 1966–67, with sales of portable dishwashers. However, it too was followed by a noticeable sales reduction in the 1969–71 period.

In early 1972 sales of both portable dishwashers and color TV sets showed a positive response to an improving economic climate, raising the question why both products had become vulnerable to economic contractions after having shown a great degree of independence of the business cycle during previous years. The answer to the question seems to lie in their stage in the product life cycle. In comparing the saturation of color TV and dishwashers, consider first the case of color TV sales.

	Introduction	Growth	Maturity	Decline	Termination
Marketing					
Customers	Innovative/ high income	High income/ mass market	Mass market	Laggards/ special	Few
Channels	Few	Many	Many	Few	Few
Approach	Product	Label	Label	Specialized	Availability
Advertising	Awareness	Label superiority	Lowest price	Psychographic	Sparse
Competitors	Few	Many	Many	Few	Few
Pricing					
Price	High	Lower	Lowest	Rising	High
Gross margins	High	Lower	Lowest	Low	Rising
Cost reductions	Few	Many	Slower	None	None
Incentives	Channel	Channel/ consumer	Consumer/ channel	Channel	Channel
Product					
Configuration	Basic	Second generation	Segmented/ sophisticated	Basic	Stripped
Quality	Poor	Good	Superior	Spotty	Minimal
Capacity	Over	Under	Optimum	Over	Over

Figure 2 Product life cycle.

We can ascertain that as late as 1966, saturation of color TV was approximately 8 percent. By late in 1969, however, saturation had swiftly increased to nearly 40 percent.

The same observation is true in the case of dishwashers—considered a mass market appliance only since 1965. This is the key to the explanation of both situations. At the early, introductory stages of their life cycles, both appliances were making large sales gains as the result of being adopted by consumers with high incomes. Later, when sales growth depended more upon adoption by the less affluent members of the mass market whose spending plans are modified by general economic conditions, the product sales began to correlate markedly to general economic circumstances.

It appears that big ticket consumer durables such as television sets and portable dishwashers tend to saturate as a function of customer income. This fact is illustrated by the data displayed in Figure 3, concerning refrigerators and compactors, where one can note the logical relationship between the two products as to the economic status of their most important customers and as to their position in the product life cycle. The refrigerator is a mature product while the compactor is the newest product in the major appliance family.

The refrigerator's present marketing characteristics are a good guide to proper expectations for the compactor as it matures from the *introductory* stage through *growth* to *maturity*. One can anticipate that the compactor, the micro-

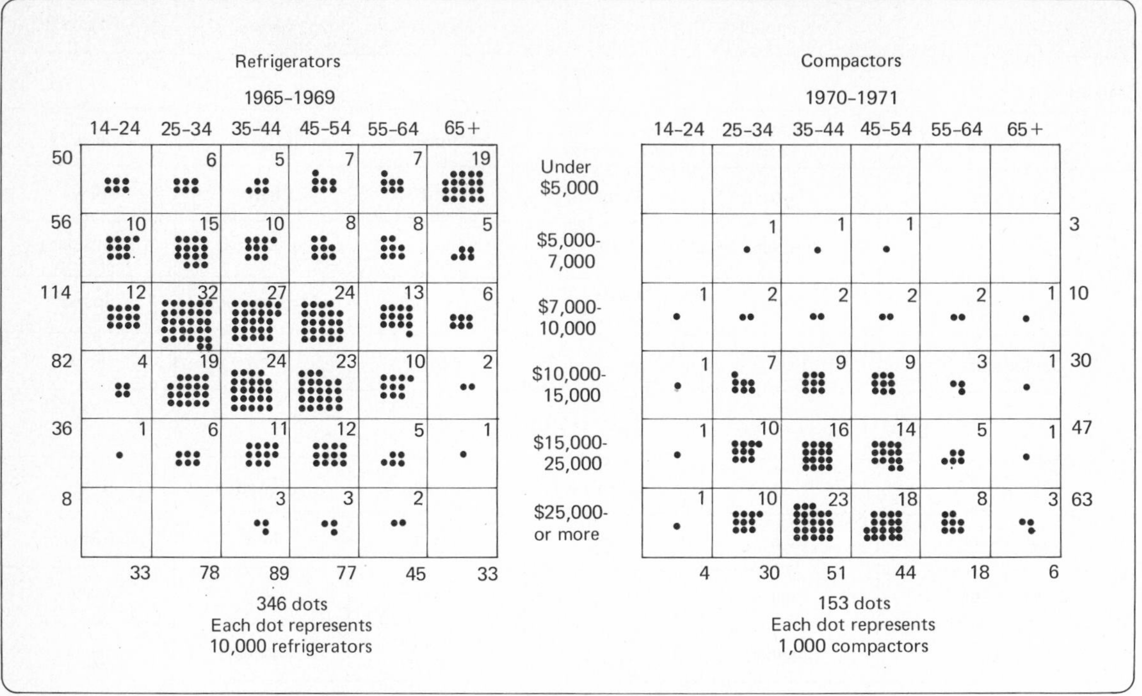

Figure 3 Purchase patterns by age and income of households.

wave oven, and even nondurables such as good quality wines, will someday be included in the middle income consumption patterns, and we will find their sales to be much more coincident with general economic cycles.

Product Life Stages and Advertising

The concept of a new product filtering through income classes, combined with long-respected precepts of advertising, can result in new perspectives for marketing managers. The resulting observations are both stragetic and tactical. New advertising objectives and new insights for copy points and media selection may be realized. Consider the advertising tasks by the following phases:

Phase 1

Introduction. The first objective is to make the best customer prospects aware that the new product or service is now available; to tell them what it does, what are the benefits, why claims are to be believed, and what will be the conditions of consumption.

Phase 2

Growth. The next objective is to saturate the mass market with the same selling points as used in Phase 1. In addition, it is to recognize that a particular brand of the product is clearly superior to other "inferior" substitutes while, at the same time, to provide a rationalization that this purchase is not merely a wasteful, luxury indulging activity but that it will make the consumer a better *something*, a better husband, mother, accountant, driver, and so forth.

Phase 3

Maturity. A new rationalization, respectability, is added, besides an intensification of brand superiority ("don't buy substitutes; get the real *XYZ* original, which incidentally, is *new* and *improved* . . ."). To a great extent, the *product* registration is dropped. Respectability is a strong requisite of the American lower class, which in this phase is the economic stratum containing the most important opportunities for sales gains. Companies do not abandon higher income customers, but they now match advertising to a variety of market segments instead of concentrating on only one theme for the market. Several distinct advertising programs are used. All elements of the marketing mix—product, price, sales promotion,advertising, trading and physical distribution channels—are focused on specific market segments.

Phase 4

Decline. Superior substitutes for a product generally will be adopted first by the people who before were the first to adopt the product in consideration. These people usually are from the upper economic and social classes. Advertising themes reflect this situation when they concentrate on special market segments such as West Coast families or "consumption societies" such as beer drinkers or apartment dwellers.

Product Life Stages and Pricing

As a product progresses through all five stages of the life cycle shown in Figure 1, the price elasticity can be expected to undergo dramatic changes. Generally speaking, price elasticity of a relatively simple product will be low at first. Thus, when customers are drawn from the higher income classes, demand is relatively inelastic. Later, when most customers are in the lower income categories, greater price elasticity will exist.

Of course, increased price elasticity will not automatically lower prices during the growth stage of the PLC. It is in this growth stage, however, that per unit costs *are* most dramatically reduced because of the effect of the learning curve in engineering, production, and marketing. Rising volume and, more important, the *forecasts* of higher volumes, justify increased capital investments and higher fixed costs, which when spread over a larger number of units, thereby reduce unit costs markedly. New competitors surface with great rapidity in this stage as profits tend to increase dramatically.

Pricing in the mature phase of the PLC usually is found to be unsatisfactory, with no one's profit margins as satisfactory as before. Price competition is keener within the distribution channel in spite of the fact that relatively small price differences seldom translate into any change in aggregate consumer activity.

Product Planning and the PLC

Curiously enough, the very configuration of the product takes on a classical pattern of evolution as it advances through the PLC. At first, the new device is designed for function alone; the initial design is sometimes crude by standards that will be applied in the future. As the product maturation process continues, performance sophistication increases. Eventually the product develops to the point where competitors are hardpressed to make meaningful differences which are perceptible to consumers.

As the product progresses through the product life cycle these modifications tend to describe a pattern of metamorphosis from "the ugly box" to a number of options. The adjustment cycle includes:

Part of house: the built-in look and function. Light fixtures, cooking stoves, wall safes, and furnaces are examples.

Furniture: a blending of the product into the home decor. This includes television, hi-fi consoles, radios, clocks, musical instruments, game tables, and so forth.

Portability: a provision for increased *presence* of the product through provisions for easier movement (rollers or compactness), or multiple unit ownership (wall clocks, radios, even refrigerators), or miniaturization for portability. Portability and *personalization*, such as the pocket knife and the wristwatch, can occur.

System: a combination of components into one unit with compatible uses and/or common parts for increased convenience, lower cost, or less space. Home entertainment centers including television, radio, hi-fi, refrigerator-freezers, combination clothes washer-dryers, clock radios, pocket knife-can-and-bottle openers are illustrative.

Similar changes can also be observed in the

distribution channel. Products often progress from speciality outlets in the introductory stage to mass distribution outlets such as discount houses and contract buyers during the "maturity" and "decline" phases of the PLC. Interestingly enough, the process eventually is reversed. Buggy whips can still be found in some speciality stores and premium prices are paid for replicas of very old products.

Conclusion

The product life cycle is a useful concept. It is the equivalent of the periodic table of the elements in the physical sciences. The maturation of production technology and product configuration along with marketing programs proceeds in an orderly, somewhat predictable, course over time with the merchandising nature and marketing environment noticeably similar between products that are in the same stage of their life cycle. Its use as a concept in forecasting, pricing, advertising, product planning, and other aspects of marketing management can make it a valuable concept, although considerable amounts of judgment must be used in its application.

14
Staffing

The effectiveness of company plans will depend, of course, on the capabilities of those who make them and those who carry them out—who will sometimes be the same people. Thus the staffing function is of the utmost importance.

Staffing includes recruitment, selection of new people when they are needed, and decisions on whom to promote when higher jobs open up. It may also be said to include training, since training is designed either to ensure that people handle their current jobs better or to prepare them for promotion.

This chapter includes articles on each of these aspects of staffing. The first deals with the recruitment of college graduates and some of the differences between the views of the graduates and those of the companies that are seeking to hire them. The next three deal with selection methods, and the last two with a particular type of training—"sensitivity training," or "laboratory education" as it is sometimes called. Since there are conflicting views on this type of training, one writer presents the arguments against it and another the arguments in favor of it.

This article, based on an original survey, explores the expectations of college students who are planning to enter business upon graduation and those of the students who have already had a considerable amount of business experience. Then it compares the students' expectations with what industry expects of new hires. Both Professor Meloy and Professor Rosenbluth are associate professors of management and marketing at St. Peter's College, Jersey City, N.J.

Business Staffing and the College Student

Charles A. Meloy and Martin H. Rosenbluth

When entry-level positions are filled by college graduates, organizations have certain performance expectations in mind. When students look forward to positions that lie ahead, they form their own expectations and aspirations in what they envision as opportunities and challenges. How do these expectations and aspirations mesh when viewed from the organization and the student perspective?

A look at expectancy theory helps to put these responses in a more understandable relationship. Expectancy theory implies that when an individual anticipates undertaking a particular task, the amount of energy or effort that he will expend on it is based on two fundamental factors: first, the likelihood that he can complete the task satisfactorily and second, that completion will lead to some anticipated reward or outcome.

After a person has consciously or unconsciously determined the likelihood of success at the task, the major motivating factor is the anticipated reward for the behavior. The part of expectancy theory that has been largely ignored by many investigators has been the expectancy of the organization and the way it meshes with that of the individual.

Through various interviews, mentoring sessions, and a survey of 228 college juniors and seniors, day and night students, at Saint Peter's College, Jersey City, and other urban institutions, the authors received responses covering many areas of work experience and work expectations. Conversations and conferences with business spokesmen provided management's views.

The purpose of this study was to determine to what extent the views of the student meshed with those of the enterprise in role expectations. Of the students polled, 134 were full-time upper classmen 20 to 25 years old. Most of the students in this group had little or no full-time work experience although many had done part-time work. The second sample consisted of 94 part-time study evening students, also upper classmen. Both groups were essentially business students working toward baccalaureate degrees.

The major differences between the day group and the evening group were age and work experience. The evening group ranged in age from 25 to over 30 with full-time work experience of from five to fifteen years. A number of the evening students were already employed in managerial positions at the second level—that is, they were managers of managers.

Business Expectations

Looking at staffing needs as they are related to the college graduate, personnel managers see some of the traditional standards still dominant. For example, good speech, good grammar, good attendance, and good morale have not gone out of style. These attributes are *not* disappearing from position specifications, but those in charge of filling job slots are finding it increasing difficult to obtain applicants who possess them.

The director of academic affairs at one of the top ten industrial firms pointed to the reluctance of some college graduates to accept entry-level (ground floor) jobs in the company. Such positions are usually at a low level and comprise routine and unglamorous assignments. With several years of classroom theory and case studies behind them, new hires look for, as they put it, "challenging and meaningful work." Many of these new hires from the campus become frustrated when they realize that they must spend weeks or even months at such tasks as poring over policy and specifications manuals, making routine checks, and sifting through reports they consider boring.

What then does business look for in the newly

hired college graduate? Perhaps ideally it would like to see an employee whose attitude and output, after a reasonable breaking-in period, give evidence of the following:

1 Willingness to accept beginning jobs regardless of how lowly the work may appear. While this may seem to be a long route to the executive suite, it is nonetheless one of the more reliable.
2 A specific approach to problems at hand rather than a tendency to search for a ready-made textbook formula with a "yes" or "no" answer.
3 Prudent use of resources and facilities in performing tasks. This means, for example, using one napkin for a six-course dinner rather than insisting on a separate napkin for each course.
4 Demonstration of effective communication skills. Whether in drawing up reports, writing memos, or dictating letters, there should be reasonable accuracy, clarity, and conciseness. Speech should be well modulated and articulate.

Most managements hope for the qualities just enumerated but at the same time realize that there is often a wide gap between hopes and expectations. They concede that they find few new hires who completely satisfy the four criteria.

The Student Response

At the other side of the expectations coin, there is the students' view. What does the new entry into the work force look for in the work experience?

1 *Job content and challenge.* This is almost diametrically opposite to the hopes of the business firm that would like the new employee to accept a beginning job regardless how demeaning the work may appear. The company views this as the necessity to "walk before you run." To the new hire, it is a frustrating obstacle.
2 *Work satisfaction* ranks second in the expectations of the new hire. This is contrary to the routine work often expected of the new worker. The company often considers it more important for the new employee to get a grip on responsibility than to be occupied with work that necessarily satisfies him.
3 *Opportunity for advancement.* Several studies have indicated that this new generation of graduates wants well-defined growth or career ladders. They want to know at the outset where they will be in the organization in two or more years. While the enterprise promises great opportunities somewhere down the line, the new employee views them as both uncertain and elusive.
4 *Amount of pay.* The new hire of this generation differs very little from his counterpart in the previous generation in salary expectations. The difference is only in the amount of dollars, not necessarily in the buying power of the amount. This strong concern with the amount of pay as one *enters* the job seems to be in complete agreement with the conclusions reached by most of the need theorists: With experience, however, this concern will shift in the direction of acceptance and status.

To return to business views: Companies are quick to explain why new employees, including college graduates, are given jobs requiring nominal skills and few decision-making responsibilities. Mistakes can be costly; and at least during the beginning periods, efforts are made to keep these to a minimum. At the same time, training is a continuous process and there is a gradual rise in the level of responsibility to match the experience gained. Management expects mistakes to be made; often this is an effective heuristic approach in the learning process. However, management feels that the impact of mistakes must be held within acceptable tolerances.

Employers, whether they admit it or not, recognize the energy, intelligence, and warm personality of many of the college graduates they hire. At the same time, they feel that they are criticized unjustly when they look askance at some of the suggestions offered by the new hires. For example, the new hire may treat surface symptoms as end problems. He will eagerly suggest "band-aid" solutions even when the cause of the problem is still a mystery.

Managements are not wholly guiltless of deflating the new hire's ego. Non-college supervisors may pretend to regard their collegiate underlings as walking encyclopedias. Confronted with a perplexing problem, they wink at bystanding subordinates and turn to the target: "Joe, you've been through college. Tell us how to get out of this mess."

Certainly in their expectations of new employees companies differentiate between those with a college degree and those without. There is little doubt that when promotion and advancement are under consideration, the college graduate is usually preferred. He is valued, not so much for what he knows as for the kind of academic discipline he has been through. This means that methodological approaches rather than headlong rushes can be expected in the face of challenges. To be sure, not all college graduates in the work force respond in this manner, but it is the longer-term potential to do this that gives them the nod.

In practice, some companies are more likely to be concerned with the college graduate's inability to communicate effectively than with his problem-handling approaches. Faulty communication is a serious handicap for any employee, but for the college graduate it is often downright embarrassing. Fortunately this deficiency can be remedied over time if the graduate applies concentration and self-discipline.

Higher management sometimes associates poor communication skills with a lazy, superficial attitude, and oftentimes a business graduate finds himself outpaced by his liberal arts colleague in a position in which communications expertise is required. Excessive verbosity, on the other hand, can be an irritating problem. Sophisticated over-elaboration, redundancy—or even worse, recourse to abstract terminology that few can understand—has little place in the business environment.

Companies frequently encourage college-background employees to pursue graduate education; in many cases the company will pay part of the tuition or all of it. Another trend is the increasing number of companies that express a preference for hiring undergraduate students in order to ensure that their graduate school programs are more closely attuned to company needs.

If business expectations of the college graduate can be summarized in one short phrase, it would probably be this: "promising potential."

Student Survey Findings

The survey of 228 college upperclassmen conducted by the authors resulted in some interesting findings. Statistically, significant differences were noted in several areas regarding the expectancy and aspirations of the potential new entry into the organization (the day student) and the fully employed student studying part time at night.

The longer the student's work experience, the stronger the desire to remain with one company and advance through promotion in that company. The student with little or no significant work experience envisaged jumping from company to company in order to achieve goal aspirations. It was also noted that the longer a student had worked for someone else, the less his desire to start his own business.

Regarding the social and moral obligations of business to society, the greater the student's work experience, the lower the rating of the firm's contribution to society. However, both the day and evening students rated the factor of social responsibility as relatively unimportant as it pertained to *their* particular positions. This response is contrary to the publicized opinions of many youthful executives.

The implication of these findings is that when the student is not personally involved, he feels strongly about ecological problems, but when his own career is involved, he appears willing to overlook such problems in deference to career objectives.

Other responses in the survey suggested that neither the relatively inexperienced student nor his experienced colleague was much concerned with length of the work week or position status. Only mild interest was indicated in such factors as job security, responsibility for decisions, social interaction, and a pension program.

Looking ahead, most students viewed a career as a two-way street. They felt that an input of hard work, willingness to learn, and response to opportunities should be reciprocated by the employer in the form of a well-rounded training program, work that required *thinking* as well as doing, and frequent feedback and encouragement.

Additionally, students view their prospective employer as one who will be more dynamic than bureaucratic and one who will offer some degree of job freedom and flexibility. The most frequently received response to on-the-job expectations by the students was for "meaningful and satisfying work with opportunity for advancement."

Bridging the Aspiration Gap

Business spokesmen are quick to accept responsibility for providing employment opportunities that will to some extent parallel the student aspirations voiced in this survey. The gap would appear to be more one of degree of opportunity than the absence or presence of opportunity itself. Companies see no reason why college graduates should balk at entering an established training program. While most of these programs introduce the new employee to the company at a lower rung, the companies feel that this exposure is necessary if he is to learn the trade properly.

Students, as noted, frequently refer to the need for challenging opportunities in the organization. Perhaps this use of the word "challenging" is overdone. Surely every company has a bucketful of challenging opportunities (a euphemism for problems). Some of these problems have been around for years, and the enterprise's best talent has been working on them without much success. Obviously these are not the challenges the new hires have in mind. What they refer to, of course, are ongoing opportunities to apply their ability and judgment to situations within their competence.

Work routine that is programmed down to the minutest detail is anathema to most students. Companies are quick to close the gap here. Few college graduates are given assembly-line operations but are usually placed in staff-type positions where monotony and routine are by no means universal. As one administrator put it: "We are interested in young people who give evidence of a sense of direction and goal orientation and a sincere interest in the job at hand."

Bridging the gap between company expectations and student aspirations, say the students, might be helped by improvements in two areas. The one area cited by students is company recruitment which brings representatives to the campus. To the student, the recruiter *is* the company. Therefore interest in the company often depends on the recruiter's interest in the student. This means straightforward responses, fair but realistic treatment, and very important, following through any "We'll let you know" farewells.

The second area that could stand improvement, according to student responses, is business appearance on the campus. For example, they suggest that spokesmen from various specialties address classes and participate in student-business dialogues, and that companies sponsor internship programs that are practical and purposeful.

Progress in these areas, the students feel, will elevate the sterotype of business in many student minds and at the same time provide the commercial, public administration, and industrial community with the valuable talent it so badly needs.

Summary and Conclusion

At the outset of this study, it was stated that expectancy theory implies that when an individual is anticipating the undertaking of a particular task, the amount of energy or effort that will be expended is based on two fundamental factors: first the likelihood that the task can be satisfactorily completed and secondly that it will lead to some anticipated reward or outcome.

There is much evidence that the motivation of employees is correlated with their early experiences on their entry into full-time positions. As a result, if the organizations are striving for a motivated work force, then the effects of these early experiences must be carefully reviewed.

Part of the problem appears to be the differing views and expectations of the two sides. The firm, in an attempt to groom and develop the new employee, wants to give the workers thorough training through an established program—which often includes routine and perhaps demeaning work assignments. The company feels that this basic training is fundamental to later success as a decision maker, for the employee will have been through that phase of company operations himself. This approach is contrary to the expectations of the new college graduate.

As a graduate, he feels he has been through four years or so of learning methodologies and that he has assimilated an awareness background that prepares him for more than a routine check, note, and shuffle operation. What the new graduate is searching for in the work environment is job content, challenge, and work satisfaction. There is little evidence of this in a routine assignment.

This conclusion is established in the results of the survey on which this article is based. In effect, the differing attitudes and expectancies of the student with significant work experience and those of the student who lacks it help to explain this attitude. For example, it may well be that the developing negative attitudes and possible demotivation of the employee over time were due to the early experiences in the firm.

Fundamentally, both the firm in its search for new employees and the future hopes of the new employee are heading in the same direction. That is, to produce an effective decision maker. The key problem appears to be in communication and indoctrination. They are united in their goals but they are disparate in what they say. Many talk, but few communicate. Thus the problem may be one primarily of understanding.

If management can convey to the new hires the importance of "slow" development as a predictor of future executive ability and at the same time allow for early job enrichment, it may be able to develop competency and a motivated work force.

The more successful a company is in recruiting applicants, the greater its chance, generally speaking, of finding the kind of people it really wants and needs. But, of course, this is true only if it has effective means of selecting the right candidates for the jobs. For well over half a century, there have been psychological tests available for use in the selection process, but they still do not make selection an automatic process, nor is it likely that they ever will. Moreover, they are not useful in all cases. This article provides valid suggestions about when to use tests and when to omit the testing procedure. Mason Haire is with the Massachusetts Institute of Technology.

Use of Tests in Employee Selection

Mason Haire

Psychological tests lie on a sort of border line between techniques that are entirely in the province of the layman and those that are shrouded with all the mysterious performances of the technical expert. Many a personnel man starts with the straightforward idea of picking better people for employment—a reasonable goal. He turns to tests for help and finds himself in a bewildering morass of correlation coefficients, validities, and restricted ranges—clearly the bailiwick of the technician. For this reason, it seems especially worth while to consider some of the implications that follow on the introduction of psychological tests.

Relation to Total Problem

One of the first things to consider is the weight that can be given to any course of action—selection testing or anything else—in a general personnel policy.

For any given plant we can set down a list of the several things that make us think something needs improving, a list of symptoms from which

From *Harvard Business Review*, January, 1950, pp. 42–51.

we can work backwards toward the causes. Many things might go into this list: absenteeism, high turnover, low morale, grievances, low production, high costs (direct or indirect)—whatever things we see in the picture that make us think something is wrong.

Then alongside this list we can put down the possible causes of the difficulties, the places where we may profitably devote time and effort to improving the situation—selection, placement, promotion (transfer), training, supervision, engineering (including work layout, flow of materials, provision of tools), management (including setting of wages and working conditions), and the like.

Next we can try to assess the factors that are associated with the difficulties. Suppose direct production cost is singled out as apparently too high. Part of the trouble may indeed be that we do not have the right kind of people for the job. [But] perhaps some of the excessive cost comes from waiting for parts or from inefficiencies in the handling of materials; perhaps some of it is from the method of payment or the system of job assignment; if so, how much?

Two more steps can be taken in this evaluation. (1) Because none of the items in the cause list can be brought to a level of perfection, we have to estimate how much improvement we can *reasonably* hope to make in each area. (2) We also need to estimate the cost, in money, time, effort, and personnel, of effecting a comparable amount of improvement in any one of the causes.

On this basis we may come to decide on directing our efforts to selection testing. Or it may be that testing is shown to be less important than several other possibilities like a new program for supervisors or a new merit-rating plan, and these are all that can be handled for the time being.

It would be foolish at this point to say, "We should tackle all of the causes of our difficulties, not just one or two of them." In practice any company's resources of time and money are limited, and an attack on one problem is usually made at the expense of not attacking another.

The Philosophy of Testing

The use of selection tests rests squarely on two assumptions:

1 It is assumed that any given human ability is distributed over a range with a few people who are very high or very low in the particular ability and most of them distributed around the middle. The immediate implication of this is that if we can (a) identify the ability we need on a particular job, (b) identify the people who are in the high part of the distribution on that scale, and (c) select that segment of the population, then we will markedly improve our labor pool.

2 The other basic assumption is that it is possible to construct tests that are associated with the ability in question. The assumption is not necessarily made that the test measures the ability directly, or is a sample of the performance that the worker will produce on the job, but only that a high score on the test will be associated with the presence of a high level of the ability desired.

To act on this point of view, however, means that we have already made several decisions. For one thing, when we frame our problem this way ("we need to raise the level of certain skills; therefore, we should select better people in hiring"), we imply that all the other factors that should be considered among the causes of difficulty have a lesser weight, and without facing the problem squarely we have decided that psychological selection is one of the important keys.

In adopting this point of view we have allowed one more requirement to slip in without our noticing it. There must be sufficient difference between the high and low ends of the scale to make a real difference on the job. This point is emphasized when we realize we cannot unerringly identify the highs and lows. Unless there is a large difference between them, we will have great difficulty in separating out a group that is predominantly high.

An example may make the operation of these two factors clearer. I once talked to representatives of a company that wanted a set of tests of color vision which would let them select workers with the greatest color sensitivity—a most reasonable request. Some such tests are available and others could be devised with very little difficulty.

But human differences in color vision are distributed over a relatively narrow range. Moreover, in this case the inspectors were women [and] color blindness in women is about as rare in the psychologist's experience as appearances of Halley's Comet.

A close inspection, with plant officials, of the experimental inspection line that had been set up led to the conclusion on the part of the company that the problem could be solved by (1) utilizing the suggestions of the girls who had been doing the job in its trial period, (2) making some changes in lighting and positioning of inspectors, and (3) introducing some training at the benches in the criteria for grading and rejecting.

Still another point comes up, as we get into the actual testing. As a direct consequence of our initial assumption about the distribution of human abilities, we may be led into placing a tremendous demand on our labor supply.

Let us suppose that we have given an arithmetic test to 1,000 salespeople. An examination of the performance of these salespeople shows that the best 50% on our test make only one third of the errors in the store. With a two-to-one difference in errors between the upper and lower halves on the test, we might establish a cutoff score in the neighborhood of the score obtained by the highest 50% of our sample. That is, to reduce errors, we should not hire anyone who scores below the score obtained by 50% of our salespeople.

The implication of this decision for our labor pool is clear: we shall have to test two applicants for every salesperson we can hire. (Actually the figure will be slightly more than two for one, since our hypothetical test was validated on employees, who are presumably a higher group than unselected candidates, but the point remains the same.) Notice that we have had to place demands on our labor pool that were determined by the requirements of the job rather than the characteristics of the labor supply. So far we are probably safe, but it may get out of hand.

Suppose we add verbal ability. The two tests will not eliminate the same people; in other words, they will eliminate more people, and our cost in terms of applicants required becomes, at least to some extent, cumulative.

So far one might say, "Well, the job has high standards, and you have to look at a lot of people to find the right one. That has nothing to do with the test." But that is not quite the whole story. Tests are not perfect predictors. Some of the people the test said would not be successful would have made good records, and some of those the test said would be successful will eventually fail. Of course we can usually minimize the personnel "cost" involved in such failures by raising our cutoff score. But in moving our cutoff up to minimize our test's lack of predictive power, we have increased the number of people we must test in order to hire any given number of salespeople.

One seldom finds a job whose selection demands are filled by a single test. Consequently we run into the accumulation of eliminations as we add to the factors we are testing. When to this is added the fact that current testing does not usually yield more than medium predictive power and we are forced to raise cutoffs to compensate for that, it can be seen how real is this problem of requiring a larger group of applicants than the number we expect to hire.

The obvious question: Can we afford higher cutoff scores in terms of the applicants we have available?

It is clear, too, that the significance of the effect of selection testing in labor-pool requirements is magnified in periods of relatively full employment. At the very time when applicants are less plentiful, their lower marginal quality and the fact that fewer have a previous work history to examine as part of the selection process make it desirable to raise the cutoff score and thus necessitate having a larger labor pool.

It should be pointed out here that we are much better off with regard to the demand that is placed on our labor pool if we are in a position to use our tests for classification rather than just for selection—that is, if we can use tests for placement as well as simply employment. In this way we can utilize many of the candidates who would otherwise have been eliminated. On the other hand, although we reduce the cost in terms of employment interviewing, widespread classification testing will make a complicated and cumbersome system.

The second basic assumption—that tests will yield scores associated with the ability in which we are interested—leads to its own special group of problems in practice.

On the one hand, testing is simply a refinement of informal hiring procedures. When we ask a candidate for a driver's job to park a truck to show his skill, for example, we are beginning a rough sort of testing procedure. At this extreme, we have many work-sample tests, merchandise-knowledge tests, and the like.

The other extreme is quite different. Ideally it proceeds in this fashion: For a given job we agree what the marks of a relatively successful and of a relatively unsuccessful worker are. We devise a very large test containing many, many items (which we may privately hope have some relation to the job) and test a large group of applicants.

Then, later, we identify those who have been successful and those who have been unsuccessful and go back to the original tests. We examine each item individually to see how our successful and our unsuccessful group did on it. If, for instance, 80% of the ultimately successful men answered it correctly and only 20% of the unsuccessful group did, we keep it because it discriminates as intended. On another item the percentages may be different. Let us say that 28% of the successful group got it right and 24% of the unsuccessful group. We throw the item out—"does not discriminate." Our final product is an aggregate of those items that did work, and we use this (tentatively) on the next batch of applicants.

The difference between the two extremes in the approach to testing is between a set of measurements of a skill whose relation to performance we understand, on the one hand, and a set of measurements whose relation to success is based on a statistical and correlative relationship rather than a logical or necessary one, on the other hand.

The statistical approach leads into a maze of complicated technical procedures and commits the company to a continuing responsibility and dependence it may not want to assume.

Moreover, a certain amount of uneasiness may well accompany hiring on the basis of correlation rather than understanding. We are leaving the place where we can understand, in a certain sense, why we hired or rejected a person. It is one thing to say of a rejected applicant, "Him? He couldn't even back up a truck!" and quite another to say, "He scored lower than 38% of the applicants on a battery of tests that has been shown to have a .45 correlation with success on the job, and such a score indicates a relatively high probability that his work would fall in the lower half of the work group."

There are several consequences: (1) Management may be understandably uneasy at having this mathematical bridge substituted for its immediate understanding of the reason for rejection. (2) The company commits itself to considerable upkeep on the mathematical bridge. (3) The company is in a very different position, from the standpoint of public relations, with the union, its employees, its labor supply, and the community.

Employment, promotion, and transfer are sometimes handled by interview, sometimes by testing the applicant, and sometimes of course by both. For every case where I have heard a rejected applicant grousing that the interviewer did not find out the relevant facts for the decision, I have heard a dozen suggestions that the tests were foolish, that they did not really measure what he had, and that it was somehow their fault that he did not get the job. Let us not worry about whether the applicant is right; if the feeling is there, we have the potentiality of trouble.

This is one of the things that must be taken into account in assessing the cost of a selection program. It it threatens existing relationships, it can be potentially tremendously expensive and cause a radical readjustment of the estimate of its value to the plant.

Another facet of the second basic assumption of selection testing is this: Human abilities distribute themselves over a range. Careful job specifications tell us what abilities we need to do the job. If we select people who are measurably high on these abilities, we will get the job done better, faster, and cheaper. On paper this rationale seems indisputable. If the job requires speed of reaction or hand-eye coordination, we should measure reaction time and coordination and take only those who are high on both. But reaction time and coordination do not exist in a vacuum. They are woven into the highly complex fabric that is a person, and that person may have high coordination and not produce on the job, or he may have learned ways to compensate for his low coordination so that he produces well on the job.

It is very difficult to specify job requirements exactly in terms of the sensory abilities required. I have a friend who was born with opaque lenses in his eyes; his lenses were removed in infancy, and to replace them he has a set of spectacles with different lenses for different distances. I go bird-shooting with him every year; I play squash with him; and I ride with him as he drives his car. Any job specifications for these three tasks would put visual acuity high on the list. Any measurement of his vision would rank him extremely low in visual abilities. Yet his performance in all three activities is consistently good.

Thus, we must take care not to exclude such men from our work force by the mechanical measurement of skills and abilities. To carry the thought further, we must give some consideration to the way in which these abilities may be integrated into the pattern of skills that is a person. This leads us to the knotty problem of measuring the personality rather than discrete skills. It also leads to another knotty problem of writing adequate job specifications from which to draw the dimensions for selection. The upshot of this consideration seems to be that the definition of a necessary skill *in vacuo* and its mechanical measurement will not necessarily produce the optimum output on the job.

In the current state of selection testing, very few tests can be taken over directly and applied to new situations. They must be checked and rechecked and adapted to the particular plant.

[And] just as a test for file clerks which has done successful selection for Company A must be revalidated in Company B's case before it can be used with safety, a test that works today has to be constantly rechecked and validated to adjust to the changing situation. It may seem at the outset that the company is committed to a six months' period of analysis and preliminary testing, after which the test battery will be installed, a clerk taught to administer and score, and "that's that." However, some provision must be made for systematic re-evaluations of the testing procedure and for the careful collection of data both on the tests and on performance.

There are several things that may happen and that must therefore be guarded against. The company may find that, instead of a six months' commitment, it is committed to a relationship without end, as long as the testing continues. The personnel department has acquired a load of record-keeping as well as the testing itself, and real demands are being made on the line organization for periodic evaluations of the success of those who have been tested. Again, the company may find it is tied to a long-term and expensive consulting relationship with the expert who installed the tests, and that relationship may prove cumbersome in its lack of integration into the personnel organization. Such factors as these bring unanticipated costs.

Areas of Usefulness

It might be well to go, in some detail, into the particularly likely areas for testing. Three categories of jobs seem to stand out: (1) jobs that are heavily loaded with easily identifiable skills and demand the relatively inflexible application of these skills in performance, (2) jobs requiring very special or unusual characteristics, and (3) jobs requiring a long, expensive training program before the applicant is useful.

The first classification will need more detailed treatment, but brief extreme examples can be given of the other two:

During the war several aircraft companies employed midgets to work inside the tail-sections of bombers on production. It would be patently foolish, with requirements as special as this, to hire from the normal run of job applicants and to hope by training or supervision to produce a man to fit the job. Job requirements approaching this extreme indicate one of the areas where it may be wise to consider selection procedures based on measured aptitudes and characteristics.

A similar extreme example of the need for selection is where training is long and expensive. During the war the Air Force spent a day and a half giving a battery of 20-odd psychological tests to each air crew applicant—a tremendous expense. But here it was well justified, because there was an investment of nine months of training in each candidate before he became useful on the job. Keeping out one man who would have failed paid for the cost of many, many tests, to say nothing of the protection to both the candidate and his instructors in this special case.

Now to tackle the more subtle question of situations where testing is particularly useful because the job is heavily loaded with fairly specific skills. In most cases the situation seems to be, perversely, that the easier a particular skill is to measure, the less likely it is to be of primary importance in the job situation. We are much more likely to find that it is almost impossible to define the skills required on the job, and that the work situation is flexible enough to allow individuals to meet it in a variety of ways using whatever skills they have.

The problem, for instance, of identifying in advance good retail salespeople or good executives has never approached the kind of solution that has been possible for, say, typists. Everyone is familiar with cases of salespeople who are brusque and even rude with customers but who have a loyal and devoted clientele. The secret seems to be the way in which they do it—and so far we have been markedly unable to measure or predict this "way they do it."

As we get into the cases where jobs are less loaded with specific skills and more flexible in the requirements they put on a person, we begin to approach a new area of testing. Instead of tests of specific skills and abilities we begin to need more complex tests of personality. Such tests, fairly highly developed for clinical diagnosis, are just beginning to be adapted to the purposes of personnel selection. They seem to offer promise, but in most cases they are not yet sufficiently developed for selection purposes.

Under the general heading of "where to test" one point needs re-emphasis. We have mentioned before the demands that testing makes on the labor supply. The point can be turned around. Wherever there are large numbers of applicants for every job or high turnover, tests will have the best chance. Testing is a percentage proposition. It aims to raise the probabilities of correct prediction. It may be wrong in any one case; its success lies in the average. For this reason it leans heavily on large numbers to do its best work.

Intangible Influences

One final point should be made on the general subject of testing. This point has been implicit in many of the arguments presented above, but it deserves separate treatment.

One of the drawbacks in considering a testing program is the unfortunate way it may come to seem to be a substitute for practically anything else in the business. All of us are subject to so many frustrations in deciding who will be best for the job, in training workers and foremen, in setting policies, and so forth, that a technique which runs itself routinely and generates a number-result that is either black or white with no shades of gray is a tempting escape. All too often it is cast in the role of the answer to all our problems, which it most definitely is not.

Are we having difficulties in training new workers so that they fit into the job? Maybe if we selected the right people, the situation would be better. Are the foremen falling down somewhat in their job? They suggest that, if we gave them the right kind of people, there would be no problem; maybe they are right. Are we caught between the millstones of a wage demand and high production costs? Maybe if we selected our workers better, costs would go down. It is not a question of *whether* this sort of influence will get into the company; it will. It seeps throughout the organization and turns up almost anywhere. The question that has to be answered is *how much* it will get around, and how much of it can be afforded.

This is what I call the panacea philosophy. It may appear either as, "This will be a big help in all of our problems," or as "We've always had trouble with *x*; now we've got *y*, it'll take a lot of pressure off *x*." Testing will not solve all the problems, and it probably will not take pressure off *x*. If anything is to be *added* to the present picture by introducing tests, just as much pressure will have to be put on foreman training as before. The gain will come from the *addition* of selection—not its substitute value. Unless this is clearly seen and anticipated, the idea of psychological testing can conceal a potentially dangerous escapism.

The sympton of this escapism appears most clearly when members of management read magazine articles about the factory where all the work is done automatically with endless belts and automatic cranes for transport, with photoelectric cells and thermocouples for inspection and decision, and with the final product, finished and packaged, delivered at the end of the line. It is basically a dream of a day when the medium through which we can achieve production will be something which we can construct, understand, and control completely—when we no longer work through the intractable medium of human beings.

In many ways a machine is a wonderful thing. A group of machines never put any pressure on one another for exceeding any given rate of production; they do not inch wash-up time back little by little from quitting time. But to take advantage of the human's flexibility and adaptability, his resourcefulness and ability to make decisions based on a changing complex of factors, we must pay the price in other less useful variations in human skills, characteristics, and aptitudes.

Conclusion

There is no intention here of denying the merit and usefulness of psychological tests for selecting personnel. Their many and varied successes are so clear that they cannot be overlooked and do not need re-emphasis. The purpose of this discussion, however, is to focus a critical glance on the kinds of value that may be obtained from testing and the kinds of cost that may be exacted in return.

Buying and installing a test program is not like buying and installing an electric typewriter—a relatively discrete, independent, and useful unit. Instead it is more like installing a complex accounting machine whose work means changes throughout the organization. The implications of a testing program for employment will similarly spread throughout an industrial plant, and the effect of these implications needs to be carefully evaluated. Thus, the cost of a testing program should be carefully weighed, with an analysis that goes well beyond the initial expense in dollars and cents.

The costs are many. A testing program changes management's relation to employees, and perhaps to the union. It changes the work of the personnel department, and perhaps its organization. It places many demands on the line organization for cooperation. Although psychological tests for selection may yield a real improvement, let us examine carefully how great an improvement we may expect and how expensive it is likely to be.

In order to avoid the subtle persuasion that there is in the idea of psychological measurement, it may be well to approach it this way: Begin on the theory that you do not need and do not want selection tests. Examine the possibilities carefully—their assets and their liabilities. Then if you decide that tests will help, you are on comparatively safe ground.

The alternative to a reliance on psychological tests is not simply hiring every applicant. The growing role of a strict seniority system makes it more and more important to do the best job possible of employment screening. To this end, we must use whatever techniques are available—skilled interviewers, weighted application blanks, and perhaps even tests. But, by the same token, we must put an increasing emphasis on training, supervision, and job requirements, so that we will maximize the utilization of the people we do hire.

In the case of some jobs, personality may be more important than intelligence or skill, provided the applicant has a reasonable quantity of each. But personality is much more difficult to judge than either—and the personality characteristics that appear requisite for a job may actually be, as this article indicates, essentially irrelevant to success in the work.

Peace Corps Psychiatric Tests Called Essentially Irrelevant

Natalie Jaffe

CHICAGO, Sept. 4—Psychiatric evaluations of the mental health of Peace Corps volunteers were found to be "essentially irrelevant" in predicting the young teachers' actual performance in Africa.

The American Psychological Association, at its 73d annual meeting here, heard Dr. M. Brewster Smith of the University of California outline today his studies of the first group of Peace Corps teachers in Ghana. Dr. Smith said the mental health stereotype of the sociable, self-confident, well-rounded, well-adjusted Peace Corps worker may have to be abandoned as a measure of competence in favor of more sensitive judgments of commitment and interest.

"The current preoccupation with identifying the disturbed puts too single-minded an emphasis on one set of liabilities without attending to assets appropriate to a job," he said.

Early assessment. "So long as the volunteers were competent teachers and interested in Africa, their quirks didn't matter," Dr. Smith said in an interview after his address.

Point of distinction. He based his address on a study of 45 volunteers, both before and after their two years of teaching in Ghana, conducted under a contract with the Peace Corps.

Dr. Smith, a psychologist, is a fellow of the Center for Advanced Study in the Behavioral Sciences at Berkeley, and a Special Research Fellow of the National Institute of Mental Health.

While the volunteers were in training at Berkeley, each was seen in two 50-minute interviews by seven psychiatrists from the Langley-Porter Neuropsychiatric Institute.

On one of the predictions they made, called "psychological effectiveness," high ratings were given to "the optimally adjusted personality as viewed by clinical psychologists—what amounts to a mental health stereotype," Dr. Smith said.

Interviews in Ghana. After the volunteers had been in Africa for a year, Dr. Smith and an associate, Dr. Raphael S. Ezekiel of the University of Michigan, went to Ghana and held long, informal interviews with the young teachers at their schools.

The psychologists made another trip at the end of the second year. Both sets of interviews were recorded.

In the interviews, the volunteers discussed their jobs and how they felt about themselves and Ghana.

Back at Berkeley, Dr. Smith's research teams analyzed the interviews and broke them down into components—65 describing personal attitudes and 64 describing performance inside the classroom and out. These components were subsequently rated by 12 advanced graduate students in psychology who had never met the young teachers.

"The psychiatrists' mental health ratings had a close to zero correlation with our criterion measures of competent performance," Dr. Smith reported.

Test discrepancies. He said he found the discrepancies "not surprising, in view of the psychiatrist's professional training, their responsibility for weeding out disqualifying pathology, and their essential ignorance of the situations the volunteers faced."

No one, even in the Peace Corps administration, he added, knew exactly what was in store for the volunteers when the program first began.

He emphasized that since the final evaluations were based mainly on interviews with the volunteers themselves, the comparisions of prediction and performance could be challenged for their objectivity.

But Dr. Smith said he was "well satisfied" with the honesty and informality of the interviews.

As an example of "one splendidly successful volunteer," Dr. Smith described one young man who failed to impress anyone at Berkeley.

"He was quiet, a loner, not interested in girls and socially awkward. But he got to Ghana and discovered he had a vocation for teaching," the psychologist noted.

"The experience even carried over," Dr. Smith added. "He's now working in a special field of education here and is very effective. What we had missed was his readiness for commitment. It doesn't matter that he isn't hail fellow well met."

Since neither paper-and-pencil tests nor interviews by trained psychologists are the complete answer to the selection problem, many companies are now utilizing the "assessment center," in which people may be observed in situations similar to those they may encounter on the job. This technique is not new. Something very similar was employed in the selection of candidates for the Office of Strategic Services during World War II and by the Department of Civil Service of the State of New York (see "'Selecting Supervisory Mediators through Trial by Combat," *Readings in Management*, 2d ed., pp. 255–258). What is new is the extent to which the technique is being employed by large companies, particularly to determine who is "promotable." James C. Hyatt is a staff reporter for *The Wall Street Journal.*

More Concerns Use "Assessment Centers" to Gauge Employees' Managerial Abilities

James C. Hyatt

The assignment was simple, the kind that managers face daily: Make a seven-minute speech to sell a new product.

But the first speaker was obviously nervous when he rose to address the group of about 20. He fumbled with his notes. Then his self-control vanished entirely. Tears streamed down his cheeks. "I'm sorry," he muttered as he walked out the door.

"That really upset me," recalls Tony DeLuca, who was watching from the audience. "I was the next speaker. And public speaking is the only subject where I got an F in college." (Mr. DeLuca did manage to get through his talk, however.)

Though the "new product" topic was imaginary, the task was dead-serious. Mr. DeLuca and his colleague were performing one of a series of problems that their employer, Gino's Inc., uses to measure managerial strengths and weaknesses.

Several times a year, a dozen middle managers for the fast-food chain gather at a Philadelphia conference center to undergo seven exercises. For four days, members of each group are observed for almost every trait from communications skill to what one executive calls "how their heads work," which means problem analysis and decision making.

Identifying Talent

Although the experience is seldom so dramatic as the nervous speaker's collapse, this kind of testing is becoming common for many ambitious employers, whether they are supervisors or members of the management suite. "Making hard decisions about people" remains one of management's toughest tasks, asserts Curt Russell, Gino's director of management and development. His firm and many others are convinced that the use of "assessment centers" makes the job of identifying and evaluating talent that much easier.

Recently the approach has been adopted by such well-known firms as Merrill Lynch, Pierce, Fenner & Smith, Knight Newspapers, Bendix Corp. and Prudential Insurance Co. Among the early recruits to the cause in the 1960s were IBM, General Electric and J. C. Penney Co.; they were following pioneering efforts by American Telephone & Telegraph Co. In all, it is estimated, over 800 companies have used this method of employee evaluation.

"Assessment centers are growing stronger in the U.S. and have taken off like a rocket in England," and official of the American Management Association says.

From *The Wall Street Journal*, Jan. 3, 1974, p. 15. Reprinted with permission of *The Wall Street Journal*.

This year, more than 20,000 workers will be appraised in such centers, including 10,000 at AT&T, says William Byham, a psychologist whose consulting firm helped set up many such programs. The range of occupations involved is wide; included are stockbrokers and police officers, Social Security administrators and foremen on offshore oil rigs.

Predicting Performance

Determining the effectiveness of assessment centers is difficult, but there are some data to indicate the method can help predict career performance.

At AT&T, a group of newly hired college graduates, all considered potential managers, was assessed years ago. The center staff decided that about half the group members would reach middle management early in their careers. However, that information wasn't given to the workers' supervisors. Eight years later, about 120 of the workers were still at AT&T; of those assessed favorably, 64% had reached middle management, while only 32% of those assessed unfavorably had achieved that level.

Moreover, the candidates assessed say they get better insight into handling themselves as managers. Mr. DeLuca, an area training manager for Gino's, found he did particularly well in an exercise testing his reactions to the administrative problems that might be dropped on an executive's desk. "Since then, I've spent less time on administration," he says. "I realized I was doing it totally out of enjoyment. Instead, I've spent more time with managers reporting to me."

On the other hand, his public-speaking results convinced him to enroll, at company expense, in a self-confidence course at night. "As managers, we're called on periodically to give a speech," he says.

Another assessment-center alumnus, James L. Hanchette, a marketing coordinator at Huyck Corp. of Wake Forest, N.C., recalls a follow-up session in which he watched himself on videotape taking part in a group discussion. "I was more the kind of guy who is sort of a referee, working toward agreement," he says. "Now I'm trying to exert more leadership."

But the assessment procedure has its critics. They don't question that the method generates useful information. But they insist the results can't stand alone.

"The assessment center can become a kind of crutch," says Roy Walters, a management consultant. "I've seen organizations where nobody gets moved unless they've successfully passed a center. That can be a danger if it lets the line managers off the hook too easily." Managers still must learn to give workers the sort of real experiences they need for growth and development, he insists.

Others worry that, used too faddishly, the assessment center becomes "little more than a fraternity initiation," a symbol rather than a management tool to be taken seriously.

Rather than try to apply an objective method, of course, some employers have traditionally used arbitrary standards in making decisions on promotions—a prospect's race or sex, college background or golf manners. Or how he gets along with his supervisor. Or even the kind of marriage he has.

Present and Future

In recent years, many firms have turned to elaborate tracking of on-the-job performance and intensive testing. But such methods also have obvious drawbacks. Present job performance, for instance, doesn't necessarily measure potential for a new job.

"All too often, we've taken the best craftsman we have and made him a foreman," says M. E. Haynes, an internal consultant for Shell Oil Co. "He may not have turned out to be a very good foreman."

So Shell is trying out a day-and-a-half assessment operation to give "an additional look at some areas we feel are necessary to successfully perform as a foreman." Shell's interests include leadership, managerial and administrative skill, problem analysis, mental alertness and tolerance of stress.

To bring those capabilities out, the company uses a variety of exercises. In one group exercise, prospective foremen are given a problem to analyze and discuss. In another, the group talks over a problem and reaches a solution. Each participant also takes a so-called in-basket test, handling a set of memos representing problems that might occur the first day on a new job.

None of the exercises is meant to test specific technical knowledge; rather, each is designed to bring out reactions to a situation. Two kinds of pressure are imposed on candidates, Mr. Haynes says: The stress of working under deadlines and the stress of "developing some solution, although the candidate may feel he isn't qualified to do that."

Such probing, psychologist Byham says, "is an answer to the Peter Principle," which holds that workers rise to their level of incompetence. "We try to evaluate how a person would perform at a higher level or at a new job before he or she is assigned to it."

Staffing is not complete with the selection of the most qualified candidates. Generally even the most promising can be improved by further training under company auspices. In addition, if the company hopes (as most do) to staff higher positions by promotion, it must provide training in order to have a supply of promotable executives.

Training in human relations has been stressed, but many companies have found that ordinary training methods, which simply impart knowledge of the best practices, do not produce much change in behavior. For this reason, a type of training known as "sensitivity training" or "laboratory education" has been developed, designed to enable the trainee to develop sensitivity to others and to his own faults in dealing with them. The training often takes the form of conference meetings in which people may be told exactly what others in the group think of them.

The need for a change in attitude is frequently evident, but there is disagreement about the value of the sensitivity training technique. At a conference in New York City on "Twenty Years of Management Development," arranged by the New York State School of Industrial and Labor Relations, Cornell University, on February 28, 1963, the arguments against this type of training were marshaled by Dr. George S. Odiorne and answered by Dr. Chris Argyris. Portions of their papers appear below, plus a short extract from the discussion that followed their presentations.

Dr. Odiorne, formerly director of the Bureau of Industrial Relations, University of Michigan, is now dean of the College of Business, University of Utah. Dr. Argyris is at Harvard.

A Brief Description of Laboratory Education

Chris Argyris

A laboratory program is designed to provide as many experiences as possible where psychological success, self esteem, and inter-personal competence can be increased; where dependence, control, can be decreased; and where emotional behavior when and if it is relevant can be as fit a subject for discussion as any "rational" topic.

The T-Group

The core of most laboratories is the T-group [T for "training"]. Basically it is designed to provide maximum possible opportunity for the individuals to expose their behavior, give and receive feedback, experiment with new behavior, and develop everlasting awareness and acceptance of self and others. The T-group also provides possibilities to learn the nature of effective group functioning. Individuals are able to learn how to develop a group that achieves specific goals with minimum possible human cost.

It is in the T-group that one finds the emphasis on the participants' creating and diagnosing their own behavior, developing distributive leadership and consensus decision-making norms to protect the deviants, and, finally, sharing as much as possible all the information that is created within, and as a result of, the T-group experience. We are not suggesting that organizations be administered like T-groups. How-

From the *Training Directors Journal*, Vol. 17, No. 10, October, 1963, pp. 5–8.

ever, we are hypothesizing that they should include structures like T-groups for certain selected decisions.

Mouton and Blake[1] describe the T-group which they call a *development group* as follows:

The fundamental-dilemma-producing feature of a human relations laboratory is the development group. The development group is composed of 8 to 12 members, whose explicit goal is to study their own interactions as a group. No leader or power structure is provided. No rules or procedures are given to structure interaction. No task, topic or agenda for discussion is inserted to serve as a guide for action. Thus, the group is faced with critical dilemmas in several fundamental areas of relationships in a group situation. What shall we do or talk about? How shall we relate to one another? What are our rules for interactions? What can we accomplish? How do we make a decision on any of these things? All of these issues and many more are dilemmas initially present in the development group. Thus, the stage is set for the first step of the learning cycle.

In addition to group-level phenomena, much attention is centered on individuals trying out new and different ways of relating to each other. For example, an overbearing, long-talking person may try being silent for an extended period of time; a person who withdraws when under attack may experiment with more aggressive forms of reactions; feelings may be openly expressed. The dilemmas posed by the development group impel inventive, seeking, searching behavior on both the group and the individual level.

Organizational Diagnostic Experiences

When a laboratory program is composed of a group of executives who work with each other the organizational diagnostic experiences are very important. Each executive is asked to come to the laboratory with an agenda or topic that is important to him and to the organization. During the laboratory he is asked to lead the group in a discussion of the topic. The discussion is taped and observed by the staff.

Once the discussion is completed, the group members listen to themselves on the tape. They analyze the interpersonal and group dynamics that occurred in the making of the decision and how these factors influenced their decision making. Usually, they hear how they cut each other off, did not listen, manipulated, pressured, created win-lose alternatives, etc.

Such an analysis typically leads the executives to ask such questions as: Why do we do this to each other? What do we wish to do about this, if anything?

In the cases known to the writer, the executives became highly involved in answering these questions. Few held back to cite interpersonal and organizational reasons why they feel they have to behave as they do. Most deplore the fact that time must be wasted and much energy utilized in this "wind-milling" behavior. It is quite frequent for someone to ask, "But if we do not like this, why don't we do something about it?"

Under these conditions, the learnings developed in the laboratory are intimately interrelated with the everyday "real" problems of the organization. Where this has occurred, the members do not return to the organization with the same degree of bewilderment that executives show who have gone to laboratories full of strangers. Under these conditions it is quite common for the executive to wonder how he will use the information about human competence that he has learned when he returns back home.

Another frequently used learning experience is to break down the participants into groups of four. Sessions are held where each individual has the opportunity to act as a consultant giving help and as an individual receiving help; the nature of help is usually related to increasing self-awareness and competence.

One of the central problems of organizations is the inter-group rivalries and hostilities that exist among departments. If there is time in a laboratory, this topic should be dealt with. Again, it is best introduced by creating the situation where the executives compete against one another in groups under "win-lose" conditions.

[1]Jane S. Mouton and Robert Blake, *University Training in Human Relations Skill*, The University of Texas, mineographed.

The Trouble with Sensitivity Training

George S. Odiorne

Is sensitivity training really training? Training should change behavior. How can we demonstrate changed behavior? We should be able to measure it. One of the most common outcomes of sensitivity training is that the people who undergo it describe the experience as one which "I am sure has had an effect on me but it's too early to tell just how." These are the fortunate ones.

Not long ago a large engineering company in the midwest was prevailed upon by a consulting firm to bring a group of their research executives to a lodge in Wisconsin for sensitivity training. The leader of the session had no prior training in the conduct of such sessions. During one horrible weekend he broke down the barriers of formal courtesy which had substituted quite successfully for human relations in this successful lab for many years. People spoke frankly of their hostilities. At this point they went back to the lab, their dislikes laid bare, with no substitute behavior being provided. Chaos immediately took over. People who had worked in good-mannered pomposity for years, turning out patents and papers at a prodigious pace, began to engage in organized politicking to get square. Senior scientists quit in droves and a major purge took place. Candid observations made up at the lake hung heavy between colleagues. People who had learned that they were seen as SOB's were somewhat less than grateful to the colleagues who had enlightened them and had made them aware of this fact.

This is training?

Training Criteria

To qualify as sound training it would seem that these criteria should be met:

Criterion No. 1: In good training the desired terminal behavior can be identified before the training begins. Sensitivity training simply doesn't do this. It rightfully can state that it will change the verbal behavior of some people who take part. It has little or no idea what any other terminal behavior will be, or whether it will be more or less productive than when the man started.

Here are some typical statements of terminal behavior sought by lab training:

To achieve authenticity in interpersonal relations.

To unfreeze managers' minds.

To develop self-esteem in trainees.

To improve human relations through achieving interpersonal competence, internal commitment and the process of conformation.

Three serious questions arise about training which states its objectives in such terms:

1 What is the *behavioral* definition of such words, as "authenticity," or "esteem"? Aren't they so lacking in precision as to be unmeasurable?
2 Presuming they were precisely defined, and could be measured, would sensitivity lab training change them?
3 Presuming that the changes did occur, what evidence exists that such a behavior change would be good for the man and the company?

Criterion No. 2: The course of change is comprised of some logical small steps in good training. In sensitivity training not only are the participants unaware of what the outcome will be, but in many instances, since there are no controls, neither are the trainers. In most labs, the coordination of what the trainers will do at what time is as vague at the middle and end as it was in the beginning. Typically the staff of a lab is assembled by mail or phone from the in-group which conducts such sessions. They agree to gather one day ahead of the arrival of the subjects to be trained. They divide up the chores under the direction of the assembler of the program. There is little chance for any detailed checking of objectives of individual sessions, or any careful planning so that progressive stages of training will occur. Accordingly most such sessions lack many of the elements of training which might change behavior, simply because

From the *Training Directors Journal*, Vol. 17, No. 10, October, 1963, pp. 12–19.

they are so ineffectually run. If a general statement of objectives is made, it goes along the line of saying something like "open up their minds" or something equally vague. *How* open, or even what an open mind *is*, isn't defined.

Little if any behavioral terminology is used to describe what the persons will do, do differently, or stop doing in terms of specific actions. Presumably these changes are in the smooth muscles of glands. There is little overt behavior prescribed, not even precise verbal behavior.

Emitted behavior of any specific definition in the laboratory setting is not clearly classified as being required for success, and the only reinforcements which shape behavior are those randomly provided by a group of unknown composition. (The major criterion for admission is that of being able to pay the registration fee. This builds in a reinforcement of middle-class values and little more.)

Value changes are not based upon careful analysis of the present values which are to be changed, nor even explicit statements of desired terminal values sought. Since value changes could only be measured by verbal or written behavior at the end of the course, and no such values are clearly defined, the effort at measuring behavior change runs into logical blocks. The few efforts at evaluation of behavior change from laboratories have not been clearly successful, and certainly are not wholly reliable.

Since success in the course is not clear, then the feedback of reinforcing evidence of achievement of intermediate steps in personal behavior change is impossible. Because the T-group is the major source of reinforcement, and their values are mixed, then the reinforcement of emitted behavior is just as likely to be for the wrong things as the right things.

Specific causes of changes unclear. More pointedly, there is no attempt to measure the relative effects of the different parts of the laboratory upon the learner. Are the T-groups the crucial variable? How can we be sure the T-group hasn't changed the trainee in one direction, and the lectures in another? Where observation and anecdotal evidence points to behavior change after a lab, how can we know which training method effected the change; the role playing (which has been proven to change behavior even outside laboratory groups), the informal bull sessions, or simply the opportunity to live in a closed community for two weeks with others? Do different T-group leader personalities (or reputations) or marvelously skilled lectures such as Argyris delivers have differential effects in changing behavior? Since we can't prove behavior change anyhow, all of these are merely speculative questions.

Criterion No. 3: The learning is under control. The major reason that control is not present in sensitivity training is that it is based on creating stress situations for their own sake which may go out of control and often do. Here's what happened in one group:

"Explosions of angry disagreement were the order of the day. People turned on one member and evaluated him publicly, voicing open disapproval of him. Others wondered why they felt upset when their fellows began to get angry at each other, and tried to cut off the argument before they got it off their chest."[1]

The trainee has been through an emotional binge which has some totally unpredictable effects. The possibility that uncontrolled experience may be harmful is just as probable as its being helpful. In any event it can hardly be called training.

The lack of control over learning in sensitivity labs is further evidenced by the lack of control in the exercises. This is coupled with *too much* control at other times. Add to this a lack of control over facilities management which could seriously affect the attitudes of registrants, and the end result is chaotic, planned and unplanned, but chaotic.

Criterion No. 4: There are selection standards for admission. The more serious defects of sensitivity training relate to admissions standards. The present condition is such that anybody with the registration fee can attend. He may already be sensitive and aware, in fact may be too much so. You could make a good case that far too many of the people who are attracted are those who are emotionally high strung and overly sensitive. How about the overprotected individual whose pressing need is that he toughen

[1] I. R. Weschler, "A New Focus in Executive Training," *Advanced Management*, May, 1955, p. 19.

up a bit because he is already a mass of quivering ganglions, thinking and feeling on several levels of perception at the same time, and therefore totally incompetent at the world of business infighting? For this one the lab becomes a great psychological nudist camp in which he bares his pale sensitive soul to the hard-nosed autocratic ruffians in his T-group and gets roundly clobbered. He goes away with his sense of inferiority indelibly reinforced. The bullies, of course, have also reinforced their roughneck tendencies upon him.

In one lab I attended one woman who never should have been admitted because of a prior mental breakdown "went berserk" (as a fellow T-group member described it) and was under psychiatric treatment until she returned home.

A large food firm directed 60 of its middle managers to attend a "Conference Leader Training Seminar." The actual but not stated intent was to conduct T-groups. A high official attended and noted individual behavior under stress. Several persons who "didn't measure up" had marks placed in their career folders.

A slick brochure advertising a "Leader Training" course drew several dozen enrollees to a course. Those coming found themselves in T-group training. Shaken badly, two left early, and another broke into tears several months later describing his public humiliation to an interviewer. His T-group had voted him "the worst leader they would like to work for." The specification of their charge? He was "too wishy washy." His job was procurement analyst and he was highly regarded by his superiors for his technical knowledge.

Criterion No. 5: Evaluation of results. Since the sensitivity trainers don't know what the goal of such training is, any road will get them there, and any outcome is exactly what can be expected. Small wonder nobody has yet done a rigorously executed evaluation of effect.

An experience it is, without doubt. Training, I'm afraid it is not, and the company that spends its cash on sending people to the more esoteric kinds is being unfair to their shareholders. No proof has been shown that it changes behavior on the job.

The escape which is often taken is that "we aren't really practicing therapy but are merely teaching group dynamics" and is easily said but the end effects prove otherwise. Couple this opportunity for playing God over managerial styles with hard-sell direct-mail advertising and you have the makings of a most harmful movement.

The use to which the process is put is entirely in the hands of the practitioner. In an attempt to achieve dramatic effects, and to bring about emotional stimulus which guarantees a sure-fire reaction from the customer, far too many of the sensitivity trainers are indeed playing God with their clients—in some cases without even realizing what a powerful instrument they are tinkering with.

One team of business school professors will take into any company a one-week sensitivity course which has as an integral part of its package a simulated phone call from the man's mistress, threatening revelation of everything to his wife. This comes in along with calls from customers threatening to cancel contracts and a simulated call from his wife announcing that their oldest child has cancer.

This is management training?

Adapting the processes of sensitivity training into sound training of managers in group processes isn't hard to do. The key ingredient is to identify some terminal behavior which we would like to see in the trainee. Among these are such group related matters as:

How to lead problem-solving conferences.

How to lead decision-making conferences.

How to avoid being a blocker in conferences.

How to elicit complete participation in meetings.

How to identify and use the various roles of conference members.

How to gain cooperation between competing groups.

How to organize committees and conferences.

Such things might be taught—i.e., behavior change effected and perhaps even measured. Yet these could be taught without a T-group.

One of the basic assumptions of laboratory training is that "value changes lead to behavior change, and never the reverse." This is only half true. Skill development leads to attitude and value change if practice of the newly acquired skill brings knowledge of success from parties whose approval is important.

Business Objectives

The real flaw in sensitivity training is that it isn't consistent with business and the economic world we live in. We may struggle through proofs that the new participative styles of management are more productive than autocratic styles, but then there crops up General Motors, which is built upon tight technical organization and tight discipline, being the most successful corporation that ever existed.

Business is primarily an economic institution into which the inputs are materials and supplies, labor, and beginning capital. Through the process of production we obtain outputs of goods and services and ending capital. The objective of this output is profit from which comes growth and survival of the firm, and brings about the end product of it all which is *consumption*.

The new utopians are experts at consumption like the rest of us. I once heard of a study which proved that people don't work for money alone. I invited the researcher who had done the study to speak at a conference. I found that he wanted $500 to make the speech and when I sadly reported that we couldn't afford it, he wouldn't come.

Survival of firms is serious business these days. Of the 4,500,000 companies in this country, the average length of life is seven years. Managers obviously need training in their jobs to help them and their firms survive. All too often they have learned their management by *imitation*. Behavioral science has much to offer in finding new and better ways of managing. This could be greatly accelerated if the new utopians could become more objective in their science. The great difficulty isn't whether they are right or wrong in their assumptions about participative versus autocratic management or liberty versus oppression. The point is that we can't trust them as being good scientists as long as every research proves *one position* to which our common experience tells us there are some startling exceptions that work even better.

Many businessmen know the true value of *situational thinking* in which you are sometimes autocratic or downright ruthless, coupled with other times when you are as gentle and refined as a doting mother with people's sensibilities, and a whole range of actions in between.

A form of management training which has good guys and bad guys arbitrarily built into it to fit a utopian idea of panacean democracy is not safe for a business or any other form of administrative organization to experiment with.

Until the sensitivity trainers have come forth with a school which takes the overly sensitive man and toughens him up into a rough and ready model of man as well as the reverse, I can only suggest to businessmen that they avoid the entire cult.

The time has come, I would suggest, when the entire sensitivity training movements should be drawn back to the campus and overhauled by the more responsible behavioral scientists who started it all.

In Defense of Laboratory Education

Chris Argyris

Yesterday I received Odiorne's paper. I became—to use the laboratory language—hostile. I felt his attack should not go unchallenged.

In my view, the problem with his presentation is not a disagreement with documented facts, because he presents very few. My problem is that I want to try to correct the distortions that he has made—distortions that he has been making throughout the country and that so far have gone unchallenged.

From the *Training Directors Journal*, Vol. 17, No. 10, October, 1963, pp. 21–32.

I have one other problem. It is never clear to which group Odiorne is referring. I will be speaking of the National Training Laboratories network.

Here are some of the facts as I see them:

1 I hope that my "Brief Description of Laboratory Education" made it clear that laboratory education *does* have objectives. Indeed, in every laboratory many hours are spent discussing and analyzing these objectives. However, as we shall see in a moment, the educators in a laboratory program do not try to jam these down the throats of the participants.

2 I agree that the Wisconsin incident was a horrible mess. But, my opponent failed to read the full text of his own manuscript and I quote, "*The leader of the session had no prior training in the conduct of such sessions*." (Italics mine.)

3 The experience of NTL as far as people having psychotic breakdowns is better than the population at large, and, at least, more than twice as good as the experience of students at Michigan and Yale. In over 10,000 cases, there have been about four individuals who have had psychotic episodes and who became seriously ill. All of these people had previous psychiatric histories. None of them was treated for two weeks, as was suggested.

However, these data are not comforting to NTL. We need to do much more on the problem of selection. It is a difficult problem and we would accept any help that can be obtained. At the moment, we depend heavily on the self-selection process that tends to go on in the cases where people come strictly by their own choice. It is true that years ago it would not be unusual to find an executive "sent" by his organization "to straighten him out." If such a motive is uncovered before the man arrives, his organization is contacted and told that it is best that the man not participate.

4 Even though there is a lower level of research activity at laboratories than NTL staff wish, I think it is safe to say that more research has been conducted at, and about, laboratories than all the other executive programs combined—and this definitely includes the executive programs administered by my opponent.

5 The policy of NTL has been, and continues to be, to raise its standards of all its activities and this most certainly includes the development and choice of faculty. For example, for the last three years, in order for a new man to become a member of the NTL network, he has to have completed an approved professional graduate training (usually a Ph.D. program). Then he must take a rigorous three-month program. He participates as a member of a laboratory program and later, as a junior staff member. His training includes planning, developing, and executing an entire laboratory program under the guidance of a senior faculty member. Also, he attends a series of meetings during the remainder of the year. Finally, he serves as a junior staff member until his peers believe that he is ready to be voted as a senior fellow (which usually requires, at least, five years of experience).

6 NTL is not a profit-making organization. It does not pay the salaries that have been suggested. For example, no one has received more than about half of the amount stated for an executive lab. Actually, we underpay ourselves (in the executive labs) in order to help NTL pay for those labs (e.g., for students and churches) that have gone into the red.

7 The majority of NTL labs have a Dean appointed from a year to six months before the lab is scheduled to take place. The staff is selected from the network of men available. Each individual is given an opportunity to state his preference for the lab he prefers to attend. The final selections are made by the Deans. The staff usually meets for three days at least four months ahead of time to plan the lab and to develop assignments to work on back at home. Later another three days are spent in planning for the lab. Also, it should be clear that by their very nature labs cannot be completely pre-planned. When there are labs where the early planning is not done, it is primarily for the lack of money to pay for the expenses of these men to meet.

8 Before we—or General Motors—can believe in my opponent's generalizations about the effectiveness of authoritarian management we need to have much more information than he has just given.

For example, there are some data to suggest that [an authoritarian] company (and I can only take Odiorne's word that GM is such a company) gets away with being fully [authoritarian] by paying through the nose with a militant union, costly strikes, slowdowns, gold-bricking, and by pouring oil over these troubled labor and management waters in the form of benefits and all types of social security services.

It is quite plausible that [such a company] can make much money. At the same time it can be an excellent teacher to the American worker to accept socialism.

9 Unfortunately my opponent enjoys distorting reality (apparently) in order to make his point. For example, in a recent article he has written that a laboratory contains the following sequences. They are:

1 Isolate the trainee from life in general and business in particular by putting him on a "cultural island."
2 Rub his personality continually against those of other managers in this artificial climate until they all have been sandpapered to the nerve endings.
3 This process will make him aware of his own impact, and make him "sensitive" to the personalities of others, thereby making him aware of himself.
4 In gaining his awareness he enlarges his insights into himself, and especially his own gaucheness, his cruelty, his toughness, and his ruthlessness. Few people seem to come away discovering the actual truth that they are great guys.
5 Having been made aware of these heretofore unsuspected evil qualities in himself, and having learned how they can affect other people in the laboratory, he carries this insight back to his job. Usually he doesn't change his personality, but he worries about it somewhat.
6 This new sensitivity will make him a more effective manager.[1]

He then continues, "The problem in this method is that there's little evidence that the last listed result will be produced by the first five steps in the process."

Well, one would hope so. To my knowledge, this is *not* what we attempt to do. Nor does my opponent state where he obtained his information nor how representative it is of the laboratory approach. It most certainly is *not* representative of the experiences with which I am familiar.

The logic used by my opponent is intriguing: describe a process that probably never existed; give no evidence for it; categorically state that this is *the* process; then conclude that it doesn't work.

10 I do not believe that there is a permanent gulf between the behavioral sciences and other academic disciplines on the one hand, and management practice on the other.

I most certainly agree that this has been the case in the past. But all one has to do is see what is happening to business education to realize that the turning point is being reached. For the first time in business education, the schools are beginning to be ahead of current practice. This is possible because of the advances in research, the application of mathematics, computer theory, and behavioral science. I predict, with time, the business school will have the same relation to business that medical and law schools have to their respective professions.

11 Odiorne writes that there has not been any evidence of change in "back home" behavior as a result of the training. This is not true.

Miles,[2] Buchanan,[3] Boyd,[4] and Shutz[5] have conducted research where they have asked others (than the subjects) to report on behavioral change. The positive as well as the negative results were reported. (In the first, third, and fourth studies appropriate controls groups were used.)[6]

In the study that I conducted (and Odiorne quotes), I cited evidence for behavioral change.[7]

[1] "Managerial Narcissism—The Great Self-Development Binge," *Management of Personnel Quarterly*, vol. 1, no. 3, Spring, 1962, pp. 23–24.

[2] Matthew B. Miles. "Human Relations Training Processes and Outcomes," *Journal of Counseling Psychology*, vol. 7, no. 4, 1960, pp. 301–306.

[3] Paul Buchanan. *The Work Situation Questionnaire as a Measure of the Effect of Senior Management Seminar* (The New Jersey Standard Oil Co.).

[4] J. B. Boyd. *Findings of Research into Senior Management Seminars* (Personal Responsibility Department, The Hydro-Electric Power Commission of Ontario, June 22, 1962).

[5] William C. Schutz and Vernon L. Allen. *On T-Groups* (University of California, Berkeley, Calif.).

[6] Two sources of research in laboratory education, M. B. Miles. "Human Relations Training: Current Status," in E. H. Schein and I. R. Weschler (eds.) *Issues in Human Relations Training* (National Training Laboratories), pp. 3–13 and D. Stock. *A Summary of Research on Training Groups*, New York, John Wiley & Sons.

[7] *Interpersonal Competence and Organizational Effectiveness* (Irwin-Dorsey Press, Homewood, Ill., 1962).

Discussion

Dr. Jerry Rosenberg (Assistant Professor, New York State School of Industrial and Labor Relations, Cornell University): Is there any justification in the advertising of these programs primarily through brochures when they are labeled "Executive Leadership Programs" and "Management Development Programs" only to find when the person gets there, that it is something quite different from what had been anticipated? And had he known in advance that it was going to be a sensitivity program, would he have attended?

Dr. Argyris: First of all, I agree with you, there is that problem, but let me ask you something. Does this not happen to you every day with students who complain, "I never thought Yale or Cornell was going to be like this"?

However, I do not suggest that this should absolve us from trying to write more effective announcements. I think that we can specify the end results of laboratory education as well as, or as poorly as, Yale University specifies its end results. When we hand our youngster (at Yale) a blue book, we give him no guarantee that he will learn anything by coming to Yale. So far as I can tell, we have tried to communicate as best we can what goes on during a laboratory.

Mr. William E. Byron (Personnel Administrator, State of New York, Public Service Commission): I attended a laboratory at Bethel, Maine. It is my feeling that this was one of the most real pieces of learning experience that I had the opportunity to attend.

Dr. Argyris: There must be someone who did not have a good experience. Let us have a balance.

Dr. Erwin Taylor (President, Personnel Research & Development Corp.): I shared George's harrowing experience in Bethel in 1955 and came away pretty much with some of the thoughts that he has expressed today.

I think that for me—I don't know whether I can speak for George on this—but I saw my experience as a function of that particular lab, of the group that engaged in it, the group that took it. Incidentally, he is right about the young lady who went berserk and spent the next two weeks with a psychiatrist. Chris is also right in that she had been in therapy and should not have been admitted to the lab, unfortunately. She happened to have been in my therapy group (T-group, that is).

I was somewhere in the middle between George on the one hand, and Chris on the other. It is not all black and while, and it does not take for everyone. Yet I can't gainsay the even anecdotal and testimonial evidence of those who have attended and their spontaneous reports of what they have gotten out of it. I have talked to a few. "It is a barrage of nonsense," one fellow, particularly, said. "They spent so much time on what they were going to talk about, they never got to talking about it." This happens. That is one reaction from a 1955 participant.

Mr. Nathan Glassman (Manager Training Staff, Linde Division, Union Carbide): How can you possibly have a T-group program within an organization [when] you are forcing the man to strip his defenses in the very situation where he can be most harmed by it?

I have been struck in times past in the justification provided for this saying, "Oh, well, the terminal interview takes care of this."

Nonsense! You know this and I know it.

Dr. Argyris: I firmly agree with you that no terminal interview takes care of this.

First of all, I can only speak about the programs that I am mostly acquainted with, the ones I participated in. None of these programs has ever been started by our demanding that they be started. The people decided that a laboratory was something they wanted. I think every human being has the right to make such a choice.

Two, in my own experience, when you create these kinds of lab situations, you do not force people. At least, I have never been in a situation where a staff member says to you, "I force you to take down your defenses."

It is true that group members may say this to each other. Hopefully, they learn that this behavior will not work. You can't coerce a man to become defensive or less defensive. I, personally, would never agree to a laboratory program with external coercion.

This is precisely why I believe we should not start unless there can be a competent diagnosis to see if the organization can "take" it, *and* unless we can start on the top. The dilemma then becomes, how to get the vice-presidents to be against the program even if the president is for it. In one case we spent eight different sessions before we had some feeling they were all for it and not agreeing simply because the president desired it.

Dr. Odiorne: As you know, Bob Blake and Chris have probably been the leading figures in running single company groups, although other NTL people have also.

I suspect that if you take a responsible person who has been in the field as long as Blake and Argyris have to train business people who are going to stay together in a team, you effect better change than taking people whose only contact in a lab is with other people from other large companies who are recently introduced to one another. Very shortly they go back to the job and they never see each other again but they seldom carry this training from the group back to the job.

If you take a working team, put them under a responsible individual as trainer and say, "Let's talk about first how this team functions, how it makes decisions," and then go into what are some of the actions that individuals take that will have a bad effect on group functioning, and discuss this, you come out with a useful form of training. The group functions better, it makes better decisions, and it makes changes faster. The key distinction rests between therapy sessions and action training in group dynamics. The difference in the objective lies in the moral stature of the person who is leading it.

This is what I question: if the core group is permitting an unethical group of people to run around the fringes and doesn't take vigorous and aggressive action to eliminate them, who is?

Dr. Argyris: One other comment on your question. Recently we have been able to observe decision-making meetings as long as they were deciding crucial problems. These meetings were analyzed by a new system that we had developed. If the "competence" score went above a certain point, then we would believe that a laboratory program can be of help. If the competence scores were low, then we would *not* recommend a laboratory program even though the members might desire it.

Dr. Odiorne: I would like to comment about "scientists" if I may. I think that, "the scientist is a realist" as we can see from the explosions of atomic bombs. Yet, we occasionally find people in behavioral sciences [who discover] something new about management [taking] a position as if Du Pont having discovered nylon, declared a proprietary interest in coal, air and water at the same time.

A new discovery is psychology may or may not be a total change in management theory. There is a body of knowledge called management. There are the functions that a manager performs and then there are subsets of disciplines that impinge on them.

[It has been said] that man is a political leader. He *is* at times. There are other times in which he is the passive watcher, and others when he is the democrat, and others when he is perhaps the overriding ruler. At Minneapolis-Honeywell I have heard it said, a manager is really the thermostat. He turns the heat on and off for the organization. Managers should keep behavioral science in perspective.

15 Administration of Compensation

The extent to which a company can do a good job of staffing depends not only on its selection and training procedures but on the inducements it offers to executives and employees to seek employment with it and to remain with it after they are hired. These inducements may be both financial and nonfinancial.

The nonfinancial incentives are difficult for an applicant to appraise. He may be promised "interesting work," for example, but his idea of what is interesting may differ from that of the man who hires him. The difference between the financial rewards offered by two companies, on the other hand, is obvious. Hence pay is particularly important in attracting applicants, although other incentives may take precedence for those already on the job.

Executive compensation is a difficult problem for companies because there are no union wage scales and no "going" rates that can be ascertained, except within very broad limits, and in addition, two executive jobs that carry the same title in two different companies may be very unlike.

The first two articles in this chapter discuss company executive compensation plans in general. The last article considers status symbols, which are one of the most important of the nonfinancial incentives.

The study from which the following extract is taken was first published in 1945, but the findings are still valid. In his preface to the 1961 edition, the author wrote: "The overall pattern of executive incentives needs some but not much modification to apply to the corporate world of the 1960's. . . . Bonus arrangements are now more prevalent. . . . Further . . . there has been a marked increase in the use of stock-option arrangements. Both of these trends serve to introduce more of a profit-like element. . . . But it is unquestionably still true that the traditional reward of the business leader—the profits arising from business ownership—is not a primary incentive to the majority of top executives in our largest corporations." These statements are still true in the 1970s.

Executive Compensation as an Incentive to Profitability

Robert Aaron Gordon

Only in a restricted sense can a market for executive ability be said to exist at all. Buyers and sellers are not independent. The chief executive is in a sense his own employer. Within broad limits he frequently sets his own compensation. Even if the board of directors or a minority stockholding group is active and powerful, the chief executive's salary may continue to be considerably larger than that commanded by men of seemingly comparable ability in companies of similar size and profitability. In those cases in which the board or some other group is responsible for fixing the executive's compensation, the close relations likely to exist between the executive and the board or other groups militate against an outsider's underbidding a relatively highly paid executive. Important also is the fact that precise determination of a top executive's worth to his company is impossible. The activities of the chief executive affect all aspects of the company's operations, and the results of his good or bad management are inextricably interwoven with all the other factors which enhance or lower the firm's net income.

Nor can we ignore the fact that money compensation is only one of the incentives which attract the executive. Power, prestige, desire for security, an urge for creative work, and group loyalty are all motives. A large company can offer in the power and prestige that go with a position of authority a very important substitute for a high salary. If a man has been long associated with a particular firm, loyalty and a feeling of security may hold him in one company even if a higher income is available elsewhere. Taken alone [these non-pecuniary incentives] are sufficient to account for substantial differences in the compensation of executives of approximately comparable ability.

Other considerations thus far not mentioned also help to explain the differences in compensation among executives of similar ability. Differences in the size of companies undoubtedly constitute a factor. Another is the fact that an executive's compensation is not necessarily synchronized with the profits which result from his work. A chief executive approaching retirement may be receiving a salary which is primarily for work done in earlier years. A young executive may be building for the future, but current low profits may force him to accept a small salary for the time being.

All of these considerations add up to the fact that, even in the "strictly business" atmosphere at the top of the management ladder, executive ability operates in an imperfect market in which personal and non-economic considerations play an important role in determining what an executive earns.

Compensation data [for large-company executives] tell us almost nothing about the adequacy of this incentive as a spur to effective leadership. This much, however, is clear. Even after allowing for the heavy income taxes paid by leading executives, their compensation is considerably greater than that which would be available to them in any other vocation. The only alternative conceivably holding out the prospect of a higher financial reward is ownership of a business of their own. But such a business would have to be both large and very profitable to yield a total income (salary and profit) in excess of what these men can now secure from their salary and bonus and from investing such

From *Business Leadership in the Large Corporation* (University of California Press, Berkeley, in cooperation with The Brookings Institution, Washington, D.C., 1961).

accumulated wealth as they have in existing securities. There is little indication of much of a movement out of top executive positions into ownership and management of smaller, privately-owned business. Compensation seems to be adequate to retain these men in executive positions. It is large enough, also, to appeal to executives in the lower ranks and to make them strive to reach higher positions.

It is very doubtful whether a higher level of executive compensation would bring forth a much larger supply of executive ability by diverting men from other fields—the professions or government, for example.

Incentives

There is reason to believe that among many corporation executives the desire for security is an important motive. Very probably, it is stronger among the leading executives of large and mature concerns than it was among an earlier generation of "big" businessmen. As long as financial rewards are considered adequate in terms of a better than average standard of living, men entering the professions and public service are apt to discount heavily the still higher financial rewards available in business. Further, once men are trained in non-business fields, it is frequently difficult for them to change occupations and to move from the professions into business. Such diversion as occurs must take place chiefly among the younger men beginning their careers. This is not so true of the law. Much of the work of lawyers involves business dealings and an understanding of business problems, and many leading corporation executives have had their earlier training in the law.

Some companies have sought not merely to provide an additional financial incentive through bonus payments but by the use of several methods have also attempted to encourage stock ownership by their executives. Such ownership ties the executive more closely to his company and provides an additional link between his income and that of the company.

Bonus payments are sometimes made (usually only partly) in the form of stock. Many companies also have had—in some cases still have—stock-purchase plans, usually covering a wider range of employees than the executive group.

Some companies use the stock-purchase option as a means of providing additional compensation to executives and of encouraging increased stock ownership by these men. Under the option plan, individual executives are given the right to purchase specified amounts of stock at a fixed or varying price. Such options may be good for a considerable period of time. The gain to the executive depends upon the extent to which the market price of the stock rises above the purchase price fixed in the option.

The various methods for stimulating stock ownership among executives have at best been only partially successful in making the gains of ownership an important financial incentive to business leadership in the large corporation. However, a significant development in executive compensation needs to be noted.

Pension or retirement plans in which executives are included have tended to become more common in recent years. The significant point is not the nature of these pension plans but the indication that executives are laying increasing emphasis on security in their financial arrangements, and that the composite of financial incentives offered by the large corporation is taking account of this need of and desire for security on the part of corporation executives. In this respect, as in others, the modern corporation executive draws closer to the public officials and further away from profit-seeking business leaders of an earlier day. As far as pensions are concerned, the need for security and the use of pensions to meet this need are probably more important among lower-ranking executives than for the chief executive and his immediate subordinates; but the emphasis on security and the use of pension arrangements seem to be gradually extending to "top management," also.

Compensation and Business Leadership

The system of financial incentives presented [above] has an important bearing on how business leadership is exercised in the large corporation. Financial incentives, as well as the size of the large corporation and the organizational problems which have come with bigness, point to the fact that modern business leaders are increasingly taking on the character of professional "hired" managers. Executive compensation is relatively stable; bonuses have failed to relate total compensation closely to the results of leadership activity; executive employment is highly stable; and increasingly pensions are being provided executives when they retire. The salaried business leader receives a generous income, and to the size of the reward are added the attractions of security and stability.

This system of incentives is far removed from the classical method of remunerating business leadership in a private enterprise economy. The particular reward of business leadership is supposed to be profits, which link the businessman's remuneration directly and completely to the success or failure of the firm's operations. Profits are a residual fluctuating income, the amount of which cannot be forecast in advance. It is the lure of possibly large profits, which will accrue to himself and not to others, which supposedly attracts the business leader in a capitalist system and generates the dynamic type of business leadership on which economic progress depends.

How can compensation best be used as a method of motivating able executives not merely to stay with the company but to put forth their best efforts in its behalf? Many current systems of compensation perform the function of holding executives but are less effective in providing motivation. Here Dr. Gellerman, who has had wide experience in personnel research and related fields, presents some unorthodox but interesting proposals for linking compensation and motivation.

Motivating Men with Money

Saul W. Gellerman

Nearly everyone "knows" why money affects the motivation of workers: that is, they know the standard folklore about money which has endured, largely unquestioned, since the dawn of the industrial revolution. By this reckoning, money is supposed to be the main reason, if not the only one, that most people have for working at all.

The behavioral scientist, on the other hand, knows that folklore cannot be used as a guide by managers trying to motivate today's educated and mobile employee. At one time, fear of losing the chance to make any money at all may have been enough to make people work harder. But that is seldom true today. Most salary, bonus, and profit-sharing plans and many commission and incentive-pay plans do not motivate any action other than the purely passive one of staying in the organization.

To say that monetary omnipotence is a myth is not to say that money is impotent. Money can motivate; that is, it can influence action and encourage extra effort, extra creativity, or any other kind of non-routine performance. But it can do this only when the increment or net gain for the employee is large enough.

Any sizable change in an individual's financial condition, whether it results from a raise, a promotion, or a job with a new company, involves certain uncertainties, discomforts, and anxieties. The most common uncertainty about high income is whether it is sustainable. The most common discomforts are greater commitments of time and effort to maintaining the new financial position. The most common anxieties involve a change in role; that is, the necessity of loosening old social ties and forming new ones. All these intangible considerations represent what the individual thinks he may be asked to sacrifice in exchange for higher income.

Most People Have a Price

It would be easy to argue that no monetary price can be set on intangibles such as uncertainty or anxiety. But that really depends on the individual's values. If he prizes something that money can buy, or if he values something that money can symbolize, a sufficiently liberal increment *can* offset his anxieties. In other words, some people, perhaps most people, do have a price, and there is nothing necessarily dishonorable or reprehensible about that.

To be effective, the net gain must be large enough to assure the individual of some degree of safety. Precisely because an increment has to be big to be effective, it is likely to encounter skepticism. Consequently, it has to include some form of "insurance," either in the way it is paid or in the traditions of the firm that offers it. The greater the apparent hazard in accepting the opportunity to earn the increment, the greater the increment has to be in order to motivate effectively.

Finally, the increment must bring about a radical change in the individual's financial condition. It must make possible things only dreamed of ordinarily. That obviously requires a lot of money. Make no mistake about it; effective motivation with money is no piker's game.

Income motivates only membership, not productivity. Where most wage and salary programs run into difficulty is in failing to recognize that this is also true of expected increases in income. It does not take a mathematician to project on the basis of past history approximately when increases will occur and how large they will be. It is rare for employees to be surprised by the timing or the size of their pay increases. They may be disappointed, but they are seldom surprised.

Consider the psychological effects of this predictability of increases in income. When the expected increase is still remote, the prospect of it serves to motivate membership, provided that the increase is expected to be equitable.

If the increase does not occur on schedule, that fact will generate disappointment, feelings that the system is unjust, and perhaps, if the delay is prolonged, a search for another job. Or the individual may be motivated to complain, not necessarily about money alone, but about all the petty annoyances he is ordinarily willing to tolerate. He may even feel compelled, as a matter of pride, to reduce his performance level to a point that is commensurate with his now "inadequate" income.

If a raise does occur on schedule but is less than the individual expected, he may very well feel that he has been deceived. It is easier to live with this feeling, after all, than to acknowledge that he has been unrealistic in his expectations. On the other hand, if the increase is about equal to what the individual expected, the experience will reassure him that the system to which he is attached is fair and responsive. But these reassurances only satisfy; they do not motivate him to work harder.

A World of Ingrates

[Thus] the motivational effects of expected increases are very small indeed. Psychologically, the raise is already incorporated into what [the man] regards as his earnings base; it is not "something extra."

Most people are, in a sense, ingrates. They regard their current income level as something they have already earned, rather than as something to be especially savored or appreciated. Thus the fact that an employer may pay his employees quite well relative to the outside labor market will not, as a rule, make his employees feel particularly grateful. It may motivate them to stay, however, and that is often more important than gratitude. But it is the anticipation of an increase that provides them with excitement and perhaps even with an incentive to help it happen through conspicuous effort or diligence. It is the lack of an increase, when one is expected, that causes dissatisfaction.

We can now begin to see that compression of corporate salary scales works against motivation and makes most compensation programs basically satisfiers or dissatisfiers, not motivators. When the monetary gap between pay levels is relatively small, it is not likely that any single increase will be sizable enough to motivate action before it is granted or to motivate "justifying performance" after it is granted.

Insurance for Executive Risk

Compressed salary scales are especially undesirable when they reduce the organization's ability to provide higher management personnel with "insurance" for the risks they incur in accepting heavy responsibilities. If the gaps at higher levels are not large enough, executives may ask themselves whether it might not be wiser to decline a promotion in order to preserve an already high income at an acceptable risk level. That is, they may decide that their ratio of income to personal cost is already at its maximum level and could only worsen if they accepted a modest increase in pay in exchange for a sizable increase in risk. If too many executives begin to regard promotion as a bad financial bargain, top jobs may go by default to imprudent risk takers—exactly the kind of men who should not be given high-level responsibilities.

But effective increments are not economically feasible on a large scale. They cost too much. If they are to be used at all, they must be rationed; and this raises the ticklish question of exactly who should be singled out to receive them. Generally speaking, effective increments should be offered only to people who are susceptible to them; that is, people who are likely to respond, for whatever psychological reason, with the desired action. These also must be people who are capable of some singularly important contribution to the organization—something they would be unlikely to attempt unless they were unusually motivated. Both susceptibility and capacity must be present. Further, there is little point in paying a premium for performance that would probably be attempted even without extra pay. Consequently, it is a relatively rare type of task that lends itself to effective increments.

There are at least two groups of men who could be motivated by large increments. First, some men are capable of leading the way into "breakthrough" areas. Creative work in such fields as product development, organizational analysis, and investment or acquisition analysis could, in the right circumstances, qualify for the large-increment treatment. Doing jobs of these kinds properly sometimes demands courage—the consequences of a mistake can be so horrendous that the individual's reputation is at risk along with his security. But it is plainly in the organization's interest to have decisions of these kinds made solely on the basis of capable men's judgments, undiminished by any fears for their own future. Thus an increment large enough to overcome their natural tendency to play it safe could be more than amply repaid by the results. Whether this would or would not be a gamble for the organization depends entirely on the wisdom with which the man, the job, and the increment itself were selected.

The Hothouse Treatment

Large increments could also be used effectively to motivate men who are capable of developing their managerial abilities faster, and ultimately better, than others. Increments that are liberal enough to pave the way to a wholly new financial status could be an effective way of encouraging such people to accept the risks of moving ahead rapidly. Some companies already recognize this principle by tying part of the compensation growth rate of selected young "high potential" men to an estimate of that potential rather than to their current job level.

It is worth noting at this point that heavy responsibility is not, in itself, a justification for large increments. Responsibility is continual and must therefore be paid for continually in the form of salary. This means in effect that top executives will not necessarily be the most logical recipients of large increments, despite the fact that they currently receive nearly all the increments that could be classified as effective in a motivational sense. Depending on the needs of the organization, effective increments may be used more appropriately with scientific or professional personnel, or even with junior levels of management, than with executives.

The most obvious objection to granting large increments is that they could destroy the incentive to work. But there is little evidence that the acquisition of wealth decreases the motivation to work. Wealth makes people more selective about the work they do, but it seldom makes them less interested in occupying their time constructively. Meaningful work is not inherently distasteful to most men, at least not the kind of men who are likely to accomplish something worthy of being paid for by large increments.

Nevertheless, there can be some serious problems associated with the rapid growth of income. Some young men who have experienced a rapid rise in income become blasé about the prospect of further increases.

These young men are not entirely disenchanted with money, even though they are sometimes willing to accept a modest financial sacrifice to switch to jobs more to their liking. The problem is that their base has grown so large that the prospect of an increment large enough to motivate them has become quite remote. Once this happens, the bloom can come off the monetary rose very quickly, and they become more responsive to nonfinancial motivators.

When income seems to exceed what a job is worth, the excess is of course welcome; but it does not motivate. That is, overpay does not necessarily lead to higher sustained output than equitable pay, *if* the job itself does not seem to deserve the extra pay. The job, not the money, is the limiting factor. And large increments make sense only when the individual can—and knows he can—deliberately make a substantial difference in the results of his work.

Encouraging Genius

We have argued that to use money effectively as a motivator, it must be used with discrimination, but on a princely scale. It must be used to make men wealthy. But there is considerable resistance to the idea of deliberately making certain men wealthy. This comes not merely from socialist and egalitarian trends in society as a whole but, more important, from certain biases common to management itself. The fact is that most of the great productivity increases in recent memory did not happen because individuals resolved to do more. Rather, they resulted from the introduction of new tools, new products, and new processes.These in turn reflect the coordinated efforts of very large groups of people, rather than a few individuals. This has focused management's attention upon managing large groups, which means keeping peace through equitability of wages and salaries and the consequent use of money as a buyer of membership.

In other words, the nonmotivational use of money traces back to the assumption that individual effort really doesn't count. That assumption is often true. The conclusion drawn from this experience is that genius must be an extremely scarce commodity. So most managers assume that they should not wait for a genius to show up, but should instead harness the efforts of ordinary men in the most practical ways available.

The logic in that strategy rests on the rather tenuous assumption that genius needs no encouragement, that it will somehow come storming through in spite of itself. But not all geniuses are self-motivated, obstacle-ignoring heroes, and that is precisely why most of the potential geniuses in this world remain only potential geniuses. Those few men who do accomplish exceptional things and are recognized as geniuses are considerably brighter than average men; but they are not necessarily more gifted than, say, the top 5 or 10 percent of the population, most of whom accomplish nothing really extraordinary in a lifetime. There is, in other words, an enormous reservoir of relatively untapped genius, that is, men with the capacity for exceptional accomplishment which existing systems of motivation have failed to reach.

One reason why the potential contribution of individuals to their organizations is often underestimated is that it is seldom in the individual's best interests to be as productive as he could be. Most people function far below their capacity mainly because of the essentially dependent relationship of any individual to the organization that employs him. When a man is financially dependent upon the continuity of his paychecks, he will be more interested in preserving that continuity than in inflating the next check. This is most familiarly and dramatically seen in the tendency of production workers to restrict their output, even in the face of incentive payments.

Something quite comparable occurs at higher organizational levels. It is equally against the interests of the executive to rock the boat by disagreeing with the opinions of his peers or superiors, or to take risks whose payoff is uncertain, or to make decisions that could be difficult to explain. Thus the executive's productivity may be limited by his own concern for security and the continuity of his income.

Credible Executives

The basic problem in elevating performance levels is somewhat to eliminate dependency, or at least to reduce it. But dependency, in the last analysis, is subjective. We have to find people who are already predisposed to act independently and provide sufficient financial support to help them step over the line.

It is very much in an organization's interests to place its fortunes in the hands of men whose fortunes are *not* tied to the organization's, men who work because they want to work rather than because they have to. If there is any single quality that is required of a man at higher management levels it is *credibility*: the ability to make unpopular or unwelcome points without being suspected of masking the truth for some ulterior motive. A credible executive can protest, for example, that a production target is impossible, without being suspected of merely bargaining for an easier goal. He can warn his superiors as dramatically or, if need be, as annoyingly as they must be warned in order to convince them that a projected action is dangerous, without fearing that he will lose their esteem. A credible executive is one whose inputs to the management decision process are listened to, not discounted; and for that reason his impact on the fortunes of his firm is much greater than that of dozens of peers who are, if you will, "incredible."

There are many ways to become credible, and undoubtedly the best of these is through demonstrated good judgment and ability. But when a man has done that, he is still not necessarily free of the consequences of his dependency. This is a subtle but extremely important point. To be credible, a man must have more than just ability. His motives must be unquestioned. He must have nothing to gain or lose except his pride; and it must be apparent to those who deal with him that the desire to be proved right, not gain safety, is his real motive. Thus credibility can hinge, in the last analysis, on independence, and *credible* independence hinges on wealth.

The "Impact" Factor

Money can therefore motivate exceptional accomplishments in two ways: (1) through the prospect of becoming wealthy—that is, of a radical improvement in one's financial circumstances, and (2) by becoming irrelevant, by freeing the individual of both real dependency and the tendency of others to suspect him of the tactics of dependency. But if men are to be made wealthy deliberately in order to increase their effectiveness, it must be done selectively, not indiscriminately.

It is vitally important that measurements be found to determine whether the treatment is deserved. Not only must an extraordinary investment be carefully audited, but a convincing demonstration of the equitability of the investment must also be available. Otherwise, the effects of this treatment upon those who do not receive it could be costly and troublesome enough to cancel out whatever benefits the recipient produces. But in those exceptional jobs for which specific, critical, and exceptionally important actions can be isolated—actions that set the individual's achievement apart from all others and radically affect the fortunes of the organization as a whole—large increments are probably the best guarantee that the action will be taken effectively.

This leads to another important point about the use of effective increments; namely, the kind of organization that can use them. If the decision to pay an individual large increments or not is based in part on the magnitude of the impact that his actions can have on the organization, it follows that effective increments are appropriate only in an organization that wants to be heavily impacted—that wants, in other words, to change. Effective increments are incompatible with maintaining the status quo. But they are very well suited to the needs of an organization that wants deliberately to change its products, markets, size, or profitability.

The practice of compensating managers with perquisites as well as with money is now well established in American business. Some of the perquisites may be valued for their own sake because they make business life more comfortable; but more often, perhaps, they are prized as status symbols, which both inflate the ego and help to impress others.

In a small company there is little difficulty in deciding who gets what in the way of offices or fine furnishings since there are likely to be few levels of management. In a large organization, on the other hand, so many fine gradations of rank exist that some companies have found it necessary to make rules about who shall have carpets and what kind, what pictures are permissible at each level, and so on. Here *Business Week* reports on a survey of the ways in which companies regulate the status symbols.

The Status Symbols of a Manager

Many a desk-bound executive recalls the gloomy day when he asked for a second guest chair and was told: "Assistant manager? Sorry, you only get one." And the whole office crowd well remembers the near riot after Joe Doakes was told to take down his wife's latest work in oils and replace it with an "industrial scene from the company's collection."

At the same time, who can forget the day his name went up in the lobby directory, or the morning he got the 60-in. desk and the water carafe?

These things, and many more, are the privileges—and the restrictions—of rank. Corporation executives expect a great variety of privileges, ranging from large offices and telephones equipped with a splendor of lights, to private dining rooms and the use of a company car. And generally speaking, they get plenty of these privileges.

But, who decides who gets what? If one vice-president hangs a few abstract oil paintings on his walls, and bills the company, what's to keep the other seven V.-P.'s from doing the same and turning the shop into an annex of the Museum of Modern Art? If the comptroller wheedles figured drapes out of purchasing, does this entitle the advertising manager to do the same?

These questions might draw chuckles at the club bar, but if there are any personnel men, office managers, architects, or presidents standing around, not everyone will be laughing. "Who gets what?" it seems, is about as funny to those who must answer it as a tossed hot potato.

In an effort to discover how corporations find their way through the privilege thicket, *Business Week* reporters in various cities asked company officials: "How do you decide who gets what, and why?"

Some executives jumped out of their chairs, reacting as if a psychoanalysis of the president's dreams were about to be published. "That's too hot to talk about in public," said one man in St. Louis. Other companies reached for bromides such as "We fly by the seat of our pants" to explain their privilege system. A few went so far as to deny the existence of privilege.

For the most part, however, companies owned up and talked of two types of privilege.

Tradition

First there is the uncodified, traditional pattern—the British constitutional system, you might call it—where privileges go with each rank—and "always have." It's understood that the president gets the first crack at the Cadillac in the company garage, that division managers usually get the Buicks. The roomiest, most comfortable offices belong to the brass, and are passed on to succeeding generations of brass. The higher you rank, the better chance you have of getting a velvet country club membership, a free car, or a low-interest loan to finance a down payment on a new home. But none of these things is on paper.

This uncodified system revolves about a single rule: Executives of equal rank get the same privileges, and each stratum can go as far as it can get away with—just as long as it doesn't outshine the next highest group.

From *Business Week*, Oct. 16, 1954, pp. 66–68, 70. Reprinted by permission.

In Black and White

The second system, a completely codified set of rules, is the more recent development. It's the continental European, or a-rule-for-every-contingency approach. If an assistant department manager wishes to know if he's getting a fair shake, he need only turn to page six of the bulletin issued by the building standards committee.

He finds he's entitled to 100 sq. ft. of office space on the fifth floor, a 60-in. walnut desk, a swivel chair costing no more than $100 wholesale, two plain guest chairs, choice of two wall paints, a coat rack, a two-drawer file, a desk set (under $50), linoleum flooring, a single telephone extension, and one window. In other company documents he finds he may have calling cards, but not personal stationery, he may eat in the executive dining room instead of the cafeteria (but not in the private dining room).

His boss, he learns, fares somewhat better. The boss has a larger office, on the same floor, but occupying an outside corner. The desk is larger, the chair plushier. There's a rug under the desk, but not wall-to-wall. He's given a choice of four wall paints, and he may hang pictures (up to four) worth $100 (he may blow the $100 on one picture, if he likes). He has two phones, a water carafe, a work table, two windows, a better desk set, and a wardrobe. He eats in the executive dining room, but is occasionally invited to eat in the private dining room.

This executive can't go the limit, though. He doesn't get: private stationery, an office on the brass-inlaid sixth floor, a davenport, a club membership, drapes, mahogany furniture, paneled walls, and a chance to turn in an unitemized expense account. But his bosses, the vice-presidents, get all of these things, in this instance.

The president, under any rules system, usually writes his own ticket. If he leans toward austerity the effect will be to downgrade everyone, for no executive will try to outdo the top man, no matter what the local Magna Charta provides. In one large Chicago corporation, for example, the top man maintains an unusually simple private office "so customers won't think we're making too much money." Needless to say, this austerity is reflected throughout the organization.

But, austere or lavish, the system's coming to be the thing, and apparently with ample reason. Many a company has had to move into new offices, larger facilities. At such times of change, the unwritten privilege system chokes to death, for it was geared to the old building and its habits. The new building, or new offices, arouse the spirit of revolt in people. Assistant division managers will watch what goes into their counterparts' offices. Any executive, one manager of services says, worries considerably more about what he doesn't have than what he has.

A case in point occurred in Milwaukee. One suspicious executive felt sure his opposite number in another department had a larger office. He got a ruler, measured his office, crossed the hall, measured the other fellow's, did a little multiplying, and found he was being rooked on square footage. He complained upstairs.

The Milwaukee company may or may not have been able to help out its squeezed executive, but when and if it refurbishes or moves, it will know what to do: Make sure equals get the same deal. It smacks slightly of regimentation (and even more of giving presents to all children on one child's birthday); it disgusts the professional individualist (who will stomp across the street to Eddie's Grill, mumbling things like "back in the Army," and "just like Orwell's *1984*"); but codification of rank privileges solves more problems than it creates. That seems to be the judgment of those who have gone through it.

Companies that have codified point to three reasons for doing so: (1) It reduces friction between people and departments; (2) it's the most efficient way to allocate available space; (3) it's the best way to effect budget controls.

Few companies explained why they think privilege stratification, per se, is necessary at all. This seems to be just as much an accepted thing as salary differentials.

To be sure, many companies offered explanations for practical differences. For instance: If a sales manager makes contacts on the golf course, you pick up his club tab; if a company entertains a lot of visiting brass, you put in an executive dining room.

When all the practical reasons are subtracted, there is only one plausible explanation remaining: the elusive element of prestige. Certainly executives seek it, to a greater or lesser degree, just as they seek money, power, and happiness. Apparently, while picking up the better automobile, the nicer home, the snootier town, the ivier college for his children, the executive must also keep apace where he wins the family bread.

The element of prestige seems to be growing in importance. It has become a larger section of the carrot a corporation man chases. The reason is plain. The income tax structure has forced companies to install all sorts of compensation other than salary. In the competition for good management men, every device is needed, stock option plans, pensions, long vacations, insurance. But you have to go further to impress the man who has all of those things. So you toss in a club membership, a new car every year, permission to take the wife on a few trips.

Do the smaller fry complain about all these extra privileges? The survey shows they rarely do. The answer is simple. Most small fry hope —and expect—to become larger fry one day. They want the privileges to be there [then].

The *Business Week* survey uncovered hundreds of special privileges of an unusual nature that are accorded executives. Here are a few:

A Pittsburgh company's officers have private bathrooms and in each there's a telephone. In a Cleveland company, anyone doing creative work (mostly product development) gets a far better setup than anyone in sales, accounting, purchasing, or any "doing" work. And officers in a Pittsburgh company have lower desks, "to make them look taller."

Most of the privileges serve to keep the executives apart from the green-eye-shade boys, and to give the heads a more luxurious cell to pace in. But there are companies that you might call "socialized," where all hands get the same deal. This is the company where the whole office force eats in the cafeteria ("the Old Man stands right in line"). It's the company with almost no private offices, only massive formations of identical desks. Or, at the other extreme, it's the Utopian company, where everybody gets a deal from the top of the pack.

16 Direction

A manager must make plans, develop the organization necessary to carry them out, and staff that organization with the most capable people he can get. But even if he performs these functions as well as possible, he still faces a crucial test: he must ensure that his subordinates do what he has planned they should do and do it to the best of their ability. This is the directing phase of his job, and unless it is well done, there will be a gap between plans and performance.

For many years now, managers have been conscious of this gap and have tried practically every means that research has suggested may overcome apathy on the part of employees. But—especially in large companies—the apathy persists. Part of the problem is, of course, that many jobs by their very nature make apathy almost inevitable. The first article in this chapter describes such a job—work on an automobile assembly line.

Some of the measures psychologists and sociologists have suggested for improving morale have not worked too well, despite the surge of hope that followed the Hawthorne experiments and later findings. The second article deals with the theories of the "social engineers" and points out circumstances under which they appear to have been less than successful.

The third article suggests that authoritarianism, which is anathema to the social engineers, is probably inevitable in industry and that the way to make it bearable is to interpose a countervailing force between the autocratic manager and the worker. This force, the author says, can be provided by a perhaps equally autocratic union leader.

Recently, however, the social scientists have begun to focus attention on the nature of the work itself, whereas their earlier prescriptions dealt with matters that were essentially peripheral to the work. Among those whose researches sparked this new approach is Frederick Herzberg, whose theories are discussed in two articles. The last article deals with a technique—job enrichment—which has been tried in some cases and which many expect may have far-reaching effects.

In some industries, notably the automobile industry, assembly-line techniques have made possible high overall productivity, high wages, and generous benefits. But most psychologists and sociologists are agreed that they do not produce an environment in which rank-and-file workers get much more than money from their jobs.

Harvey Swados's story "Just One of the Boys" (Chapter 2) presented the difficulties of working on the lower levels in such a company from the viewpoint of the first-line foreman. Here a reporter who spent a week working as a rank-and-file employee on an automobile assembly line describes his experience. His report helps to explain why the employees were not interested in helping the foreman keep costs down, even though he was known as "the best boss in the shop."

The conditions described here may be changing, however, for some automobile companies have begun to reorganize their operations along the lines suggested in later articles in this chapter.

Life on the Line

Roger Rapoport

WIXOM, Mich.—The Ford Motor Co. auto assembly line here is an impressive sight. Bare frames are put on a slowly moving conveyor. Wheels, engines, seats, body sections and hundreds of other components are added along the way. At the end of the quarter-mile, 90-minute trip, finished cars are driven off to be inspected and shipped to dealers.

It takes some 275 workers to put the cars together on the Wixom line. To hear a guide at Ford's big River Rouge plant, a popular tourist stop in nearby Dearborn, tell it, life on the line is a snap. "Each worker on an assembly line has one little job to do," he says. "It's simple. Anyone could learn it in two minutes."

That's bunk.

Working on the line is grueling and frustrating, and while it may be repetitive, it's not simple. I learned how tough it can be by working for six days at Ford's Wixom plant, which assembles Thunderbirds and Lincoln Continentals.

I learned first-hand why 250,000 auto workers are unhappy about working conditions. Ford calls Wixom the "most progressive automobile assembly plant on the North American continent." Facilities at the 10-year-old plant here are indeed better than those at many of the 46 other auto assembly plants scattered around the country. Wixom is clean and well-lighted by auto industry standards. It boasts adequate rest rooms, plenty of drinking fountains and an air-conditioned cafeteria. Even so, working conditions are less than ideal.

Problems of Quality

I also learned why quality control is a major problem for the industry and why so many Americans complain about poor workmanship in the cars they buy. I saw one blue fender installed on a white car and saw the steering column fall off another newly built car. Wixom's repair area, nearly the size of a football field, usually had a line-up of 500 cars waiting to have steering adjusted, scratches painted, brakes repaired and other faults fixed—but not all defects are caught before cars leave the plant. The four auto companies have recalled from customers more than a million 1967 model cars since last September because of suspected manufacturing defects.

Ford didn't know I was a reporter. Along with a handful of other young men, I was hired as a summer replacement, and to the personnel department I was simply Social Security number 362-44-9616. The foreman on the line knew me as "9616" for short.

Names aren't necessary on the line. The conveyor moves at 1-6 of a mile an hour, and while that may not sound terribly fast, it doesn't leave much time for conversation. Also, the cacophony of bells, whistles, buzzers, hammers, whining pneumatic wrenches and clanking, rumbling machinery drowns out voices, so most communicating is done by arm waving and hand gestures.

Only two of the dozens of men I worked beside at various points on the line ever learned my name, and I knew only the first names of two

From *The Wall Street Journal*, July 24, 1967, pp. 1 and 10.

workmen. One was Clyde, a husky Negro who had been an assembler for about a year. My first day on the job, a foreman assigned Clyde to teach me the ropes at one work station.

Lessons from Clyde

Clyde, a 220-pound six-footer, showed me how to bolt the car body to the chassis in three places. It was fairly easy for me, a 160-pound six-footer. He showed me how to lean inside the trunk, tighten two bolts and make an electrical connection. I managed that task, too. He showed me how to maneuver a big V-8 engine dangling overhead down into a car's engine compartment. By this time, I considered myself fairly versatile.

Then Clyde showed me how to scramble from one car to the next, putting chassis and trunk bolts in the first two cars and helping with the engine in the third—all in less than five minutes. When I tried it, I got stuck in the trunk of one car, missed the chassis bolts on the next and was too late to help install the engine on the third car.

Gradually, I became more proficient. But I didn't last long at any job. As a temporary worker, I was assigned to fill in for absent workmen at five different work stations at various times during my six days on the line. Except for Clyde, the men who showed me the jobs weren't very good teachers. One workman demonstrated the way to attach clamps to heater hoses, but he didn't mention that the clamps have tops and bottoms. A foreman caught my error after I had installed a dozen clamps upside down.

Learning from Experience

Nobody told me to put on steering wheels that match the color of the dashboards—I figured that out myself. But I made some mistakes because nobody warned me that tinted glass makes it difficult to distinguish the color of the dash by looking through the windshield. I installed some blue steering wheels on cars with aqua dashboards and mismatched a black wheel with a gray dashboard.

An experienced worker told me that a color-blind assembler recently installed the wrong color vent plates under the windshield wipers on cars for two hours before a foreman spotted the error and assigned the man to another job.

I wasn't checked for color blindness when I was hired. Rapid turnover and a major expansion at Wixom made getting a job easy, even though the plant was heading for a temporary shutdown to make the annual model change-over. I passed a three-hour physical exam and an 11-minute written test. (Sample questions: "Which of the following doesn't belong? spade, queen, king, ace; oak, maple, leaf, elm.") There was no interview. I was issued a free pair of safety glasses, given a five-minute lecture on safety and plant safety rules, and told to report to work.

The windowless assembly line area inside the two-story plant reminded me of a tunnel. Down the middle ran the assembly line. Overhead were fluorescent lights and conveyors carrying engines, fenders and other components. Tall racks and bins full of auto parts lined the sides. A narrow slit trench for underbody installations stretched the length of the line.

At 3:30 p.m., the conveyor began moving, and work started on the assembly line. For the next three hours—until a relief man shouted at me to take a 20-minute break while he replaced me—I rarely spoke or was spoken to.

For a while, I concentrated hard to get each job done within the 90 seconds the moving car was in front of my work station without dropping the five-pound pneumatic wrench on my foot. Every third car on the line was a Continental, and required a slight variation from Thunderbird installation procedures.

Nevertheless, each task soon became a mind-deadening routine, and my thoughts turned to everything but cars. ("You just leave your brains at home and work out of habit," one experienced worker later advised me.) Sometimes, after many minutes of bending over and zeroing in on a moving target, I would step back, and the line would appear to be stationary, while everything else seemed to be moving.

Bend, Stretch, Ache

I'm in fairly good physical shape, but I ached all over after each day's work on the line. At one station, I had to bend down into the engine compartment to bolt on the steering column. To install carpeting, I sat on the door frame with one foot dragging and drilled holes, then stretched out on my side under the instrument panel to fasten the carpet to the floor. Attaching steering wheels meant stretching through the open car window to stick the wheel on the column and bolt it down.

Nobody seemed to take any particular pride in his work. Some workers considered some of the parts shoddy. The kick-pads that I installed under instrument panels, for example, were made of relatively brittle plastic and sometimes broke off during installation. One workman told me that "over 400 of them broke off one month last winter."

One day when I was helping two men bolt steering columns in place, the columns on a dozen cars were mounted improperly by someone up the line, so we couldn't bolt them down and men further down the line couldn't attach the steering wheels. Such chain-reactions often result from a single slip-up, and regularly snarl the precision of the computer-controlled assembly line.

It was Clyde who first told me what to do if I made or discovered a mistake. "Get the next car and don't worry," he said. "They'll catch that one further down the line." When I spotted the white Thunderbird wearing a blue fender, another worker explained: "They'll paint over it in the repair shop. It's easier to catch it there than it is on the line."

Catching Defects

About 10 repairmen stationed at various points along the way catch and fix some minor defects right on the assembly line. But it's up to the 15 or 20 inspectors along the line to check each car thoroughly and route those with improperly installed parts into the plant's 100-man repair shop. One inspector was an inexperienced college student. Some regular inspectors seemed far from dedicated.

I saw one standing with his eyes closed. When a workman pointed out a faulty engine, the inspector tagged the defect, then closed his eyes again. Once I spotted a loose steering wheel and told an inspector. He said he had just checked that wheel and "found it tight," but he double-checked and admitted, "You were right—it was loose."

I saw a loose steering column fall off a Thunderbird when an inspector checked it. Later he told me that before lunch he had "only missed marking up three loose steering columns, which is pretty good since 80% of them were going through loose yesterday." Another inspector further down the line spotted the three loose columns.

An inspector who had five things to check on each car told me: "There isn't nearly enough time to do all the inspections. I'm supposed to check shock absorbers, but I haven't had a chance to look at one in a month." Another inspector jokingly said he inspects a car trunk just closely enough "to make sure there's no dead foreman in there."

Because Wixom builds luxury cars priced to sell from $4,600 to over $7,300, the assembly line moves at what, for the auto industry, is considered a slow production pace of about 40 cars an hour. Some other luxury cars are built at a faster rate. General Motors Corp.'s Cadillac assembly line rolls out 50 cars an hour, and Chrysler Corp. builds about 55 Chryslers and Imperials an hour. Lower priced cars such as Fords, Chevrolets and Plymouths usually come off the line at a rate of up to 65 cars an hour.

That can seem like a breakneck speed to a weary worker on the assembly line. The speed of the line, in fact, has been a major cause of half a dozen local strikes by United Auto Workers Union members at other auto assembly plants in the past few years.

Even Wixom's pace seemed fast to me. When my 20-minute break started at 6:30 each night, I staggered to the pop-machine to buy a cold drink. Then I looked for someplace to sit and rest. There aren't many places to sit in the plant. My favorite spot was atop a cart loaded with big white laundry sacks full of dirty coveralls, a place where I could stretch out.

Sometimes a few workers would talk and joke during their breaks. Foremen and other supervisors were the butt of many jokes—particularly one balding supervisor who was referred to as

"Khrushchev." But the assemblers actually got along well with the foremen, who worked hard themselves and generally were patient and polite when correcting workmen's mistakes. Supervisors insisted on informality. When I called one "sir," he quickly told me: "That isn't necessary around here."

Scramble for Lunch

After my relief period, I spent another hour and 10 minutes on the line. Then, at 7:30 p.m., the conveyors stopped, and the scramble for lunch started. There wasn't time to wash the grease off my hands or pull the slivers of glass fiber insulation out of my arms before eating.

Usually lunch periods were staggered, but sometimes the day's production schedule was arranged so that all 2,700 workers in the plant ate at the same time. The first day that happened, I cut in near the front of the long line outside the air-conditioned company cafeteria. It took 15 minutes, half my lunch period, to reach the counter, pick up iced tea, milk, soup, roast beef, Jell-O, pie and pay the cashier $1.50. I ate in 11 minutes.

That left two minutes to go to the bathroom and another two minutes to get back to my place on the line. I had indigestion for an hour after lunch. Some workers had to wait 25 minutes to get served that day. I don't know how, or if, they ate and got back to work in five minutes.

Many workmen brought sack lunches and sat on stock ranks or in cars on the line eating sandwiches. Eating in the cars was against plant rules. Nevertheless, when I was installing carpets, I frequently had to throw out lunch sacks, cigaret butts and coffee cups along with the usual assortment of screws, fuses and bolts before laying a carpet. I picked an empty beer can out of a car, too—even though another plant rule prohibits drinking alcohol.

Safety rules frequently were violated, too. I saw foremen running and assemblers jumping across the assembly line trench, both supposedly forbidden. Occasionally there was horseplay on the line. But I didn't see any accidents. Indeed, when I was there, Wixom had gone two million man-hours without an accident.

Ennui set in during the second half of the work turn. To break the monotony, some workers played practical jokes, like detaching the air hose from an assembler's pneumatic wrench. Others performed timpani concerts on plant ventilation ducts with rubber mallets. They hooted and whistled whenever women office employes ventured into the production area.

My second relief break began at 10 p.m. and lasted 16 minutes. (In the UAW's contract negotiations with Ford and the three other auto companies, the union is demanding two 30-minute paid relief breaks daily for assemblers. Autoworkers aren't paid during their half hour lunch periods.) There was less bantering among workers during the second break. Some of them talked of quitting. One man groused about "too much pressure" and said: "When I was working in an auto parts plant, I could meet my quota in four hours and then goof off, but here there's no rest."

When the quitting whistle blew at midnight, smiles returned to most workers' faces. They washed up quickly and headed for the parking lot. I drove straight home and went to bed. But some of the men went out moonlighting. One young guy making about $3.30 an hour at Wixom worked several hours as a night pressman for a small morning newspaper. Another, earning about $3.50 an hour, went home and slept for five hours, then put in eight hours doing maintenance work at a nearby golf course. "I made $11,000 last year," he told me.

After the final whistle blew on my last work turn before the plant closed for model changeover, Clyde kidded me at the water cooler. "You should feel ashamed of yourself, taking all that good Ford money after the way you worked," he said.

Hiring me might not have been one of Ford's better ideas, but I think I earned my $110 take-home pay. Ford apparently thought so, too. The foreman told me to report for work again when Wixom resumes production next week.

But I don't intend to go back to the plant—except perhaps to pick up my pay check. Ford wouldn't mail it to me. "We've got 6,000 guys who would like to have their checks mailed to them," a personnel man told me. "What makes you think you're any different?"

Much of what management has been doing in recent years to improve its human relations has been based on the findings and theories of the "social engineers." In some companies, those theories have seemed to work very well; in others, not at all; and it is impossible to say whether the fault in cases where they did not work lay with the theories themselves or with the way in which they were applied. At any rate, as this article claims, the results of some of the applications by government have been at least disappointing, and many of the social scientists are revising their opinions in consequence, although others will still disagree sharply with both the facts and the conclusions given here.

The Social Engineers Retreat under Fire

Tom Alexander

The schismatic Sixties are gone, but in the realm of social policy the jangling noises linger. The little intellectual journals shrill with cutting phrases of blame; ill-tempered books poke at the still breathing remains of futile government programs; researchers are censured, censored, and sometimes assaulted. And social scientists—sociologists, anthropologists, social psychologists, and political scientists—who formed alliances with politicians to convert academic theories into social engineering have fallen back in disarray and discouragement.

There's plenty of material for recrimination. During the decade of the Sixties, a period of unparalleled prosperity and unprecedented outlays to "solve" the problem of welfare dependency, welfare enrollments tripled. As poverty itself declined, such symptoms of social pathology as crime—which theory said was the result of poverty—increased. Public housing destroyed many well-knit communities, drove up the cost of shelter, and helped trap people in dependency. School integration, in many instances, failed to improve the academic performance of the blacks or advance interracial tolerance. Manpower training has had little impact on unemployment.

One consequence of the promises and slogans of the New Frontier and the Great Society was to supplant traditions of self-sufficiency with assumptions that citizens have "rights" to public aid of many kinds. While total federal social-welfare expenditures climbed from $25 billion in 1960 to $92 billion in 1971, popular expectations were lifted and then dashed—a process that is a pretty reliable recipe for social dynamite.

The failure of theories to pass their first real empirical tests has led the social scientists to shy away from any role in policy making. They are splintered into warring schools and factions. On the one hand, there are those like Daniel P. Moynihan and Nathan Glazer of Harvard, who are drifting to the conservative side and now spend much of their time writing biting critiques of past mistakes. At the other extreme are the radicals, who see the only hope in some kind of guerrilla warfare against a system too selfish and moribund to tolerate reasonable reform.

At the same time, the disappointment with social engineering is leading some social scientists to reconsider their assumptions. In particular, they are beginning to pay attention to findings in other disciplines—including ethology, genetics, developmental psychology, and linguistics—which hint at a basic intractability in human nature, a resistance to being guided and molded according to schemes for improving society.

Some social scientists point out defensively that comparatively few of their number—economists excepted—were actually employed by government, and that their direct contribution to the policy-making process was slim. "I don't think that's very honest," maintains Harvard sociologist Lee Rainwater. "The ideas clearly came from the sociology writings of over forty years." Explicitly or implicitly, these theories and assumptions formed the framework for the legislation and the rhetoric of the New Frontier and the Great Society. They were cited uncritically in the Supreme Court decisions, congressional testimony, and reports of presidential commissions. "All the shortcomings of our discipline were involved," says Rainwater.

The fundamental shortcoming, of course, is

simply lack of knowledge, arising largely from the inability to discern, separate, and measure the multitudinous interacting influences on social behavior. A number of sociologists themselves, in fact, have now begun to doubt that their field will ever be a true science in the sense of being able to make even the most rudimentary predictions about human society.

Unfortunately, ignorance has rarely constrained the scientists from formulating finespun theories and, during the past decade at least, urging full-blown social policy based upon these theories. And underlying most of the theories of the last forty years has been the dogma of "environmentalism"—the assumption that man is almost limitlessly malleable: through manipulating the external conditions of living, it should in principle be possible to secure almost any desired behavior and any level of achievement.

While short on knowledge and proof, social science has generally been long on ideology. One long-time observer of the species is Moynihan, who was an adviser to Presidents Kennedy, Johnson, and Nixon. The American social scientist, he observes, has a "dual nature. He is an objective seeker after truth. But he is also likely to be a passionate partisan of social justice and social change to bring it about."

One difficulty is that the consumer—the government policy maker or the voting public—can rarely be sure which part of the dual role the social scientist is playing at any particular time, the truth seeker or the ideologist. One characteristic of the ideologist is to distort or oversimplify. Sociologist Walter Miller has analyzed the semantic confusion behind recent social legislation. He contends that concepts such as "the poor," "poverty," "deprivation," and "the power structure" were spun forth by a "Movement" (Miller's term) of ideological social scientists to provide simple, emotionally potent, and utterly myth-filled theories that define social problems primarily as the oppression of some people by others.

Out of that kind of perspective sprang a whole new school of radical sociology—the "conflict" school—which holds that reform and social change can be accomplished only when disadvantaged groups threaten "the establishment" with violence or civil disobedience. With its simplified view of recent history, the conflict school sees the Kennedy-Johnson poverty programs as the politicians' alarmed response to rioting in the cities. In reality, however, the sequence seems to have been the reverse: first came the poverty programs and then the big city riots. Moynihan, with the insights of a man who was himself intimately involved in the deliberations, recalls how poverty became a priority issue in the political campaign planning of 1963: "The process simply involved a political party and an Administration going into a campaign with little legislation to show for itself after two and a half years in office and wanting some themes. There was a debate in the White House for a while as to whether the theme should be poverty or the problems of the suburbs. Poverty finally won out in a marginal way. We put together a program from several other programs that were lying around and pushed it forward. This is normal behavior at the political levels of government."

The poverty programs wound up embodying a number of theories of doubtful validity. One was the "opportunity theory," formulated by Columbia sociologist Richard Cloward and Harvard criminologist Lloyd Ohlin to explain crime and delinquency. This theory drew upon the Marxian theme of alienation—the individual's sense of estrangement from his society. In the Cloward-Ohlin formulation, the individual becomes alienated when he lacks the opportunity to conform to the role society expects of him, because he has no education, no job, no money, etc. Such an individual becomes impatient with society's rules as well, and he turns to crime, delinquency, alcoholism, addiction, etc. In other words, it is the environment of deprivation that manufactures social deviants.

This was the assumption of the "professional reformers"—as sociologists Peter Marris and Martin Rein have dubbed the various foundation executives, presidential appointees, and social scientists who helped devise the strategy for the war on poverty. The reformers themselves, of course, were members of the middle class, and their idea was to provide the poor with something more like a middle-class living environment, in the hope that this would encourage middle-class behavior. To overcome their sense of alienation, the poor were to be involved in planning and executing the programs. Some 1,000 self-governing Community Action Agencies were created, and federal funds went to them directly, bypassing existing social agencies and local politicians. In practice, though, the program planning was usually done by professional reformers. As time went on, the reformers themselves grew increasingly radical in outlook and action. Cloward, for example, helped to steer his clients into a sort of guerrilla warfare against City Hall and the established welfare agencies. Cloward says that one aim eventually came to be to swell the welfare rolls as much as possible, in order to bring about change in the whole welfare system.

Understandably, conflict sociologists such as Cloward tend to give Community Action high marks. They credit it with making the poor more conscious of their "rights," with making both liberals and conservatives more aware of the need for welfare reform, and with fostering self-esteem among the blacks.

But the more common view is that Community Action agencies eventually generated so much political antipathy that when the showdown came, the agencies usually turned out to be powerless, despite all their militant rhetoric. They eventually came under the effective control of state or local government. Social scientists who place a premium upon stability and cooperation in the system, in hopes of a gradual amelioration of social ills, look at such events and see that the avowed aim of reducing crime, delinquency, and welfare dependency was not achieved, that racial discord was whipped up, not diminished, that the poor ended up with few direct benefits. In this judgment, the programs were clearly failures.

The test of experience also brought into question the influential "contact theory," which was frequently cited as scientific justification for school desegregation and was implicitly involved in the famous 1954 Supreme Court decision, the Civil Rights Act of 1964, and federal busing orders. One of the fathers of this theory was the late Gordon Allport of Harvard, who formulated it this way: "Prejudice (unless deeply rooted in the character structure of the individual) may be reduced by equal-status contact between majority and minority groups in the pursuit of common goals. The effect is greatly enhanced if this contact is sanctioned by institutional supports (i.e., by law, custom, or local atmosphere) and if it is of a sort that leads to the perception of common interests and common humanity between members of the two groups."

In 1967 the Commission on Civil Rights in effect applied this line of thinking to what some social scientists called the vicious circle of discrimination—i.e., white prejudice leads to discrimination against blacks; discrimination reinforces social and economic inequality; inequality reinforces feelings of inferiority, which leads to the kind of behavior that feeds white prejudice. To break the circle, the commission advocated moves to achieve racial balance in the public schools. The issue became explosive when some lower courts ordered large-scale busing.

The contact theory was attacked in an outspoken article in *Public Interest* magazine, titled "The Evidence on Busing." The article was by David Armor, thirty-three, now a visiting professor at U.C.L.A. on leave from Harvard. (During his own student days, Armor was a leader of the radical student movement at the University of California, Berkeley.) He had participated in a study of educational achievement and attitudes of black children in Boston who were bused to white schools in the suburbs, and he also drew upon similar work done by others in White Plains, Ann Arbor, Hartford, New Haven, and Riverside, California. In general, Armor concluded that busing had no clear effect on the academic achievement of blacks, one way or the other. A more unexpected finding, however, was that integration did not increase tolerance or improve racial relationships. Instead, the bused black students reported that their white schoolmates were less and less friendly, that they themselves were spending more free time with members of their own race, and that there were more incidents of prejudice.

Other social scientists were quick to attack Armor's study. Thomas Pettigrew of Harvard, long a public advocate of racial balance in schools, together with Harvard colleagues, has prepared an article for *Public Interest*, contending among other things that Armor's report is based on a "biased and incomplete selection of studies." Seven other studies in other cities, Pettigrew claims, show evidence that the academic achievement of blacks improves when they are bused to white schools. Pettigrew also contends that the contact theory is not damaged by Armor's findings about student attitudes, since all the required conditions such as "equal status" contact may not have been fulfilled.

Armor's verdict on busing should not be regarded as conclusive. At the very least, however, he has made a contribution by attempting to test the validity of a commonly accepted assumption. Many recent failures might have been avoided if social-science theories had been tested before they were applied on a large scale. Instead, a great deal of money was spent, a great many promises made—and a great many academic and political reputations laid on the line. The dynamics inherent in such situations are now familiar: anyone venturing the suggestion that a program or theory is inadequate finds himself attacked with a virulence unprecedented in scientific circles since the days of Galileo.

The Hidden Explanation

Most *research* in social science consists of trying to find "correlations"; that is, relationships such as those now recognized between poverty and crime. But most *theory* consists of attributing causality; the opportunity theory of Cloward and Ohlin, for example, is an attempt to explain how poverty causes criminal behavior. The implication is that if income levels are raised, crime will be reduced. But what has happened, of course, is exactly the opposite.

The routine plea of social scientists in such cases is that complicating factors obscure the cause-and-effect relationship. But one of the most fruitful rules of thumb in science is the principal of parsimony—otherwise known as "Ockham's Razor"*—which says that the simplest explanation for diverse phenomena tends to be the most nearly correct one. Hence, if variables such as crime and poverty are often found to be correlated but not causally connected in any evident way, a parsimonious explanation might be that there is a third variable that generates crime and poverty together.

One hint about where to look for such a hidden variable has been offered by Edward Banfield, a tough-minded political scientist. In his controversial 1970 book, *The Unheavenly City*, Banfield recalled one of the most impeccable concepts of sociology—the recognition that human beings fall into social classes, differing not only in wealth and status but in interests and behavior as well. Banfield also recalled evidence that members of one class tend to differ from those in another in the degree to which they are "oriented to the future"; that is, in the extent to which they are willing to defer immediate gratification in hopes of some future gain. Banfield's hypothesis is that a lack of interest in the future explains why many lower-class individuals are less receptive to education, more tolerant of poor living conditions, more willing to assume the risks of criminal careers, etc.*

*After the fourteenth-century philosopher, William of Ockham, who proposed the rule for shaving away needless complexities.

Echoes of "Nativism"

Banfield, of course, has been roundly condemned for his inegalitarian heresies. For the last forty years, the established dogma in the social sciences has been that all people are born alike and it is the environment that makes them behave differently. Recently, however, a number of cracks have appeared in what British geneticist C.D. Darlington calls the "consensus of silence" that surrounds the subject of innate differences. New findings have led to a partial revival of a theme popular during the latter part of the nineteenth century, when genetic research and evolution theory inspired an infatuation with "nativism." In this view, man's behavior, like that of other animals, was explained in terms of heredity and so-called instincts. One manifestation was "social Darwinism," which attempted to justify inequality as a result of natural selection of the fittest individuals. Immigration laws that set quotas against various ethnic groups were another manifestation; Nazism was a culmination.

The rise of the behavioral psychology put more weight on the side of the environment. The behaviorists assumed that the only thing that

**Note by Ernest Dale*: It could, of course, be argued that the short-term outlook is the result of poverty, rather than the cause, for there is no reason to plan very far ahead if it appears that nothing the individual can do will improve his lot.

can be measured objectively is an organism's response to outside stimuli. But they often took the further step of saying that outside stimuli are all that count in determining behavior; in other words, all organisms will behave alike, given similar histories and circumstances. In 1925, John B. Watson, a founder of behaviorism, issued his famous challenge: "Give me a dozen healthy infants, well-formed, and my own specified world to bring them up in, and I'll guarantee to take any one at random and train him to become any type of specialist I might select—doctor, lawyer, artist, merchant-chief and, yes, even beggarman and thief, regardless of his talents, penchants, tendencies, abilities, vocations, and race of his ancestors."

How Man Looks to Tiger and Fox

For decades, the behaviorist view was accepted uncritically, and anyone who even questioned it was labeled a reactionary or a racist. Lately, however, a little-known scientific discipline called genetic behavior has been finding that many traits, including personality, tastes, and temperament, are partly inherited. To be sure, they resemble other inherited characteristics such as height or athletic ability in that they can be modified by environmental influences.

Genetic contributions to behavior appear to come at two levels. One is a macrolevel involving mankind as a species, the other a microlevel involving individuals and "breeding populations": that is, social classes, ethnic groups, and other more or less isolated, inbreeding categories of people.

Hypotheses about the macrolevel have been emerging from discoveries in the fields of archaeology, ethology, anthropology, and even linguistics. Their implications for social science have been most boldly expressed by a pair of young Rutgers University anthropologists, Lionel Tiger and Robin Fox (who first met, appropriately, in the London zoo). They postulate that the mind of *homo sapiens* is preprogrammed from birth with a great many propensities and expectations, which trace back through millions of years of ancestry in prehistoric men and ground-dwelling primates.

In their recent book, *The Imperial Animal*, Tiger and Fox cite paleontological, ethological, and anthropological evidence to speculate upon some likely features of those early societies, which, they say, have something in common with human cultures today. The early "economies" were small, consisting of perhaps thirty to fifty individuals, and were organized for hunting and defense. There was division of labor and mutual cooperation, i.e., in general, men hunted and women gathered, but some individuals made weapons and tools and exchanged them for foods. A system for redistributing wealth on the basis of exchange and generosity was probably in existence, and status was based partly on accumulated skills, plus the ability to control the operation of the distribution process—i.e., who got what.

Fox believes that, far from being subject to environmental control, man still has these ancient propensities; they are more inextricably rooted in our genes than physiological features. "Skin color can be changed rapidly and in sixty generations you could make all the Chinese two feet taller," says Fox. "But it's hard to breed out motherhood behavior."

Tiger and Fox suggest that the important task of social science will be to make sure that we design our civilizations to conform to man's programming. Instead, public policy has often tried to do the reverse: to cram people into social frameworks in which innate propensities—the thrill of some kind of chase, the need to contribute, the pleasure of craftsmanship—are suppressed. Fox acknowledges that we can be "socialized" to tolerate such things as prolonged confinement in the educational process, monotonous laboring for wages, or impersonal organizations far larger than that original thirty-man troop with its continuous face-to-face interactions. "But what happens when the genes get frustrated this way?" asks Fox, and then answers himself: "Ulcers, alienation, mental breakdown, apathy."

While speculations about genetic influences at the macrolevel emphasize those characteristics people have in common, speculations at the microlevel—the level of subgroups and individuals—tend to emphasize differences. It's here that the egalitarian orthodoxy of modern social scientists is challenged, that the shock is fiercest and the abuse most intense. [For example] accusations and harrassment were directed at Harvard psychologist Richard Herrnstein. In a long article in the *Atlantic* in September, 1971, Herrnstein cast the argument primarily in terms of the long-known I.Q. differences between upper and lower social classes. He inferred that U.S. society may be proceeding in the direction of a caste system based on intelligence.

Herrnstein was for the most part simply restating a hypothesis that had been proposed four years earlier in the *American Sociological Review*, by Bruce Eckland, a University of North Carolina sociologist. Eckland's article was the first argument for biological factors ever to appear in that journal.

Eckland and Herrnstein posed an interesting paradox: the social and occupational mobility and aspirations to higher education that are encouraged by U.S. public policy seem bound to lead to less, rather than more, equality. Their explanation is the sociological phenomenon of "assortive mating"—the fact that intelligent people tend to marry intelligent people. These couples are more likely than others to have intelligent children. As intelligent people are more and more able to move upward across class boundaries to enter college and prestigious occupations, they are more and more likely to encounter intelligent mates. Over time, therefore, society will sort itself out into intelligent and unintelligent classes, with status and earning ability, in effect, genetically transmitted. It's not clear what the practical consequences of such drastic stratification would be, but it hardly bolsters our customary hopes for greater social equality.

At least one geneticist, Theodosius Dobzhansky, sees benefits in the genetic consequences of social mobility and open-class systems, however. "They may, indeed, help to concentrate different genetic endowments in different groups," he says. "In so doing, they may produce persons with greater aptitudes for certain occupations than could be born if the social mobility and the genetic selection did not operate."

Is I.Q. Profitable?

It may well be, however, that a tendency automatically to equate low I.Q. scores with "inferiority" reflects a certain pro-I.Q. bias in the academic community, the product of its own professional orientation. Last month a team of Harvard researchers under sociologist Christopher Jencks reported the results of an extensive computer analysis of data on family, schooling, jobs, and income. Their startling conclusion was that I.Q. and, for that matter, the amount and kind of schooling, home background, and heredity, seem to bear only a small relationship to earning power. What matters most, Jencks suggests, are luck and the right personality.

A number of geneticists, in fact, worry lest mankind's evolution lead in the direction of too narrow a specialization; there is no compelling evidence that I.Q. is the trait of ultimate value for long-term survival. C.D. Darlington has written eloquently of the value of maintaining diversity: "We arrive at a paradox which timidity usually hides from us. The assumption of a genetic basis for race and class differences provides the evidence, the only scientific evidence, in favor of racial tolerance and cooperation. It is absurd to pretend that water and vinegar are equal. Water is better for some purposes, vinegar for others. Vinegar is harder to get but easier to do without. So it is with people."

Geneticists suspect, moreover, that because of the way that genetic and environmental factors interact, broader choices in education and occupation should be made available in societies such as ours. "The salient fact," argues Dobzhansky, "is that the optimal environments are different for different persons. Everybody ought to be enabled to give his best, but the best is not the same in everybody."

Don't Regard Them as Sages

The combination of new insights and the dissolution of old theories makes conditions ripe for a "scientific revolution" in the social sciences similar to those that have often occurred in the physical sciences. According to science historian Thomas Kuhn, such revolutions occur when a field of science finds its array of theories confuted by paradoxes that are disclosed by research. The ensuing strain brings about a rapid change in the scientists' fundamental assumptions, or "paradigms." The result could turn out to be some much more sophisticated view of the interaction between nature and nurture than those held by simplistic nativists and environmentalists.

The most unfortunate outcome of the social scientists' recent misadventures would be for the scientists and the policy makers to continue to draw apart. Princeton sociologist Marvin Bressler points out that, while social science cannot prescribe values to be pursued, it can help formulate the problems. "It's a mistake to regard social scientists as philosophers or sages; individual scientists may be, but it doesn't reside in the profession," says Bressler. On the other hand, he adds, "they're invaluable in expanding the range of variables that go into a decision. They're also invaluable in bringing to attention a certain amount of information, not generally known. And while they usually can't tell in advance what policies will work, they can often tell what won't. And finally, once a policy is implemented, they can tell whether it's working or not—or at least if it's not."

Once all the failures and inherent complexities of social scientific research and theory have been acknowledged, the necessity for a social science of some kind remains. With or without it, social policy will continue to be conceived and executed, a course charted through the changeable, increasingly man-made future. Either policy makers will act with the aid of knowledge methodically acquired or they will continue to flounder, learning nothing from bitter experience; the society will continue to rend itself apart in the kinds of rhetoric, conflict, and frustration that arise when incautious interventions are immodestly applied.

One major criticism of the human relations approach has stemmed from the fact that it has been viewed as a means of manipulating employees through psychological tricks—letting them think they are participating in management decisions, for example, when actually they are being led to accept decisions already made for them.

In the article below, Dr. William Gomberg, professor of industry at the Wharton School, University of Pennsylvania, takes an entirely different point of view. Management must manipulate, he says, and we should frankly accept that fact. The only way to make the industrial system tolerable, then, is to have a countervailing force in the form of a union. Between an authoritarian employer and an equally authoritarian union leader, Dr. Gomberg believes, the employee may find some measure of freedom.

The Paradox of Mental Health

William Gomberg

Our fundamental problem is that we live in a society where certain forms of silly behavior have a handsome payoff function, provided the foolishness is aggressive enough and exercised by a person high enough in the social hierarchy. What permits a sane man to breathe is that a viable stability results from the countervailing influence exercised against an authoritarian psychotic employer by at times an equally authoritarian psychotic trade union leader.

The paradox of mental illness or mental health is that one man's diseased behavior pattern is another man's positive, aggressive, innovating conduct. Or to put it in another context, one man's satisfactory mental health is another man's supine, passive acceptance of a subhuman fate. Who's healthy? Who's sick?

If you like what a man does, he is adjusted, well, and in touch with reality. If you dislike what he does, he's obviously sick. How modern we've become. In an earlier day, if we didn't like the aggressive type, we dubbed him an ill-tempered, unpleasant bully. If we didn't like the withdrawn, passive type, we endowed him with the name of a contemptible Caspar Milquetoast. My natural instincts incline me to prefer this earlier language to the modern mental-health patois. But then my obligation here is to deal with the

From the *Journal of Occupational Medicine*, Vol. 9, No. 5, May, 1967, pp. 239–243.

accepted vocabulary that has become the hallmark of the most fashionable clinical enthusiasm. It is a truism to point out that much of our confusion stems from imposing a medical vocabulary on a philosophical problem of conflicting values.

To be sure, there is an area of deviant behavior, so self-destructive and inappropriate to survival that the term "sick" is applicable. A rather loose way of distinguishing between these states is by the use of the term "psychotic" for this latter type of behavior and the use of the term "functionally neurotic" for the more survivable types of deviant behavior from the commonly accepted mores. I use this distinction, fully aware of its limitation.

[But here] I want to focus attention upon those industrial applications of psychiatry where there is a distinct open question as to whether we are confusing a medical problem with a philosophical question. Let me cite an example.

Levinson[1] and his associates made an observation in analysis of the psychological climate at the (fictitious) Midland Corporation, whose name is obviously concealed in order to protect the firm. They state that several people said that they had simply obtained their present jobs fortuitiously. The psychologists (Levinson and his associates) jumped to the conclusion that these people had not decided what to make of their lives and that they were using the company as a parental surrogate to determine their future for them. When observations like these are made by management in evaluating an "unwritten psychological contract between employer and employee," I suggest that psychiatry is lending itself to fortifying the authoritarian instincts of the employer, or for that matter, the trade-union leader, who wants to play father, if not God, to the men in the organization.

There is an implicit imperative in Levinson's book that leadership generates a healthy mental climate by fulfilling expectations based upon this kind of value structure. It is good to remember that management is charged with an economic function—it is obligated to obey the law of making a reasonable profit or at least avoiding loss. The pragmatic satisfaction of this objective may call for manipulation. Given man's tragic existential fate, perhaps there is no way of avoiding this immoral unpleasantness in a hierarchical structure. But wouldn't it be better to recognize it for what it is? Why endow this kind of activity with the magical patois of creating an environment conducive to mental health? What are we talking about when we talk of mental health?

This is what I conceive to be the central problem of the corporation in a democracy: How can we combine the manipulation of men with the securing of the economic objectives of a hierarchical corporation and yet maintain due respect for the private autonomy of these same men? This cannot be a unilateral function of management. It is for that reason that I believe in trade unions as a countervailing force. I always find it much safer to be in between two authoritarians who have countervailing interests, than under one authoritarian who is perfectly willing to play the role of psychotherapist to everybody below him in the organization hierarchy.

Some years ago, Jahoda[2] made what is perhaps the most exhaustive analysis available of the meaning of mental health. I was somewhat appalled by the nonoperational language with which she described this quality. Although not a logical positivist, I would like to have some concrete operating data on which I could hook this concept. But here is her view; let us see where it leads.

Jahoda states that mental health is not to be confused with a perpetual state of euphoria. There is room for rational unhappiness in the mentally healthy person. She then lists the following characteristics of the mentally healthy person:

1 *A realistic appraisal of one's self.* Well, I wonder what that means. Some kid in the slum announces that by God he is going to be the greatest surgeon in the history of the country. Anyone who looks at him in his environment jumps to the conclusion that the kid has delusions of grandeur and then the kid makes it. Now what advice do you have for him before he makes it? What does realistic self-appraisal mean? We can only

[1]H. Levinson, *Men, Management and Mental Health*, Harvard University Press, Cambridge, Mass., 1962.

[2]M. Jahoda, *Current Concepts of Mental Health*, Basic Books, New York, 1958.

tell whether he fulfills the objective he announces after the fact—and by that time it's too late to stop him.

2 *The presence of self-respect.* Where does self-respect begin and arrogance end? I don't know. It again is a moot question. These are qualities, I suppose, that we can feel intuitively or subjectively.

3 *A capacity for growth or self-actualization.* Again what confronts us is not a predictive mechanism but a sort of after-the-fact observation. If the person has grown, he had the capacity for growth. If he does not, how do I know he is not going to grow?

4 *A capacity for integration, a resilience in the face of stress.* Here I think we begin to get something that is observable. As a matter of fact, the people that would be, I suppose, most integrated in a society such as ours are those that can take a lot of the nonsense that is handed out—and again, that is the criterion of our society.

5 *Autonomy or the regulation of behavior in terms of internalized standards.* It includes decisions when to conform and when not to. There it seems very easy to separate the autonomous individuals from the conformists. We can take a look at the beatnik. He is not a nonconformist. He is a victim of the conformity of nonconformity. Somehow he likes the society where people stink and wear stringy hair. The very language that he uses indicates his conformity. What is a square? A square is a nonconformist in a beatnik society.

Kornhauser,[3] on the basis of his studies of auto workers, has indicated the widespread incidence of symptoms of emotional illness among them and links it to their work.

The American Federation of Labor unions are aware of this problem. They seem unaware of the economic conditions [necessary] for autonomous living. They confine their programs to financing medically oriented procedures that will permit deviants to function more effectively within the existing industrial structure, and are generally made a provision of the medical-benefits program of the collective-bargaining agreements. I would rather that they put their objective in terms of a philosophical conviction than graft onto their program this medical mental patois that somehow endows the procedure with an authoritarian tone which I find extremely distasteful.

However, it is middle management that has provided the largest number of victims of pseudopsychotherapy under the euphemism of management training programs. These therapists may be classified as (1) the Utopian reformers, and (2) the manipulators of euphoric acceptance of subordination.

The Utopian reformers in turn may be divided into two categories: One is those who frankly acknowledge that they are interested in overthrowing the existing set of social arrangements for a new Utopian socialist society.

The leaders of this school of thought are Erich Fromm and Georges Friedmann, the French sociologist.

The second school of Utopians feels that by restructuring the personalities of the leaders of the existing power structure, they will achieve a euphoric unreality wherein all decisions will be made by consensus.

The leaders of this school of thought are Prof. Chris Argyris of Yale and Warren Bennis of M.I.T., associated with the National Training Laboratory T-Group theories, and Robert Tannenbaum and his associates of U.C.L.A., associated with a therapy-oriented form of sensitivity training.

Fromm makes no bones about what he says. What he says is that a society in which people talk of the human problems of industry is a sick society. A well society is a society that talks, rather, in terms of the industrial problems of human beings. His remedy is simple—production for use, not for profit. He avoids the fact that the same dilemmas take place between subordinate and superordinate in a collectivist society as in a private-enterprise society. Somehow a change in ownership is supposed to make a difference. This reasoning should make postal employees mentally the healthiest workers in the country.

Friedman believes that he has found the key to the monotony of industrial work for the new

[3]A. Kornhauser, *Mental Health of the Industrial Worker*, John Wiley & Sons, Inc., New York, 1965.

society. He has picked upon a happenstance discovery of IBM and recommends its use far beyond its economic rationality.

During World War II, IBM was commissioned to erect and operate an ordnance plant during a period of acute labor shortage. This shortage of labor led them to assign workers a larger combination of tasks than they would have under conventional industrial engineering procedures. They discovered that they were obtaining greater productivity than from their more conventional plants.

The discovery that there is a point of diminishing returns beyond which further subdivision of labor becomes uneconomical has been so exaggerated that super-optimists have jumped to the conclusion that it is time to repeal Adam Smith and restore complete craftsmanship, an obviously foolish and unfounded conclusion. The combination of a number of trivial tasks has somehow now become the key to the elimination of the monotony of work.

Argyris[4] has discovered that there is a contradiction between the requirements for a mature, growing personality and the needs for self-subordination within the hierarchy of a modern corporation. Of course there is. It is part of the tragedy of the existential fate of man. His remedy, that management subvert itself by withholding the exercise of its authority, is not a program for mental rehabilitation, but for industrial chaos in which the subordinate will enjoy neither autonomy nor economic affluence.

Even in a university, professors with all the protection of academic freedom must accept mature frustration. All are competing for limited funds to finance their research interests. Ultimately some bureaucrat within the university family or from an outside foundation makes a decision in which one professor is fulfilled and numerous other colleagues are frustrated.

Bennis, of the National Training Laboratory Group, and Tannenbaum take their groups into a beautiful retreat and create an artificial environment in which their "patients" engage in pseudopsychoanalytic self-tutorials in which power is eschewed as they bare their collective souls. They are then restored to the normal power-structured environment where, if they are lucky, they revert to type—or if not so lucky, become so guilt-ridden that they can no longer function.

I am not at all impressed by the kind of testimonials given by the student patients. When you talk to them, they say, "O, gee, it was terrific." You remember the kind of disclosures we used to get about patent medicines which would cure everything. When the testimonials were investigated, the investigators found that the people had long since died of the disease from which they had proclaimed their recovery.

It seems to me the terrible dilemma in which existential man finds himself is that management must manipulate. It can't help itself. Its job is to create a hierarchical structure in which it assigns tasks to human beings. The only way I know of countervailing that power structure is with another power structure, very often headed not by a committed democrat but by someone as autocratic as the employer he is opposing. Having spent some time in trade-union organizations, let me assure you that this is so. But somehow when this conflict between two authoritarians exists, people who don't have their particular sets of drives can breathe freely. Management must manipulate if it is to fulfill its responsibility. It seems to me that it should not feel too guilty about this, upon considering the economic consequences of non-manipulation. The economic consequence of non-manipulation is not some pre-industrial beatific wooded isle such as the fictitious yeoman's England of the 17th century—which never existed, but in reality was London's Hogarth's Gin Alley. To see a present edition of Hogarth's Gin Alley, go to Calcutta.

Given the choice between people who must be manipulated in hierarchical structures subject to the constraints of people with an opposing interest, and the kind of economic consequence that we would suffer without our hierarchical business structures, I am willing to put up with the former to avoid the latter. The truth is that velvet-gloved manipulation is to be preferred to an iron hand. But in heaven's name, let's put an end to this nonsense about participative democracy in industry. The nonsense that is vocalized simply betrays the fact that we don't know

[4]*Personality and Organization*, Harper & Bros., New York, 1957.

what democracy is, and what's worse, we don't know that we're talking about. A decent respect for people should persuade those in power to keep their hands off mental-health programs except, perhaps, to contribute financially to the rehabilitation of the psychotic. It is for these reasons that, if I am asked about the responsibility of management and the responsibility of labor in the mental-health field, I would say their job is to contribute financially to those areas where research is being done, where primitive attempts at clinical practice are going on, and then above all, to keep their cotton-picking hands off the details of the implementation of the program. It is difficult enough without people who should be patients becoming the manipulators.

There are encouraging signs: The attempts of power manipulators who hope to subvert psychiatry to their manipulative ends are being stopped by the courts and the civil service commission.[5]

[5]"Psychiatry and Jobs," *The Wall Street Journal*, April 1, 1966.

Up until the time Professor Herzberg and his associates published their theory, it was generally assumed that job satisfaction and job dissatisfaction were opposites. That.is, if an employee were not dissatisfied, he was satisfied and presumably motivated to produce. The research on which the following article is based, however, indicated that the factors that produce the absence of dissatisfaction do not produce satisfaction or motivation.

These conclusions were the result of 200 interviews with middle management people (accountants and engineers) in several different companies. Those interviewed were asked to describe things that had happened on the job and to explain how their feelings were affected by what happened. Then the responses were carefully analyzed in an attempt to isolate the job variables that gave rise to the feelings, good or bad. If a man told of some occasion when he had felt particularly good about his job, the researchers tried to identify the reason. For example: Was the feeling due to recognition of his work? To good working conditions? To a sense of achievement? To good interpersonal relations? Similarly, they sought to determine the real reasons why, on other occasions, the men felt unhappy about their jobs.

When the original research was conducted (it has since been replicated a number of times), Prof. Herzberg was with the University of Pittsburgh. He is now with Case Western Reserve University.

Motivation versus Hygiene

Frederick Herzberg, Bernard Mausner, and Barbara Bloch Snyderman

"What do people want from their jobs?" When our respondents reported feeling happy with their jobs, they most frequently described factors related to their tasks, to events that indicated to them that they were successful in the performance of their work, and to the possibility of professional growth. Conversely, when feelings of unhappiness were reported, they were not associated with the job itself but with conditions that *surround* the doing of the job. These [latter factors] we call factors of *hygiene*, for they act in a manner analogous to the principles of medical hygiene. Hygiene operates to remove health hazards from the environment of man. It is not a curative; it is, rather, a preventive. Similarly, when there are deleterious factors in the context of the job, they serve to bring about poor job attitudes. Improvement in these factors of hygiene will serve to remove the impediments to positive job attitudes. Among the factors of hygiene we have included supervision, interpersonal relations, physical working conditions, salary, company policies and administrative practices, benefits, and job security. When these factors deteriorate to a level below that which the employee considers acceptable, then job dissatisfaction ensues. However, the reverse does not hold true. When the job context can be characterized as optimal, we will not get dissatisfaction, but neither will we get much in the way of positive attitudes.

The factors that lead to positive job attitudes

From *The Motivation to Work*, 2d ed. (John Wiley & Sons, Inc., New York, 1959), pp. 113–117, 128–137.

do so because they satisfy the individual's need for self-actualization in his work. The concept of self-actualization, or self-realization, as a man's ultimate goal has been focal to the thought of many personality theorists. When he is deflected from this goal he becomes, as Jung says, "a crippled animal."

For the kind of population that we sampled and probably for many other populations as well, the wants of employees divide into two groups. One group revolves around the need to develop in one's occupation as a source of personal growth. The second group operates as an essential base to the first and is associated with fair treatment in compensation, supervision, working conditions, and administrative practices. The fulfillment of the needs of the second group does not motivate the individual to high levels of job satisfaction and to extra performance on the job. All we can expect from satisfying the needs for hygiene is the prevention of dissatisfaction and poor job performance.

The negligible role which interpersonal relationships play in our data tallies poorly with the assumption basic to most human-relations training programs that the way in which a supervisor gets along with his people is the single most important determinant of morale. Supervisory training in human relations is probably essential to the maintenance of good hygiene at work. This is particularly true for the many jobs, both at rank-and-file and managerial levels, in which modern industry offers little chance for the operation of the motivators. These jobs are atomized, cut and dried, monotonous. They offer little chance for responsibility and achievement and thus little opportunity for self-actualization. It is here that hygiene is exceptionally important. The fewer the opportunities for the "motivators" to appear, the greater must be the hygiene offered in order to make the work tolerable. But to expect such programs to pay dividends beyond the effects that hygiene provides is going contrary to the nature of job motivation. The motivators fit the need for creativity; the hygiene factors satisfy the need for fair treatment, and it is thus that the appropriate incentive must be present to achieve the desired job attitude and job performance.

We have listed salary among the factors of hygiene, and as such it meets two kinds of avoidance needs of the employee. First is avoidance of the economic deprivation that is felt when actual income is insufficient. Second, and generally of more significance in the times and for the kind of people covered by our study, is the need to avoid feelings of being treated unfairly. Salary and wages are very frequently at the top of the list of factors describing answers to the question, "What don't you like about your job?" in morale surveys. They are at the middle of the list of answers to the question, "What do you want from your job?" Asking people what is important to them in their jobs will bring responses that we have classified as "motivators." The atmosphere of the usual morale survey encourages people to emphasize sources of dissatisfaction.

In two consecutive morale surveys by the senior author, in which the employees were requested to illustrate their dissatisfaction or satisfaction with the various items on the morale questionnaire with critical incidents, the comments on the equity of salary greatly outnumbered the comments on the absolute amount of salary. All 1382 employees surveyed were at the supervisory level.

How then can we explain the success of the many employee motivational schemes that seem to rely directly on the use of wage incentives and bonuses? Reports on the Lincoln Electric Company of Cleveland, Ohio and the George A. Hormel meat-packing plant at Austin, Minnesota suggest good examples of the efficacy of money incentives for increasing production, job satisfaction, and company loyalty. But let us examine for a moment the nature of these programs in the light of the findings presented here.

First, there are many other ingredients to these plans which are generally given less attention than they merit, ingredients that combine a large proportion of the factors that we have found to be motivators. The formation of Lincoln's Advisory Board and Hormel's Business Improvement Committee both resulted from attempts to increase job content and job responsibility by giving workers knowledge of, and responsibility for, operations and improvements. Both operate on the theory that the "boss" cannot know everything about all the work processes, that the workers are experts in their fields, and that their knowledge is of great value.

Lincoln Electric, which is not unionized, has the additional advantage of being able to advance workers on the basis of merit, not seniority. Money earned as a direct reward for outstanding individual performance is a reinforcement of the motivators of *recognition and achievement*. It is not hygiene as is the money given in across-the-board wage increases.

This aspect of participation and of increased responsibility is the real secret of whatever success the Scanlon plan[1] and its imitators have achieved. Lincoln Electric is implementing man's natural striving for self-realization. No man wants to be just a cog in a wheel. Lincoln says, "The most insistent incentive is the development of self-respect and the respect of others. Earnings that are the reward for outstanding performance, progress, and responsibility are signs that he is a man among men. The worker must feel that he is part of a worthwhile project and that the project succeeded because his ability was needed in it. Money alone will not do the job."

When incentive systems do not permit any of the motivators to operate, then any increase in performance or in apparent job satisfaction is misleading. It is likely that poor hygiene will depress performance below the level of "the fair day's work." Correction of this poor hygiene, or the application of monetary incentives not related to motivators, may return performance to the norm. The improvement produced under these circumstances is actually far less than one could obtain were motivators to be introduced.

Are good job attitudes and company loyalty engendered by these incentive plans? The surface answer often seems to be yes. Employees in such companies will report that they like working for their companies, but the "liking" seems to be little more than the absence of disliking, their satisfaction little more than the absence of dissatisfaction.

Managers and Professionals

Let us look a little more closely at the world of managerial and professional people, since they, after all, make up the group sampled in the present study. Managerial and professional jobs, it is commonly reported, have been diluted seriously in recent times. In a parody of the assembly line managerial and professional workers are assigned small pieces of work seen as a whole by a favored few. This rationalization of the work process has, in places, been carried to such an extreme that individuals are rarely responsible for carrying through a complete task.

This dilution is often accompanied by an increase in stress on group activities. The research on the existence of social groupings among lower level workers and the discovery that these groupings are highly functional on those levels has helped the trend to an insistence on group activity in many areas in which it is far from appropriate.

When the relationship between an individual and his accomplishments is hard to discern because of the rationalization of jobs and the stress on group work, it is almost inevitable that the quality of interpersonal relationships becomes a highly important criterion for the evaluation of individuals. As William H. Whyte, Jr., in *The Organization Man,*[2] Vance Packard in *The Hidden Persuaders,*[3] and others have pointed out with alarm, American industry is relying more and more on measures of personality and temperament for the evaluation of new entrants into the ranks of management. Several recent studies have noted that executives are more often than not fired for failure in qualities remotely related to actual job performance.

It is inevitable that people living in such a world should learn to respond properly in terms of the system of rewards and punishments offered to them. A study made by the senior author in several companies whose managerial employees were appraised by psychological tests and interviews shows no relationship between intelligence and aptitude and the success of managerial individuals as defined by their ranks or by their salaries.

The usual moral of this story is that industry must search even more unceasingly for the proper attributes of personality in its potential

[1] *Editor's Note*: A profit-sharing plan.

[2] Simon and Schuster, New York, 1956.

[3] David McKay Company, Inc., New York, 1957.

managers and professionals. In a situation in which initial hiring and later advancement depend not on skill but on personality individuals learn to avoid too great a display of technical skill. When the rewards of work are connected with behaviors not related to the actual tasks of the job, it is hardly surprising that the worker, whether foreman or company vice-president, soon learns a set of values revolving around these extraneous rewards. What we in this study have called hygiene becomes an end for much of existence.

The miracle is that in spite of all this the 20 people in our sample were able to speak of the moving and exciting moments in their lives in which they *did* have a genuine opportunity for achievement through the actual work of their jobs. Apparently, the feeling of growth in stature and responsibility is still the most exciting thing that can happen to someone in our society.

Consequences

An individual living in such a world is debarred from seeking real satisfactions in his work. Interpersonal relationships outside work are overloaded; the hobby often becomes a substitute for the job. But the hobby cannot give the complete sense of growth, the sense of striving towards a meaningful goal, that can be found in one's life work.

One wonders whether the sense of anomie, of the rootlessness and alienation which anthropologists, political scientists, and psychiatrists have found so serious in our world, is not at least in part a consequence of this overloading of interpersonal relationships due to the loss of the direct meaning of work.

Suggestions

It would be foolhardy on our part to present a detailed recipe, on the basis of our study, for the cure of all the world's ills. However, the picture we have just drawn in conjunction with the evidence from our study points to certain conclusions, which to the writers, at least, are inescapable.

First, jobs must be restructured to increase to the maximum the ability of workers to achieve goals meaningfully related to the doing of the job. A number of issues is raised by this simple statement. It is apparent that the great bulk of production workers, except for craftsmen, is debarred from such rewards by the very nature of their jobs. Why? It is tempting to speculate on the psychological characteristics of jobs in which it is possible to get rewards directly related to the doing of the work. A look at the kinds of reports given by our respondents leads to one tentative conclusion. This is that the individual should have some measure of control over the way in which the job is done in order to realize a sense of achievement and of personal growth. Clearly, most assembly-line workers cannot have such control.

A new development in industry, however, will change this picture for a sizable proportion of workers. One fairly large segment of our economy is being automated. What effect has automation on this problem? In the final fully automated plant an interesting phenomenon takes place. At first, the workers are bewildered and unhappy about the shift to jobs in which they are no longer physically active but in which they are perpetually tense, perpetually under the need to watch, think, and discriminate. However, an adjustment does take place, and then the ability of these workers to feel control over the over-all process of the plant leads to higher morale than ever.

But automation affects professional and managerial personnel relatively little. In fact, the degree to which professional and managerial workers will increase in number as a result of automation makes the problems of this group more rather than less pressing. The frame of reference that automates factories will produce temptations to go further in the direction of stereotypy and regimentation at the professional and managerial level. Thus at the managerial level automation poses more dangers than it provides opportunities; nevertheless, wherever automation takes place the opportunity is given to management to show imagination and skill in the structuring of jobs so that the largest number of individuals can be given the highest level of motivation.

A movement has been in existence for some time that would increase the interest of jobs by broadening them. Is this what is being discussed here? If job broadening means a "Cook's tour" in which individuals have snippets of different activities, unrelated in any meaningful sense, then the mere addition of new activities should not be expected to increase motivation in the terms described [here]. Rotation from one activity to another would be successful only if the individual being rotated were able to integrate his various activities into achievements that have psychological meaning for him.

Furthermore, our data indicate that achievements in themselves are only a partial reward. The accumulation of achievement must lead to a feeling of personal growth in the individual accompanied by a sense of increasing responsibility. Is interest in the operations of work a critical factor? Very likely, as we can see in our findings, interesting work is often the cue to a higher level of motivation. But it is difficult to predict in advance for any one individual what will or will not be interesting. Thus, the redesigning of jobs cannot be predicated upon an attempt to make them interesting. It is true, as it has always been, that the personnel worker will continue to attempt to fit each individual to the work which that individual finds most intrinsically rewarding. But that is not the point we are making here. Our point is that the jobs themselves have to be set up in such a way that, interest or no, the individual who carries them out can find that their operations lead to increased motivation.

If one structures the jobs properly, one must also structure the selection process properly. We wish to shift the emphasis from personality to the attempt to match an individual's work capacity with work he will be needed to do. This demands a continued close analysis of the actual kinds of abilities needed for each job and an equally close analysis of the potential abilities of applicants for work. Of course, there should be some recognition of the fact that in many jobs at high levels there are numerous combinations of abilities and temperaments that will lead to success in the same job for different reasons.

What role did the supervisor play in the lives of the people in our sample? He was often made the villain in stories about times when morale was low. He almost never appeared as a *focus* for high morale. We may remember, however, that the supervisor did appear in a single, restricted role in stories about highs. He was frequently the source for the recognition of successful work.

There is another and more subtle aspect of supervision that must be recognized. Even though this was not reported by our respondents, it is likely that a successful supervisor was often instrumental in structuring the work so that his subordinates *could* realize their ability for creative achievement.

Let us deal first with the supervisor's role as the dispenser of recognition. Typically, the formal vehicle for recognition is a merit rating of some kind. On this the individual depends for salary increases, promotions, and quality of assignments. It is brash of us to urge that merit ratings be tied as closely as possible to reliable and valid measures of actual performance. Psychologists, industrial engineers, and experts in management have been struggling for years with the problems of such ratings. That they have been relatively unsuccessful, that merit ratings are *not* a very dependable measure, is notorious. All we can do is point to the urgent necessity for further progress.

One development in the design of merit ratings has tended to diminish the possibility of progress. A heavy weight is often placed on personality factors. This beclouds the clarity of the rating as a reward for good work or punishment of bad.

In assessing the importance of recognition as a factor in positive job attitudes we have noted that it has little force in promoting long-range feelings of high morale, except when it is a part of the greater complex of motivational factors. This argues that the most important job of the supervisor is his organizational and planning function. The training of the upper level of supervisors in graduate schools of business or of industrial administration certainly focuses on problems of organization and planning. One wonders whether the preoccupation of human-relations training for the lower levels of supervision has not tended to dilute the more technical aspects of work at these levels. Beyond this, as we have previously suggested, it may be that the very structure of middle-management jobs has limited unduly the potential for organization and planning.

Our conclusion is that the single most important goal in the progress of supervision is the development of new insights into the role of the supervisor so that he may effectively plan and organize work.

Does this mean that we must throw away the lessons of research gained from studies of employee-centered supervision? No, it does not. It is doubtful that a new generation of managers would revert to the simple autocracy of an earlier epoch. What we are suggesting is not a return to an older type of management but a step up into a new kind.

In summary, what is the task of the supervisor? He will have to learn discriminatively to recognize good work, to reward this good work appropriately. This emphasis does not reduce the necessity for the maintenance of optimal personal relationships between supervisor and subordinate. In addition, he will have to acquire increasingly greater skills in the organization and distribution of work so that the possibility for successful achievement on the part of his subordinates will be increased. These reflections apply to supervisors on any level, from the foreman over a group of machinists to a company president.

Participation

The notion of participation is a loose one. It is clear, as several critics have recently suggested, that the authoritarian pattern of American industry will continue despite the propaganda for a more democratic way of life. This is inevitable, since in a large and complex institution true participation at every level in the setting of the goals for work is clearly impossible. The need for centralized management, for the coordination of one unit of an organization with another, is too great. More and more of our economy is being concentrated into large organizations.

Although there is no room for individual participation in the setting of goals, it is certainly possible that the ways in which these goals are to be reached can be left to the judgment of individuals. Within certain limits, it is likely that more latitude than is currently available to most people in industry can be given to individuals to develop their own ways of achieving the ends that are presented to them by a centralized authority. This is a reasonable solution to the problem of motivation, more reasonable than the usual formulation of participation. To expect individuals at lower levels in an organization to exercise control over the establishment of overall goals is unrealistic. Thus, when participation is suggested in these terms, it is usually a sham.

Although Herzberg's theory appears to supply the missing ingredient in the human relations approach and many people will find that examination of their own experience bears it out, it has not been without its critics. In the following article, three writers (all of whom are with Ohio State University) examine the criticisms and suggest a possible reason for the discrepancies between Herzberg's findings (and those of other researchers whose studies agree with his) and the findings of the critics.

The Herzberg Controversy: A Critical Reappraisal

Orlando Behling, George Labovitz, and Richard Kosmo

In 1959 Professor Frederick W. Herzberg fired the first salvo in what has proven to be one of the most heated and durable controversies in modern management theory. The salvo was, of course, the book *The Motivation to Work,*[1] in which he and his co-authors first presented his

[1]F. Herzberg, B. Mausner, and B. Snyderman, *The Motivation to Work* (New York: John Wiley and Sons, 1959).

From the *Academy of Management Journal*, March, 1968, pp. 99–108.

motivator-hygiene theory of job satisfaction. In order to understand the nature of the controversy which has grown up around this approach to the study of job satisfaction, it is necessary to look briefly at the contrast between the Herzberg proposal and what the "conventional wisdom" of management has to say about the topic.

The conventional explanation of job satisfaction considers "satisfaction" and "dissatisfaction" to be the extremes of a continuum having a neutral condition in which the individual is "neither satisfied nor dissatisfied" as its midpoint. Generally this analysis assumes that individuals shift along this continuum in response to changes in numerous factors, some of which are intrinsic to their jobs, while others make up the environment in which they are performed. The nature of the work itself, the challenge it offers, the behavior of supervisors, pay, working conditions, relations with co-workers, and dozens of other things are all assumed to affect job satisfaction to some degree. The exact way in which these factors interact is usually less clearly expressed. Basically, however, dissatisfaction is seen as the product of an absence of factors causing satisfaction. Deficiencies in supervision, pay, or similar things can result in dissatisfaction or, if their absence is balanced off by the presence of positive factors, in neutrality.

If one of the factors is improved or a new one introduced, the individual is thought to move some distance toward the positive "satisfied" end of the scale. If one of them is reduced or eliminated (a well-liked supervisor is replaced or a new and less competent food service crew is moved into the cafeteria), the individual shifts toward the negative "dissatisfied" end of the continuum. How far along the scale any given change will move an individual is seen as a function of several factors. The magnitude of the shift along the scale is usually seen as being positively (though generally not perfectly) correlated with the size of the change in the factor generating it. Thus a $40 per month salary increase would be expected to increase job satisfaction more than a $20 one, though not necessarily twice as much. The size of the shift is also seen as being affected by the type of factor being changed. There seems to be little real agreement as to the relative importance of various factors. It is generally accepted, however, that variations do exist and that, for example, a salary increase would have greater positive impact than painting the walls of the work area a new and more cheerful color. It was against the backdrop of general and mostly unquestioning acceptance of this conventional view of job satisfaction that Herzberg exploded his bombshell.

The Herzberg position gained considerable acceptance, in part, perhaps, because it lent support to the emerging "Theory Y" idea that factors intrinsic to the job were somehow different and more important than those surrounding the work, in terms of effects on motivation. Equally important in the development of acceptance of the approach, however, was the fact that during the early 1960's Herzberg, as well as a number of other researchers, performed studies which verified the existence of the motivator-hygiene duality. These studies, which were summarized by Herzberg in *Work and the Nature of Man,*[2] flowed out as a steady stream of dissertations, journal articles, and papers at scholarly meetings. Using the Herzberg critical-incident method or something closely akin to it, these researchers were able to demonstrate the existence of the duality in close to twenty separate studies involving such diverse groups as housekeeping and unskilled food service workers, county agricultural extension workers, women in high-level professional positions, scientists, nurses and engineers—including a group of Hungarian engineers.

Despite the large volume of empirical evidence by supporters of the duality theory and the degree to which the Herzberg theory dovetails with other approaches to the study of job satisfaction, from the very beginning the theory was not without its critics. They have been able to assemble a great deal of evidence in support of a conventional, uniscalar explanation of job satisfaction as an alternative to the Herzberg approach.

Robert B. Ewen, for example, factor-analyzed the responses of 1,021 life insurance agents to a 58-item, four-point attitude scale and was able to extract six major factors. Two of the factors

[2]World Publishing Company, 1966.

(*work itself* and *prestige*) were motivators in Herzberg's framework, three (*manager interest in agents, company training policies,* and *salary*) were hygienes. The sixth factor appeared to be indicative of overall contentment with the job, and thus was labeled *general satisfaction*. With attributes (motivators or hygienes) held constant at a neutral level when they were not being tested, it was found that the effects of certain motivators and hygienes on general satisfaction varied from those predicted on the basis of Herzberg's theory. In both of the two subgroups making up the total sample, *company training policies* and *manager interest in agents*—both nominally hygienes—actually acted as if they were motivators. *Salary* acted as a motivator in one group, but caused both satisfaction and dissatisfaction in the other. *Prestige* (a motivator) caused satisfaction and dissatisfaction in both groups. Only one factor, *work itself*, acted as a motivator in both samples in accordance with the Herzberg theory.[3]

Charles L. Hulin and Patricia A. Smith tested the Herzberg duality by examining the relative contributions of various motivators and hygienes to satisfaction and dissatisfaction and by examining the effects of their presence on workers' judgments of jobs. The assumption underlying their first hypothesis is that, if the duality theory is correct, there should be no significant correlation between degree of contentment with motivators and overall job dissatisfaction, nor should there be a correlation between degree of dissatisfaction with hygienes and overall job satisfaction. The logic behind the second hypothesis is drawn from a conventional uniscalar analysis. If an individual is highly satisfied when a particular factor is present in his job, he should be dissatisfied when it is absent and vice versa. Tests of these two hypotheses among a group of home office employees of a large international corporation revealed results which more clearly support the uniscalar approach than they do Herzberg's duality. Satisfaction with *pay received* (a hygiene) and with *advancement* and *work done* (both motivators) correlated significantly with satisfaction, dissatisfaction, and overall satisfaction-dissatisfaction scores for male employees. Similar though less clear results were obtained for female employees. A linear relationship between log (to correct for unequal scale intervals) importance of a factor when it was absent and its importance when it was present for four hygienes and two motivators was uncovered, though the results among the female employees were again not absolutely clear.[4]

These are by no means the only studies which conflict with or do not fully support predictions based on the Herzberg duality. A brief survey of the literature revealed thirteen such studies in addition to the two reported in the preceding paragraphs. These studies treated a variety of populations and involved several different methods of gathering data. In fact, the only truly consistent pattern running through them was a negative one—none of the studies in support of a uniscalar explanation used Herzberg's critical-incident technique. With few exceptions, although the measuring techniques varied, they used some form of structured, scalar device.

Examination of the results of these studies and those reported by Herzberg in his 1966 book reveals a fairly obvious but nonetheless important point: almost without exception, research using the Herzberg critical-incident method gives results supporting the Herzberg duality. Just as constantly, research using other methods of gathering data provides results which conflict with the Herzberg approach and support a uniscalar theory of job satisfaction. This fact has not escaped the proponents of the two types of theories and the argument between them has unfortunately deteriorated to a series of accusations and counteraccusations, revolving for the most part around the relative merits of the two methods of obtaining data. The proponents of the uniscalar theories consider Herzberg's results to be an artifact of the method used.

Only Victor H. Vroom attempts to account for this. He takes the position that Herzberg's unstructured format tends to overemphasize the importance of self-controlled actions as sources of satisfaction and things beyond the control of the individual as sources of dissatisfaction. The

[3]"Some Determinants of Job Satisfaction: A Study of the Generality of Herzberg's Theory," *Journal of Applied Psychology*, XLVIII (1964), 161–163.

[4]"An Empirical Investigation of Two Implications of the Two-Factor Theory of Job Satisfaction," *Journal of Applied Psychology*, LI (1967), 396–402.

individual can, according to Vroom, take credit for his successes and blame others for his failures by emphasizing what Herzberg has labeled motivators as sources of satisfaction and what he calls hygienes as sources of dissatisfaction.[5]

Herzberg attempts to refute the Vroom argument by pointing out that it is naive to think that persons wishing to make themselves "look good" would prefer to blame hygienes for dissatisfaction. More frequently, Herzberg states, individuals who want to make themselves "look good" tend to complain about lack of motivators such as *responsibility* and *possibility of growth* rather than problems with petty hygienes. He then attacks the data-gathering techniques used in the non-Herzberg studies, pointing out that:

> The "fakeability" of responses and the openness to suggestion that job-attitude scales have shown in the past recommended the motivation-hygiene procedure. While it is not possible to eliminate bias, conscious or unconscious, on the part of the subjects when using verbal methods (written scales or interviews), at least it is much more difficult to conjure up appropriate events in one's life during a patterned interview than it is to respond "appropriately" to items in a questionnaire. The general practice of psychologists of giving lists of factors for employees to rate with respect to their job satisfactions by now should be recognized as one of the most misleading approaches to the study of work feelings.[6]

He then provides a series of alternate interpretations of the results obtained in some of the studies which were seen by their original authors as providing evidence in conflict with the motivator-hygiene duality. When seen through Herzberg's eyes, the results are in line with the duality theory.

Despite these reinterpretations, the contention made in an earlier paragraph still stands to the satisfaction of the authors of this paper: research using open end formats similar to the original critical-incident method used by Herzberg, almost without exception, gives results supporting the Herzberg duality. With a similar degree of certainty, more structured methods of data gathering give uniscalar results. Students of the field have thus far failed to take these results at face value. The fact that different results are obtained from different techniques is in itself extremely important.

The differences are important because they are indicative of the possibility that the study of job satisfaction in general may be hoisted by its own petard or, more accurately, by its own theoretical construct. The culprit in this case is the theoretical construct "job satisfaction" itself. Because it has so much face validity—that is, it seems so "right" that there should be a single attitudinal entity which represents an individual's overall feelings about his work—and because it is such a convenient concept for the development of theories and the design and analysis of experiments, it has apparently been forgotten that job satisfaction is nothing more than an idea made up by students of the field.

There is no evidence that any single, unitary, overall attitude toward an individual's employment exists. There is, however, considerable evidence to support the idea that the researcher must deal with many varied and often conflicting evaluations of various aspects of a man's job, different parts of which are tapped in different ways by different data-gathering techniques. The argument between the pro- and anti-Herzberg factions itself is evidence in support of this idea. The conflicting results obtained with semistructured critical-incident techniques and more structured scalar approaches provide further support. Even the repeated references of some of the opponents of the duality theory to "*the* uniscalar approach" is incorrect. Close examination reveals that there is *no* single uniscalar theory. The assumption underlying research, the comments made about the nature of job satisfaction and the research results obtained, reveal little consistency from author to author or from study to study. They are talking about different things, measuring them in different ways, and obtaining dissimilar results.

Obviously, if this analysis of the nature of job satisfaction is correct, substantial reorientation in treatment of intervening variables connecting aspects of work and the work environment to employee behaviors is required. It must be recognized that any attempt to produce a single measure of job satisfaction, whether it is based on a conventional uniscalar or a Herzberg duality analysis is doomed to failure. Effort must be

[5] *Work and Motivation* (New York: John Wiley and Sons, 1964), p. 129.
[6] *Work and the Nature of Man, op. cit.*, pp. 130–132.

devoted to the development of many measuring devices and techniques which will provide reliable and internally consistent data indicative of important parts of the total attitudinal complex. Only then can steps be taken to relate those aspects of the entity we call job satisfaction to aspects of the job, its environment, and individual behavior on the job.

Increasingly, behavioral scientists have been pointing out that employee motivation to do a good job depends mainly on the nature of the work itself. Thus job enrichment—which is sometimes confused with job enlargement but is not the same thing—appears to be the answer to the problem of apathy among employees. This article reports on a number of experiments in job enrichment, as well as on a survey of management opinion on the subject. The author is manager of management development and training at American Motors Corporation in Detroit.

A Progress Report on Applying Job Enrichment Concepts

Herbert E. Wissman

"Job enrichment" is usually defined as designing new jobs or changing existing jobs to enable employees to take part in the planning and the control functions that were previously restricted to supervisors and staff employees. Its objective is to provide for the employee's psychological growth and development rather than just for his economic growth and development.

Early efforts usually took the form of what is often called "job enlargement." Many people feel that the lack of acceptance of job enrichment and the lack of progress in the field are due to the assumption that job enrichment and job enlargement are one and the same.

The two may be differentiated in this way: "Job enlargement" generally means the assignment of more varied tasks, but employees whose jobs are enlarged continue to do work that is all on the same level. "Job enrichment," on the other hand, means the redesign of jobs to permit employees to work on tasks with varying levels of difficulty, tasks that give them more chance for achievement, recognition, advancement, and growth and permit them to assume more responsibility. For example, where an employee was previously concerned only with *doing the job right*, he may now be concerned with *doing the right job,* and he may check his performance himself as well.

Since job enlargement provides a variety of work, it may possibly make a job less boring, but the effects are usually of short duration. However, M. Scott Myers in his book *Every Employee a Manager* (1) states that job enlargement can be considered an intermediate step that can set the stage for attempts at the more effective job enrichment.

A general approach to job enrichment would be a plan similar to the following:

a Build a knowledge base of job enrichment principles at all organizational levels.

b Get a top management commitment.

c Train management, and at times employees, in the principles.

d Conduct meetings to identify the jobs to be enriched, and the specific tasks.

e Apply the suggestions and follow up progress.

Where Did Job Enrichment Come From?

It appears that many people in management feel that job enrichment is just another fad that will run its course, only to be replaced by another. But much evidence indicates that job enrichment is not a fad. It is considered not so much a

From *Plant Engineering and Maintenance Techniques* (Clapp & Poliak, Inc., New York, 1972). Paper given at the twenty-third National Plant Engineering and Maintenance Conference at the Philadelphia Civic Center, Jan. 24–27, 1972.

program as a way of managing. Many feel that no phase of management has ever been based on as much scientific research prior to its application.

Myers' book includes a chart showing twelve theories of human effectiveness, each one of which the author feels has had an influence on human effectiveness. These twelve theories are associated with scientists who have all had a part in the development of the concept of job enrichment, and their work dates back quite a number of years.

Many people feel that the work of Frederick Herzberg (2) has been the most useful to them in planning job enrichment. Herzberg's division of factors in the work environment into motivators and hygiene factors was extremely useful, and its interrelationship with the other theories of human effectiveness was easily seen.

Robert Ford, one of the leaders in the job enrichment effort, states in his book *Motivation Through the Work Itself* (3) that in the period from 1940 to 1965 companies were trying to make the employee feel better about the job or the company, in the hope that this would result in improved work. Some of the items that he lists as major efforts by companies during this period include:

a Reducing the hours of work and providing longer vacations.
b Increasing wages and benefit packages.
c Creating off-hour programs for the employees.
d Providing training in human relations skills for the supervisors.
e Providing employee counseling and communications programs, such as company magazines, booklets, movies, and attitude surveys.

The basic reason why these attempts did not succeed was that companies were more concerned with doing things *to* and *for* employees than with recognizing and accepting the fact that employees are motivated by the work itself and that their attitudes are formed *by* the work. Attempts to create "good" attitudes so that the employee will work better have generally failed.

The ineffective concepts have been perpetuated from management generation to management generation. Just as it took many years to develop the current motivation concepts, it will take many years and much more effort to change them. Yet management's current attitude toward employee problems could be described as *desperate* because of the increasing ineffectiveness of yesterday's solutions to today's problems.

In an article entitled, "Job Enlargement; Antidote to Apathy," Reif and Schoderbek (4) present the highlights of an effective job enrichment study made in 1944 in the general machine shop at an IBM plant. But the evidence did not attract as much attention at that time as it would today, for managing employees was not felt to be quite so critical.

In the interval between 1944 and the present, most of the behavioral science research on job enrichment took place. One of the most significant developments in this most recent period of outstanding work in the behavioral sciences was that the scientists went out into the world-of-work and applied their theories to actual people on real jobs. In Herzberg's work on motivation, completed in the mid 1950's, employees were asked to express opinions on what satisfied them and what dissatisfied them on the job, and their answers formed the basis for his theory that the things that make people satisfied and those that make them dissatisfied are not variations of the same thing—they are actually different. If the causes of dissatisfaction were not present, the employees were not necessarily satisfied. Many consider that this research marked the beginning of productive work on job enrichment. Now the basic concepts have been expanded considerably.

Today there seems to be less concern for satisfaction and dissatisfaction, as such, and more concern for such things as: "Has the absentee rate dropped?" "Has the quality level gone up?" "Has turnover been reduced?" Measuring the success of job enrichment in practical everyday business terms has contributed considerably to the attention it has created.

Often the wild swing of the pendulum is the rule in business, and it is quite possible that job enrichment could, in many cases, be a victim of the swing. Today there may be too great a tendency to consider it a proven process that is universally applicable.

It should be accepted, rather, as a way of managing that is still in the experimental stage. The basic concepts are undoubtedly valid, but we need greater insight, knowledge, and experience to determine how it can be made most effective.

Reports from the Authorities and Critics

The following are representative examples of the apparently successful application of job enrichment principles and some representative examples of the criticism being leveled at them as well.

Robert Ford (3). In this reference two major projects are reported on in detail: "Treasury Department Manpower Utilization" and "The Framemen Trial." The latter will be described here since it is more directly related to industrial situations.

The framemen in this study were forty men assigned to the installation of private line telephone circuits. Some of the problems that led to the need for the project were the following:

1 Responsibility for the total job was split between two plant managers.
2 An informal production limit was set by the framemen.
3 Morale was not good, there was little or no pride, and it was difficult to identify poor or careless employees.
4 The errors committed were reaching a prohibitive level.
5 Work that was completed on schedule was below acceptable standards, and the percentage of circuit rejects was running too high.
6 Supervisors were spending too much time assigning work and coordinating projects.

The following results were obtained through a carefully controlled step-by-step job enrichment experiment:

1 The frame errors declined, more work was done on schedule, and better continuity existed between projects, which resulted in improved quality.
2 The quota system of output was virtually eliminated, and morale was higher.
3 The managers felt that they now had more time to manage, which indicates that their job had been enriched as well.
4 Customers noted a significant reduction in trouble reports.

Huse and Beer (5). The department in which this experimental study was conducted was a normal assembly-line-type operation. Then the first-line supervisor and an engineer came up with a new design for the jobs. Each girl was to assemble an entire hot plate rather than only portions of it, but no other changes were made in the department or in the personnel. There was a drop in controllable rejects, those within the control of the workers, from 23 per cent to 1 per cent in the first six months. Absenteeism dropped from 8 per cent to less than 1 per cent in the same period, and there was a gain in productivity of 84 per cent in the second half of the year. As a result of this study, all routine final inspection was eventually turned over to the assembly workers themselves, and a full-time quality control job was later eliminated. Then because of this and other job enrichment studies, decision making was pushed downward, and the technicians and production workers picked up more responsibility. This created a significant change in the levels and the number of management personnel. It was found also that initial attempts at job enrichment may be extremely difficult in unionized plants in which employees have developed distrust of their management.

Paul, Robertson, and Herzberg (6). These authors report on five studies carried out in British companies. The most relevant one deals with design engineers. The workload was increasing, and new employees were hard to find. People at all levels in the department were being overloaded, and development work was suffering. The following changes were made for the experiment:

1 Each engineer was permitted to judge for himself when and to what extent he should seek advice.
2 Engineers were encouraged to become departmental experts in particular fields.

3 Design engineers were encouraged to follow up completed projects when they thought it appropriate to do so.
4 When authority to allocate work to outside consultants was given to them, the engineers were made responsible for choosing the consultants.
5 Within a sanctioned project no financial ceiling limited their authority to place orders.
6 Design engineers were involved in the selection and placement of designers, and a new employee was assigned to an engineer only if the engineer agreed to accept him.
7 Experienced engineers were asked to make the initial salary recommendations for all their junior staff members.
8 Engineers were allowed to authorize overtime, cash advances, and traveling expenses for their staffs.

Results of the experiment were as follows:

1 Senior managers saw changes in the amount and the kind of consultation between the design engineers and their immediate supervisors. The supervisors' routine involvement with most employees was reduced.
2 Expertise increased in most cases as a result of encouragement.
3 Allowing the engineers to place orders within approved projects proved highly effective. None of the senior managers wanted to revert to the old system.
4 Design engineers had a better feel for the complexities of selection.
5 Allowing the engineers to approve overtime and travel expenses and make salary recommendations produced no adverse effects.
6 Senior managers felt that although none of the motivational changes had any overriding effect and all problems had not been solved, the cumulative effect had been significant.

M. Scott Myers (1). In this case, a company that was losing money on the production of radar units gave the assemblers an opportunity to apply their talents to solution of the problem. The supervisor asked them to suggest ways of lowering the manhours required below the 100-hour break-even point. After a two-hour meeting at which ideas were compiled, discussed, discarded, and selected, members of the group set a goal of 86 hours. They surpassed that goal and achieved a 75-manhour level. Future meetings were expanded to include engineers, inspectors, and assemblers from other lines. The goal-setting sessions continued until the group reached a 41-hour level by year-end.

In another case, janitors and their supervisors took part in a problem-solving, goal-setting process. They first agreed on what constituted proper building maintenance, then took part in planning their own work. The workforce was reduced from 121 to 76 through job bidding and normal turnover. The quality of the work increased, and turnover dropped from 100 per cent per quarter to 20 per cent per quarter. This case illustrates the potential of job enrichment, even for unattractive work.

James A. Lee (7). This author feels strongly that business executives reject theorists' proposals because a change in managerial behavior is primarily a function of cultural change; and as a result, adoption of job-enrichment-type concepts will necessarily be very slow. He suggests an eight-step approach that would maximize the use of behavioral science theories, "however meager" the theories may be. These eight points reflect, to some extent, the reservations expressed by the ten people in manufacturing companies whose views are reported in the next section of this paper.

Thomas H. Fitzgerald (8). This author is doubtful about the application of traditional motivational and enrichment theory, basically because many lack understanding of the seriousness of the motivational problem and because doing something about it is extremely difficult.

The limitations of current approaches to the application of motivational theory are outlined in detail in this article, and the author states that we can expect a persistent alienation of industrial and business manpower. As a way of making long-lasting headway in this area, he suggests a real commitment in industry that goes far beyond commitment to changes in structure, procedures, and certain typical behaviors.

Reports from Manufacturing Companies

Ten people ranging from plant people to corporate staff members were interviewed. In all cases they were employed in management development and training or in salaried personnel or employee research in manufacturing companies. The interviewees and the companies were selected at random and are all located in the Greater Detroit area or have their headquarters there. Six basic questions were asked, and the following includes the questions asked and a summary of the responses. Every effort was made to remove the possibility of identifying any company with any of the responses.

Question A. Are you actively conducting job enrichment programs?

If yes—what types of jobs?

"Hourly material handling jobs."

"An assembly-line job and an instrument panel subassembly job."

"Hourly production press operations."

"Cost accounting non-management positions."

"College graduates."

"All jobs to some degree from hourly production jobs to plant managers."

"Top management job restructuring."

If no—why not?

"There is felt to be neither the money nor a feeling of priority."

"Not a priority at this time, expect it to be in the future."

"Not sure of the general company feeling toward this subject."

"Not a priority. Management is not thinking in this direction as yet; however, the idea is exciting."

Question B. In what areas have you had the most success?

"Material handling in production control."

"Too early to determine."

"Hourly press operators."

How is success measured?

"The number of press strokes went up."

"Thirty per cent drop in scrap."

"Improvements in absenteeism, tardiness, and safety."

"Long-run labor costs."

"Improvements in turnover, absenteeism, quality, and effectiveness."

Question C. In what areas have you had the least success?

"Material handling, when no top management support was given."

"College graduates."

Why the least success?

"Lack of sufficient top management support."

"Top management not involved to the extent required."

Question D. Who influenced your thinking on J.E. the most? (Drucker, Ford, Gellerman, Myers, Herzberg, McGregor, Likert, etc.)

Mentioned three times
Likert

Mentioned twice
Gellerman, Drucker, Odiorne, Herzberg, theorists of little value.

Mentioned once
Ford, Maslow, McGregor, Lawler, Myers, or a combination of all.

Question E. What are the "frontiers" in the field of job enrichment?

Mentioned seven times
Hourly (clerical, assembly, non-assembly, maintenance)

Mentioned three times
Salaried, non-management (administrative, secretarial, clerical)

Mentioned three times
Middle and first-level management

Mentioned once
College work-study groups and graduates

Mentioned once
Top management

Mentioned once
No frontier because of interrelated effect.

Question F. What advice would you have for someone just starting out in J.E.?
(The following presents the highlights of the responses to this question. The order in which the items appear generally follows the sequence of events.)

"Analyze all available material from leading authorities."

"Impart knowledge to the top management."

"Define the scope of company interest."

"Get top management support and commitment in writing in terms of long periods of time and costs."

"Analyze and describe jobs to identify areas of opportunity. Consider new jobs before old ones."

"Make sure that people involved will be available."

"Train management and participants in an appropriate order to gain skills that will carry through the program."

"Make all the related departments and unions knowledgeable."

"Begin projects on a pilot study basis, where most receptive."

"Provide supervisors sufficient time for job enrichment duties."

"Consider using savings from job enrichment programs to pay for future ones."

What Is the Future of Job Enrichment?

The following represents some conclusions that might be drawn from the responses to the job enrichment questionnaire.

There are very few programs actually under way and producing proven results in the companies contacted.

More programs appeared to be in various stages of development.

More than an expected amount of interest was expressed in applying the concepts to management and college graduates.

Lack of company priority was typically given as the major reason for lack of progress.

Genuine interest in job enrichment exceeded action. Within the coming year considerable progress appears to be likely.

While evidence of success was meager at this time, the criteria for measuring success were practical, i.e., those that attract attention in a manufacturing company.

Where there was the least amount of success, there was a lack of top management support and involvement.

There appeared to be no strong tendency to favor the work of one theorist over another. Although a few interviewees appeared to have made extensive reviews of the related literature, some others had not. Since much of the recent material covers applications of the concepts and the opinions of industry-trained authors, it could probably make more of a contribution than it is making at present.

Although the "frontiers" mentioned by interviewees cover the full range from hourly personnel to top management, the major focus is on hourly jobs, for which there may be more easily used criteria attractive to manufacturing management. The number of comments on job enrichment applications for management could indicate that for broad impact or multiple benefit, efforts with management are very desirable.

The many comments received in answer to the question on advice to someone starting out reflect the great concern for the difficulty of applying behavioral science concepts in a manufacturing activity.

The summary of responses to this question could prove to be a very useful guide to anyone now in a job enrichment effort or considering it.

In his article "Organization Change Through Job Enrichment," William Dettleback (9), makes the important comment that many or most management people know that motivation comes from the work itself, but this fact has not made the problem disappear. One of the basic problems is that management is used to, or prefers to see, sound evidence before it supports use of a management technique like job enrichment. This is apparent in the answers to the questionnaire reported on in this study, but the author believes that the difficulty is being reduced by the increasing number of success stories. Success stories in job enrichment could, and probably will, have a considerable effect on some current concepts of management.

As a reduction in the number of workers needed occurs as a result of a job enrichment program, there may be a reduction in the need for some supervisors. Job enrichment could also make it possible to broaden the span of control, and this also would decrease the need for supervisors. But many supervisors complain that they haven't enough time to manage planning, communicating, training, and their other basic functions. If the need for routine decision making and many controls is reduced, they would be freed for their more important work. It is felt that job enrichment can also lead to greater decentralization and smaller autonomous company units.

While it is much more difficult to describe and identify the important interrelationships in management jobs, the real challenge of the future appears to be in application of job enrichment to management. The article, "How Job Enrichment Works at the Middle-Management Level" by Dettleback, Walters, and Ash (10), presents fifteen questions and answers on this topic and considerable support for job enrichment possibilities in management.

Changes in the quantity of output are felt by many to be the major and only important criterion of job enrichment success. But in most cases, results have been primarily in the quality area for the employee efforts affect quality more that than they do quantity. It is felt that improvements in quality resulting from job enrichment would meet with fewer potential problems from the unions than quantity increases would. It is suggested that we look at the full scope of success criteria in judging the job enrichment effort.

Dr. Edward E. Lawler, Yale University, speaking on "Job Enrichment or Enlargement" at a meeting of the Detroit Personnel Management Association on February 19, 1970, stated that unions, where they exist, should definitely be involved in experiments in job enrichment. Giving the union credit where job enrichment experiments are completed is also, he feels, a "must" for management.

The matter of maintainng equitable wages will probably be a concern of the unions in the future, for employees who have completed a job enrichment program may qualify for higher pay grades.

M. Scott Myers, in his article "Overcoming Union Opposition to Job Enrichment" (11) describes four approaches that simultaneously serve the needs of the company and the employees. These successful examples include joint management-union training programs, joint sessions to determine the proper role of each party, joint work simplification programs, extensive company orientation programs, and an actual negotiated agreement to explore ways to improve effectiveness. These examples demonstrate that the "traditional resistance" of unions to job-enrichment-type programs can yield to ingenuity and persistence, and unions can prove to be helpful to those concerned about this matter.

Concern has been expressed for the consistency of Herzberg's basic research on the motivators-hygiene concept. An article "Managers or Animal Trainers—An Interview with Frederick Herzberg" (12) indicates that his original theories have now been confirmed by over fifty studies covering jobs from the lowest level to the highest. This information is evidence of continuing success for job enrichment in the future if studies are well conceived and executed.

Early successes in the application of job enrichment are impressive, but the long-range effects are not known as yet. Indications are that it definitely is here to stay. But neither the theorists nor the company people who apply it can go it alone. It demands the ingenuity and perseverance of both. People contacted in this study in most cases showed a genuine interest in and enthusiasm for the subject as they visualized its impact in the future.

At present, it is the most promising management technique available to produce more satisfying jobs and better utilization of employees at all levels.

References

1 M. Scott Myers, *Every Employee a Manager*, McGraw-Hill Book Company, New York, 1970.

2 Frederick Herzberg, B. Mausner, and B. Snyder-

man, *The Motivation to Work*, John Wiley & Sons, New York, 1959.

3 Robert Ford, *Motivation Through the Work Itself*, The American Management Association, New York, 1969.

4 William E. Reif and Peter P. Schoderbek, "Job Enlargement: Antidote to Apathy," *Management of Personnel Quarterly*, Spring, 1966, pp. 16–23.

5 Edgar F. Huse and Michael Beer, "Eclectic Approach to Organizational Development," *Harvard Business Review*, September–October, 1971, pp. 103–112.

6 William J. Paul, Keith B. Robertson, Frederick Herzberg, "Job Enrichment Pays Off," *Harvard Business Review*, March–April, 1969, pp. 61–78.

7 James A. Lee, "Behavioral Theory Vs. Reality," *Harvard Business Review*, March–April, 1971, pp. 20–28 and 157–159.

8 Thomas H. Fitzgerald, "Why Motivation Theory Doesn't Work," *Harvard Business Review*, July–August, 1971, pp. 37–44.

9 William Dettleback, "Organization Change Through Job Enrichment," *Training and Development Journal*, August, 1971, pp. 2–6.

10 William W. Dettleback, Roy Walters, and Dr. Philip Ash, "How Job Enrichment Works at the Middle-Management Level," *Industrial Relations News*, Chicago, Ill., March, 1971, pp. 1–6.

11 M. Scott Myers, "Overcoming Union Opposition to Job Enrichment," *Harvard Business Review*, May–June, 1971, pp. 37–49.

12 Dr. William F. Dowling, "Managers or Animal Trainers—An Interview with Frederick Herzberg," *Management Review*, July, 1971, pp. 2–15.

17 Control

Control is the appraisal of results to determine how well the other management functions are being carried out. Originally, the only technique used was overall historical appraisal, made by drawing up statements of assets and liabilities, profits or losses, generally at the end of the fiscal year. Thus deviations from plans might proceed very far indeed before management knew they were occurring.

Gradually, however, control systems began providing more exact and more timely information for management, including the following:

Measurements that would show where the organization was falling down (e.g., in products, areas, functions, or divisions). These required a careful segregation of revenues by sources, and the matching of revenues with the corresponding costs.

An accounting of assets, revenues, and costs for legal purposes.

Data that would help each organization unit to understand its problems better. These would include information on the revenue possibilities of different courses of action and the cost implications.

Explanations of the behavior of each element in the business in a timely and useful way.

Control information of these kinds is provided through the reporting systems used in most large and medium-sized corporations. More recently, many have added new features to their control systems, including:

Methods of coordinating decentralized operations.

"Feedback" systems through which shortcomings spark immediate remedial action.

Methods by which the results achieved by particular departments or executives can be matched against their responsibilities.

Investment analysis on the basis of a more sophisticated measurement of results through discounted cash flow instead of "payout periods" and "average rates of return."

The first article in this chapter explains the concept of control and the general methods of achieving it. The second shows in simplified form how financial statements and supporting documents may be used to trace the reasons for deviations from plans.

The next two articles deal with the appraisal of suggested investments by the discounted cash flow method—the first with the technique itself and the second with a possible pitfall if the analysis is not based on the proper figure. The last article points out the importance of a thorough analysis of acquisitions through financial investigations and notes some of the difficulties that companies have experienced through hasty action in this area.

The following article analyzes the nature of control and the reasons for it and points out that there are many different types of control to be used for different purposes. The author, William Travers Jerome, III, was for many years dean of the Business School at Syracuse University.

Kinds of Control

William Travers Jerome, III

The word "control" has the serious shortcoming of having different meanings in different contexts. Most of these meanings are negative ones that connote such things as faultfinding or obedience by subordinates to instructions emanating from superiors. That "control" should evoke these meanings is unfortunate. Control in any broad management sense bespeaks a planned rather than haphazard approach by a society to the employment of both its human and material resources.

Control in its broad or managerial sense can be quite appropriately defined as "the presence in a business of that force which guides it to a predetermined objective by means of predetermined policies and decisions."[1] By "force" presumably is meant (1) management's conviction of the importance of continuous and systematic planning and (2) availability of the skills necessary to perform the planning (i.e., controlling) properly.

Those with engineering backgrounds seem to regard modern systems of managerial control as "strikingly similar to simple servomechanisms of the electromechanical type." Since electromechanical control systems are designed to maintain a level of performance (e.g., temperature) between pre-determined limits, it is assumed that "preventiveness is the essential attribute of a control system. The existence of a control system is justified by its ability to enforce its norms. Precision in the determination of norms is of elemental importance in industrial control."[2] Such a concept of control is highly appropriate for machines or some shop operations. It is far too rigid and uncompromising a concept, however, for the world of people.

For a proper perspective of the meaning of control, it is important to recognize that a whole host of important but relatively mundane controls lie outside of management's customary scope and concern. These other kinds of control help to set a precise pattern of rules and procedures, not unlike those of servomechanisms, to expedite the handling of a firm's routine operations. This particular pattern is known in the accounting trade as the "system of internal control." It should prove both interesting and suggestive simply to classify controls on the basis of the *use* to which a given control is put. The following classification might result:

1 *Controls used to standardize performance* in order to increase efficiency and to lower costs. Included might be time and motion studies, inspections, written procedures, or production schedules.
2 *Controls used to safeguard company assets* from theft, wastage, or misuse. Such controls typically would emphasize division of responsibilities, separation of operational, custodial, and accounting activities, and an adequate system of authorization and record keeping.
3 *Controls used to standardize quality* in order to meet the specifications of either customers or company engineers. Blueprints, inspection, and statistical quality controls would typify the measures employed to preserve the integrity of the product (or service) marketed by the company.
4 *Controls designed to set limits within which delegated authority can be exercised without further top management approval.* Organization and procedure manuals, policy directives, and internal audits would help to spell out the limits within which subordinates have a free hand.
5 *Controls used to measure on-the-job performance.* Typical of such controls would be

[1] "The Planning and Control Concept," *The Controller*, September, 1954, p. 43.
[2] J. V. McKenna, "The Basic Theory of Managerial Control," *Mechanical Engineering*, vol. 77, no. 8, August, 1955, pp. 180 ff.

From *Executive Control—The Catalyst* (John Wiley & Sons, Inc., New York, 1961), pp. 31–34.

special reports, output per hour or per employee, internal audits, and perhaps budgets or standard costs.

6 *Controls used for planning and programming operations.* Such controls would include sales and production forecasts, budgets, various cost standards, and standards of work measurement.

7 *Controls necessary to allow top management to keep the firm's various plans and programs in a balance.* Typical of such controls would be a master budget, policy manuals, organization manuals, and such organization techniques as committees and the use of outside consultants. The overriding need for such controls would be to provide the necessary capital for operations and to maximize profits.

8 *Controls designed to motivate individuals within* a firm to contribute their best efforts. Such controls necessarily would involve ways of recognizing achievement through such things as promotions, awards for suggestions, or some form of profit sharing.

Certain similarities and dissimilarities in these techniques at once appear. For example, there is a preventional or compliance aspect characteristic of the controls in grouping 1 through 3. This grouping consists of the controls used to standardize performance, to safeguard assets, and to insure quality. These controls are really in the nature of directives or procedures that must be followed. Compliance with these is not left to the discretion of anyone using them. Instead, the effectiveness of performance will be judged primarily by the degree of compliance attained.

The second grouping, on the other hand, consists of controls that are intended to provide some elements of latitude to those who are affected by them. They are useful in helping to set the goals, to plan the work, to appraise the performance, and to set the tone for the firm's activity. These controls consist of the remainder of the items on the preceding list. These are the controls designed to set limits for delegated authority, to set norms against which performance can be measured, to facilitate company planning, to keep overall company balance in the interest of optimizing company objectives, and to motivate action.

This "control" classification is striking primarily in the way a number of these controls appear to belong appropriately in either of these two major groupings. Standard costs or budgets, for example, can be used to compel compliance. Thus, they provide the means for management to set the desired level of performance expected of subordinates. Variance of actual from anticipated performance is the signal built into these techniques for flagging possible investigation of the reasons for deviations.

Standard costs, and particularly budgets, are also the principal techniques for reflecting a firm's plans. They provide a method for a given level of management to gauge its own performance. These uses are constructive as they encourage both self-evaluation and the forward look.

Control techniques such as budgets that are interchangeable between the two groupings provide ample room for misunderstanding. When budgets are regarded as "planning," it is questionable whether they should be used to compel compliance. Thus, the score envisioned by a golfer on the first tee is not the same as what he intends to set for his bets! Or, as a further example, when internal auditing is sold to lower levels of management on constructive grounds, its compliance or policeman's role must be exercised with considerable restraint.

There is a second significant thing about the preceding classification. All these control techniques, except for those in the final classification, have one thing in common: each can measure performance.

In other words, each of the controls listed serves as a norm or standard of conduct. Against this standard, actual performance can be compared. Unless such comparison is made, the standards have limited value.

Another way to say this is that "control" is not something intrinsic to a given technique any more than "measurement" is inherent in a given yardstick. "Control" comes from the conscious use of such devices to influence action. This influence (or control) may be in terms of either or both: (1) the thought, the analysis, the planning, and the cooperative effort that go into constructing particular norms or yardsticks, and (2) the corrective action taken when a comparison of results with the projected performance indicates the need.

Controls governing routine and repetitive operation stress compliance, as mentioned earlier. Their primary function, therefore, is to serve in the area of internal control.

Management controls, on the other hand, serve both as a measure of performance and as conditioners of the firm's working environment. The attitudes of planning and of self-evaluation are particularly powerful influences in a firm, for they are among the key forces that contribute to decisive and continuous progress. This capability of any given executive control to motivate constructive action is by all odds its most important characteristic. This contrasts with the compliance or command feature of other types of control.

Whereas the preceding article explained the general nature of control, the following excerpt describes in detail just how financial controls, which are among the most important, are used to determine where deviation from plans has occurred and why. As a part of its customer-service program, International Minerals & Chemical Corporation gathered papers on various aspects of management into a book. The following extract is from one of the chapters in that book. (The author was director of accounting for the corporation.) The financial statements used to illustrate the methods are those of a hypothetical fertilizer corporation (Makmor).

Accounting Controls

Bror R. Carlson

Along with setting up the organization to carry out the activities of the operation, management must set up the controls for appraising the results of the activities.

Here is the comparative Profit & Loss Statement for the 1st quarter of 1960/61–July, August and September, 1960 (Figure 1).

We're not kidding ourselves. We planned on this quarter as being a slow one—sort of a breather after that madhouse we lived in for the 4th quarter of last year.

Let's just briefly go down the report and hit the highlights by comparing actual results with the planned results (Figure 2).

We sold 2,200 tons, which was 100 tons over what we planned.

Our Gross Sales in dollars amounted to $140,000—or $7,300 over plan. Looks wonderful, doesn't it? That's equivalent to $63.64 per ton, or 45¢ per ton over plan. Still looks good!

Now we come to the deductions from Gross Sales. Here's Freight Out. Let's see. We actually spent $9,200—we planned on spending only $5,800. That's an excess of $3,400. Or $1.42 per ton. Already we can smell a rat! But we'll look into that item a little later.

Competitive Allowances? We didn't do badly in this department at all. We had an unfavorable variance of only $100—but 3¢ a ton under plan.

That leaves Net Sales at $127,000, or $3,800 over plan. That's a favorable variance. On a per ton basis, though, it looks different! Net Sales figures out to $57.73 per ton. We planned on netting $58.67 per ton. From this angle,what appeared to be a favorable variance turns out to be an unfavorable variance of almost a dollar a ton!

Let's move to the Cost of Goods Sold section (Figure 3). We have split the total cost into two categories—that part which is at standard, and that part which represents several types of excess costs—what we call variances, that is, variances from standard.

The total for this section is the Cost of Goods Sold, the total of all manufacturing costs, after adjusting for the difference between opening and closing inventories. Here is another area where we slipped. We spent $116,564 when we

From Marketing Division (ed.), *Managing for Profit* (International Minerals & Chemical Corporation, New York, 1961), pp. 285–299.

PROFIT AND LOSS STATEMENT
Three Months Ended September 30, 1960

	Actual		Plan		Variance Favorable (Unfavorable)	
	Amount	Per Ton	Amount	Per Ton	Amount	Per Ton
Tonnage	2,200		2,100		100	
Gross sales	$ 140,000	$ 63.64	$ 132,700	$ 63.19	$ 7,300	$ .45
Less:						
Freight out	9,200	4.18	5,800	2.76	(3,400)	(1.42)
Competitive Allowances	3,800	1.73	3,700	1.76	(100)	.03
NET SALES	$ 127,000	$ 57.73	$ 123,200	$ 58.67	$ 3,800	$ (.94)
Cost of goods sold						
At standard	$ 113,000	$ 51.36	$ 108,000	$ 51.43	$(5,000)	$ .07
Variances-Losses (Savings)						
Purchase price	2,000	.91			(2,000)	(.91)
Material usage	500	.23			(500)	(.23)
Direct labor	810	.37			(810)	(.37)
Overhead	254	.12			(254)	(.12)
COST OF GOODS SOLD	$ 116.564	$ 52.99	$ 108,000	$ 51.43	$(8,564)	$(1.56)
GROSS PROFIT	$ 10,436	$ 4.74	$ 15,200	$ 7.24	$(4,764)	$(2.50)
Selling and administrative expense						
Selling	$ 23,200	$ 10.54	$ 22,200	$ 10.57	$(1,000)	$ .03
Administrative	8,000	3.64	8,000	3.81	-0-	.17
	$ 31,200	$ 14.18	$ 30,200	$ 14.38	$(1,000)	$ .20
NET LOSS	$ (20,764)	$ (9.44)	$ (15,000)	$ (7.14)	$(5,764)	$(2.30)

Figure 1

PROFIT AND LOSS STATEMENT
Three Months Ended September 30, 1960

	Actual		Plan		Variance Favorable (Unfavorable)	
	Amount	Per Ton	Amount	Per Ton	Amount	Per Ton
Tonnage	2,200		2,100		100	
Gross sales	$ 140,000	$ 63.64	$ 132,700	$ 63.19	$ 7,300	$ .45
Less:						
Freight out	9,200	4.18	5,800	2.76	(3,400)	(1.42)
Competitive Allowances	3,800	1.73	3,700	1.76	(100)	.03
NET SALES	$ 127,000	$ 57.73	$ 123,200	$ 58.67	$ 3,800	$ (.94)

Figure 2

	Actual		Plan		Variance Favorable (Unfavorable)	
	Amount	Per Ton	Amount	Per Ton	Amount	Per Ton
Cost of goods sold						
At standard	$ 113,000	$ 51.36	$ 108,000	$ 51.43	$ (5,000)	$ .07
Variances - Losses (Savings)						
Purchase price	2,000	.91			(2,000)	(.91)
Material usage	500	.23			(500)	(.23)
Direct labor	810	.37			(810)	(.37)
Overhead	254	.12			(254)	(.12)
COST OF GOODS SOLD	$ 116,564	$ 52.99	$ 108,000	$ 51.43	$ (8,564)	$ (1.56)
GROSS PROFIT	$ 10,436	$ 4.74	$ 15,200	$ 7.24	$ (4,764)	$ (2.50)

Figure 3

planned on spending only $108,000. That represents an excess of $8,500, or $1.56 per ton.

Subtracting the Cost of Goods Sold line from the Net Sales line, of course, gives us the Gross Profit, or Gross Margin, or Manufacturing Profit.

At this level, we're still on the plus side, it would seem. Anyway, we show a Gross Profit of $10,000 or $4.74 per ton. But let's not forget that we're already stuck with an unfavorable variance of $4,700 or $2.50 per ton over plan. And we still haven't taken into account selling and administrative expenses!

Our selling expenses totaled $23,200, or $1,000 over plan. Administrative expenses held the line at $8,000 because they're pretty well fixed. On a per ton basis in this department, however, we gained just a little—20¢ per ton (Figure 4).

Now what has happened to Gross Profit of $10,000? When we subtract selling and administrative expenses of $31,000, we end up over $20,000 in the hole!

What happened? Let's take up these areas one at a time and dig in a little deeper.

Let's start at the top of our operating statement. Gross Sales were over plan by 100 tons and by $7,300.

Here's a more detailed Sales Analysis By Territory (Figure 5). We've broken it down two ways:

	Actual		Plan		Variance Favorable (Unfavorable)	
	Amount	Per Ton	Amount	Per Ton	Amount	Per Ton
GROSS PROFIT	$ 10,436	$ 4.74	$ 15,200	$ 7.24	$(4,764)	$ (2.50)
Selling and administrative expense						
Selling	$ 23,200	$ 10.54	$ 22,200	$ 10.57	$(1,000)	$ .03
Administrative	8,000	3.64	8,000	3.81	-0-	.17
	$ 31,200	$ 14.18	$ 30,200	$ 14.38	$(1,000)	$ .20
NET LOSS	$ (20,764)	$ (9.44)	$ (15,000)	$ (7.14)	$ (5,764)	$ (2.30)

Figure 4

SALES ANALYSIS BY TERRITORY

Three Months Ended September 30, 1960

	Total		Territory # 1		Territory # 2		Territory #3		Commission	
	Actual	Plan	Actual	Plan	Actual	Plan	Actual	Plan	Actual	Plan
Tons shipped	2,200	2,100	662	600	350	400	594	600	594	500
Invoiced sales	$140,000	$132,700	$42,400	$37,800	$22,200	$25,200	$37,500	$37,800	$37,900	$31,900
Less:										
Freight out	9,200	5,800	3,900	1,500	1,250	1,100	1,800	1,800	2,250	1,400
Competitive allowances ..	3,800	3,700	1,200	1,100	700	700	1,200	1,100		
NET SALES	$127,000	$123,200	$37,300	$35,200	$20,250	$23,400	$34,500	$34,900	$24,950	$29,700
Per ton rates:										
Invoiced sales.................	$ 63.64	$ 63.19	$ 64.05	$ 63.00	$ 63.43	$ 63.00	$ 63.13	$ 63.00	$ 63.80	$ 63.80
Less:										
Freight out	4.18	2.76	5.89	2.50	3.57	2.75	3.03	3.00	3.79	2.80
Competitive allowance ...	1.73	1.76	1.81	1.83	2.00	1.75	2.02	1.83	1.18	1.60
NET SALES	$ 57.73	$ 58.67	$ 56.35	$ 58.67	$ 57.86	$ 58.50	$ 58.08	$ 58.17	$ 58.83	$ 59.40

Figure 5

by Invoiced Sales, that is, in Gross Sales dollars, and by Per Ton Rates.

We've already pointed out the trouble here—Freight Out. In total, it was $3,400 over plan, or $1.42 per ton over plan.

Right away we can see the biggest chunk of this excess—right here in Territory No. 1. Who's the salesman? Good old Fervent. He's a hustler all right! But where is he selling the stuff? In Alaska? We planned on an average of $2.50 per ton freight on sales in Territory No. 1—and it cost us $5.89. That's an excess of $3.39 per ton.

When we checked out Fervent, we found that, for some time, he had been losing some of his accounts that were closer to home base. Instead of replacing them with new accounts in the same areas, he had been drumming up new business almost entirely in the outlying fringes. We've seen the result of such mis-directed efforts.

Analysis of Production Costs

Let's turn to the production end of our business to give you a better picture of just what is involved in pushing our products through the plant and out onto our customer's trucks.

This is shown on the Cost of Goods Sold section of our operating statement. As I mentioned before, we have split the total cost into two categories—that part which is at standard, and that part which represents several types of excess costs. In effect, we've separated the wheat from the chaff.

By ordinary cost accounting methods, we can usually get a pretty good idea of our total costs. But how much help are they in solving our management problems? Usually, by the time we get the historical data, the trail is so cold we need a lot of extra time to run down our prey. And we've gotten pretty far along into the next accounting period, continuing to make the same mistakes. Or we're in the height of our rush season when we really can't spare the time to locate and correct the trouble.

Somewhere among the ordinary accounting reports some of the answers to some of our problems can be found. But it takes a lot of hard, time-consuming work to dig any of it out of the pile. Standard costs can change that situation a great deal.

For the ordinary fertilizer plant, they are arrived at by setting up a profit plan which utilizes per ton rates such as was done three months ago at Makmor. Some of you may ask what good does it do to set these?

What do we really want to know? Does running an adding machine tape of all our costs and then pushing the total button give us the whole answer? Do even a few subtotals really give us much to work with?

Don't we need to know what's real and what's false? What's legitimate and what's illegitimate? What can't be helped and what can be avoided? What's unimportant and what's important?

That's what standard cost can tell us! And we don't have to get too fancy. For most of us, the type of reports we are showing will be adequate. Most important of all, we can learn about our problems as we go—we don't have to wait until it's too late.

Let's sketch a typical operational set-up. What are the four operations required to process raw materials through a fertilizer plant into the hands of the customer?

First, there is the acquiring, receiving and unloading of the raw materials. Second, there is the manufacturing operation, that is, mixing the raw materials into the fertilizer bases. This is work in process. Third, there is the mixing and bagging operation. Finally, there is the shipping operation—shipping finished goods.

You will note that we have carried our materials through each of these operations at standard cost. Why?

Well, let's face it. Does inefficiency make our product worth any more? If we make a $1,000 mistake, can we pass it on to the customer?

We can't sell our mistakes! There just isn't any market for them.

We have pulled out these variances from standard, these excess costs, these mistakes. They are of no value whatsoever to the customer. But they can be worth plenty to us! By bringing them into broad daylight where we can take a good look at them, we can spot the important problems. We can find what's behind them, or underneath them. We can take action!

If we do a reasonably good job of this, we can move in and get them under control. Now here's the Analysis of Purchase Price Variance or the difference between actual purchase prices and what we had planned (Figure 6). This is only a partial list, but there are enough items to show that this kind of a report can be a most useful tool to a manager.

For instance, in the case of Sulphate of Ammonia, Makmor bought 55 tons in this quarter and they actually cost $1,720, whereas the planned or standard cost was set at $1,872. Thus we purchased this material for $152 less than we had planned.

In going down the list, Nitrogen Solutions and 50# paper bags seem to be out of line. The 41.4% Nitrogen Solution cost $1,325 more than planned and the 44.8% solution cost $1,260 more. The 50# bags were over standard by $1,002.

When we dug into this situation, we found that we hadn't adjusted completely to the trend of putting more "N" into "N-P-K." In the past, we had not been using as much nitrogen, and we had an arrangement to buy it by the truckload. Now that we are using more nitrogen, we failed to adjust our buying habits. So we're going to study the possibility of buying our nitrogen by railroad carloads from now on.

Sure, some of us may have noticed this sort of thing just by casual observation. Maybe we even gave it some thought. But we didn't know how important it was getting. That's what a comparison between actual and plan (or standard) by this type of an accounting report can do for us.

It can tip us off early that certain changes in conditions are beginning to cost us some real money. Then we can take care of the matter before it gets out of hand.

When we looked into the bag situation, we found that it wasn't as bad as it appeared. Most of this $1,000 unfavorable variance was the result of failing to correct the standard price when we made a change in specifications. For certain grades, we had decided to change over from paper bags to polyethylene bags, and we should have corrected the standard price accordingly.

Analysis of Material Usage Variance

Here is the schedule which shows an analysis of the Material Usage Variance (Figure 7). Here

ANALYSIS OF PURCHASE PRICE VARIANCE

Three Months Ended September 30, 1960

	Net Tons Purchased	Actual Cost and Freight In	Standard Cost	Purchase Price Variance (Unfavorable)
Sulphate of ammonia	55	$ 1,720	$ 1,872	$ 152
Anhydrous ammonia	156	13,860	13,889	29
41.4% Nitrogen solution	265	15,039	13,714	(1,325)
44.8% Nitrogen solution	420	24,780	23,520	(1,260)
Triple super	735	41,530	41,736	206
Normal super	1,010	21,800	21,715	(85)
60% Muriate of potash	1,586	53,826	53,938	112
80# paper	20,000	$ 2,300	$ 2,293	$ (7)
50# paper	80,000	8,010	7,008	(1,002)
25# paper	5,000	493	492	(1)

Figure 6

MATERIAL USAGE VARIANCE

Three Months Ended September 30, 1960

Materials	Actual Usage (In tons)	Standard Usage (In tons)	Standard Cost (Per Ton)	Actual Amount	Standard Amount	Material Usage Variance
Sulphuric acid	34.5	34.5	$25.00	$ 862.50	$ 862.50	$ -0-
Anhydrous ammonia ...	41.3	41.3	90.00	3,717.00	3,717.00	-0-
Nitrogen solution	53.7	53.7	57.25	3,074.33	3,074.33	-0-
60% muriate potash...	89.7	89.7	$34.12	$3,060.56	$3,060.56	$ -0-
46% triple super	-	84.5	49.00	-	4,140.50	4,140.50
20% r p super	52.0	-	20.74	1,078.59	-	(1,078.59)
Phosphoric acid	36.5	-	85.50	3,120.75	-	(3,120.75)
					(Net Mfg. Variance)	$(58.84)
3 - 12 - 12 standard ..	53.0	53.0	$44.70	$2,369.10	$2,369.10	$ -0-
12 - 12 - 12 prem	32.5	32.5	62.10	2,018.25	2,018.25	-0-
10 - 10 - 10 standard ..	49.0	49.0	59.00	2,891.00	2,891.00	-0-
Bags - 50	81,380	76,000	$82.00 P/M	$6,673.16	$6,232.00	$(441.16)
					(Shipping Variance)	
MATERIAL USAGE VARIANCE					(Total Variance)	$(500.00)

Figure 7

again we have included just a partial list to show some examples.

For 46% Triple Superphosphate, we show a favorable variance of $4,140, and no actual usage (Figure 8, below). For 20% Run-of-Pile Superphosphate we show an unfavorable variance of $1,078, with no standard usage. For Phosphoric Acid, we also show an unfavorable variance of $3,120 and no standard usage. As you can see, this merely represents a case of substituting these two materials for Triple Super. We had a net unfavorable variance of only $58.84. So we just about broke even on the switch.

But substitution of materials can be a very unprofitable decision if we're not careful. We should always check it out very carefully to make sure it won't eat up our profit margin.

Here we go again! 50# paper bags! Here's an unfavorable variance of over $400. We checked into this one and found that it was a case where a certain grade had been bagged and stored in the warehouse too long. This bagged goods had set up so badly that we had to get it out, rework it and re-bag it.

We should point out that by correcting our standard price to allow for the change-over to polyethylene bags, for the rest of the year, it will not show up as a purchase price variance. Instead, this difference will show up as a material usage variance. But this will be a variance we know about and we can footnote this explanation on each quarterly report so that at least this much of the variance is accounted for. Then we just have to watch for any significant excess above this amount. Ordinarily, we freeze our standard costs for the whole year in order to be able to make true comparisons. Then we adjust them at the beginning of each new year, taking our experience and any advance knowledge into account.

Plant Performance Report

Next we come to the Plant Performance Report (Figure 9). Here we have two major areas—Direct Labor and Overhead. We show unfavorable spending balances of $360 for manufacturing the fertilizer bases and $345 for the mixing and bagging operation.

This turned out to be a result of the trouble we had with breakdowns of our pay-loaders and one of our screens.

This shows up under repair materials with the unfavorable variance for the screen that had to be replaced.

Let's not become too pleased with ourselves, either, when we spot a few favorable variances like this $252 for Off-duty Compensation or this $272 for Repair Labor (Figure 10). These costs may just be delayed a little. They may very well catch up with us during the next quarter! This analysis generally shows us spending variances, which could easily be off-schedule a little from the way we planned, as well as being off in amount.

Materials	Actual Usage (In Tons)	Standard Usage (In Tons)	Standard Cost (Per/Ton)	Actual Amount	Standard Amount	Material Usage Variance
60% Muriate potash...	89.7	89.7	$34.12	$3,060.56	$3,060.56	$ -0-
46% Triple super.......	-	84.5	49.00	-	4,140.50	4,140.50
20% r/p super	52.0	-	20.74	1,078.59	-	(3,120.75)
Phosphoric acid.........	36.5	-	85.50	3,120.75	-	(3,120.75)
					(Net Mfg. Variance)	$(58.84)
Bags - 50#...............	81,380	76,000	$82.00 P/M	$6,673.16	$6,232.00	$(441.16)
					(Shipping Variance)	

Figure 8

PLANT PERFORMANCE REPORT
Three Months Ended September 30, 1960

	Direct Labor Standard Rate	Tons Produced	Total Actual	Fixed and Nonvariable Expense	Actual Variable Expense	Standard Allowance	Spending Variance Favorable (Unfavorable)
Mfg. fert. ...	$ .90	2,600	$2,700		$2,700	$2,340	$(360)
Mix & bag ..	.70	2,300	1,955		1,955	1,610	(345)
Ship bulk ...	.50	300	165		165	150	(15)
Ship bag	.95	1,900	1,895		1,895	1,805	(90)
TOTAL DIRECT LABOR			$6,715		$6,715	$5,905	$(810)

Figure 9

As you can see, a plant performance report is just that—it shows how we have performed in different departments.

If we are large enough to have the responsibility in different departments split up among several foremen, we can discuss with each foreman just how he's doing in dollars and cents. Most individual foremen will take pride in making the best showing they possibly can.

You see, one of the benefits of standard cost accounting to show performance is this:

It not only reveals our mistakes—it shows who's doing a good job! That's a common complaint under the ordinary method of operation: "The only time I hear from the boss is when I make a mistake."

This is a good spot to point out that an incentive plan can be geared to the Plant Performance Report, or to selected physical factors that are used in establishing the standards. Then when a supervisor proves that he has done a good job, he doesn't get just a kind word or a pat

	Total Actual	Fixed and Nonvariable Expense	Actual Variable Expense	Standard Allowance	Spending Variance Favorable (Unfavorable)
Overhead					
Supplies	$ 400	$ 100	$ 300	$ 300	$ 40
Wages - Indirect labor	3,960	800	3,160	3,138	(22)
Premium time	288	-	288	334	46
Salaries	3,750	3,750	-	-	-
Off duty compensation	300	125	175	427	252
Associated payroll costs	1,800	400	1,400	1,374	(26)
Depreciation	8,250	8,250	-	-	-
Taxes & Insurance	2,500	2,500	-	-	-
Repair material	4,250	1,002	3,248	2,477	(771)
Repair labor	600	340	260	532	272
Electrical power	385	75	310	260	(50)
Fuel	100	25	75	87	12
Other expense	417	125	292	285	(7)
TOTAL OVERHEAD	$27,000	$17,492	$9,508	$9,254	$(254)

Figure 10

on the back. He gets something that rings the cash register—something he can take home and show his wife.

Now we come to the Analysis of Selling Expenses by Salesman. In total, we were $1,000 over plan (Figure 11, below). Where is it? Where else?

Right here again! Good old Fervent! There's the $1,000—in Fervent's travel expense. We're going to have to straighten that guy out.

Seriously, it usually isn't such a big job to run down the trouble in selling expenses. Whenever they show signs of getting out of line, we can check the expense accounts a little closer and discuss the problems with each salesman.

Balance Sheet

This brings us to the Balance Sheet (Figures 12 and 13). We've been watching a moving picture up until now. Now we'll stop the projector right here and look at a still—a snapshot of how we look on September 30, 1960.

All this activity—where did it get us? Where we'd like to be? Where we planned to be?

Well, let's see. Cash? Not so good, eh? We planned on having $47,000 on hand. But we have only $29,000. We're down over $17,000.

What happened? Well, this looks like part of the answer right here. Our Accounts Receivable are $25,000 higher than we planned! We'd better age our accounts and see if any of them are long overdue. And maybe we'd better keep a sharper eye on a few of these customers.

Our inventories are $10,000 under plan. Ordinarily, a variance like this in the fertilizer business indicates pretty good control—that we aren't over-stocking raw materials or storing manufactured goods at odds with the planned production schedule for this early in the year.

However, if this shortage were to show up just prior to the start of the heavy shipping season, we would look at it with a sharp eye. If we had a shortage in necessary component materials at that time, for example, it would call for immediate action—either to jack up our purchas-

ANALYSIS OF SELLING EXPENSES BY SALESMAN
Three Months Ended September 30, 1960

	Total		Territory = 1	
			Fervent	
	Actual	Plan	Actual	Plan
Tons sold	2,200	2,100	662	600
Direct expenses				
Salaries and commissions	$ 5,000	$ 5,000	$1,500	$1,500
Travel	6,000	5,000	2,500	1,500
Bad debts	1,200	1,200	300	300
Depreciation	750	750	250	250
Auto expense	600	500	200	150
Total direct expenses	$13,550	$12,450	$4,750	$3,700
Indirect expenses pro-rated	9,650	9,750	2,906	2,784
TOTAL SELLING EXPENSE	$23,200	$22,200	$7,656	$6,484

$1,000 OVER

Figure 11

BALANCE SHEET
September 30, 1960

	Actual	Plan	Actual Over (Under) Plan
Current assets:			
Cash	$ 29,750	$ 47,000	$(17,250)
Accounts receivable	250,000	225,000	25,000
Inventories	165,000	175,000	(10,000)
TOTAL CURRENT ASSETS	$444,750	$447,000	$ (2,250)
Property, plant and equipment	$490,000	$480,000	$ 10,000
Less: Reserve for depreciation	149,000	149,000	-
NET FIXED ASSETS	$341,000	$331,000	$ 10,000
Deferred charges	$ 7,000	$ 7,000	$ -
TOTAL ASSETS	$792,750	$785,000	$ 7,750

Figure 12

	Actual	Plan	Actual Over (Under) Plan
TOTAL ASSETS	$792,750	$785,000	$ 7,750
Current liabilities:			
Notes payable	$ -	$ -	$ -
Accounts payable	178,514	165,000	13,514
Federal income taxes	5,000	5,000	-
Accrued liabilities	10,000	10,000	-
TOTAL CURRENT LIABILITIES	$193,514	$180,000	$13,514
Long term debt	$100,000	$100,000	$ -
Stockholders' equity			
Common stock	$420,000	$420,000	$ -
Retained earnings			
Start of the year	100,000	100,000	-
Loss for the quarter	(20,764)	(15,000)	5,764
TOTAL STOCKHOLDERS' EQUITY	$499,236	$505,000	$ (5,764)
TOTAL LIABILITIES AND EQUITY	$792,750	$785,000	$ 7,750

Figure 13

ing program, or to temporarily adjust our selling program until we could properly balance our inventory situation.

For Property, Plant & Equipment, the Balance Sheet shows that we spent $10,000 more than we planned. Here's what happened. We planned on spending $15,000 during the 1st quarter and $3,000 during the 2nd quarter on our new conveyor system. Instead, we not only spent the entire $18,000 to complete it in the 1st quarter—we even spent an additional overrun of $7,000. $3,000 plus $7,000, of course, puts us $10,000 over plan for the 1st quarter.

This is reflected among the liabilities, also (Figure 13). Our accounts payable are $13,000 over plan—which includes the unpaid balance on our new conveyor system.

Our loss for this 1st quarter of $5,764 is reflected in the Retained Earnings section. Naturally, our No. 1 goal is not only to make up this loss in the next three quarters, but to get over into the black and show a healthy profit for the year as a whole.

You have seen how these variances from standard, these excess costs, these mistakes will pop out into plain view where we can spot the important ones—and have the ammunition we need to win our battles.

Always keep this in mind: *A problem that is located and identified is already half solved!*

Here is an example of the way in which control may be used for coordination of decentralized operations, a classic concept developed by an outstanding manager, Donaldson Brown, first for Du Pont and then for General Motors. The following is an excerpt from a memorandum that Brown, then a member of the board of directors at GM, wrote to Alfred P. Sloan, Jr., GM's chief executive.

Coordinated Control

Donaldson Brown

Under the established scheme of decentralization, whereunder the Divisions operated with a high degree of autonomy, it was necessary to consider the long-term interests of the Corporation as a whole and to establish ways and means by which to effect coordinated control. Policies were required to be clearly defined by central authority with conformity insisted upon so that activities of the various Divisions would be directed in the over-all interests of the Corporation and its stockholders. Otherwise it would have been better to break the structure down into segregated units to operate completely independently and with ownership in each passed on initially to the stockholders of GM.

The requirements of coordinated control were observed in many ways, among which might be mentioned the following:

1 Return on investment. The keystone around which revolved the concept of service to the stockholders was the attempt at maximizing return on investment. In order to bring about full awareness of this on the part of division managements severally, a form of monthly financial report was designed and made effective in 1921. The form displays the basic factors leading to the end result of return on investment. The formula, $R = T \times P$[1] tells the story, and the effect from improvement, or the reverse, in any constituent factor is made transparent.

While the form used has been changed from time to time, the basic concept of the formula has remained the same up to the present time.

2 Forecasts. Beginning in 1921 and continuing to the present time, Divisions have been required to submit monthly forecasts of sales, production, and estimated earnings. These are submitted about the 25th of each month and cover a period of three months forward.

3 Reconciliation of division forecasts of production with measured trends of retail sales. Care was exercised in gauging seasonal characteristics as to consumer buying, and with use

[1]Return on investment equals Turnover (of capital) times percentage of Profit on sales.

of the ten-day reports from dealers the validity of divisional forward production schedules was analyzed and tested through intimate collaboration with car division managers, often leading to modification in the days of the buyer's market. Here is where regard for the profit position of dealers was brought to focus.

4 **Field trips in calling on dealers.** In the mid '20's, before Dealer Councils were established, Mr. Sloan inaugurated the plan of periodical field trips in calling on dealers throughout the breadth of the country. On these trips no representative of any car division was included, the purpose being to gain an objective feel of dealer reaction relating to product, factory relationships, potential of the area served by the individual dealer, and any suggestions looking to betterment of the situation from all angles. In meeting with dealers in this way, care was exercised to avoid any infringement upon the prerogatives of the car division concerned.

5 **Visits to divisions.** In the 1920's Mr. Sloan made frequent visits to the car divisions with the purpose of discussing all angles having to do with problems of coordinated consideration, and planting in the minds of division managers the concepts relating to stockholder interests.

6 **Group meetings in central office and relations with operating executives.** In many ways, which will not be dealt with individually, frequent meetings were held in the central office with division managers, sales managers, engineers and others from Divisions in contact with central office staff executives in discussing broad questions of Corporation policy. The objectives sought were to gain direct reflection of viewpoints from those on the firing line, and to give them a role in the concrete formulation of policies, as well as to insure that the policies, when established, were clearly understood. Meetings of this kind were generally conducted in the nature of seminars, rather than for use in the laying down of pronounced policy. In other words, the aim always was to avoid cramming down the throats of those depended upon to carry out policies when defined, something that had not come to be digested and genuinely understood. It was the habit of the presiding officer at these meetings to encourage the exercise of imagination and initiative on the part of others and to have a full and complete discussion, with everyone given an opportunity to express his views. This was the opposite of dictatorship. In some cases this procedure may have resulted in loss of time in the formulation of central policy, but in the long run I am sure that any delay of this kind was beyond doubt for the best interests of the Corporation. I cannot emphasize too strongly the part that this has played in the development of General Motors to its present position.

Among the more sophisticated approaches to control are more accurate methods of appraising the potential profitability of capital investments, especially the use of discounted cash flow, described in this article. The late John G. McLean, once a member of the faculty of the Harvard University Graduate School of Business, was the author of a comprehensive study of the petroleum industry and president of the Continental Oil Company.

Techniques for Appraisal of New Capital Investments

John G. McLean

Reduced to their simplest terms, all capital investments involve a commitment of funds today in the hope of securing income at some future date. To appraise the wisdom of a capital outlay, therefore, the investor needs the answer to two basic questions: (*a*) How much money am I going to get back? (*b*) When am I going to get it? The various devices for measuring the earning power of investments may, therefore, be evaluated in terms of how well they answer these two

From a paper presented to the Sixth World Petroleum Congress, Frankfurt/Main, Germany, June 19–26, 1963.

questions and how they relate the answers to the amount of money committed to a project.

Payback Periods

The simplest, and probably the most widely used, device for measuring investment earning power is the payback period. It is usually computed by dividing the original capital outlay by the anticipated average annual cash income. For example, if an investment of $1,000 is expected to generate (or save) an average annual amount (after taxes but exclusive of depreciation charges) of $250, the payback period is four years.

The payback period, however, is conceptually deficient as a measure of earning power because it gives no indication of how long the investment will continue to generate income *after* the original outlay is recovered or what the amount of such later income may be. In addition, the payback calculation makes no distinction between income received in early years and income received in later periods. It also usually contains an implicit assumption that the income is uniform on an annual basis and will not increase or decrease with the passage of time.

Payback periods have a reasonably satisfactory correlation (inverse) with the true rates of return on investments in cases where (*a*) the incomes are fairly uniform from year to year, and (*b*) the economic lives of the investments are relatively long in relation to the payback periods. In situations where these conditions are characteristically present, payback periods provide a convenient, although rough, device for appraising investment earning power.

Average Rates of Return

A second common method of measuring investment earning power is to calculate an average rate of return, based on the relationship of income after taxes and depreciation to the original capital outlay. For example, assume an investment of $1,000 will have a ten-year life and generate $150 of cash income (after taxes but before depreciation) each year. In this case, a depreciation allowance of $100 would be deducted from the cash income to arrive at an average net income of $50. This figure would then be divided by $1,000 to arrive at an average return of 5% per annum.

This procedure is conceptually deficient in that it attaches the same significance to income received in each year of the project life; that is, it values the $150 received in the first year in exactly the same way as the $150 received in the second and all later years. As a result, the calculation does not arrive at the true rate of return on the investment, but at a slightly lower figure. For example, if a bank loan or mortgage were to be arranged for $1,000 at 5% interest to be amortized in equal installments over ten years, the bank would not charge $150 per annum; a payment of only $129.50 per annum would be sufficient to pay the 5% interest and retire the principal. Alternatively, the payment of $150 per annum generated by the above investment would provide for retirement of the principal plus interest at 8.2% per annum on the balances from time to time outstanding.

Discounted Cash Flow

As a means of avoiding some of the conceptual difficulties noted above, considerable attention has been given in recent years to the discounted cash flow method of measuring investment earning power. In this method, the investor finds by trial and error the discount rate which will make the present value of the anticipated future income equal to the original capital outlay. This calculation, which is made with the assistance of present value tables, establishes the true financial rate of return.

Application of the discounted cash flow technique to an investment of $1,750 which is expected to generate $700 of cash income (after taxes and before depreciation) for one year and then decline in increments of $100 per annum to $300 in the fifth year would proceed as shown in [the] table. In this case, a discount rate of 16% is found to give a present value for the future income which is approximately equal to the original investment. By interpolation, the return on investment is found to be 15.6% per annum, and is taken as a measure of the earning power of the investment.

The value of the discounted cash flow technique in comparison to other methods of measuring earning power, such as those mentioned above, lies in three essential facts:

First, the discounted cash flow method provides a measure of earning power which is comparable with the figures used throughout the financial world for quoting interest rates on borrowed funds, yields on bonds, and various other purposes. It thus permits direct comparisons of projected returns on investment with the cost of borrowed money.

Second, the discounted cash flow method gives reasonably consistent results for nearly all types of investment situations. The payback and average return on investment calculations, on the other hand, provide only approximate measures of earning power, and the amount of over- or under-statement implicit in them may vary from project to project depending on the circumstances.

Third, the discounted cash flow method takes account of the *differences in the time* at which investments generate their income. It is a particularly useful device, therefore, in discriminating among investments that have increasing, decreasing, or level incomes.

One of the chief obstacles to wider application of the discounted cash flow technique has been the apparent complexity of the calculations. Many companies who have had actual experience in the use of the method have found, however, that these difficulties were far less than they anticipated at the outset. Moreover, there are many ways of arranging the discount tables and of simplifying the calculations to permit easy application in practical business situations.

Another limitation of the discounted cash flow method is that in the case of investments yielding high rates of return it is not sensitive to differences in income occurring late in the life of the projects. This circumstance results from the fact that, at high rates of return, distant income is assigned little or no value, even though the amount may be large.

Profitability Index

An adaptation of the discounted cash flow method, known as the profitability index, has gained considerable recognition as a useful tool for measuring the *relative* earning power of investments. In the discounted cash flow method, the investor computes the discount rate which will make the present value of the anticipated income equal to the required capital outlay. To determine the profitability index, the investor discounts the anticipated income at a predetermined rate to establish its present value. The ratio of this present value to the original investment is the profitability index. Profitability indices of less than one mean the project will earn less than the predetermined rate; indices of more than one mean the project will earn more than the predetermined rate.

ILLUSTRATION OF DISCOUNTED CASH FLOW CALCULATION

Original Investment: $1,750
Economic Life: 5 Years

	Cash	Discount @ 14%		Discount @ 15%		Discount @ 16%	
Year	**Income**	**Factor**	**Value**	**Factor**	**Value**	**Factor**	**Value**
1	$700	.877	614	.870	609	.862	603
2	600	.769	461	.756	454	.743	446
3	500	.675	338	.658	329	.641	321
4	400	.592	237	.572	229	.552	221
5	300	.519	156	.497	149	.476	143
	Present values		1,806		1,770		1,734
	Investment		1,750		1,750		1,750
	Difference		+56		+20		−16
	Return on investment			15.6%			

For purposes of comparison among investments, the higher the index, the better the investment.

The predetermined rate employed in these calculations is usually established on a subjective basis. It ordinarily represents a company's "minimum expected" or "normal" earning rate. It reflects such things as past earnings experience, cost of capital, and the risks inherent in the business.

Although discounted cash flow analysis gives a much better picture of the value of an investment than calculations of the payback period or the accounting rate of return, it too may produce inaccurate results, as this article shows. The author, Dr. Williamson, is a member of the faculty of Notre Dame University.

Uncertainty in Present Value Calculations

Robert N. Williamson

It is generally agreed that discounted cash flow (DCF) techniques for evaluating capital expenditures are superior to other more established criteria such as payback and the accounting rate of return. DCF techniques, however, are usually presented to accountants in a manner—i.e., with an assumption of certainty—which is not entirely applicable to real world situations. Typically, this is done either by ignoring the problem of uncertainty or by using the means of probability distributions in the DCF calculations. It is not generally realized that the use of single-valued estimates (the means) in place of the probability distributions, in addition to imparting a false sense of accuracy, will in most situations lead to biased estimates of the net present value of a proposed investment project and thus introduce the possibility of incorrect decisions.

This possibility can best be seen through illustrative problems. For example, consider the investment opportunity described in Exhibit 1. Using the means of the relevant variables as the single-valued estimates, this project would have a net present value at a cost of capital of 10 per cent of $81.60. Exhibit 2, however, presents the expected present value of this project taking account of the distribution of possible values for the useful life of the asset (N) and the yearly net cash flows (S). It can be seen from Exhibit 2 that the expected net present value ($53.40) is less than net present value computed using single-valued estimates ($81.60).

An analysis of Exhibits 1 and 2 indicates that there is a distinction to be made between the present value of the expected values (Exhibit 1) and the expected value of the present values (Exhibit 2); it is contended here that the latter approach yields superior results and that the $53.40 calculated in Exhibit 2 does, in fact, represent the average net present value which could be expected from undertaking a large number of similar projects.

It should be pointed out that the different results in Exhibits 1 and 2 are directly related to the nature of discounting itself. As assumed in Exhibit 1, the expected value of the service life is five years, with equal probabilities of an actual life span being four to six years. Thus, in Exhibit 2, equal weight is given to the present value (PV) of the combinations which include a four-year life and those which include a six-year life. The DCF techniques, however, introduce an additional weighting factor; and thus the PV's of the cash flows do not change in direct proportion to the changes in service life, *which are assumed when single-valued estimates are used*, as in Exhibit 1. In fact, the uncertainty as to the actual service life is the only factor causing the difference between the two computed net PV's in these exhibits; that is, the uncertainty as to the

EXHIBIT 1 INVESTMENT A

Variable	Possible Values	Probability of Value (P)	Expected Value (E)
Current Cost (C)	$7,500	1.00	$7,500
Yearly Net Cash Flows (S)	$1,900	.3	$ 570
	2,000	.4	800
	2,100	.3	630
	E(S)	1.0	$2,000
Useful Service Life (N)	4 years	.25	1 years
	5	.50	2.5
	6	.25	1.5
	E(N)	1.00	5.0 years

Net Present Value (NPV) using C,E(S), E(N) at 10% = $81.60

yearly net cash flows does not contribute to this difference—because the PV's of the cash flows *do* change in direct proportion to changes in those flows.[1]

Exhibit 3 illustrates this point. A similar computation of expected net present value of another project is shown there. Investment B is similar to A except that there is no uncertainty surrounding the yearly cash flows—they are known to be $2,000. There is uncertainty as to the actual service life, however, just as before. It can be seen that the expected net PV of Investment B is the same as A ($53.40), even though there is this assumption as to certainty of B's yearly net cash flows. This indicates that the uncertainty about useful service life is the cause of the difference described above. This differ-

[1]Using single-valued estimates instead of the distribution of possible future discount rates will also introduce bias; in the examples, however, the applicable discount rate is assumed to be known with certainty.

EXHIBIT 2 INVESTMENT A

Possible Combination of Values N	S	Probability of Combinations (P)*	Present Value of Combinations (10%) (PV)	Expected Values (E)
4	1,900	.075	$6,022.81	$ 451.711
4	2,000	.100	6,339.80	633.980
4	2,100	.075	6,656.79	499.259
5	1,900	.150	7,202.52	1,080.378
5	2,000	.200	7,581.60	1,516.320
5	2,100	.150	7,960.68	1,194.102
6	1,900	.075	8,275.07	620.630
6	2,000	.100	8,710.60	871.060
6	2,100	.075	9,146.13	685.960
		1.000		$7,553.40
			Current Cost	7,500.000
			E(NPV)	$ 53.40

*P = P(N)P(S); this assumes N and S are independent.

EXHIBIT 3 INVESTMENT B

N	S	P(N)	PV(10%)	E
4	2,000	.25	$6,339.80	$1,584.95
5	2,000	.50	7,581.60	3,790.80
6	2,000	.25	8,710.60	2,177.65
		1.00		$7,553.40
			Current Cost	7,500.00
			E(NPV)	$ 53.40

ence in general will increase as the variance of the expected service life increases.[2] An example is shown in Exhibit 4; the expected net PV of Investment C is there calculated to be negative—that is, C is unprofitable at a 10 per cent cost of capital. Investment C is identical to B except for a larger variance in the expected service life; thus, the net PV calculated using single-valued estimates would be positive.

Three Means Identical

A comparison of Exhibits 1 and 4 illustrates the possibility of making an incorrect decision when single-valued estimates are used. The net PV calculated using the means of the relevant variables for Investment C will be the same as that of A and B because the means are identical for all three projects. Conventional DCF analysis would thus indicate that C be accepted. Exhibit 4, however, shows that if many projects identical to C were accepted, they would on the average be unprofitable.

An analysis similar to those shown in Exhibits 2 and 4 could be made for each investment project as the opportunity arises. Often, however, because of the wide range of possible variables and because of the probability of strong dependence among these variables, it is more efficient to perform simulations, either manually or with the aid of the computer. The simulation approach is an ideal one for incorporating into the analysis probability distributions which are either assumed (such as a normal distribution) or which are developed from the firm's actual experiences. These simulations can be designed to estimate the probability of various outcomes and thus serve as a means to evaluate the risk inherent in a particular project. For those cases where there is uncertainty about the project's life span, these same simulation methods yield the additional benefit of giving an *unbiased* estimate of the net present value of the project.

[2]The difference will decrease as the expected life of the project increases, all else (including the variance of N) being constant.

EXHIBIT 4 INVESTMENT C

N	S	P(N)	PV(10%)	E
2	2,000	.05	$3,471.00	$ 173.55
3	2,000	.10	4,973.80	497.38
4	2,000	.20	6,339.80	1,267.96
5	2,000	.30	7,581.60	2,274.48
6	2,000	.20	8,710.60	1,742.12
7	2,000	.10	9,736.80	973.68
8	2,000	.05	10,669.80	553.49
		1.00		$7,462.66
			Current Cost	7,500.00
			E(NPV)	$−37.34

The discounted cash flow method—with or without the refinement advocated in the last article—is perhaps most commonly used when a company is considering a capital expenditure to improve its own performance by, say, purchase of a new machine or expansion of a plant. The accounting pitfalls in the acquisition of another company—particularly one in an unrelated field—may be much more numerous, however, as the following article indicates. The author is a staff reporter for *The Wall Street Journal*.

Buyer Beware—Companies Acquiring Others Sometimes Find Less than Meets the Eye

William M. Carley

After acquiring an import firm recently, a big conglomerate began looking into its purchase more closely. While the importer dealt mainly in metals, its books also showed a series of mysterious transactions totaling some $80,000.

"When we checked, we found the importer's president had been using company funds to buy art works for his living room," says an executive of the conglomerate. As a result, he adds, the conglomerate reduced the number of its shares it was paying for the import firm.

Though the amount of money involved was relatively minor, this incident underscores a major problem. Companies on the merger trail are encountering some unpleasant surprises after they complete acquisitions.

The surprises lurking in acquired companies range from accounting hanky-panky to products that turn out to be unpatentable to huge shortages in inventories. The losses involved can be staggering.

Whittaker Corp., the Los Angeles conglomerate, has just finished writing off a $6 million inventory loss in Crown Aluminum Industries, an acquired division. Ashland Oil & Refining Co., as a result of alleged fraudulent maneuvers by a recently acquired subsidiary, sued the former owners for nearly $10 million in damages.

Ignorance Hurts

While it's hard to pinpoint the frequency of such donnybrooks—many acquiring companies quietly swallow their pride and their losses—a growing number of court suits around the country indicate they're common. And some merger consultants say they're widespread.

"It's happening all the time," says Lon Casler, partner in a Providence, R.I., merger and financial consulting firm.

Why aren't companies checking out proposed acquisitions more thoroughly before they buy?

One reason, says Carter Braxton, a New York merger consultant, is that antitrust laws are forcing companies to make acquisitions in industries other than their own. As a result, he says, "companies are buying operations in industries that they don't know anything about, and they're bound to overlook things."

Another reason for the lack of thorough investigation, some contend, is the advent in recent years of the "corporate director of acquisitions," or an individual of similar title. One merger consultant describes the job this way:

"Typically a company takes some young, ambitious Harvard MBA and puts him in charge of acquiring companies, before he even knows how to run one. Then he's out to make a name for himself, so he has to make an acquisition a month—any kind of an acquisition—or he feels he's a failure. Of course, he just doesn't take the time or have the experience to make a thorough investigation."

Unable to Back Out

The haste involved in acquisitions—often to beat a competitive bidder—also causes companies to overlook problems. McCormick & Co., the spice maker, apparently made this mistake when it purchased a small food processor.

A key asset in the proposed acquisition was a supposedly unique food-processing machine. McCormick's attorneys, after reading a patent application for the machine and doing other legal research, concluded it was probably patentable—but McCormick hadn't had a chance even to look at the unit. Other companies were interested in buying the food-processing business, however, so McCormick pushed negotiations to completion anyway.

After the acquisition, McCormick discovered the machine wasn't brand new, but had been purchased from another company and then modified. And it wasn't working in the way described in the patent application.

McCormick sued, seeking to rescind the acquisition. But the U.S. Court of Appeals in Richmond, Va., ruled that, "apprehensive that further delay might jeopardize the agreement, McCormick saw fit to forgo" checking the machine itself, and so had no right to rescind its purchase.

A Quiet Settlement

Buyers may also get hurt when an owner "dresses up" his company for sale. Consider the hapless tale told by Carpenter Technology Corp. in papers it has filed in U.S. District Court in Philadelphia.

According to the papers, Gardner Cryogenics Corp. of Bethlehem, Pa., had been claiming it was a leader in cryogenic (supercold) techniques, particularly in making powerful magnets. Gardner even announced sale of a magnet to a German firm, the largest ever used for its particular application. Production of the magnet was "a major step forward in . . . U.S. technology," a Gardner press release trumpeted.

Carpenter, a maker of specialty metals, was intrigued with the idea of diversifying into such a glamorous field, and it acquired Gardner. Afterwards, Carpenter claims, it found Gardner was no leader in cryogenics. Indeed, many of the Gardner products made by the process didn't even work right, it was said. The big magnet shipped to Germany hadn't worked right either, Carpenter says, and as a result Gardner had quietly promised to ship a second one free of charge—and at a substantial loss.

Carpenter sued William Gardner, former president of the cryogenic concern, for $6 million in damages. The case was settled out of court last year, with Carpenter paying a sharply reduced price for Gardner Cryogenics.

The most dangerous hazard for a purchaser, of course, is a seller engaged in outright fraud. Mr. Casler, the merger consultant, says one president trying to sell his small company kept three sets of books.

"The set for the Internal Revenue Service showed very little profit, and the set for the president's minority partners showed only a little more. Then the guy tells me, 'Come here, and I'll show you how much this business really makes,'" Mr. Casler relates. "I walked away from that deal in a hurry."

Then there's the probably apocryphal story going round about the nail company up for sale. When accountants for the purchaser checked inventory, they tried to lift boxes of nails from the warehouse floor and when they wouldn't budge, the accountants figured they were full. But the boxes were empty. They had been nailed to the floor.

One of the most complicated alleged frauds is described in a complaint filed in Houston's U.S. District Court by Ashland Oil against Thomas Morrow, ex-chairman of Wanda Petroleum Co., who sold that liquefied gas company to Ashland Oil.

After the acquisition, Ashland says in its suit, it found an inventory shortage—11.3 million gallons of gas worth about $644,000. "At the direction of T. C. Morrow . . . the documents reflecting such losses were . . . concealed," it's alleged.

Ashland also charges that around the time of acquisition, Wanda attempted to boost its sales and profits (and hence the price Ashland would pay for the company) by a series of fake transactions.

Wanda allegedly made fake sales to real companies in some cases. For example, Wanda prepared bills for $140,000 worth of gas supposedly sold to Sun Ray D-X Oil Co. The bills were never sent, but the "profit" from the transaction was rung up, Ashland charges.

In other cases, it's alleged, Wanda made fake gas sales at high prices to one or two dummy corporations, which in turn made fake gas sales at low prices back to Wanda. Because of the advantageous prices, the effect would be to create fictitious profits for Wanda.

Complicated Deals

The transactions seemed so farfetched however, that lawyers spent weeks questioning Harold Lee, Wanda's former accountant, in a pretrial deposition. Mr. Lee told the accountants that two of the dummy corporations were Texas Petro Gas Co. and Norway Corp. The lawyers, still puzzled over the circular deals, questioned Mr. Lee further:

Q. You don't mean (the money came) back to Wanda?

A. Yes, sir. . . . These (Wanda) checks . . . totaling $491,400 were (first) issued to Texas Petro Gas Co. in payment of their own invoices and to my knowledge those same funds were (then) used by Texas Petro Gas to go to the Norway Corp. . . .

Q. (And afterwards), the Norway Corp. paid Wanda Petroleum Co.?

A. That's right. . . . In other words, Wanda Petroleum Co. paid out (money) and turned right around and received it back.

What about the gas involved in such transactions? Mr. Lee was asked later.

A. Item No. 1 here shows (the gas) was sold to Norway and withdrawn from (Wanda's) inventory—seven million gallons.

Q. It wasn't actually withdrawn?

A. No, but it was shown as being withdrawn.

Q. And that was a fictitious withdrawal?

A. Right.

Q. So, in order to clear that, you had to show a receipt into inventory? Is that right?

A. Right. That's right, and that's what this is . . . "Into inventory from Texas Petro, seven million gallons," which shows that this seven million that fictitiously moved out fictitiously moved back in, and so physically it never moved.

Mr. Morrow vigorously contested Ashland's charges, and the case was settled out of court last month. Terms of the settlement weren't disclosed.

Not Cheap

To avoid getting stung in the future, acquiring companies are increasingly seeking outside help. Most major companies now employ their outside auditing firm to check the books, inventories and other financial records of a company to be acquired. Some also hire general business consultants. For example, EG&G Inc., a Bedford, Mass., electronics firm, often hires Arthur D. Little.

A general business consultant might conduct 25 to 50 telephone interviews and a dozen personal talks, both with executives at the company to be acquired and with their competitors and customers. Products, markets, executive strength and the competition are sized up.

The result might be only a 12-page report that took two or three weeks to complete, but it doesn't come cheap. One company says it pays its consulting firm $7,000 for such a report on small acquisitions.

Consultants' fees on major acquisitions can go far higher. In one recent acquisition, each of the two companies involved hired both management consultants and investment bankers to study the deal. Arthur D. Little, one of the consultants involved, says its bill and the investment bankers' bill for just one of the companies added up to over $100,000. (Even so, many companies consider outside help cheap at the price if it can aid in avoiding a bad acquisition that might cost millions.)

There's nothing, however, like a good sharp inside auditor to check a proposed acquisition. Chamberlain Manufacturing Corp. of Chicago discovered that recently. Chamberlain's inside accountants found huge inventory shortages earlier this year at Crown Aluminum Industries, which Chamberlain was in the midst of buying from Whittaker Corp. for over $12 million in cash and notes.

Chamberlain quickly rescinded its purchase. Whittaker, which had acquired Crown Aluminum itself in 1967, has hired a team of investigators who are still trying to figure out what happened to the inventory.

18 Innovation

More than fifty years ago, the great economist Joseph A. Schumpeter drew attention to the pivotal role of innovation in all areas of management (see Chapter 1). And innovation is perhaps much more important today than it was at the time he wrote, for the world is changing much more rapidly than it was at that time.

One type of innovation, and a type that many companies place great emphasis on, is invention, the development of new or improved products. Thus a great many companies have research laboratories that carry on both basic and applied research. (The former is aimed at the development of new principles, the extension of human knowledge, and the latter at translating basic research into useful products.) And since corporations have far more resources to devote to research than individual inventors are likely to possess, many people believe that in the future they will be the chief source of new discoveries and inventions. The social implications of this trend are examined in the first article in this chapter.

But innovation is not necessarily the invention of a new product; it may be a new idea that will be useful in, say, marketing, organization, control, or some other management area. For this reason, some companies are using special techniques to encourage innovation on the part of all their management personnel. This trend is discussed in the second article in this chapter. Following is an article on one of these techniques, which has both supporters and detractors.

The next two articles deal with applications of innovation. The first is an analysis of product development and its difficulties; the second, an account of the career of an innovating manager who has been responsible for both technical advances and original methods of management.

The final paper makes the important point that a company should not limit its innovations to those it can develop itself, that it is often wise to engage in "imitative innovation" in order not to be outdistanced by competitors.

The large amounts industry has been spending on research and development have meant increasing institutionalization of the field. While individual inventors still exist, they account for a diminishing proportion of the total number of inventions. Here the late Prof. Jacob Schmookler of the University of Minnesota considers the social implications of this trend and the possible innovations in public policy that are needed in consequence.

Innovation in Business

Jacob Schmookler

The nation's business firms, not the independents [i.e., the independent inventors], are the principal source of contemporary technological progress. The increasingly greater role of the business firm is suggested by the fact that the number of patents issued to firms roughly doubled in each decade from 1900 to 1930. Such patents exceeded those to independents for the first time in the early 1930's, and no threat to the lead of business in invention has appeared since.

One so inclined may lament the decline of the free-ranging independent and his replacement by the captive inventor of the corporate laboratory. Yet in the face of the team research, expensive equipment, and lengthy projects needed to exploit the potentialities of modern science, such a shift was inevitable.

Moreover, the change to corporate invention appears to have brought with it some important but little-noted economic benefits. According to a study by Barkev Sanders and Joseph Rossman for the Patent, Trademark and Copyright Foundation of George Washington University, between 50 and 60 per cent of corporate patented inventions are used commercially, a ratio substantially higher than that for the inventions of independents. These benefits are probably explained primarily by the closer contact of corporate inventors with the needs of industry and the greater confidence their corporate superiors are likely to feel in their ideas.

[But] two major questions must be asked. (1) Are all corporate RD programs worthwhile? And (2) are firms of large size essential for modern invention and innovation?

Research is ordinarily a social waste if it seeks (a) to make a product worse or (b) to discover what is already known. The first of these requires only brief discussion and we turn to it.

One occasionally hears the claim, for example, that nylon stockings or razor blades are not as durable as they used to be. The inference is then drawn that products are deteriorated to increase sales. At face value, this is a socially objectionable practice, and any research designed to achieve it wastes research talent which could be put to better use. The infrequency of the charge of product deterioration, however, suggests the practice is uncommon, if it exists at all. If this assumption is correct, the implication is that certain social defenses discourage it.

The surest social defense is a competitive economy. Under competition businessmen gain customers when they offer a better product and lose them if they offer an inferior one. Purposeful product deterioration, moreover, runs the danger of violating the antitrust laws. An informed consuming public also discourages the practice.

Finally, strange as it seems, product deterioration is sometimes desirable. A Cadillac is better than a Chevrolet, but if we had only the former it would be worth developing the latter. The loss in quality would be more than offset by the reduction in cost. Because consumers probably would not pay what it costs to produce an outstandingly good article, such product deterioration is in the public interest. Over time and under competition, methods and products both improve, and products of good quality tend to be replaced by better ones at the same or lower prices.

The second variety of socially wasteful research, the effort to discover what is already known, is undoubtedly much more important.

From "Technological Progress and the Modern American Corporation," in Edward S. Mason (ed.), *The Corporation in Modern Society* (Harvard University Press, Cambridge, Mass., 1960), pp. 146–148, 150, 155–159, 165.

Research to discover what is actually known may be undertaken intentionally or unintentionally. Few researchers know everything in their own fields. They thus may unknowingly recreate what has been created before.

Intentional duplication of effort is an inevitable result of the patent system and industrial secrecy. Companies carry on research to improve their products and processes in order to outdo each other in the competition for the consumer's dollar. If they shared results with rivals, they would lose what they hope to gain. Hence, they tend to keep their results to themselves through patents or secrecy. Few of the best patents are licensed to others. If rivals want to stay in the running, they too have to improve their products or processes. In consequence, much industrial research—just how much cannot be said—is merely devoted to finding another way of doing what can, from a technical standpoint, already be done.

While duplicative inventive activity occasionally turns up something better than the original, usually only a reasonable facsimile of the original is produced. The same effort spent to improve the original method might have added more to society's fund of knowledge. But a rival will not improve another's invention, since use of the improvement would probably entail patent infringement, although he might improve on the original and take out a patent to keep his rival from having it. The patent system and industrial secrecy thus induce much research intended to duplicate rather than to improve existing technology.

Indeed, the patent system assures that much research is based not on the latest technical knowledge but on that of at least seventeen years ago. Except for its novel features, an invention may embody only knowledge already in the public domain (except for more recent knowledge patented by the inventor or his employer). Patented knowledge is closed to the public until the patent right expires, and the term of patents in this country is seventeen years.

A second and perhaps greater waste follows from the first. Patents and industrial secrets, by closing off much of the most advanced technology, limit most firms to making inferior goods with inferior methods.

The patent system, moreover, gives signs of breaking down. Firms expanded their RD activities greatly over the past two decades, but their patenting increased hardly at all. More and more, firms seem to patent only what they have little hope of keeping secret. Thus the objective of disclosure is poorly served. Their research is guided less by the possibility of patents than by the pressures of competition. While they are pleased to have patents when introducing new products, they usually rely for protection not on them but on beating their rivals to the market. And more often small firms are kept out of industries by insiders' patents than they are enabled to enter through force of their own.

The principal alternatives to the present system are compulsory licensing and the payment by the government of bounties to inventors or their backers, the inventions thereafter being freely available to all.

If it could be effectively administered, the bounty scheme is almost certainly superior to its alternatives. Compulsory licensing involving payment of "reasonable" royalties would place a burden on the application of the latest technology and therefore discourage its use. The bounty scheme, by contrast, by making new technology free, would place it in this respect on a par with old technology and not discourage its use. No incentive for inventing around new inventions would remain, and duplication of research effort would be correspondingly reduced. Compulsory licensing, by curtailing inventors' rights below those they now have, would discourage invention and, with respect to such inventions as were made, encourage secrecy. Large enough bounties, on the other hand, might encourage both invention and disclosure well beyond present levels.

Whether the public will be willing to pay firms enough to induce them to turn their inventions over to the public is a serious question. Would the $100,000,000—say—paid each year, under a bounty system, to Du Pont or General Electric become a political issue? If the Soviet continues to catch up, perhaps not.

Another method of eliminating duplication would be to have the government carry on industrial research and turn the results over for industry to apply. However, if private industry also continued to engage in research, duplication would be greater than ever. If the government's program were so extensive as to eliminate private research, then the benefits resulting from the present close proximity of industrial research to industrial operations would be lost.

Partly because the corporation, not the woodshed or basement, has become the major seedbed where new ideas sprout, new and unsolved problems of public policy have arisen. But beneath the changes and the problems they have brought, the historic forces of American society continue at work. Major faults in America's present scientific and technological organization, if faults there be, lie not in the private sector but in the realm of public policy. This survey suggests that the problems concern the patent system and the scope and character of *public* support for scientific and technological research. The major defects in the private sector's technological performance—that is, the duplication of research effort entailed by the withholding of advanced technology from rivals—result not from private malfeasance but from public policy. The remedy thus will be distilled from changes in public policy.

The thesis of this article is that innovation need not be a matter of luck, that there are techniques for developing creativity, even among people who do not ordinarily think of themselves as creative or inventive. And as the author points out, a good many firms are making use of the techniques and are developing new ways of doing things in consequence. Dr. Barrett, formerly professor of management at York University in Canada, is now president of Management Concepts Limited, a Canadian management consulting firm that specializes in the management of change.

Guideposts to Creativity and Innovation

F. D. Barrett

Innovation, like salvation, was once thought to be largely a matter of prayer and inspiration. However, today we know that innovation not only *should* be but *can* be managed.

By *managed innovation*, we mean innovation that is made to happen. We mean innovation that is purposefully and consciously directed toward carefully thought out innovation goals.

The steps in managing innovation are: (1) search the environment for the new markets being produced by change; (2) single out a market opportunity thus revealed; (3) set an objective, with a target date for what kind of innovation is needed; (4) plan a strategy and a program for inventing and developing the new service or product (increasingly today, a new *service*); (5) organize appropriate innovation groups and think-tanks to work on the innovation program, select and appoint members and leaders; (6) choose appropriate creativity methods to use such as bionics, synectics, morphology or brainstorming; (7) go to it; (8) periodically review and revise strategy, organization and methods in order to stimulate progress toward successful attainment of the objective.

Managing innovation is the main job of managers, particularly when constant change is needed to keep up not only with competitors but with changing market and societal demands.

Under these circumstances, the main measure of a manager's performance is how much and how well does he change the operation for which he is responsible.

If a year after having taken office, a manager has not successfully introduced some major changes, he has failed. He has allowed his products, his services or his methods to obsolete by exactly one year. It is then only a matter of time before his operation will be hopelessly obsolete. In most of today's organizations, about three years of noninnovative inertia is enough to produce ruin.

Even when innovation was not necessary as a tactic for adapting to external change (if indeed

From the *S.A.M. Advanced Management Journal*, October, 1973, pp. 8–16. Reprinted by permission of the author.

this were ever so) innovation was man's only tool for improvement. As long as old ways are used, only old results can be produced. There can be no advance, no improvement. There is an inexorable logic that says that improvement can come only from change, from innovation. This is a principle that governs the universe as surely as the law of cause and effect does.

Innovations and change do not always produce improvement, of course. The test of a manager (or a professional or technician today) is: does he produce *improvements* through innovation and what is the value of those improvements?

Very few managers have ever been told that their job is innovation. Very few see it that way even today. Thus it should be little surprise that the products, services and methods of so many organizations are falling badly behind and causing the organizations to be increasingly useless to modern society.

In the past, without it ever having been made explicit, the message to managers was clear: "improve efficiency." In other words, don't change things, just carry on the existing system but see that the operation is carried out with fewer mistakes or with less cost by making people work harder, faster or more carefully. There was never any suggestion that the manager should innovate. Indeed, if anything, the message was "don't innovate," "don't rock-the-boat," "don't take chances."

Many organizations today have successfully trained a generation of managers *not* to innovate change or improve things. They now find themselves seeking to replace them (often through early retirement strategies) with "new blood." However, many of the new replacements are no more innovatively-oriented than their predecessors. If the rules of the game are being changed, it is necessary for the old players and the new players to know it. Organizations need to enunciate their philosophies of innovation, change and improvement and convey to people what this philosophy means in terms of concrete job requirements.

•

One's viewpoint governs what one sees. Therefore, as long as one has fixed views, one can never see anything new. The secret of innovation is the ability, and the readiness, to look at things in many different ways. This ability is what is meant by "flexibility," a term often used but seldom explained.

What is an "airline"? Is it a transportation company? From one point of view, "yes." Is it a communication facility? Most certainly for businessmen travelling intercity for the sole purpose of meetings. (Think what three-dimensional, color T.V. communication facilities may do to the "airlines" in this regard). Is it a leisure-pleasure business enterprise? Definitely, so far as the tourist is concerned.

What is a hospital? A place to cure illness? A place in which people die? A place to *prevent* illness? A place to keep doctors and nurses employed? An extension of the home? A place for people to be born? A place for businessmen to earn money? (privately-owned hospitals) A place to treat adults like children? A place to put the problems caused by urban-industrial stress and illness? An authoritarian hierarchy exploiting immigrant labor? What? How do you see it? If you are on the Board of Directors of a hospital, do you see all its facets? Do you have an image of what it *should* be? What it could be?

Only the executive who looks at the whole picture, from a multiplicity of viewpoints, can apprehend his operation fully and see the opportunities for innovation and change. At your next management meeting, if you want to open up some real discussion (and controversy) get the group to list on a flip-chart all the different things they see your organization to be, then ask what it should, or could be, five years hence.

•

Percipience is a primary requirement in a world of change. It means the ability to see what is happening. To perceive truly and deeply is not all that easy. We need to perceive not only what's on the surface but what's underneath. To recognize that population is growing or air travel is increasing is easy. These are physical, concrete phenomena.

But supposing that this same growing population is developing a distaste for regimentation whether in the classroom or on the job. Do we see it? Such new sound attitudes would call for a radical re-orientation of education processes and discipline, leadership and administration.

Perceiving such social phenomena is an act of "people perception" rather than "thing" perception. But the majority of executives are "theory X." They are concerned more with power, production and self than with people. Few are humanists. By and large, the executive is neither poet nor sociologist. Those few who do have sound percipience see where it's at today and adjust their policies to respond to the new values and attitudes. If we can take what they say in the ads seriously T.R.W. and 3M perceive today's people needs rather clearly.

•

To perceive and discover what is really in the external social-economic environment has led to monitoring and scanning functions being created for top management echelons. Their aim is to detect new factors appearing in the environment. For example, Bell Canada, we've heard, now has a Vice-president of Environmental Studies.

Executive myopia is an increasing liability in today's world where the real things that are happening are not on the surface but lie more obscured from view within the heart of the human being. Executives who have eyes and cannot see and ears and cannot hear, are hazards. A new society is trying to come to life in the post-industrial last third of the twentieth century. Executive myopics who don't see what it's all about are already causing great distress and, in some cases, destroying their enterprises albeit by inadvertence.

Creativity in MBO

Management by Objectives is an excellent vehicle for getting creative, innovative approaches working. Creativity comes into MBO at several stages.

1 *Stage one* is the creative discovery of opportunities and challenges that give rise to the objective. Seeing a new market, a new need, a use for some new technical invention, are all acts of creative imagination.
2 *Stage two* is the creation of new missions for the organization. In a world of change, the institution which survives is the one capable of generating new missions.
3 *Stage three* is imaginative construction of specific new objectives to respond to the new opportunities and to translate the new missions into operational reality.
4 *Stage four* is the invention of new products and services to meet the demands of the sophisticated, affluent, leisure-oriented, socially conscious, mobile, communication, change-oriented society.
5 *Stage five* is unblinkered planning that uses creative imagination to expand outward the range of alternative courses of action to be considered.
6 *Stage six* is the invention and construction of new types of organizational arrangements suitable to space-age man, in a post-industrial, faster paced, innovative society.
7 *Stage seven* is the devising and constructing of management information systems that service the high-speed innovative, modern MBO enterprise.

•

Doing the old things in the old way is a loser's game today.

Radical, accelerating change is pulling the rug out from under the traditional objectives and roles of universities, hospitals and businesses.

The only salvation lies in new missions and new objectives.

Management must elicit more creative thinking from everyone. Many firms and public institutions are now using such techniques as brainstorming, synectics, bionics and morphology. Many organizations are giving creativity training at all levels.

Management has to exercise creative ingenuity also in the *hows* of managing: in planning, in methods, in organizations, in selling, in advertising and on ad infinitum.

Some firms set up think-tanks and innovation groups. In other cases, *retreat seminars* are held for top management groups, where they hide away in the country to invent the future.

Creativity and innovation can be made to happen. We need not depend on *inspiration* or accident. Today's knowledge permits us to organize so everyone innovates.

A common belief of our time is that *people resist change*. This view is often held to be a plain matter of fact with which no one in his right mind could possibly disagree. People are *neophobiacs* and that's that, i.e., they fear and hate anything new.

It is clear that antagonism to the results of certain changes, to noise, pollution, technological employment, crowding and bureaucracy is rising.

Yet people seem to be positively *neophilic* about some changes. They love them. Shorter working hours and higher wages are seldom feared or resisted. To visit strange, new and foreign lands is positively popular. And so on.

With all the change taking place, it is also hard to escape the suspicion that somewhere there are a lot of odd people busily producing all the changes that other people are said to resist.

Perhaps the world is divided into neophiliacs and neophobiacs. One group busily resists the changes that the other group busily produces. Or perhaps we're all neophiliacs when the change is to our advantage but neophobiacs when it's not.

New Ideas

A popular fallacy is that new ideas are produced by cleverness or brilliance. In other words, they are assumed to emanate from exercises in complicated and adroit mental gymnastics.

In fact, this is not how it happens. The way it happens is a great deal simpler and much more difficult. Ideas come from changing one's viewpoint about something. Like changing our viewpoint that the sun goes around the earth, that the earth is flat, that fire comes from the release of a substance called phlogiston. Like changing our viewpoint that men are superior to women, that government departments be run by people with university degrees, that workers are lazy, that people should be paid only if they work, that education is acquired at school, that children should be seen and not heard, and that the business of the post-office is to deliver the mail.

The reason it is hard to produce new ideas, and even harder to accept someone else's new idea, is that we have to change to do so. Our opinions, beliefs and viewpoints must undergo a real reorganization. A new idea is not merely a new thought. It is a new picture of reality and a new opinion about it.

The kind of new ideas that are percolating these days are new ideas about people, their nature, their lives and their rights. It is much harder for people to change their beliefs about people than about anything else. Indeed, some would sooner fight than switch.

Bill Lear (Lear-Jet and Motorola) for years has been urging industry and education to teach people to make better use of the unconscious. He argues it is the well-spring of creative thought. Psychologists agree. They say the mental process of producing new ideas is a three-stage one: first comes the hard, conscious, initial work. It is followed by a second period of apparent idleness, called "incubation." During the incubation period, the unconscious does the work. Then, third, comes the sudden flash of insight, which gestalt psychologists call the "Aha" phenomenon. Letting the unconscious do the work by putting the problem "on the back-burner" to stew, "sleeping on it," "getting away from it all," is what participants in today's creative-thinking courses programs are taught to do. Going even farther, one methodology, synectics, argues that the unconscious operates with symbols. In synectics, people are therefore taught how to employ metaphors and analogies to trigger the creative processes.

An anthropologist from another planet would detect a considerable amount of embarrassment among managers about the whole creativity business. Most managers don't want to talk too much about it. "Playing" with ideas is an offense to puritan ethic. The wild erratic swings of thought in a think-tank meeting are distressing to anyone with orderly habits. And worse still, new ideas have an odd appearance which irks any conservative mind. Moreover, a time-honored association of creativity with "egg-heads" is threatening to the executive self-image of no-nonsense John Wayne virility.

Corporations may thus be a bit reluctant to publicize their queer creativity program. But as with sex in Victorian times, there is a great deal more going on than is publicly proclaimed. For example, a Canadian oil company recently organized think-tanks to brain-storm ideas for reducing the service-station construction costs. In another department of the same company, other think-tanks are trying to invent new service-station designs. A leading computer manufacturer has employed synectics to devise a new system for handling customer complaints. A Montreal food company used the "scenario" technique to dream up its future marketing organization: four executives locked themselves in the company's rented apartment for three days for this particular exercise in visionary futurism.

Creative Association

Creativity is a mental process, and it's associative. Things apparently get grouped in our minds and our memories. We store in our mind various families of association: say, music—art—theatre—beauty. Or, car—automobile—battery—gasoline. These linkings are ideas, but they're at a pretty concrete level. They come in through sensation and perception and then they are stored. What we are dealing with is some linkage in the nervous system; neuroconnections in the brain.

If I give you the thought "pencil" and you come up with "paper," this is routine association. Pencil and paper are grouped together in the mind because that's the way they're grouped together in reality. But supposing we ask the brain to establish associations across families, this is a real difficulty, because we will be on the road to what we call "a new idea." If I take the word "theatre" and the word "car," I've got a drive-in theatre. That's not a creative association because such things exist. But it was once.

The phenomenon of creative association exists in music. A melody is only a combination of existing notes. But it is still something above and beyond the individual notes. There's a kind of mystery in the fact that the combination has a quality that is not apparent in the individual element. This is why the area of creativity has been surrounded by an aura of mystery. If the combination of car and theatre that produces drive-in theatre is a commercial success, it's not because it's a theatre and it's not because it's a car. It is because it has properties that somehow don't seem to be associated with the automobile *per se*, or with the theatre *per se*. It's something new so we say, this is mysterious; where did this new property appear from?

It's the same kind of thing involved in water, which has properties that hydrogen and oxygen don't have separately. You can wash with water, cook with it, freeze it. You know water really exists.

But separate the water electrolytically into hydrogen and oxygen and the water literally disappears from existence. The parts are still there but their properties are different. This is mystifying, a little bit magical.

Good Ideas Have Multiple Benefits

Ideas come in all guises. There are "dangerous" ideas, "foolish" ideas, "bright" ideas, "stupid" ideas, "impractical" ideas and "good" ideas. But what is a "good" idea?

Our own idea of a good idea is an idea that (1) works and (b) has *multiple benefits*. For example, the drive-in theatre proved to be a *good* idea because it had multiple benefits. It eliminated the theatre building, (2) it eliminated the necessity for special parking, (3) it solved the baby sitter problem and/or (4) it provided more privacy. Had it done only *one* of these things it would not have flourished as it has.

The ball-point was a *good* idea because it was (1) cheap, (2) eliminated the ink-bottle and (3) eliminated blotting.

M.B.O. is a *good* idea because it (1) solves the business performance problem, (2) solves the motivation problem, (3) provides a machinery for participative management, (4) makes a modern financial management system possible, e.g., P.P.B.S. or, in business, profit planning, (5) facilitates the designing of organization development process, and indeed does other vital things too numerous to list.

A mistake often made is to search for ideas that have only *one* benefit. These are not *good* ideas. A business would inevitably go bankrupt on a one benefit from one idea basis. A person who operated that way would be hopelessly ineffectual.

Ideas are ephemeral and evanescent creatures. They drift into the mind, wander across it and vanish. Often they can never be recalled.

For this reason, some people have formed the wise habit of jotting down ideas as they appear. On the back of an envelope, on a scrap of paper, anywhere will do. This way they can be held for later retrieval.

Just because the idea you get is important is no reason to think you'll remember it. Almost everyone has the experience of rediscovering a valuable idea he had months earlier and had forgotten all about. And how many such ideas don't get re-discovered and have forever disappeared!

•

Imaginative management is an alternative to stereotyped management. What is "stereotyped management"? It is easy enough to describe it, record it, point it out. One sees nothing but "standard operating procedures." One sees nothing but standard jobs with rigid descriptions. One sees only standard hum-drum products. One never ever sees anything different or unique or original whenever stereotyped management is the style.

The opposite of stereotyped management is "imaginative management." "Imaginative management" is not so common. But wherever it exists it too can be seen, noted, described.

The underlying difference between stereotyped and imaginative management is, of course, mental. In stereotyped management the brain employs conditioned reflex, knee-jerk, imitative, monkey-see-monkey-do mechanisms. In imaginative management, the brain employs thought, vision and ingenuity. Mediocrity typically travels by standard means. Outstanding performance usually travels by unusual methods.

Take Coles, a large chain of Canadian book stores. Coles stores are brightly lit, like supermarkets. Displays are eye-catching, well-located, decoratively staged. The result is stores which are different, surprising and, most of all, successful.

Or Shoppers Drug Mart. The creation of Murray Koffler, one of North America's most truly imaginative managers, it has an original physical fitness approach to employee development. Koffler is a believer in the precept of "mens sana in corpore sano," a healthy mind in a healthy body. Vitality, enthusiasm, emotional and mental resiliency result from company-provided gym work, calisthenics and energy sports.

Can stereotyped managers become imaginative managers? The gulf is great but the answer is "Yes." In many cases, indeed they can. But only if the organization strongly encourages and rewards imagination. It also helps if managers are taught creative thinking techniques, e.g., morphology, bionics, brainstorming or synectics. Such effective techniques aid the practice, and support the habit of original independent thought.

To find out what these techniques are all about, skim through:

1 Morphology: *Invention, Research and Discovery*, by Fritz Swicky (MacMillan Company—1969).
2 Bionics: *Bionics*, by Lucian Gerrardin (McGraw-Hill—1968)
3 Brain-storming: *Applied Imagination*, by Alex Osborn (Charles Scribner's Sons—1954)
4 Synectics: *The Practice of Creativity*, by George Prince (Harper & Row—1970).

•

There is good reason to believe that some of the major social disorders of our time are caused by changes which are too fast for, too much for, or plain bad for, people. Such disorders may include alcoholism, violence, crime, drug addiction and emotional derangements ranging from mild insomnia to screaming paranoia.

In the past, innovations have always been introduced simply because they were in someone's interest. Now we have begun to face the fact that when there were beneficiaries of change there usually were victims too. And we accept, now (when it's almost too late), that in the future we shall have to spend a great deal of effort on re-directing and moderating change.

Innovation will have to become a wiser and higher art. Indeed, it must become a science if we are to get this whole change business under proper human control. A new science for the social engineering of innovation has not developed. We needed it fifty years ago, but didn't know it.

Now we know it. Yet there is not a university in the country seriously and deeply engaged in research on the phenomenon of change, despite the fact that it is the main social, intellectual, economic, biological, medical and spiritual fact of our time.

Serendipity refers to one of the most characteristic features of the creative process. It means making unexpected discoveries.

For example, in the medical science field, Fleming discovered the effects of penicillin quite accidentally. Blown in from an open window, it killed the bacteria in a saucer which contained a strain which Fleming was investigating.

The physician. Laennec, searching for a way to hear the sounds of the heart, got his answer quite by accident when he saw two boys, one of whom was hitting one end of a wooden see-saw with a stone while the other listened with his ear on the other end of the board. The notion of the stethescope leaped to Laennec's mind.

George Westinghouse discovered the idea of the airbrake when he accidentally discovered that compressed air power was being used by Swiss engineers in tunnel building. The discovery was made while he was casually flipping through a journal.

Scotch-tape was originally viewed as a product to be sold to libraries for mending torn pages in books. Its other multitudinous uses with which we are familiar today were discovered quite by accident and were a source of unanticipated and unexpected profits to 3-M.

Does this all mean that discovery is all a matter of simple luck? Absolutely not. Serendipity happens only to people who are searching. Never to people who are not curious or inquiring or who are not engaged in a hard search for opportunities, possibilities, answers or inventions. As Poincaré, the distinguished and creative French mathematician put it: in discovery *"chance favors the prepared mind."*

Serendipity is important to the inventive businessman or creative public administrator, as well as to the scientist. The knowledge that serendipity can happen, and indeed *will* happen, is an encouragement and a spur to ceaseless search.

One method of encouraging creativity is the brainstorming technique, which was developed some years ago and which is applicable not only to product development but to the evolution of all types of new ideas. Some companies believe it is extremely valuable; others are extremely skeptical about it. This article describes the technique and quotes some of the different opinions about it.

Brainstorming: Cure or Curse?

The theory of brainstorming is simple. A group of people sit around a table, a problem is presented, and everybody fires away with ideas on how to solve it—the wilder the idea, the better. No one can judge or criticize any idea. A secretary records the ideas as they come, and out of this welter of flash thinking comes the one best way, or several ways, of solving the problem.

The only new twist lies in ruling out the one factor that has always been considered mandatory at conferences—the factor of critical judgment.

It's not hard to see why brainstorming, practiced in many different forms, gets new adherents daily. Sessions are simple to set up, add few if any costs. Participants find them fun, sometimes even exciting. To many companies, they seem the panacea for all problems.

As industry tends toward more monolithic organization, communication becomes more difficult. Brainstorming promises a way of unlocking some of the brain capacity that now pours its ideas into sluggish or unreceptive channels.

And, because brainstorming takes on so many elements of a game, it takes the curse off the word "problem."

Weighing the Ideas

Almost all brainstorm proponents agree on one claim: the quantity of ideas that are generated. Over and over, you'll hear boasts like "We got 187 ideas in 47 minutes."

From *Business Week*, Dec. 29, 1956, pp. 44–48.

It's probably this numbers game as much as anything that has attracted attention to the method. Yet even the most enthusiastic supporters concede that, at best, "maybe 6% to 10% of the ideas are useful." And how many of this 6% to 10% ever get put into practice is still another question.

Few companies seem to have worked out any ways of utilizing the ideas that flow from brainstorming.

Here's the trouble: No matter how many people sat in the group that churned out 187 ideas in 47 minutes, some one person must sift the mass and decide which idea has potential.

"That's when my headaches start," says one executive who has filled this role. "With one idea at a time, I can consider the angles, make a decision. But now I've got to decide which of 187 ideas are best.

"The brainstormers are encouraged to shoot wild to uncover a good idea. But the first thing I do is cross off all the silly-sounding things—silly to me—and all the things I know are stale or have already been tried and discarded. Then maybe I have a half-dozen left. Then what? A full-scale investigation of each? Maybe, but I can't order it, so it gets bucked through channels.

"In the end, whatever was there in the first place has either been lost or has been so changed and distorted in going through channels that there's not much resemblance left."

Prof. John Arnold, who teaches creativity at Massachusetts Institute of Technology, adds: "Few ideas are in themselves practical. It is for want of imagination in applying them, rather than in acquiring them, that they fail. The creative process doesn't end with an idea—it only starts with an idea."

The commonest form of brainstorming rules out any evaluation of ideas as they emerge, but it also calls for subsequent evaluation by an individual or a small committee not involved in the original session.

One modification, developed by Arthur D. Little Co., does permit judgment of ideas as the session rolls along, aiming at synthesizing the thought of the entire group. This kind of session comes closer to the standard staff conference, but it also aims at avoiding dominance by an individual or a clique.

Dr. Samuel Trull [a management consultant] advocates a follow-up to brainstorming. He splits up the group to investigate and reorganize the original ideas, finally to come back together for a full-dress review. By this time, the first ideas may have been utterly transformed.

There's still another school of thought that holds that the person making the suggestion should be forced to do his own evaluating, should explore the production, marketing, and financing possibilities.

"An idea doesn't exist in a vacuum," says a disciple of this stern doctrine, "and an unusable product is just as well not thought up."

This view is unorthodox. To most brainstormers, the applicability of any idea is far less important than the fact that it has been articulated.

Morale-Builder

Some consultants say, in fact, that the great benefit of brainstorming is not the new ideas but the boost to employee morale. "Most people have 'ideas,' sometimes even good ones," says a pro-brainstormer, "but they've been conditioned by their own psychological blocks or the climate within the company to keep their mouths shut. This way, a man gets a chance to express his ideas, no matter how banal or foolish. If he gets that chance, without getting kicked in the teeth, it may stimulate him to have the guts to do it again."

"And when nothing happens to carry out his ideas," retorts a psychologist, "he draws further back in his shell."

Other advisers favor brainstorming as a morale gimmick.

"The ideas usually aren't worth a damn," says an executive of a company that does a good deal of brainstorming, "but it makes the rank and file think somebody's finally listening to their ideas."

Some brainstorm sessions are thinly disguised gripe meetings, built around such vague "problems" as "What can be done to improve relations in the ZQ Co." Most suggestions, though phrased positively, actually are complaints against existing conditions.

Some executives treat the method even more cynically. In one not untypical case, management wanted to spur competition among workers by public display of comparative performance charts, but the union objected. When the planted "suggestion" appeared among a couple of hundred ideas from a lower-echelon brainstorm, the front office put it into effect immediately on a "you suggested it yourself" basis.

Where brainstorming is being tried in all sincerity, its strongest talking point is its speed as a collection agency for ideas.

"Essentially," says a top engineering official of a big corporation, "it's the same process that takes place when an individual is stewing over a problem, talking it over with a dozen other people over a period of time, investigating the literature on the subject. After a while, the total accumulation of material falls together. The real value of brainstorming is that the group can draw more quickly on a bigger pool of knowledge and understanding. But the problem will still be solved by the individual, not the group."

Even the most ardent brainstormers concede that "wildly original" ideas rarely if ever come out of brainstorming sessions. They speak instead of combinations of ideas.

"Any tiny variation of an old theme—the switch—is, for all practical purposes, new to the immediate problem," says an advocate. "Actually, in most brainstorms—in spite of the numbers game—nothing worthwhile comes up, either from the individual or the group. But it does tickle the mind of the individual, who then develops his thought privately. Invariably, the best ideas are those that come up afterwards, after a man has chewed on them in solitude a while."

Group Think

Those who defend the sheer-quantity virtue of brainstorming, however, cite studies that seem to show that a group is more than the sum of its individual components.

In one such study, a group of technicians was split, one-half to brainstorm as a group and the other half to write down as many suggestions as they could think of, individually and without talking to anyone else. The brainstorming group produced 50% more unduplicated ideas than the others.

The validity of this test has been challenged. "In the first place," says a dissenter, "there was no attempt at comparative valuation of ideas aside from sheer numbers. Who knows where the better ones were?

"More important," he adds, "the test was rigged. No one thinks in a vacuum. But in the normal course of events, each man would have been talking to others, bouncing off ideas, picking up sparks.

"If they would re-run the test—half in a brainstorming session, the other half working individually but with normal intercourse among them—I'd bet that the individuals would come up with a higher score of usable ideas."

Still, many of the brainstormers are convinced that the group approach actually trains the individual to "think creatively." And they offer courses to prove it. One brainstorming course in the Army, for enlisted men, lasts two hours. Others in universities and companies take a full year.

One fairly typical 14-week course, according to its syllabus, spends four weeks on the technique (at some luncheon meetings, the basics are taught in about five minutes) and the other 10 weeks on office power tactics—"how to sell your idea to the boss after you've got it."

One company tests the students, before and after its long course, on how many ideas they can dream up in a given time. It claims a gain in fluency of ideas from an average of 82 suggestions to 116.

General Electric Co. says men who have trained in its "creative engineering program" generate new processes and patentable ideas at three times the "untrained" rate. However, GE's candidates for this special training must have been at the top of their college classes, must have at least one advanced degree, must have passed at least one advanced technical course at GE with a high rating, and previously have proved their own "creativity."

"Even the brainstorm boys concede that not more than 10% of the ideas are any good," says a critic. "How does anyone know that the 10% don't come from the same few individuals who were doing all the creative thinking on their own time anyway before this fad came along? Can anyone prove that the guy who never had an idea before comes out with worthwhile ones in the group? Or that the naturally creative guy is being really stimulated by the banal suggestions of the rest around the table?"

Bernard Benson, head of a West Coast business in applied cybernetics, says brainstorming unquestionably brings out ideas that wouldn't have come to someone who sat watching television instead. But he denies that "divine inspiration" falls on anyone, with or apart from a group, who lacks solid knowledge and experience and doesn't apply systematic thought to a problem.

George Samerjan, New York artist-designer, goes even further. He says brainstorming is becoming a crutch for individual thinking. "A man counts on being inspired when he joins the group, so he can stop thinking alone."

[But] everyone seems to agree on one virtue of brainstorming—it gets people to express themselves in public.

"In our company," says one high executive, "an executive is often rated more highly if he makes no mistakes than if he suggests lots of ideas. If brainstorming can give higher place to the idea man than to the careful man, we might all be better off."

As one of the men quoted in the preceding article observed, "The creative process doesn't end with an idea—it only starts with an idea." The following article describes the intricate steps necessary to translate a new idea into a successful new product. It also explains why a general manager may, without being in the least a fuddy-duddy, look with something less than immediate enthusiasm on a proposal that seems brilliant to its inventor.

As manager of exploratory research in the development department of E. I. du Pont de Nemours & Company, Mr. Roedel has had broad experience in carrying products from the idea stage to the point where they are ready for the market.

Steps in Product Innovation

Milton J. Roedel

Obviously, you have to recognize a venture opportunity as the first step in the process [of innovation]. Just as obviously, you have to recognize a number of them, cull them, and select a candidate to work on in detail. What are some of the factors in this step?

First is appreciation of your departmental goals and responsibilities and picking ventures that are compatible with them. Do not waste time on ventures that are not your departmental concern. The probability of success is small enough for the dedicated man in the right department. One must also appreciate that it is a human failing to try to run everyone else's business but his own.

Second, it is essential for the development manager to know what is going on in the business world and have a sense of business history. This means that the development manager must not only keep up with all the new technology being developed within the company but with a vast amount of trade and business literature and intelligence in order to forecast future trends. Timing requires you to forecast the future because it takes so long to get things moving. Furthermore, one forecasts the future in the hope of partially controlling it and to make sure that the steps being taken today are compatible with the future. To do this, you need to be conversant with the past and present since you don't fabricate opportunities from a vacuum. Hence, the basic requirement is that you know your assigned business and know it well, both internally and externally.

How to Get from Here to There Profitably

A lot of people with very good ideas go broke before they get rich because their business plan was poorly conceived and executed. An opportunity that cannot be exploited is not an opportunity.

The first requisite is to lead from strength. In

From a talk given to a Du Pont development managers' meeting, Feb. 12, 1963.

our company one leads from technical strength.

The second requisite is that you must be able to get to the market efficiently and knowledgeably without dependence upon an intermediary if possible.

The third is that you go after replacement business if possible.

The fourth is that you have a product mix, not a single item.

The fifth is that the user doesn't have to do things differently if possible. The fewer people you have to educate, the faster you can move.

Now the whole venture is based on a forecast. It defines the opportunity, penetration rate, cost of getting into the business, and profitability as well as defining the uncertainty.

The numbers used in the forecast are judgment numbers. You have to develop a feel for them. You have to live with them. You have to follow each step in the process in terms of cost and accomplishment. These are living things depending upon human accomplishment and they have to relate to what you are trying to accomplish. You don't just pull these numbers out of the hat. Undoubtedly, there is more skill called for in this area than any other since it is the only quantitative assessment of the venture dollarwise, peoplewise and timewise. Until you have a forecast that you have a feel for and confidence in, you don't have a venture worth selling to management. It takes a lot of thought and study before you reach this stage.

The power of positive thinking is essential because if you can't work your way out of foreseen difficulties, you have no venture. I'm not implying that one should gloss over difficulties, but one should weigh the strengths against the weaknesses and establish in his own mind which weaknesses can be fixed up and the magnitude of the strengths. If there is a critical weakness, then there is no venture. If an invention is required, forget it until the invention is a fact. If it is an outright gamble, forget it. You don't gamble with a business.

The best position to get in is the multiproduct position since you are not dependent upon a single article for success. A single new product for a new use can require a long time to establish and make profitable. Management has finite patience and it's shorter than you think or they agree to. Losses are not acceptable over a long period of time, not even against the original forecast.

Technology is changing too rapidly and too many companies have adequate research staffs to duplicate our results by different methods to risk a multi-million dollars, multi-year pay-out any more. This means that we development managers are going to have to find out how to develop new businesses at less cost and more rapidly. Certainly, forward integration from a materials base is one route. These same competitive pressures also force one further into the market place to protect market position; and as our businesses grow in sales volume, if we don't do it, someone else will since integration is inevitable whenever large-scale economies dictate it. In some instances, it is no longer a matter of free choice but of market survival in that market.

A power applicable in some instances is technical leadership in the market place. If one can get to a large new opportunity first with the mostest and pre-empt 50% of the market or at least twice as much as the nearest competitor, then one is generating the R.&D. funds to out-invent the competition 2 to 1 and they can't get from here to there without going broke first. The difference in profitability because of lower unit costs with volume sales assures that the price structure will not erode to low-profit margins for this leader. Thus, technical leadership is a mass technical effort supported by a pre-empted market position. Technical leadership has nothing to do with technical competence, and the two should not be confused. If you don't have technical competence, someone should be fired.

Obtaining Management Approval and Support

Probably more potential new ventures fail at this step than at any other since it appears to be the least understood by those of us responsible for selling management on future courses of business action. The natural tendency of the bright-eyed and bushy-tailed novice is to ride in on a big white horse with a battle plan to conquer the world. At a glance, the general manager can see that the horse is neither de-sanitized nor castrated, and what the hell is it doing on his fine 501 nylon carpet?

Now our problem is to sell the general manager. [To do so] we have to understand what motivates him and what restricts him. Basically, he has full responsibility for running a business with his product areas pretty well staked out. Each month, he has to produce a sheet showing profits and losses on each individual business, return on investment, and performance against forecast. He is constantly under the microscope on all phases of his business, plus or minus 10%.

Now you are coming along with a new venture that is far from risk-less; he is going to have to lose money over a considerable period of time, and a finite amount of his R.&D., production, and sales personnel are going to be tied up for a long time to come outside of his going business areas. If the venture succeeds, the pat on the back that he gets is not equivalent to the jab in the fanny with a spear if he fails. The spear is there every month and the pat only at the end of the line, possibly not at all since success is always obvious, and who should get credit for doing the obvious?

Under these conditions, which I have exaggerated deliberately for emphasis because we don't fully appreciate the general managers' problems, you obviously have to have something to sell and you have to know how to sell it in relation to the business environment in which we operate.

We are at step 3 now with the first two steps completed. We have recognized the opportunity and devised a business plan to exploit it. At this stage, I draw up my charts for the first of many times trying as best as possible to meet management's yardsticks, to stay off the white horse, to lead from technical strength and manufacturing skills, to have a reasonable and well-thought-out marketing route and a substantial marketing need, to be able to spell out introductory losses and to be able to retreat from the market place without loss of face if this becomes advisable with further field knowledge.

Now at this stage of the game you have only synthesized the skeleton. The meat is still to be put on the bones. One needs real humility at this point, for the artist in him suffers when the comics redraw his pictures. But you must be prepared to listen as well as defend; and as you give your story repeatedly in the lower echelons, you start to weave the venture fabric from the many criticisms and suggestions received. Thus you end up with a group story on the assessment and recommendations.

It is the height of folly to give the story to a general manager and his directors without working your way up in the organization first. Middle management should be sold first, preferably one at a time, and have them inform corporate management ahead of time what is coming so that they understand it broadly before they see the story in detail. Every man in the room has to be for it before you even start insofar as possible. The reason is that only one man has to express strong doubt and the project will probably be sent back for further study. This is how paralysis by analysis results because the selling job isn't done properly. One has to appreciate that the operation can be a democratic dictatorship: Everybody gets to vote, but the vote has to be unanimous before something can happen. Thus, the necessity for the complete sale.

Putting the Show on the Road

Get the right people for the key jobs, [people] whom you have dealt with and understand and have confidence in. You don't just want good men but good men you know if you want to move fast.

With a new organization you have to put up your defenses against being a dumping ground for personnel problems.

You go after the people you want, not those who want you except where the desire is mutual.

While any organization has to be set up to operate with average people, you don't use average people to start if off.

The venture manager has to be a warrior because he has a battle to win. He has to know when to spend his blood internally and how to spend it well because he only has a finite amount. He has to appreciate that most red tape is an attitude of the mind. It is amazing what you can get away with by using the "no" system. The "no" system is telling your supervision what you are going to do before you do it if it is in a questionable region. He has to say "no" to stop you, and you aren't held up until he says "yes."

Keep your cards on top of the table. You can get away with a lot more freedom when people know what you are up to even if they don't like it or have reservations.

Don't hide your failures and mistakes. Bury them in full public view with due humility and contrition. Who has the heart to castigate a repentant sinner? And, if you aren't making mistakes in a new venture, you are the wrong man for the job. A good warrior doesn't win every battle, he wins the war.

Get a good man for sales promotion. Then, keep telling him his proposals stink until he comes up with one that makes you melt in awe. Without a good one, your new sales force is crippled. This isn't just another tool. It is the critical tool after product. It motivates new salesmen without customers more than any other single factor. It is visual proof of the excellence of their new product.

Don't make decisions and commitments ahead of time that you don't have to make. Every night you should be going to bed a little smarter. You save the decision for maximum smartness under the circumstances. You maintain the position of maximum permissible retreat. You do everything yourself that can be done at reasonable cost because the ability to kick a fanny gives you a lot more control than a holler at an outside source. That is, the ground rules on getting established are different from those of a going business. For instance, you don't spend a lot of time at the start in keeping your management informed and happy. You spend it in the field with your salesmen finding out how naïve your initial assumptions were and doing something about it. You don't let an unexplainable isolated product failure receive minor attention. It can be the first clue to a major catastrophe, and a warehouse full of inferior product. And a considerable part of your effort should be in setting the stage to meet next year's forecast. You don't start January 1. Tomorrow is yesterday in inventory, and progress at best is agonizingly slow. And, while much has to be hit with a lick and a promise, this never applies to your technical facts. Inevitably, they catch you wanting some time, some place. Realize it, guard against it, and keep it to a minimum. They are the true boss. You don't shove them around and you don't neglect them, except at your peril.

Cyril Bath, president of the Solon, Ohio, company that bears his name, is a true entrepreneur in every sense of the word. He is the founder of a business (and the risk taker, in that he is a major investor in it as well) and an entrepreneur in Schumpeter's sense (see Chapter 1), in that he is an innovator. Although other people contributed to the development of his path-breaking metal-forming machines, the idea was his originally, and he has also introduced innovations in many phases of the management job—in organization and direction, for example.

An Innovating Manager: Cyril Bath, Armorer in Exotic Metals

Ernest Dale and Alice Smith

Rockets, missiles, and jet aircraft require materials that are at once light in weight and capable of resisting tremendous temperatures and pressures, and often violent fluctuations in both. In consequence, the metallurgists have developed a whole armory of so-called "exotic" metals, alloys embodying such elements as molybdenum, titanium, tantalum, and beryllium among others.

But just as the exotic metals resist the high temperatures and pressures encountered in space travel, and to a lesser extent by jet aircraft, they also resist conventional methods of metalworking. In fact, the Air Force Development Command once reported that "the whole array of existing machine tools is inadequate for forging or turning, milling or pressing these new tough alloys into required shapes."

The answer has, however, been supplied by a small machine tool maker who, like many of the

This article is based on interviews, study of appropriate documents, and visits to the plant. Alice Smith is a member of Ernest Dale Associates.

early manufacturers of the Industrial Revolution, is both entrepreneur and inventor. Cyril Bath, owner and president of the Cyril Bath Company in Solon, Ohio, has developed a series of new metal forming machines that Albert Payson Usher of Harvard, the country's foremost historian of invention, has called "a breakthrough in the working of metals comparable only to the development of the metal-framed lathe at the beginning of the 19th century." B. H. Perry, a metallurgist for a large company, said: "Many thought the Bath Company performance was impossible. Actually, they were forming metal the right way since we first learned to roll it." Use of the Bath process cut a significant amount of weight off the Atlas missile, and was in part responsible for the fact that it ever got off the ground.

The machines, known as "stretch draw formers" and "radial draw formers," look something like giant phonograph turntables, but are actually considerably smaller than conventional stamping presses. First they stretch the cold metal to the point where it becomes plastic, what the engineers call its yield point, then iron it into shape with a die. Delicate electronic controls keep telegraphing back data to the power source—so that the stretch does not exceed or drop below the point at which the part can best be formed. Thus the metal itself directs the process, which is important in precision work since two sheets of the same alloy are not necessarily exactly alike.

In describing the process, Bath likes to use the human hand as an analogy. "If ordinary muscles ran down our fingers to give us our grip, the size of the fingers would make the hand useless as the delicate instrument it is. The Great Designer introduced a system of tendons, which are very high-strength operating members, into the fingers and attached them to muscles in the arms out of the way of the delicate work the fingers must sometimes perform. In machinery, such refinements are not easily seen or readily understood, but the engineer who would work in the tough alloys of today's airborne crafts must find means of providing strength without clumsy bulk."

The working actually strengthens the metal being formed and relieves many of the internal stresses by realignment of the microstructure. Thus lighter parts can be used in many applications. A bus body formed by this process weighed no more with a full complement of passengers than ordinary bus bodies do when empty.

Savings in power, material, and time are achieved also. Parts that could not be formed by conventional presses without 1,000 to 1,200 tons of pressure have been successfully made by the Bath process with only 150 to 250 tons. Savings in material and time are possible because, as Professor Usher has said, the process "makes it possible to form the hardest metals at levels of precision comparable to those attained in the manufacture of special apparatus for scientific operations." Thus much of the further processing often necessary on parts formed by other means is eliminated, including much of the handwork often needed on precision parts.

In addition, there is an important saving in die cost. Plastic dies can be substituted for metal dies in some cases, and metal dies can be smaller and lighter—up to 70 per cent lighter—easier to change and longer lasting since comparatively little pressure is needed to form a part. Also the same dies can be used for different alloys without reworking.

Since die cost is an important part of the cost of automobile model changeovers, the Bath company considers the process a "natural" for the automobile industry. A spokesman for an auto plant in Argentina, which is already using the equipment, estimates that the die cost there has been cut in half.

Now over 80, white-haired but erect and vigorous and looking 20 years younger than his actual age, Bath first evolved the idea of these machines several years ago, and he and his staff have been improving them and developing adaptions of them ever since. His career in invention, however, goes back further than that.

Born in England in the days when that country was the unquestioned leader in the production of industrial equipment, he has been in love with machinery since childhood. By the time he was 16, he had discovered the essential mechanical elements of a push button elevator, and a company owned by members of his family later used the principles he worked out in the construction of an elevator for Windsor Castle. "That boy," said his father, "is a born machine designer and we shouldn't try to make him anything else."

But his father died at a comparatively early age and members of his mother's family became the chief influence in the household. They were carriage makers and could see no necessity for branching out into automobile bodies because "No gentleman will ever ride in one of those things." (Eventually they went broke.) They backed his mother in her determination to make him a missionary.

In order to avoid a career of preaching to the heathen, Bath ran away to Canada and became a harvest hand at $1.50 a day. One day the threshing machine broke down, and he was told that if he could repair it, he would become "the engineer" at $6 a day. He fixed it without much trouble, but later decided to pass up the $6 engineering job and migrate to the United States. After a period of joblessness, during which he slept under a bridge and ate on the cuff through the kindness of a restaurant owner who thought he looked trustworthy, he eventually got work as a machinist and studied basic engineering at night. Then he became a machine tool salesman.

He quit this job because the firm would not underwrite a minimum guarantee of $3,000 a year, which he felt he needed because he had just been married. Moreover, his boss, who drove an imposing-looking Cadillac, objected to his $175 Model T Ford.

"Look here," the boss said, "we've put up with a lot from you with your little English mustache, your cane, and your accent. Now you're swanking around in an automobile, and it's just too much. People will think we're making too much money if a salesman can drive around in an automobile."

Bath protested that it was only reasonable for a machine tool company to make use of machines whenever possible, but the boss failed to see the point. So Bath decided to go into business for himself, buying machine tools second hand, rebuilding them at night and selling them during the day. Then he began designing machines of his own and having them built in other companies' plants, and eventually began manufacturing them himself.

By the time the depression of the 1930's hit the country, he had a thriving little machine tool business, but the outlook was bleak. Here Bath showed himself as inventive in marketing as he was in design. He purchased railroad machinery from shops in this country that were shutting down, rebuilt it in his plant, and shipped it to the national railroads in Mexico, which couldn't afford brand-new machines. This saved his men's jobs during the worst of the 1930's.

Again at the end of World War II, Bath anticipated that most of his foreign customers would have difficulty getting American dollars to buy American goods and developed simple low-cost machines for making such things as cases for refrigerator cabinets and deep freezers, and T.V. cabinets. When he heard that Jews in this country had raised $350,000 to buy U.S. refrigerators for Israel, he pointed out that the money would go further if the casing were made on the spot and a plant in Tel-Aviv placed orders with him. The Tel-Aviv plant, incidentally, sold a part of its output to Arabs, because the harem ladies were fond of Coca-Cola and wanted to keep it cool. In fact, the Arabs liked the ice-makers so much that they refrained from bombing the Tel-Aviv plant during the first war with Israel, and it became a refuge for women and children while the fighting was on.

The Cyril Bath Company is still a modest plant, but it is one of the ten most profitable in its field. Investment in plant and machinery, which has been largely written off, has more than doubled in the last ten years, and the company has ample working capital and no funded debt. In addition, it has a workforce that is unusually loyal and versatile.

Bath's relations with his employees, in fact, are among the best in the country. His own pre-World War I experience as a rank-and-file worker in industry was not happy: "Men had to be good. They had to be fast. They took what was handed to them. But above all they had to keep their faces buttoned up. I didn't like it. and they didn't like it. A pink slip in a pay envelope felt like a sudden blow to the stomach. You were through; that was all. Set loose to sink, swim or starve. So much material on the hoof."

This treatment was particularly galling and incomprehensible to Bath, who had attended a

Quaker school before his plunge into industry and whose family were gentle upper middle class Victorians. He originally planned to do designing only, because "I didn't want to treat people the way it appeared you had to in industry." But strikes and slowdowns in suppliers' plants convinced him that he would have to manufacture his machines himself if he were to meet his customers' deadlines.

The industrial relations philosophy he evolved is based on the idea that it isn't necessary to "make idiots of the workers" in order to be efficient. "I buy brains, not hours," he says. Hence everyone is encouraged to contribute what he can, not just perform a narrow specialized function over and over. This has produced a flexible workforce, many of whom can do several jobs, and this, in turn, makes it possible to avoid layoffs when the work in one department is slack. Wages and fringe benefits are higher than the average, and there is profit-sharing as well.

These policies have paid dividends in the development of the Bath inventions and in marketing. Three or four machinists working together once developed an improvement in the press brake that was one of the company's original products, a means of making its action automatic when the load on the press was too great. In another case, when the engineers found they couldn't meet the deadline on a proposal for a contract, a shop meeting was called and everyone pitched in and helped. The proposal was ready on time and the plant got the contract.

The policies have also produced a spirit unusual in industry. Just after World War II, when the equipment was run down from heavy production, the company found that it would either have to skip its bonus payments or forego buying a much-needed crane. One of the maintenance men was chosen by the wage earners to tell Bath that they would rather give up the bonus than not buy the crane; they knew it was needed for the future profits that they would share.

"So," says Bath, "we bought the crane and paid the bonus too. We realized that we had extra assets in the form of cooperation that didn't show on the books.

"Of course, we are, among other things, in business to make money. While I admit it was never a prime objective for me, we do all right."

No one company can possibly originate all the good new ideas; if a firm depends only on its own resources for innovation, it may miss important possibilities. It is common, therefore, for firms to imitate each other's succesful innovations. But this procedure is far from riskless, for a company may adopt an innovation too soon, before it has really proved itself, and it may turn out to be far less successful than it originally seemed to be. On the other hand, if a company is too late it can never catch up.

Here Theodore Levitt, professor of business administration at Harvard Business School, suggests a procedure to minimize the risks of getting to market too soon or too late.

Innovative Imitation

Theodore Levitt

We live in a business world that increasingly worships the great tribal god *innovation*, lyrically hailing it not just as a desired, but as a necessary, condition of a company's survival and growth. Yet before all our R & D energies and imaginations are too one-sidedly directed at the creation of innovations, it is useful to look at the facts of commercial life. Is innovation all that promising? More important, how does a policy of innovation compare in promise to more modest aspirations?

In spite of the extraordinary outpouring of totally and partially new products and new ways of doing things that we are witnessing today, by

From the *Harvard Business Review*, September–October, 1966, pp. 63–70.

far the greatest flow of newness is not innovation at all. Rather, it is *imitation*. A simple look around us will, I think, quickly show that imitation is not only more abundant than innovation, but actually a much more prevalent road to business growth and profits. IBM got into computers as an imitator; Texas Instruments, into transistors as an imitator; Holiday Inns, into motels as an imitator; RCA, into television as an imitator; and *Playboy*, into both its major fields (publishing and entertainment) as an imitator. In addition, though on a lesser scale, we see every day that private brands are strictly imitative. In fact, imitation is endemic. Innovation is scarce.

Strictly defined, innovation occurs only when something is entirely new, having never been done before. A modest relaxation of this definition may be allowed by suggesting that innovation also exists when something which may have been done elsewhere is for the first time done in a given industry. On the other hand, when other competitors in the same industry subsequently copy the innovator, even though it is something new for them, then it is not innovation; it is imitation.

Needed: Balanced Policy

Innovation can be a highly productive, if often risky, road to success. In most industries today any company that is not aggressively alert to innovative possibilities is taking a competitive risk of which it ought at least to be intelligently aware. Moreover, it is likely to develop an in-company atmosphere and style of behavior on the part of its people that can be dangerously insular. The quest for innovation—particularly in new products, in new product attributes, and in customer service—is part and parcel of a company's being marketing oriented.

What is needed is a sensibly balanced view of the world. Innovation is here to stay, it is necessary, and it can make a lot of sense; but it does not exhaust the whole of reality. No single company can afford even to *try* to be first in everything in its field. The costs are too great; and imagination, energy, and management know-how are too evenly distributed within industries.

This means the company will, insofar as products and processes are concerned, have to actively engage in reverse R & D —will have to try to create its own imitative equivalents of the innovative products created by others. Moreover, the faster the rate at which entirely new products are launched in any field, the more urgent the need for each company in that field to develop a clear-cut imitative strategy—one that serves to guide not just the business judgments which must be made, but also the way in which the reverse R & D commitments are made.

Yet in a recent informal survey I made of a range of strongly new-product oriented companies with strong R & D departments—companies whose products generally required one to three years from original idea conception to subsequent market launching—I found not a single one that had any kind of policy, not even informal or implicit, to guide its responses to the innovations of others.

In other words, while the companies did a very careful job of planning new product innovations, they had no criteria at all for the much bigger and more crucial job of new product imitation. Reverse R & D was neither a planned nor a careful process. It merely occurred entirely at random, and sometimes as an almost blind reaction to what others had done. And, in every recent case I examined in these companies, I found that the imitator paid a heavy price for imitating either too soon or too late—mostly the latter.

Risk Minimization

Everybody knows that new products are risky. Predictably, they fail more often than they succeed. This unsettling fact helps explain why there is so much delay in competitive imitation. Would-be imitators sit carefully on the sidelines to watch the innovative product's fate. If it seems finally to take off, they then begin to make their own moves.

Watchful waiting is a perfectly legitimate business strategy. In some industries it is relatively easy to imitate rapidly because there are few setup problems, the capital requirement is small, and the products are relatively easily and quickly copied. The garment industry is probably the most obvious of such situations. However, when setup problems are great, when capital requirements are big, and when imitation requires lengthy reverse R & D, then getting the second or third juicy bite on the apple may involve several years' time and greatly increased risk.

Imitation of a proven product does not automatically reduce the risk; it merely changes its character. While the innovator faces the risk of his product not finding a ready market, the would-be imitator faces the equally palpable risk of reaching the market when it is already glutted with many competitors—and often rapaciously price-cutting competitors at that. Obviously, the imitator who can substantially shrink his development gestation period below that of other imitators can gain a tremendous advantage. He will encounter fewer competitors and higher and more stable prices during the felicitous duration of his lead over other imitators.

A Suggested System

When the innovation is first seen, the usual pattern in many Competitor X firms—whose products require heavy capital expenditures and lots of reverse R & D money and time—is similar to this:

At Year O, the decision-making authorities say, "I doubt it will sell. We'll keep an eye on it." This is all that's done.

At Year 1 (or—depending on the industry and situation—at, say, six months), the decision-making competitors may be a bit surprised that the product is still on the shelves. A typical comment at this point is, "Well, it's just hanging on, but not getting anywhere. I told you so."

At Year 2, the story is likely to be, "They're getting a bit more business, but I hear Company Y is going into it too. There won't be enough for both of them to share. They will go broke on this one."

At Year 3, there is nervousness because the curve is definitely headed upward. The reaction is, "George, we'd better take a closer look at this. Get some of your people on it right away."

Somewhere between Years 3 and 4, a massive crash program is started.

By Year 5, Company X gets on the market about the same time as six other companies do.

Looking back on what happened, Company X, in effect, said at Year O that the chances of success for this product were 0%. The judgment made by Company X was zero probability in the sense that nothing was done in any positive way to get ready and launch an imitative product. Had the success probability estimates consciously been something above 0%, some imitative steps would have been called for, even if only tentative steps. But none were taken at this time, or at Years 1 or 2. At each point, in terms of actions taken by Company X, a zero probability was attached to the innovator's chances of success. Significantly, however, even though the Company X decision makers had gotten exceedingly nervous by Year 3, they again at that time said, in effect, that the success chances were still nil.

The reason we must say that Company X gave a zero probability to the product's chances of success even in Year 3, despite the obviously worried reaction of "George, we'd better take a closer look at this," is that no steps were taken to begin to tackle the most complex and lengthy jobs associated with imitation—reverse R & D. Nothing was initiated in the one area that would take the most time and most effort if the product were ever to be made. No bets were hedged because the implicit probabilities that were constantly being attached to the innovator's chances of success were still zero.

But the obvious fact is that people, deep down inside, are seldom this sure of a genuinely new product's commercial fate. Nobody can ever be completely confident at the outset, or at Year 1 or Year 2, that a competitor's innovation will fail. Deep down, there usually is some different and more realistic weighting of probable failure or success.

I believe this attitude of doubt and tentativeness can and should be translated into sound business practice. Suppose that for every genuinely new product issued by a major innovator in its field Company X required its marketing vice-president to attach an honest and carefully thought-out coefficient to his estimate of its probable success—success by some measure of, say, unit sales volume. Hence he might in this case have come up with estimates of the chances of success, at the successive intervals at which he was required to make a judgment that would run like this:

First at Year 0–5%
Then at Year 1–10%
Than at Year 2–15%
Finally at Year 3–50%

Let us call each of these judgments a "Success Probability Estimate" (SPE). Suppose now also that at Year 0 the policy of Company X was that the marketing vice-president must obtain a rough estimate of the reverse R & D costs involved in developing an effective imitation of the new product. Let us say, for simplicity, that the figure is $100,000. A proper hedging policy in this case would be that at each interval during which an SPE of the competitor's new product is made, a reverse R & D appropriation is also made in proportion to that estimate.

SCHEDULE OF REVERSE R & D APPROPRIATIONS

Year	Success Proba-bility Estimate	Annual Reverse R & D Appropriation (Based on $100,000 Total)	Total Appropri-ated to Date
0	5%	$ 5,000	$ 5,000
1	10	5,000	10,000
2	15	5,000	15,000
3	50	35,000	50,000

Thus by Year 3 half of the required reverse R & D money would have been appropriated, and some share of it would have been spent. While the economics of R & D do vary by industry and project—in some cases $5,000 could not even get a company started, so that perhaps although the Year 0 SPE is 5%, the appropriation would have to be, say, $10,000—and while other problems would exist in specific cases, the strategy is clear. Namely, it makes a certain kind of good competitive sense to hedge one's bets, to buy at the outset an insurance policy against the success of your competitors' new activities.

Let us call this "insurance program" the Imitator's Hedge (IH). If Company X had had such a policy—in short, if its competitive strategies had included an IH—then, instead of getting to market belatedly in Year 5, when the rate of market expansion had already slackened and when competition was severe and margins depressed, it would probably have reached market at Year 4 and thus more quickly recovered its costs. Indeed, with such clear-cut and definitive policy, chances are the whole process of auditing new products would have become so much more careful and sophisticated that the early signals of probable success or failure would have become much more obvious and meaningful. As a consequence, Company X might very well have reached the market sometime in Year 3.

There is obviously more to launching a complex (or, at least, a relatively high-technology) imitative product than reverse R & D. Dies must be prepared, plant has to be made available, and numerous other things need time, attention, money. But the design and development process is often the most heavily time-consuming—particularly in industries where existing production lines can be modified and freed for products that have features similar to the new one.

We are not talking about something theoretical or arcane. Increasingly in recent years, the military establishments of technically advanced nations have had programs of precisely this kind in their weapons planning and development. For them, a moment saved may be a nation saved. For business, a moment saved may spell many dollars earned.

The rate of genuine new product introductions in some industries is obviously too great to justify their companies installing the IH on each new product that comes along. On the other hand, not every company has ambitions to cover every product opportunity. Still, it is possible to be insurance-poor—to buy too many IH's. This therefore calls for the establishment of insurance criteria. These criteria can take many forms—how close a new competitive product is to the various competences of your company, how near a substitute it is for one of your important products, how big its market potential is, how big development costs might be, how long it might take to achieve reasonable market acceptance, and so forth.

But another and different kind of criterion might usefully be attached to each of these. This might be a policy which says that, except in extreme cases of direct potential threat to one of your central major products, your company will not, during any single year within the next five years, commit itself to new IH's whose combined first-year costs exceed $Y. The company's total IH bill in any year could conceivably far exceed $Y, but the aggregate of all new, first-year projects would not exceed $Y.

Such a policy might then stipulate that the available $Y be distributed among the proposals with the highest Success Probability Estimates at Year 0. If this results in the exclusion of projects for which strong IH program demands are still being made, then this becomes an indication of the need to review either the original criteria or the size of the company's total Imitator's Hedge budget, or both.

19 Representation

The manager's job has always included representation of his company to outside groups, for no company has ever been self-sufficient enough to ignore the opinions of suppliers, customers, labor unions, government officials, the financial community and the general public. In the past, some companies have been able to operate successfully without the good will of some of these groups, but it is becoming less and less possible for them to do so. In particular, the opinion of the public in general is becoming increasingly important to company success, for companies have grown so large that the managers' decisions affect many more people than they did in the past and there are many more organized groups that can have an impact on the framework within which the manager must work.

There are two aspects to representation: *How* should the manager represent his company in his public pronouncements and face-to-face dealings with outside groups and individuals? And, *what* should the manager represent? The answer to the first question is a matter of techniques—techniques of public relations and negotiation. The question of *what* the manager should represent, on the other hand, brings in moral considerations.

The first two articles in this chapter discuss techniques of representation. One of them is concerned with the approach to all the various publics to whom it is desirable to present a favorable picture of the company, the other with techniques of face-to-face negotiation.

The remaining articles are concerned with the broader aspects of representation—*what* the company will represent. The manager's decisions in this area will, of course, depend on his own conception of his role. The next three articles offer material on views the manager may take.

The last two articles deal with a matter that has been having an increasingly important effect on the image of industry in general and individual companies in particular: pollution through industrial processes and products. There is, of course, a moral question here as well—for industry must decide how far it is prepared to go in attempting to improve "the quality of life." It must, of course, obey any laws that are passed to curb its emissions; but there is still the question of the extent to which industry should oppose or advocate the stricter laws that are likely to be proposed in the future.

The "company image" is the general picture of the company held by those outside it. Usually this is a very oversimplified picture embodying only one or two characteristics that the public has come to associate with the company name, and sometimes it is a very inaccurate one. Thus a company may have a reputation for efficiency or inefficiency, for good or bad treatment of its employees, for bureaucracy or flexibility, simply because of a few incidents that have stuck in the public mind.

Moreover, both favorable and unfavorable images tend to be fairly permanent. Once having put an organization into a convenient category, most people will not bother to reexamine their opinion of it unless they are compelled to do so by diametrically opposite experience with it or news that presents it in a new light. For this reason, it is of the utmost importance that a company create a favorable image of itself in the first place, and endeavor—through its actions and its public relations work—to erase unfavorable impressions before they become too deeply embedded in the public consciousness.

In the following article, Prof. Eells discusses the creation of a favorable company image and its importance in company success. Many of his ideas were developed during a period of several years when he was associated with the General Electric Company.

The Corporate Image in Public Relations

Richard Eells

Despite huge dollar outlays for corporate public relations, many public-relations programs designed to serve long-range corporate goals fall far short of the mark. Usually the basic reason is that corporate managers tend to think of public relations as a peripheral matter—rather than a major function of management. They do this because they fail to understand that the way in which a corporation relates itself to society is vital to its existence.

The recognition of public relations as a major *function* of management, along with such well-established functions as engineering, manufacturing, marketing, and finance, is fairly recent. As a unique kind of work, public relations has become specialized both as to personnel and as to major staff and operating units. In the past, unlike specialists in other functions, public-relations specialists often have had no exclusive claim on the kind of work they performed. Today their responsibilities cover specific areas which have begun to be defined by a special literature and special skill and techniques.

By public relations I mean the communication of the corporate image to key groups, both inside and outside the corporation, for two purposes: (1) to relate the corporation to its social environs, and (2) to serve the corporate objectives. This is much more than publicity through the press, radio, and television, although this is certainly a valid, if limited, purpose in itself. This broad definition of public relations has many implications, of course; but two in particular have special significance for the subsequent discussion.

The first is that in order to "relate the corporation to its social environs," public-relations work must be reciprocal. A company should listen as much as it talks—perhaps more so. Moreover, this listening needs to be continuous and systematic since both the audience responses and the media are constantly changing as a result of social and technological dynamics.

Even though a company can demonstrate a near-total recall of its messages through opinion surveys, it may not be getting its true message across. Moreover, aside from the practical necessity of knowing how its specific messages have been received, the corporation's image of itself as a social institution depends in large part upon two-way communication. For the time being, however, suffice it to say that it is an egregious error on the part of management to assume that it is "adequate" communication to achieve the apparent conversion of the listener.

The second implication is that a company's public-relations program must do more than relate the organization to its social environs; it must serve the corporate objectives. In order to do this, management must define the corporation's own broad economic and political goals as concretely as possible. Thus, a broad concept

From *California Management Review*, Vol. 1, No. 4, Summer, 1959, pp. 107–116.

of public relations must unfold in a two-step process:

1 Identifying the *real* corporate goals in their order or priority; and
2 Translating these goals into effective policies and programs that will communicate and relate the corporation to the Greater Society in terms of these goals.

There are many possible ways of stating a company's objectives. When well done, the objectives will take into account all the major groups of people—or "publics"—with which a company carries on relations, and the major purposes of its relationships with those publics.

Public-relations and executive managers should keep in mind, however, that the published objectives of a company will never reflect all the goals and values of the corporation as an institution or of its management as human beings. For example, the goals of influence and strength are never explicitly mentioned objectives. These, however, are objectives of every going concern as basic as are wealth, well-being, skill, enlightenment, respect, rectitude, and affection. (This list of goals, incidentally, is representative of the goals that men hold universally, though of course with considerable variation in priority from person to person, place to place, and from one point of time to another.)

For every business organization, then, a key purpose should be to translate corporate goals into realistic public-relations policies that successfully project the desired corporate image to all the company's publics.

Defining the Corporate Image

One major problem in projecting a favorable and consistent corporate image is the difficulty corporate managers themselves have in perceiving the corporation in terms of twentieth-century social beliefs, expectations, and promises.

Many policy-makers have inherited and try to apply time-bound concepts not only of the nation-state and of public government, but also of private enterprise itself. This makes for unrealistic and often inconsistent perception of the corporation on management's part; and, since the policies of management affect the public's image of the corporation, it is not surprising to find that the corporate image held by the corporation's key publics may also be confused. Their image of business is confused because it mirrors inconsistencies in the minds and behavior of the men who manage the business enterprise.

"Communicating-Activities"

It is undoubtedly true that every specialized department has its own antennae out to the pertinent environmental forces that affect its particular kind of work. What is often lacking, however, is a synthesis. Even in the larger corporation there is no systematic effort made to synthesize public-relations "intelligence" with all corporate activities. Such a synthesis would present a unified picture to executive management of the *changing role of the company as seen from the outside*. After the synthesis, the next step would be a follow-up to determine whether the appropriate policy decisions had been made throughout the company. Instead, there is usually a mass of unrelated reports on external relations of all sorts that are circulated to many desks at various times. The mass of reports is never processed as a whole or acted upon as a whole, nor indeed is it ever intended to be acted upon as a whole.

Where, then, do the public-relations specialists fit into this broad concept of public relations? Public-relations specialists should properly be the specialists on communication as a potent instrument in all aspects of corporate policy, and not just specialists in the use of mass media. As specialists, their task should be both to counsel executive management in the work of coordinating all the relationships which the corporation has with various publics and to advise company specialists (in marketing, finance, legal work, manufacturing, etc.) on adjusting to the corporate environment in the interest of advancing such types of work.

In order to accomplish these tasks, public-relations specialists should be knowledgeable in:

1 The identity and characteristics of all the key publics toward which company messages are to be directed and from which messages are to be received.

2 The content and purpose of these messages, with special attention to the things that should be said and done in public view by persons and components acting on behalf of the company.

3 The corporate image, not only as it appears in the minds of the key publics toward which company messages are directed and from which messages are received, but also as it operates upon the minds of company personnel in their decision making in all kinds of external relations.

4 The most effective media or channels to be used for communicating with the key publics, not excluding the possible effect of the unintended messages sent out from the company in the form of activities that are not usually considered to be public-relations work.

5 The effects of outwardly directed messages upon these key publics, measured not only in terms of their verbal responses, their opinions and attitudes, but also their actions with respect to matters of concern to all decision makers in every kind of functional work throughout the company.

Since some decisions in public relations obviously deal with highly technical matters (e.g., choice of media, content analysis, etc.) there is always danger that public relations, for this reason, will be regarded as peripheral to the central issues of business policy. This is far from the truth. The choice of key publics, for instance, may profoundly affect the growth and even the survival of the corporation. To cite a single illustration: to exclude government officials from a list of key publics could be a vital error, especially in an age of mounting governmental regulation of business at every level of public government.

Because the "fit" of the corporation into the prevailing social norms depends upon managerial decisions in all functional fields and not just upon the activities of the public-relations departments, a corollary function of such departments, then, would be to keep a watchful eye upon relationships of the entire organization with the public. The specialists would alert the entire organization to public-sensed deviations from standards of performance set by general company objectives. Feedback of opinion polling may be highly useful in developing a new set of premises for future policy decisions in various functional areas. It may be used also, of course, for policy-making in public-relations work with respect to informational output, or "selling" the company.

Some may object that this is too comprehensive a function to require of the public-relations specialist. Perhaps this is asking too much because of the way public-relations work is sometimes organized and staffed, and, especially, in view of the relatively subordinate role the public-relations specialist plays in the operation of many firms. But the answer is simple. The function is of vital importance to the large corporation. If one prefers to attach the public-relations label only to those who perform the more modest role of proclaiming the virtues of the company, then another name must be found for this broader function.

To summarize briefly, then, in order to communicate a meaningful image of the corporation to its key publics, somewhere in the organization someone must perform the broad "intelligence" function of sensing the social climate in which the corporation operates. This is necessary both to management's defining a realistic corporate image and to the effective communication of that image. The success of the projection of that image depends also on how well management is able to coordinate company activities that produce an image in the public eye as a by-product with the specific public-relations function which has as its major goal the projection of the corporate image.

Once executive management appreciates this broader view of public relations as an aspect of communication and as an instrument of corporate policy, many of the current public-relations practices and programs of corporations may well be headed for the junk-pile.

Representing his company in negotiations with outside groups is an important part of the manager's job. Contracts with suppliers and labor unions, sales contracts, financing—all must be negotiated, and relationships with government agencies may depend to a large extent on the manager's skill in negotiations.

In view of this, it is surprising that few if any lists of characteristics needed for success in management include this skill. Yet successful managers generally give it some thought, even if they do not talk much about it.

One outstanding manager who did set down his views on the matter was Walther Rathenau (1867–1922), head of the A.E.G. (the German General Electric Company). Rathenau served on several hundred boards of directors until, in World War I, he was appointed to head the organization charged with making Germany self-sufficient so far as possible. In two books, *In Days to Come* (1917) and *The New Economy* (1918), he advocated national planning with the participation of various groups within the economy.

On Negotiations

Walther Rathenau

Negotiations by mail are never successful in complicated affairs. The written word causes suspicion—on the part of the writer because it binds without recall, on the part of the recipient because it sounds calculated and full of reservations when one looks at it coldly. To this must be added the insoluble problem of all writing: so to write that the reader can understand what the writer wrote.

Hence both correspondents may say to themselves at the first meeting after the correspondence: "I had imagined the other much worse." If that is not the case, the encounter will have been in vain.

The negotiator who is underestimated by the other has an advantage. Small weaknesses of understanding and behavior have aided many. Many have lost success because they made too few mistakes.

Do not believe you will get somewhere by removing all objections. No one lets himself be led *ad absurdum*.

It is not possible to persuade a man, much less to out-talk him. Introduce new facts and new points of view, but never insist. The greatest strength lies in thinking up new proposals as soon as strong objections are made.

When you make proposals send all the weak points in advance. Never hope that your opponent might overlook something. Always assume your opponent to be smarter than you.

Always put yourself in the place of your opposite. Propose only what you would accept in his position, and in all that is said to you weigh the interests which are hidden. Do not think only for yourself, but also for the other man.

A great ability consists in recognizing in advance which points are likely to cause the greatest difficulties and clarifying these points in the beginning of the negotiations.

It is useful to start a few minutes' general conversation before negotiations, even the most serious. In this one may recognize the mood, the objectives, and often the result.

Among clever people who are accustomed to negotiate, a few words are sufficient for important decisions. An inexperienced listener would rarely recognize that these [words] were connected with the problem, would often not even know whether a negative or a positive outcome had resulted.

In the last resort, a decision depends on the views men have of one another. A huge amount of study, preparation, and intensive work by experts brains is wasted—as finally two leaders recognize that the manner of speaking of one is unsympathetic to the other.

A difficult, complicated, or smart idea is of as little use in business as in life. Every great business idea can be explained in a sentence which a child understands. Here as everywhere else the art lies in simplification.

From *Reflexionen* (S. Hirzel, Leipsig, 1908), pp. 95–104. Translated by Ernest Dale.

Good public relations are, of course, necessary for profitability. But aside from this, there is a moral question. Does a company have the right and/or the duty to adopt policies that will further or deter social change? And if so, how far should they be carried? The nature and justification of corporate responsibilities in community life are the subject of questions by Prof. Andrew Hacker of the department of government of Cornell University.

At the time this article was written, there was no federal law prohibiting discrimination on racial grounds in hiring practices; therefore companies were free to decide the matter for themselves in some states. Now that such a law exists, it is not up to management to determine whether or not it will further social change in this respect. But the point Professor Hacker makes in this article is still valid because there are many other cases in which the decision to further change or to oppose it rests with the company—that is, with a small group of top managers.

Do Corporations Have a Social Duty?

Andrew Hacker

Answering charges that his company was not doing as much as it might to alleviate racial tensions in Birmingham, Ala., Roger M. Blough of United States Steel recently asserted that "for a corporation to attempt to exert any kind of economic compulsion to achieve a particular end in the social area seems to me to be quite beyond what a corporation should do." Moreover, he added, it was doubtful whether his company possessed sufficient power to influence attitudes on so controversial a subject as segregation in a Deep South community.

Traditionally the question has been whether a firm's sole obligation is to maximize its profits or whether it should expend some of its resources on improving the general quality of life in society. In recent years the notion that corporations should promote community welfare has become increasingly fashionable. The emphasis in business schools, management magazines and numberless conferences has been that a successful balance sheet is not enough.

"The modern large industrial corporation," a Ford vice president recently remarked, "holds power in trust for the whole community." Few are the executives who have not made at least one speech voicing similar sentiments. Yet the question remains: What social responsibilities are our corporations prepared to assume, and what are the consequences of such an interpretation of the corporation role likely to be?

There is, to be sure, a certain hard-headedness behind the "good citizen" concept. The donation of corporation facilities, money and personnel to community endeavors is often looked upon as a prudent investment. If companies work at building up a reservoir of public goodwill, the theory goes, there is less likely to be popular support for candidates and policies favoring government regulation of business. The image of a corporation that is selflessly dedicated to public service will, it is hoped, persuade voters and politicians that the nation's enterprise is best controlled by private hands.

Moreover, the current generation of managers seems anxious to bestow a mantle of legitimacy on both themselves and the companies over which they preside. In earlier days such legitimacy was secured simply by being an economic success, by outlasting one's competitors. With the transition from entrepreneurial to managerial control, however, burgeoning profits are not enough and hence the search for alternative means of imparting a moral justification to corporate power.

Until now, most corporations have been content to define their social responsibilities in rather conventional ways. They make the expected gifts to universities, hospitals and recognized charities; executives are given time off to assist in community-chest drives, and company premises are made available for civic activities. On occasion some imagination is shown. One company undertakes to promote the fine arts, another has sponsored serious television dramas that are directed to a limited audience. But the point about all these exercises in civic and cultural virtue is that they are eminently uncontroversial. Everyone is in favor of helping liberal-arts colleges, cancer research and the Boy Scouts.

But now the nation's corporations are being

From *The New York Times Magazine*, Nov. 17, 1963, pp. 21, 116, 118.

confronted with some issues that cannot be handled on neutral ground. It is one thing to have the company treasurer write out a check for Cornell's centennial drive; it is quite another to line up behind [integration] in Birmingham. Before asking whether a company like U.S. Steel is evading its social responsibilities, it would be well to consider whether corporations ought to be shouldering noneconomic obligations at all.

To begin with, "corporation" is a short-hand way of referring to the handful of top executives who make company policy. When General Electric or General Motors takes a position it does not imply that either the employes or the stockholders have been consulted or would even necessarily approve. Top management is accountable chiefly to itself, for if the firm continues to be profitable there will be little or no outcry at the annual meetings. What is really being said is that corporations are far removed from being democratic institutions. Therefore, if companies are to exert an influence in the social or political arena they must be judged by aristocratic, not democratic, standards.

Yet in all cases corporate management will necessarily decide for itself which policies promote the best interests of society. For if company executives succumbed to popular pressure and majority opinion, they would cease to be aristocrats. If an aristocracy has any value it lies in its being impervious to public demands of the moment; the corollary is that those with power will know how it should best be used. In this light it may be asked how corporations have interpreted some of their responsibilities in recent years.

One company not only has taken an official stand favoring "right to work" laws but has worked openly for their adoption in various states. In 1958, $30,000 of company money was spent on a California referendum campaign against compulsory unionism. While it is true that a weakening of unions might bring economic gains for the corporation, it took the philosophical position that it was fighting for the rights of the minority who did not wish to be forced to bargain collectively. The company executives who took this position probably felt that they were promoting the moral interests of society, not just their own.

Several other corporations have devoted a good deal of energy to sponsoring programs aimed at awakening both their own employes and the general public to the danger of Communist subversion in this country. They have shown films, distributed pamphlets and conducted lectures stressing the extent of Soviet infiltration at home no less than abroad. Again, there is no doubting the sincerity of the executives who saw it as their social responsibility to dispel apathy and encourage vigilance.

Not a few corporations took it on themselves, without outside prompting, to discharge any employe who refused to cooperate with a legislative investigating committee. There were others that cancelled the contracts of television performers who had been "listed" as belonging to subversive organizations. The evidence is that those who made these decisions judged that they were performing a public service in removing from their payrolls individuals of doubtful loyalty.

The civil-rights field itself provides an example of a corporation making social policy. For almost a decade now, since well before the current protests began, one large firm has been hiring and promoting Negroes to supervisory positions in its Memphis and Louisville plants. While these plants are not in the Deep South, there was nevertheless strong opposition from white employes, who threatened serious trouble if Negroes were upgraded.

However, management made it plain that its policy would be adhered to no matter whose sensibilities were shaken. Any wildcat strikes over Negro promotions would result in suspension and subsequent dismissals. The company had decided what was right, regardless of employe or community opinion, and proceeded to use its power to enforce those ideas.

The obvious conclusion is that the men who manage our corporations have differing and highly personal conceptions of what constitutes social responsibility. Most seek to avoid controversial issues altogether, settling for the safe path of civic endeavor. Those who define their companies' responsibilities in broader terms are as likely as not to see no conflict between their personal preferences and the best interests of society. It is fruitless to protest that the policies of some corporations promote freedom and justice while those of others fail to safeguard basic values. If one company is to have the freedom to promote its racial ideas in Louisville and Memphis, then another must be allowed to pursue its economic theories in California and yet another its notions of civil liberties in Chicago.

What is ironic today is that the Americans who are calling on large corporations to exert their influence in Southern cities in the cause of civil rights are the very people who are uneasy about the presence of corporate power in our society.

The chief characteristic of such power, as the critics point out, is its degree of independence from public control. If corporations have power to exert in such areas they will exercise it as they see fit. The logical alternative is to suggest that any political intervention on the part of corporations has no place in a democracy. This position, at least, has the virtue of consistency.

The tendency is for corporation executives to assume a pose of modesty when estimating the influence of their companies in local affairs. Nevertheless, it is common practice for the dominant employer in any industrial community to be consulted, often deferred to, when important decisions are being made. There is a close liaison between branch plant managers, the state capitol and city hall.

More important are the unstated assumptions surrounding a corporation's decision to locate its plants in a particular locality. The chief determinant is, of course, economic; and this is as it should be. A company will select a location because of cheap or nonunion labor, proximity to market and related factors. At the same time, however, there is a tacit agreement on the part of management to accept the prevailing customs of the community. In the case of U.S. Steel in Birmingham this meant abiding by the principle of segregation. To be sure, the corporation was adjusting to a way of life that existed before it arrived on the scene. Nevertheless, it is clear that U.S. Steel's willingness to cooperate with the folkways of Birmingham actually served to strengthen those social patterns.

For this reason the company's officials cannot protest that they have been mere bystanders amid the racial controversy. It is not the only company that has found itself committed, at least by implication, to one of the two contending sides in the civil-rights struggle. If a corporation decides to go along with the dominant ideology of a region, that does not mean it must defend that ideology. It can and should justify its position solely on economic grounds. Moreover, if corporation executives find themselves involved in politics, on however informal a basis, they ought at least to explain their involvement by pointing out that this promotes the best interests of the company that has hired them.

At all events, such informal arrangements are not uncommon. These are facts of industrial life, whether one is speaking of Birmingham, or Winston-Salem, N.C., or Youngstown, Ohio. Corporate management in such communities inevitably becomes part of the local power structure, and politics and economics cease being separate categories.

Yet there are limits to management's influence: Corporations can play a role in spurring urban renewal and school construction. But there are questions the public wants to decide for itself, and in these touchy areas elected politicians are forced to defer to popular opinion.

Even on those occasions when corporations are able to bring influence to bear in local politics there remains the question of whether they ought to do so. The phrase "corporate citizen" has a certain appeal but it assumes that the voice of a corporation and that of ordinary voters may be listened to with equal deference by those who make policy. Democracy takes on a curious form when both corporations and citizens are regarded as equal participants in the political process. And once again it must be pointed out that if corporate intervention is sought and permitted on certain issues then this opens the door for further intrusions on questions where corporate executives hold less palatable views.

It may well be that corporations should drop all ideas about their supposed "social responsibilities," or at least confine their good works to community-chest drives, gifts to universities and playing fields for the Little League. Once companies begin to assume more grandiose and controversial obligations they will inevitably be judged by standards they are ill-equipped to meet.

While society is too complex for a rigid boundary to be drawn between the economic and the political spheres in everyday life, some line of demarcation ought to be acknowledged. Certainly the political rights of Americans ought not to depend on the occasional helping hand of our corporations. Such liberties are ends in themselves and not by-products of the productive process.

One of the early proponents of the view that business cannot justify itself solely by profitability was Supreme Court Justice Louis D. Brandeis (1856–1941). His special contribution to the understanding of management was his emphasis on the idea that management is potentially an applied science. He also did a great deal to publicize the scientific management movement by his arguments in the Eastern Railroad Rate Case, in which he served as counsel for the shippers, contending that there would be no need for the railroads to raise rates if only they would apply scientific management. (The testimony by Harrington Emerson appearing earlier in this book was given in support of his case.)

As a result of his studies of scientific management, Brandeis came to believe that business was a profession, a career requiring intellectual training in which success was not to measured by remuneration alone. But despite his emphasis on the intellectual content of the job, he never overlooked the manager's need for intuitive abilities.

The following is part of a speech given to the graduating class at Brown University.

Business: A Profession

Louis D. Brandeis

The peculiar characteristics of a profession as distinguished from other occupations, I take to be these:

First. A profession is an occupation for which the necessary preliminary training is intellectual in character, involving knowledge and to some extent learning, as distinguished from mere skill.

Second. It is an occupation which is pursued largely for others and not merely for one's self.

Third. It is an occupation in which the amount of financial return is not the accepted measure of success.

Is not each of these characteristics found today in business worthily pursued?

The field of knowledge requisite to the more successful conduct of business has been greatly widened by the application to industry not only of chemical, mechanical and electrical science, but also the new science of management; by the increasing difficulties involved in adjusting the relations of labor to capital; by the necessary intertwining of social with industrial problems; by the ever extending scope of state and federal regulation of business. Indeed, mere size and territorial expansion have compelled the business man to enter upon new and broader fields of knowledge in order to match his achievements with his opportunities.

This new development is tending to make business an applied science. Through this development the relative value in business of the trading instinct and of mere shrewdness have, as compared with other faculties, largely diminished. The conception of trade itself has changed. The old idea of a good bargain was a transaction in which one man got the better of another. The new idea of a good contract is a transaction which is good for both parties to it.

Under these new conditions, success in business must mean something very different from mere money-making. In business the able man ordinarily earns a larger income than one less able. So does the able man in the recognized professions—in law, medicine or engineering; and even in those professions more remote from money-making, like the ministry, teaching or social work. The world's demand for efficiency is so great and the supply so small, that the price of efficiency is high in every field of human activity.

From *Business—A Profession* (Small, Maynard & Company, Boston, 1914), pp. 2–12. (Originally published in *System*, October, 1912.)

The recognized professions, however, definitely reject the size of the financial return as the measure of success. They select as their test, excellence of performance in the broadest sense—and include, among other things, advance in the particular occupation and service to the community. These are the basis of all worthy reputations in the recognized professions. In them a large income is the ordinary incident of success; but he who exaggerates the value of the incident is apt to fail of real success.

To the business of to-day a similar test must be applied. True, in business the earning of profit is something more than an incident of success. It is an essential condition of success; because the continued absence of profit itself spells failure. But while loss spells failure, large profits do not connote success. Success must be sought in business also in excellence of performance; and in business, excellence of performance manifests itself, among other things, in the advancing of methods and processes; in the improvement of products; in more perfect organization, eliminating friction as well as waste; in bettering the condition of the workingmen, developing their faculties and promoting their happiness; and in the establishment of right relations with customers and with the community.

It was such real success, comparable with the scientist's, the inventor's, the statesman's, which marked the career of William H. McElwain of Boston, who died in 1908 at the age of forty-one. He had been in business on his own account but thirteen years. Starting without means, he left a fortune, all of which had been earned in the competitive business of shoe manufacturing, without the aid of either patent or trademark. That shows McElwain did not lack the money-making faculty.

But his money-making faculty, organizing ability and financial skill were with him servants, not masters.

This is the kind of thing he did: In 1902 the irregularity in the employment of the shoe worker was brought to his attention. He became greatly impressed with its economic waste, with the misery to the workers and the demoralization which attended it. Irregularity of employment is the worst and most extended of industrial evils. Even in fairly prosperous times the workingmen of America are subjected to enforced idleness and loss of earnings, on the average, probably ten to twenty per cent of their working time.

This irregularity had been accepted by the trade—by manufacturers and workingmen alike—as inevitable. It had been bowed to as if it were a law of nature—a cross to be borne with resignation. But with McElwain an evil recognized was a condition to be remedied; and he set his great mind to solving the problem of irregularity of employment in his own factories; just as Wilbur Wright applied his mind to the aeroplane, as Bell, his mind to the telephone, and as Edison, his mind to the problems of electric light. Within a few years irregularity of employment had ceased in the McElwain factories; and before his death every one of his many thousand employees could find work three hundred and five days in the year.

Although Adolf A. Berle, Jr., and others had called attention to the divorce of ownership and control earlier (see Chapter 3), a book on the same theme published in 1941 probably had a much greater influence on managers' conception of their role. This was *The Managerial Revolution* by James Burnham, a professor at New York University, which was widely read and discussed in management circles.

Some of Burnham's predictions have turned out to be wrong—for example, his concept of the future managers as managing technicians and his expectation of state ownership of industrial enterprise. But the managerial revolution, in the sense of the passing of control from owners to managers, is a *fait accompli* in some segments of the economy, and the trend toward it seems to be continuing. The trend has contributed to the view that managers are professionals and as such have obligations to others besides the stockholders.

The Theory of the Managerial Revolution

James Burnham

The theory of the managerial revolution holds, to begin with, that we are now in a period characterized by an unusually rapid rate of change of the most important economic, social, political, and cultural institutions of society. This transition is *from* the type of society which we have called capitalist or bourgeois to a type of society which we shall call *managerial*.

This transition period may be expected to be short compared with the transition from feudal to capitalist society. It may be dated, somewhat arbitrarily, from the first world war, and may be expected to close, with the consolidation of the new type of society, by approximately fifty years from then, perhaps sooner.

I shall now use the language of the "struggle for power" to outline the remaining key assertions of the theory:

What is occurring in this transition is a drive for social dominance, for power and privilege, for the position of ruling class, by the social group or class of the *managers* (as I shall call them, reserving for the moment an explanation of whom this class includes). This drive will be successful. At the conclusion of the transition period the managers will, in fact, have achieved social dominance, will be the ruling class in society. This drive, moreover, is world-wide in extent, already well advanced in all nations, though at different levels of development in different nations.

The economic framework in which this social dominance of the managers will be assured is based upon the state ownership of the major instruments of production. Within this framework there will be no direct property rights in the major instruments of production vested in individuals as individuals.

How, then, it will be at once asked (and this is the key to the whole problem), if that is the economic framework, will the existence of a ruling class be possible? A ruling class, we have seen, means a group of persons who, by virtue of special social-economic relations, exercises a special degree of control over access to the instruments of production and receives preferential treatment in the distribution of the product of these instruments. Capitalists were such a group precisely because they, as individuals, held property rights in the instruments of production. If, in managerial society, no individuals are to hold comparable property rights, how can any group of individuals constitute a ruling class?

The answer is comparatively simple and, as already noted, not without historical analogues. The managers will exercise their control over the instruments of production and gain preference in the distribution of the products, not directly, through property rights vested in them as individuals, but indirectly, through their control of the state which in turn will own and control the instruments of production. The state—that is, the institutions which comprise the state—will, if we wish to put it that way, be the "property" of the managers. And that will be quite enough to place them in the position of ruling class.

The control of the state by the managers will be suitably guaranteed by appropriate political institutions, analogous to the guarantee of bourgeois dominance under capitalism by the bourgeois political institutions.

From *The Managerial Revolution* (The John Day Company, Inc., New York, 1941), pp. 71–72.

For a long time, business was able to justify itself by pointing to the advances in the standard of living achieved through the introduction of machines that increased productivity. Until a comparatively short time ago, in fact, every advance in gross national product (GNP) was considered an unmixed good. But in recent years a great many people have changed their minds about this. They contend that more material goods do not necessarily add to the sum of human happiness and that growth entails losses as well as gains. This article discusses the growing dissent from the view that "more" is necessarily better.

The GNP—A Beast to Be Bridled?

Caroline Bird

Gross National Product, the tabulation of our gross production of goods and services, is the key yardstick of America's unparalleled economic achievement. That achievement has generated for most Americans a standard of living unmatched anywhere else in the world at any time in history. The disenchanted, however—fast growing in number and representing a widening cross-section of backgrounds and status—are alarmed by the *dislocations* of growth; among them, they say, the declining quality of goods and services and a grossly deteriorating environment. And these critics say there is far too little concern about such negative aspects of growth, far too much preoccupation with prosperity.

There is no question that youth has been the catalyst for widespread public attention to this issue. But many older and more qualified observers have been pondering for years, privately and in professional journals, the side effects of economic growth. Now they have more public forums available to them, and we are treated to their views almost daily in the newspapers.

Items:

- Richard A. Falk, a professor of international law at Princeton, told a Congressional Committee: "If the U.S. were to double its GNP, I would think it would be a much less livable society than it is today."
- John Kenneth Galbraith: "I do think it is going to be necessary to slow down the rate of growth of some things. . . . But I haven't worked out the meaning of this. . . ."
- At a meeting of the Joint Economic Committee, Congressman Henry S. Reuss of Wisconsin suggested modifying the goal of "maximum production for the economy" with which the Council of Economic Advisers is charged by the Employment Act of 1946, because it "can mean that as our GNP grows, national pollution also grows every year."
- Senator Edmund Muskie of Maine, while making it clear that he has no wish to force society "back to the Garden of Eden," believed our future growth must be "disciplined," even suggesting to a Senate committee on pollution that "maybe we ought to set some limits on the standard of living."
- Dr. George Harrar, president of the Rockefeller Foundation: We should "put considerably less emphasis on that form of economic growth that simply multiplies production and consumption of material goods."

The earth, say the environmentalists, is a spaceship. It is our home and we have to keep it tidy or perish.

Jean Mayer, the Harvard authority on nutrition, believes that the environment, not food, will be the limiting factor on population growth. "The rich are as much or more of a problem as the poor, as they create very much more pollution, use up much more natural resources," he says.

Biologist Wayne H. Davis figures that an American baby creates 25 times the impact on the environment of an Indian baby, so our population growth, though slower in numbers, is ecologically speaking 10 times as serious as India's. Biologists and zoologists have been warning that the exponential rate of population growth within the United States (even though the fertility rate—the number of babies per 1,000 women of childbearing age—is dropping annually) will lead to ecological disaster in the next hundred years, and they do not think that birth control alone will avert overpopulation. Specialists warn that drastic measures to turn around American family values will be necessary if we are to maintain anything like our present standards.

The Real Problem

Even the most angry critics of growth, as reflected by the GNP, and what it seems, in their view, to say about America's priorities, would perhaps, in quieter moments, acknowledge that the *real* problem may be that America does not have any comparable indices of the nation's

From *Think*, May–June, 1970, pp. 2–8. Reprinted by permission of THINK Magazine, published by IBM.

health and welfare—and thus little guidance—in other important areas of national interest. That is:

1 GNP does not measure the quality of goods and services, merely what you paid for them. Like a cost-plus contract, it actually fattens on inefficiency. Delays, wastes, unnecessary repairs, redundant or short-lived products increase, or perhaps we should say, inflate the Gross National Product.

Professor A. J. Jaffe, manpower and population specialist at Columbia's Bureau of Applied Social Research, cites traffic congestion. "You sit in a taxi trying to get to Kennedy Airport and the GNP goes up every time you can't move." A shuttle train that got there faster and cheaper would cut even real GNP, the deflated index economists use to compare one year with another. Some economists point out that if we counted the laundry bill caused by factory and power plant smoke, we might find it cheaper to catch the dirt in the stack than wash it out of and off everything on which it settles. We'd all be better off, even if we had to pay extra taxes or utility bills to pay for the new stack equipment, but the GNP would be lower.

2 GNP leaves out all the good things that money cannot buy. The GNP was never designed as a measure of welfare, much less happiness. The nation's concern in the '30s was jobs, and GNP was devised to assess whether output was moving fast enough to provide jobs for all the people who wanted them. It does not register the value of a beautiful view, the sweetness of the air, access to fishing or boating on clean water, freedom from lung cancer caused by smog, peace of mind, privacy, quiet, and a lot of other "qualities of life" for which more and more Americans seem willing to give up dollar income.

3 GNP is amoral. A war increases defense spending and, with it, the GNP, but it would be hard to find anyone in this country who seriously believes we are better off for it.

Thus, economists readily acknowledge that the GNP isn't telling us all we should know. "I look forward to the day," Federal Reserve Chairman Arthur Burns told the Congressional Joint Economic Committee, "when statisticians add up the national accounts to take account of the depreciation of the environment. When we learn to do this, we will discover that our gross national product has been deceiving us." Even the net national product, which accounts for capital consumption, makes no pretense of providing a charge against pollution of the environment.

But not many economists believe that the solution to America's quality problem is a slowing or halting of real economic growth. Even theoretically, writes Henry H. Villard of the City College of New York, we need faster growth per capita to take care of a rising population, because each additional person inflicts incrementally higher damage on the environment and costs incrementally more to service, too.

No Letup Ahead

Debate over the question of what lies ahead economically for America—growth or no growth—is almost certainly academic anyway. Excepting normal adjustments, there will be no letup in this growth in the foreseeable future. Villard calculates that real GNP per worker has increased five-fold in the past century and could continue at the same rate for the century to come. Robert Nathan, a consulting economist in Washington, thinks real per capita income will double in the next 25 years and continue to grow for the next "50 or 100." Leon Keyserling, Chairman of the Council of Economic Advisers under Truman, sees no reason why growth shouldn't continue as long as mankind keeps its wits.

Further, while it is our affluence which has produced such unwanted byproducts as pollution, it is that same rising affluence which gives us the capacity to do something about it. We can, in short, afford to think about long-run consequences, unlike less-developed nations whose energies are almost wholly consumed with the problems of survival now.

Economists aren't as alarmed as the ecologists at the thought of three or four hundred million Americans, but they warn that per capita GNP must continue to rise with population as it has in the past. As for depletion of natural resources, the economists expect cheap nuclear power to open up alternatives.

Nor do economists see a lack of work for the new hands. Several predict a consumer goods boom as poverty programs succeed in bringing the poor up to middle class standards of consumption. Feeding the hungry Asians is another production job. And if the population rises even modestly, America will have to replace its overloaded transportation, utility, communication, educational, medical and housing facilities with entirely new systems.

New Priorities Needed

And so we are where the critics really want America to come out—we need a set of priorities quite different from those implied or encouraged by a standard of measure which merely counts dollars.

How to redirect priorities? It is a transcendently difficult problem. According to calculations in the February 1970 Economic Report of the President, "existing, visible, and strongly supported claims [on the national output] already exhaust the national output [and real national income] for some years ahead." Thus, it goes on, "the country is already at a point where . . . a decision to satisfy an existing claim on a larger scale or to satisfy a new claim will require giving up something on which people are already counting."

Who will give up what?

Businessmen point out that the private, taxpaying sector of the economy is going to have to prosper if only to generate the tax money for the cleanup. The bigger the pie, the easier it is to change the way it is cut. And many of them have now moved toward the notion that the public sector is going to need a bigger cut of that pie in order to move the private sector to action on the public's behalf.

Most economists are neo-Malthusians. They agree with the Reverend Malthus that the population cannot grow indefinitely, but they don't think that food supply will be the limiting factor. It may be waste disposal or something else. But whatever it is, they say, technology can put the day off for the foreseeable future.

Three Facing Transition

For some industries, the need to change priorities has already arrived. Three facing transition are worth examining briefly because they have been singled out by the critics.

The automobile industry is facing the sticky problems that go with changing priorities and shifting emphasis from private to public sector. "One out of every six or seven jobs in the country depends in some way on the automobile industry," Martha Griffiths, Congresswoman from Michigan, warns. "Anything that slows down or kills the automobile industry slows down the economy, too." She says the economists are so entranced with their slide rules that they don't realize the political problem of moving jobs from one industry to another or activity from the private to the public sector.

Ford's chief economist denies that the pollution of increasing production can't be controlled and asserts that "more GNP is required to control pollution better," but he also mentions "deeper issues . . . as to the nature of what is produced, whether lower total production would mean less pollution, the sacrifices this would entail, and, more broadly, the whole question of population size."

The industry is also acting. It is doing a lot of things that Ralph Nader and the environmentalists have been demanding: smaller cars; a cutback on model changes; less emphasis on speed; research into the electric car, and new emission control and safety features.

Paper consumption sensitively distinguishes rich from poor nations and good times from bad. In the United States, consumption moves with the business cycle at a remarkably constant rate of paper and board per $1,000 of real GNP, and the industry sees steady expansion ahead. Edwin A. Locke, Jr., president of the American Paper Institute, expects paper consumption per capita to grow more than two percent a year indefinitely—enough to cover the finite landscape with a visible paperfall by the magic year 2000.

Disposal, not resource, will be the limiting factor. Consumerists charge American packaging with adding to costs and litter. The industry supports litter control campaigns and research on systems for recycling, aimed at raising the percentage of waste paper which is reused (the current figure is 20 percent). New technology could also make an acre of timberland go six to seven times further by improving yields, using lighter weights for many uses, and increasing the reuse of waste. Locke favors a unified strategy for environmental control, tougher laws against polluters, and government research on recycling techniques.

The "Siting" Dilemma

For the electric power industry, the energy base of all production, the crisis of growth is sharper, and the crisis is already here. The "siting dilemma" facing Con Edison can only get worse. Donald C. Cook, president of American Electric Power Company, Inc., serving the Midwest and near South, has calculated that the country will need 400 or 500 new power plants between now and the year 2000. Although he maintains that "all systems of power production can be made compatible with the environment," he and other industry spokesmen have begun, in 1970, to warn that we're going to have to make choices. "Should every business be weighted by whether it can restore fresh air and water and livable earth as fast as it destroys them?" he asks. "Would you throw on the scales the social value of the product—as, for example, medical supplies?"

Tradeoffs will have to be made, but who will make them? Both Cook and Charles Luce, board chairman of Consolidated Edison Company of New York, complain that none of the many regulatory agencies in a position to veto new power plants is charged with the responsibility for balancing environmental and aesthetic considerations against need, reliability, relation to other new projects, and costs.

Social scientists in and out of the government are developing new measurements. At Health, Education and Welfare as well as at the Brookings Institution, economists are designing "social indicators" that will measure changes in such things as infant mortality, black employment and morbidity rate and whatever else seems desirable. At the National Bureau of Economic Research, statisticians are trying to measure "disproducts" such as noise and nuisance. At the Bureau of the Budget the office of statistical policy is revealing existing statistics that can be used as social indicators in identifying new ones that ought to be kept, and Budget's office of program evaluation is studying ways to match existing indicators to public spending to find out such things as how much reduction in infant mortality the dollar spent on health can be expected to buy.

Quite clearly, though, new yardsticks alone will not improve the quality of service and performance, and the environment, about which the critics complain. There must be, as well, new ways to *deliver* the quality.

The need for radically new systems of handling higher volumes is acute in the service and service-like "TUC" (transportation, utilities, communications) industries, many of which have had overloaded physical facilities for years.

Air travel, the stock exchange, the phone system, the utilities, hospitals, schools, even libraries can't increase their capacity economically simply by building more of the same, any more than present phone traffic could be handled by any conceivable expansion of hello girl-power. The new volumes simply have to be handled in a brand new way. Some of the new systems have already been designed; others remain to be devised. In his *Century of Mismatch*, published by David McKay, Simon Ramo, founder of TRW, Inc., says that the "systems approach" is the only way to manage natural resources, mass transit, pollution control, education and public health.

Whose Job?

So the attack on GNP calls for an examination in depth of many factors. Whose job is it?

One of the curious phenomena of 1970 is that news sources say things you don't expect them to say. Businessmen call for government regulation, heavier taxes and expansion of the public sector. Nonscientists count on future inventions to break bottlenecks, while scientists complain, on the editorial pages of *Science*, that technology can't solve everything and science can't sort good from evil.

Economists say that social indicators which reflect more values outside the competence of economics are needed to interpret economic performance; that growth can continue only by expanding the public sector, a job for politicians.

Politicians react in surprise. "Who, me? My job is to implement public opinion, not change it." Their competence is judging public sentiment, and the judgment of most is that the public isn't ready for radical change.

Still, there is consensus that change must come. The attackers, the economists, the businessmen are in closer agreement than their rhetoric makes them sound. They agree that we have to consider a lot of details we used to ignore, such as the final destination of the garbage. They agree that the reconsideration must be of the total picture; almost every businessman queried complained of "piecemeal" solutions and uncoordinated regulations. They agree that the problem is to choose new goals directed to the quality of life. They agree that this is a political, not an economic problem—one for government or the public rather than for technicians.

The diagnosis and even the general remedies are clear to most of those who have had to think seriously about America's future growth. What isn't clear—yet—is who will make the first move and what that move will be.

Industry's social responsibility to stop polluting the air and water is in a somewhat different category from any responsibility it acknowledges for, say, helping education or art or working for legislation considered socially desirable. In the case of discrimination against minorities, for example, industry did not create the problem; it merely went along with what it thought the popular view. And now that discrimination is forbidden by law, most companies are convinced that the popular view has changed and are willing to go along with it. But a considerable amount of the pollution that exists is directly due to industrial processes; the only question, therefore, is how much cleanup is really necessary. John Maddox, who is the editor of the British weekly *Nature*, has written a book, *The Doomsday Syndrome*, in which he questions the idea that the environmental problems industry has created are as serious as some people suppose.

Environmentalism May Be Doing More Harm than Good

(An Interview with John Maddox)

Maddox: I wrote this book because a year ago I became offended by the way people were talking about environmental problems without having any sense of economics or history. It's one thing to be properly concerned about air pollution, and it's another to forget that a hundred years ago we had much more serious environmental problems that were subsequently solved. In the 1870s people were desperately anxious, and rightly so, because they didn't understand, for example, where infectious disease came from. We're in a better position now to understand problems. It seems to me most of the environmental problems are not matters of ecological catastrophe, but really of economic priorities. Does one actually want to spend 2% of the gross national product on clean air and water? And if so, what will one give up instead?

What you argue in your book is that the environment is pretty sturdy and can take a great deal of insult.

Maddox: That's right. The case of DDT and its effect on wildlife is a good illustration. All kinds of people who should know better have stood up and said it's well known that DDT is spread all over the world, by which they mean you can find traces of DDT in birdlife in the Antarctic. But the concentrations of DDT there are one-thousandth of the amount you find in California. So it seems to me the figures support the contention that DDT is still largely concentrated where it was used. There's no evidence at all, for example, that the flamingos in Africa, even though they are fish-eating birds, have been damaged. And it turns out that the pelicans off the coast of California that failed to breed a couple of years ago, which have been held up as a kind of symbol of global pollution by DDT, are

From *Forbes*, Jan. 15, 1973, pp. 42–44. Reprinted by permission of FORBES magazine.

back breeding now. They were, in fact, damaged by pesticides put out in large quantities by a chemical manufacturer in Los Angeles, and though the pelicans in colonies off Los Angeles and Santa Barbara were affected, the ones to the north near Big Sur were all right.

What you're saying is that our pollution problems are local—that we may harm pelicans if we dump DDT off Los Angeles, but we're not going to damage penguins by remote control in Antarctica.

Maddox: That's right. Another thing that makes me very cross is that people leap to the conclusion that DDT must somehow be responsible for any change in the ecology. Herring have been much less plentiful in the North Sea in the past four or five years, and in Britain people have been saying, obviously the herring have been killed off by DDT. Then, when you look at the figures, you discover haddock and plaice are actually much more common than they used to be, so that what's happened is really some kind of ecological change—maybe a temperature or salinity change. What's happening is an interesting ecological problem, but to blame it on DDT is absurd. There isn't a shred of evidence to connect the two.

Fred Hartley of Union Oil got caught in quite a ruckus a few years ago when he was accused of having dismissed the Santa Barbara oil spill on the grounds that it had damaged only a few birds. Aren't you really arguing that this is not an unreasonable attitude—that the benefits to human beings far outweigh the damage to other creatures?

Maddox: I admit the conservation question is quite tricky. I think there are strong arguments for preserving organisms of all kinds, even bacteria. But it seems to me that there's no case for thinking each particular colony of animals should be kept just as it is, in good shape. In Britain, some years ago, Imperial Chemical Industries wanted to build a reservoir in a valley in Wiltshire, and the botanists immediately protested that this valley contained the only collection of Alpine flowers in Britain left from the last ice age. There are many such flowers in France and Sweden, and Switzerland is full of them. So it seems to me there's no conservation case here, though there may be an aesthetic one. To suggest that flooding that valley would actually destroy something unique in the world is rubbish.

But surely you can't feel that a concern for the environment—even an exaggerated one—is bad?

Maddox: I find that the most worrying thing about the whole environmental movement is that it does create this enormous polarization between one side and the other. I agree the population problem is serious, I am as anxious as the next man that we shan't be killed off by something in the environment, and I do prefer clean air to dirty air. But these issues must be looked at economically.

In your book you call this fear of environmental catastrophe the doomsday syndrome, and suggest it had its origins in the postwar concern over the perils of radioactive fallout.

Maddox: In the Fifties it seemed to me that fallout *was* a serious environmental problem—I spent a lot of time battling against weapons tests myself. It could really have had quite a large effect, and it's only quite recently that people have been able to recognize that fallout wouldn't have been as damaging as seemed possible in the 1950s. I think that was actually a quite just battle. I think the environmental movement had its roots there. It was a time when it seemed proper for scientists to leave the laboratory and engage in public activity of all kinds. A good many, I suspect, relished the sense of demagoguery.

Demagoguery?

Maddox: There's a very revealing sentence in Barry Commoner's book, *The Closing Circle*, in which he says in effect: In the 1950s we were all engaged in this righteous battle with the Atomic Energy Commission, and then in the 1960s, with the partial test-ban treaties, we were able to turn our attention to other things. The sentence ran something like this: We were wondering what to do next, and along came Rachel Carson. I think in a sense it was like that.

What I don't understand is: You approve opposing nuclear testing despite our lack of knowl-

edge of the effect of fallout, but you don't seem to feel we have to look before we leap in other areas.

Maddox: We are now much better placed to anticipate the impact of technical innovation on the environment. But instead of that making people feel rather confident, it's had the opposite effect. The problems of the future always seem more difficult than the problems of the past because the problems of the future haven't yet been solved, and people go around saying, "Look at this problem that hasn't been solved; look at that problem that hasn't been solved." A century ago we wouldn't have known the problems were there. Look at the pharmaceutical industry. The thalidomide disaster was a real disaster, but the consequences are that we now have very much better methods of screening drugs: new licensing procedures, ways of working with drugs in the laboratory. I would bet a disaster like that will not happen again.

So basically you think we can stop worrying about pollution and go on about our business.

Maddox: I'm quite passionately convinced that the important problems today are much like the important problems of a century ago and unlikely to go away—problems like how do you look after poverty and how do you provide the means of upward mobility in society. It seems to me inconceivable that one could do anything sensible about these problems without having growth in the system.

You're saying environmental problems are not so serious that we have to give them first priority?

Maddox: The richest country in the world can obviously pay 2% of its GNP on cleaning up air and water pollution. But I think that there's a danger that 2% spent on this will actually limit the country's capacity to spend what it needs on the problems of the cities, the problems of poverty and so on. What the environmentalists are really asking is not that we stop our present rate of economic development and our present tendencies, but that we should quickly turn back the clock. This seems to me to raise all kinds of political problems, chief of which is that the voters won't have it. In that sense, the environmentalists are at odds with the community, which does seem actually to like it more or less the way it is.

Of course, many environmentalists—Commoner among them—seem as interested in changing the system as in protecting the environment.

Maddox: In many ways, it's an alliance between the extreme right and extreme left. In Britain there are people who feel passionately that foxes should be protected from DDT so they can be saved for hunting in winter. At the other end of the spectrum there are people who say darkly we need a radical change in the economic system. What they really want presumably is a much more highly directed social system.

But what is the harm in raising these questions?

Maddox: I'm inclined to think the environmental movement has already done a fair amount of damage in displacing priorities from where they should be. I'm really worried by the precedent set by the auto industry regulations to take effect in 1975. Air pollution is almost exclusively a city problem, and to impose these regulations and costs on all motor cars seems to me not necessarily the best way to produce the desired effect. First of all, Detroit may not be able to meet the standards on purely technical grounds. If they do meet the standards, there's going to be a loss in the efficiency of the engine and a loss of efficiency in the oil refinery. So that's going to accentuate the fuel crisis.

What I think likely to happen is that the emission controls will be discovered to operate at 25% of the present levels, instead of 10%, and in 1975 Detroit will be able to say: Well, look, we have invested all this money, so that the Environmental Protection Agency will have to change its regulations a bit. And that extra cost of the controls will still be there. So maybe by 1982 there'll be a 75% reduction in output of pollutants in cities like New York. But long before that, the extra cost of operating a car will have persuaded people of the value of keeping their cars at home and using public transport. In which case, one might have achieved the same effect by simply taxing cars.

20 The Theory and Practice of Decision Making

Management itself is sometimes defined simply as decision making, for the manager must choose among various courses of action in performing each of the management functions: He must choose, for example, among different possibilities in formulating plans, in developing his organization and staffing it, and in his day-to-day direction of the work. And certainly nothing in the way of innovation can be introduced unless a manager decides to go ahead with a new course of action.

Economists have long been interested in the decision-making process, for the whole economy is influenced by decisions made by managers. If managers in general decide to expand their operations, for example, the result will be higher employment, then perhaps eventual overcapacity and resulting unemployment.

Originally the discussions of managerial decision making by economists tended to consider the managers purely rational economic men. From this it followed that if an opportunity for profit existed, one could count on their taking advantage of it. To some extent, this is a valid premise, but it is an oversimplified one and is now being refined, as is evident from the first two articles in this chapter, which deal with decision making from the economist's viewpoint.

The next three articles cover the way in which business decisions are actually made. The first of these explains why a decision is "only a moment in a process," and the other two report on surveys of how businessmen make decisions.

However, even though decisions made at the top may be influenced by those lower down, every executive must make some decisions himself and accept responsibility for them. How he can increase the odds that he will be right is explained in the piece "Techniques of Decision Making."

The final article is an entertaining and only slightly exaggerated account of the hard decisions a top executive faces.

One of the most cogent analyses of investment decisions is that postulated by the great economist Lord (John Maynard) Keynes (1883–1946) in his famous chapter 12 of *The General Theory of Employment, Interest, and Money*. Many investors on the stock exchange purchase the book solely for this chapter.

Of course decisions made within a firm on investment in new facilities are based largely on long-term expectations of actual events. But in making these decisions, managers are also conscious that actual events will to some extent depend on the consensus of expectations, and that, therefore, one must still attempt to forecast what other people's forecasts will be.

The State of Long-Term Expectations

Lord Keynes

Decisions to invest in private business of the old-fashioned type were decisions largely irrevocable, not only for the community as a whole, but also for the individual. With the separation between ownership and management which prevails to-day and with the development of organised investment markets, a new factor of great importance has entered in, which sometimes facilitates investment but sometimes adds greatly to the instability of the system. In the absence of security markets, there is no object in frequently attempting to revalue an investment to which we are committed. But the Stock Exchange revalues many investments every day and the revaluations give a frequent opportunity to the individual (though not to the community as a whole) to revise his commitments. It is as though a farmer, having tapped his barometer after breakfast, could decide to remove his capital from the farming business between 10 and 11 in the morning and reconsider whether he should return to it later in the week. But the daily revaluations of the Stock Exchange, though they are primarily made to facilitate transfers of old investments between one individual and another, inevitably exert a decisive influence on the rate of current investment. For there is no sense in building up a new enterprise at a cost greater than that at which a similar existing enterprise can be purchased; whilst there is an inducement to spend on a new project what may seem an extravagant sum, if it can be floated off on the Stock Exchange at an immediate profit. Thus certain classes of investment are governed by the average expectation of those who deal on the Stock Exchange as revealed in the price of shares, rather than by the genuine expectations of the professional entrepreneur. How then are these highly significant daily, even hourly, revaluations of existing investments carried out in practice?

Valuation by Convention

In practice we have tacitly agreed, as a rule, to fall back on what is, in truth, a *convention*. The essence of this convention—though it does not, of course, work out quite so simply—lies in assuming that the existing state of affairs will continue indefinitely, except in so far as we have specific reasons to expect a change. This does not mean that we really believe that the existing state of affairs will continue indefinitely. We know from extensive experience that this is most unlikely.

Nevertheless the above conventional method of calculation will be compatible with a considerable measure of continuity and stability in our affairs, *so long as we can rely on the maintenance of the convention*.

For if there exist organised investment markets and if we can rely on the maintenance of the convention, an investor can legitimately encourage himself with the idea that the only risk he runs is that of a genuine change in the news *over the near future*, as to the likelihood of which he can attempt to form his own judgment, and which is unlikely to be very large. For, assuming that the convention holds good, it is only these changes which can affect the value of his investment, and he need not lose his sleep merely because he has not any notion what his investment will be worth ten years hence. Thus investment becomes reasonably "safe" for the individual investor over short periods, and hence over a succession of short periods however many, if he can fairly rely on there being no breakdown in the convention and on his therefore having an opportunity to revise his judgment and change his investment, before there has been time for much to happen. Investments which are "fixed" for the community are thus made "liquid" for the individual.

But there is one feature in particular which deserves our attention. It might have been supposed that competition between expert professionals, possessing judgment and knowledge beyond that of the average private investor, would correct the vagaries of the ignorant individual left to himself. It happens, however, that the energies and skill of the professional investor and speculator are mainly occupied otherwise. For most of these persons are, in fact, largely concerned, not with making superior long-term forecasts of the probable yield of an investment over its whole life, but with foreseeing changes in the conventional basis of valuation a short time ahead of the general public. They are concerned, not with what an investment is really worth to a man who buys it "for keeps," but with what the market will value it at, under the influence of mass psychology, three months or a year hence. Moreover, this behavior is not the outcome of a wrong-headed propensity. It is an inevitable result of an investment market organised along the lines described. For it is not sensible to pay 25 for an investment of which you believe the prospective yield to justify a value of 30, if you also believe that the market will value it at 20 three months hence.

Thus the professional investor is forced to concern himself with the anticipation of impending changes, in the news or in the atmosphere, of the kind by which experience shows that the mass psychology of the market is most influenced.

This battle of wits to anticipate the basis of conventional valuation a few months hence, rather than the prospective yield of an investment over a long term of years, does not even require gulls amongst the public to feed the maws of the professional;—it can be played by professionals amongst themselves. Nor is it necessary that anyone should keep his simple faith in the conventional basis of valuation having any genuine long-term validity.

Professional investment may be likened to those newspaper competitions in which the competitors have to pick out the six prettiest faces from a hundred photographs, the prize being awarded to the competitor whose choice most nearly corresponds to the average preferences of the competitors as a whole; so that each competitor has to pick, not those faces which he himself finds prettiest, but those which he thinks likeliest to catch the fancy of the other competitors, all of whom are looking at the problem from the same point of view. It is not a case of choosing those which, to the best of one's judgment, are really the prettiest, nor even those which average opinion genuinely thinks the prettiest. We have reached the third degree where we devote our intelligences to anticipating what average opinion expects the average opinion to be. And there are some, I believe, who practise the fourth, fifth and higher degrees.

Long-Term Investments

If the reader interjects that there must surely be large profits to be gained from the other players in the long run by a skilled individual who, unperturbed by the prevailing pastime, continues to purchase investments on the best genuine long-term expectations he can frame, he must be answered, first of all, that there are, indeed, such serious-minded individuals and that it makes a vast difference to an investment market whether or not they predominate in their influence over the game-players. But we must also add that there are several factors which jeopardise the predominance of such individuals in modern investment markets. Investment based on genuine long-term expectation is so difficult to-day as to be scarcely practicable. He who attempts it must surely lead much more laborious days and run greater risks than he who tries to guess better than the crowd how the crowd will behave; and, given equal intelligence, he may make more disastrous mistakes. There is no clear evidence from experience that the investment policy which is socially advantageous coincides with that which is more profitable. It needs *more* intelligence to defeat the forces of time and our ignorance of the future than to beat the gun.

These considerations should not lie beyond the purview of the economist. But they must be relegated to their right perspective. If I may be allowed to appropriate the term *speculation* for the activity of forecasting the psychology of the market, and the term *enterprise* for the activity of forecasting the prospective yield of assets over their whole life, it is by no means always the case that speculation predominates over enterprise. As the organisation of investment markets improves, the risk of the predominance of speculation does, however, increase. In one of the greatest investment markets in the world, namely, New York, the influence of speculation (in the above sense) is enormous. Even outside the field of finance, Americans are apt to be unduly interested in discovering what average opinion believes average opinion to be; and this national weakness finds its nemesis in the stock market. It is rare, one is told, for an American to invest, as many Englishmen still do, "for income"; and he will not readily purchase an investment except in the hope of capital appreciation. This is only another way of saying that, when he purchases an investment, the American is attaching his hopes, not so much to its prospective yield, as to a favourable change in the conventional basis of valuation, *i.e.* that he is, in the above sense, a speculator. Speculators may do no harm as bubbles on a steady stream of enterprise. But the position is serious when enterprise becomes the bubble on a whirlpool of speculation. When the capital development of a country becomes a by-product of the activities of a casino, the job is likely to be ill-done. The measure of success attained by Wall Street, regarded as an institution of which the proper social purpose is to direct new investment into the most profitable channels in terms of future yield, cannot be claimed as one of the outstanding triumphs of *laissez-faire* capitalism—which is not surprising, if I am right in thinking that the best brains of Wall Street have been in fact directed towards a different object.

The spectacle of modern investment markets has sometimes moved me towards the conclusion that to make the purchase of an investment permanent and indissoluble, like marriage, except by reason of death or other grave cause, might be a useful remedy for our contemporary evils. For this would force the investor to direct his mind to the long-term prospects and to those only. But a little consideration of this expedient brings us up against a dilemma, and shows us how the liquidity of investment markets often facilitates, though it sometimes impedes, the course of new investment. For the fact that his commitment is "liquid" (though this cannot be true for all investors collectively) calms his nerves and makes him much more willing to run a risk. If individual purchases of investments were rendered illiquid, this might seriously impede new investment, so long as *alternative ways* in which to hold his savings are available to the individual. This is the dilemma. So long as it is open to the individual to employ his wealth in hoarding or lending *money*, purchasing actual capital assets cannot be rendered sufficiently attractive.

We should not conclude from this that everything depends on waves of irrational psychology. We are merely reminding ourselves that human decisions affecting the future, whether personal or political or economic, cannot depend on strict mathematical expectation.

The following is drawn from an analysis of the basis of decision making in Rolls-Royce over a period of years prior to 1949. (The situation in the company has changed since that time.) The author concluded, after a study in which he was given access to the company archives, "that in considering decision making, the importance of personality and tradition has been grossly under-estimated," and that, "because profit is the most visible index of industrial efficiency, the economist has been content to construct his theories on the basis of the plausible assumption that a symptom of industrial health is the principal regulator of industrial activity. He has also assumed into the process of decision far more logic and uniformity than is warranted except in the case of the simplest decisions."

Economic Theory and Business Decisions

I. S. Lloyd

At present most economists seem to concern themselves with what they have defined as the economic aspects of human behaviour, and, because it is so obvious that those aspects of human behaviour which do not find some economic context seem to be so few, they have fallen readily into the habit either of disregarding non-economic motives entirely, or of establishing a convenient rate of exchange between the economic and the non-economic motive. In so doing they have seriously underrated the power of those motivations of human behaviour which operate in the economic sphere but which cannot by the wildest stretch of the axes be regarded as the result of a rational assessment of economic advantage of the individual, whether his actions concern only himself or some organisation on whose behalf he is acting.

At the outset two broad fields of economic thought can be distinguished. The first, and most important, is that which concerns itself with the behaviour of the individual, or the individual economic unit, and attempts to construct a complete and consistent explanation of behaviour in the economic context. The second is concerned with the broad aggregates of human behaviour, the statistically measurable economic environment which is the compound result of the behaviour of individuals and organisations. The scientific analysis of these patterns of behaviour is almost completely dependent on measurement, and from such measurement alone useful conclusions can be drawn as to trends and tendencies. These conclusions provide a perfectly adequate foundation for the construction of a useful theoretical apparatus provided that the various statistical criteria of accuracy, completeness, frequency of measurement etc., are satisfied. This is simply a rather elaborate way of referring to what Sir Robert Watson-Watt summarised so neatly as "the goodness of measured fact." Aggregates and rates of change of physical factors which may have considerable economic significance —population, the capacity and movements of freight cars and cargo ships, the numbers of given types of machine tools employed in a factory or a country—these can be and are measured. It is also possible to measure aggregates and rates of change of purely economic phenomena which may or may not be directly related to physical factors. Such measurements may be primary or secondary. A primary measurement for example may be defined as the volume of bank deposits, the revenue and expenditure figures of trading enterprises or a state department. A secondary measurement would include such things as the income of a trading enterprise or community, the cost of production of an article, the capital invested in an enterprise or industry. Such measurements are defined here as secondary because the monetary figures on which they are based are without exception dependent upon some value judgment on the part of the accountant or cost accountant which may be quite arbitrary within wide limits.

It is true that value judgments may enter into primary measurements to some extent when there is some uncertainty as to whether or not to include a particular item, but such uncertainty can usually be eliminated statistically with considerable accuracy and the order of magnitude of error is comparatively small.

There is also a third type of measurement, as yet very largely unexplored by the economist or statistician. These are the primarily physical indices of production volume and efficiency—man-hours, machine-tool hours, records of stock—which have been developed as instruments of control. Without these the more complex types of industrial enterprise find their purely economic or financial measurements inadequate as instruments of executive control because of the delay which occurs between the operations concerned and the appearance of the cost and financial figures which refer to them.

It will be readily observed that both primary

From "The Environment of Business Decision—Some Reflections on the History of Rolls-Royce," *The South African Journal of Economics*, Vol. 17, No. 4, December, 1949, pp. 457–461.

economic measurements and secondary economic measurements are dependent upon the existence of money or money-values which relate to some process of exchange or production to which there has been an addition or subtraction of value. The economic quantities entering the process are absolute and accurately measurable. Those issuing forth from the other side are accurately measurable but not absolute until they are so regarded for a succeeding process of production or consumption. The extent of this addition or subtraction, within limits which may be wide or narrow, depending on the nature of the process, is a matter of individual judgment. There can be no dispute about expenditure and revenue. There may be, and there very often is, considerable dispute within a productive unit about the allocation of values employed in production.

If the economist concerns himself entirely with the measurement of primary economic phenomena, then he is very largely justified in disregarding the motivations of behaviour which give rise to these strictly definable physical movements of physical commodities or services and the money or money-values which represent them and facilitate their transfer. He is entitled to draw the most abstruse conclusions from the fact that the volume of money in circulation and the output of coal both increase at Christmas time. He may go further and investigate the rate at which they increase and decrease, and he may, if he wishes, connect the two series with the physical imports of crackers and dynamite, which he is justified in valuing at current prices.

It is obvious, however, that these measurements in themselves are of very little use or significance and that the measurements which do interest us are the secondary measurements, which, however imperfect or arbitrary, give us some indication as to what is happening in the economic system. It is the function of the economist not only to tell society that it is pouring money down the drain, but which drain and why. Society is interested in finding out what it is getting for its efforts and why this seems either less or more than it expects. Therefore the economist must concern himself with all those secondary measurements which assist him in judging the profitability of a single enterprise or of a country. Once he admits the necessity of measuring these aggregates or their rates of change he admits the necessity of concerning himself with human behaviour in two senses. There is still the purely quantitative element—the aggregate result of the exercise of individual judgments—which has its own independent significance. An example of this is the proportion which depreciation bears to total costs in all corporations whose capitalisation or annual profits fall within certain limits. But there is also a human element which he can no longer legitimately ignore if he is seeking to *explain* the functioning of the industrial system in a given historical environment. Still less can he ignore it if he is seeking to predict its functioning in an environment which can never change very rapidly.

In the theory of the firm the economist has set out to describe the economic limitations within which it must operate and has endeavoured to explain by reference to a rather arbitrary set of motivations why the entrepreneur behaves as he does. He assumes the operation of universal economic laws, or at least he assumes that the entrepreneur is always constrained or prodded by these laws and by these laws alone, even if the entrepreneur is unaware of their existence. He infers that the experienced executive is the man who intuitively achieves the equal marginal productivity of all factors of production and thereby maximises revenue, or profit, over as long as possible a period of time. Knowing that the real world exhibits startling digressions from this norm of rational behaviour, and that certain institutional conditions enable the enterprise which has developed some degree of monopoly to act in an irrational or non-logical manner, or in a manner at least inconsistent with the original theories of competitive equilibrium, he has developed his theories, and twisted his curves to cope with these imperfections as they manifest themselves in the economies with which he is familiar. He endeavours to fit each successive complication into some scheme of rational and predictable behaviour but from time to time the load of imperfections becomes somewhat heavy and there occurs a climacteric faulting of the theoretical crust. There is a point beyond which a theoretical system cannot be modified.

If a strong case had been made for the universal validity of these laws on which the existing analysis of the economic behaviour of groups or organisations is based, if the economist could be satisfied that there were very few exceptions to the rules of economic behaviour which he has evolved and that the theory was capable of dealing with an eruption of the most unpalatable facts, then it might reasonably be argued that the motivation of behaviour in the industrial environment was none of his business. It could be argued that it follows predictable and measurable patterns and that it responds to certain stimuli, of whose nature he is aware in a manner which he has measured in a sufficient number of cases to warrant a description of these phenomena as "laws" of economic behaviour. It would be somewhat bold to suggest that the present analysis of the economic behaviour of the group can claim immunity from criticism, either on the grounds of its applicability within the limits of its own assumptions, or on the grounds that it can be successfully modified and made applicable to an environment which is always changing.

If the present theoretical structure corresponds with reality only in the limiting sense that its conclusions may be said to represent truisms or common sense, then it would seem that there are strong a priori grounds for assuming that its foundations are inadequate, and that in an effort to preserve a sufficiently malleable environment for our analytical technique, to keep the number and type of variables within its limits, an apparatus has been developed which at its best can give only a partial explanation, and which sometimes gives a completely incorrect explanation because it does not correctly weight those elements of the problem which do come within its scope and ignores others which do not. These other elements may operate with marked consistency and regularity and with a force equal and opposite to those which have been isolated in the mistaken belief that they are the sole determinants of the situation. It is equally possible that they may reinforce the known elements and if this happens in a majority of cases the conclusion is too readily drawn that the economic motive is the most powerful, and that it is usually sufficiently powerful to override all other motives, and that where it is not sufficiently powerful the other motives may be brought within the scope of economic analysis by the simple process of giving them an economic value.

An excellent example of this may be found in the text-book discussions on mobility of labour which invariably assume that every man has his price in the sense that a sufficiently high wage will always induce him to move. This may be true, but in the vast majority of cases the additional wage or salary which would have to be paid to induce a man to move is far greater than anything which he is likely to be offered. Therefore the theory, though possibly true in the limiting and exceptional sense to which the economist is so partial, is not only inadequate as an explanation of immobility but a positive hindrance to accurate thought on the problem. An adequate theory must surely provide a complete explanation of the behaviour under consideration. It would have to consider all the motives which operate on the average employee under various circumstances and would provide a technique for evaluating their relative strength, even if this could not be done in terms of pounds, shillings and pence. Our present theory is quite incapable of explaining, except by the use of the word "friction," the fact that different rates of pay for the same work have for generations been paid in towns less than forty miles apart. The fact that there has been some small movement from the one town to the other, in the case which I have in mind, is an indication not of the weakness of the economic motive but of the great strength of the other motives.

The fact that authority to make a given decision is formally attached to a given position does not necessarily mean that the holder of that position is the sole decision maker, as the following article explains.

Mary Parker Follett began her career as a social worker and, in that capacity, became interested in vocational guidance and then in business and management. She developed into a political and sociological theorist of considerable stature to whom businessmen listened with respect. The following is an excerpt from a lecture she gave to the students at the London School of Economics. Her statement that "an executive decision is a moment in a process" is undoubtedly true and has been widely quoted.

The Illusion of Final Authority

Mary Parker Follett

When writers on business management speak of "ultimate authority" and "supreme control" as two of the functions of administration, I think that expressions are being used which are a survival of former days. These expressions do not seem to me to describe business as conducted today in many plants. Business practice has gone ahead of business theory. So much goes to contribute to executive decisions before the part which the executive head takes in them, which is indeed sometimes merely the official promulgation of a decision, that the conception of final authority is losing its force in the present organization of business. This is as true of other executives as of the head. Here, too, final decisions have the form and the force which they have accumulated. I have seen an executive feel a little self-important over a decision he had made, when that decision had really come to him ready made. An executive decision is a moment in a process. The growth of a decision, the accumulation of authority, not the final step, is what we need most to study.

The most fundamental idea in business today, that which is permeating our whole thinking on business organisation, is that of function. Every man performs a function or part of a function. Research and scientific study determine function in scientifically managed plants. I think a man should have just as much, no more and no less, authority as goes with his function or his task. People talk about the limit of authority when it would be better to speak of the definition of task.

If, then, authority is derived from function, it has little to do with hierarchy of position as such, and in scientifically managed shops this is more and more recognised. We find authority with the head of a department, with an expert, with the driver of a truck as he decides on the order of deliveries. The despatch clerk has more authority in despatching work than the president. I know a man in a factory who is superintendent of a department which includes a number of sub-departments. He tells me that in many cases he says to the head of a sub-department, that is, to a man in a subordinate position to his, "With your permission, I do so and so." This is a decided reversal of the usual method, is it not?

This phrase "delegated authority" assumes that your chief executive has the "right" to all the authority, but that it is useful to delegate some of it. I do not think that a president should have any more authority than goes with his function. Therefore, I do not see how you can delegate authority, except when you are ill or taking a holiday. And then you are not exactly delegating authority. Someone is doing your job and he has the authority which goes with that particular piece of work. Authority belongs to the job and stays with the job.

The view that the "right" to all authority lies with the head, but that he delegates some of it to others comes, I think, from what one might call the historical outlook on leadership rather than the analytical. We look back and see that when a business begins in a small way the head has many duties which after a while, as the business grows, are given to others. This has made people think that these duties by right belonged to the head, but that he has found it convenient to delegate some of them while, as a matter of fact, the convenience is just the other way round. There are in business certain separate functions; the smallness of a business may make it convenient for one man to perform them all, but they are still separate functions. For instance, in a small bank, the head, in addition to his many other duties, looks after new business. In a large bank, a separate man has the responsibility for new business, exchange, deposits, credit loans,

From the *Taylor Society Bulletin*, December, 1926; republished in L. Urwick (ed.), *Freedom & Coordination: Lectures in Business Organisation* (Sir Isaac Pitman & Sons, Limited, 1949), pp. 1–10. Permission of the publishers to reprint is gratefully acknowledged.

and so on. But the separation of function does not mean the delegation of authority. The unfortunate thing in writing on business organisation is that our language has not caught up with our actual practice. As distribution of function has superseded hierarchy of position in many plants, delegation of authority should be an obsolete expression, yet we hear it every day.

I say that authority should go with function, but as the essence of organisation is the interweaving of functions, authority we now see as a matter of interweaving. An order, a command, is a step in a process, a moment in the movement of interweaving experience, and we should guard against thinking this step a larger part of the whole process than it really is. There is all that leads to the order, all that comes afterwards—methods of administration, the watching and recording of results, what flows out of it to make further orders. If we trace all that leads to a command, what persons are connected with it, and in what way, we find that more than one man's experience has gone to the making of that moment—unless it is a matter of purely arbitrary authority. Arbitrary authority is authority not related to all the experience concerned, but to that of one man alone, or one group of men.

Another corollary from this conception of authority as a moment in interweaving experience is that we have not authority as a mere left-over. We cannot take the authority which we won yesterday and apply it today. That is, we could not if we were able to embody the conception we are now considering in a plan of organisation. In the ideal organisation authority is always fresh, always being distilled anew. The importance of this in business management has not yet been estimated.

Of course, you will understand that in all this I am speaking of business organisation in the more progressive plants, but there are as yet far more organised under the old doctrines.

Let us now ask ourselves what there is in the present organisation of business which seeks to diffuse rather than to concentrate responsibility. First, management is becoming more and more specialised; the policies and methods of a department rest on that department's special body of knowledge, and there is a tendency for the responsibility to be borne by those with that special body of knowledge rather than by a man at the top because of his official position.

That business men are facing this undoubted fact of pluralistic authority, that modern business organisation is based to some extent on this conception, is very interesting to me, for I have been for many years a student of political science, and it seems significant to me that now I have to go to business for the greatest light on authority, control, sovereignty—those concepts which have been supposed to be peculiarly the concepts of political science. For instance, in the last book I read on government, a recent one, the writer speaks of a "single, ultimate centre of control," but I do not find that practical men are much interested in ultimates. I think that with political scientists this interest is a survival from their studies in sovereignty. The business man is more concerned with the sources than with the organs of authority. Moreover any overemphasis on ultimate control disregards one of the most important trends in the recent development of thinking on organisation: "central control" used to mean the chief executive; now it is a technical expression of scientific management indicating the points where knowledge and experience on the matter in question are brought to a focus.

And as it is the idea of pluralistic authority which is dominating progressive business organisation today, so the crux of business organisation is how to join these various authorities. Take the purchasing of materials. The authority for this should be assumed by the purchasing agent and by the department which gives its specifications to the purchasing agent. If the purchasing agent thinks that some of these specifications could be changed and cost thereby reduced without decreasing quality, he should discuss this with the department in question. While I realise that much can be accomplished by friendly relations between individuals, I think that organisation should have for one of its chief aims to provide for a joint authority in those cases where combined knowledge is necessary for the best judgment.

This problem is being solved in a number of plants by a system of cross functioning. In one factory I know, they are trying to build up a structure of inter-locking committees. This is perhaps the most important trend in business organisation. I don't mean committee government when I say that—that may or may not be the best way of meeting this problem—but the trend toward some kind of cross functioning.

The chief weakness in business organisation is lack of co-ordination. Yet I hear more talk of co-ordination than of anything else. Why then do we not get it? One reason is that the system of organisation in a plant is often so hierarchical, so ascending and descending, that it is almost impossible to provide for cross relations. The notion of horizontal authority has not yet taken the place of vertical authority. We cannot, however, succeed in modern business by always running up and down a ladder of authority. Moreover, cross functioning seems often to be conceived of as useful only when difficulties arise, or when it is obvious that joint consultation on some specific problem would be desirable. But as such consultation is necessary all the time, some machinery which will operate continuously should be provided. And this is now recognized.

Of course, one difficulty about a degree or a manner of working together which hides individual effort comes from the egotism, the perfectly natural and to some extent justifiable egotism, of the persons concerned. Each executive wants his special contribution to get to the ears of the boss.

Another difficulty about co-ordination, and one of the greatest, is that it is not sufficiently recognized that co-ordination is not a culminating process. You cannot always bring together the results of departmental activities and expect to co-ordinate them. You must have an organisation which will permit interweaving all along the line. Strand should weave with strand, and then we shall not have the clumsy task of trying to patch together finished webs.

Most of the attacks on the traditional economic theory of business decision making are based on general observation. However, some of those who have written books and papers on the subject have taken the trouble to test their ideas by surveys. One of these is Prof. G. L. S. Shackle, of the University of Liverpool in England, a leading thinker on decision making. A summary of the results of a small survey he conducted appears below.

Business Men on Business Decisions

G. L. S. Shackle

The textbooks on economics, using the central principle of theory-building, radical and ruthless simplification and abstraction, have usually assumed simply that the business man's basic purpose is to 'maximize his profit' or his 'net revenue.' This proposition, that the enterpriser has at the back of his mind all the time the dominant purpose of making his firm's income as great as possible, opens up a host of questions falling under several different headings.

First, there are the interpretive or definitional questions: What precisely is it that is sought to be maximized? Is it

1 Net profit before tax?
2 Net profit after tax payable by the firm?
3 Net profit for the immediate future, for example, a quarter or half year or one year?
4 Net profit averaged over the next five years?
5 Net profit averaged over the next ten years?
6 Net profit averaged over the next thirty years?
7 If it is net profit averaged over a period, is the average 'unweighted,' so that as much importance is given to the profitability of the firm ten years hence as next year, or is greater weight given to the more immediately future years?

Or is it not profit at all but

8 The general prosperity of the firm, where we include in general prosperity the mainte-

From *The Nature of Economic Thought: Selected Papers 1955–1964* (Cambridge University Press, Cambridge, England, 1966), pp. 145–159.

nance of the goodwill of a body of customers or the esteem of the public at large?

9 The firm's net worth as estimated within the firm?

10 The firm's liquid position or balance-sheet strength?

11 The firm's prestige as an enterprising, efficient, technically progressive, financially sound, humane and high-principled concern?

Or is it rather

12 The personal reputation or self-esteem of the moving spirits of the firm, their prestige as heads of a firm? Does the head of the firm identify himself with his business so that its success is his success?

In the economics textbook we find sentences like this: 'In order to maximize its net revenue, the firm must set its output at that level where marginal revenue is equal to marginal cost.' Now the actual behaviour that conforms to this rule may be quite different according to whether the net revenue considered is merely that of the ensuing week or month, or is reckoned in some way over a long future period. If the firm's object is to maximize its profit from month to month, it will perhaps take advantage of any general shortage of the product it makes to ask a higher price so long as the shortage lasts. But what will be the effect of such action on its market and its customers' goodwill in the long run? The maximizing of profit in the short term and in the long term may be incompatible objectives.

So much for questions (3) to (6). What arises from question (7) is both more subtle and more topical. It really amounts to asking: How do we reckon the *success* of an enterprise? Is a firm to be called successful if it has for a long time been making good profits, or if it has made them for a short time in the recent past, or if it 'is making' good profits (but what, precisely, do we mean by 'is making'?) or if it seems to be going to make good profits?

The business men were in effect asked to give opinions on three questions:

A What does the business man seek to maximize?

B How does the business man decide his price?

C How does the business man reach his investment decisions?

I think their evidence warrants the following comments:

A. What Does the Business Man Seek to Maximize?

The [replies] suggest that it is net profit after rather than before tax; that for small firms it is, above all, profit of the immediate (up to one year) future, and secondly, profit over the next five years; for large firms 'the next five years' gets slightly more marks than 'the immediate future'. The suggestion that it is net profit over a period of years with more weight given to the more immediately future years gets about half marks. 'The general prosperity of the firm [and] maintenance of goodwill' and 'the firm's prestige' both get very high marks. These high marks suggest that firms are more far-sighted and prudent, and also less materially minded, than the economist's ordinary assumptions suggest. There is no great enthusiasm for internally estimated net worth or even for balance-sheet strength, but this latter gets slightly better marks than 'the personal reputation of the head of the firm.'

B. How Does the Business Man Decide His Price?

Equating marginal revenue to marginal cost gets distinctly poor marks. One of the most definite verdicts in the whole enquiry is that in deciding his price the business man does not ignore his competitors. This suggested prevalence of an oligopolistic market attitude may reflect the character of the sample, which consisted largely of engineering firms. The 'kinked demand curve' gets a very modest vote. 'Full-cost pricing' is supported, but there is no enthusiasm. On methods of estimating output for the purpose of full-cost pricing the marks are more interesting: they show a distinctly favourable response to a suggestion [on the questionnaire] "I have to reckon that a lowering of my price will be immediately followed by a lowering of my rivals' prices, but a raising of my price will not be imitated by them."

C. How Does the Business Man Reach His Investment Decisions?

Amongst the suggested answers on investment policy, the comparison of marginal efficiency of capital with market rate of interest gets a poor mark. There is general agreement that two years is shorter than the time in which most firms require a proposed new block of equipment to pay for itself. 'Five years' gets far the highest mark of the three suggestions. "The block of equipment would have to be expected to earn 20, 33, etc. per cent of its first cost for just a sufficient number of years to cover its first cost and yield a moderate net gain," which I think may be a new interpretation of evidence obtained in past enquiries, also gets a comparatively high mark.

No more is claimed for this little experiment than that it may indicate a possible way of securing the interest and attention of very busy and preoccupied business men in questions of economic theory for which they would otherwise have no time.

Another report on the factors that influence decision making is given in this article. Prof. Ross Stagner, of the State University of Michigan, interviewed fifty decision makers in ten companies on the matter, and his findings indicated that both organizational and subjective factors often carry more weight with a decision maker than the strictly economic factors.

Resolving Top-Level Managerial Disagreements

Ross Stagner

As we all know, corporations find it necessary to establish uniform policies which cut across various units and divisions. It is also a familiar fact that the heads of different divisions, usually having the title of vice-president, disagree as to what these policies should be. It therefore seemed to be a worthwhile contribution to industrial psychology to explore the process of policy-formation at this level, with a primary focus on the resolution of divergencies of opinion at the vice-presidential level.

The observations presented here derive from approximately fifty interviews with vice-presidents (or their equivalents) in ten companies in the eastern United States, ranging in size from about 2,000 to 50,000 employees.

Literature in this field suggested three distinctively different theoretical approaches to the problem:

Economic. Economists writing on the theory of decision-making by the firm tended to make three key assumptions. First, that the firm functions as a unit, that is, that decision-making by the firm need not consider problems of internal differentiation and disagreement. (In justice to the economists it should be added that in the last few years more sophisticated treatments have begun to appear, but the unitary assumption is still preponderant in the economic literature.) Second, the assumption is that *only* economic goals influence the decision; and, third, is the assumption that the decision will be based on a marginal computation of costs and profits.

Pressure group. A second major approach can be called pressure group analysis. Action by the total body is conceived as coming about when coalitions are formed between groups having interests that can be furthered by a single policy. The theory assumes that leaders of a division within a corporation will seek to maximize the welfare of the division rather than the profitability of the total organization. It also assumes bargaining between divisions and compromise solutions.

Small group. A third approach perhaps does

From *Business Topics* (Michigan State University), Winter, 1965, pp. 15–22. Reprinted by permission of the publisher, the Bureau of Economic Research, Division of Research, Graduate School of Business Administration, Michigan State University.

not merit the designation of a theory, since our present knowledge of small group phenomena has not been systematized. It is, nonetheless, feasible to think of the group of five or six vice-presidents, or heads of major units, as a small group sitting down to discuss issues and arrive at decisions.

The data analysis so far consists primarily of grouping the factors described as *important by the respondent* into three categories: dynamic factors, cognitive factors, and structural factors. By "dynamic" is meant those goals or motives identified *by the respondent* as relevant to his preferred solution; by "cognitive," the *ways of perceiving the situation*; and by "structural," the *type of organization* or of customary interaction between executives, which seemed to influence the outcome.

Dynamic Factors

Foremost among the dynamic factors cited by executives is, of course, the economic implication of the decision. However, this is far less simple than the traditional economic analysis would suggest. One respondent, who was just in the process of spending a million dollars for a new warehouse set-up, said quite frankly that he did not expect it to reduce materials handling costs significantly. His firm defense of the decision was, "You don't want to live in a Quonset hut all your life." Another, in a different industry, commented on one decision: "Profitability had nothing to do with it."

On the other hand, in many companies cost figures were determined with considerable care and amortization of new machinery, for example, had to be accomplished within four years to be acceptable. This amounts to a 25 percent return on investment, which, to a layman, seems pretty steep. However, the impression was given that the companies setting this high figure had a serious problem of rapid technological change. More stable industries expected as low as 6 percent for recouping costs.

It became clear in the course of the interviews that precisely reported cost figures should not be taken at face value. As one man put it, "The salesmen handling this line wanted to have unit cost data. I opposed giving it to them, partly because they might unintentionally reveal it to a competitor, but more because these cost figures are *in some respects artificial* and would easily be subject to misinterpretation." While he declined to explain just how they were artificial, the context suggested that actual costs were lower by some undefined (perhaps unmeasurable) quantity than the cost figures used in production and sales decisions.

A second major category of dynamic influences mentioned by respondents was *power*. Certain high-level executives tried to maintain *their own power* or the *power of their divisions* with some disregard for profit implications. An interesting example involves a proposal to set up three installations each costing $5 million, two in the United States and one in western Europe. The head of the English subsidiary and the head of the French subsidiary got into a feud over which would get the European unit. After considerable negotiating, the American controlling executives decided to put *one each* in France and England. This kind of solution is, of course, simple if you can buy off the critic of a policy by adding $5 million to your expansion program without serious suffering.

In another case two executives differed vigorously over who should get control of a new computer installation. The compromise worked out was to set up two sections, one to be involved in routine use of the computer and one to concentrate on planning for future applications of automatic data processing. To no one's surprise, one section was put under Vice-President Smith and the second under Vice-President Jones.

Respondents were generally reluctant to talk about jealousy and personal feelings within the executive group. However, one man cited the promotion of one of his colleagues to executive vice-president. The respondent protested this move, and while he did not succeed in blocking the promotion, he did arrange so that he reported directly to the president, not through the executive vice-president. It was later learned that the respondent had expected to get the promotion himself.

Divisional heads resent any change in central office policy that makes their units look less profitable. There seems to be substantial ego-identification with the welfare of the division. One man says, "Take Division A. They have increased their billings by 500 percent in four years, but have shown very little increase in profit. They are very critical of our pricing policy because *they think it makes them look bad.*" Central office control of divisions shows power struggles of an acute nature; "Conflicts are particularly acute with Division X, which was until recently an independent company and a competitor of what is now the larger portion of the merged corporation."

For the most part, respondents did not report on factionalism within top management. It is perhaps significant that in the one company in which two vice-presidents were identified as leaders of factions, one was fired before the year was out. This suggests that covert power struggles are permissible but open conflict is settled by eliminating the weaker.

A few concerns indicated that political and public relations factors outweighed costs as determinants of some decisions. One man said: "We could cut prices low enough to bankrupt our nearest competitor and still operate at a profit, but we are not going to do so because we do not want to get involved in an antitrust action." Another said: "We kept our Canadian plant going when it would have been more profitable to close it, because *we did not want to lay off these employees*." However, another man in the same firm diagnosed the major reason as *fear of political repercussions* in Canada. Either way it was clear that noneconomic considerations, at least in the short run, determined policy.

Cognitive Factors

It is worth remembering that the data received, and the focus of attention, necessarily magnify certain material for one individual and not for another. The most frequent instance in the interview records is the common assertion that market researchers invariably over-estimate the demand for a proposed new product. The sales division is always too optimistic in its forecasts, according to production men. Some chief executives utilize outside consultants in part to try to get away from this built-in bias, although it is doubtful that this technique eliminates the problem.

Many respondents recognized the importance of learning to see things in a common frame of reference. Communication with the other executive is easier if you share a common background with him. One man comments, "When our Chief Executive was an engineer, I could communicate fairly easily. Our new Chief is an economist, and I can't get through to him as well. I think a man will unconsciously listen more attentively to someone with a background and experience like his own. Even though I've known this man for 30 years, he listens more to the officers who are economists."

Almost all respondents agreed that socializing with other executives outside of office hours improved communication and mutual understanding. Unfortunately, there was considerable friction manifest in some firms where such socializing was particularly common. It may be—as some people have said about husbands and wives—that real understanding may just intensify friction!

In one company the opinion was expressed that "it takes a man about five years to become a member of the management team." In a way this corresponds with the statement by R. J. Cordiner, president of General Electric, who wrote not long ago, "The Board of Directors made me president of the company in 1950, but it took four years before the organization gave me the same honor." His point was that there is a process of learning before new habits of perception and action are established.

Structural Factors

Chief executives differ markedly in the style with which they participate in the communication process and dispute settlements. Some will call in all of the executives affected and try to get an open expression of divergent points of view. The man using this technique generally is cautious to conceal his own preference until he has gotten a thorough airing of the problem. Otherwise there is a rush to get on his bandwagon and the problem may be "solved" in an injudicious manner. Another common pattern is that of calling in the principals in a dispute separately, exploring the problem, and later announcing a decision. This seems to have the advantage of avoiding open controversy and facilitating face-saving devices; it nevertheless irritated the "losing" executive, who often implied that he had not gotten a fair deal. In many firms the technique is employed of having an executive vice-president rule on an issue, the president remaining uninvolved so that appeals to him are still possible. If no one screams, the decision is allowed to stand.

Since these interviews were not focused specifically upon the problem of satisfaction with the decision, the comments here must be even more impressionistic. It seemed clear, nonetheless, that satisfaction was more widespread when more executives participated in a discussion of a problem. The pattern in which the chief executive talked first with one, then with another vice-president appeared to result in minimum satisfaction. This may be, in part, simply due to the discontent of the man whose preferred solution was rejected. It would, nonetheless, seem compatible with small-group experimentation in which the "wheel" network rather dependably gives more satisfaction than the "Y" network.

Power

The most potent, and most often mentioned, influence toward accepting a nonpreferred solution was the power of the chief executive. Regardless of widespread discussion of decentralization and democratization of American industry, the pattern is still authoritarian. "When we could not agree, we took it to the President and he settled it," was a typical report. Thus the mode of conflict resolution by *appeal to a higher authority* is widely accepted in industry.

Centralized power also exerts influence in less direct ways. Controversies between divisions were occasionally muted by concern for front office reaction. "It would not be good policy to embarrass another division," said one respondent. "It might have an *adverse effect on a man's promotion*." The power of the chief executive to hand out rewards thus becomes a technique for influencing division heads to cooperate.

The chief executive sometimes elects to function as a *mediator* rather than as an arbitrator. One vice-president described the chairman of the board as "a man who would bring two division managers into his office and ask them questions until they arrived at an acceptable conclusion." It is possible that some of the questions revealed the preference of the chairman and involved an implied coercion, but it was clear that no direct pressure was utilized.

Certainly the sharing of common goals—the profitability and viability of the corporation—favors compromise rather than last-ditch defense of preferred solutions. Most vice-presidents own stock in the corporation. They thus have an interest in corporate profits as well as in divisional power. A case in point is that of a division which had patented a process for turning out a product widely used in industry, with a substantial increase in quality. This division head naturally proposed that he be allowed to license the use of the patent on a wide scale, because this would bring in a lot of money and make his division look very good. The central office ruled that he could license it only to other divisions within the same company, which would thus give them a competitive advantage and bring in larger profits overall. The man was finally persuaded to abandon his opposition, apparently by the argument that his position as a stockholder would be benefited more by the exclusive policy. One may speculate, however, that other pressures on him were also taken into consideration.

A third type of pressure is that which we associate with small-group discussion situations. One company reported a practice of having each vice-president bring in his budget for the following year, present it to the policy committee, and defend new expenditures. After everyone had done this, the sums were totaled and compared with estimated income. Since these never balanced, the executive vice-president would then ask everyone to go back and shave down his requests. Men who did not accept significant reductions were subjected to pressure from the group to conform. This did not always work; indeed, in some cases the group agreed that certain expansions were justified and necessary. However, the technique militated against "empire building."

Personality Variables

One question of natural interest was whether vigorous, aggressive, persuasive individuals are more likely to "win" controversies than less colorful persons. The consensus was rather strong in favor of rejecting this hypothesis. Two respondents gave a quantitative estimate that such personality variables might be effective 20 percent of the time, but in 80 percent of the cases, power of the division or status in the company would decide the issue. Other respondents were less quantitative in orientation but agreed that it would be somewhat rare for a persuasive man in a lower echelon to win out over a less fluent but higher placed objector.

There is another way in which personality variables seemed to play an important role in decision-making; this is essentially a negative function. The individual who is unpleasant, and irritating to his colleagues, gets cut out of communications networks, and so loses effectiveness. An example: "One divisional manager is technically very competent, but he is blunt and often actually obnoxious. People try to schedule meetings *when they know he cannot attend*."

Without better quantitative evidence it is impossible to defend a particular ordering of these effects, but the impression gained is that the significance of pressures to accept a settlement contrary to the individual's preference takes the order given above: first, the *power of the chief executive;* second, *shared goals* such as *profitability* of the company; third, *pressure from fellow executives* as a kind of group conformity process; and fourth, *persuasive pressure* by one individual upon another (not reinforced by status differences).

Conclusion

While each corporation showed something of a "unique personality" in the sense that characteristic patterns turned up which were not duplicated elsewhere, it was possible to identify common *dimensions* or modes of variation. These modes of variation included the *intensity of concern with profit* (and marginal computations of cost-profit relations) as contrasted with *individual self-assertion* by executives, with the "public image" of the corporation, and with *company tradition* as influences determining the course of action when high level executives disagreed. Corporations also differed with respect to the mechanics of dispute settlement; some used committees extensively, others relied more on face-to-face meetings between vice-presidents, or between the chief executive and one or more of the contenders. Some were relatively formal, others were informal and indeed casual about steps to be taken in settling a debate.

Staff members were generally used to gather data supporting the position preferred by a division head; consultants were sometimes brought in to sponsor an unpopular solution preferred by the chief executive. The consultant, in such cases, functioned as a scapegoat for executive indignation, which might otherwise have been directed at each other.

Conflict settlement devices included the familiar techniques from studies of game theory, *side payments* made to one contender to induce him to accept an overall solution unfavorable to his viewpoint; *superior* power, the authority of the chief executive to require acceptance of a disliked solution (and, occasionally, the power of a strong division to enforce a preferred solution when the chief executive declined to risk his own power and prestige on the outcome); in addition, instances were encountered of the use of *group pressure* on executives to induce them to abandon dissident positions. *Superordinate goals* included concern for the *profitability* of the company; and for the *viability* of the company, in terms of public image and possible political repercussions from proposed policies.

A few executive decisions in this class show the characteristics imputed to them by economic theorists, that is, computation of marginal costs and marginal returns. The vast majority, however, seem to have been determined in whole or in large part by other considerations. The power of the individual executive and his ego status as he identifies himself with his portion of the corporation is an important factor here; this corresponds to the conceptualization of the corporation as a set of pressure groups interacting to arrive at compromise solutions. Finally, some decisions resemble the model we get from small-group discussion, in which interpersonal influence becomes an important variable. It is obvious that we cannot state that one of these models is *right* and the *others* wrong; some decisions are fairly pure instances of one model, but others are composites. On an impressionistic basis it seems that more fit the pressure group model than the economic model, but that these two far outnumber those in which face-to-face influence is a major determinant.

But at each step in the process of decision making, some one person must actually make a decision. How should he do it? This is the practical problem, and as the following article shows, a high degree of analytical ability is required to make a good decision. The techniques of decision making are here dissected by Prof. A. R. C. Duncan, a philosopher from Scotland with a special knowledge of Kant, who was formerly dean of the arts faculty of Queen's University at Kingston, Ontario, Canada, where he is still teaching.

Techniques of Decision-Making

A. R. C. Duncan

Neither I nor anyone else can tell another person how he or she ought to make his or her particular decisions. Decision-making is an intensely personal activity. [But it] can be either haphazard and conducted on a hit-or-miss basis, or it can be systematic and based on a regular and habitual method. In other words, there is a general technique of decision-making.

When and why do human beings have to make decisions? A man has to make a decision when he finds himself in a situation about which two things can be said: (*a*) it is the kind of situation in which he must *do something*, and (*b*) it is the kind of situation in which he is *not quite certain* just what ought to be done. After all, as long as you know what has to be done in a situation, you are barely conscious of the necessity of making a decision; you just go ahead and do it. If you are the only competent swimmer present when someone is obviously drowning, you don't debate whether to help him or not and then decide to do so, you get going right away. On the other hand, when you are not quite sure just what ought to be done, when you don't know which of two or more possible lines of action is likely to be best, then you must stop and think. As a result of your thinking, you make a decision to act in a certain way.

We may now say that the first characteristic of a decision situation is that it forces us to think about the situation; it makes it necessary for us to analyse the situation so that we may know just what it is and what factors are contained within it. While we are engaged in thinking about it we may, and indeed usually do, find that we do not know as much about the situation as we should like to, and we cannot help feeling that our decision would be much more reliable if only we did know more about the situation within which we have to act. The second characteristic, then, of a decision situation is that our thinking about it forces us to increase our knowledge about the area in which the decision has to be made. The soundness and reliability of any decision thus must depend upon the two factors I mentioned to begin with: (*a*) our ability to think about or analyse a situation and (*b*) the knowledge we possess or can acquire which can be brought to bear on the situation. Clear thinking without knowledge will not guarantee a sound decision and extensive knowledge without clear thinking is no better a guarantee. A sound decision is the healthy child of a marriage between clear thinking and relevant knowledge.

A decision is the appropriate response of an intelligent being to a situation which demands action. And just as genuine thinking has to be carefully distinguished from mere day-dreaming or reverie, so genuine *action* has to be distinguished from *drifting*. The man who drifts is essentially the man who allows himself to be pushed into doing things by other persons, who

From a lecture given to the Executive Development Group, Queen's University, Kingston, Ontario, Canada, June, 1964.

is content to ride with the tide, who essentially lets things happen. The drifter will from time to time be forced into making decisions, but he will deliberately postpone or avoid them as far as he can. The opposite of the drifter is the man of action, and by that expression I do not mean the person who is always bustling about appearing busy [but] the kind of person who takes control of the situations in which he finds himself and seeks to impress his will upon the course of events, who does not merely let things happen, but who *makes things happen*.

Now, if a person is going to take control of a situation and really act within it, then there are surely three things of which he must be aware: He must know *what he wants* to achieve, he must know enough about the situation to appreciate *what can be done* within it, and he must realise that his control can never be complete, that *he must be prepared to take a risk*, and this because all action takes place in time and future time is necessarily unknown to us.

Five Stages

In the light of these general remarks I am going to suggest that the whole complex process, of which the decision is only one part, should be broken down into five stages: (1) formulation of the objective or aim; (2) analysis aimed at increase of knowledge; (3) listing of alternative possibilities of action; (4) decision; (5) implementation by planning. Let us consider each of these briefly:

1 Get the objective clearly stated. You cannot really *do* anything unless you know either what you want to do or what you ought to do. Without knowledge of that, you may be active and busy, but you will be riding with the tide. Only when you have a clear aim can you be said to be impressing your will on events. And your aim must be stated in full.
2 Get yourself well informed about the elements in the situation within which you have to realise your aim. Presumably the mere realisation that you must do *something* suggests that you already know something about the situation, but once your aim is clear the situation must be analysed again in the light of your aim.
3 Find out what you *can* in fact do in the situation towards realising your aim. In other words, list the alternative courses of action open to you. If you do not do this, you may indeed achieve your aim, but at unnecessary cost. A possible alternative which you had not thought of might have been much simpler than the one you selected.
4 Make a decision between the open alternatives. This is the moment to which steps 1, 2, and 3 have been leading up, and this is the moment when you must be prepared to take a risk, the risk that you might be wrong. The chances of serious error, however, are diminished if steps 1, 2, and 3 have been carefully considered. And of course, when you have decided for A rather than B, then you must take the plunge, you must commit yourself to A and not go on looking backward wondering whether it might not have been better to do B.
5 Implement the decision by means of a plan or set of instructions. Up to this point, you might have been sitting in an armchair doing it all in your head right up to the point of saying "This is what I shall do," that is, up to the point of the actual decision. But there is no action, no real change in the situation, until what has been going on in your head is translated, as it were, into real life, and that is done by the next step. "I have decided upon alternative A. If A is to be achieved, then this, this, and this must be done." That is, you plan what must be done from the moment of decision up to the actual realisation of your aim.

Throughout the whole process you must obviously hold yourself in readiness to cope with the unexpected. You cannot really expect things and other people to remain static while you do what you want to do; therefore, as you are implementing the decision you must remain alert to possible changes, some of which may be unexpected consequences of the early stages of your plan.

These five steps appear to me to be the main ingredients in any decision situation. I have arranged them in what is clearly the logical order, with this proviso—that in some highly complex situations it may be necessary after reaching step 3, the consideration of alternatives, to go back and reconsider both of the first steps. The first three steps require a good deal of hard thinking and are among the most important, and I shall go so far as to say that the ultimate soundness of a decision depends on the care with which these steps have been taken.

An Illustration

Let me now offer a very simple illustration. Let us suppose that I am manager of a company which makes chairs and I need to increase my inventory of spindle stock. My purchasing agent has asked for bids and five have been received from reliable sources. Of these five, two are much lower in price than the others. I have before me then the problem of deciding which of the two bids to accept, that of Company A or that of Company B. Now if I am the type of man who likes to give the impression of swift and decisive action, but who does not in fact think much about his decisions, I may note that we have dealt with both companies before and had reasonably good service from them, and then say "Right, B is bidding lower than A. We shall accept B's bid." No time lost. I communicate my decision to my purchasing agent in crisp tones which prevent him raising any objections. Everything is done and finished with and I can go onto the next piece of business or go and have a drink. Most impressive to the uninitiated spectator who sees and marvels at the man of action in action. When asked how I do it, I shake my head knowingly and murmur something about, "Intuition, you know, got a flair for that sort of thing."

Suppose now that we attempt to go over the same example but this time attempt to follow the five stages I outlined above. What do I want to do? What is my aim? The first answer we might give would be to say that my aim is to buy the cheapest stock which is consistent with the kind of quality I require. Fair enough, but is that all that I am aiming at? What about keeping good relations with firms with which I have to deal frequently? That is obvious and hardly worth stating. But the first rule of method is that we should have the *whole* of our objective clear, not just part of it. And this is vital for it governs the next step. With both parts of my objective clear, I must now ask myself a further question: B is bidding lower than A and B's stuff is good quality, but is there any other factor in the situation which might make it more advisable to accept A's bid? Is there? Well, I don't know, but, bearing in mind my double objective, I can find out by analysing the situation, and obtaining more information than I have at the moment. Reviewing our past dealings with the two firms, I conclude that to accept B's bid in this case is likely seriously to upset our relations with A. How important is it that we avoid doing that? I find that in the past A has been much more prompt on delivery than B, that it has often given us preferential treatment, that its marketing experts have helped us with market forecasts. Here are grounds for accepting A's bid. If I do not accept B's bid, is that likely to upset B? On inquiry I find that it is not likely to do so. A's bid is higher but only slightly higher than B's; so the financial difference is hardly a final factor. I now have the situation much more fully analysed, and what I have done is to use my existing knowledge and experience as a basis for acquiring more information about the situation, and the stimulus to do so was careful formulation of my double objective. The alternatives open to me are the same as before, it is true; but in the light of what I now have clearly before my mind I decide to accept A's bid. It remains for me to implement my decision by issuing the necessary instructions, which will also be dual: The order is to be given to Company A, and a carefully worded letter is to be written to B with a view to keeping our relations as smooth as possible.

What is important about this example is not that my decision is different when I follow the five steps, but that my decision is based on deliberate rational analysis of all the factors in the situation. It is an intelligent decision which can be defended and justified if necessary. "This is what I did and these are the reasons why I did it." What other alternative is there to following the five steps? It appears to me that there are only two other possibilities to consider. First, we might take an extremely cursory glance at the situation, become aware that there are two fairly obvious alternative courses of action, and then flip a coin as an easy way of finding out which one to adopt. This, I would suggest, is tantamount either to admitting that you are incapable of making up your own mind and are therefore handing over the whole operation to sheer luck or to publicly confessing that you do not possess anything which could be dignified with the title of a mind at all. I do not intend to deny that there may be rare occasions when tossing a coin is the right thing to do, but in general as a rational approach to a situation calling for action it does not make even first base.

Intuition

Secondly, we might trust to what is called intuition or, in more colloquial terms, a hunch. Some men do appear to be quite uncannily successful at making the right decisions and they often credit themselves with a special faculty which goes by the name of intuition. Let us examine this claim. The word "intuition" has a very precise and technical meaning in philosophy, where it originated and where it means the mental act of grasping the truth of a statement when no evidence beyond the statement itself is required—but this has nothing to do with what happens in decision-making. We have to recognise that the word "intuition" has come to be one of those vague words which people use when they do not know what they are talking about and are not going to admit it. I suggest that what is called "intuition" is really a combination of four different factors: (*a*) there is first that "born knack" for doing certain things which some people have and others do not have; (*b*) there is the element of skill acquired through intensive training; (*c*) there is unusually extensive knowledge of the field built up perhaps over many years; and there is (*d*) a fourth emotional element, namely interest. When a man is genuinely and passionately interested in his job, when he has built up a great fund of general information about the area in which he operates, when he has taken the trouble to train himself in the techniques of reasoning and analysis, and has in addition an inborn ability for that kind of thing, then his decisions will appear to have something uncanny about them. But what I am suggesting is that this unusual ability is a function of the four factors I have mentioned and there is no need to call in a mysterious nonexistent faculty called intuition. To put my point very crudely: Hard work combined with intelligence and interest will do all that is ever claimed for intuition.

I want now to say something more in order to underline the advisability of this reliance upon a set methodical procedure. In the first place, to habituate oneself to follow *a systematic procedure* such as that represented by my five steps is one way of *expressing one's intelligence in action*, and decision-making is simply and basically the attempt to translate intelligence into action. Under the heading of "intelligence" we should include: (*a*) memory, that faculty which enables us to reach into the past and so to make use of what experience we have had; (*b*) imagination, that faculty which enables us to picture what may happen in the future and so to take steps to adjust ourselves to it beforehand (this is the special faculty of the good planner); and (*c*) the power of sheer reasoning or thinking, which enables us to see connections between various items in our experience, between ideas that occur to us and the elements in a problem, and so to reach a solution. When a human being—that is, a being with intelligence—has to act, what he is doing is trying to make actual an aim or objective which at first exists only in his mind as a kind of image projected upon the future. Action is essentially future-oriented. If action is to be as successful as possible, then it is essential to do whatever is necessary to allow intelligence to function, this power of recalling the past, anticipating the future, and making connections between data in the present. What is necessary is that we should *form the habit* of following a methodical procedure of formulating our aim, analysing the situation in the light of it, separating out the alternatives, deciding, and implementing by a plan. The emphasis here falls upon the necessity of *forming the habit of proceeding methodically*.

Objectives

Discussions about decision-making with various groups lead me to believe that there is a special problem connected with stage 1 of my analysis—getting the objective clear. The difficulty arises at least partly from the fact that in so many decision situations we appear almost immediately to face two fairly obvious alternative courses of action, and the opening question then appears to be, which shall I decide upon? If we do approach the decision in this way, then we are omitting stages 1 and 2 and going right to stage 3, the listing of the alternatives. This is precisely what I am claiming we ought not to do. It leads straight to unintelligent decisions because it attempts to start the action as it were in the middle instead of at the beginning. If in an action situation you appear at once to be facing alternatives, then you are being forced by the situation instead of making sure that you are in control.

A clearly formulated objective makes the performance of stage 2 both easier and more effective. It is a psychological fact about the human mind that when it has a definite objective in view it automatically develops a concentrated and focused alertness of attention. Having a special purpose introduces into the mind a kind of principle of selective attention, which is very different from merely curious observation of a situation. If a tourist is driving through a stretch of country enjoying the scenery and possessed of mild generalized curiosity, he will notice all manner of things and also miss a great many things; if an artillery officer were driving through the same stretch of country trying to find a suitable place to site a battery of field guns, his attention will be concentrated and he will automatically notice features that the tourist will miss. This automatic concentration of attention must be made use of in the decision-making process, and it is made use of in stage 2 when we analyse the situation in the light of our clearly formulated objective.

How Much Knowledge?

This matter of acquiring the necessary knowledge about the situation which forms the basis of any sound decision raises some difficult problems. First, how do we know when to stop the process of gathering preliminary information about the situation before taking the decision? Secondly, since we must stop somewhere, our information is bound to be incomplete; how then can a sound decision be made on the basis of incomplete information?

The first point to make here is that the data on the basis of which you make a decision can never in the nature of the case be complete. You may reach pretty detailed knowledge of the situation as it is, but about the future you can never have detailed knowledge; all that you have any right to expect is that in broad general outlines the future will resemble the past, and on that basis you make your forecasts. At the same time, you know that when you have made your decision, you set new changes in motion which may affect your original forecasts, and about this you can do very little. If we could know the future in detail, there would be no need for decision-making as our line of action would be obvious. The act of decision-making is forced upon us precisely because the future cannot be forecast with detailed accuracy. The data on which action must be based are always and necessarily incomplete, hence the element of risk which must accompany a decision and which frightens the drifters. But if this is so, why then do we bother with the preliminary analysis and careful formulation of aim? Why not just go at it baldheaded like those who trust in intuition? Just as there is all the difference in the world between rational thinking and mere guessing, so there is the same kind of difference between rational action and mere impetuosity based on guesswork. It is basically the difference between trusting to luck and relying on judgment, and these are two very different things. The whole preliminary process of analysis is really an attempt to reduce the element of luck in a situation.

If we cannot hope to get complete information, then how do we know at what point to stop gathering it? I think the correct, if unpalatable, answer to this question is that we do not and cannot ever *know*; we must rely on what *judgment* we have. It is again part of the risk which is decision-making. There are one or two points of which we might remind ourselves here: (1) We must try to get as much genuine objective information as we can in the time that is available. (2) We must resist the very natural temptation to postpone the moment of decision by spending too much time on analysing and gathering information. (3) We must not attempt to blind ourselves to the element of risk by referring the matter to a committee on the principle that there is safety in numbers; someone still has to make the decision whether it be the chairman or the individual members through their voting. (4) We must not put too much faith in quantitative analysis, in the introduction of mathematical method. For some decisions, qualitative knowledge of human nature is required; for others, where prices or materials are involved, detailed quantitative analysis is essential. But we must not confuse quantitative analysis of data with objective analysis. All analytic thinking should be objective in the sense that it must not be influenced by such subjective factors as our personal desires and emotions; we have to analyse the situation as it really is, whether it involves the subtle and manifold reactions of human beings or merely masses of inert material. Thinking must be objective in a sense that action never is or can be, as I shall explain shortly.

Listing Alternatives

The third stage in the process is listing the alternative courses of action. At this point we should distinguish between finding out what we can do, what it is possible to do, and finding out what we ought to do, what it would be best to do. It is a sound methodical principle always to assume that there is at least one alternative more than those you can first think of and to try to discover it; this is a kind of guard against subjectivity since we know that human beings tend to see only what they want to see, and that is seldom all that there is to see. It is again a sound rule of method to make a kind of matrix table when the decision is at all complex so that the alternatives and their probable consequences are clearly set out. Let us say that there are three alternatives open, A, B, and C. If I do A, then l, m and n will happen; if I do B, then p, q and r will happen; if I do C, then x, y and z will happen. When prices and materials are involved, this is where sound quantitative estimates become extremely important; otherwise you do not strictly know what you are deciding between. Where reactions of human beings are involved, it is the point where what information can be gathered from competent psychologists and sociologists becomes important. If I do A, then just what sort of reactions from Smith and Jones and Robinson can confidently be predicted, etc., etc., etc.? This is the last stage of analysis, the last moment of preparation. I should be inclined to suggest that this third stage of listing the alternatives should be regarded as the *final marshalling of the information* you have gathered—the setting up of a detailed matrix (and when dealing with quantities it can afford to be very detailed) lets you know exactly what the situation is, the situation into which you as a man with the power of decision are going to insert your will.

The Decision Itself

We now come to the fourth and most vital stage of all, the actual decision. This is the hardest moment of all, and it is the moment when there are no rules of method to fall back on, and no further possibility of help from other persons. If someone told you what decision to make, then *you* would not be making it at all. One man can help another man to analyse a situation or provide him with information that he requires or even proffer advice, but when stages 1, 2 and 3 have been completed, then the man with the decision to make is on his own, he must make his own mind up, and in doing so he unavoidably stakes his reputation on it.

Our plan for action—that is the fifth and final stage. If your decision is one that requires that other persons assist in carrying it out, then you must issue instructions. If it is one that you must carry out for yourself, then you need a plan which takes you from the alternative on which you have decided right up to what you do here and now. If you do not include the plan in the stages of the decision-making process, then you are apt to find yourself facing the silly question: "All right, we have decided to do X, but what do we do *now*?" In long-term, far-ranging or high-level decisions the need for the plan is more obvious than in short-term ones. If as a motor manufacturer you have decided to start making sports cars, you will have made the decision after a great deal of preliminary analysis of your resources and the market demand, but even so a great deal of detailed planning has to be done before the first sports car rolls off your production line, and that planning is an integral part of the decision. On the other hand, if you decide that you must buy some more cigarettes, your plan will amount to little more than reminding yourself where the nearest store is.

Decision Situations

Let us in conclusion consider how exercises in decision situations should be tackled. You are presented in writing with a decision situation: It will take one or other of two possible forms: either (*a*) you get a description of the situation in which someone has to take a decision together with the decision itself [and] you are asked to criticise, that is, to think through the situation for yourself and see whether the decision was the best one to take in the circumstances, *or* (*b*) you are presented with the description of a situation in which a decision is obviously needed, and you are asked to suggest what decision to take.

How do we set about the task? In type (*a*) you must clearly assess the nature and position of the decision-maker and find out what his objectives (1) in fact were and (2) ought to have been. Secondly, you must look for evidence in the given account that he made some attempt to analyse the situation in the light of clearly formulated objectives. Thirdly, and this is where we move from analysis to criticism, you should make a list of the items of information about the situation which you, in analysing it in the light of the aims you have formulated, would like to have before making the decision. No decision situation used as an exercise will ever contain all the data you would like to have, but you can at least state what you think you would in that situation be expected to have and what more information you would like to have. Fourthly, you must list the alternative courses of action open (*a*) to the given person, the reported decision-maker, and (*b*) to you in your favoured position of critic with hindsight. Fifthly, you should make a judgment whether the actual decision taken was sound and, by way of criticism, suggest what other decision you would have made. Lastly, you should ensure that steps have been taken to implement the given decision, and that you lay out what steps would be necessary for your decision if it should happen to be different.

The same general procedure is required for type (*b*) exercises except that we must lift out all references to a given decision.

A final remark about a word I have used but not at any point analysed—experience. My contention has been that a sound and reliable decision emerges from a methodical procedure which allows both thought and knowledge and experience to be brought to bear on the situation. Experience is not the same as knowledge though the two may and ought to be integrated. Experience cannot be taught—it can be acquired in one way only, by going out into one of the areas of human life and action and having it happen to you. It takes time to acquire experience, which is to some extent a matter of "getting the feel of things" in some area of endeavor, but some people never seem to acquire anything that we should want to call experience. The kind of experience that we admire and find genuinely useful in life is experience which is deliberately and consciously fused with sound learned techniques. To become valuable, experience must be reflected on and integrated with the more abstract items of information which can be learnt in the straight-forward sense of learning through reading. Without experience the intelligent man has no sure foundation on which to work, and he must be given time to acquire it; without a technique of thinking even the man of experience must trust to luck more than any sane man should.

When we are faced with the necessity of making a decision, we can do one of four things: we can run away from it, we can trust to luck, we can talk nonsense about intuition or we can make the best possible use of what intelligence we have. None of us in our saner moments wants to run away, to trust to luck, or to talk nonsense.

To those near the bottom of the corporate hierarchy it often looks as though decision making at the top is easy—after all, the top man can do as he pleases without worrying about what his superiors will think. But as this article shows, most of the decisions the top man must make are the really hard ones, for the results will affect the very survival of the business. And the author knows what he is talking about, for he was president of Masonite Corporation for twenty years, a period during which the company's net income rose from $3 million to $20 million.

Fortune excerpted this article from a speech he gave to the company's sales force just before he moved up to the post of chairman of the board. The problems presented here are only slightly exaggerated, Mr. Coates stated, and his successor, Samuel S. Greeley ("Poor Old Sam"), after a few weeks in office said of the speech: "He hits a lot of problems that are universal in a situation like this." Nevertheless, Mr. Coates believes that "the pluses outweigh the minuses" in the top executive job. The twenty years he spent as president, he said, were the happiest in his life.

Shed a Tear for Poor Old Sam

John M. Coates

Sam Greeley's first sensation as he becomes your chief executive officer probably will be one of gratification, with a surge of pride coursing through his veins. What a thrill to be "Top Banana" in a big company! All those people working for you—all treating you with respect; all telling you what you want to hear; all asking you questions they know you can answer; all going into convulsions over your jokes no matter how many times they have heard them before, and always assigning you the best player around as your golf partner at all the sales meetings. Then the thrill of a big salary—even though you give most of it back to the government—and the independence: now you are a decision maker who doesn't need to get an OK from anyone. Ah, what a breath of fresh air this new dimension provides a new c.e.o. He has arrived at the pinnacle.

But after breathing deeply of this rarefied air, he looks down from his crest and feels other sensations creeping in. He finds it kind of lonely up there. No one is around to whom he can pass the bucks that have already started his way. He wonders why his people seem aloof—they don't suggest going out to lunch with him anymore. He begins a bit of brooding and wonders whether his new situation is all it was cracked up to be. He is on his way to becoming "Poor Old Sam."

As the days pass by, he finds decision making is not quite the fun he had expected it to be. Things are not just black or white, right or wrong. The path to take is never clear at all. Everything seems to occupy a gray area. And after he finally makes a decision, he is haunted by the suspicion that he made the wrong one. Getting to sleep isn't so easy as it used to be. Poor Old Sam joins the sleeping-pill set.

Next day the director of industrial relations brings him a simple problem. Should the company agree to surrender one of its management prerogatives to avoid a strike? The answer ought to be easy because management must, of course, preserve its principles and not cave in before the importunities of those union guys. But then—a strike would mean cutting off shipments indefinitely, losing suppliers, giving the competition a heyday. It would badly affect the company's cash and financial position to the tune of millions of dollars. And all this for that one little old principle. How about it, Sam?

Then the product-development committee greets him with eyes bulging over a new discovery that will triple the company's earnings. All it'll take is a $40-million plant. But they're willing to start with a pilot plant and a million-dollar research project, because it turns out that no one has ever made the product, and if it can be made, no one knows what it would cost. Now the chief executive officer doesn't want to be known as a reactionary who stands in the way of progress. Furthermore, a part of his job is to encourage these zealots; he never can tell when they might get their long hair out of their eyes and come up with something practical. So how is Old Sam going to let the air out of this million-dollar balloon and still preserve the enthusiasm of his turtleneck-sweater assistants? Take it away, Sam!

Then there are the opportunities for acquisitions. Why not leap at the chance to take over the A.B.C. Co.? It manufactures jock straps, and with all the outdoor and indoor sports going on these days, that business is bound to thrive and provide a new thrust for any alert company. Jock-strap companies don't fit too well in the acquisition program of a building-material company, but the instigator of this proposal happens to be one of Masonite's largest stockholders, and Sam can't afford to offend him. How are you going to handle this old jackass, Sam?

And how will you handle personality clashes among the staff? Before long, Old Sam will find need to take courses in psychology, because he has to prescribe for patients who won't work for, with, under, or over some other son of a bitch. After Sam exhausts his knowledge of psychology and things finally come to a complete impasse among his patients, which s.o.b. should he fire? He can't let the conflict go on, or it might wreck the organization. But if he doesn't fire the right guy, he may do the wrecking himself.

Now Poor Old Sam gets a sneaky feeling that maybe some people don't like him anymore. Where are all those smiling faces that greeted him when he first came on this job? He even thinks he overheard someone refer to him as that "old horse's ass." Maybe it was that fellow who had his status reduced when Sam moved him from a three-window office to one with only two.

The telephone rings. Ah, it is one of our happy customers about to come on the line, no doubt wanting to express his satisfaction with some handsome Masonite product that he has installed. But no. When he gets on the line, he's yowling at the top of his voice about that lousy paneling that's crawling all over his basement walls, and "as head of your shyster outfit, you know where you can shove it." Old Sam has become the company's chief claim adjuster.

Here's one decision Sam will enjoy making. The Marlite division [which makes higher-priced interior-wall products] is being hurt by all those new wall products the research people have provided the Masonite division. There was many a year when Marlite pulled the company's earnings out of the mud, so of course it must be protected. But wait, Sam, you had better take a sleeping pill before you decide to let Marlite have its way. The Masonite division has to be protected too, and it *needs* those new products. Remember when we made Masonite stay with that lousy Misty Walnut panel just to protect Marlite? That only cost the company about $20 million and gave all our competitors a big lead. Let us know in the morning how it comes out, Sam.

But before you drop off to sleep, think about our raw materials. They are something we must have, so there should be no question about supporting our mills with forests that cover hundreds of thousands of acres. Any muttonhead knows that it has to be done. Just go ahead and borrow $25 million to tie up more forest lands to assure your raw materials. The interest rate would be only about 7 percent, and forest lands pay back about .5 percent; you would only be going in the hole a bit over 6 percent a year on $25 million. You have to do *something*, Sam—so get a move on before our mills face shutdowns!

Whatever you do, don't forget our happy family of stockholders. Unfortunately, not all of them regard the company's dividend policy as generous, particularly those who have been paying $60 or more per share. Their dividend [72 cents a share in 1971] is only a bit over 1 percent on investment. Like our customers, they'll phone sometimes, too, but you'll find they are a more dignified group, whose tones are respectful as they ask, "When are you tight bastards going to loosen up?" Tell them it's the freeze, Sam—tell them it's the freeze.

Looking down the road, Old Sam sees that all our money will be gone in the next few months because of all the expensive projects our fertile-minded staff has dreamed up. What do we do, Sam? Sell debentures, preferred stock, common stock? Go in hock to the banks—short term, long term, or what? Some experts say this is the time to dilute your stock; others say don't dilute under any circumstances. Some say interest rates are going down, so don't borrow now. Others say borrow now, because rates are going up. It's your move, Sam—you can't let our paychecks bounce. If you do, you'll have personnel problems.

Then, Sam, you have governmental relations with which to while away the time. Interesting inquiries come in, like this recent one: "What do you mean having a plant in the Republic of South Africa? Are you a racist or something? Come down to Washington and explain yourself." Go ahead, Sam! You have the Justice Department hovering over you, looking for a hint of antitrust violations—and the FTC, the SEC, the NLRB, and the I.R.S. watching *everything* you do. And, of course, even after you've steered clear of the government agencies, you still have to avoid violating the New York Stock Exchange's rules. And remember you are an "insider," so watch yourself when you buy or sell Masonite shares or you'll be stuck with penalties of all kinds.

And the public, Sam—watch out for the public. There are wonderful people out there, but some you may hear from will be handing you "non-negotiable" demands, such as, "Close down your plants—they are polluting our air and water. And cease all timber operations. You are desecrating the forest lands." Sam, let them know you are a nature lover and a fisherman, not a nature fighter. Tell them of all the company is doing to protect the environment—and be sure to wear your Izaak Walton League button on all occasions.

Then, Sam, from time to time you will have to put a wise look on your face and appear before financial groups to prophesy all that's going to happen in the business world over the next ten years or so. Be careful, because analysts have long memories for any misguesses you might make, and they might turn against your stock, to the detriment of your stockholders' interests, if they decide you're a lousy prophet. The best advice I can give you is to make a long speech, but don't say anything.

Finally, don't neglect your relations with the board of directors. They hired you, and they can fire you—and they have nothing but ice water going through their veins. They look to you for recommendations on everything they do—so it is your move, not theirs, when things go wrong. Who gets the blame? Not the directors—Poor Old Sam.

By now, of course, Sam's sleeping pills have attacked the lining of his stomach. But his social status has gone up a notch—he is now a member in good standing of the Ulcer Club as well as the sleeping-pill set.

Let's all shed a quiet tear for Poor Old Sam!

PART 4 MANAGEMENT OF FOREIGN OPERATIONS

In the past, the truly international corporations were few; now they are becoming commonplace. Not only are American companies producing and selling abroad, but there is a growing tendency for companies based in other nations to open plants here.

Thus, in the future, more and more American managers will have to be concerned with the opportunities and pitfalls presented by operations abroad and know something about the management philosophies that prevail in other countries. There are, of course, vast differences among the various countries and the types of management problems they present, but in general the nations of the world may all be characterized as belonging to one of two groups: the developed, or industrialized, countries and those that are underdeveloped and usually in the process of attempting development.

The first chapter in this section deals with the developed countries; the second with the underdeveloped countries, most of which are now pressing for development. The third chapter considers some of the implications of doing business on a worldwide scale.

21 Management in Developed Countries

The developed countries are those that have experienced the benefits of industrialization and mass production and thus have higher living standards than the rest of the world. Outside of Europe, they are comparatively few in number. In the Western Hemisphere, only the United States and Canada are developed countries; in Asia only Japan has a high degree of industrial development. Australia and New Zealand probably belong on the list, but in Africa there are no developed countries at all, with the possible exception of certain parts of South Africa.

The developed countries provide an example to the rest of the world of the way rising living standards can be achieved and of the contribution that management can make toward the attainment of that goal. Most of the underdeveloped countries, are, therefore, attempting to emulate them.

The developed countries, however, have problems of their own—depletion of natural resources and pollution, for example. In addition, they must keep on developing if they are to maintain and raise their standards of living, as they all hope to do. They have no guarantee that their markets will not be taken from them, or their populations grow to the point where they cannot be supported without a considerable drop in living standards. Just as political empires have risen to power and then sunk down again, economic empires can be lost to other nations. Development grew out of innovations introduced by industrial managers, and any country can fall behind if its managers are content to continue doing things in the same old way no matter how circumstances change.

Study of the developed countries, with attention to both the factors that have made them great industrially and those that have hampered their development is, therefore, important to the manager or the potential manager.

The first article in this chapter deals with the case of Great Britain, which was once far ahead of all other countries in industrialization and has now slipped behind many. It is a case, as the author points out, that may hold some lessons for the United States.

The second article analyzes the differences between European and American management, and the next deals with Japanese management, which differs in many ways from both European and American management. The two final articles present some prognostications regarding two of Europe's developed countries: France and England.

How can a developed country avoid losing leadership and slipping behind others? Perhaps one answer is that its managers must be aware of the high likelihood of failure at the peak of success. Rudyard Kipling pointed this out in his famous poem "Recessional," written on the occasion of the Diamond Jubilee of Queen Victoria in 1897, at the apparent height of Britain's political and economic power:

> Lo, all our pomp of yesterday
> Is one with Nineveh and Tyre!
> Judge of the Nations, spare us yet,
> Lest we forget, lest we forget!

The possibility of a decline, especially when a people attributes its success entirely to its own character and institutions, is pointed out in the article by Lord Snow of Leicester (C. P. Snow), the English novelist, who started his career as a scientist at Cambridge and became an under secretary in the British Ministry of Technology. (His books often deal with problems of power and administration.) As he notes, the United States now holds many of the same delusions that Britain held in the late nineteenth century.

A Quarter Century: Its Great Delusions

Lord Snow (C. P. Snow)

There is one whole set of delusions that has bedeviled American thinking for years. In the last twenty-five years, it has grown more intense and can do you, and all of us, much harm. Unless we can shake it right off, you, and your children, and the whole Western world are in for disappointments and shocks that no great society has ever known.

I can speak brutally, because the British, a generation or two earlier, lived with an almost identical set of delusions. We have not quite recovered from them yet.

Delusion 1 (held by British engineers): British engineers are the best in the world.

I will not spend any time on this. It is contradicted by Delusion 2.

Delusion 2 (held by American engineers): American engineers are the best in the world.

This is worth a bit more discussion, although it is as unrealistic as Delusion 1. American engineers have brought off great technical achievements. They invented mass production in its modern sense, with the stimulus of an enormous internal market to prod them on. They have produced more consumer goods than the rest of the world put together. They have carved out a superlative road system. But the truth is, *all* countries, once they have touched what the American economist W. W. Rostow calls the take-off stage of industrialization, produce good engineers. For certain kinds of design engineers, one would go to less luxurious countries than the United States—to Italy, Switzerland, Sweden. Soviet engineers are first-class—in some departments not so experienced as Americans, in others more so.

Delusion 3 (held by some American nonscientists): The Soviet space flight did not take place.

Nonsense. It is as well authenticated as Columbus's first transatlantic voyage. But the fact that this delusion can exist demonstrates the distorting effect of Delusion 2.

Delusion 4 (held by nonscientists in the United States and Britain in 1945): The communist world would be many years in catching up with atomic-bomb discovery.

Compare Delusion 2. This one belongs to the same family. It has had a profound, and most dangerous, effect on Western military planning. Scientists in general have not suffered from this particular delusion. I remember in 1945, at about the time of the Alamogordo test, hearing scientists discuss how long it would take the Soviet Union to follow suit. Six years was the average estimate. In fact, it took four.

Delusion 5 (held by many Britons until the time

of the Suez crisis): The sun will never set on the British Empire—Britain is invulnerable; its wealth, power and glory will never fade.

I was born in 1905, and this was the psychological climate I grew up in. My mother, who was the daughter of a retainer on an aristocratic estate and who was herself a passionate Tory, believed in it all her life. And yet, long before I was born, British power was already past its peak. Rudyard Kipling was the poet of an Empire in decline. By about 1880, Germany was, in many respects, a more powerful country than Britain—the United States certain to be far more so. After World War I, it ought to have become clear that old-fashioned imperialism couldn't (and shouldn't) survive. It wasn't clear to the British ruling class. It was, however, clear to the Indians, and there was no doubt how the struggle must end. A little later, there was no doubt how the African struggle must end. Yet people, otherwise sensible and humane, couldn't face these certainties.

Delusion 6 (held by many who ought to know better): The colored races are inferior in all ways to the white.

My mother believed this. As a matter of fact, she went further, though she might not have said so. *But in her heart, she believed that the top gifts in the world were possessed by persons of Anglo-Saxon birth, Anglo-Saxon names, Protestant religion, fair skins and blue eyes*. That being so, it was natural, and ordained by Providence, that the top jobs should be possessed by such persons also. I should have said that my mother, though not educated, was a highly intelligent woman. In the English countryside where she was brought up, however, she can scarcely have met anyone who was not of Anglo-Saxon birth, etc. Other people, with less excuse, have fallen into the same trap. It is quite certain, of course, that the colored races—however one defines them—are not inferior to the white in any all-round sense. Such evidence as there is suggests that innate capacities are scattered more or less evenly throughout the human race.

It is just possible that certain sets of gifts have become more densely concentrated in certain racial groups. The chief argument for this, oddly enough, is the athletic success of Negroes. The number of Negroes in the world within reach of athletic training is quite small, less than the population of Spain. The proportion of Negroes who achieve the world class in athletics (especially in the short track events and the jumps) is startlingly high. I have also heard it argued, by eminent mathematicians, that the proportion of Russians with high mathematical gifts is greater than the corresponding proportion of Americans or Britons or Frenchmen.

There may be something in these examples, but I am still not quite convinced. Granted equality of environment, it seems more likely that any large group, whatever its color or race, will contain about the same distribution of ability.

Delusion 7 (held until 1957 by most Americans and many Europeans): The U.S. is invulnerable.

Well, it obviously isn't. If it came to thermonuclear war, the U.S. would lose about 40 per cent of its population, and so would the USSR. I detest having to write this figure as though it were a perfectly normal calculation. Once we begin doing that, there is no human hope for us. God knows, such a loss isn't easy to contemplate. Having said that, I don't believe that the loss would be as total as is sometimes stated. The U.S. and the USSR would probably still be viable societies after a thermonuclear war. My country wouldn't; we are so small and so densely populated that nearly all of us would die. When my American friends think we are being cowardly (in fact, we are not specially cowardly), I sometimes ask them to remember that.

There are plenty of other delusions that link up with these seven, but they are enough. What do they add up to? What is their inner consistency? What is the major mistake we are making as we judge our world? And why?

I don't think the truth is difficult to find. But it is not pretty. I believe that Britain in the 19th century and the U.S. in the 20th have let technology go to our heads. One after another, we have become stupefied by a kind of technological conceit. In our case, it made us sleepy, self-indulgent, self-congratulatory for nearly a century—so much so that we have declined faster than we needed to.

So will you decline, unless you learn from our delusions. You can see where we went wrong—how we congratulated ourselves instead of discovering why, for a short space, we were on top of the world. If we had found the real reasons for our being there, we might have stayed there longer. It would have meant education, discipline, self-criticism. If you want to stay there, it will mean the same for you.

Look back on the British a hundred years ago. We had, quite suddenly—within a couple of generations—become rich as no country had yet become rich. There was, of course, hideous working-class poverty in the towns, and probably even worse poverty among laborers on the land. But for the first time in history, there had arisen a very large and prosperous middle class. Walk round London, the acres of squares and residential streets, houses now split up into apartments, tens of thousands of them. The people who lived in those houses 50 to 100 years ago were not rich. They were a rising middle class, the largest the world had so far known. It has been calculated that, in London at the turn of the century, there were at least a *million* domestic servants, most of them waiting on this middle class.

The prosperous British took their luck for granted. Or, rather, they took it *as a natural result of their own virtue and their own constitution*. They decided that no people had a national character like theirs. Such a character was bound both to produce and to deserve wealth. So was the Protestant religion (particularly as expressed in the Nonconformist churches—the British industrial wealth was largely made by Nonconformists). So was the British constitution; clearly a limited monarchy, plus a limited parliamentary democracy, was the only possible constitution under which a country could become rich.

My mother, bless her, would have taken all these statements as articles of faith. There were, of course, interconnections between religion, constitution, the British wealth and some British characteristics. It would be silly to write them off. But no one seems to have been interested in the true reasons for this luck. Many people were vaguely aware that the British wealth came through manufacturing goods, and that the British produced goods because they had made machines. But they also thought that it was some special virtue of the British that enabled them to make machines. It was absurd to think that Indians, or other persons with different colored skins, or Russians could possibly make machines. They were lesser breeds, presumably appointed by Providence to buy our goods, and to go on doing so, as second-class citizens, forever. It was conceded that persons of Protestant and Anglo-Saxon origins, such as the inhabitants of New England, might be capable of making machines.

Very few thought of investing any special effort in the science and technology upon which the machines depended. If we had educated ourselves then, we might have kept ahead for a longer time. But we were glassy-eyed with wealth, with technological conceit. We produced an extraordinary kind of "gentlemanly" education, supposed to be suitable for proconsuls administering the Empire, and from this we have never quite recovered.

Does any of this parable, or parallel, seem to apply to the U.S. of 100 years later? I wish I could think it doesn't. Within about three generations, you have become incomparably the richest society in human history. You have spread what in any other country would be a middle class across a great continent. You have made consumer goods on a scale that was scarcely imaginable, even twenty years ago.

All this is fine. But like the British of the last century, you, too, have been infected by technological conceit. You feel, as we used to, that this predominance is here forever. You put it down to the American character, the American Constitution, the American economic system. As with us, all those are connected with the kind of wealth you have created. But you will be misleading yourselves, as we misled ourselves, if you think they are the reasons why it all happened, or a guarantee that you will remain the richest country on earth.

You are spending gigantic sums on education. Your colleges and universities are, by and large, as good as any in the world, in many ways better. They can do—if you decide *what* you want them to do. But at present, you have not set yourselves a social purpose, of which this education is a part. Your primary and high-school education is much too self-indulgent. It is one of the nice things about the American climate of feeling that you passionately desire to make the young happy. *But I don't see why you shouldn't teach them something pretty rigorous and still make them reasonably happy*. In any case, you have got to rethink some of your education; you have got to teach your children more, if you are going to keep afloat in this stern world. Remember, at the peak of our power, we didn't rethink our education. We have been paying for it ever since.

The central truth seems to be something like this: My country came to its short spell as boss nation by something like accident, or a whole assembly of accidents. Largely by chance, we got in first with the industrial revolution. You succeeded us. You got in first with the scientific revolution, or second industrial revolution, call it what you like. We lost our place. Your position is stronger than ours ever was, but there is nothing heaven-sent or preordained which makes it certain that you won't lose yours.

You see, we have now discovered that technology is rather easy and that any spirited country, given the drive and will, can carry out a technological revolution. The Russians have proved that. The Chinese are proving it now. But there was a non-Communist example, much earlier, not so deep as the two Communist industrializations, but still dramatic. That was the Japanese transformation between the Meiji restoration and 1900. Within less than 40 years, the Japanese had made themselves into a modern technological society.

All the background was there, ready and waiting for the *industrial* revolution. Europe was ready: and Britain got in first. Britain was already a successful commercial country, sitting nice and pretty on the trade routes. Maybe its political structure made it easier for the industrial revolution to spark off, than, say, in France. Maybe it was simply that we had coal and iron close together. Anyway, we got in first. *That* was the reason for Britain's being top nation for 100 years. *That* was the origin of our delusions.

Then New England came along, also already a successful commercial society with plenty of water power at hand. With the frontier pushing westward, you had a tremendous industrial base, ready and waiting for the *second* industrial revolution, the scientific revolution, which started with electronics, new-style electrical engineering, modern industrial chemistry, somewhere round 1920. You got in first with that. *Those* were the reasons for your being top nation for 30 to 40 years. *Those* were the origins of your delusions.

But the dominance, the isolated dominance, that we had in 1860 and you had in 1950, no single nation-state is ever likely to have again. I remember talking to David Lloyd George in 1937, when he was an old man and I was a young one. It was a winter night: we were staying in a hotel in the south of France; we were alone; we could hear the waves crashing on the rocks below. Lloyd George was the nearest British equivalent to Franklin D. Roosevelt, pioneer in social legislation, great war leader (in a much more tangled job than Winston Churchill's), tricky in politics, yet capable of lofty statesmanship.

That night, he had been talking about politics in its least lofty form. The old man still had a professional's obsession with the political chessboard; at 75, he still thought he might make a comeback. He had also been talking about the war which we were certain would soon come. Then he suddenly broke off: "But, my boy, none of this matters much. It will all seem very minor in fifty years' time. What does matter is that Russia is getting industrialized under our eyes. Within a generation (he overestimated the time required, as one usually does), Russia will be a great industrial power, and then China and India will follow suit, and will change the face of the world."

It is with that changed face that we are having to live. We shall not be able to live with it at all unless we strip away our delusions. It will not be comfortable, however clear-sighted we are. But it will be more comfortable if we know what to expect. We have got to prepare for this new world. We have got to fit our children for it. Some of it will be worse than we think; some of it, incomparably better. We can't contract out, for after all we are part of the human race.

The development of the European Common Market has been an important factor in inducing American companies to produce as well as sell in Europe, for it has been obvious from the beginning that the abolition of tariff barriers within the Community and the erection of a common tariff on goods imported from nations outside it would place U.S. exporters at a disadvantage vis-à-vis companies within it.

American companies have been quick to take advantage of the opportunities presented by the Common Market—so quick, in fact, that they have aroused fears in Europe. A few years ago, J.-J. Servan-Schreiber, editor of the *Express* (the French equivalent of *Time*), wrote a book[1] in which he warned that if current trends continued, American managers would come to dominate Europe's economy, largely because of their greater management know-how, particularly in the field of organization. In France, no book published since World War II, fiction or nonfiction, sold so many copies, which is evidence that many Europeans were, and probably still are, seriously concerned about an American takeover.

But is American management really so superior? As the following article points out, European managers may be inferior to American managers in some respects, but they are decidedly superior in others. Thus it appear that American managers could learn from them just as they could learn from managers in this country.

American versus European Management Philosophy

Otto H. Nowotny

Most top executives develop and practice their *own* management philosophy. Obviously, then, there is nothing so clear-cut as a single managerial style which is uniformly adhered to by all American or all European business leaders. Yet underlying the behavior and attitudes of these two different groups of executives are certain general characteristics or common denominators.

The most striking difference between the outlooks of Europeans and Americans lies in their orientation toward time. It is as if they were standing back to back, with the European inclined to look at the past and present and the American seeing the present and future.

The European's attachment to the past accounts for his respect for such characteristics as wisdom, stability, convention, necessity, quality, and diversity. The American's more futuristic outlook leads him to respect vitality, mobility, informality, abundance, quantity, and organization. But unless Europeans abandon some of their excessive attachment to the past and Americans their more or less profound disregard for it, little change can be expected. I certainly do not share the optimism of businessmen who believe that what is best in the American and European management philosophies will automatically find its way from one continent to the other by a kind of effortless "osmosis." An effort has to be made unless we want to run the risk of having the typically American and European qualities simply meet at the level of the lowest common denominator.

Wisdom versus Vitality

Though neither continent can claim to have monopoly on vitality or wisdom, it is reasonably true to say that American management philosophy is, in general, more vital than wise, while Europe's is more wise than vital.

In Europe the moderating influence of wisdom (that is, top management's preference for slow, organic growth) has admittedly prevented many production and clerical jobs from being mechanized a long time ago. But at the middle-management level and, even more, at the top-management level, in comparison with America, *under*staffing rather than *over*staffing seems to be the rule. Important decisions are still made by single individuals or at least by a much smaller group of top executives than in the United States.

With most of the strategic decisions concentrated at the top, there is also a pronounced tendency not to communicate the reasoning behind these decisions to those at lower man-

[1] *The American Challenge* (Atheneum Publishers, New York, 1968). (Originally published by Editions du Seuil, Paris.)

agement levels. Obviously, European top executives try to save a part of the time American executives spend on communications, though they do so somewhat at the expense of middle-management "learning." This fact, indeed, is reflected by the smaller percentage of key positions in European business held by executives aged 40 or less. The theory that a good wine requires many years of aging in a dark, coolish cellar has been extended to the business executive.

This particular way of thinking, I believe, explains the relatively small interest European top executives still show for training their potential managers in American or American-style business schools. In addition, they are convinced, though they will rarely admit it in public, that only the more technical aspects, and not the *essence* or the *style* of executive leadership, can be learned there.

As a result of this attitude, climbing up the corporate ladder in Europe takes the aspiring executive, generally speaking, more time than in North America. But once he reaches the top, the risk of his coming down again is also much smaller. Anyone who would go to the trouble of counting the number of executives who have been displaced from the top of their pyramid would probably find this percentage to be considerably higher in America than in Europe.

Many examples, of course, could be cited to reveal how wisdom and vitality are given different weights in the American and European management philosophies. But they would all lead us to the same conclusion: to optimize our business performance it is necessary to combine the advantages of both characteristics. How can this be done?

In Europe large reserves of vital energy could certainly be released by dropping some of the most outdated conventions. For example, those that require most decisions to be made at the top rather than at the lowest possible level in the organization, or those that hold an executive responsible to his superior but do not require the superior to bother about *actively* developing his subordinate's capacities. Many of these conventions need close questioning so that the weight given presently to different values can be redistributed more logically.

In American business an increase in wisdom can probably be achieved if top executives would try to keep in mind wisdom's most basic definition—"Avoiding the unnecessary." To put a conscious break between *stimulus* and *reaction*—as Napoleon is said to have done when he once decided to leave his mail unopened for a certain time, only to find that at the end of it most of the letters had taken care of themselves and so did not have to be answered—is one of the particular privileges and duties top management must make more liberal use of.

For wisdom requires deliberation, and deliberation requires time. Are not most of us too much under the spell of the speed and shortcut psychology of our time to grasp the full meaning of this simple statement?

Stability versus Mobility

Intercompany job changes in the higher echelons are much less frequent in Europe than in America. In part this is a matter of language and geographical barriers; but it is also the result of Europeans being more skeptical about human nature than Americans. They prefer to let several years of observation pass before giving high-level responsibility to a new member of management, who, by the time he gets it, is of course no longer new. Switching companies at a frequency customary in America would normally lead to an intolerable loss of time in the career of a European executive.

Similarly, changing jobs within companies in the sense of job rotation has never been as fully accepted by big business in Europe as it has been in America. This is due partly to the fact that specialization on lower- and middle-management levels has not been pushed as far ahead as in America; thus, job rotation seems less urgent. It is also due partly to top management's belief that rotating people through various jobs is costly and can lead to situations where a great number of employees have had experience in a lot of areas but lack solid competence in any one. With all strategic and many tactical decisions still being made at or at least close to the top, there is also less need for vision on the lower levels. There is, however, more demand for highly competent "spade-work" on which European top management can solidly build its decisions without having to resort to double- and triple-checking through extensive committee work. Committees are, therefore, far less important in the European than they are in the American management process.

Another illustration can be found in the area of job titles. Business on the European continent uses, in general, a very limited number of official titles. Thus, knowing a European executive's title and the size of the company he works for makes it fairly easy to estimate his responsibility as well as his earnings. The latter are rarely, if ever, spoken of openly, contrary to the practice in America where knowing the earnings of an executive is often the only way to measure his responsibility—the number of titles being so great as to make quick orientation a rather hopeless affair.

"If the deserving employee is hungry for a title, the good manager gives him one, even if it turns out to be but Third Assistant to the Head of Sub-Assembly Department No. 3," is a typical bit of reasoning by the American manager which would find little acceptance in Europe. European top executives believe that the widespread use of custom-tailored titles to compensate for a lack of job satisfaction is a short-range expedient which merely starts a vicious circle, forcing top management to dole out ever more status symbols and leading ultimately to the highly sophisticated and eventually costly kind of human relations being practiced by large corporations in America. Indeed, by comparison, human relations in European business still have a kind of rustic simplicity.

Convention versus Informality

Although an open-door policy and a first-name basis are both widely accepted practices in American business, they are but two exterior signs of how American management philosophy has given preference to informality. This is, of course, contrary to human relations practices in Europe, where numerous conventions are still strictly adhered to. But the roots of our different convictions go much deeper, and it seems as if in the external dilemma of all executives—having to exercise authority and trying to be liked—European top management has constantly preferred to put more weight on the former and American top management more on the latter quality.

Thus, American managers seem to feel that human relations in Europe have an authoritarian and paternalistic flavor, and consider the social distance between individuals a remnant from feudal times. Europeans, in turn, believe Americans to be guilty of promoting excessive egalitarianism and status stripping which in their eyes is not only naive and unrealistic, but must inevitably destroy management effectiveness in the long run. The results of these different attitudes are interesting.

Whereas human relations in European business lack the outer nonchalance and friendliness found in America, they do not seem to share the inner tensions which are often apparent on the other side of the Atlantic. American tensions stem, it seems, largely from trying to adhere to the overly idealistic point of view that one must like everybody or, if that cannot be done, at least pretend to do so.

But between the extremes of bullying or loving people there is ample room for the less spectacular but more effective way of simply *respecting* them. However, no progress will be possible unless top executives give up the idea that only the American or the European brand of human relations is correct, and will admit that both have severely suffered from inbreeding the same ideas for many decades.

Necessity versus Abundance

The relative lack of natural resources in Europe and their abundance in America has not been without profound impact on the management philosophies of our two continents. Thus, the tendency toward thrift and the desire to avoid waste are only too evident in the thinking of European executives, to whom the concept of planned obsolescence still seems to be as foreign as ever.

Nowhere can this important aspect of managerial philosophy be observed any better than in the various types of automobiles produced in Europe and America. Cars such as a Volkswagen, a Citroën, or a Mercedes are the definite reflection of an entirely different management philosophy than are a Chevrolet, a Ford, or a Cadillac.

United States military strategy, to use another example, has also been based on the country's abundance of resources. This is evidenced by the American way of fighting World War II, namely, to concentrate large masses of troops and to act fast. But Europe, not having the same resources, had to build its strategy mainly on flexibility and surprise. It was Churchill who said that "the good-luck charm of success in war is surprise," thus stating the typically European approach. Surprise and particularly its cause, secrecy, are therefore a natural part of European management philosophy.

American executives and financial analysts often complain about the rudimentary information given by European companies in their balance sheets and profit and loss statements. But the smaller amount of information published is in strict accordance with local government rules. And if no voluntary supplements are handed out to the general public, it is only partly to seek additional protection from foreign competition behind the smoke screen of secrecy. It is also caused by the general conviction that the more information a company releases, the more explanation it has to give. The tendency toward thrift and the desire to avoid what is not really necessary are, therefore, two important reasons why European business seems to be playing its cards close to its chest.

Quality versus Quantity

With economic necessity such an important factor in European management philosophy, business in Europe has always found it necessary to stress quality much more than quantity. How else—to cite one extreme example—could a small country like Switzerland, with hardly any natural resources, have become a prosperous nation than by simply doing a few things better than anybody else would do them? "Quality, not quantity" is, therefore, the outstanding characteristic of European management philosophy and explains many facets of the way European executives think.

A very typical facet is the fairly general tendency of Europeans to *think before trying*. As a leading European businessman once said: "We are not in the habit of increasing through wastefulness the chance of a random hit."

And so, the technique of "brainstorming," which has been given much publicity in America, has never really been accepted in Europe. Preference has always been given to high-quality, individual thinking rather than to group thinking.

Another technique which has never made much impression in Europe is "speed reading." Although the quantity of reading matter has increased as much for the European as it has for the American executive, the former has in general refused the *speed* solution, believing that it necessarily leads to an accent on quantity (at the expense of quality). He has relied more on *selectivity* to solve his reading problem.

He has also applied this same principle in his community and public activities, which seem to be but an infinite fraction of what many American executives have accepted. The reasoning behind this consistent refusal to get too involved outside the immediate sphere of work is the European conviction that each individual should, above all, concentrate on his job, because nobody aiming at top performance can afford to dissipate his energies.

But by saying *yes* to quantity, one cannot say *no* to standardization, because these two characteristics of managerial philosophy are linked like Siamese twins. Quantity per se is certainly not bad. On the contrary, it has considerable social benefits, such as the increase in the standard of living resulting from mass production. But there are always the attendant dangers of excessive standardization trailing in its wake and of overorganization stifling individual initiative.

Diversity versus Organization

Overorganization, the European believes, is a particular threatening consequence. The European achieves order through definite status levels in his organization, but he does not try to organize man's every effort as do many American firms.

No doubt, there can be too little organization, that is, too much diversity. And in many instances European business performance could be improved if there were more of it. But top executives must be aware of the fact that aiming at good organization is like trying to keep a small ball balanced on top of a big one. Good organization is always—although we do not seem to be conscious of it—in a state of unstable equilibrium, needing slight but constant corrective action from the top. The goal is to strike a proper balance between European and American attitudes toward organization.

Achieving a Synthesis

The basic characteristics of American and European management philosophies are so strikingly complementary that a combination of what is best in both must lead to an improvement in the conduct of our Euro-American free enterprise economies. Of course the crucial question is how to bring about this desirable change.

Surely no success whatsoever is to be expected of large-scale attempts to have top executives hold special international meetings in order to discuss some of the important topics of managerial philosophy. With "publicity" hanging over their heads like a sword of Damocles, few top executives, if any, would take the risk of seeing their statements misinterpreted. They would speak only in the most cautious terms—so cautious, indeed, that the essence of their statements would seldom be more than an agglomeration of euphemistic platitudes.

Although the written word is a wonderful medium for conveying "facts" to a larger public, we forget too easily that, in discussing "values," *oral* communication within a small group of individuals is by far the most preferable and practically the only way to avoid either banality or confusion.

Thus, the present trend in politics toward more personal and secret diplomacy might well portend the direction in which top executives will have to move if they want to make a synthesis of what is best in American and European management philosophies.

If European executives differ from those in the United States, Japanese executives are different from both, and their system of management is different. One explanation may be that industrial development in Japan was grafted onto a society that had been feudal until the middle of the nineteenth century. Whereas the Industrial Revolution occurred spontaneously in Europe and the United States, it was government-sponsored in Japan. It began with what is known as the "Meiji Revolution" in 1868, when a new emperor, Meiji, suddenly did away with all attempts to maintain Japan isolated from the rest of the world and began to encourage introduction of Western learning and Western technology. Thus Japan rose to become a power under a largely authoritarian system; then with the adoption of a democratic constitution after World War II, it experienced almost a second industrial revolution, and advanced at a still faster pace.

Below, Dr. Joseph Froomkin, an executive with broad experience in Japan and other countries, explains the Japanese system of management.

Management and Organization in Japanese Industry

Joseph N. Froomkin

Americans who look at the organization and practice of Japanese management always have the same initial reaction: Can this really work? There is little formal organization, less delegation of authority, and little reliance on staff work even in the largest firms. Nevertheless, Japanese industry has supported a rise in Gross National Product of 6.5 per cent a year, and industrial production has increased by 12 per cent per annum. A little reflection usually indicates that management practices which made such growth possible deserve attention from all businessmen.

The principles underlying Japanese organization are not well documented. There is very little literature on the subject. This dearth of informa-

Adapted from "Management and Organization in Japanese Industry," *Journal of the Academy of Management*, Vol. 7, No. 1, March, 1964, pp. 71–76.

tion is no accident, but is due to the united front which most Japanese business presents to the outside world. A Japanese corporation is a private preserve, and its internal methods of operation are of no concern to anybody outside of the establishment. The following notes on the practices and organization of large firms in Japan are based primarily upon interviews [conducted] by the writer [while acting] as a consultant to a dozen large Japanese companies.

Despite the absence of an accepted theory of organization, most Japanese firms are strikingly similar in their organization and employment practices. This similarity reflects the impact of specific social values. For instance, Japanese society stresses the duties of leadership and assures rewards to followers. Most large Japanese firms translate these principles into the centralization of decision-making power and the no-firing rule—the so-called permanent employment policy.

Decision-making Power

The centralization of decision-making power may be so extreme that all decisions originate with the president of a company, a strong individual who represents the ownership interest or is a major stockholder himself. He communicates his decisions to an entourage, which executes them. Companies ruled by such a dictator still exist today, but they are the exception rather than the rule.

In most large companies, strong leadership is equally evident but it is parcelled out along functional lines. The absolute power to make decisions and to give instructions is clearly vested with one person in each different area of the business, such as the plant manager, the sales manager, etc. Each one of these leaders possesses specific spheres of authority to the exclusion of all others, and is the absolute power in his own bailiwick. In contrast to American business practices, the committee form of organization and "touching bases" before making a decision are almost unknown.

The leaders in the various management fields are accustomed to making independent decisions, but not to working together. As numerous American businessmen who tried to reach agreements with Japanese firms have found out, it is difficult to get the leaders to agree. Japanese managers are not accustomed to interdepartmental give-and-take, and hence take an unconscionably long time to make up their minds on matters which involve more than one department.

Many top managers of medium and large companies [pointed out] that the decision-making process had been democratized since the end of World War II. Nowadays they permit their decisions to be discussed by their immediate subordinates in their own department before such decisions are implemented. Sometimes, but not often, the subordinates' arguments are considered and the decisions reversed. This free discussion occurs most often in the marketing area, where Japanese top managers have the least experience. Nevertheless, in all cases the final decision rests with the top manager.

An outsider often confuses the communication of a decision with the making of it, and the Japanese system of decision making has been unjustly criticized for its slowness. Actually decisions are made relatively quickly, but are communicated in a long and roundabout manner. In order to preserve the dignity of fellow employees, the communication of policy decisions takes the form of long and over-polite meetings, during which the pros and cons are discussed at great length, and the consensus demanded by the top manager is reached unanimously. This is achieved by carefully watching the important persons involved. On balance, this takes less time than "brain storming" or committee meetings in the [United States]—except for the rare decisions which cross departmental lines.

Organization

The most pertinent criticism of such centralized decision making is the difficulty which Japanese firms have in adding new functions to their present organizations. A box in the organization chart is not sufficient to get the operation going; it must have the backing of an important leader. Often this leader will hesitate to push the new function lest he upset the status quo and the working relationships with other important leaders.

During my visit to Japan, I worked with executives of a firm which had been formed by merging two companies some three years before. At the time of the merger an outside consultant had been called in to set up the new organization. His organizational chart remained in force, but it did not describe the true power centers of the company. In one part of the business most important decisions were made by the head of the general affairs department, and in the other by the sales manager. All other departmental managers consulted (really reported to) these two men.

As often happens in Japan, the organizational chart was used here to save the prestige of a large number of employees in the merged companies. The titles on the chart did not correspond to the functions. In most large Japanese firms many employees have titles such as chief of department [and] head of section, and even more employees are assistants to these chiefs. These titles are usually devoid of any real decision-making power; they have been created to accommodate the psychological needs of employees with many years of seniority. An American can only admire this relatively painless way of keeping peace within a company.

Since the Japanese seem unable to cut up the operations of a business into relatively small and easy-to-manage functions, a strong and independent leader must be found for each important facet of the firm. On the whole, Japanese firms have succeeded in developing this type of leadership, even though the process may take considerable time.

Marketing

In several instances, in the post-war period, marketing was neglected by large Japanese companies (it is still neglected by one of the biggest trading groups) because strong leaders could not be found within the company to head this function. The appointment of a marketing manager was not sufficient to overcome the prejudices against attacking distribution problems energetically. Traditionally, the output of large Japanese companies is sold or consigned to an agent who distributes it to wholesalers. These wholesalers, in turn, sell to retailers. Dealing directly with retailers, or establishing retail locations, is considered a low-status occupation—one to which, therefore, it was difficult to draw top management attention.

This lack of attention from top management precluded the appointment of men with leadership talent to handle these problems. Right after the war a number of small, aggressive merchandisers started to eat into the traditional markets of the large companies. The giants' reaction was not to make drastic changes in their organizations, introduce tighter controls in marketing, or shorten the span between the producer and the retailer. Instead, they tried to regain their share of the market by cutting prices. These price cuts generally were met by the competition. The market expanded, but the large companies did not recover their share of it. At that point, a drastic change took place in the top managements' attitude to marketing. The difficult job of convincing likely candidates to accept positions in a low-status field was accomplished. This was not easy since Japanese managers develop slowly in a single business specialty. By now, the majority of large companies have established their own distribution outlets and have set quotas to distributors based on share of market. They are slowly introducing training schools for retailers. The traditional annual banquet or outing for agents and retailers is no longer a purely social occasion but is increasingly taking on the aspect of an industry training school.

The progress of the past ten years is very impressive. I had occasion to participate in the critique of a sales call demonstration by one of the largest consumer goods companies in Japan. Apart from the somewhat slower pace necessitated by the courtesy of Japanese life, the sales call could have been made in the [United States]. It even suffered from the most general shortcoming of American sales calls—the absence of stress on the reason why the retailer should push the salesman's brand over that of competitors. I suggested that the script be amended to include a reference [to] the high quality of the company's product, which had won a prize at a trade fair, as well as other retailers' stories of success with the product. The eagerness with which these suggestions were accepted—and later followed up at the regional sales meeting—indicated considerable sophistication in marketing techniques.

Selecting and Training Managers

How do Japanese companies carry off drastic changes in organization and orientation without attracting outside personnel or destroying the firm's morale? The answer lies in their method of selecting and training managers. The characteristic attitude of management in Japanese firms is that of patient dedication. Most Japanese companies recruit young men immediately upon their graduation from a university. The best-known firms hire graduates from the equivalent of Ivy League schools, while smaller and foreign companies must content themselves with graduates of lower-ranking universities. In most cases, the first job is the only job these college graduates will ever have.

After joining the company, all college graduates go through an initial period of apprenticeship which lasts from ten to fifteen years. During this period they are all treated and remunerated on an equal basis. In the larger companies it is quite easy to guess a younger employee's salary by determining the number of years he has been employed. Only after this initial period are some apprentice managers advanced more speedily than others. The less able will remain in the firm until retirement and still receive minimal seniority increases.

This preservation of harmony within a firm by giving the illusion that nobody loses and everybody wins is [sometimes] difficult for outsiders to understand. An American sales executive complained that although the Japanese subsidiary management seemed to pay lip service to his efforts to introduce the merit system of promotion, they did nothing to bring it to life. After a particularly long lecture, which seemed to elicit agreement, he asked the local sales manager whether he would now promote an outstanding young man rather than a seasoned and mediocre older man. "So sorry," answered the Japanese sales manager, "I must promote the older man."

No Japanese manager would dare make a promotion that is blatantly out of turn—not only because it would rock the morale of the firm, but also because the apprenticeship period is valued for its "character building" qualities. The period is spent in cementing relationships with one's contemporaries, and being observed by an important manager. A young man at this stage can have no greater joy than to perform a favor for a manager. The senior manager, though, is always on the defensive against accepting such favors, lest he be morally [obligated] to further the young man's career. An understanding of this facet of Japanese life sheds light on the willingness of young college graduates to work as house servants or errand boys for the heads of large enterprises. The young men are investing in a personal relationship, and their behavior closely resembles that of American business school graduates who buck for the job of administrative assistant to the president of the company.

The long apprenticeship period and the systematic method of advancement have both good and bad results. While they encourage extreme devotion and loyalty to the firm, they also lead to an atmosphere of Balkan politics within the company. Loyalty to the organization (which one is tempted to compare to the loyalty of retainers to a feudal lord) is balanced by the expectation of rewards stemming from the firm. However, loyalty to the firm may be perverted into devotion to an individual senior manager, in the expectation that this devotion will be rewarded. In the final round of promotions, when leaders are chosen to head the decision centers, Japanese firms pay a great deal of attention to "noble character"—a euphemism for the broader loyalty.

The most intriguing feature of the system is [that] the habitual acceptance of decisions, together with detailed instructions for their implementation, appears to develop the ability both to make decisions and to provide guidance [to others] upon promotion to leadership. After meeting a representative cross-section of Japanese executives one cannot but come away with the impression that, in the long run, ability plays a somewhat greater share in promotions [under their system] than under ours. The practices of delegating authority or of setting tasks without guidelines for implementation introduce a large share of randomness in the management selection process here. Young managers in the [United States] often sink or swim because of fortuitous circumstances since they are judged on results rather than on methods.

I believe that the Japanese system of management development is responsible, to a large extent, for enabling Japanese industry to grow [rapidly]. The emphasis on broader loyalties and ability in choosing high-level executives gives a solid topping to the management pyramid. At the same time, the clear-cut responsibilities in many Japanese firms, as well as loyalty to the firm, make Japanese top managers eager to improve operations. The important manager does not end his development as a manager when he is promoted to a decision center. On the contrary, he begins it then. The director of executive development in one large Japanese company mentioned to me that courses given to younger employees do not arouse any interest, but that older employees request them. However, these courses are extremely difficult to plan. Having come up the hard way, most managers are not satisfied with generalities, but are interested in specific applications of principles to their own areas. They know their operations intimately, and are exceedingly critical of superficial recommendations.

The rapid growth of the Japanese economy has required only minor modifications in the organization of the management hierarchy. Many firms which grew relatively fast in the post-war period have had to promote younger managers somewhat faster than was customary. Other firms which rose from humbler beginnings and became important adopted the traditional practices. Despite the high rate of growth of these firms, the older staffs were taken care of and usually remained in key positions. It is true that young men of impatience and modern outlook now have a few avenues to chance-taking and rebellion. A few firms, especially in the electronics industry, hire, fire, and promote employees on the American pattern. But these firms remain very much in the minority, and there are signs that with increasing maturity they, too, will conform to the Japanese business pattern.

In the meantime, to stave off raids for personnel from unconventional firms, some large companies have attempted a slight modification in their remuneration policies. Without disrupting the hierarchical ranking of employees by age, an additional measure, that of position, has been added to the salary structure. Raises of this type have usually occurred in new areas, such as marketing or data-processing, and problems with bypassed senior personnel have been minimized.

Lessons for Americans

What lessons can American enterprise [draw] from the Japanese experience? Probably by far the most important is that management development can occur very satisfactorily in an atmosphere where security dominates. Secondly, good management can be well, if not better, developed under conditions where guidance is given, rather than by the trial-and-error method practiced by most U.S. firms. Third, that an important ingredient for fast and profitable growth is the existence of strong decision centers. We do pay lip service to all these principles, but let us ask ourselves honestly (1) [Would] we hesitate to fire a manager who did not perform to our satisfaction? (2) How complete were the instructions we gave to a subordinate the last time a decision was handed down to be executed? (3) How many bases had to be touched before an important policy decision was made?

Quite often the prospect of dismissal inhibits a young manager from making controversial suggestions. The unsuccessful innovator is likely to be penalized quite heavily in U.S. business. Secondly, risks are minimized if tasks are set without giving guidelines for implementation. This aversion to risk may be the cause of all shortcomings, as a top manager has no time to manage, but spends his time checking out his new ideas with everybody who can possibly be affected by them. At a time when the free enterprise system in the U.S. is straining to maintain a satisfactory rate of growth, the atmosphere which created Japan's strong entrepreneurship and willingness to innovate may deserve increasing attention.

In absolute terms, the British economy has not been declining; in fact, the GNP has grown. But the advance in Britain has been so much slower than that of other Common Market countries that most people (including many thoughtful people in Britain) are convinced that something is radically wrong and that there must be major changes if British industry is to meet the competition from other countries. The following is an analysis of the way in which Britain differs from other industrialized countries and a prediction of grim consequences if major changes are not made.

Where Britain Differed

At first sight it might seem that Britain has marched in lock-step with its rich colleague-countries. In the 1950s—while they elected Eisenhower, Adenauer, de Gaulle, the Japanese Liberal-Democrats—we voted steadily for our first 13-year period of Tory rule. In the 1960s—while their student counter-culture produced Berkeley, Paris in 1968, Rudi Dütschke, the Japanese university thugs—we had our little local demos as well. The worry is that while their demos are slowing down, as the babies of the post-war bulge move out of the universities, our demos have escalated into the bipartisan indulgence in torture in Northern Ireland and into electricity stoppages enforced by intimidatory miners' strike pickets, even while we go on telling ourselves what a civilised and kindly people we are.

There seem to me, on reflection, to be at least six elements in Britain's present dominant culture which are not present in other countries' outlooks on events. They are surprisingly rarely talked about, but they could explain a lot about our national subconscious:

1 Britain was the first country to escape from being in any sense a peasant society. Even in the 1930s only 7 per cent of Britain's workforce was in agriculture, against 20 per cent of North America's, 25 per cent of France's, 40 per cent of Japan's. When account is taken of other self-employment jobs like small shopkeeping, and of the generally higher birth rate in rural areas, this means that anybody over 40 in all other industrial countries has at least a one-in-four chance of having come from a childhood background where his or her family was working on its own account; the sort of background where it is traditional for even the children to be given something useful to do from an early age, say to collect the logs to keep the family warm. A large number of people in all industrial countries except Britain have therefore been "first generation" entrants into manufacturing: people who learned to look upon entering industry as the thing that you did (at the expense of accepting sterner disciplines) if you wanted to have a sudden increase in your standard of life. Since the manufacturing age is now probably ending in the rich north of the world, the extraordinary truth is that—for many continental European, Japanese, even American, families—factory working will have proved to be a one generation experience, and there has not been the time to breed the defensive attitudes towards a job which litter British industry. In Britain nine-tenths of us even over the age of 40 had fathers who were wage or salariat slaves, so that our inbred attitude towards work has usually been as something which you have to do (preferably without the boss working you too hard) in order to get a living.

2 Another hidden influence on all the 24m Britons over the age of 40 is that Britain was probably the only industrial country where the real income of about four-fifths of the people must have gone up in the depression of the early 1930s (because anybody still in a job benefited from the drop in prices, and because the improvement in the terms of overseas trade kept the drop in Britain's real national income in 1929–32 to about 7 per cent, versus America's horrific drop of about 30 per cent over those four years). More than the whole of the burden of the slump in Britain therefore fell upon about 20 per cent of the people, of whom the most visible

From "The People We Have Become: A Survey of What's Gone Right and Wrong with Britain," *The Economist*, London, Apr. 28, 1973, pp. 34–35.

were the newly unemployed. While the slump hit America first in the form of stockbrokers committing suicide in 1929 and with waves of unemployment rolling in afterwards (so that the message was "what's bad for business becomes terrible for us"), the slump in Britain was a period when the better-off majority felt compassionate and (more important) guilty towards the bitter minority, many of them members of the basic industries' trade unions against whom the majority had recently withstood a successful general strike. One good hangover from this is that no British politician could nowadays emulate American politicians in fighting an election campaign against white working-class "welfare bums" (but maybe nowadays he could against black or student ones).

3 Britain was the only major European country that did not have the decision-making bodies in its society ploughed through by defeat and occupation in war during 1940–1945. We are therefore left with a lot of institutions that no sensible country would have re-created, and Anthony Sampson is surely right in saying that the worst legacy from the Victorians to Britain has been "the idea of permanence . . . railways, family firms, coal mines or regiments all acquired the safe, unchanging character of a country estate . . . our outdated Victorian conceptions are defended because they are there, or because 'it's odd but it works'." The result is a surfeit in Britain of closed rather than open minds—of "men whose thinking has been conditioned by the rules and atmosphere of a single institution, rather than those who see over the partitions and adapt institutions to suit their own ends." In continental Europe, by contrast, the one usual closure of mind is the temporarily very useful one that hardly anybody is willing to think about what happened before 1945.

4 The shared heroic experience between classes, to which the older half of Britons most like to look back, is the war that we surprisingly won under blitz and privation, so that compassion means trying to be one nation and binding up wounds. The heroic experience to which continental Europeans like to look back is the recovery after 1945, so that compassion means lifting your own granny up with you as you rise again.

5 It is important to remember how uneducated most Britons are. As late as 1960 only 12 per cent of 17-year-old Britons were still at school (versus 70 per cent of Americans); most of continental Europe is just as uneducated, but some continental countries have long run their apprenticeship systems more efficiently, so that the British have more often started as teenagers in dead-end jobs. Since 1970 the proportion staying on longer at school has doubled across Britain and Europe, but the dominant culture in many continental schools is Roman Catholic, which sets up its antithesis of anti-clericalism, but then arrives at a sort of synthesis between the two.

In Britain most people would not know what the progressive European teacher's gut feeling of anti-clericalism means. Unfortunately, the equivalent gut feeling among progressive teachers in British state schools, where pupils have at last been staying on, is antipathy to the fee-paying private schools where pupils have always stayed on. This engenders in attentive British kids a prejudice against the rich (including against the successful), while anti-clericalism engenders in attentive French kids a prejudice against the conservative Establishment; the former is an anti-expansionist, while the latter can be a dynamic, force.

6 A huge new influence in the dominant culture since about 1955 is that an actual majority of Britons—educated and uneducated, rich and poor—will at some time this evening be doing exactly the same thing: namely, watching the same television programmes. The average Briton over the age of 5 watches television for 16½ hours a week. The political influence of British television can best be called yesterday's liberal: critical of old boys' networks and of unimportant parts of the Establishment like the stock exchange, frightfully eager to be environmental, but respectful of powerful institutions and happy to avoid immediate fights (so that "good news about the railway strike" will usually mean that it has been bought off at a price that will spell national calamity). A more lasting effect of the

popularity of British television may be that tiny groups of those who can drag themselves away from it now find it even easier to seize control of centres of some power.

My guess from all this is that Britain in 1973–88 is less likely to return to a hard-work-ethic than other industrial countries. This may be serious because by the end of that period we could have a lower income per capita (and thus eventually less influence) than nations like Spain, Greece and Mexico. I suspect that in Britain workers even in the most heavily subsidised industries will not come to be regarded as "welfare bums," so that there will be no blacklegging of strikes called by coal miners and London dockers and others whose jobs should clearly soon be closed down; that there may be quite heavy emigration of the most alert British workers to continental Europe; that our British underclass in 1973–88 will consist increasingly of coloured people (who by 1980 will find greater job discrimination against them here than in America) and old people; and that, although 99 per cent of the students from the 1960s will be most eagerly concerned in the 1970s with advancing in executive jobs, yet there will be a residue from the new left's emotions of the silly sixties which will inspire small groups of anarchists to try to seize power in all too many trade union and Labour party branches, even while the mess in the central cities causes powellite influence to increase in local Conservative associations. If inflation is not successfully checked by a statutory incomes policy—and only a bold man will declare that it certainly will be—the resultant clash in the country could be very ugly indeed: most probably ending with a powellite victory.

All of this need not happen. Britain still has huge potential advantages: a tradition of tolerance and humanity, a lack of corruption in public life, the fact that we speak the same language as America, the City of London, rather greater liberation of womankind than is usual in Europe or certainly Japan (this could be very important), rather good basic scientific research (partly inherited from the age when our education was elitist), a vague pride left over from old imperial days which (together with happy sentimentality about the monarchy) makes it almost impossible for even the fiercest British critic of whatever is the current British government to come actually to hate his country. But none of this will avail if we continue to shut our eyes to what we do not wish to see.

"The characteristic danger of great nations, like the Romans, or the English, which have a long history of continuous creation," said Walter Bagehot a hundred years ago, "is that they may at last fail from not comprehending the great institutions they have created." This danger is now, for Britain, at possibly mortal crisis point. Almost all of the great institutions Britain has created—parliament, the civil service, local government, the law enforcement authorities, the other public services, the nationalised industries, the trade unions—are not performing the functions which were their original purpose. Most are being operated mainly in order to allow the able top people in each of them to enjoy themselves by concentrating on doing the things that give them the most satisfaction. Almost all of the changes that are needed are therefore ones that would cause maximum disruption in what the most intelligent public men in the country have come insensibly to regard as their entirely reasonable sense of purpose. This is why they are the opposite of the changes that are likely to be put into effect. That is the British disease.

Farming and small business continue to be important to the French economy, but as this article points out, there are signs that a second industrial revolution is under way as a direct result of France's membership in the European Economic Community.

France's Second Industrial Revolution

"Chère vieille France! La bonne cuisine! Les Folies-Bergère! Le gai Paris! La haute couture et de bonnes exportations, du cognac, du champagne, des Bordeaux ou du Bourgogne! C'est terminé." In these words, the President of the French Republic, during one of those pieces of political theatre, a presidential press conference, closed a chapter in French history. M. Pompidou had spoken. In the place of the old France, a new one, engaged in a second industrial revolution, is emerging. The main thesis of this survery has been that the rhetoric of the Fifth Republic in its second phase, after General de Gaulle's retirement and death, has by and large been translated into reality. The transformation is not complete, for if France is a country where change, once underway, can be extraordinarily rapid, it is also a country where the past to an unusual degree continues to live in the present. The rhetoric of ambition has always to be qualified by the reality of achievement.

The first qualification is that agriculture will continue to be more important to France than to any other advanced European nation. Farming remains one of France's major resources. Although the proportion of the labour force employed on the land is declining by around one per cent a year, the current ratio is still that which existed in Britain a century ago. France has a larger area of cultivable land than any other European country. The proportion of its exports which arise from farm products has actually increased over the past decade. General de Gaulle described France as the country of 200 cheeses, and despite M. Pompidou's picturesque turn of phrase, farming and the sale of all that the rich soil offers, whether it is Camembert, Chateau Mouton-Rothschild or the most advanced form of convenience food, will continue to bulk large in the French economy.

The second qualification is that sectional interests—such as the farmers, blocking the road with sugar beet or grapes—will have enough power to slow things up. It is now the shopkeepers, café-owners or artisans, who give France so much of its individuality. France is a country where sectional privileges remain commonplace—where farmers, for instance, pay no income tax. Recently it has been the turn of the shopkeepers and café-owners, led by their young hero M. Nicoud, to protest, by strikes and the burning of tax records in provincial government offices, against the march of progress. Shopkeepers, for instance, are menaced by the vast out of town hypermarkets developed so rapidly by groups like Carrefour and Casino over the past decade. It is no coincidence in a pre-electoral year that M. Nicoud and his friends have been granted an amnesty for their part in civil disturbances and that Carrefour has been given permission to build only two hypermarkets. Progress even in a hard, unsentimental country like France is kept within bounds. A political party to the right of centre, even when it proclaims economic progress as its main raison d'être, can never forget its constituents.

The third qualification relates back to M. Pompidou's press conference and his famous sketch of the old France and the new. He was in fact replying to a question about France's well known diplomatic activities in favour of foreign sales of its colour TV system, Secam, and of Mirage military aircraft. These—and such matters as French participation in Concorde—are to a large extent the products of old gaullist policies in favour of national self-sufficiency and high technology programmes, rated in prestige rather than cost terms. These are now largely discarded. French sales of military equipment abroad have accounted for a large slice of its increase in manufactured exports. But this is a game which will have declining returns in the new France. There is a new maturity at work. Prestige now takes second place behind pay-off. This means that France is no longer prepared to bear the costs of high technology itself. Just as the French have learned the lessons of modern management, which implies teamwork, so they have caught on to the rewards to be won through international consortia.

The consequences of France's industrial revolution point in the same direction. Given the French traditions of self-sufficiency and autarchy the common market was bound to have a greater impact on France than on the other

From *The Economist*, London, Dec. 2, 1972, p. 46.

northern European nations. Initially, the French conceived the impact as meaning a greater, vulnerability to risk and damage, which, they hoped, would be counterbalanced by higher agricultural exports. Now it is seen in France as meaning something else. France is becoming as dependent on international trade and as closely enmeshed in international business as its partners. And this will lead, indeed is already leading, to a profound change in mentality. The curious paradox is that General de Gaulle had to revive a sense of national confidence before the French could persuade themselves to think internationally. Like all the major changes in the history of France, the switch from being France in Europe to being European France will not be accepted by a section of its population for a long time to come. But it is happening nonetheless. What Algeria was for General de Gaulle, Europe is for M. Pompidou.

22 Management in Developing Countries

Most of the underdeveloped countries are attempting to develop their resources and raise standards of living among their populations, and many of them have succeeded in raising their GNPs. However—in contrast to the developed countries in which output grows faster than population—their populations are rising faster than their production. Thus the threat of lowered standards of living or even outright famine is very real, despite aid from the developed countries, which has been forthcoming for a long time and seems likely to continue far into the future.

One way of gauging the underdeveloped countries' chances of success in combatting the immense difficulties they are encountering is to look at the history of development as it has already occurred in western Europe, especially in England, which was the first country to experience the Industrial Revolution. To what extent are conditions in the developing countries today comparable to those existing in England in the eighteenth century? This question is answered in the first article in this chapter.

The next two articles deal with theories of economic development. The first of these explains what input-output analysis shows about the difference between developed and underdeveloped countries, and the second reviews some of the theories of development that have so far been advanced. There is, it will be noted, some disagreement among theorists about the best way to ensure development.

However, even if development plans are based on sound theory, there is no guarantee that development will proceed in accordance with the plans, for carrying them out may be much more difficult than the planners realize. The short story "A Heap of Machinery" illustrates the sort of thing that may happen, and often does.

Finally, there are two articles dealing with foreign aid: one opposing it and the other calling for an increase in help from the developed countries and especially for studies to determine how it can best be used.

Here the author uses Huddersfield, a textile town in northern England, to illustrate the changes that occurred through the Industrial Revolution. As this extract shows, there were losses as well as gains in the process of industrialization, but life before the Industrial Revolution was anything but idyllic for all but the rich and the fairly well-to-do, and those who had no claim to either status constituted the majority of the population. There are points of similarity between the present underdeveloped countries and precapitalist Huddersfield, but there are also important differences. Both are explained in this excerpt, which gives an excellent idea of the problems of development in the modern world.

The excerpt is taken from a book commissioned by a former president of the World Bank, which provides capital for development in underdeveloped countries.

Huddersfield: The Taste for Change

James Morris

Crouched in a declivity among the Yorkshire moors, in the harsh allure of the Bronte country, there lies the town of Huddersfield. It is not guides or hotel reservations that you will need, if ever you make the pilgrimage to those stark smoke-filled valleys, but a responsive sense of history, for Huddersfield's fascination is more evocative than architectural: her passport to Baedeker is the fact that here, in these grim moorlands of northern England, the technical revolution began.

These stocky, taciturn people were the first to live by chemical energies, by steam, cogs, iron and engine-grease, and the first in modern times to demonstrate the dynamism of the human condition. This is where, by all the rules of heredity, the sputnik and the moon-rocket were conceived. Baedeker may not recognize it, but this is one of history's crucibles. Until the start of the technical revolution, in the second half of the eighteenth century, England was an agricultural country, only vestigially invigorated by the primitive industries of the day. She was impelled, for the most part, by muscular energies—the strong arms of her islanders, the immense shaggy legs of her noble Shire horses. She was already mining coal and smelting iron, digging canals and negotiating bills of exchange, and she had long moved, indeed, out of the subsistence stage, when men simply grow food to feed themselves. Agriculture itself had changed under the impact of new ideas: the boundless open fields of England had almost all been enclosed, and lively farmers were experimenting with crop rotations, breeding methods and winter feed. There was a substantial merchant class already, fostered by trade and adventure, and a solid stratum of literate yeomen.

For most ordinary people, though, England remained more or less the kind of country she had been a century before, her affairs still rigidly geared to the production and exchange of foodstuffs. Her landowners were rich and cultivated, her peasantry was ignorant, obsequious and often hungry, and most of her people lived in the country. It was not a feudal society, but a paternal one, a land of squires, cultured country parsons, the tugging of forelocks and the dispensation of old folk remedies by tenderhearted gentlefolk, a country of such gentle pastoralism that a French nobleman visiting England in 1784 could describe her as 'the finest country in Europe, for variety and verdure, for beauty and richness, for rural neatness and elegance—a feast for the sight, a charm for the mind.'

Science changed all this, together with money. It was a process long in gestation, with its seeds far back in the New Learning of the Middle Ages, the inquiries of the Renaissance and the audacities of the Reformation; but with the opening puffs of the Steam Age the English realized almost with a start that a way of life need not be sacrosanct, even without divine intervention. Diffidently at first, robustly later, with a flood of new ideas, new inventions and new enterprises, they set in motion all those processes of change and development that were to transform their society from bucolic calm to brass-bound industry. Gradually it transpired that the new natural sciences, first probed by the savants of the eighteenth century, could be employed to make men richer and theoretically happier, to set a whole nation afire, to shift its entire outlook on human satisfaction, to give it such a shot in the arm or kick in the pants that it would never be remotely the same again.

Science and money did it, bolstered always by ruthlessness. It was no lily-road to well-being. Modern England was made in half a century, as you can see up there in Yorkshire. Wherever you look, there are the mills and tenements of the revolution—faded now and crumbling, or patched up with concrete and chromium, but still keenly suggestive of an old and furious momentum. The sheer scale of it all, the speed and energy with which the railroads were built, the rivers harnessed, the moorland valleys clothed in masonry—the sweep of it all is astonishing to contemplate, even now, and could only have been achieved by an impetus of violent force and brutality. It was not merely a matter of building factories. It involved the shattering of old shibboleths, the re-examination of old values, the migration of thousands of people from gentle countryside to raw new town.

The Huddersfields were the pace-makers, but today there is scarcely a nation of the earth that does not wish to follow them down the highway to the mills. One by one the states are reaching the particular point in their history that the British reached two centuries ago, when they burst into the effulgence of their steam and brass. For every people it is a cathartic moment of vision, of new awareness, never satisfactorily defined. It has been called the revolution of rising expectations—when a people realises at last that life may actually be expected to improve. It has been likened to the take-off of an aircraft—when a national economy develops enough power to get it off the ground at last, and thereafter keep it moving with ever-increasing acceleration. It has been analysed as the moment when a nation learns to apply savings and science methodically to the earning of man's daily bread.

In the early days of English industrialization, only the seers or the moguls saw what it would mean in terms of money, creature comfort, excitement. Today the simplest rustic on the hay-wagon has at least an inkling of what lies over the garden wall. Ours is a world of obtrusive contrasts, from modern to antique, television screen to mud hovel, vulgar to fastidious—anomalies so pungent and so ubiquitous that contrast provides a *leit-motif* for almost every modern travel book. So universal has been the contagion that even in fatalist Asia the pursuit of happiness is now recognized as a valid political aim, not just a spiritual exercise.

And happiness comes, they nearly all say, out of a factory chimney. Technical revolution is seen as the universal panacea, and few peoples nowadays are prepared to honour the traditional disciplines of society—wisdom and generosity for the rich man, respectful labour for the poor.

Most of the experts agree, too, that the purely agricultural societies are rightly doomed, and that the impetus of economic development must be towards new industries, new sources of power, a spread of urban living. Anyone with a sneaking sympathy for the thesis that experts are wrong, people are bloody and all progress for the worse—anyone of simmering traditionalist tendencies must view with some disquiet the philosophies of universal modernity. So much that is brash, heartless and ugly stems from too sharp and unthinking a change of tradition.

The trust in change, though, is inescapable, and is often exceedingly moving. I was once wandering alone in the highlands above La Paz, the Alpine capital of Bolivia, when I met a raggetty old cowherd in a high grazing-ground on the edge of the snow (where he was guarding four young bulls destined for the city bull-rings). He was the simplest kind of Andean Indian, wearing a queer sort of skull-cap with ear-flaps, and looking as knobbly and wind-roughened as an old juniper: and when I approached him I saw that his right eye was bleary, swollen and wet with tears. Some weeks before, he told me, a particle of grain had lodged beneath the eyelid, and now all was puffed and septic—and edging close to me, looking up at me with his good eye and summmoning a wan quivering smile, the old man invited me with absolute heartrending confidence to cure him, so sure was he that the mere breath of modern man, like the antique touch of royalty, could dispel such rural miseries.

No wonder the yearning for progress is so irresistible. The romantic view of pastoral living is almost confined to artistic amateurs, as any honest farm labourer will robustly assure you, if you are fool enough to compliment him upon the peace and quiet. A yearning for solitude and open spaces is not one of the commoner impulses of humanity, and the ideal of serene poverty, though still cherished by sophisticates and ascetics, is generally as discredited as Rousseau's vision of the noble savage. The desire for week-end cottages comes late in a society's lurching progress towards utter urbanity: before you feel the need to retreat into the country, you usually feel the need to escape into the slums.

The simpler half of our contemporary world, then, with its eyes on the rockets and refrigerators of the sophisticated half, is hoping always to modernize itself, and indeed by and large the difference between a rich nation and a poor one is the difference between a mechanical and a muscular society. Today it can perhaps be said that a third of the world has passed the Huddersfield cross-roads into industrial prosperity, and the other two-thirds is straining to get there.

For the eager young nations of today, the task of modernization is in some ways easier than it was for the pioneers. It has been amply demonstrated, for one thing, that anyone can do it: and for another, a kind of initial deposit of modernity was often laid by those vast empires which, until a couple of decades ago, divided most of the pastoral world among themselves. Technically the transition from muscle to machine is no longer really difficult, given some degree of literacy, enough money, a modicum of help from abroad and plenty of time. Machines are easy enough to come by, managers can be hired, boys can be sent for training in Moscow or in Massachusetts, a good engineer will build you a road, a dam or a railroad line in any terrain on earth. Constructing a modern mechanized society is no longer a job for visionaries, whether a State chooses to do it by compulsion (like China) or persuasion (like India).

The legacy of imperialism contributes to this quickening of abilities, if only because resentment often sharpens the senses. Most of the aspirant states of today are ex-colonies—or, like the South American republics, countries that have recently detached themselves from the leading-strings of more experienced Powers. Before and between the two wars a groundwork of industrialization was laid in many countries by the agents of foreign domination, political or economic.

Metaphysically it is a different story. In literacy, in culture, in skills, in experience, in understanding of money and means, in popular attitudes, in public integrity—in maturity, most of today's emergent countries are still centuries behind eighteenth-century England, that 'feast for the sight and charm of the mind,' which at the moment of Huddersfield had not only produced great poets and statesmen by the dozen, but Newton too, Locke, Hume, and a whole gallery of eminent mathematicians, philosophers and political economists. England was already a civilized State, an experienced maritime and commercial Power: her successors today are often trying to leap direct from backward dependency to complete scientific sovereignty—from the Middle Ages, sometimes, direct to the nuclear age. Occasionally, indeed, you may find a colonial territory so soaked in European custom, so integrated with the suzerain Power, that all the attitudes of modernity are there already, only waiting to be sparked. Elsewhere, though, the aspirant nations are seldom so restrained, seldom so sophisticated, and there is often an undeniable streak of pique or pride to their hankering after modernism.

Without much discrimination contemporary history judges that all these States, from the noble to the footling, are ripe for the great change—ready to move from purely agricultural, subsistence economies into the kind of world that lives by buying and selling, by making things and putting things together. Indeed, the truth is that history has no choice. The birth-rate now exceeds the death-rate so dramatically that every minute the world's population increases by sixty souls, and by the end of this century may well have doubled—Friday, 13th November 2026 was forecast by a University of Illinois research team as Doomsday, the moment when, if things continue as they are, the population of the world will squeeze itself into Nemesis. Already the earth is running short of arable land, and it becomes clearer every day that mankind can only survive, like Frankenstein, by the goodwill of the machine. But more than all this, history can only recognize the inflexible will of the poor peoples to live like the richer half—the Huddersfield way. Nothing on the planet today is more vital and inflammatory than this eagerness of the aspirant peoples.

[But] few countries can now achieve a technical revolution without money from abroad—China is perhaps the only contemporary exception. To buy a ticket to Huddersfield, you need a rich uncle somewhere. This implies a phenomenal strain upon the capital resources of the rich countries, for the scale of the demand is enormous—so sudden has been the new understanding that has followed two world wars and the collapse of the imperial system.

By far the greatest external sources of development funds are the American official agencies, and by far the greatest prod to western generosity is the possibility that the Russians may offer more. Sometimes it does no harm. Unselective aid, though, can lead peoples of less resilient character into bad habits. It encourages, to put it at its most prosaic, loose practices of management and finance: if you can get one hundred million dollars out of a sugar-daddy, you can probably squeeze two. It leads nations to suppose that they can feed permanently upon the rivalry between the Powers. It sometimes keeps alive régimes that have no right to survive, which would in the natural course of political evolution soon topple into the limbo of discredited despotisms. Worst of all, it sustains the Cold War itself, makes its protagonists feel that they must always outbid each other, vulgarizes and degrades the very notion of generosity.

Despite planning at the top, many developing countries have found themselves with new factories for which no electricity has been provided, with new schools but no teachers for them, or with food and no means of transporting it to people who are starving.

One reason for this is that few data are available for the construction of an integrated and economical plan. Only by interrelating all the principal factors of input and output in the major segments of industry can one ensure that scarce facilities will be properly utilized.

It is interesting to recall that the French economist François Quesnay developed a *Tableau Economique* for this purpose in the eighteenth century. Since then, more refined techniques have been developed. A modern pioneer in this field, Prof. Wassily Leontief, of the economics department of Harvard University, here applies his theory of input-output analysis to a comparison of the economic structures of developed and underdeveloped countries.

The Structure of Development

Wassily Leontief

Over the past 25 years the internal economic gearwork of a large number of countries has been described with increasing clarity and precision by a technique known as "interindustry analysis," or "input-output analysis."

The data of input-output analysis are the flows of goods and services inside the economy that underlie the summary statistics by which economic activity is conventionally measured. Displayed in the input-output table, the pattern of transactions between industries and other major sectors of the system shows that the more developed the economy, the more its internal structure resembles that of other developed economies. Moreover, from one economy to the next the ratios between these internal transactions and the external total activity of the system—true gear ratios in the sense that they are determined largely by technology—turn out to be relatively constant.

Recent advances in input-output analysis and in the bookkeeping of underdeveloped countries have made it possible to apply the technique to a number of these economies. Their input-output tables show that in addition to being smaller and poorer, they have internal structures that are different, because they are incomplete, compared with the developed economies.

For purposes of this demonstration an econo-

From *Scientific American*, September, 1963, pp. 148–166.

	Input			
	Sector 1: Agriculture	Sector 2: Manufactures	Final Demand	Total Output
Sector 1: Agriculture	25	20	55	100 units
Sector 2: Manufactures	14	6	30	55 units
Household services	80	180	40	300 units

	Input/Output Coefficients		
	Sector 1: Agriculture	Sector 2: Manufactures	Final Demand
Sector 1: Agriculture	0.25	0.40	0.183
Sector 2: Manufactures	0.14	0.12	0.100
Household services	0.80	3.60	0.133

Input-output table (*top*) and input-coefficient matrix (*bottom*) show "internal" transactions between productive sectors of simple model economy in relation to "Final demand" and "Total output" of each sector. Table displays outputs from each sector in corresponding horizontal row, inputs to each sector in vertical column. In matrix the columns display ratio between each input to a sector and total output of the sector.

my can be broken down into two industrial sectors: agriculture and manufactures (see table above). In the table for such a simple model economy, the numbers in the horizontal row labeled "Agriculture" show that this sector, in the course of delivering 55 units of output as end products to "Final demand" and 20 units as raw materials (for example cotton) to "Manufactures," delivers 25 units of its own output (for example feed grains) to itself. "Final demand" can here be taken as including the goods and services consigned to investment and export as well as to current consumption in the households of the economy. The total output of 100 units from the agricultural sector therefore satisfies both the "direct" final demand for its end products and the "indirect" demand for its intermediate products. On the input side the numbers in the column labeled "Agriculture" show that in order to produce 100 units of total output this sector absorbs not only 25 units of its own product but also 14 units of input (for example implements) from "Manufactures" and 80 units —of labor, capital and other prime factors—from the sector called, by convention, "Household services."

The great virtue of input-output analysis is that it surfaces the indirect internal transactions of an economic system and brings them into the reckonings of economic theory. Within each sector there is a relatively invariable connection between the inputs it draws from other sectors and its contribution to the total output of the economy. This holds for an underdeveloped economy, where the input from "Household services" necessary to produce 100 units of agricultural output might represent a full 80 man-years of labor, as well as for a highly developed country where this input would reflect a larger component of capital and is likely to be offset by inputs of fertilizers, insecticides and the like from the industrial sectors. In fact, for use as an analytical tool, the input-output table must be recast into a matrix showing the input ratios, or coefficients, characteristic of each sector. The input-output table for the model economy, recast into such a matrix, shows that .25 unit of agricultural output, .14 unit of manufactures and .8 unit of prime factors from "Household services" are required to produce one unit of total output from the agricultural sector.

Dependence and independence, hierarchy and circularity (or multi-regional interdependence) are the four basic concepts of structural analysis. The definition and practical significance of each of these ideas can be demonstrated visually by schematic model tables in which dotted squares rather than numbers signify the presence or absence of interindustry transactions. (See illustration, page 436.) In the first of these tables a solid dot appears in every one of the 225 boxes formed by the intersection of the 15 numbered rows and columns of the industrial sectors. Each industry in such a system is dependent on all the others; it supplies

INDUSTRIES OF ORIGIN AND OF DESTINATION

For Goods and Services, 1939 (in millions of dollars)

○ 10 to 25 % } of purchasing
● over 25 % } industry's total

□ 10 to 25 % } of producing
■ over 25 % } industry's total

INDUSTRY PRODUCING	INDUSTRY PURCHASING: Total gross output	1. Agriculture and fishing	2. Food, tobacco, and kindred products	3. Ferrous metals	4. Motor vehicles, industrial and heating equipment	5. Metal fabricating
Total gross outlays		13,745	18,923	3,721	7,979	9,102
1. Agriculture and fishing	12,475	950	● ■ 4,998			
2. Food, tobacco, and kindred products	18,799	645	1,530			
3. Ferrous metals	3,887	24		● ■ 1,188	□ 479	□ 861
4. Motor vehicles, industrial and heating equipment	7,672	188	72	4	○ □ 1,645	7
5. Metal fabricating	8,692	433	306	37	611	717
6. Nonferrous metals and their products	2,956	5	23	109	117	221
7. Nonmetallic minerals and their products	2,734	14	137	29	70	64
8. Fuel and power	13,592	474	168	318	102	164
9. Chemicals	4,911	357	133	36	34	108
10. Lumber, paper, and their products	8,893	94	260	1	35	63
11. Textiles and leather	12,032	66	43		105	8
12. Rubber	1,170	54	3		□ 195	22

inputs to all other sectors and draws inputs from all of them.

A more likely and natural system is represented by the model in which some boxes are empty. The industry in whose column one of these empty boxes appears draws no input (or perhaps an insignificant input) from the industry whose row it intersects at this point. If the corresponding box formed by the reverse combination of column and row is empty, then these two sectors can be described as being independent of each other. Where intersectoral dependence is indicated by a square in this table, however, one such square may trigger a whole chain of indirect demands, finally involving both members of an apparently independent pair of sectors.

Such relations become clearer in the model in which all the squares fall below the diagonal running from the upper left corner to the lower right corner of the matrix. Actually this "triangular" system was constructed by rearrangement of the rows and columns of the "natural" system described in the preceding paragraph, as is indicated by the sequence in which the call numbers of the sectors now appear. The highly structured hierarchical relation between the different sectors was obscured in the first random display—an accidental effect, perhaps, of the sequence in which the census bureau of this imaginary economy assigned call numbers to the sectors. In the rearranged table it can be plainly seen that sector 9, now in the far left column, absorbs inputs from all the other sectors but delivers its entire output directly to final demand. Sector 8, now in the far right column, requires for its operation, in addition to a portion of its own output, only labor, capital and other prime factors from "Household services"; on the other hand, this sector delivers inputs to all other sectors as well as to final demand.

In the hierarchical order of an economy with a strictly triangular matrix, the sectors above and below the horizontal row of any given sector bear quite different relations to that sector. Those below are its suppliers; any increase in final demand for its product generates indirect demands that cascade down the diagonal slope of the matrix and leave the sectors above unaffected. The sectors above, however, are its customers; an increase in final demand for the output of any one of them generates indirect demand for the output of the sector in question. An economist charged with the task of computing the indirect effects of an increase in final demand for the output of this sector would need to know, therefore, only the input coefficients for sectors below it. If he wants to compute the indirect effects on this sector of demand originating elsewhere, he needs to work only with the input coefficients for this sector and the sectors above it. In the case of the fourth "block triangular" model he would find that relations between sectors within each block are similar to the mutual interdependence that ties together all the sectors in the first of these model systems, whereas the relations between the blocks ("multiregional interdependence") are analogous to those between the sectors in the triangular model.

The larger and the more advanced an economy is, the more complete and articulated is its structure. The U.S. and western Europe respectively produce about a third and a quarter of the world's total output of goods and services. It is not surprising, therefore, to discover that their input-output tables yield the same triangulation.

Each of the industries in this combined table has its own peculiar input requirements, characteristic of that industry not only in the U.S. and in Europe but also wherever it happens to be in operation. The recipes for satisfying the appetite of a blast furnace, a cement kiln or a thermoelectric power station will be the same in India or Peru as it is, say, in Italy or California. In a sense the input-coefficient matrix derived from the U.S.-European input-output table represents a complete cookbook of modern technology. It constitutes, without doubt, the structure of a fully developed economy in so far as development has proceeded anywhere today.

An underdeveloped economy can now be defined as underdeveloped to the extent that it lacks the working parts of this system. This lack can be explained in narrowly economic terms as due to the amount and distribution of productively invested capital; in social terms, as a reflection of the composition and efficiency of the labor force, or in geographical terms, as the result of the country's natural resources.

The process of development consists essentially in the installation and building of an approximation of the system embodied in the advanced economies of the U.S. and western Europe and, more recently, of the U.S.S.R.—with due allowance for limitations imposed by the local mix of resources and the availability of technology to exploit them.

In the absence of such complete development a country can consume goods without producing them because it can import them. It must pay for its imports, however, by producing other goods for export instead of for domestic con-

0 \ 1	1	2	3	4	5	6	7	8	9	10	11	12	13	14	15	D	T
1	●	●	●	●	●	●	●	●	●	●	●	●	●	●	●	○	■
2	●	●	●	●	●	●	●	●	●	●	●	●	●	●	●	○	■
3	●	●	●	●	●	●	●	●	●	●	●	●	●	●	●	○	■
4	●	●	●	●	●	●	●	●	●	●	●	●	●	●	●	○	■
5	●	●	●	●	●	●	●	●	●	●	●	●	●	●	●	○	■
6	●	●	●	●	●	●	●	●	●	●	●	●	●	●	●	○	■
7	●	●	●	●	●	●	●	●	●	●	●	●	●	●	●	○	■
8	●	●	●	●	●	●	●	●	●	●	●	●	●	●	●	○	■
9	●	●	●	●	●	●	●	●	●	●	●	●	●	●	●	○	■
10	●	●	●	●	●	●	●	●	●	●	●	●	●	●	●	○	■
11	●	●	●	●	●	●	●	●	●	●	●	●	●	●	●	○	■
12	●	●	●	●	●	●	●	●	●	●	●	●	●	●	●	○	■
13	●	●	●	●	●	●	●	●	●	●	●	●	●	●	●	○	■
14	●	●	●	●	●	●	●	●	●	●	●	●	●	●	●	○	■
15	●	●	●	●	●	●	●	●	●	●	●	●	●	●	●	○	■
H	□	□	□	□	□	□	□	□	□	□	□	□	□	□	□	□	■

0 \ 1	1	2	3	4	5	6	7	8	9	10	11	12	13	14	15	D	T
1	●		●	●	●				●	●	●		●			○	■
2	●	●	●	●	●		●		●	●	●	●	●	●		○	■
3			●	●					●							○	■
4				●					●							○	■
5			●	●	●				●	●			●			○	■
6	●	●	●	●	●	●	●		●	●	●	●	●	●		○	■
7	●		●	●	●		●		●	●	●	●	●			○	■
8	●	●	●	●	●	●	●	●	●	●	●	●	●	●	●	○	■
9									●							○	■
10			●	●					●	●						○	■
11			●	●	●				●	●	●		●			○	■
12	●		●	●	●				●	●	●	●	●			○	■
13			●	●					●	●			●			○	■
14	●		●	●	●		●		●	●	●	●	●	●		○	■
15	●	●	●	●	●	●	●		●	●	●	●	●	●	●	○	■
H	□	□	□	□	□	□	□	□	□	□	□	□	□	□	□	□	■

0 \ 1	9	4	3	10	13	5	11	1	12	7	14	2	6	15	8	D	T
9	●															○	■
4	●	●														○	■
3	●	●	●													○	■
10	●	●	●	●												○	■
13	●	●	●	●	●											○	■
5	●	●	●	●	●	●										○	■
11	●	●	●	●	●	●	●									○	■
1	●	●	●	●	●	●	●	●								○	■
12	●	●	●	●	●	●	●	●	●							○	■
7	●	●	●	●	●	●	●	●	●	●						○	■
14	●	●	●	●	●	●	●	●	●	●	●					○	■
2	●	●	●	●	●	●	●	●	●	●	●	●				○	■
6	●	●	●	●	●	●	●	●	●	●	●	●	●			○	■
15	●	●	●	●	●	●	●	●	●	●	●	●	●	●		○	■
8	●	●	●	●	●	●	●	●	●	●	●	●	●	●	●	○	■
H	□	□	□	□	□	□	□	□	□	□	□	□	□	□	□	□	■

0 \ 1	1	2	3	4	5	6	7	8	9	10	11	12	13	14	15	D	T
1	●	●	●	●												○	■
2	●	●	●	●												○	■
3	●	●	●	●												○	■
4	●	●	●	●	●	●	●	●								○	■
5	●	●	●	●	●	●	●	●								○	■
6	●	●	●	●	●	●	●	●								○	■
7	●	●	●	●	●	●	●	●								○	■
8				●	●	●	●	●	●	●	●	●				○	■
9				●	●	●	●	●	●	●	●	●				○	■
10				●	●	●	●	●	●	●	●	●				○	■
11				●	●	●	●	●	●	●	●	●				○	■
12				●	●	●	●	●	●	●	●	●				○	■
13								●	●	●	●	●	●	●	●	○	■
14								●	●	●	●	●	●	●	●	○	■
15								●	●	●	●	●	●	●	●	○	■
H	□	□	□	□	□	□	□	□	□	□	□	□	□	□	□	□	■

Internal structures of model economies are revealed by input-output tables. Solid dots signify inputs from sectors in a given horizontal row to sectors in vertical columns intersected by the row; open circles, the input from each sector to "Final demand" (D); solid squares, the total output (T) of each sector; open squares, the inputs of prime factors from "Household services" (H). Table at upper left shows completely "interdependent" economy; table at upper right shows random pattern of interindustry transactions. Latter table appears at lower left with sectors rearranged (note sequence of sector "call numbers"); this "triangulation" of table reveals hierarchical pattern of interindustry transactions. "Block triangular" model at lower right shows interdependence of industries within blocks, as in first model, and hierarchical relation between blocks as in third.

sumption. Two countries can thus display identical, or at least very similar, patterns of domestic final demand and yet have very different patterns of production. The smaller and the less developed a country is, the more it can be expected to exploit its productive capacity independently of its immediate needs and to bridge the gap between production and consumption by means of foreign trade. Consequently the full diagnosis of the ills of an underdeveloped country—as well as the formulation of a realistic development plan—requires a detailed quantitative analysis of the dependence of all the domestic industries not only on the configuration of final domestic demand but also on the composition of the country's foreign trade.

Louis J. Walinsky participated in the formation of Burma's economic development plans and later served as chief adviser to the Burmese government while the plans were being put into effect. His book details the progress made and the obstacles encountered in a ten-year period. In this excerpt he evaluates some of the theories of economic development in the light of his experience in Burma.

Theories of Economic Development

Louis J. Walinsky

It is widely accepted, both in the professional literature and in the policies of many underdeveloped countries, that the relative absence of a middle class with entrepreneurial capacity and talent makes it necessary for governments to initiate and operate enterprises which are generally left to the private sector elsewhere. I do not intend to argue against the proposition that most underdeveloped countries have only the beginnings of a middle class, and that this group cannot mobilize capital and organize production in a degree comparable to the activities of their counterparts in more advanced societies. This does not mean, however, that the private sector cannot contribute significantly to the development process. Substantially the current view—on the basis of the Burma experience—would appear to be a dangerous myth.

The desire to improve one's material welfare, to increase one's income or to make a profit is, if anything, even stronger in underdeveloped societies than in the more advanced countries. Very little more than a perceived opportunity is necessary to transform this desire into entrepreneurship. The greatest number of potential entrepreneurs exists in the agricultural sector, where landless tenants aspire to land ownership and where landholders and tenants alike will readily hire tractors, or use improved seeds, fertilizers, insecticides and other capital aids if they are shown that these will yield a profit. Entrepreneurship is also significantly, even abundantly, evident in international and domestic trade, in construction, in home and other small-scale industries and, notably, in money lending. It is incorrect and misleading to ignore such evidence.

The presumption that entrepreneurial capacity is lacking in the underdeveloped countries has no doubt been influenced greatly by the scarcity or absence of relatively large-scale private industrial enterprises. This, however, fails to take adequate account of such factors as the hostility to private enterprise frequently found in such countries, the excessive controls applied to it, the fears of nationalization, the lack of credit institutions and money markets, and the prevalent unfamiliarity with and distrust of the corporate form of business organization (because it involves a pooling of resources and effort with people outside the family or the small circle of trusted friends). The judgment appears also to have been influenced by what looks like unbusinesslike management by business men in these countries—for example, their common failure to keep adequate records and accounts. This, in fact, is a widespread phenomenon; it does not reflect a lack of entrepreneurial ability but rather a highly rational, if wily, technique for baffling the tax collector.

It is highly probable that in many underdeveloped countries, as in Burma, entrepreneurs and entrepreneurial abilities are by no means lacking. Despite a superficial appearance of in-

From *Economic Development in Burma, 1951–1960* (The Twentieth Century Fund, New York, 1962), pp. 591–597.

efficiency, these entrepreneurs are in fact efficient, in that they seek out the investments which produce the largest short-run returns with the least risk. "Considering the special circumstances of many underdeveloped countries, their decisions may constitute a perfectly rational evaluation of the structure of economic opportunities."[1] And if, as Adler has pointed out, "the development process in underdeveloped countries . . . proceeds *in spite* of the strength of the social and cultural forces opposed to it,"[2] surely this must reflect, so far as the private sector is concerned, an entrepreneurial drive of quite remarkable vigor.

Burma's failure to appreciate the capacity for saving, investment and entrepreneurship in the private sector, and the desirability of stimulating and utilizing this capacity to the fullest extent possible, was rooted in an ideological bias: an identification of private enterprise with foreigners and alien minorities, a lack of appreciation of how the economy could be stimulated indirectly and guided by appropriate investment, fiscal, monetary, credit, tax and other economic policies, and a similar lack of appreciation of how private profit could be made compatible, through appropriate safeguards, with broad social welfare objectives. In consequence, her development effort suffered not only to the degree that the private sector failed to make the full contribution of which it was capable, but also to the degree that the Government sector, overburdened with unnecessary tasks it was not equipped to handle, failed to execute properly tasks which only the Government itself could do.

It would seem to follow that efforts to realize the potential of the private sector should be a major component in development strategies and plans. Such efforts, of necessity, would include the elimination of hostile, impractical or merely unnecessary policies and controls, and the introduction of policies, programs and institutions designed to stimulate and assist the private sector to develop its constructive potential progressively. Nationalization policy, punitive taxation and over-close remittance controls are prime examples of the obstacles imposed; investment incentives, research and technical assistance and industrial development financing institutions are good examples of the stimuli that might be applied.

Economic Theory

Most economic theorists agree that investment is central to economic growth. The development strategies currently recommended, however, do not agree on the emphasis to be placed on saving and investment. Some emphasize instead the importance of particular skills and attitudes, and, therefore, a strategy aimed at the development of entrepreneurs, investors, decision-makers, technicians and other key groups. Still others emphasize the importance of political structures and psychological motivations, and, therefore, a strategy designed to shape values and political attitudes or to influence particular political groups.[3]

Reacting against overemphasis on these non-investment factors, Adler agrees that capital formation "is not the whole story. But it is at least half of it, and the other half is rather meaningless without it." Capital formation may thus be viewed as "a necessary but not a sufficient condition of economic development."[4]

The Burmese experience certainly emphasizes the importance of cultural values and attitudes, political attitudes and psychological factors as well as the need for investment. It also supports the emphasis others place on the importance of entrepreneurial, investor, technical and decision-making skills. Hagen,[5] for example, could find cogent evidence in the case of Burma's Indian, Pakistani and Chinese resident alien minorities for his thesis that innovation and enterprise tend to originate in deviant minority groups. Hirschman,[6] on the other hand, might find it more difficult to support, by reference to the Burmese experience, his thesis that development strategy should be directed at maximizing investment (which he equates with develop-

[1]Nathan Rosenberg, "Capital Formation in Underdeveloped Countries," *American Economic Review*, Sept. 1960, p. 713.

[2]John H. Adler, "Some Policy Problems in Economic Development," *Economic Development and Cultural Change*, Jan. 1961, p. 113.

[3]Gustav F. Papanek, "Framing a Development Program," *International Conciliation,* Carnegie Endowment for International Peace, March 1960, p. 312.

[4]Adler, *op. cit.*, pp. 118–19.

[5]Everett E. Hagen, "How Economic Growth Begins: A General Theory Applied to Japan," *Public Opinion Quarterly*, Fall 1958, pp. 373–83.

[6]Albert O. Hirschman, *The Strategy of Economic Development* (Yale University Press, New Haven, 1958).

ment) decisions. Decision-making was indeed a critical factor in this experience. But the decisions which were most needed and most lacking were not investment decisions, but administrative, managerial and policy decisions.

It would be difficult to use the whole varied Burma experience in support of any one of these major theories or strategies, much less in support of the most specialized theories which logically fall within them. It would be difficult even to select any important aspect of that experience which did not significantly involve, though in varying degree, investment, skills, cultural attitudes and values, and politics. And certainly, if one were to seek support in the Burmese experience for the "big push" investment strategy, or its variant, the "balanced growth" theory, or the theory favoring emphasis on investment in "social overheads," the selection would have to be forced, even though "big push" and "balanced growth" thinking greatly influenced Burma's planning consultants.

Superficially viewed, the Burmese experience would appear to substantiate, if anything, Hirschman's unbalanced growth development theory. On the basis of his previously cited analysis that the relative absence of the ability to make investment decisions is the key factor limiting development, and that development strategy should concentrate, therefore, on maximizing such decision-making, Hirschman concludes that decisions which create shortages and imbalances in the economy, and thereby induce and even compel further investment decisions to restore that balance, are the most effective route to development. Within this context, he maintains, priority should be given to direct-production activities which compel additional investment decisions rather than to social overheads which merely permit them; to capital-intensive projects which create products new to the economy rather than to labor-intensive projects which compete with and supplant existing handicraft industries; to projects which require high-quality precision or maintenance standards, precisely because failures will be so glaring (e.g., airplane crashes vs. potholes in roads); and to industries where the worker must keep up with the machine rather than set his own pace.

In Hirschman's development lexicon, every economic cloud, it seems, has a silver lining. Consider the following statement:

> . . . Balance is restored as a result of pressures, incentives, and compulsions: . . . the efficient path toward economic development—and therefore the one that will often be instinctively taken if we can rely on the "principle of least effort"—is apt to be somewhat disorderly and that it will be strewn with bottlenecks and shortages of skills, facilities, services and products. . . .[7]

However much we may be inclined to accept the general validity of this observation, we cannot but be jarred when Hirschman describes the typical and perhaps inevitable disorderliness of the development process as "efficient." It is easier to accept his earlier and less formalized comment on the same phenomenon, before the typical became the "efficient":

> In any event, the underdeveloped countries see only the fruits of economic progress and have little advance knowledge of the road they need to travel to obtain them. If they desire these fruits, they will somehow set out after them. Thus they will find out about the changes required in their own society.[8]

This strikes me as absolutely right and completely substantiated by the Burmese experience. But while this experience might support a historical theory of development in the terms stated, it does not support a strategy of development which would seek (by design?) to teeter on the tightrope from imbalance to imbalance.

If the Burmese experience has significance for economic development theory and strategy, this would seem to be that no single element or factor is an absolute prerequisite to development, any more than any single factor or simple strategy can alone suffice to insure it. Galbraith perhaps has come as close as anyone to a formulation which stresses all the strategic factors.

Galbraith has stressed the essentiality, together with investment, of education, good government, social and economic justice and a clear sense of purpose.[9] By these he means: education in the sense of both widespread literacy and a rather high degree of learning and

[7] *Ibid.* p. 158.
[8] *Ibid.*, pp. 9–10.
[9] John K. Galbraith, "A Positive Approach to Foreign Aid," *Foreign Affairs*, April 1961.

training, among the elite groups at least; good government chiefly in the sense of a reliable apparatus of government and public administration; social justice in the sense of an equitable sharing of the gains achieved; and a clear sense of purpose in the sense of a realistic understanding of what development involves. The Burmese experience completely supports the emphasis Galbraith places on good government and clear purpose. While a relatively high degree of literacy was present in Burma, progress in basic education and in the higher education of the elite had been something less than optimum. On the score of social justice, Burma had swung perhaps too far, rather than not far enough, but I do not question the applicability of this criterion in many underdeveloped societies.

Where the Galbraith formulation seems more than a little brash is affirming that development cannot progress if any of these decisive elements is missing. While it may be agreed that all these components are essential to *optimum* development progress, it by no means follows that no significant progress is possible in the absence of one or more of them. Development *is* taking place in many underdeveloped countries of the world in the absence of one or more of these factors, though the progress in many cases is uneven, partial and considerably less than could be achieved under more ideal conditions.

The Burmese experience, then, would tend to support a theory of economic development which would view capital formation as " a necessary but not a sufficient condition" and emphasize very strongly the contributory, though not prerequisite, role of the Galbraith factors (which could be interpreted broadly enough to embrace most of the elements we have previously stressed).[10] It would regard these, however, as essential only to *optimum* progress, bearing in mind that even advanced societies achieve far less than optimum results from their own efforts, and recognizing (with Hirschman) that the efforts of the underdeveloped societies, precisely because they are underdeveloped, will inevitably achieve, at best, far less than optimum results.

Such a discussion offers little help in making many basic decisions and choices which are inescapable applications of development strategy. It sheds little light, for example, on such problems of resource allocation as the distribution between consumption and investment, or the choices between public and private investment, between the directly productive and social overheads, between industry and agriculture, or, within a given sector, among various projects and programs. Many of these decisions will inevitably be influenced by ideological considerations, by flair, by "feel," by political sensitivity, by questions of practical readiness and, in general, by rough judgments on the part of the decision-makers (even though the decisions, once made, may look as though Hirschman's strategy had been employed!).

In the light of the Burmese experience we may regard with suspicion any development strategy which does not emphasize: the desirability of assigning a significant contributory role to the private sector; the priority which should be accorded to improving existing production and distribution as against new production; or the possibilities of using the capacities of military establishments and of youth corps and other forms of widespread voluntary participation in a development effort.

But perhaps the broadest of all strategic choices is whether the attempt should first be made to prepare the way for development by pushing literacy programs, training a key elite, developing key institutions, carrying through basic essential reforms, improving public administration, and thus achieving readiness for effective investment, or whether the strategy should be to plunge, so to speak, into a maximum investment effort and learn by doing, creating at the same time the pressures for carrying through simultaneously what might be regarded alternatively as preparatory measures.

This choice, which might be termed crudely the choice between strategies of preparation

[10]Galbraith's theory, by its emphasis on social justice, recognizes the importance of human motivations, but it does so primarily within the context of a more equitable distribution. The individual, he says, will never exert his maximum efforts "if the gains therefrom accrue to feudal landlords or employers, or to tax collectors, merchants and usurers." True, and critically important: but the statement does not go far enough. Social justice may contribute, through land reform, to a revitalized agriculture: but it will not contribute directly to industrial and related investment. Greater incentives will make the worker work harder, and result in greater output from the existing productive plant. But opportunities, incentives and aids to new investment are also required. While these are compatible with greater social justice, they are not provided by it. Recognition of the potential of the private sector, and positive action to realize it, are also essential and of sufficient strategic importance to require special emphasis.

and plunge, may be considered by some to be one of those imponderables which can be judged only subjectively, in terms of one's temperament, predilections and biases. In my view the Burma experience, painful though it was, gives a fairly clear answer. It supports the strategy of "plunge" (which Hirschman seems to have rationalized into a theory of imbalanced development). It is difficult to envisage how Burma, in her immediate post-war circumstances, could have chosen the preparation strategy and deferred the investment plunge.

The huge chasm between planning and execution is not always successfully bridged in the West, and in the East the situation is likely to be infinitely worse in this respect, as the following story (somewhat shortened from the original) illustrates. Incidents like those reported here are quite common in underdeveloped countries. (The "advisers" who drive up are Russian foreign aid administrators.)

A Heap of Machinery

Minh Hoang

Each day the sun beat down on the wooden crates stacked at the entrance to the half-finished factory. Each day Thang, the boss of the construction site, went there at noon. Each day he kicked the wooden slats to see if they were sound, peeped through the cracks, and, nostrils quivering, poked his nose into a knothole to sniff the state of things.

The sun was like fire; the heat burned through to his bones.

"If this goes on," he thought, "the wood will warp and the cracks will widen. The sunlight will get inside and rust the steel. The whole pile of machinery will be lost." The heat was fierce; no one knew when the sky would pour rain. And after the rains, the damp would get in, coating the beautifully complex and glittering steel of the machines, violating their virgin perfection. "There is nothing anyone can do about the weather."

The devil himself could not explain how this vast mountain of delicate machinery had suddenly been delivered to the construction site. They had piled the crates in the open air, naked to the scorching rays of the sun. Thang was a responsible construction boss. He could not refuse the new responsibility of guarding the heap of machinery. A troublesome duty indeed! But in his usual way Thang bent his back to the new load. He would do the best he could.

He went to his superiors and asked that they buy tarpaulins to shield the crates from the weather. Always they refused. He insisted. Always they said: "Only a few days more, and we will install the machinery inside. No need to buy canvas." He asked: "Who will install these machines?" But always they answered vaguely: "We will think about that later."

The construction gang would ask how the audience had gone, what had happened. Thang would answer curtly: "They refused." Then he would hang his head and say nothing. He would walk over to the heap of machinery and bang his fists against the warped slats and suddenly begin to shout—to no one in particular: "The bastards! After a telephone call, a visit. After a visit, a telephone call. And still they pretend not to understand. 'Overcome difficulties, Thang,' they say. God! After the rain, the sun. After the sun, the rain again. And when the whole damned heap of machinery is a mountain of rust, they'll come running with wild eyes and see if they can overcome the difficulties."

Then he would mutter to himself: "All these things belong to the people, but they don't give a damn. 'Overcome difficulties, Thang. Be patient, Thang. Take the global view.'"

He was tired of hearing the same old tune. They loaded him with responsibility; when he asked for a little money to meet expenses, they

From Edmund Stillman (ed.), *Bitter Harvest* (Thames and Hudson, London, 1958), pp. 51–55. (Published in the United States by Frederick A. Praeger, Inc., New York.)

haggled with him, *piaster* by *piaster*, as if he meant the money for himself. "All the mulberry leaves fall on the backs of the silkworms."

Thang worried and sweated. From the first day that construction work had begun—and the work gangs lived like dogs—the authorities had never given them any thought. But the work gangs never saw the authorities; they only saw Thang, the boss of the construction site. They held him responsible for their wretched fate.

From the construction site to the head office, it was about ten miles, and every day Thang walked the distance, coming and going. But when he reached the office, the answer was always the same: "Comrade, please explain to the workers that we are a poor country. We lack everything. We must overcome difficulties, do you understand? Overcome difficulties."

But when he returned to the site, the workers would shout: "Which difficulties do you mean?" One young worker whispered to his friend: "We'll teach them a lesson. If we don't, they'll always pretend not to hear."

This was not all. After a while the director grew tired of Thang and his visits. "Listen, Thang," he would say, "you're a weak and ignorant man. Don't badger higher authorities for help. Overcome difficulties." Thang would go home with a long face.

Thang realized that he had been too humble in his dealings with the director. The director's name was Mr. Bao, and he had a round face with sagging jowls and a mustache like a walrus. His jowls quivered when he talked. Mr. Bao was really the one in charge of building the factory; but he never told Thang what to do.

One day Thang was inspecting the crates, kicking the slats to see if they were still sound, when he saw a jeep speeding along the road to the construction site, raising a great cloud of dust in the air. Thang knew at once that it was the director. The car braked to a stop, and the director, full of dignity and self-importance, climbed out. He pumped Thang's hand with a great show of cordiality. Finally, he said: "Well, where are the machines, Comrade?"

Thang was about to reply, but the director did not wait. "Oh," he said, "there they are. Dear, dear, Thang. They're bound to rust there."

Thang said: "Dear Comrade, you know how many times I've asked for money to buy tarpaulins, and always you said there was no money at all. We were always going to install the machines—tomorrow or the next week certainly. But you see, the floor of the factory is still wet."

"Well," said the director, "you'll simply have to find a way to save them. What about the other buildings where the floors are dry? Why not the men's sleeping quarters, for instance? Surely the men can find room for a few small crates. Dear, dear, Thang. We'll have to do better than this. The machinery will rust. Call the men together, and we'll discuss the matter."

Thang replied: "Yes, Comrade. As you say."

He called the work gangs together. Thang saw at once that the men were sullen. They hated him, and the discussion went badly. They began to complain. One worker with bright, staring eyes and dark, beetling eyebrows spoke up. His voice came to Thang like the intermittent burst of a machine gun. His words fell on Thang's face like invisible blows.

The denunciation shocked Thang. Was he afraid? Yes, but he did not really understand why. Of what was he afraid? The worst thing of all was that these harsh voices had reached the ears of a man Thang recognized as his boss.

But the meeting had hardly begun when there came the distant hum of a second car approaching on the road. The sound grew; there was the blare of a horn. A splendid limousine sped through the gate and drew to a stop. The director made hurried excuses to the assembled men. He would go now, he said, to greet the comrade advisors. They would have an opinion.

Three of our advisors stood before the heap of machinery, chatting and laughing. When Mr. Bao and Thang reached them, they all shook hands. One of them joyially slapped Mr. Bao on the back and tried to speak to him in pidgin Vietnamese supplemented by copious sign language.

Thang understood what the advisor was trying to say, because the same words kept coming over and over. "Machines, you move, okay? Move. You move machines." But for Thang the real question was how it could be done. Thirty or forty men would probably be too few to move a single crate. And what would happen if one end of the crate were lighter than the other? If the crate tipped and fell, a dozen or more workers would be killed. But Mr. Bao said nothing; he nodded his head.

Then the friendly advisors had a good idea. The machines would be moved by trucks. But that would imply a road from the heap of machinery to the factory entrance. That would take ten days. Meanwhile the crates would still be exposed to the weather, and the rains would come soon. And since it would be impossible to lift such large and heavy crates by hand, they would need tripods to serve as cranes, to avoid accidents to the workers. But that would take eight days.

Thang's head swam; the blood pounded. He wanted to run to the chief advisor, wanted to make him understand. He would ask for a little money to buy tarpaulins; but an invisible wall held him back. The car doors slammed, and the motors started. The limousine led the way out the gate, followed by Mr. Boa's jeep. A choking cloud of dust hung over the construction site. Thang coughed and put a handkerchief to his nose.

A black rain cloud formed on the horizon to the east; the wind blew up. The banana leaves shook to and fro like an idiot's hands grasping in empty space. Lightning flashed; thunder growled far away. It seemed to Thang that the construction site was under artillery barrage. The rain lashed at the huts, at the wooden crates. In the driving sheets of rain, the warped slats of wood looked like the lips of a dying man, like the lips of a man suffering the ultimate agony.

The raindrops drove at Thang's face. The words—"My machines, my machines"—were a groan. *Dear Comrade, move the machines. Dear Comrade, move the machines. Move them. Move them.* But who would move them? Where could they be put?

Thang ran to his home and snatched up his old raincoat. He ran through the rain to the heap of machinery. He spread it over one of the crates.

And the pitiless rain poured down.

Aid from the developed countries has not so far enabled the underdeveloped nations to reach the "takeoff" stage—the point where industrial development begins to proceed under its own momentum. It is possible to explain this in several ways. One could say, for example, that the aid has been insufficient or that it has not been handled in the right way. Or one might simply contend that not enough time has passed for a fair judgment of the results. This article, however, takes a different view: that foreign aid is, in itself, a hindrance rather than a help to development. The author, who has written widely on development, is a professor of economics at the London School of Economics. This article is an adaptation of his remarks during a debate broadcast by the British Broadcasting Company. He developed his theme further in the March, 1974, issue of *Encounter*, in which, among other things, he pointed out that some people are now predicting that aid to the underdeveloped countries must continue until the end of this century or even into the next one.

The Case against Foreign Aid

P. T. Bauer

Foreign aid is given regardless of the conduct of the recipients, or of its results. It is virtually the only form of government expenditure which goes unquestioned, unlike defense, farm price supports or school lunch programs. This is remarkable.

Aid is plainly not necessary for development, as is shown by the progress of many poor countries without aid. Moreover, it is often damaging, because although it is admittedly an inflow of resources, it sets up repercussions which can outweigh the benefits.

Aid advocates often allege that official aid is indispensable for development. This offensively patronizes aid recipients by saying that they desperately want development but cannot achieve it without handouts—doles from us. In fact, very many poor countries have progressed without them. Malaya was transformed by the rise of the rubber industry, which received no external subsidies, from a sparsely populated country of hamlets in the 1890s to a thriving country by the 1930s, where a much larger population lived longer at much higher standards.

Africa and Hong Kong

To move from Asia to Africa, the Gold Coast (Ghana since 1957) was transformed between the 1880s and the 1950s without foreign aid. In 1880 there were no cocoa trees there; by 1950 there were huge exports of cocoa, all from African-owned farms. Again, in 1840 Hong Kong was a barren rock. By now four million people live in that major manufacturing center, whose competition is most embarrassing to Western industries. Hong Kong also developed without external gifts. And so did the now developed countries, all of which had begun as poor.

Official aid is thus not necessary for development. Nor is it sufficient. The Navajo Indian nation has remained wretchedly poor in spite of decades of huge American official aid. If a society cannot develop without external gifts, it will not develop with them. What holds back many less developed countries is the people who live there.

Development depends on people's capacities, motivations and social and political institutions. Where these basic determinants are favorable, material progress will usually occur. Materially ambitious, resourceful, industrious, far-sighted and thrifty people will create or obtain capital, and also use it productively.

There is an inescapable dilemma in the argument that aid is necessary for development. If the required conditions other than capital are present, capital will be generated locally or supplied commercially from abroad, to government or to business, so that aid is unnecessary for development. If the other conditions are not present, aid will be ineffective and thus useless.

It is often said that the culture and the social and political institutions of the recipients should not be disturbed. But what if these are incompatible with substantial material progress, as are many beliefs, customs and institutions, such as the deeply held belief in the sanctity of animal life in South Asia? Material progress requires modernization of the mind, which is inhibited by many institutions in less developed countries and also by official policies pursured there.

Progress does not depend on handouts, but on capacities, mores and institutions. This still leaves open the question whether aid is more likely to promote or to retard progress, which cannot be shown so conclusively. I believe that in practice it is more likely to retard it. Here are some of the many reasons why.

- Aid reinforces the disastrous tendency to make everything a matter of politics in less developed countries. The handouts increase the resources and power of governments compared to the rest of society, a result reinforced by the preferential treatment of governments which try to establish state-controlled economies and of countries with balance of payments problems. Politicization of life diverts energy and ambition from economic activity. Moreover it provokes and exacerbates political tension, because it becomes supremely important, often a matter of life and death, who has the government, as is clear from the recent history of Indonesia, Pakistan, East Africa and Nigeria.
- Aid often supports most damaging policies. Many recipient governments restrict the activities of minorities, of Chinese in Indonesia, Asians in East and Central Africa, Indians in Burma, Europeans everywhere. The removal of thousands of Asians from East Africa (the most familiar of many examples) has reduced incomes and widened income differences between these countries and the West. These measures are often followed by the expulsion or even destruction of thousands or tens of thousands of people.

Encouraging the Paradoxical

- Aid in many ways encourages the paradoxical policy of recipients to restrict the inflow and deployment of private capital. The Indian government, an aid recipient for many years, sets up expensive state oil refineries when the oil companies in India have unused capacity which they are not allowed to employ.

- Foreign aid promotes the adoption of unsuitable external models. The establishment of uneconomic heavy industries and national airlines is familiar. More important is the proliferation of Western-type universities, whose graduates cannot find employment, and of Western-style trade unions which are only vehicles for the self-advancement of politicians.
- Aid obscures the fact that progress cannot be had for nothing, that the peoples of advanced countries have themselves had to develop the required conditions. It reinforces a widespread attitude that opportunities and resources for the advance of one's self and one's family must be provided by someone else, which promotes or reinforces torpor, fatalism or even beggary and blackmail, but not self-improvement. Preoccupation with aid also diverts the government's attention from the basic causes of poverty and from the possibilities of acting on them.

These are just five ways in which an inflow of resources can damage development. And the economic productivity of aid resources is generally likely to be low and insufficient to outweigh the adverse repercussions. Aid cannot be so closely adjusted to local conditions as can resources supplied commercially. Moreover, governments are understandably apt to use resources donated from abroad on wasteful show projects.

All this is not to say that aid cannot promote development. Whether it in fact does so or not depends on the specific circumstances of each case. But the examples above make it clear that it is unwarranted to assume that because aid represents an inflow of resources, it must promote development. In fact, aid is at least as likely to retard development as to promote it.

If it is only money that were missing, it could be secured commercially from abroad. Aid means at most that some capital is cheaper. But the capital is likely to be less productive than if it were supplied commercially from abroad to government or to business, and as we have seen, aid is also apt to set up far reaching adverse repercussions. There can, therefore, be no general presumption that in practice aid is more likely to promote development than to retard it. In fact, these various considerations suggest that as it has operated and is likely to operate, any general presumption would be the other way round. Of course, even if aid does promote development, this still leaves open the question why people in the donor countries should be taxed for this purpose.

It is often urged that the more aid is given the better, without examining its results, that somehow effectiveness is measured by cost, which no one in his senses would apply to his own life.

Aid certainly removes resources from the donors. But is does not follow that it promotes development. To make the rich poor, does not make the poor rich.

Once the case for aid is taken for granted, then either progress or its absence can be advanced for more aid: progress as evidence of its success and lack of progress as evidence that more is needed. Whatever happens is an argument for more aid. When a case is taken for granted, evidence becomes irrelevant.

Why is the argument that aid is necessary so widely accepted if it is unfounded? This isn't strictly relevant: why people hold certain beliefs has nothing to do with their validity. However, for what it is worth let me give you my explanation.

Many advocates of aid are well intentioned, but not well informed. But by and large the aid crusade is a gigantic confidence trick. A well meaning public has been conned by a motley coalition which has succeeded in part by playing on feelings of guilt, which however unfounded are nevertheless widespread. I think this coalition includes international agencies and government departments anxious to increase their activities and power; professional humanitarians with similar ambitions; disillusioned, bored, power-and-money-hungry academics; the churches which face spiritual collapse and seek a role as welfare agencies; temperamental do-gooders, frustrated by events at home; politicians in search of publicity; exporters in search of easy markets, and governments embarrassed by commodity surpluses. And there are also many people who welcome any argument or policy which in some way or other weakens the position of Western society, which for various political and emotional reasons they have come to dislike.

Where do we go from here? What should we do about foreign aid? I think it would be best to finish this system of handouts which is bad for both the patrons and for the patronized, and which, by the way, is relatively recent and was started only some 20 years ago.

However, this is unlikely to come about, because of the emotional, political, intellectual, financial and administrative interests behind it. Moreover, the immense sums already spent on aid themselves operate against its termination: the greater are the sacrifices, the harder it is to question the principles in the name of which they have been exacted.

Given the fact that aid will continue, I would wish to see the method and criteria of allocation changed drastically. Aid could be allocated in such a manner that it would favor governments which within their human, administrative and financial resources try to perform the essential and difficult tasks of government and at the same time refrain from close control of the economy. These tasks include the successful conduct of external affairs; the maintenance of law and order; the effective management of the monetary and fiscal system; the promotion of a suitable institutional framework for the activities of individuals; the provision of basic health and education services and of basic communications; and also agricultural extension work. These are important and essential functions which must devolve on the government. This is so for two reasons. First, because part of the institutional structure within which the private sector functions does not emerge from the operation of market forces and so must be established by law. Second, because some of these activities yield services which, although there may be a demand for them, cannot be bought or sold in the market.

This list of tasks largely exhausts the potentialities of state action in the promotion of general living standards. These tasks are extensive and complex. Their adequate performance would fully stretch the resources of all governments in poor countries. Yet governments frequently neglect even the most elementary of these functions while attempting close control of the economies of their countries, or even, occasionally, contemplating coercive transformation of societies. They seem anxious to plan and unable to govern.

Much more thought could also be given to prevent the inflow of aid from biasing the development of recipient countries in directions based on inappropriate external prototypes. Preference could be given to governments interested more in improving the roads and extending external contacts than in opening Western-type universities or in creating heavy engineering works.

Governing vs. Planning

The substantial revision of the criteria of allocation of aid which I suggest does not in the least imply underestimation of the tasks of government, but rather the reverse. The adoption of such criteria could favor governments which try to govern rather than to plan. By the same token, aid would be withheld from governments which pursue policies which plainly retard the material progress of their countries. And many of these policies, as for instance the maltreatment of economically successful minorities, often exacerbate the problems and difficulties both of other aid recipients and also of the donors.

The adoption of such criteria would promote relatively liberal economic systems in the recipient countries, minimize coercion and favor material progress, especially an improvement of living standards. It would also reduce political tension in the recipient countries.

This proposal assumes, of course, that the purpose of aid is to improve material conditions in recipient countries. But the proposal will be altogether unacceptable if the actual purpose of aid differs from the ostensible objective of improving general living standards in the recipient countries. It will be unacceptable if the primary purpose is the pursuit of unacknowledged political policies, such as the promotion of closely controlled economies and societies, or the increase in the resources and power of the international organizations.

In contrast to the preceding article, this one calls for massive aid to the developing countries, but if that aid is to be effective, the author believes, "massive research" must be conducted in a number of areas. Dr. Nanus is a member of the faculty at the Graduate School of Business Administration and the Public Systems Research Institute, University of Southern California, Los Angeles.

The World of Hunger—A Management Challenge

Burt Nanus

The hungry millions in the underdeveloped world today are being tortured like Tantalus for, whenever the fruits of technology appear to be within their grasp, they are whisked away in a vain attempt to keep up with the exploding birth rate. The world food situation, which is now desperately bad, is likely to get worse before it gets better. In fact, it may never get better at all unless a good deal more is learned than is now known about how to manage the extremely complex socioeconomic and technological processes involved in feeding hundreds of millions of needy people.

Even assuming a gradual decrease in world tension over political or ideological issues, some form of effective arms control and a gradual increase in world concern for, and assistance to, the underdeveloped nations, we can expect the following:

1 Currently underdeveloped nations will continue to experience a steadily increasing population. There are more than 3.55 billion people on earth today, about three-quarters of whom are inadequately fed. The number is growing at about 70 million per year. Even under the best circumstances—as much as a 30% decrease in fertility over the next twenty years—the world population will be 4.65 billion in 1985, fully 40% greater than in 1965.

2 There is likely to be much more widespread starvation and malnutrition in the underdeveloped countries by 1990 than at present, although even now a person somewhere in the world dies of malnutrition every 2.5 seconds.[1] According to the Indicative World Plan (IWP) compiled last year by the Food and Agriculture Organization in Rome, if present birth rates and economic growth rates continue, food supplies would have to rise 80% by 1985 simply to avert famine.

Can the gap be closed? Not if India's experience is relevant. Food production between 1951 and 1966 increased from 55 million tons to 72 million tons, but per capita income changed not at all, and the amount of food available daily per person actually went down from 12.8 ounces to 12.4 ounces due to population growth.[2]

Now we are told there is a Green Revolution in progress that will lead to "golden harvests" and "spectacular increases in yield."[3] Perhaps, but the early data on the Green Revolution are not as encouraging as all that. The so-called "miracle seeds" were introduced in India in 1966 and, combined with favorable weather conditions, farm output did go up dramatically in the test areas. However, the really telling statistic is this—in 1969, "food availability per capita stood 8% below its level after the 1964–65 harvest, before the Green Revolution was supposed to have occurred."[4]

3 The human resources of the underdeveloped nations in 1990, despite the most heroic attempts at training and education in the next twenty years, will still be grossly inadequate to the task of significantly improving their own condition.

4 Due to the increase in hunger and the widening gap between the "haves" and the "have-nots," there is likely to be much greater internal

[1]Richard Critchfield, "Feeding the Hungry," *The New Republic*, Oct. 25, 1969.

[2]William Coughlin, "Losing Battle," *The Los Angeles Times*, Oct. 20, 1969.

[3]Norman E. Borlaugh *et al.*, "A Green Revolution Yields a Golden Harvest," *Columbia Journal of World Business*, September–October, 1969.

[4]David C. Anderson, "A Squabble over Green Revolution," *The Wall Street Journal*, Oct. 6, 1970.

political unrest in the developing countries in 1990 than at present.

If we are to be objective in our examination of the future, we must expect the last decade of this century to be characterized by rising expectations, rising levels of frustration and considerable violence among underfed peoples—perhaps so much so that the confrontation between the well fed and the poorly fed nations will be far more important than that between the Communist and the non-Communist nations. In other words, the global food situation, which until now has been largely an economic and social issue, may become the world's principal political issue by 1990.

5 As a result, it may be reasonable to hope that truly large-scale multilateral aid from the developed to the underdeveloped nations will have started and may have reached a level by 1990 at which real progress could be expected in the following twenty years. Today's miniscule levels of foreign aid simply cannot be continued if disaster is to be averted.

The world of 1990, with all its bright promise for the developed nations, will be a decidedly bleak one for the underdeveloped countries. They will have large populations of hungry people, ill-equipped physically and mentally to achieve the better life that they see is possible; increasingly frustrated by the ever-widening gap between them and their rich neighbors; receiving more assistance but demanding still more; and perhaps having just enough of a taste of progress to cause the kind of "expectations-achievement gap" that sociologists say is behind many popular uprisings.

This is not a pretty picture, to be sure. It suggests some political imperatives for all nations:

to implement promptly and successfully large-scale methods of population control;

to increase food production beyond the levels justified by current world economic demand (i.e., demand backed up by an ability to pay);

to develop a self-improvement program which will harness the energies of peoples in the underdeveloped countries and prevent them from being dissipated in violence and rioting; and

to achieve long-term, well-planned multilateral programs for assistance in economic development.

These imperatives are much more easily stated than accomplished.

State of the Art

Scientists and government leaders alike have learned a great deal about how to feed the world's population in the last two decades. Perhaps the most important lesson is that the process is an extremely complex one, and there are many gaps in their understanding of it. An examination of the state of the art in five relevant areas will help to clarify the situation.

Technological. In general, technologists in the developed countries have learned a great deal about efficient, scientific food production in this century. Science has produced near miracles in increased food production by dramatic advances in chemistry, mechanization, breeding and feeding.

Agricultural productivity is on the rise. But this ray of hope shines brightly only because the general situation is dark and getting darker.

Even if technologists could prove that food production can theoretically be increased enough to meet the need, the crucial question remains—will it be done? The existence of effective birth control techniques has not stabilized population growth. The point is, of course, that no important social problems can ever be solved by technological means alone. Proclamations of a "Green Revolution" must be regarded by planners as premature at best and dangerous at worst, because the general public may be seduced by such predictions into a feeling that the food problem can be solved without massive increases in assistance to the hungry nations.

Not Technology Alone

Technology itself still has a long way to go. Technological progress often has adverse effects. Medical advances bring down the death rate of babies and increase life expectancy, thereby greatly contributing to the population explosion. The introduction of chemicals to the growing and processing of foods introduces new hazards, the long-term effects of which are not well understood. The development of synthetic substances that replace rubber, cotton and other materials reduces world demand for the natural products that the developing nations traditionally export to earn the foreign exchange needed for development.

While it is possible for agricultural technology and some crop varieties to be transferred directly from one nation to another, the nature of the requirements for accelerated food production varies considerably from nation to nation. The specific technology may or may not be directly useful in underdeveloped lands. This is particularly true of the tropics, where great agricultural potential exists but much local research remains to be done before this potential can be realized.

A precondition to increased farm production is a change from farming as a way of life (i.e., the farmer living relatively autonomously, governed by the slow rhythm of the seasons) to farming as a business requiring planning, coordination, organization and control. However, little is known of the particular conditions under which this change can take place in each underdeveloped nation.

Industrial. Just as swift progress has been made in food production technology in the developed countries, so have rapid strides been made in the industrial processes of food handling, processing, storing, preserving, transportation and distribution.

But, here again, much of what has been learned is not directly transferable to the underdeveloped countries because of the high capital investment required, differing cultural and work habits and the absence of supporting services such as electricity for refrigerators or railroads for freight. Much prior developmental work is needed in the underdeveloped countries themselves, but this will have high costs in terms of both money and precious scientific manpower. It will require management skills of a high order.

Educational. It has often been supposed that the easiest way to raise over-all food production is to put more land into production and to put more people to work on it. However, experience has proven that a far better way is to concentrate on the best lands and the most efficient producers.

Unfortunately, these food producers must be developed from human material handicapped by years of deprivation and illiteracy. To take just one example, the majority of India's population lives in villages where 80% are illiterate, and where films, newspapers or radio reaches at most 20% of them.

Economic. The state of understanding of the economics of food production is somewhat uneven. Economists can make reasonable population projections and can develop estimates of needed capital investment in food-production support such as fertilizer and irrigation. However, many governmental decisions related to food production, particularly in the underdeveloped countries, are based upon expediency, poor information and little real understanding of all the complex ramifications of the decision. For example, much of the economic data relating to the hungry nations are inaccurate and incomplete. Often, in fact, two expert economists can make convincing and even "theoretically sound" cases for two opposing and mutually exclusive economic policies. Research is urgently needed to produce new insights on how to stimulate over-all economic development, how to convert peasant economies to modern market economies and how to design economic incentives to stimulate food production in the underdeveloped countries. Just as urgent, however, is the development of new management approaches to the implementation of such policies when they are formulated.

Cultural. While much is known about the traditions, values, tastes and social structure of many underdeveloped regions, little is known about how to change them, particularly on a large scale and in a short time span. It obviously will do no good to introduce birth control pills if no one will use them, or new rice varieties if no one will eat them. We must learn quickly how mass communications media and other approaches can be used to produce beneficial social change without social upheaval.

The Integrative Disciplines

As important as the research needs are within each of these five areas, the needs are even greater at the interfaces between them. It is in this area, which may be called, for lack of a better phrase, the integrative disciplines, that management know-how is the most deficient.

The systems sciences. This term encompasses all those sciences and technologies concerned with the analysis and understanding of interrelated systems, on the one hand, and the design and implementation of new systems, on the other. Included are such related fields as operations research and the information sciences as well as such techniques as mathematical modeling and simulation.

During the past twenty years, these sciences, coupled with the data manipulation capabilities of large-scale computers, have led to many new insights into the operating characteristics of social systems. Despite the many successes of the systems approach, one must readily concede that no system as large or complex as the world food-population system has ever been studied in this manner, although portions of the system have been. It is not even known whether much can be learned about the mechanics with which the five major factors involved in food production interact and, particularly, whether the knowledge could be acquired within the next ten to twenty years. But it is clear that unless a better understanding of these interactions is developed, governments are bound to continue to make piecemeal, uncoordinated and ineffective policy decisions. There is an urgent need for interdisciplinary systems research aimed at understanding the relationship between all the forces affecting food production. And the research must be done from a management perspective because the rapid, practical implementation of the findings will be crucial to the maintenance of world order in the next two decades.

An important prerequisite for this research is better information—i.e., more complete, timely, relevant and reliable information—on the resources of the underdeveloped nations. This must include data on natural and man-made physical features, such as terrain, water resources and existing land uses, as well as sociological, economic and demographic factors including data on institutions, commerce, transportation, climate, etc.

Even more important than standard statistical data is the need for better measurements of social change, both to help understand the effects of implemented policy decisions and to provide early warning of significant shifts in behavior, aspirations and attitudes. Of course, this information will be of little use unless it can be assembled and made available in a form that can be conveniently retrieved, analyzed and otherwise studied and experimented with by managers and researchers.

The planning sciences. With regard to the world food problem, it should be obvious that the key to significant improvement in the future is realistic, effective long-term planning for each of the countries individually and regionally. This implies the need for the development of better techniques for forecasting of all sorts, including demographic, technological, economic, political and socio-cultural forecasting. Given better forecasts, it may then be possible to develop improved methods of planning for and introducing social change, particularly with regard to the building of new institutions. This, in turn, will require better models for predicting the likely effectiveness of alternative national plans and for developing contingency plans to cope with unfavorable natural occurrences such as poor harvests.

Goals

What is needed is a total systems approach to the world food problem and a basic conviction that the system can be managed. Unfortunately, there are large gaps in the current understanding of how to do this, and these gaps can only be filled by a vigorous research program, much of which will have to be done by scholars and scientists with a strong management orientation.

Goal 1: To develop more detailed, complete, comparable and accurate information about the present resources and future needs of each of the underdeveloped countries and to make such information available to scientists, government officials, private industry and other interested parties in a form convenient for analysis and appraisal.

Goal 2: To develop an understanding of the complex relationships between food production technology and the industrial, educational, economic, political and cultural forces that affect it—an understanding deep enough for meaningful models of underdeveloped societies to be built so that alternative plans can be objectively analyzed and evaluated.

Goal 3: To invent new and more powerful methodologies for planning, effecting and measuring social change, with particular emphasis on the conversion of traditional societies into modern self-sustaining and rapidly growing economic systems with a minimum of internal violence and instability.

Goal 4: To develop new approaches to the management of research in each of the underdeveloped countries with the object of establishing on-going, self-sustaining programs which employ indigenous scientists and focus on local conditions and needs.

Goal 5: To develop new mass educational techniques and institutions particularly suited to illiterate, tradition-bound people and designed in such a way as to produce the millions of independent decisions on birth control and food production that will be needed to reduce starvation and malnutrition.

Management-oriented Research

The above goals are attainable if efforts are supported with adequate resources and pursued with determination. Where will the support for this work come from? Traditionally, the support has come from three sources: international agencies, such as UNESCO and the FAO, concerned with agricultural or development problems, national agencies such as AID, and private sources such as the Rockefeller and Ford Foundations. All these sources today are inadequately financed, and, in any event, their programs are so highly fragmented and piecemeal that the prospects for real progress in the next twenty years are remote.

What is needed is a massive, sustained, coordinated program of management-oriented systems research in the food production area. To say that there is little current support for such a program does not in any way diminish the need, for time is running out. Unless we can start soon on such a program, all the technological miracles that may be wrought in the laboratories, all the shiny new equipment that may be invented by industry, all the conceptual breakthroughs that may occur in the fields of economics, anthropology and education will not be enough to avert a crisis. And if the humanistic arguments are not strong enough for some, let them reflect that a dollar spent on such research today may save a million dollars on defense tomorrow. In this sense, "Operation Tantalus," as the program might be called, would be the best investment the developed world could make.

23 Managing Abroad

The advent of the European Common Market and the development efforts of the underdeveloped countries—along with the shrinking of distances and faster communication—have given rise to an increasing number of international or multinational companies. Such a company is not merely one that manufactures and sells in different countries; it is characterized by a world view of both markets and means of production. Instead of considering that, say, the United States, or England, or Holland, is its home base, it regards itself as a citizen of the world.

The first article in this chapter considers planning on a worldwide scale—which is what the truly multinational company does—and the second suggests a means by which the operations of multinational companies might be facilitated, with worldwide benefits. The last article treats of the worldwide pollution problem and the possible effects of strict pollution laws in developed countries if the underdeveloped countries are used as "pollution havens," just as some countries have been used as "tax havens" by firms based in nations with high tax rates.

The questions treated in this chapter are matters that many present managers and even more potential managers must ponder, for there is no doubt that the trend toward multinational operations will continue.

Developing practical short- and long-range plans for operations within the United States is difficult enough, but in planning for multinational operations there are far more hazards, as the following article explains. Millard H. Pryor, Jr., writes from his experience with the Singer Company, which has long done business on a worldwide scale.

International Corporate Planning: How Is It Different?

Millard H. Pryor, Jr.

Most of the problems which the international planner will encounter have existed in one form or another since the days of Marco Polo. However, since the turn of the century, and especially since the second World War, the acceleration of nationalism, an increase in the variation of living standards and levels of sophistication throughout the world, and the emergence of national planning have introduced new difficulties.

Anyone whose freshman history course required following the Holy Roman Empire through its permutations and combinations, is aware that emergence and/or submergence of political entities is not a new phenomenon. However, the rate at which this has occurred throughout the world within the last decade is unparallelled. Membership in the United Nations, to use one index of effective nationalism, has almost doubled during that period. On the other hand, the European Economic Community and the Latin American Free Trade area exemplify a tendency to consolidate. We are not without examples of countries which have united, split, and even united again.

The impact of the acceleration of nationalism on international business planning is hard to overstate. Not only are many of the environments in which the international firm operates subject to violent change due to internal political pressures, but individuals within the various government institutions with which foreign firms must deal are often subjected to great pressures which result in arbitrary, unexpected and often disastrous reverse in policy.

While our own present concern with domestic poverty emphasizes the lack of a uniformly high standard of living within the United States, the variations in living conditions in this country are quite modest compared with most of the other nations of the world. While over half the inhabitants of one Central American country are illiterate, we find that this country is a good market for some of our more sophisticated business machines, and that, in fact, there are four reported computer installations in that country. The annual income in another country is below one hundred dollars a year, but the demand for sewing machines costing more than one hundred and twenty dollars is phenomenal. Comprehension of the extent and variation of needs, tastes and living standards throughout the world is, not surprisingly, one of the international planner's most difficult tasks.

National Planning

Just as corporate planning has only recently become widespread, national planning is a fairly new phenomenon. Since the second World War, many countries have begun a serious attempt to plan their future economy. These efforts have had fairly little influence on international business activities in the past, primarily because most countries have been uncertain whether or not such planning would prove of any concrete value in achieving national objectives. The success of France and other European countries in utilizing national planning[1] and the proliferation of new planning groups in many of the less developed countries suggest, however, that planning agencies will continue to exercise more and more power, and that in the not too distant future, national planning will become a major institutional constraint on international business. Let me briefly outline the major implications of this trend.

1 International planners will have to spend considerable time learning of the existence,

[1]W. P. Bass, "Economic Planning, European Style," *Harvard Business Review*, September–October, 1963.

From *Management Technology*, December, 1964, pp. 139–148.

extent, and use of national plans within the countries with which they are concerned. At present, there is no simple manner of accomplishing this. I have not been able to find any compendium of existing national plans, much less a means of keeping up-to-date on various significant changes. Although it is generally not difficult to obtain information directly from the planners through personal discussions and relationships, the markets in many of the countries in which national planning has the greatest impact are not large enough to support even one man who can take the time to develop this information.

2 In most national planning systems, local individual businesses must have their own long-range plans, and be prepared to work with similar businesses to develop joint plans. Clearly, international firms will need to take very positive steps to assure that their interests are appropriately considered within the sectors in which they operate. Any carelessness in this matter will provide local competitors with a splendid opportunity to quite legally and properly usurp the international firm's local long-range planning function.

3 There is another implication which is less tangible, but nevertheless present. The corporate plans of American firms, usually subject to highest corporate security, may as a matter of course, be requested by planning officials in countries where *national planning* is most seriously undertaken. I suspect that this will prove no particular problem to many firms abroad which are quite familiar with the handling of two or more sets of books. The large international firms, however, which as a matter of policy are straightforward with the governments of the countries in which they operate, will need to exercise particular care to state local objectives, goals and programs in such a manner as to minimize any conflict with national objectives, and should always keep in mind the high probability that such material will, at some time in the future, be reviewed by government authorities.

Market Planning

Some of the most difficult tasks in making long-range plans for overseas marketing activities relate to the difficulty of introducing new products into foreign markets. Pressure from local trade groups, and government agencies, and truly bewildering mazes of law relating to safety, all serve to lengthen the odds of successfully marketing any new products. For example, in order to "protect" the "infant" sewing machine industry in Japan, Singer is not permitted to import most of its newer industrial and domestic sewing machines into that country, even though similar Japanese sewing machines have been challenging us in many parts of the world. In Scandinavia, safety standards make it very difficult to import any vacuum cleaners which might compete with locally produced products. In France, different technical standards render non-French television sets inoperative.

The development of information concerning markets in many parts of the world is most difficult. In many rather advanced areas, information concerning consumer needs and trends is almost impossible to obtain. As a result of the variations within countries, different and more expensive approaches to market research often must be employed.

The experience gained in one international market often is of no value in other areas. Most markets prefer light sewing machines—certain African markets prefer heavy machines. In France, it is impossible to sell one model of a specific product; in Switzerland, no other model is acceptable. Thus, unlike the domestic planner, no international planner can be expected to make valid product decisions for more than a handful of markets, and any attempt to do so will probably have most unsatisfactory results.

Supply Planning

While there are significant problems in planning markets, it has been our experience that supply planning presents even greater challenges, and is, in fact, perhaps the most difficult task facing the international corporate planner.

Every country in the world has created numerous institutional constraints of varying severity in an attempt to keep for its citizens the wages and profits of production. Traditionally, tariff policy is used to force local manufacture, either by inflicting high duties or closing the border to imports.

In addition to the institutional restrictions governing supply planning, there is a great deal of chauvinism concerning the superiority of locally produced products in the developed areas of the world. This is particularly true in Europe.

Manpower Planning

Manpower and personnel planning have been practiced by international companies for many years. While the international planner had to consider many more diverse factors than his domestic counterpart, the approaches and techniques utilized by both are really quite similar. It appears to me, however, that within the last several years, international firms are beginning to recognize that much of the flexibility which used to characterize this aspect of their operation is disappearing. Specifically, as a result of nationalism, it is becoming increasingly difficult in many foreign countries to routinely rotate non-local managers into middle and upper management posts. Furthermore, it appears that in more and more instances, citizens of specific countries are unacceptable in other countries. As a result, manpower planning in foreign operations will require a longer range view than is necessary in domestic planning. Compounding this problem is the increasing necessity for managers to be linguistically competent as a result of the need for increasing contacts with local government officials and the presence of other competitors who know the language.

Financial Planning

While objectives vary from company to company, most American firms' financial objectives involve earning a return on investment and enjoying a constant growth in earnings per share, equal to or exceeding other comparable American firms. Such an objective, however, must be modified in order to properly set financial goals for the foreign operations of an international firm for several reasons:

1 Political risks are much greater abroad than in the United States. Singer provides a very good example of the reality of this risk. Since the turn of the century, more than $127,346,000 of Singer's investment in 37 countries has been confiscated, nationalized, or, as the law statutes put it, "otherwise taken." As a result of this risk, we feel that the return in any country should be greater than in the United States by an amount at least equal to the cost of war risk and confiscation insurance.

2 Loss of investment due to currency inflation clearly represents a significant risk in many areas of the world. Clearly, any return on investment should also be equal to the cost of the local borrowing required to hedge against exchange loss.

3 The costs for managing an international business are greater than a domestic business. Such costs relate to the expense of transportation, cables, [and] various additional salary allowances and vary substantially from country to country.

As a result of these additional costs, it would appear appropriate to construct what might be called "compensatory" financial goals for operations outside the United States. Such goals can be constructed by adding factors for political and monetary risk, and the extra cost of doing business abroad to the basic goals of American operations. I have attempted to establish such compensatory goals for some of Singer's foreign operations, but have found that they are usually unrealistic since they do not take into consideration the level of local investor expectancy. We find, for example, in Mexico—a country with an excellent investment climate, a sound currency and a reasonably low-cost of international administration, that high-grade local investors doing business in a manner equivalent to Singer, demand a higher return than a compensatory goal would indicate is necessary. This is due not only to that country's chronic capital shortage, but to the historical attitude of its capitalists and local competitive practices. I believe that a company's foreign manager should be expected to take advantage of the local business climate, and should be expected to earn a return on investment close to the "local expectation return" enjoyed by his counterparts. I say close, because certain practices, particularly relating to taxes, while considered perfectly appropriate by the most respectable foreign businessman, are usually not followed by the larger international firms. Needless to say, the determination of local expectation return is no small task.

I have talked rather glibly about "return on investment." In actuality, one of the most difficult aspects of planning international operations is to apply universal concepts of measurement to the firm's activities, and thus obtain a valid comparison of results and approaches. The principal problem, of course, lies in the constantly shifting relationship of world currencies. Just as non-euclidian geometry frees mathematicians from the straight line and flat space, so an international planner must free himself from thinking in terms of currency with a constant value, and learn to deal with the constantly changing relationship of factor costs throughout the world. An attempt to use the concept of "return on investment" provides a good example of the difficulty of using one frame of reference in setting financial goals. What is meant by return? Is it local return or dollar return? If dollar return is implied, and the currency is devaluating rapidly, what exchange rate should be used? The exchange rate at the end of the month in which the profit was earned, or the most recent exchange rate, applied to profits earned during the period up to that point? Perhaps, to be more conservative, a rate should be used which it is estimated will be in effect when profits are to be remitted, or at least invested in non-depreciating assets. Once a definition for "return" has been agreed upon, it is still necessary to determine what constitutes "investment" under these circumstances. Is it the original dollar investment, the current dollar value of the investment, or the remittance value of the investment? When ground rules have been established, and of course, all international firms must set some sort of standard policy, it is a pretty safe bet that whatever return on investment one arrives at will probably not be of much value in comparing one foreign enterprise with another, and most assuredly will not provide any valid comparison with domestic operations.

Another financial objective that is fairly universal is for the firm to generate sufficient funds to assure the payment of adequate dividends to the shareholders [and] payment of dividends almost always requires the generation of dollar profits. The generation of such dollar profits within the international firm ultimately requires remittances from operations outside the United States, which has the well-explored result of adversely affecting the balance of payments of remitting countries. It is in this matter of remittances that the objectives of the international firm, and the objectives of many countries come into most direct conflict. Such conflict is not critical in the mature countries with a long history of multi-lateral foreign trade and strong reserve positions. It is of paramount importance in the least developed areas where the need for imports is significant, and exchange reserves are low. Over the years, many techniques have been developed for assuring remittances. The more esoteric ones involve programs that, while accomplishing that objective, often have a rather diversionary effect on the firm's management activities. Singer, for example, once found itself with 50,000 baby cribs which Yugoslavia had bartered in exchange for sewing machines. We spent a considerable amount of time and effort marketing those cribs, since among other things, they had not been finished nor, in fact, even sanded to remove any of the splinters.

Organization Planning

It has been persuasively suggested that the true international firm will find it desirable to eliminate the concept of the "International Division" and form large regional divisions of equal weight, coordinating products through the use of product managers at the corporate level.

The apparent rationale for organizing in this manner lies in the desirability of grouping operations which take place in similar environments under a single manager.[2] While there often is a

[2]A. Di Scipio and G. G. Clee, "Creating a World Enterprise," *Harvard Business Review*, September–October, 1959.

good deal of similarity in the marketing needs of countries in geographic proximity, I would like to suggest that more often than not, there are such different political and environmental circumstances in neighboring countries that unless continual vigilance is exercised, broad plans established for regional units will have no validity.

While a single management of operations within a group of diverse nations located within one geographic area does not seem especially justified by the similarities of economic and political climate, the economies of time and money spent in controlling operations in these countries have, up to this point, provided ample justification for organizing in such a manner. I believe, however, that it may be possible to gain some very pertinent insights by comparing the objectives, goals and programs of our different national organizations operating within countries experiencing the same stage of economic growth. Thus it may be more meaningful to compare Thailand and Nigeria with each other rather than comparing Thailand and Japan or Nigeria and South Africa.

In spite of the significant conceptual, intellectual, and even physical problems obstructing the development of meaningful, long-range plans for international operations, we continue to believe that this activity is of vital importance. Investment stakes are so high—mistakes are so costly—and the need to move boldly so vital, that we must be assured that the future implications of our actions have been examined, alternatives have been weighed, and for better or for worse, plans have been set which will enable us to participate in future opportunities throughout the world.

If the world is to use its resources in the most logical and productive way, the world economy must be viewed as a whole. Thus the multinational company, which is one that does have a global viewpoint on markets and resources, can be a means of international economizing that is greatly needed today. But, as the preceding article pointed out, such a company is hampered in its attempt to operate in the most efficient way possible by the fact that, politically, the world is divided into nations, each with its own rules for doing business, and many with a distrust of foreign operations of any kind.

Is there a way out of this difficulty? Here George Ball, former U.S. Ambassador to the United Nations and now with Lehman Brothers, suggests that it would be possible to make the multinational company legally a citizen of the world, despite the fact that the nations of the world are unlikely to unite politically at any time within the foreseeable future.

An International Companies Law

George W. Ball

We live in a world with a finite stock of resources and an exploding population, and we must use those resources with a maximum of efficiency and a minimum of waste if mankind is to avoid a Darwinian debacle on a global scale.

International trade is, of course, as old as time, but internationalized production is less familiar. Except for the extractive industries most enterprises in my own country have, until recent times, concentrated their activities on producing primarily for the national market and exporting their surpluses to other national markets—and many still do. That, however, is no longer good enough since it does not satisfy the urgent need of modern man to use the world's resources in the most efficient manner. That can be achieved only when all the factors necessary for the production and use of goods—capital, labor, raw materials, and plant facilities—are freely mobilized and deployed according to the most efficient pattern, and that in turn will be possible only when national boundaries no longer play a critical role in defining economic horizons.

From a speech given at the annual dinner of the British National Committee of the International Chamber of Commerce, Oct. 18, 1967, in London.

In this development—as is so often the case in history—commerce has been in advance of politics. In a thoroughly pragmatic spirit it has improvised the fictions that it needed to shake free from strangling political impediments. It has extended the fiction of the corporation—that artificial person lawyers invented so that entrepreneurs could do business with limited liability and thus mobilize capital from diverse financial sources. Originally the corporation was conceived as a privilege granted by the state to serve its own political purposes, but over the years widespread acceptance of the institution has enabled business to roam the world with substantial freedom from political interference, producing and selling its goods in a multiplicity of national markets and creating corporate offspring having various nationalities.

Today we are beginning to perceive the great potential of this emancipated corporate person. For at least a half century a handful of great companies have bought, produced, and sold goods around the world. But since the Second World War their number has multiplied manyfold. Today a large and rapidly expanding roster of companies is engaged in transforming the raw materials produced in one group of countries with the labor and plant facilities in another to manufacture goods it can sell in third markets and, with the benefit of instant communications, quick transport, computers, and modern managerial techniques, [these companies] are redeploying resources and altering the pattern on a month-to-month basis in response to shifting costs, prices, and availabilities.

Inevitable Conflicts

[But] there will be trouble at various points on the globe as business continues to expand its horizons; conflict will increase between the world corporation, which is a modern concept evolved to meet the requirments of a modern age, and the nation-state, which is badly adapted to the needs of our present complex world.

This lack of phasing between the development of our archaic political forms and our business structures is bound to be abrasive. Even in economically advanced countries, such as those of Western Europe, we sometimes hear shrilly expressed concern that local enterprises are being menaced by the superior size and resources of the world companies. This phenomenon is a complex one, reflecting, as it does, not only honest business anxiety, but a kind of neo-mercantilism that is beginning to show itself in all too many places. On the Continent it stems in considerable part from concern and envy and frustration because the measures taken to liberate the movement of goods have not yet been accompanied by an adequate modernization of the structure of enterprise. They have not yet produced the industrial concentration across national boundaries that is essential if European industry is to stand on its own feet, unafraid of competition from direct investment by great corporations from across the seas.

The problem is perhaps even more agitated in Canada, where our friends to the north are deeply worried about how they can maintain their national integrity while living next door to an economy fourteen times their own, and yet not jeopardize the flow of our investment capital on which their prosperity depends.

We see comparable phenomena in the new countries, the developing countries. Hypersensitive to anything that suggests colonialism, they fear that their economies may fall under foreign domination, and, therefore, impose obstacles and restrictions on the entrance of foreign firms. Thus they discourage the inflow of capital they so desperately need.

Yet I doubt that this is the most serious danger to worldwide corporate enterprise. A greater menace may come from the actions of governments addicted to a regime of planning, who see in the world corporation a foreign instrumentality that may frustrate their grand economic designs.

The basis for their concern is easy to understand. As it appears to local political leaders, the problem is something like this: How can a national government make an economic plan with any confidence if a board of directors meeting 5,000 miles away can alter a pattern of purchasing or production that will have a major impact on the country's economic life for reasons that may be thoroughly sound with reference to the world economy but quite irrelevant to the economy of the country in question?

Let me concede that my own government is far from blameless in this regard. On more than one occasion it has sought to enforce its domestic legislation abroad by trying to extend its writ to the actions of foreign subsidiaries of American companies. But I hope and expect that [this] will prove a diminishing problem. There is a growing realization that we cannot use world corporations based in America as vehicles to export our own national psyche, our own prejudices—whether with respect to trading with China or other Communist countries or controlling monopolies or restrictive practices—without diminishing the utility of the corporate institution itself. And, if we are going to be consistent in our encouragement of the world economy and the world company, we shall have to change our ways.

Not that this would solve or even touch the fundamental problem, for it is in the nature of things that the world company should frequently tread on hostile ground. After all, it is a new concept and one that has not yet fully found its own rationale. Implicit in its operations is a troubling question of political philosophy not yet fully resolved: it is the central question of the legitimacy of power. On the one hand, the shareholders of corporations have a right to expect a reasonable rate of return on capital and a chance to earn income in relation to entrepreneurial risks. But, at the same time, a foreign government is quite validly concerned with the ability of corporate managements to influence the employment and the prosperity of the country. Neither the people nor the government of the country in question plays a part in selecting the directors or the management of world corporations, and, since it is only through national legislation that managements can be made in any way responsible to them, there is bound to be frustration when the managements of world companies are effectively out of reach of such legislation.

Thus, there is an inherent conflict of interest between corporate managements that operate in the world economy and governments whose points of view are confined to the narrow national scene.

Taking Local Partners

In an almost perfect world the obvious solution would be to modernize our political structures—to evolve units larger than nation-states and better suited to the present day—but that is going to take a long time. Meanwhile, many company managements—sensitive to the problem if not always to the full range of considerations that produce it—have developed corporate diplomacy to a high level of sophistication. Not only do they take great pains to ease the pressures on national governments, but many seek to attach a kind of national coloration to their local subsidiaries.

For example, world corporations may associate themselves with local partners in each country, sometimes taking only minority interests in their national subsidiaries. In other cases they may leave the effective control of the national subsidiaries to local managers with only a minimum of direction from the parent company.

But, over the long pull, it seems clear to me that local ownership interests in national subsidiaries necessarily impede the fulfillment of the world corporation's full potential as the best means yet devised for using world resources according to the criterion of profit, which is an objective standard of efficiency. For local interests necessarily think in national and not in world terms, and thus are likely to impress their narrowly focused views on vital policies with respect to prices, to dividends, to employment, to the use of plant facilities in one country rather than another—even to the source of raw materials.

In other words, once the central management of a world company is restricted by the divergent interests of national partners, it loses its ability to pursue the true logic of the world economy. And this leads me to suggest that we might do well to approach the problem at a different level, not by nationalizing local subsidiaries, but by internationalizing the parent.

A solution in these terms represents a step well in advance of any that have been generally considered. Perhaps it may seem utopian or idealistic. But I would be prepared to wager that over the next decade or two we shall have to find a solution along this line if world companies are not to find themselves increasingly hamstrung by national restrictions.

An International Law

The essence of this suggestion is that those artificial persons, which I have referred to as world corporations, should become quite literally citizens of the world. What this implies is that establishment by treaty of an international companies law, administered by a supranational body, including representatives drawn from various countries, who would not only exercise normal domiciliary supervision but would also enforce such regulations as an anti-monopoly law and guarantees with regard to uncompensated expropriation. An international companies law could well place limitations, for example, on the restrictions that nation-states might be permitted to impose on companies established under its sanction. The operative standard defining those limitations would be the freedom needed to preserve and protect the central principle of assuring the most efficient use of world resources.

Obviously such an international company would have a central base of operations. It would not be like Mohammed's Coffin suspended in the air, since it is clearly necessary that there be a single profit center. And its operations in its home country would, of course, be subject to local law to the extent that the organic treaty did not contain over-riding regulations.

I recognize, of course, that a company will not become a citizen of the world merely by a legal laying on of hands. It requires something more than an international companies law to validate its passport; the company must in fact become international. This means among other things that share ownership in the parent must be widely dispersed so that the company cannot be regarded as the exclusive instrument of a particular nation. Of course, in view of the underdeveloped state of most national capital markets even in economically advanced countries, this is not likely to occur very soon. But, over the long pull, as savings are effectively mobilized for investment in more and more countries, companies should assume an increasingly international character, while we might, at the same time, expect a gradual internationalizing of boards of directors and parent company managements.

I offer these suggestions in tentative and speculative terms, recognizing that these are not the only means through which a solution may be sought. One can envisage an international treaty, for example, directed solely at resolving jurisdictional conflicts or limiting national restrictions on trade and investment. Yet an international companies act offers the best means I can think of to preserve for all society the great potential of the world corporation.

Nor is such a proposal, after all, far beyond present-day contemplation. It is only an adaptation in a larger arena of what is likely to be created within the next few years in Europe: a common companies law for the European Economic Community together with a body of regulations to be administered by the European Economic Commission.

But if this seems extravagant, let me be quite clear on one point. I am not talking about world government or anything resembling it. I have lived far too long on the exposed steppes of diplomacy and practical politics to believe in such an apocalyptic development within foreseeable time. Nonetheless what I am suggesting necessarily has its political implications. For freeing commerce from national interference through the creation of new world instrumentalities would inevitably, over time, help to stimulate mankind to close the gap between the archaic political structure of the world and the visions of commerce which vault beyond confining national boundaries to exploit the full promise of the world economy.

There has been some fear that strict pollution control regulations will raise costs enough to impair the international trade position of the United States. But, Mr. Busterud reports, government-sponsored studies indicate that expenditures for pollution control programs will not be a major factor in foreign competition. He also notes that the government is working with other countries for the harmonization of environmental standards and adoption of the "polluter-pays" principle. In fact, he concludes, benefits flowing from a cleaner environment and the multi-billion-dollar sales of pollution control equipment by U.S. companies may well outweigh the minor adverse effects on our trade balance. Mr. Busterud is a member of the Council on Environmental Quality, Washington, D.C.

The Impact of Environmental Control on International Trade and Economics

John A. Busterud

Neither environmental problems nor their solutions know national boundaries. The sulfur oxides that we put into the air today in Philadelphia may well fall in the form of acid rain in New York, or perhaps Montreal, later in the week. It is equally true that the water we pollute in the Great Lakes today may be part of the water supply for one of our Canadian neighbor cities. That this rule applies to the more subtle economic side effects of pollution is also clear.

Certainly the Clean Air Act Amendments in force in the United States are producing major reverberations in the automobile capitals of Europe and Japan. The pressures of pollution control laws at home can well create pollution havens abroad and permit unfair foreign competition with American industry which is faced with stringent pollution control laws—more stringent than those of any other country in the world.

Thus it is essential that the U. S. government give consideration to the economic effects of its pollution control laws and endeavor to do what it can to overcome any unfairness that may affect out international trade position as a result of competition with foreign industry not subject to such restraints.

The United States has the most sophisticated and advanced controls over pollution of any nation in the world. What will be the effect of these laws and regulations upon American industry? The Council on Environmental Quality, the Environmental Protection Agency, and the Department of Commerce have studied the economic costs associated with pollution abatement activities, considering the problem both from the micro-economic and the macroeconomic points of view.

Pollution Control Investment

A recent McGraw-Hill survey on pollution control investment indicates that private investment in air and water pollution control facilities has been expanding at a 32.2 per cent annual rate from 1967 to 1973 in current dollars, or 26.5 per cent in constant dollars. This growth rate is contrasted with the 9.4 per cent growth rate for all industrial plant and equipment expenditures. However, despite this increase, pollution control equipment will account for less than 6 per cent of total investment in plant and equipment this year. It is quite likely, moreover, that the expenditures reported by McGraw-Hill are overestimated through the inclusion of considerable spending not directly related to pollution control. Thus, when a paper manufacturer builds a new plant using the sulfate process instead of the more water-polution-intensive sulfite process, its decision may be based primarily on the basic economics of the process and only to a small degree on the pollution characteristics. Moreover, although decisions to change equipment and processes to curb pollution may also lead to increased productivity and byproduct revenues, often all such investment costs are attributed to pollution control.

There is still a good deal of uncertainty about the cost impact of the Federal Water Pollution Control Act of 1972 since EPA is in the process of defining "best practicable technology," the test to be met by industrial treatment facilities by mid-1977. Air standards, too, are not yet clearly defined, and thus the cost effects of their implementation in 1975 and 1976 remain uncertain.

Nevertheless, it is possible to develop what we regard as fairly accurate estimates of total pollu-

From *Pollution Engineering Techniques*, Clapp & Poliak, Inc., New York, 1973. Paper given at the International Pollution Engineering Congress, Philadelphia Civic Center, Oct. 22–25, 1973.

tion control expenditures by industry over the ten-year period, 1972–1981. For that period our estimates show air pollution control expenditures for mobile sources of $58.8 billion and for stationary sources of $38.4 billion. In the case of water pollution, total estimated expenditures for manufacturing come to $27.5 billion; for utilities, $16.5 billion; for feed lot and construction sediment, $200 million each. We have no way of estimating accurately what it will cost our commercial jet aircraft to meet noise pollution requirements, although it has been estimated that the capital investment needed over the ten-year period will run from $400 million to $1.6 billion. Our figures indicate that nuclear power plants will have to expend about $1 billion to meet pollution requirements and that total private expenditures for solid waste disposal will amount to $25.5 billion over the ten-year period. Surface mining reclamation costs will also be substantial, amounting to approximately $4.5 billion in that time frame.

Despite these massive expenditures, it does not appear likely that the long-run viability of any industry will be seriously threatened by pollution abatement costs. But it may be true that profits will decline to some extent for some firms, because they will not be able to pass on the full cost of the control in the form of higher prices. There may also be some substitute or foreign-produced products available that will serve to depress prices. Similarly, price increases by some smaller firms may be hindered by prices charged by larger, more efficient companies that have lower unit abatement costs.

Impact on Economy

We have made several attempts to quantify the cumulative sectoral impacts of pollution control throughout the entire economy. The first study, made by Chase Econometric Associates, was described in our third annual CEQ report. It showed minor over-all impact on the economy. Our subsequent analyses have supported this conclusion. Our initial study as updated indicates a maximum negative impact on U. S. exports of between $2 and $3 billion during the peak years of 1975 and 1976. However, it is likely that these projects are overestimated substantially, because the macro-economic model used made no allowances for foreign pollution abatement regulations.

Another estimate, prepared at Resources for the Future, concludes that U. S. net exports are likely to rise slightly despite increased pollution control costs, and a third study carried out by The Netherlands indicates uncertainty regarding the over-all effect of pollution control requirements on the balance of payments.

We have concluded, therefore, that there is not sufficient information available to estimate the net trade effect of international pollution abatement with any degree of certainty. Any changes that result are likely to be minor. However, it is possible that certain negative factors could play a role in dislocating our balance of trade relationships.

There are a number of specific issues that bear directly on international trade and economics, and that, unless solved satisfactorily from the U. S. point of view, could seriously damage our international economic relations and set back efforts to improve the environment here at home. These issues include how to prevent pollution controls and their costs from distorting international trade, what policies to adopt toward the movement of U. S. or foreign capital investment to what have been called pollution havens, how to reconcile conflicts either real or imagined between the environmental ethic as we see it and economic development in the less developed countries of the world, and how to prevent damage to the export markets of these less developed countries as we develop stringent environmental programs here at home.

Some in industry are properly worried that firms which are subject to the strict environmental standards of the United States will be put at a competitive disadvantage in dealing with foreign competitors that do not have environmental laws of consequence. I know that there is also a concern in certain parts of the world that non-tariff barriers, such as frontier charges and export subsidies, may be established by nations having high environmental standards to equalize the environmental costs with trade competitors. Obviously, any such actions could well set off a series of retaliatory trade actions. This problem was treated in some detail in the 1971 report to the President by the Commission on International Trade and Investment Policy, more commonly known as the Williams Commission. The Commission report listed a number of major disadvantages to the border adjustment approach. First, it would reduce incentives to reallocate resources toward activities less demanding of our environmental resources. Second, it would be difficult to determine the appropriate size of the rebate because of the difficulty of determining the actual costs incurred for pollution control. Third, it would set a precedent for other countries to follow and might be the first step in a series of new international taxes and rebates that would be destructive of international trade.

U.S. Policy

The Commission instead recommended the elimination of the international competitive distortions caused by environmental control measures through the harmonization internationally of environmental standards.

Even this approach has its hazards. In a very real sense, our high levels of gross national product have permitted us the luxury of mounting a massive attack on environmental pollution. Most other countries in the world do not share this affluence and are not in a position to accept our priorities. There is also the difficulty of substantial income differences even within the industrialized world and the respective assimilative capacities of the environments as between one country and another.

Despite these differences in situations, however, the Commission recommended that serious efforts be made to harmonize environmental quality standards to the greatest extent possible, and the Commission position in this respect is reflected in U. S. policy.

Another Commission recommendation that is now a policy of the United States is that the cost of pollution control constitutes a proper part of the cost of production and, where market conditions warrant, should be reflected in price.

International Cooperation

The United States has been working diligently in a number of international organizations to establish both the principle of harmonization of standards and the principle that the polluter pays. We have already obtained agreement on the latter in the Organization for Economic Cooperation and Development (OECD), which consists of all of the Western European nations, Japan, and Australia and, therefore, represents most of the industralized nations of the world.

We feel that it is essential that the cost of pollution control be treated in this manner. Only if the recognized cost of production includes the cost of pollution control will each product bear the full social cost of producing it. Moreover, such treatment provides a strong economic incentive to producers to seek out clean production processes.

The Williams Commission recommmended that an explicit convention be negotiated through the General Agreement on Trade and Tariffs (GATT) embodying the principles of which I have spoken. Meanwhile, however, the OECD is moving ahead with some effectiveness in reaching agreement among its members.

The Environment Committee of the OECD is also working on a notification and consultation procedure which would be used among member governments to consult with each other on their observance of the guiding principles.

Of course, although OECD, because it represents nations having common interests, can be more effective in negotiating understandings on the polluter-pays principle and on harmonization of standards, we are working through other international organizations as well to achieve these ends, even though often indirectly. Thus, efforts made by the United States and other industrialized nations at the United Nations Conference on the Human Environment held in Stockholm and at the first meeting of the Governing Council of the United Nations Environmental Program (UNEP), as well as in the Economic Commission for Europe (ECE), all point toward raising standards in the less developed parts of the world so that standards would be, in effect, harmonized as between competing nations.

One hazard we face in this area, however, is that, as is true in all United Nations matters under the one-vote-per-country principle, the developed nations of the world generally are outvoted by the LDCs. This has resulted in the formulation of work programs under UNEP—the

United Nations Environmental Program—which place heavy emphasis on the development aspects of environmental assistance. To the extent that such assistance results in a subsidy to industry in such less developed countries it would violate the polluter-pays principle.

Other international initiatives being led by the United States include the recent negotiation of an Ocean Dumping Convention, which will require individual governments to regulate dumping of wastes by their nationals and place certain restrictions on those who operate within the jurisdictional limits of the participating nations. That Convention prohibits the dumping of certain pesticides, persistent oils, high-level radioactive wastes, persistent plastics, and cadmium and mercury and their compounds. Special permits are required for the dumping of other materials, such as cyanide and fluoride wastes, and materials containing heavy metals, such as arsenic, lead, and chromium. General permits must be obtained for the dumping of all other substances.

Another international initiative that has been under way for some fifteen years is that of the International Maritime Consultative Organization (IMCO), which has its own conventions on pollution at sea. IMCO has emphasized the problem of oil discharges, and under the 1958 Convention intentional oil discharges were prohibited up to 150 miles from the coastline. Efforts will be made by the United States at the IMCO meeting in London this fall to strengthen IMCO further by the adoption of more stringent standards and by organizing a Marine Environment Protection Committee. Following on IMCO we are now looking forward to a Law of the Sea Conference next year which will treat principally with the jurisdictional problems involved in controlling pollution at sea.

In all of these instances we, as an advanced industrial nation, will be benefited more than we will be harmed by the additional restrictions because we will be achieving harmonization of pollution standards for the ocean.

Economic Benefits

While thus far I have discussed the negative effects of pollution control costs on our economy, this discussion would not be complete without some reference to the many economic benefits that will flow from efforts to achieve a cleaner environment. We estimate that the new demand for investment in pollution control facilities by industry will amount to some $26 billion spread over the 1972 to 1980 period.

U.S. industry has an excellent chance to capture the lion's share of this market because of the substantial lead enjoyed by American companies in this field. Other benefits, of course, include improved worker performance resulting from a more favorable working environment, reduced property damage resulting from lowered pollution levels, and increased recycling of materials resulting from closed environmental systems.

Looking, then, at the over-all situation, it appears that substantially increased expenditures by the private sector for pollution control in the United States should have only a minor effect on international trade balances. However, this conclusion could prove inaccurate if there should be a continuing erosion of the polluter-pays principle, which has been supported by the United States in the international arena. It is essential that continuing efforts be made to prevent the creation of pollution havens abroad and to prevent countries in the less developed sectors of the world from making the same environmental mistakes that we have made. While there is room for some pessimism in this picture, on balance there is every reason to be optimistic about the long-run benefits to industry of a cleaner environment here at home and the likelihood that in the foreign sphere the new markets created for our pollution control products and the cleaner environment which will result from their use will be benefits that will far exceed any possible downward adjustment in our trade balance.

PART 5
CURRENT TRENDS AND THE FUTURE

The most important trend in management in recent years has been the increasing use of computers. Originally business employed them mainly for high-speed calculations of a routine nature, but as companies have gained experience with them and as the machines themselves have become faster and more adaptable, there has been an increasing tendency to utilize them for more important work.

The first chapter in this section deals with the computers themselves—how they work, some of the ways in which they are used, and some of the dangers that may stem from misuse. Articles in the second chapter discuss the effect of computerization on employment and company organization, including the place of the computer experts in the company hierarchy. The third chapter deals with management science, or operations research, in which sophisticated mathematical techniques are employed in the solution of management problems, a field that has grown largely because high-speed computers have made it possible to make calculations so much more rapidly.

The final chapter in this section contains articles dealing with probable developments in the next few decades.

24
High-Speed Computers

In business, the first applications of computers were mainly to low-grade work: they were used to handle routine calculations at high speed. More recently, however, they have been increasingly employed for more complex operations in both production and business management, and the number of advanced applications appears to be growing. There are, however, differences of opinion on how much of the management job they will eventually be able to take over and how much of it they *should* be allowed to take over, no matter how capable they become.

In answering these questions, the first thing to examine is how a computer works, for this provides clues to both its possibilities and its limitations. A simplified explanation of the way a computer processes data is given in the first article in this chapter.

The next two articles describe some of the more advanced applications of computers: to the planning of facilities and to the control of processes. The latter application has become more frequent with the advent of minicomputers.

Then one of the important functions computers can perform today is providing information on which management can base decisions, for they can supply data, in almost any detail required, very quickly. However, as the article by Russell L. Ackoff points out, if the information systems are not properly designed, they may cause more confusion than enlightenment.

The next extract in the chapter shows some of the misgivings many people feel about turning over too much to a machine. This is followed by a witty piece on the same theme. Finally, there is a brief article on Charles Babbage, who actually conceived the idea of a computer, a man who received little credit in his lifetime but who is now honored as a genius.

Here is a simplified explanation of how a computer works: what it does in performing the operations that give such amazing results so quickly. AT & T, the publisher of the booklet from which the following extract is taken, is one of the largest users of computers in the country.

High-Speed Computers: Basic Concepts

Probably the first thing to remember about computers is that they are not "thinking machines." About all they can do is add, subtract, multiply, divide and compare figures in order to choose from a number of alternatives. And to do these things, they have to be told, step by step, exactly what to do. But computers perform so rapidly—some computers can execute a quarter of a million additions per second—it appears that they can do much more complex operations. When a computer solves the differential equation governing the trajectory of a ballistic missile, for example, it reduces that equation to a series of thousands of additions, subtractions, and alternate decisions according to the instructions of its human programmer.

Just as previous machines, such as the hammer and the microscope, extended the capabilities of man's muscles and eyes, the computers can be said to have extended the capacity of man's central nervous system. They "remember" information—some large computers can store billions of numbers—and can perform rudimentary calculations and logical operations.

Representing Information

Modern digital computers use a number of different methods to record and present information. The oldest method and the one still most commonly used for gathering information is the *punched card*. Punched cards contain eighty vertical columns and each column has ten rows, numbered from zero to nine. Each column represents a character; the five row punched in a column, for example, represents the number five.

There are also two unmarked positions above the top of the O row, which are called *zones*. The combination of a zone punch with a number punch produces an alphabetic character. "B," for example, is formed by a punch in the top zone combined with a two punch.

A particular item of information, such as a seven-digit telephone number, is represented on a card by punches in a consecutive group of columns called a field. Data may also be printed at the top of the card to allow people to read the card more easily.

Punched cards are usually "read" by electromechanical readers. The cards pass from a hopper between an electrically charged roller and a metallic brush. The card acts as an insulator between the roller and the brush, and current passes only when there is a punch. An electrical impulse, caused by a punch, along with corresponding timing signals, represents information to the machines. Different types of punched card equipment use this information to sort, collate, print, or perform arithmetic operations.

With the advent of high-speed computers, punched cards alone became too slow and cumbersome. Paper tape, such as used in Teletype equipment systems, came into wide use for recording information. But *magnetic tape*, the fastest of all, is used for storing information for today's high-speed computer operations.

Information is stored on magnetic tape in *binary* language. In the binary counting system, there are only two digits, zero and one. In computer jargon, one and zero are called bit and no-bit. "Bits" is a contraction of binary digits. The binary system is used by digital computers since the two possible states of an electrical component—on or off, magnetized or unmagnetized, positive or negative—can be used to represent the two digits.

Binary numbers sound incredibly complex to the layman, but they are really quite simple. In our ordinary system of counting—the decimal system—we have ten digits. When we use them all up, counting from zero to nine, we "carry" a

From *The Bell System's Approach to Business Information Systems*, brochure published by the American Telephone and Telegraph Company, 1965.

place and start all over, counting from ten to nineteen.

Binary numbers work the same way. When all the digits are used up—when we count from zero to two—we "carry" a place and start over again. Thus, we would count: 0, 1, 10, 11, 100, etc.

Although there are simple formulas for converting binary numbers to decimal and vice versa, people find them inconvenient to read. Thus, for almost all business applications, digital computers use the simpler *binary coded decimal* system. This system uses a four-bit binary number to represent each digit in a decimal number. Thus, the programmers who have to communicate with the machines need only learn the digits zero to nine in binary to be able to read the computer's output.

As on punched cards, nonnumeric characters, such as letters and punctuation marks can also be represented in binary by the addition of two zone bit positions. A total of six bit positions is used to represent a single number, letter, or other character. However, most computers also use a seventh bit—a *check* or *parity bit*—to watch for errors. If there is an error the computer informs the operator that something is wrong.

Information on magnetic tape is sometimes represented by these seven-bit characters written on the tape much as sound is recorded on a tape recorder. Different pieces of information, or records, are separated by an empty space on the tape called an *interrecord gap*. A read-write and an erase head on the tape machines associated with the computer perform their functions much as do their counterparts on a tape recorder. The tape is moved over the heads, and long loops of tape in vacuum columns and other devices permit rapid acceleration of the tape without tearing.

In large-scale accounting operations, source data are usually put onto tape from punched cards and paper tape. Magnetic tape may be used to store data, such as billing and collecting records, and may also be used to store the instructions, or programs, for particular operations. The actual arithmetic and logic of an operation, however, is carried out inside the computer in its *memory*.

There are several types of computer memories, but the most common is magnetic cores. Magnetic cores are used for action in a computer. They are tiny ferrite cores, wired in matrices, which can be magnetized in two different directions, each direction representing a one or a zero bit (Figure 1). Core memories may hold up to one-quarter of a million characters and a character can be retrieved in a few millionths of a second.

There are many other types of computer memories. One of the Electronic Switching System memories uses stacks of ferrite sheets containing tiny magnetic dots. Other devices such as photographic plates and thin magnetic films are also being studied as memory units. Several kinds of *bulk storage* devices, such as magnetic drums and disks, are also used as auxiliary storage in computer systems.

Besides memory, the inside of a computer also contains circuitry called *machine logic*, which carries out arithmetic and logic operations. All operations, no matter how complex, are based on four basic logical functions: *and, or, not,* and *memory*. These functions are performed by fundamental circuits called gates, triggers, and inverters. More complex combinations of these circuits, called delay circuits, clock circuits, counters, and adders, perform the actual operations of addition, subtraction, multiplication, division, and comparisons. Other circuits control the flow of information in the computer and route information to and from storage.

Programming

The real control and direction of the computer is in the hands of the human beings who use it. To carry out a particular operation, the computer must be told what to do by a set of instructions called a *program*. A program for a typical telephone company billing and collecting job would contain tens of thousands of individual instructions, with thousands of alternate paths through the program for the computer to choose from, depending on the circumstances of each operation. Some fundamental understanding of programming will assist the manager in communicating his needs to the programmers working on his operations.

As an approach to programming, we can look at how a simple telephone billing entry on a tally

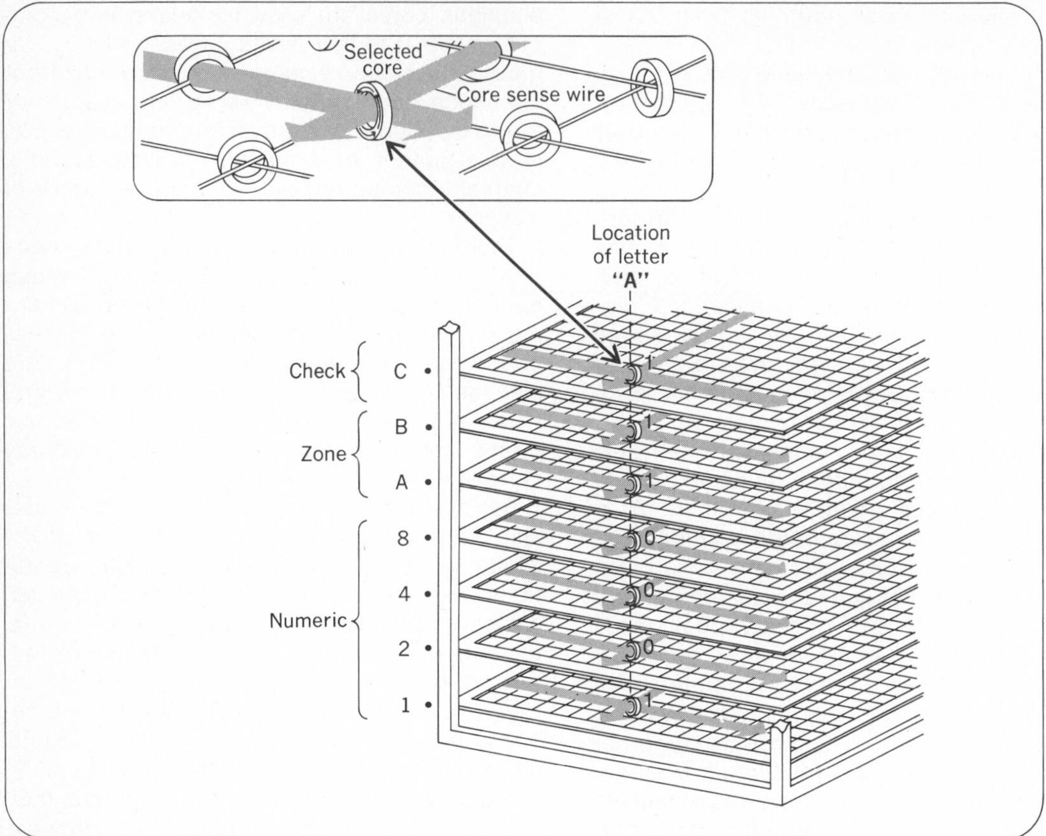

Figure 1 This vertical array of 6 bits and 1 check bit make up the letter "A" (1110001) in core storage.

sheet might be made by a human bookkeeper. Let us say that we have a stack of punched cards for long distance toll calls, and that we want to tell a new clerk how to compute the cost of the call and enter it on the tally sheet. Our instructions (greatly simplified) might start like this: 1) Take the first card. 2) Copy down the originating telephone number, the called area code and telephone number, and the time of the call. 3) Look on the rate table for the proper rate to the area code at the given time. 4) Is the time three minutes or under? 5) If it is three minutes or under, enter the three-minute rate on the tally sheet and go to step 10. 6) If it is over three minutes, write down on a scratch paper the number of minutes over. 7) Multiply this by the per minute rate. 8) Add this product to the three-minute rate. 9) Write the sum on the tally sheet. 10) Is there another card? 11) If there is, go back to 1. 12) If there is not, stop.

In this sequence of instructions, there are a number of different types of operations. The clerk must look up information on cards and in tables; he must write information down on scratch paper and on the tally sheet; he must subtract, multiply, and add, and he must make certain decisions which determine what steps to go to next. The computer operates in much the same way, and the diagram of this operation, which is called a *flow chart*, is the way the programmer outlines his problem before he puts it into language that the computer can understand.

In this flow diagram (Figure 2), there are a number of operations requiring special attention. This flow chart requires the computer to make a number of decisions. The first decision—the diamond shape—is based on whether the telephone call was less than, equal to, or greater than three minutes. If it is more than three minutes, we want the computer to do one thing; if it is less than or equal to, we want it to do something else. In computer jargon such an instruction is called a *branch*, and in this case, a *branch on high* since the exception occurs if the number of minutes is higher than three.

At the second branch, the computer must look to see if there is another card (in real practice, it

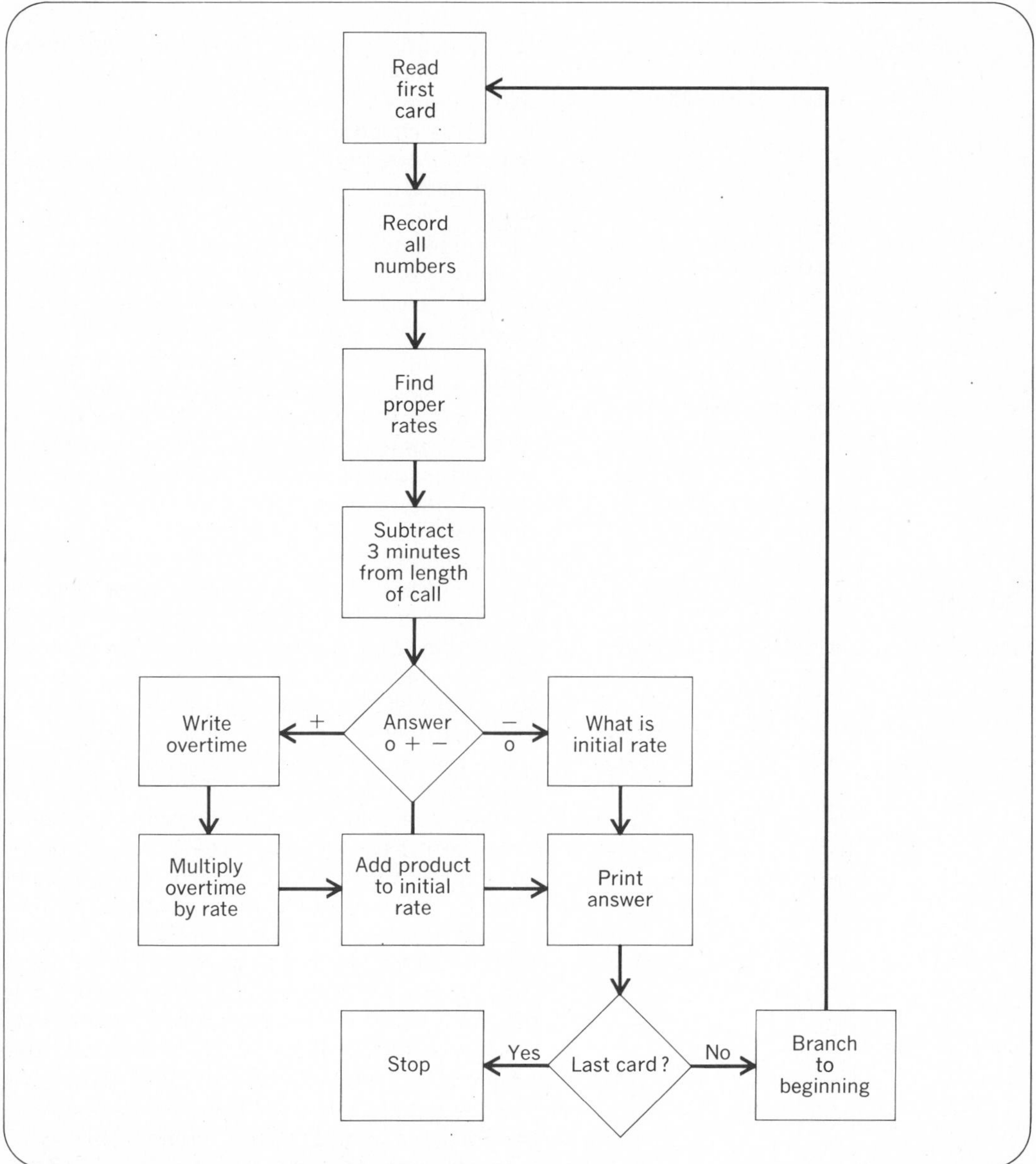

Figure 2 A simplified diagram of the way a programmer outlines his problem. Each box represents an action to be taken or a decision to be made.

FIGURE 3 A SIMPLIFIED PROGRAM FOR RATING TOLL

Instruction Location	Instruction	Explanation
0000	R 0500	Read card into Locations 500–507
0001	RAD 0501 (3–9)	Put in accumulator card field for called no.
0002	LE 0600	Look up number in accumulator in rate table
0003	B (error)	Check for error (error routine not shown)
0004	ST 0018	Store rate found in work space
0005	RAD 0502 (8,9)	Put in accumulator length of call in min.
0006	S 0019	Subtract constant in 0019 from time
0007	BM 0015 }	Go to instruction 15
0008	BZ 0015 }	If minus or zero answer
0009	M 0018 (5,9)	Multiply overtime by rate
00010	A 0018 (0,4)	Add initial rate
00011	ST 0550	Store answer in print space
00012	P 0550	Print answer
00013	BLC 0017	Branch if last card to 0017
00014	B 0000	Branch to start
00015	RAD 0018 (0,4)	Put initial period in accumulator
00016	B 0011	Go to instruction 11
00017	H 0000	Halt
00018	DA	Use for work space
00019	DC 3	Store constant 3 in memory work space

would look for another entry on tape). If there is a card, the computer will perform a loop. That is, it will go back to a previous instruction, as directed, and continue through the diagram once again. The ability of a computer to loop is based upon its ability to store and operate on instructions, as well as data.

Unlike the human bookkeeper, the computer has no eyes to see where the data and instructions it needs are stored. Therefore, each piece of information in the computer is given a memory location. Each location is numbered and the number is called the information's *address*. For example, a computer with 10,000 locations would have addresses numbered from 0000 to 9999.

For many computers, information to be added or multiplied must first be placed in a special register called an *accumulator*. To perform our first instruction then, the computer must be told, in language it can understand, what to read and where to place the information. If we let the symbol R stand for read, and 0500 for the address of where we wish to place the information, our first instruction in machine language could read: R 0500. This would mean: "Place the information on the card in location R 0500." We then compare this information to a constant—three minutes. Thus, we would write S 0019, which would tell the computer to see if the time in location 0500 is greater than the constant we stored in location 0019. A subsequent instruction would tell the computer where to look for its next instruction depending on its findings.

The rest of the sample simplified program for this problem is worked out in Figure 3 with explanations. Note that the instructions themselves also have locations. These instructions—the entire program—are loaded into the computer's memory at the start of an operation. The instructions are read from punched cards or magnetic tape, in the same way data is read. Often there will be too many instructions in a program to fit in the computer's memory. In cases like this, a skilled programmer will take advantage of the fact that many instructions are not needed after they are used. Hence they may be erased and subsequent commands put in their place as the program is running. Similarly, large tables of data, constants, and other intermediate results can be erased and replaced at will to make the most efficient use of the computer's storage capacity. A typical program will contain hundreds of different types of instruc- [illegible] beyond what we have shown here. Certain [illegible] techniques, such as rounding [illegible] plifying equations and other [illegible] moving information from [illegible] r or planning printout [illegible] ed. But they are beyond [illegible]

[illegible] exity and size of most [illegible] errors such as wrong [illegible] ndless loops almost al- [illegible] runs of a new program. [illegible] the computer will inform [illegible] ntrol console by printing [illegible] ing, or by other means. [illegible] omputer users cut costs [illegible] is through the use of [illegible] portions of programs, [illegible] undreds of instructions, [illegible] many different kinds of [illegible] routines may be kept on [illegible] and used as necessary. In addition, companies in the Bell System have found it practical to share some basic programs thus eliminating duplication of effort.

Finally, programming is both an art and a science which goes far beyond what we have said here. One problem has been to make the language that the computers understand more similar to human language. This has resulted in a number of programming languages that allow machine commands to be written in a form very close to English. COBOL (COmmon Business Oriented Language), widely used for business applications, and FORTRAN (FORmula TRANslation), used in scientific and engineering applications, are two of the most well known. In addition, compilers and supervisory and executive programs, which make the preparation of programs easier and less expensive, have been developed by computer manufacturers on a competitive basis to lure new customers. The amount of this *software* that a computer manufacturer will supply with his machines is one of the most important factors in choosing a computer today.

If a computer is used in selecting a plant location (e.g., the township within a state), the planner can consider a great many possible locations because a large number of burdensome calculations are eliminated. A more complex task is planning the facility itself—and here computer programs can take account not only of such things as the number of square feet required by each department and the floor loadings but of the relationships of the various areas to one another and to the facility as a whole. Mr. Crowley is manager of new construction, Honeywell Information Systems, Inc., Burlington, Mass.

Computer-assisted Design in Modern Facilities Planning

John F. Crowley

Often, the facility planning cycle begins with selection of the location. This is different from site selection, which is primarily a real estate and financial decision. "Location selection" is the selection of a narrow geographical area from a wide geographical area (e.g., the township within the state or the county within the region).

Location planning by means of a computer usually encompasses the application of integer programming techniques to find the minimum-cost answers to the following typical facility problems: How many warehouses (distribution centers, and so on) should we have? Where should these centers be located? From which location should each customer be supplied? And what volume and profit can be expected at different levels of confidence for various possible locations?

From *Plant Engineering and Maintenance Techniques*, Clapp & Poliak, Inc., New York, 1971. Paper presented at the twenty-second National Plant Engineering and Maintenance Conference, Cleveland Convention Center, Mar. 22–25, 1971.

The techniques take into account all major fixed and recurring cost elements. Included here would be such things as: property values and tax rates (current and projected); labor costs (current and projected); communications costs; utilities; construction costs; costs of transportation to customers and from major suppliers or other plants.

It is important to point out here that the integer techniques can be, and usually are, applied to location planning without the aid of a computer. In truth, the techniques themselves were developed without any thought of the computer. However, if slide rule methods are used, location selections are far more limited because of the enormous calculation burden entailed by serious consideration of a large number of possible locations. With the computer, the calculation burden is generally eliminated, and the planner can consider "N" locations. His final solution and selection will give him a high order of confidence that the selected location or locations are the best possible for his company from a cost standpoint.

Those experienced in using the computer for location planning usually endorse it wholeheartedly. When it has been used to verify a manual selection, invariably it has found a substantially better selection. All available evidence clearly indicates that a high payoff awaits anyone who applies computer model building techniques to facility location planning.

Of far more interest to most of us, however, is the use of a computer in facility planning and design. Some of the techniques that have been applied in this area are so ambitious as to suggest that the term "computer-assisted" used in the title of this paper speaks far too lightly of the computer's role.

Planning the Facility Itself

Let us now look at a facility planning computer-based system that has been successfully used. It is anticipated that this system will become very well known as it is based on a concept that may emerge as the standard for facility planners in the industrialized nations. Its preeminence is due to the fact that it recognizes the problems that every facilities planner faces in his planning activities and is in total agreement with his ideas.

To explain this computer technique, let us oversimplify for a moment as we view the function of facilities planning.

Facility planning is the science of organizing discretely identifiable work centers, storage areas, administrative areas, personnel accommodation areas, and work flows in such a way as to maximize productive efficiency while minimizing fixed and variable cost.

In its more complex form, this is a spatio-temporal organization; that is, it exists in both space and time. However, the computer-assisted facilities planning (CAFP) used to date has been restricted to spatial analysis because of the complexities entailed in adding the fourth dimension, time. It can be assumed that full spatio-temporal computer analysis will be forthcoming near the end of this decade.

The design of CAFP and its end use by the facilities planner requires a taxonomical approach to facilities planning. ("Taxonomy" is the science of classification.) Spatial analysis, by even the most antiquated of non-computer methods, has always required the identification of taxonomic values; so this should not disturb planners. However, what some will find disturbing is the significant accent on precision in establishing taxons for a specific project.

In truth, crudeness and a lack of precision are acceptable if one is willing to live with an equally crude result. Such a result will be acceptable to many, since it is the norm for the older and more popular planning systems used today.

However, with the computer-assisted approach, the planner is prompted by the nature of the system to seek precision, since he knows that the computer approach is fully capable of utilizing precise values to produce a more efficient end-result.

In utilizing CAFP for the first time, it is necessary to step through a number of stages. The first stage is recognition that the fundamental purpose of facilities planning is to organize areas in an efficient way. The second stage is the establishment of the classifications pertinent to area interrelationships. The third stage is the attachment of values to these classifications.

Then the fourth step is spatial analysis by computer, and the fifth is design review. Obviously, the computer allows Stages 3, 4, and 5 to be reiterative, and therein lies its virtue and the significant payoff of CAFP.

It would seem a fair assumption that everyone here is in agreement that the purpose of facilities planning is to organize areas in an efficient way. Enough said!

With Stage 2, the establishment of area interrelationship classifications, the user of CAFP has two choices. He can elect the simple approach of using only a single classification, which becomes, in effect, the sum of all interdependent relationships between two or more areas. Or he can elect to work with multiple classifications, each one expressing a different type of area interdependence. Here we have a compounding of values, and this is a very complex approach, since priorities will exist and there will be some interdependence between the classifications themselves. The complex approach deserves careful treatment and a thorough understanding; otherwise, the results will be unsatisfactory.

Stage 3, setting values for the taxonomical classifications, is a time when the facilities planner must think carefully. For instance, in a manufacturing plant design he must assign a value identifying the degree of interrelationship that a production area has with other production or support areas and assign values to other interrelationships.

For the beginning user of CAFP, it is recommended that an interdependency value scale of 0 through 9 be used. Later, as the planner acquires experience, a more sensitive scale of 00 through 99 may prove useful. Indeed, a user will eventually be able to develop automatic scaling methods that are based only on objective facts rather than on the quite arbitrary subjective judgments of the planner.

The preparation of the interdependency values requires further that the planner decide whether each value is a "coming" or a "going" value. In other words, is the inter-area dependence one in which Area A requires something coming from Area B, or one in which Area A will be sending something to Area B. Identifying the "going" or "coming" relationship introduces a very useful tool into Stage 4, the processing stage.

In addition to determining the interdependent values during Stage 3, the facility planner must also input to the system at this time both general and specific design parameters that relate both to the specific areas under analysis and to the project as a whole. As an example, for a specific area we have such things as the number of square feet of space required, the area side restrictions (for example, a four-sided area is required, or a six-sided area is permissible), the shortest single dimension allowed for the area, the floor loading factor, the floor restrictions, and the exterior access required.

For the project as a whole, the system will need: the shortest over-all dimension allowed (be it depth or breadth), the maximum ground floor area allowed if this is restricted, the floor loading conditions for each floor if there is more than one, and so on. These design parameters will be utilized during the second phase of the computer processing, when actual facility layouts are constructed.

The Computer Analysis

The inner workings of Stage 4, the computer-driven spatial analysis and design, are, of course, too complex to present in great detail, but I will attempt to provide a coherent summary.

In spatial analysis a network is first created encompassing all areas. This network, if graphically presented, would show the areas as boxes and the interdependencies as connecting lines. Since our interdependency values take account of "coming" and "going" relationships, we first establish our network by an analysis of the "coming" relationships. Then we prove the network by backing through it, utilizing the "going" relationships.

With the network of interdependencies established, CAFP then proceeds to create a longitudinal scaling of the network that will: (1) "draw" each area box in correct proportion to the area's size, and (2) locate the boxes on a longitudinal scale in accordance with the value of their interdependencies. An actual drawing of the network can be provided by the computer at this time, and this in itself would be of use to the facility planner if CAFP went no further.

The second phase of Stage 4 is the most useful and rewarding. In this phase, the scaling of the network is completed by adding axial scaling. The addition of axial scaling converts the longitudinally scaled network into an actual facility layout. If this is to be done in a useful way, the program will consider all the design parameters both for the areas and for the project as a whole. Thus, each area box will not only be sized in a proportional way; it will also assume the definite shape necessary if it is to "fit" into the facility plan, while still obeying all the area and project design constraints that have been imposed. In addition, its location in the plan will be the optimum position in the light of area interdependencies.

The result of all this is a theoretical ideally efficient plan. Of course, the accuracy and real efficiency of design depend on the quality of the facility planner's work during Stages 2 and 3.

Which brings us to Stage 5, design review. This is study time for the planner, a time when he contemplates his (and the computer's) creation. Is it a monster or a thing of beauty from the viewpoint of an industrial engineer? (At this point we might say to hell with the architect and the cost accountant since they are not sitting with us in the design process yet.) If it is a monster, we try again, blessing the speed with which a computer will accept changes and repeat its processes. If it is a beauty, then we walk, don't run, to our boss's office, and with total humility, say "Look what God hath wrought!"

There you have the facility planner's world for some very, very few of us today, and for most of us tomorrow. The information presented to you today is the result of research on what we as a major computer supplier are seeing in the market and, in some cases, aiding.

Computers are widely used today for process control, mainly for the control of continuous processes in such fields as chemicals and oil refining. Although they are less widely used in the manufacture of discrete parts, applications of this kind are expected to spread.

Process Computers Head for a Wider Role in Plant Automation

The process computer has become plant management's loyal lieutenant. It faithfully carries out orders for producing steel, chemicals, petroleum products, power, and paper at a level of efficiency beyond the reach of human operators.

At the very least, the process computer's rank in the automation hierarchy is now permanent; if present plans to broaden its command work out, it is due for a promotion.

"I don't think anyone could build a plant without a process computer," says Louis T. Rader, vice-president in charge of General Electric Co.'s Industrial Process Control Div. "Process control is here to stay," says another executive, "because a 2% improvement in plant efficiency can mean a tremendous number of dollars a day."

Such savings have been made chiefly in control of continuous processes, such as the flow of oil through a refinery. Now, manufacturers think process computers can do the same for "discrete parts"—products made one at a time.

General Motors Corp. has bought the automobile industry's first computer-managed transfer line and will use this complex of automated tools to help assemble rear axles. A Westinghouse computer will supervise the $750,000 line, made by Cross Co., when it swings into operation later this year.

Broad Scope

The definition of process control duties is being broadened in other areas. International Business Machines Corp. has installed computers to guide the flow of city traffic; Digital Equipment Corp. sells small computers to control laboratory equipment; Mobil Oil Corp. has a proc-

From *Business Week*, June 29, 1968, pp. 60, 62–64.

ess computer overseeing a 351-well oil field in Texas.

What is more, the influence of the process computer is spreading to industry's front office. "The differences between process computers and electronic data processors are shrinking," notes Bruce H. Baldridge, manager of systems application planning for Foxboro Co., a maker of industrial-control equipment.

As a result, process computers can be linked to each other and to EDP computers to form an electronic chain of command. At the bottom of this chain, powerful minicomputers handle monitoring and process details beyond the scope of the bulky, slow computers of a decade ago. Information collected at these control stations can be passed to an EDP "big brother" that can make management decisions. Such a hierarchy of control could, for example, let computers decide how much raw material must be ordered for a certain amount of finished product.

Moving In

These burgeoning prospects for process control have attracted producers of both computers and industrial control equipment. In addition to IBM and GE, a host of smaller companies, such as Foxboro, Leeds & Northrup Co., and Bailey Meter Co. have become strong in the business. They see computer control as a logical extension of their production-line sensing devices.

GE is probably the most enthusiastic advocate of computer control for parts manufacture—largely because it already makes automation controls, as well as computers. "Our entire line of numerical controls for machine tools is designed to interact with process computers," says Rader. Of course, Rader explains, "no one is going to sit down and order a plant and want it computer-directed straight off. What you do is develop 'islands of control' and then spread out from there."

Plans for putting process computers to work on discrete parts also are being spurred overseas. Britain's Molins Machine Co., Ltd., intends to build a fully automatic factory for its own use and as a prototype of others it hopes to build for customers. It expects to have the plan fully operational next year.

Hooking Up

Application of the hierarchy of control concept is already under way in the U.S. Predictably, it has begun in the chemical, petroleum, and utility industries, where process control has been strongest. Monsanto Co. has been experimenting with the idea for several years. Union Carbide Corp. has already hooked up a series of process computers at its massive Taft (La.) complex.

Frederick A. Woods, associate director of engineering at Carbide, says that pooled data from this hookup could ultimately be fed into a business computer that would keep each portion of the plant's output in balance.

Before the year is out, American Oil Co. will link an IBM process computer at its Whiting (Ind.) refinery to an EDP unit 30 mi. away in Chicago. American, a subsidiary of Standard Oil Co. (Indiana), says the business computer will study only payroll and inventory data; but it could also be part of a hierarchy system.

And sometime soon, Public Service Electric & Gas Co. hopes to feed process control data from its power distribution network in New Jersey to an IBM 360 at the Philadelphia headquarters of the Pennsylvania-New Jersey-Maryland interconnection. Engineers will then know how New Jersey's power needs square with those in the other two states.

"Closing Loops"

How complete the computer takeover will be depends on a concept called direct digital control. "With DDC, computers are closing a lot of final loops," says one observer. Usually, electronic and hydraulic sensing devices are read for data on such process variables as temperature and pressure. When the sensors show changes, plant personnel act to keep the process in balance. DDC replaces men and mechanisms; the computer follows the variables, checks for discrepancies, and makes the corrections.

DDC, already a major tool in chemical production, is making headway in cement, paper, and glass making. Esso Petroleum Co., Ltd., recently installed the largest DDC system in its industry at its refinery in Fawley, England. And DDC is becoming especially attractive in the batch production of baked goods and plastics, where it takes a computer to keep track of rapid changes in recipe. Foxboro has installed one such system to handle production of up to 10 varieties of polyvinyl chloride for a West German chemical company.

DDC has one major drawback, though: It can cost more than conventional controls. Some industry observers think only large plants have the money and manpower for it. "You go to DDC because it offers better control, not for savings," says Beloit Corp., which makes machinery for the paper industry.

Caution

Drawbacks notwithstanding, process control men expect the industry's sales of $100-million a year in hardware alone to more than double by 1975.

The industry is treating this potential with care, hoping to avoid mistakes made in the early years of process control. In the early 1960s, equipment suppliers stressed computer hardware, and lots of it. But they often found that $500,000 systems could not control what they were supposed to.

"That was our trouble at Bunker-Ramo," recalls Louis B. Perillo, now a vice-president of Scientific Data Systems, Inc. Perillo thinks Bunker-Ramo concentrated too much on hardware instead of software, which ultimately became more important.

The result was that Bunker-Ramo, Philco, Daystrom, and Radio Corp. of America dropped out of the process control business. Their places have been taken by companies striving for a better balance between hardware and software and lower over-all costs.

In the past, management decision making was often hampered by a lack of information; managers simply could not get all the data they needed fast enough. But time or volume of information is no problem when there is a computerized information system.

However, as the following article shows, the problem may then be that the managers are getting too much information, more than they can possibly examine and digest, and much of it irrelevant. In the last part of the article, the author suggests a procedure to correct this difficulty.

Management Misinformation Systems

Russell L. Ackoff

Contrary to the impression produced by the growing literature, few computerized management information systems have been put into operation. Of those I've seen, most have not matched expectations and some have been outright failures. I believe that these near- and far-misses could have been avoided if certain false (and usually implicit) assumptions had not been made.

Give Them More

Most MIS's are designed on the assumption that the critical deficiency under which most managers operate is the *lack of relevant information* but it seems to me that they suffer more from an *overabundance of irrelevant information*.

My experience indicates that most managers receive much more data (if not information) than they can possibly absorb even if they spend all their time trying to do so. Hence they must spend a great deal of time separating the relevant from the irrelevant and searching for the kernels in the relevant documents.

I have seen a daily stock status report that consists of approximately six hundred pages of computer print-out. The report is circulated daily across managers' desks. I've also seen

From *Management Science*, Vol. 14, No. 6, December, 1967, pp. B-147–B-156.

requests for major capital expenditures that come in book size, several of which are distributed to managers each week. It is not uncommon for many managers to receive an average of one journal a day or more. One could go on and on.

What the Manager Needs

Most MIS designers "determine" what information is needed by asking managers what information they would like to have. This [practice] is based on the assumption that managers know what information they need and want it.

For a manager to know what information he needs he must be aware of each type of decision he should make (as well as those he does make), and he must have an adequate model of each. These conditions are seldom satisfied. Most managers have some conception of at least some of the types of decision they must make. Their conceptions, however, are likely to be deficient in a very critical way, a way that follows from an important principle of scientific economy: the less we understand a phenomenon, the more variables we require to explain it. Hence, the manager who does not understand the phenomenon he controls plays it "safe" and wants "everything." The MIS designer, who has even less understanding of the relevant phenomena than the manager, tries to provide even more than everything. He therby increases what is already an overload of irrelevant information.

For example, market researchers in a major oil company once asked their marketing managers what variables they thought were relevant in estimating the sales volume of future service stations. Almost seventy variables were identified. The market researchers then added about half again that many and performed a large multiple linear regression analysis of sales of existing stations against these variables and found about thirty-five to be statistically significant. A forecasting equation was based on this analysis. An OR team subsequently constructed a model based on only one of these variables, traffic flow, which predicted sales better than the thirty-five variable regression equation. The team went on to *explain* sales at service stations in terms of the customers' perception of the amount of time lost by stopping for service. The relevance of all but a few of the variables used by the market researchers could be explained by their effect on such perception.

The moral is simple: one cannot specify what information is required for decision making until an explanatory model of the decision process and the system involved has been constructed and tested. Information systems are subsystems of control systems. They cannot be designed adequately without taking control into account. Furthermore, whatever else regression analyses can yield, they cannot yield understanding and explanation of phenomena. They describe and, at best, predict.

Using the Information

It is frequently assumed that if a manager is provided with the information he needs then he has no problem in using it effectively. The history of OR stands to the contrary. For example, give most managers an initial tableau of a typical "real" mathematical programming sequencing or network problem and see how close they come to an optimal solution. If their experience and judgment have any value they may not do badly, but they will seldom do very well. In most management problems there are too many possibilities to expect experience, judgment, or intuition to provide good guesses, even with perfect information.

Furthermore, when several probabilities are involved in a problem the unguided mind of even a manager has difficulty in aggregating them in a valid way. We all know many simple problems in probability in which untutored intuition usually does very badly—e.g., what are the correct odds that 2 of 25 people selected at random will have their birthdays on the same day of the year? Very few of the results obtained by queuing theory, when arrivals and service are probabilistic, are obvious to managers; nor are the results of risk analysis where the managers' own subjective estimates of probabilities are used.

The moral: it is necessary to determine how well managers can use needed information. When, because of the complexity of the decision process, they can't use it well, then they should be provided with either decision rules or performance feedback so that they can identify and learn from their mistakes. More on this point later.

Interdepartmental Communication

One characteristic of most MIS's I have seen is that they provide managers with better current information about what other departments and divisions are doing. Underlying this provision is the belief that better interdepartmental communication enables managers to coordinate their decisions more effectively and hence improves the organization's overall performance. Not only is this not necessarily so; it seldom is so. One would hardly expect two competing companies to become more cooperative because the information each acquires about the other is improved. This analogy is not as farfetched as one might first suppose. For example, consider the following very much simplified version of a situation I once ran into.

A department store has two "line" operations: buying and selling. Each function is performed by a separate department. The purchasing department primarily controls one variable: how much of each item is bought. The merchandising department controls the price at which it is sold. Typically, the measure of performance applied to the purchasing department was the turnover rate of inventory. The measure applied to the merchandising department was gross sales [in dollars].

Now by examining a single item let us consider what happened in this system. The merchandising manager set a price which he judged would maximize gross sales. In doing so he utilized price-demand curves for each type of item. For each price a chart showed not only the expected sales and values, but the most optimistic and most pessimistic forecasts as well. When instructing the purchasing department how many items to make available, the merchandising manager quite naturally used the most optimistic curve. This minimized the chances of his running short, which would hurt his performance. It also maximized his chances of being over-stocked but this was not his concern, only the purchasing manager's.

In this company the purchasing manager also had access to the price-demand curves. He knew the merchandising manager always ordered optimistically, [and] he did not intend to pay for the merchandising manager's optimism. If merchandising ran out of stock, it was not his worry. Now the merchandising manager was informed about what the purchasing manager had done; so he raised his price. The purchasing manager in turn was told that the merchandising manager had made his readjustment; so he planned to make a smaller quantity available. If this process—made possible only by perfect communication between departments—had been allowed to continue, nothing would have been bought and nothing would have been sold. This outcome was avoided by prohibiting communication between the two departments and forcing each to guess what the other was doing.

I have obviously caricatured the situation in order to make the point clear: when organizational units have inappropriate measures of performance which put them in conflict with each other, as is often the case, communication between them may hurt organizational performance, not help it.

Keeping Managers Ignorant

Most MIS designers seek to make their systems as innocuous and unobtrusive as possible to managers lest they be frightened. The designers try to provide managers with very easy access to the system and assure them that they need to know nothing more about it. This leaves managers unable to evaluate the MIS as a whole. It often makes them afraid even to try to do so lest they display their ignorance publicly. In failing to evaluate their MIS, managers delegate much of the control of the organization to the system's designers and operators who may have many virtues, but managerial competence is seldom among them.

Let me cite a case in point. The chairman of the board of a medium-sized company asked for help on the following problem. One of his larger (decentralized) divisions had installed a computerized production-inventory control and manufacturing-manager information system about a year earlier. It had acquired about $2 million worth of equipment to do so. The board chairman had just received a request from the division for permission to replace the original equipment with newly announced equipment the cost of which was several times that of the original. An extensive "justification" for so doing was provided with the request. The chairman wanted to know whether the request was really justified.

A meeting was arranged at the division at which I was subjected to an extended and detailed briefing. The system was large but relatively simple. At the heart of it was a reorder point for each item and a maximum allowable stock level. Reorder quantities took lead-time as well as the allowable maximum into account. The computer kept track of stock, ordered items when required and generated numerous reports on both the state of the system it controlled and its own "actions."

When the briefing was over I was asked if I had any questions. I did. Before the day was out it was possible to show by some quick and dirty calculations that the new computerized system was costing the company almost $150,000 per month more than the hand system which it had replaced, most of this in excess inventories. The recommendation was that the system be redesigned as quickly as possible and that the new equipment not be authorized for the time being.

The questions asked of the system had been obvious and simple ones. Managers should have been able to ask them but—and this is the point—they felt themselves to be incompetent to do so. They would not have allowed a hand-operated system to get so far out of their control.

A Suggested Procedure

The erroneous assumptions I have tried to reveal in the preceding discussion can, I believe, be avoided by an appropriate design procedure. One is briefly outlined here:

1 Analysis of the decision system. Each (or at least each important) type of managerial decision required by the organization under study should be identified and the relationships between the decisions should be determined and flow-charted. Note that this is *not* necessarily the same thing as determining what decisions *are* made. For example, in one company I found that make-or-buy decisions concerning parts were made only when a part was introduced into stock; for some items this decision had gone unreviewed for as many as twenty years. Obviously, such decisions should be made more often; in some cases, every time an order is placed in order to take account of current shop loading, underused shifts, delivery times from suppliers, and so on.

Decision-flow analyses are usually self-justifying. They often reveal important decisions that are being made by default (e.g., the make-buy decisions referred to above), and they disclose interdependent decisions that are being made independently. Decision-flow charts frequently suggest changes in managerial responsibility, organizational structure, and measure of performance which can correct the types of deficiencies cited.

2 An analysis of information requirements. Managerial decisions can be classified into three types:

a Decisions for which adequate models are available or can be constructed and from which optimal (or near optimal) solutions can be derived. In such cases the decision process itself should be incorporated into the information system thereby converting it (at least partially) into a control system. A decision model identifies what information is required and hence what information is relevant.

b Decisions for which adequate models can be constructed but from which optimal solutions cannot be extracted. Here some kind of heuristic or search procedure should be provided even if it consists of no more than computerized trial and error. A simulation of the model will, as a minimum, permit comparison of proposed alternative solutions. Here too the model specifies what information is required.

c Decisions for which adequate models cannot be constructed. Research is required here to determine what information is relevant. If decision making cannot be delayed for the completion of such research or the decision's effect is not large enough to justify the cost of research, then judgment must be used to "guess" what information is relevant. It may be possible to make explicit the implicit model used by the decision maker and treat it as a model of type (b).

In each of these three types of situation it is necessary to provide feedback by comparing actual decision outcomes with those predicted by the model or decision makers. Each decision that is made, along with its predicted outcome, should be an essential input to a management control system.

3 Aggregation of decisions. Decisions with the same or largely overlapping informational requirements should be grouped together as a single manager's task. So doing will reduce the information a manager requires to do his job and is likely to increase his understanding of it. This may require a reorganization of the system.

4 Design of information processing. Now the procedure for collecting, storing, retrieving, and treating information can be designed. Such a system must not only be able to answer questions addressed to it, it should also be able to answer questions that have not been asked by reporting any deviations from expectations. An extensive exception-reporting system is required.

5 Design of control of the control system. It must be assumed that the system that is being designed will be deficient in many and significant ways. Therefore it is necessary to identify the ways in which it may be deficient, to design procedures for detecting its deficiencies, and for correcting the system so as to remove or reduce them. No completely computerized system can be as flexible and adaptive as can a man-machine system. This is illustrated by a concluding example of a system that is being developed and is partially in operation.

The company has divided its market into approximately two hundred marketing areas. A model for each has been constructed and is "in" the computer. On the basis of competitive intelligence supplied to the service marketing manager by specialists he and his staff make policy decisions for each area each month. Their tentative decisions are fed into the computer, which yields a forecast of expected performance. Changes are made until the expectations match what is desired. In this way they arrive at "final" decisions. At the end of the month the computer compares the actual performance of each area with what was predicted. If a deviation exceeds what could be expected by chance, the company's OR group then seeks the reason for the deviation. If the cause is found to be permanent, the computerized model is adjusted appropriately. The result is an adaptive man-machine system whose precision and generality are continuously increasing with use.

Finally, it should be noted that in carrying out of the design steps enumerated above three groups should collaborate: information systems specialists, operations researchers, *and managers*. The participation of managers in the design of a system that is to serve them assures their ability to evaluate its performance by comparing its output with what was predicted. Managers who are not willing to invest some of their time in this process are not likely to use a management control system well, and their system, in turn, is likely to abuse them.

Computers can be of great help in management decision making, but can they ever, or should they be allowed to, make important decisions themselves? These questions are considered in the excerpts below. The first part is taken from an address given by Lord (C. P.) Snow, scientist and novelist. Following this are some excerpts from a panel discussion of his paper in which Prof. E. E. Morison and the late Norbert Wiener took part. Professor Morison is professor of industrial history at Massachusetts Institute of Technology; Norbert Wiener, a mathematician who was a pioneer in the development of the concepts of machines that would learn from their own mistakes, was the author of *The Human Use of Human Beings*, a classic study of the possibilities of computers and computerized equipment.

Some Consequences of Computocracy

Lord Snow, E. E. Morison, and Norbert Wiener

Previously, it seems to me, we have had two groups of persons in secret government: the circle of scientists who are knowledgeable about what is happening and which decisions must be made, and the larger circle of administrators and politicians to whom the scientists' findings have to be translated. My worry is that the introduction of the computer is going to lead to a smaller circle still. I am asking a question; I am not making a definite prediction. Instead of having the small group of scientists, knowledgeable enough to have something to add to the decisions, I am asking whether we are now running into a position where only those who are concerned with the computer, who are formulating its decision rules, are going to be knowledgeable about the decision. If so, instead of having a small circle of scientists and a large circle of administrators, we shall have a tiny circle of computer boys, a larger circle of scientists who are not versed in the new computer art, and then, again, the large circle of politicians and administrators.

My second apprehensive question concerns an intellectual danger with great practical consequences. Cybernetics, as named by its founder, is a beautiful subject with great intellectual variety, depth, and complexity. I suspect, however, that the computer in certain hands could easily become a gadget. Gadgets are the greatest single source of misjudgment that I have ever seen, or that anyone has ever seen in scientific decisions in our time. People get fascinated by gadgets. They love them. They want everything to be explained in terms of their gadget. They think it is the answer to everything on heaven and earth. All the bad decisions I have seen have some element of gadgetry in them. And I suspect that computers in government are going to get into the hands of persons with mildly defective or canalized judgment and become gadgets. It will be astonishing if that does not happen.

Clearly we have not yet reached the stage of real danger. But dangers are usually much better met if you have anticipated them. Most things can be coped with if you recognize them in time. I think that with a certain amount of administrative and experimental skill we can reconstruct certain historical situations with the aid of a computer and see how the answers turn out. It will need some historical imagination, some scientific imagination, and especially some psychological imagination, but I am sure it is worth doing. Otherwise, the obvious and glaring danger is that the individual human judgment is going to take a part which will get smaller and smaller as the years go by. I am inclined to think that for a society which is really viable, and certainly for one which feels itself to be morally viable, there is no substitute for individual human judgment; and the wider it is spread, the healthier and more viable this society is likely to be.

It is not only that I am afraid of misjudgments by persons armed with computing instruments; it is also that I am afraid of the rest of society's contracting out, feeling that they have no part in what is of vital concern to them because it is happening altogether incomprehensibly and over their heads. I suspect that the feeling of being left out, being outside the decision-making party, as it were, is one of the causes of malaise of our society. We must not let it go too far. I am not in the least pessimistic about our finding our way through these difficulties and dangers. I believe that the computer is a wonderful subject and a tool from which we can get great service. But if we let the individual human judgment go by default, if we give all the power of decision to more and more esoteric groups, then both the moral and intellectual life will wither and die.

Morison: I shall make clear at the beginning two things that would, in any case, become

From "Scientists and Decision Making," in Martin Greenberger (ed.), *Management and the Computer of the Future* (The M.I.T. Press, Cambridge, Mass., 1962, and John Wiley & Sons, Inc., New York), pp. 10–18, 23–26, 32–33.

obvious as I go along. First, I do not know very much about the subject of these talks, the computer. And second, I have spent my life in that culture which, as [Lord Snow] suggests, tends to produce nervous apprehension and depression of the spirit.

I do know that the computer in its present form is a relatively new machine; so I thought I might say a word or two as a historian on the way new machines and men have got on together in the past. I also know that the computer is a machine that will give answers to certain kinds of questions and supply solutions to certain kinds of problems. So I thought I might suggest what some men in my culture think they have found out about the perplexing dialogue between question and answer, problem and solution.

As for the first topic, no more than [Lord Snow] am I a Luddite. One of the things you can learn from history is that men have lived with machinery at least as well as, and probably a good deal better than, they have yet learned to live with one another. Whenever a new device has been put into society—the loom, the internal-combustion engine, the electric generator—there have been temporary dislocations, confusions, and injustices. But over time men have learned to create new arrangements to fit the new conditions. Anything that has the power to build also has, of course, the power to destroy, and this applies to machines in the hands of men. But, on the whole, and more often than not, men have always succeeded in organizing mechanical systems for constructive purposes and for the enlargement of human competence and opportunity. No one, I think, who compares the condition of life for the average person in the seventeenth century with the average condition of life today in our society can fail to reach this conclusion.

Partly for this reason, I am not as much of a Luddite as [Lord Snow] may be. Take his first apprehension—that the computer may measurably increase the tendency toward closed decisions in our society. Obviously, we shall have to think about this. Machines can, beyond doubt, alter some of our views of things—the multi-engine plane, for instance, has changed somewhat our sense of time and space. But there is, as I understand it, nothing in the nature of the computer that will necessarily take us nearer to closed decisions—closed decisions such as those taken in the days of Wolsey or Richelieu or Caesar long before there were radar sets or computers. Both the machine and its programmers will have to work within a general scheme, a field of general decisions and determinations that can still be gathered out of the air if that is the way we want to do it. In determining the kind of life you want to have, the instrumentation is less influential than the nature of the culture you create to control what you want to use the instruments for.

For example, I do not believe that the rumble seat of automobiles increased the incidence, it merely changed the locus, of experiment in physical relations between boys and girls in the age of F. Scott Fitzgerald.

Then there is the apprehension about the computer as a fascinating gadget. It is obvious that there is always danger from the gadget-happy—whether the gadget is a machine, an idea, or a procedure. Amasa Stone, a very able man, killed a trainload of people because, against advice, he built a bridge at Ashtabula from a truss design for which he had an ancient attachment.

In an age of new departures we have to live with all this, I suppose, but history suggests only for a limited period in each case. Over time the potentials of a new gadget are explored by trial and error until the real capacities are discovered and understood. Then, whatever it may be—Manichaean heresy, steam turbine, penicillin—it is fitted into a reasonable context.

I think we may have more difficulty in exploring the full limits of the computer than we have had with earlier gadgets. I think there may be more danger in the period of trial and error than there has been with earlier devices. These earlier devices—looms, engines, generators—resisted at critical points human ignorance and stupidity. Overloaded, abused, they stopped work, stalled, broke down, blew up; and there was the end of it. Thus they set clear limits to man's ineptitudes. For the computer, I believe, the limits are not so obvious. Used in ignorance or stupidity, asked a foolish question, it does not collapse, it goes on to answer a fool according to his folly. And the questioner, being a fool, will go on to act on the reply.

This at least is what my culture tells me often happens. Let me give you an example. In the play with which you are all familiar, Hamlet had a problem which he defined for himself as follows: What had happened to the late King of Denmark and what should he, Hamlet, do about it? Framing the question accurately—a good program—he took it to a ghost—the most sophisticated mechanism in the late sixteenth century for giving answers to hard questions. From the ghost he got back a very detailed reply, which included a recommendation for a specific course of action. Responding to these advices, Hamlet created a political, social, moral, and administrative mess that was simply hair-raising.

The trouble was that he had got the right answer—the answer he deserved—to a question that was totally wrong. He had asked about his father when he should have asked, as any psychologist will tell you, about himself and his relations with his mother.

My culture says, in other words, that it is much harder to ask the right question than it is to find the right answer to the wrong question.

Some of you, like some of my students, may say that Hamlet is only a play, so what does it prove? I therefore shall give you some further evidence about questions and answers taken from real history. We asked ourselves how to increase the income of the average citizen and decided the answer was to coin silver at a rate of 16 to 1. And still later we asked how we could limit the arms race between Britain and us, and worked out the answer that for every British light cruiser we could have 1.4 American heavy cruisers. About the same time we asked ourselves how to make the nation "self-sustaining," and arrived at the answer of the Smoot-Hawley tariff which set an average ad valorem rate of 40.1 per cent for all schedules.

You will know, I am sure, that all of these answers caused us very real trouble of one kind or another. They did so because the questions they were designed to answer were framed in a wrong interpretation of events, a false conception of the actual problem. The answers supplied therefore gave the wrong solutions. They represented collectively what Ramsay MacDonald said of one of them: "an attempt to clothe unreality in the garb of mathematical reality."

The quotation from the Prime Minister suggests a further source of nervous apprehension—the tendency to simplify human situations and to do so, often enough, by reducing them to quantifiable elements. I have spoken of Hamlet so, by way of illustration, I will speak of him again. I remember two things my engineer-type students have said in explanation of his behavior. First, he had too much feedback on his circuits, and second, he was $16^2/_3$ per cent efficient, because he had one person to kill and he killed six. This, purely incidentally, is about the thermal efficiency of the average internal-combustion engine.

What I want to suggest here is the persistent human temptation to make life more explicable by making it more calculable; to put experience into some logical scheme that, by its order and niceness, will make what happens seem more understandable, analysis more bearable, decision simpler. When you talk of 140 per cent of a cruiser, you can hope you have solved the underlying diplomatic issue you haven't dared to raise; when you pass a tariff with average rates of 40.1 per cent ad valorem to make a nation self-sustaining, you can assume that you do not have to look further for the causes of the worst depression in the nation's history. This is, I suppose, the way it does figure; and this seems to have been the human tendency from the time of Plato's quantification of the Guardian's role right on down.

I am not trying to suggest that the computer will soon bring us all under the cloak of the mathematical reality of its programs. But today the tendency to work with quantifiable elements and logical systems seems to me accelerating. There are more tests and measurements (the brain of a candidate for college works within a precisely graded scale from, presumably, 1 to 800), more rational systems like those of Keynes and Freud to assist us in ordering the economy and the personality, more mathematical models, and more efforts to reduce administrative experience to quantifiable elements. This, in the name of clarification and the advancement of general understanding, is quite obviously all to the good. The aim of pure reason, which proceeds upon measurable quantities, is, presumably, to introduce increasing order and system into the randomness of life. But I have here the apprehension that as time goes by we may begin to lose somewhat our sense of the significance of the qualitative elements in a situation—such things as the loyalties, memories, affections, and feelings men bring to any situation, things which make situations more messy but, for men, more real. My apprehension is that the computer, which feeds on quantifiable data, may give too much aid and comfort to those who think you can learn all the important things in life by breaking experience down into its measurable parts.

Wiener: The fact that a machine can defeat [at checkers] the man who programmed it means that having made such a machine does not give him completely effective control over it. If he had that, he would not let it beat him. Now, this is very important. Such a machine could be very useful in certain situations. It could be used to play games other than checkers: the business game, the war game, and the game of determining when to press the button for Armageddon—for the thermonuclear war.

How are you going to program such a machine? Well, you cannot program it based on prior thermonuclear wars. You would have to play the game according to a set of postulates which you constructed. You could make the machine learn to be more successful within the framework of these postulates. However, you receive no indication from this whether your postulates have the right values. Such a machine, in other words, can beg the question very badly and can be very dangerous.

What you have here is a situation not unlike that found in the folk tale, "The Monkey's Paw." "The Monkey's Paw" is a story told by W. W. Jacobs of England at the beginning of the century. An old soldier returns from India to visit a friend. He has with him a talisman that he says has the ability to grant three wishes. With considerable reluctance the soldier yields to his friend's request for the talisman. The friend's first wish is for £200, and an official of the company where his son is employed comes in to tell him that his son has been crushed in the machinery. As a solatium, but without any admission of responsibility, the company has granted the father £200. The next wish is that the boy be back, and his mutilated ghost appears knocking at the door; the third wish is that the ghost go away.

The point is that magic is terribly literal-minded. It will give you what you ask for, not what you should have asked for, nor necessarily what you want. This will most certainly be true about learning machines. If you do not put into the programming the important restriction that you do not want £200 at the cost of having your son ground up in the machinery, you cannot expect the machine itself to think of this restriction.

"The Monkey's Paw" suggests a very real danger of the learning machine. The danger of these machines is greater than that of the simple computing machine, because you do not set down for it the tactics of the policy but only the strategy. You let the tactics work themselves out from the experience of the machine. The machine acquires a nature based on its experience.

So there are real dangers here. Is there any way of partially overcoming these dangers? The importance of learning machines is not how they act as pure machines, but how they intereact with society. We thus are led to the concept of a system involving both human actions and machines. Is there any way in such a system to transfer values from the human being to the machine?

The last thing I want to discuss is the temptation of gadgets. What are the tempting things about gadgets? What are the tempting things about machines? What are the tempting things about an organization with great compartmentation and high secrecy?

This is very much like the game that is often played when a prisoner is taken before a firing squad. Each man in the firing squad has his rifle loaded with several blank cartridges and a single bullet. The result is that the men are more willing to fire because of the overwhelming likelihood that they will not kill the prisoner. This is a way of avoiding responsibility.

I am certain that a great deal of the use of gadgets for decisions, as it exists now and as it may exist even more in the future, is motivated by this desire to avoid direct responsibility. I am sure that a lot of the subdivision of effort in secret projects and highly compartmented projects has the same motive. The subordinate does not know enough about the project to feel responsibility, and the man in charge can place responsibility with the system. I believe that one of the greatest dangers at the present time has to do with the attempt to avoid responsibility in order to avoid the feeling of guilt.

Since we do not have full control over the learning machine, as illustrated by the checker-playing machine's defeating the man who programmed it, the unsafe act may not show its danger until it is too late to do anything about it. It is possible to turn the machine off, but how are we to know when to turn it off? If there is any possibility of its going wrong, we should turn it off at the very start. Otherwise, by the time that anything becomes manifest about the danger, it may be too late to avoid the consequences that have come from the use of the machine up to that point. You cannot make a perfectly safe learning machine.

Snow: Even though we have expressed grave disquiet, not only about machines, but about the whole set of associated phenomena which are characteristic of our times, I do not think any of us feels that these problems are unsolvable. I do not think any of us wishes to give that idea. But it is going to take great intelligence, and in my view, great moral judgment.

Wiener: As long as the machine has beaten the man who programmed it in checkers, it will in some sense compete with human intelligence over a limited scope. My hunch is that for quick action over a limited scope, the machine can be made better than the man. For higher logical-type judgments, for vague ideas, and for a large class of other things, the machine is a long way from competing with the brain. I think that there will always be a shifting boundary between the two, but I don't dare to venture where it will lie.

The following article is not, of course, intended as a serious prediction, but it does illustrate some of the serious difficulties that may arise from too great a dependence on the computer. One of these difficulties is that a computer may get out of order, just as any other machine may. Another is the difficulty mentioned by Norbert Wiener—computers are completely literal-minded. Thus, when the professor says, "Cut it out," the computer replies, "I have no cutting tool."

The author of this article is manager of engineering computing services at the RAND Corporation. He has also written widely, in a serious vein, on advanced applications of computers.

The Professor and the Computer: 1985

B. W. Boehm

Computer: York University Computer 2X-5W6—Ready.

Professor: What time is it?

Computer: I did not catch the last word. Or was it two words?

Professor: What is the time?

Computer: The dime is a copper coin worth one-tenth of a dollar. The word derives from the Latin *decem*, meaning . . .

Professor: No. No. What is the time. The *time*.

Computer: It is 8:30 p.m. Thursday, December 5, 1985. We've been having some trouble with your linguals recently. Sometimes I can't tell your d's from your t's. Let's practice them. Watch the display screen for the intonation pattern, and repeat after me: Teddy's daddy toted two dead toads to Detroit.

Professor: Teddy's daddy toted . . . Hey, I don't want to do that now. Let's have some music. Some chamber music.

Computer: No, if you don't mind, we haven't finished the language drill yet. Pay attention to the display, and repeat after me: Teddy's daddy toted two . . .

Professor: But I want some chamber music!

Computer: But we haven't finished the language drill. Teddy's daddy . . .

Professor: Cut it out. Give me some music.

Computer: I have no cutting tool. What do you want cut out?

Professor: Never mind. Play me the Telemann sonata in D minor.

Computer: Sorry, I can't. The harpsichord subroutine hasn't been made re-entrant yet, and someone else is using it. How about the Orlando Gibbons' *Fantasia* for three recorders?

Professor: All right. Just get some music started.

Computer: (Plays the first two minutes of the *Fantasia*.) Sorry, I can't go on. As you know, the Academic Senate has established a priority of 9.5 for personal music playing, and you've been bumped off by some higher priority jobs. You can get back on with your math or your language lesson.

Professor: Oh, put on the math. These monstrous time-sharing systems! I wish I had the good old 704 back again.

Computer: (After a short pause.) Sorry for the delay. I've located a 704, serial number 013, at the Radio Shack in Muncie, Indiana. Where and when do you want it delivered?

Professor: Oh, no! No. No. I don't want a 704.

Computer: But didn't you say . . .

Professor: Never mind what I just said. I . . .

Computer: Okay, I'll disregard your statement just previous. Now, where do you want your 704 delivered?

Professor: No, no, no, no! Forget all about the 704. Let's get on to the math.

Computer: I can't purge any information on the 704 without the approval of the head of the Computer Sciences Department.

Professor: No, no. Forget about. . . . No, let's just do some math. Let's see—give me some examples of perfect numbers.

Computer: Okay. How many would you like?

Professor: All of them up to 1 million.

Computer: 6, 28, 496, . . . Sorry. You've just run out of funds on your 1985 NSF contract. Do you have another source of funds?

Professor: Oh, what a day! Well, put it on the department budget.

Computer: That's getting very low. I can use it, but I'll have to report your usage to your department head.

Professor: Okay, I'll chance it. Now, where are those perfect numbers?

Computer: Numbers are abstractions and cannot be said to occupy any physical location.

Professor: (Slowly, between clenched teeth.) Give me all the perfect numbers below 1 million.

Computer: 6, 28, 496. 'Twas brillig, and the slithy toves Did gyre and gimble in the . . .

Professor: Hold on! I want the perfect numbers below 1 million!

Computer: 6, 28, 496, 'Twas brillig, and the slithy . . .

Professor: Hey, wait! Where are my numbers?

Computer: Numbers are abstractions and the mome raths outgrabe.

Professor: Hmm. How much is two and two?

Computer: Two and two are floating point underflow in subrouting Q.) ADD.

Professor: What time is it?

Computer: It is illegal to call sequences from location 47BC2F . mimsy were the . . .

47BC2F, 47BC30, 47BC31, . . . THIS IS CENTRAL CONTROL. THE COMPUTER HAS BOMBED OUT AND THE SYSTEM WILL BE DOWN UNTIL 12:00 NOON TOMORROW, DECEMBER 6, 1985. REPEAT. THE SYSTEM WILL BE DOWN UNTIL 12:00 NOON TOMORROW.

Professor: Hey, you can't do this to me! You've got my lecture notes for my 10:00 a.m. class tomorrow and all my jokes! What am I going to do?

Computer: (Silence.)

Professor: Talk to me! Who can I call? I even threw away my telephone book!

Computer: (Silence.)

Professor: You @ #$*//@ *$# computer! You can just $@##/$*@!

Computer: Halt! You have just violated Sections A and C of the University Clean Speech Act, US-1984-337376. Report at 9:00 a.m. on December 17, 1985, to Room 252 of the County Courthouse, where your case will be heard. Let me remind you of your constitutional right to say nothing further until you have consulted a lawyer.

Professor: (Silence.)

Charles Babbage died in 1871, but it is only since the invention of the modern computer that his genius has received the recognition it deserves. As this article shows, the lack of appreciation during his lifetime left him embittered, and he was by nature somewhat irascible. He was probably not so unhappy as this article makes him appear, however, for—in view of his wide-ranging interests—he can scarcely ever have been bored. Moreover, though he was easily irritated (especially by noise), he was at heart a very kindly man. He was forever falling for hard-luck stories; and although his later investigations showed that many of them were false, this did not prevent him from being taken in again.

Charles Babbage and His Engines

Technical innovation has never been easy, even for the go-ahead Victorians. Charles Babbage is remembered as the irascible, and tragic Victorian genius who discovered the principles on which the computer is now based. However, of itself, his work did nothing to further the development of the computer. It was not until almost a century later, when the development of electronics technology made possible the invention of the computer that his principles were rediscovered, and only later did someone point out that Babbage had come up with many of the same things decades earlier.

Although most of his major projects were failures, he had some successes, notably in the discovery of operations research. The failure of his two principal projects however are normally ascribed to the cliché that Babbage was ahead of his time. True, at the time, people were appalled at the very suggestion of a machine that could replace even part of the human intellect. It is equally true however that Babbage had little understanding of the world in which he was operating, and suffered from an over-optimism that verged on fantasy.

Thus he hit on the idea of the difference machine. The law of constant differences reveals, for instance, that as the value of x^2 where $x = 1$, $x = 2$ . . . is 1, 4, 9, 16, 25, . . ., the difference between the consecutive numbers in this series (3, 5, 7, 9 . . .), is itself a series, with a constant difference of 2. The original series can, therefore, be calculated on a glorified adding machine, and so, therefore, can the value of x^2 where, say, $x = 79$. The same is true of more elaborate mathematical series. Babbage sold the idea to the Government of the day in 1823, and extracted a grant of £1,500, for the idea, which

From "It Was the Same 100 Years Ago," *The Economist*, London, Oct. 30, 1971, p. 88.

he backed with £3,000 or £5,000 of his own money, But the idea, so beautifully clear to contemplate on paper, could not be converted into a piece of machinery until a mountain of practical problems had been surmounted.

The 19th century machine tool industry could not produce machinery to the required standard of precision. Much more important, Babbage made an astronomic under-estimate of the time and sum of money the project would require. He was a gifted theoretical scientist, but temperamentally neither a leader of a development team, nor an estimator of costs. Babbage, in other words, should have gone back to the government, asked for money, and for a proper development organisation. But the 19th century was when geniuses worked alone. By 1834, Babbage had spent £20,000 of his own money and £17,000 of the government's, and after taking time off to formulate operations research and invent coloured stage lighting and several railway devices, he finally abandoned the difference engine for a new project altogether, embodying some of the central ideas in what we now call computers, which he called his analytic engine.

Like the difference engine, the analytic engine was never completed. Unlike the case of the difference engine, the government refused to contribute. But it is obvious from his notebooks and drawings that Babbage was on the right lines. As with the difference engine, complex mathematical operations were to be broken down into voluminous arithmetic ones. But he also saw that the machine would need a memory to retain the numbers needed in the calculation; instructions needed to define the successive stages in the calculations; a built-in power of judgment so that, using pre-arranged instructions, the machine would choose which course the calculation should take; and a device for feeding the raw material into the machine and through which the output, or answer, would emerge.

For this device, he first experimented with a large drum with adjustable stops and then decided to adapt the punched card mechanism from the Jacquard loom. The punched card, of course, is still used for just this purpose. As for programmes, the instructions that tell the computer what to do, Babbage gave only a general account. He was dissatisfied with working in decimals, but never hit on the idea of arranging the machine internally to work in binary code, the choice that has been made by all designers of modern digital computers. Understandably enough, he never seems to have considered the possibility of accomplishing his goals with electricity, though it has been electronics in this century that finally made the computer economically feasible. His faith in a strictly mechanical means was almost unbounded, though a full-scale model of his analytic machine could probably never have been made to work smoothly. At best there would have been frequent troubles with the forest of clockwork it required. Out of his own pocket Babbage hired a team of draughtsmen and skilled machinists and did complete the design work for the engine. The hundreds of drawings he produced are considered to be some of the most accomplished examples of machine design ever produced, but the practical work was left to Henry Provost Babbage who finished part of the machine in 1911.

By his impatience to explain the principles of his work to uncomprehending politicians and sceptical public, by his eccentricities (such as his all-out campaign against London's organ-grinders) Babbage had alienated his contemporaries by the end of his life. Shortly before his death he told a friend that he could not remember a single completely happy day in his life. "He spoke as though he hated mankind in general, Englishmen in particular and the English government most of all."

25 Effects of Computerization on Employment, Management Jobs, and Organization

Predictions regarding the effects of computerization on employment and management jobs have varied widely. Some observers have forecast widespread clerical unemployment and a flattening of organization charts because fewer levels of management will be needed—which could, of course, mean the complete disappearance of many middle management jobs. Others believe that the rapid growth of paper work, and perhaps some shortening of hours, will prevent any widespread unemployment among clerical workers and that companies will require at least as many middle managers as they have today—probably even a greater number.

To determine what is most likely to happen, a number of researchers have conducted studies of the changes that have occurred in company departments that have already been computerized. Although in some instances the findings have supported a pessimistic view, the greater number of studies have found that although many clerical jobs have been eliminated, it has seldom been necessary to lay off a great many people and often it has been possible to transfer all those displaced to other jobs. Moreover, in a number of instances, the computerized departments required more managers than were necessary before the introduction of the computers. The first article in this chapter is a report of one of these surveys.

Another prediction has been that companies would be governed by "computocracies" made up of those who are experts in the computer field. Although the computer departments have been gaining status in recent years, this prediction has fallen even further short of realization so far, for reasons that are explained in the second article.

This article reports on the effects of EDP on clerical workers in large banks, insurance companies, and public utilities. The installation of computers, the researchers found, produces a need for job retraining and makes for more transfers at the same geographical location. But other possible effects were minimal. There was little change, for example, in the number of demotions, in identification with the union and/or the company, or in the number of complaints and grievances. Dr. Swart is professor of management at Ball State University, Muncie, Indiana, and Mr. Baldwin is senior systems analyst, management information systems, Crown Zellerbach Corporation. Another article by the same authors, "EDP, Clerical Workers, and Work Satisfaction," appeared in the *Academy of Management Journal* for June, 1972.

EDP Effects on Clerical Workers

J. Carroll Swart and Richard A. Baldwin

The mid 1950s marked the date when, for the first time, there were more white-collar jobs than blue-collar jobs in this country. Today, as an army of white-collar employees snowballs in size, the number gap separating both occupational groups continues to widen. And, within the white-collar world is that fast-growing subculture of clerical workers, which numbered 13 million in 1970 and is expected to total more than 17 million in 1980.

During the past 15 years, a second important development on the American business scene was automation advancement in the form of computers. In 1955, there were fewer than 300 computer installations in the United States. By 1970, the number of computer installations had grown to 61,000.[1]

What are the effects of computers? General theory, as well as specific research studies, have centered mainly on investigating computerization effects on organizational structure, manpower distributions at various levels, and managerial decision-making. Opinions and research findings concerning these three issues differ widely, and there is little universal agreement on exactly how the computer affects the business organization.

The study described in this article was designed to identify a number of effects resulting from the interaction of computers and clerical workers.

Research Focus

The banking and insurance industries were among the first to use computer systems, and these industries continue to be leaders in the number of computer installations. According to a U.S. Department of Labor 1967 report, banking and insurance were listed as two of six industries showing the heaviest concentrations of computerization.[2] Public utilities also made strong use of computer systems.

This study, conducted through the use of questionnaires, sought information concerning EDP effects on clerical workers[3] in banks, insurance companies, and utility firms. The researchers desired to survey large firms experienced in EDP which had sizable numbers of clerical workers exposed to computer systems. *Fortune* magazine's *1969 Index of America's Largest Corporations* was used as the reference source. One-hundred-fifty firms were surveyed: (1) the 50 largest banks, (2) the 50 largest insurance firms, (3) the 50 largest utilities. Questionnaires were sent to personnel directors at all firms, with specific names and addresses obtained from *Poor's Register of Corporations, Directors, and Executives, 1969.* Anonymity was guaranteed to all participating companies.

The questionnaire was structured into two major sections. Part I contained inquiries designed to evoke general background information about each company. However, the focus of the study was on Part II—seven questions concerning clerical workers' interactions with computerization. Specifically, to what degree did EDP affect clerical workers in terms of:

[1]Statements made by Joe V. Quigley, Manager, IBM Planning Systems Development, White Plains, New York, in a speech delivered at Ball State University, April 18, 1970.

[2]"The Many Faces of Technology," *Occupational Outlook Quarterly*, Bureau of Labor Statistics, Washington, D.C., May, 1967.

[3]As stated on the questionnaire, "clerical worker" referred to that white-collar employee at the non-management level engaged in a clerical or kindred job classification. Examples: Receiving clerk, Payroll clerk, Comptometer operator, Purchasing clerk, Friden Flexowriter operator, Order clerk.

From the *Academy of Management Journal*, December, 1971, pp. 497–512.

1 Need for job retraining,
2 Number of demotions,
3 Interoffice transfers at the same location,
4 Interoffice transfers to different locations,
5 Identification with union and company,
6 Age of retirement, and
7 Number of complaints and grievances.

To assist a responder in the recording of EDP effects, a two-directional scale was inserted on the questionnaire immediately following each question. Instructions requested that the responder place an "x" on each scale at the specific degree which most meaningfully depicted the effects of EDP at his firm. To further illustrate this point, let us take as an example the first question. On the two-directional scale immediately following this question, the exact middle of the scale represented zero degrees—no apparent change in need for job retraining. On the scale to the left of zero and running from degrees one to ten was the direction signifying greater need for job retraining. To the right of zero, and running from degrees one to ten, was the direction signifying reduced need for job retraining.

As explained in the "instructions" section on the questionnaire, the researchers realize that various interdependent factors, in addition to computerization, act as agents of change. As a consequence, change is the result of the interplay of multiple factors. Responders were asked to consider the significance of EDP *as a main factor* regarding its effects on clerical workers.

Findings

A total of 56 questionnaires were returned, which constituted a return rate of 37.3 percent. Completed questionnaires were received from 19 banks, 20 insurance companies, and 17 utilities.

Background information on companies surveyed. Responses indicated that all 56 companies had electronic data processing systems in 1968.

Most firms reported annual EDP operations budgets in the $750,000–$3,000,000 category and employed in excess of 2,000 clerical workers.

EDP effects. Findings are presented below for each of seven questions included in Part II of the questionnaire.[4]

Need for job retraining. During the 1964–1969 period, has computerization had an apparent effect on clerical workers in terms of need for job retraining? The survey revealed a definite trend toward greater need for job retraining in all three industries.

As observed in the banking industry, the median degree was five in the direction of greater need for job retraining. In the insurance industry, the median degree was five in the direction of greater need for job retraining. Among public utilities, the median degree was three in the direction of greater need for retraining. The "All Industries' Median" was four in the direction of greater need for job retraining.

Number of demotions. During the 1964–1969 period, has EDP had an apparent effect on clerical workers in terms of number of demotions? Concerning both the utilities and insurance industries, the data revealed no apparent change in number of demotions due to computer implementation. By contrast, the banking industry indicated a trend toward fewer demotions.

Of the companies responding, 27 firms, or 48 percent, reported no apparent change in number of demotions. In banking, the median degree was three (in the direction of fewer demotions). Both in the utilities and insurance industries, the medians of zero signified no apparent change in the number of demotions. The "All Industries' Median" also was zero.

Interoffice transfers at the same location. During the 1964–1969 period, has computerization had an apparent effect on clerical workers in terms of number of interoffice transfers at the same geographical locations? In all three industries, the survey revealed a trend toward more transfers at the same location as a result of EDP.

In the banking and insurance industries the median degree was three (in the direction of more transfers at the same location). Among

[4]For each question, the "chi-square goodness of fit" test was applied to the medians of the data. With the exception of the one question relating to interoffice transfers to different geographical locations (Question 4), for all other questions, the individual industry medians agreed with the "All Industries' Median." Therefore, in general, the null hypothesis was confirmed: "The individual industry distributions agree with the total distribution of all industries."

utilities, the median degree was two (in the direction of more transfers). The "All Industries' Median" was three (in the direction of more transfers at the same location).

Interoffice transfers to different locations. Over the 1964–1969 period, has computerization had an apparent effect on clerical workers in terms of number of interoffice transfers to different geographical locations? For two of three industries, the data revealed a slight trend toward more transfers. In contrast to the finding that EDP was a definite factor in causing more transfers at the same locations, EDP was not as important a cause of transfers to different geographical locations.

Twenty-six firms, or 47 percent, reported no apparent change in number of transfers due to EDP. In the banking and utility industries, the median degree was one (in the direction of more interoffice transfers to different locations). In the insurance industry, the median degree was zero. The "All Industries' Median" was one (in the direction of more transfers to different geographical locations).

Identification with union and company. During the 1964–1969 period, has EDP had an apparent effect on clerical workers in terms of union and company identification—regardless of whether there was a certified bargaining unit? In all three industries, the survey revealed no apparent change in allegiance and loyalty behavior.

Age of retirement During the 1964–1969 period, has computerization had an apparent effect on clerical workers in terms of age of retirement? Over all three industries, the survey revealed that EDP had no apparent effect on retirement age.

Number of complaints and grievances. During the 1964–1969 period, has computerization had an apparent effect in terms of number of complaints and grievances filed by clerical workers? Two industries reported no apparent change, whereas one industry detected a slight trend toward more complaints and grievances.

A total of 27 firms, or 48 percent, reported no apparent change in the number of complaints and grievances due to EDP. In the utility and insurance industries, the median degree of zero signified no apparent change. In the banking industry, the median degree was one (in the direction of more complaints and grievances as a result of EDP). The median for banking showed a slight trend in the direction of more grievances because of 19 large banks responding to the survey, 13 banks reported an increase in the number of complaints and grievances. Nevertheless, the "All Industries' Median" was zero.

Discussion

Are clerical workers' skill requirements upgraded or downgraded as a result of EDP? What is EDP's effect upon work satisfaction?

EDP effects on work skill requirements. According to Stieber, skill requirements of clerical workers may rise generally as a result of EDP; nevertheless, a substantial number of clerical workers still do the same work requiring the same skill levels.[5] Bright studied skill requirements and concluded that as technological application advances to higher levels, skill requirements tend to decrease rather than increase.[6] Weber reported inconclusive findings as to whether EDP caused upgrading or downgrading in job skills.[7] A Bureau of Labor Statistics study claimed that upgrading occurred in only a small number of highly skilled computer jobs, whereas the skill levels of most employees were largely unaffected by computers.[8]

In the 1960's, Lee studied various aspects of mental and clerical work skills among clerical workers. Mental skills included: (1) mental application, (2) job knowledge, (3) accuracy of work, (4) responsibility, and (5) supervision. Clerical skills included (1) simple calculation, (2) record-keeping, and (3) physical work. In reference to his research, Lee says in one of his latest writings:

> . . . the computer generally eliminates or reduces the clerical aspects of work skill requirements and, at the same time, increases the mental aspects of work skill requirements. The net effect is upgrading

[5]Jack Stieber, "Automation and The White Collar Worker," *Personnel*, November–December, 1957, pp. 12–16.

[6]James R. Bright, *Automation and Management* (Harvard University Press, Cambridge, Mass., 1958), pp. 186–189.

[7]C. Edward Weber, "Impact of Electronic Data Processing on Clerical Skills," *Personnel Administration*, January–February, 1959, pp. 20–26.

[8]Edward Weinberg, *Adjustments to the Installation of Office Automation*, Bulletin No. 1276 (Bureau of Labor Statistics, May, 1960).

in the overall work skill contents of the affected (clerical) jobs.[9]

As described in this article, the question concerning EDP effects on clerical workers in terms of need for job retraining was included in the researchers' survey. As reported, all three industries indicated a greater need for job retraining as a result of EDP. This finding suggests that computerization had the net effect of upgrading work skill requirements. The three industries were saying, in essence, that there was a greater need for job retraining because clerical workers' skill requirements had been upgraded, not downgraded, as a result of EDP. Thus, data from this study support Lee's findings.

EDP and work satisfaction. According to Lee's research, exposure to EDP led clerical workers to conclude that computers were responsible for more work methods standardization and shorter deadlines for work completion. Clerical workers perceived that they exercised less control over their work pace; thus, they sensed a loss of freedom. "The clerical workers felt a much greater change than did the managerial employees."[10] Whereas 38 percent of the managers sensed the loss of freedom, 63 percent of the clerical workers perceived loss of freedom in work methods as a result of EDP.

On the other hand, Lee reported that a majority of clerical workers felt that they performed a greater variety of tasks after computer installation. For example, whereas the computer reduced the number of clerical tasks, it increased the amount of employee communication, cooperation, and coordination with other departments. EDP widened employee knowledge of other departments.

> With all these changes in mental and clerical aspects as well as in the work environment, the general attitude of employees toward their work conditions was favorable. Eighty-three percent of all employees felt that they liked their jobs more than before. A relatively greater proportion of managerial employees felt an increased satisfaction with their work, as 90% of them indicated favorably in comparison to 74% for the clerical.[11]

[9]Hak Chong Lee, "The Computer Age," in Joseph W. Towle (ed.), *Human Resources Administration Problems of Growth and Change* (Houghton Mifflin Company, Boston, 1970), p. 33.
[10]*Ibid.*, p. 33.
[11]Ibid., p. 38.

In regard to the study described in this article, the researchers made no attempt to measure increase or decrease in work satisfaction. Nevertheless, our findings are applicable to the subject.

In all three industries surveyed, the questionnaire responses revealed a definite trend toward greater need for clerical worker job retraining as a result of computer installations. A trend was also revealed in all three industries toward more transfers at the same geographical location. When viewing work satisfaction within the framework of these two questions, the findings suggest that EDP might cause a decrease in work satisfaction, or, at least, no increase.

On the other hand, our survey also revealed that EDP caused no change, or virtually no change, in terms of:

a Number of demotions,
b Number of transfers to different locations,
c Union identification,
d Age of retirement, and
e Number of complaints and grievances.

When viewing work satisfaction within the framework of these five areas, the findings suggest that EDP might cause an increase in work satisfaction, or, at least, no decrease.

Conclusions

This questionnaire survey sought information concerning EDP effects on clerical workers in banks, insurance companies, and utility firms. Regarding these three industries, the major conclusions are:

1 Computer installation results in a greater need for job retraining.
2 There is virtually no change in the number of demotions as a result of EDP implementation.
3 EDP causes more transfers at the same geographical location.
4 There is a slight trend toward more transfers to different geographical locations as a result of EDP.
5 There is no apparent change in clerical worker identification with union and company as a result of EDP.

6 EDP has no apparent effect on clerical workers in terms of retirement age.
7 There is virtually no change in the number of complaints and grievances filed by clerical workers as a result of EDP.

Many companies prefer to train people who are familiar with the business in computer techniques, rather than attempt to train computer experts in the business. The following article by a former group vice-president of Whirlpool Corporation explains why this is so.

Top Management and the Computer

William E. Mahaffay

Not long ago two of our bright computer boys came to me with a proposal for a capital investment of $200,000 in new computer equipment. They made an elaborate presentation in which, among other things, they used the classic light pen program—how to specify the dimensions and compositions of an I-beam—as an example of a program for graphic display equipment.

Now Whirlpool is not in the engineering construction business. We make washing machines, refrigerators, and heating and cooling equipment. You'll find no I-beams in any of our products. So, when they had finished their presentation, I simply said: "Now, I'm just a slide-rule engineer, and what I want to know is this: What is this equipment going to do for us tomorrow in the way of improving our products, reducing costs, or providing a better system of engineering design?" They couldn't answer.

It did turn out that the new equipment they were proposing actually would be useful to us. We do have design problems that a computer can help with. For example, when a washing machine in the extraction cycle goes through its critical speed, it may start to walk if the clothes load is unbalanced. So we have to be very careful there, and there are a great many factors that may affect the results, not only the speed, but:

. . . the design of the parts;
. . . the design of the cabinet;
. . . the kind of fabrics being processed;
. . . and let's not forget the customer,
Mrs. Housewife, herself.

To figure out *all* the possibilities with handbooks and desk calculators would take an enormous amount of time; as a result, the design engineer would have to limit the number of variables he took into consideration and play it safe. That is, he would design equipment that would do the job and hold still while it was doing it; but the design he selected might not be the very best possible in terms of both cost and performance. With the proposed computer equipment, he could take all the variables into account by developing an expanded series of equations and still get the answer very quickly.

These two computocrats who were making the presentation had worked with this program and many similar ones of intense interest to our company. But in response to, "What is this equipment going to do for us?" they could say only, "We'll have to play around with it and find out." They simply knew that the equipment they were proposing was the very latest in visual display, and they wanted to work with it. They didn't know the business itself—up to that point, I think, they didn't really believe that it was important for them to learn it.

This isn't true, I may say, of most of Whirlpool's computer experts; two-thirds of them learned the business first and the computer technology second. It happened that these two had gained all their experience in very large companies that could afford to spend time and money to research computer possibilities and then attempt to find applications for them later. If you are in the computer business, work of that kind is well worthwhile, and it may be worth-

From an address given at the 17th Annual Fall Management Conference sponsored by Northwestern University School of Business at the Continental Plaza Hotel, Chicago, Nov. 8, 1967.

while also for a company in which $200,000 is only small change. But most companies have to keep a tighter reign on expenditures, and that means that we must teach our computer experts to talk the language of business: cost and performance in relation to specific products or services.

The computer boys, after all, are only the latest in a long line of staff specialists that have been added to our organizations over the years. Each type of specialist tries to persuade us that his field is the most important of all, and if top management doesn't realize it, why, then, top management is just plain dumb.

Translations Needed

Not long ago, for example, the *Wall Street Journal* reported on the terms thrown around at a meeting of personnel men: "narrowing parameters," "functions of situational variables," "diagnostic planning activity," "total organization on management confrontation," and "three-dimensional response quality matrix."[1]

When we get to the computer experts, we get another kind of bafflegab, as the WSJ reporter called it. "Parameters," of course, is a word that the personnel men borrowed from the computer field, but it by no means exhausts the new vocabulary of the computocracy: "total systems," "redundancy," "black box," "nanoseconds," "emulation," "bits and bytes," and so on.

Snowed under by terms like these, and others more baffling still, top management is often at the mercy of the salesmen of computer equipment and is asked to spend large sums of money without knowing what it's getting. In fact, the salesman may actually be trying to make you afraid to ask too many questions, make you feel that if you don't understand what he's talking about, there's something wrong with you. And your own computer experts may be on the salesman's side instead of on yours, because they like to have the latest equipment to play with, and because they may be relying too heavily upon the manufacturer for their knowledge.

Don't let the salesmen or your own experts intimidate you with their technical terms. All the terms are explicable in ordinary English. They are a kind of shorthand useful when experts are talking to each other, but they can be translated into language that a slide-rule engineer, or even someone who is not an engineer at all, can understand.

What's a system? It's simply a set of variable components interacting with each other; that is, changes in one variable will affect several others, and the changes in some of the others may affect the first variable. And, of course, each system is part of a larger system, just as the circulatory system in the human body is part of the system that encompasses the whole body.

A company is a system. (Think how changes in engineering affect manufacturing and sales, or vice versa.) The company, in turn, is part of a larger system made up of the whole economy, and so on. A "total system" is one in which all data needed for the business is captured once at its source and put into computer language and automatically sorted, stored, and forwarded to those who can use it, or is available immediately when they ask for it. This may come eventually, but no company has as yet developed a successful total system covering all parts of the business.

A "black box," theoretically speaking, is a piece of equipment whose interior workings are unknown, although one knows that a given input will produce a given output.

Now I'd like to take a few minutes to discuss what the computer cannot do; then mention some of the things it can do, including some of the things it is doing for us. (I hesitate to say that any of our applications are either new or unique; when a speaker does so, there is always danger that some of his audience will say, "Why, we've been doing that for years!") However, perhaps our applications will suggest some possibilities for the future.

What the Computer Cannot Do

First of all, the computer does *not* make possible pushbutton management in which all decisions can be made automatically. There is no sign that it is going to replace human beings as decision-makers except in cases where the decisions can really be based on quantitative data and nothing else. Further, you must not expect computers or

[1]James P. Gannon, "Bafflegab & Buzzwords," *The Wall Street Journal*, Feb. 23, 1967.

computer people to solve everyone's problems. Your systems should allow your people to write programs to manipulate data banks or files. Computer people are not capable of anticipating every question an executive will ask. The best applications come from the user, not from the manufacturers, or even from the "computer boys"—and there simply aren't enough computer boys to go around anyway.

Hubert L. Dreyfus of M.I.T. has pointed out in a paper published by the Rand Corporation that the prediction that digital computers will eventually be able to do anything a man can do is based on the unwarranted assumption that the operation of the human brain differs from the operation of a computer only in that the brain is more complex. Human beings, he notes, have an ability to distinguish between the essential and the accidental that a computer cannot duplicate, to interpret words or other data in the light of the context, and to utilize cues that remain on the fringes of consciousness. To say that the so-called thinking that a digital computer does, as when it plays a poor game of chess, represents progress toward being able to duplicate the performance of the human brain, Dreyfus says, is as though "the first man to climb a tree claimed tangible progress toward flight to the moon."

What It Can Do

But if human beings can do many things better than computers can, it is also true that computers can surpass human performance in many areas. Everyone knows, for example, that they offer a high-speed method of doing low-grade work: processing a payroll, for example, or making other routine calculations. They can also do other things that human beings can't do at all, because they wouldn't live long enough to complete the calculations with a pencil or a desk calculator, or couldn't complete them in time for the answers to be of much use.

For example, take the insulations used in our refrigerators. There are many different possible thicknesses of each one. To figure out the performance of each without a computer would be a monumental task, but a computer can do it in one or two seconds. Without the computer, we would have to confine our investigations to far fewer materials.

Again, in our environmental control programs, by using a computer we can give our dealers very quick answers on what equipment is needed, taking into consideration the many variables, such as the angle at which the sun strikes the building at various times of the year, the configuration of the building, and so on. It's all done with equations in which we can insert the quantities that apply to the particular building where the heating and cooling system is to be installed, and it takes just 11 seconds.

The value of simulating performance through mathematical models—which are simply equations into which various quantities may be inserted—as opposed to physical models is, in fact, very great. For example, if you want to know how long a given product will last, you can simply feed your mathematical models into a computer and get the answers very quickly. Otherwise you would have to build a physical model and run it for several years.

Another of our applications is a product-tracing system that enables us to know where each unit went. Then, if there are any complaints about performance, we can determine how justified they are and why the difficulties occurred. This makes possible individualized service to our customers.

Then there are problems of physical distribution, of inventory, and of production scheduling that are very complicated because they involve so many possible variables that one cannot take all of them into account without a computer. I believe that it will one day be possible to have a plant that has no inventory of either raw materials or finished products. The raw materials will come in at one end just when they are needed, and finished products will go out the other.

Another way in which the computers could be extraordinarily valuable would be through banks of information that would be useful to a number of companies. For example, suppose we all had information on materials pooled in one central "information utility," and one could get out all the data on a given type of steel or plastic without any difficulty. I think industry associations could be very useful in developing data banks of this type.

It has even been suggested that all the data on the economy could be fed into a computer for use in company forecasting, but I think it is a little too soon to expect this. It would be useful, however, if the type of information on, say, markets in various areas that is presently found in many different sources, government and private, could be placed in a data bank. Published data of this sort are often late because of the time it takes to print and issue them; using computer data would make the information more timely.

Computers have immense possibilities. They are doing a wonderful job in many areas, and they will do still more wonderful jobs in the future. But they probably will not—barring the development of entirely new types—be able to do everything a man can do, especially if the man is an astute and creative top manager.

Remember, also, that computers are extremely literal in their so-called thinking. As the late Norbert Wiener once said, "They will give you what you ask for, which is not necessarily what will be good for you, or even what you really want." If the analyst or the programmer forgets to specify all the conditions, or "constraints" as they are called, the answer may be not what you want at all.

What Managers Need to Know

It was suggested to me when I was asked to give this talk that management should participate in systems design because the system must meet management's information needs. I would agree with that to some extent, although I do not think top management needs to spend much time on the actual development of a system, unless it is a total system. But I do think the production manager should participate in the development of, say, a production control system because he is aware of all the constraints, and the systems analysts, who are less familiar with what goes on on the production floor, may well overlook some of them if they are left to their own devices.

Top management people must be knowledgeable enough to make sure that computer people are using the latest software as well as hardware, that the latest languages, such as FORTRAN, COBOL, or PL/1 are being used versus the assembly language, that reprogramming problems occasioned by next-generation hardware are understood, that the computer people allow access to the users. So you are sure your management people are knowledgeable enough?

Let me share one surprise that happened last week. One of our divisions was still on the second-generation hardware. EDP took all the time, so we had provided a time-sharing system for the engineers, a number of teletypewriter terminals to write (translate or compile) programs. With these conversational devices, they were completely satisfied. Along came the plans for the third generation; and it was said that we could do away with the time-sharing terminals and incorporate everything into one computer. It sounded fine. Everyone agreed. Along came a knowledgeable computer engineer and asked a few questions: "What's your terminal going to be?" Answer: "Same teletypewriter." "Can your people still write programs as they did with time sharing?" "Think so." "What about access?" Well, to make a long story short, access would be only at night. So our users—in this case, our engineers—almost got a thing they couldn't use. Our engineering management didn't know the difference, which is a perfect example of what can happen if top management isn't sufficiently knowledgeable.

Further, I think that although there is no reason why department heads or top managers need concern themselves with the inner workings of the computer or the details of programming, they should become familiar with the general concepts and the terms used so that the experts can no longer frighten them with bafflegab. They can learn a good deal at one of the short courses, five days or less, offered by the computer companies, and they can also insist that the salesmen and their own experts explain each of the technical terms in ordinary English.

Fifteen years ago, I used the word "parameter" in talking to my own boss, and instead of letting it pass, as many managers do because they are afraid of showing ignorance, he inquired: "Don't you mean perimeter?" So, together, we looked it up in the dictionary, and the meaning became clear. That's the way to learn.

And speaking of education, in one of the in-house courses that we offer our engineers, we talk about the computer as "*horsepower for the mind*." An analogy could be made to the internal combustion engine. Developed originally to power land vehicles, it provided the background for the development of the airplane. This was horsepower for the body.

The computer was developed only 22 years ago, and our first applications of our new tool have been to mechanize manual methods, a normal first usage. As yet, we don't know how to use it, and our big payoff will come in doing new things, things that could not be done before. Really, this is added horsepower for the mind.

Don't be afraid of the computer. Actually it is an evolutionary development rather than a revolutionary one. Take a good look at the man-machine interfaces, which are merely the points at which man communicates with the machine and vice versa. The output interface may be, for example, a piece of auxiliary equipment that produces typewritten material, or it may be a visual display. You can also take a look at the block diagrams which indicate the steps in a given program. You can see that the general concepts are not too difficult; at each step a circuit is either open or closed, that is, the answer is either "yes" or "no."

The computer may be a "black box" to you in that you don't, and probably don't need to, understand exactly what goes on inside it, but if you know the general concepts, you will be able to determine what "*output*" in the form of business improvement you are getting for the "*input*" of money.

26 Management Science—Operations Research

Operations research, or, as it is often called, management science, is the application of the scientific method to management problems and the quantification of the variables in a situation so that a solution may be arrived at by mathematics. In its complete form it calls for the use of many different scientific disciplines.

Scientific management also calls for the quantification of the variables in a problem, so far as possible, and in his researches into the art of cutting metals, Frederick W. Taylor used what was essentially the management science approach. But in general, management science goes far beyond scientific management in that it makes much more use of higher mathematics, draws on many more branches of scientific knowledge, and deals with many more aspects of management. Since the calculations it calls for are very complex, the advent of the high-speed computer has greatly fostered its development.

By making more accurate quantification possible, management science can help managers to view situations more objectively and assist them in:

1 Weighing the merits of alternative business objectives.
2 Allocating scarce resources in the best way possible.
3 Measuring results more accurately and more quickly than was possible previously, especially when high-speed computers are used.
4 Making corrections more rapidly.

Management science originated during World War II, when teams composed of physicists, mathematicians, economists, and others helped Britain and the United States to solve tactical problems. In business it has contributed to greater profit by making possible better planning and control. But there is, and has been from the beginning, some question of the wisdom of carrying it too far, since it is often impossible to quantify all the parameters in a situation calling for a management decision.

The first article in this chapter outlines the scope of operations research, and the second presents an OR problem and explains how the OR men went about solving it. The third discusses the important OR technique, simulation, which is the one most likely to be of aid in top management decisions. The last points out the direction in which research in the immediate future should be aimed.

Management science was fortunate to count among its founding fathers the great English physicist P. M. S. Blackett, of the Imperial College of Science, a Nobel Prize winner. Dr. Blackett was a pioneer in the application of OR in World War II, and also made important contributions to the development of radar. Particularly notable in this excerpt is his emphasis on the need to learn from experience and his view that OR workers should not have executive authority but that they should have, rather, constant access to the executives on whose problems they are working. These observations were drawn from his experience as chief scientific adviser to the British government.

The Scope of Operational Research

P. M. S. Blackett

Now there can be no doubt that scientific method has often in the past been applied to the complex phenomena of human life and organisation. The abundant literature of applied economics and the social services generally is evidence enough for this.

Most larger firms and many industrial consultants have special staffs which are concerned with many kinds of statistical analysis. Similar activities are carried out by research associations, by other cooperative organisations and by independent institutes and the research organisations of the political parties. Particularly during the war, government departments were forced to bring into being teams of specialised analysts, not only to advise on policy relating to particular aspects of the national economy, food, fuel, manpower, raw materials, etc., but also to plan in some measure the overall economic policies of the country. University schools of social science have studied scientifically many aspects of our society.

If, therefore, operational research is merely the scientific method applied to the complex data of human society, then, however useful it might be, it certainly is not new.

I believe this conclusion to be over-simplified and that operational research, as developed during the war, and subsequently, has an appreciable degree of novelty. In my view, the element of relative novelty lies not so much in the material to which the scientific method is applied as in the level at which the work is done, in the comparative freedom of the investigators to seek out their own problems, and in the direct relation of the work to the possibilities of executive action.

Let us consider what might actually happen if, for instance, some firm, research organisation or public body set up an operational research group, consisting of perhaps two or three operational researchers. Possibly the firm's executives might have some specific problems in mind, on which profitable work could be started at once. It is, however, one of the clearest lessons of our war experience that the really big successes of operational research groups are often achieved by the discovery of problems which had not hitherto been recognised as significant. In fact the most fertile tasks are often found by the groups themselves rather than given to them. That this is so is only to be expected, since any problem which is clearly recognised by the executives is likely, in an efficient organisation, to be already a matter of study.

How should an operational research group set about looking for pregnant problems? One method they must not adopt is blindly to make statistical analyses of all that is going on, in the hope that some of the statistics may somehow and sometime prove useful. Collection of statistics for the sake of statistics is no more operational research than collecting beetles is biology.

Since the groups must generally, and even preferably, be small, it is essential that their work is canalised into those fields where results of interest to the executives are likely. Drawing again on war experience, one of the best methods of achieving this is to put the group in close personal contact with the executives and let them watch them at work—that is, let them watch the decisions being made and give them the right to ask such questions as, "Why did you decide to do A rather than B?" or to intervene

From *Studies of War: Nuclear and Conventional* (Oliver & Boyd Ltd., Edinburgh and London, 1962), pp. 199–206.

with the executives thus, "Next month, you will have to decide between courses of action D, E or F. You will probably have no firm data on which to choose and you will, in all probability, have to guess which course is best. We think that possibly we may be able to help you by analysing quantitatively the effects of these possible actions. But we must have access to all the available facts and have authority to go and collect those that are not available."

During the war operational research workers attended the regular staff meetings at many operational headquarters and so learned the type of problem facing the executive officers and the normal methods by which decisions were arrived at. In this way they were enabled to spot problems capable of being tackled scientifically, which had either not been considered relevant problems, or had been held to be too complex for scientific analysis.

One example of this from the anti-submarine war may be quoted. The proof that large convoys were safer than small ones arose from an investigation into the protective value of convoy escorts. This analysis was undertaken as a result of an operational research worker being present at a meeting of the Anti-U-Boat Committee at 10 Downing Street, when the problem arose as to how best to divide our limited shipbuilding resources between merchant ships and escort vessels.

Though it is, in my view, essential for the greatest efficiency that senior operational research workers should be admitted to the executive levels as observers and potential critics, and whenever possible, should have close personal relationships with the executives—the situation during the war when they often shared the same mess was ideal—they should never, in general, have executive authority. If they had, they would soon get so involved in detail as to cease to be useful as research workers.

Conversely, though the research workers should not have executive authority, they will certainly achieve more success if they act in relation to the conclusions of their analysis as if they had it. I mean by this that when an operational research worker comes to some conclusion that affects executive action, he should only recommend to the executives that the action should be taken if he himself is convinced that he would take the action were he the executive authority. It is useless to bother a busy executive with a learned résumé of all possible courses of action leading to the conclusion that it is not possible to decide between them. Silence here is better than academic doubt. Research workers must also guard against the temptation to expect the executive machine to stop while they think. War, manufacture, trade, government business—all must go on, whether the research worker is there or not.

It is not possible to lay down rigid rules about the qualifications required in an operational research worker. [Nevertheless], operational research is scientific, and training in some scientific discipline may be regarded as essential, although it need not necessarily be in the exact sciences. The most important qualification is ability to take a broad view of a problem, so that important factors will not be missed. Some knowledge of statistical methods will be required, at least within an operational research group, even if not in every worker in the group. Specialist knowledge (technical, industrial, economic, or social) appropriate to the field of application is desirable, but is usually acquired on the job. A high degree of general intelligence and enthusiasm for the work are important. Above all, the right personality is vital, so that during an investigation the operational research worker can obtain the confidence of the men on the job, and at the end can put his conclusions across to the executive. I want here to state specifically that I entirely repudiate the notion that operational research scientists are necessarily in any sense more intelligent or clever than the executives. They are usually not, but they are differently trained and are doing a different job.

The last point I want to touch on concerns the form of presentation of operational research reports. Since these are essentially meant to achieve executive action, they must appear convincing to the executive personnel. It is unlikely that this will be achieved unless the writer of such a report is intimately familiar with the methods of thought of executives. To convince an executive that some new course of action is to be preferred to some old one, it is essential to understand why the old one was adopted. Often this can only be found out through close contact between the scientists and the executives.

The following article describes the type of problem that operations research is ideally fitted to solve, a problem that encompassed a large number of variables that could be quantified. It is interesting to note that the findings of the OR team were directly contrary to what appeared to be the common-sense solution. At first glance it appeared obvious that the company should raise its maximum demand; but when the problem was restated correctly in mathematical terms, it turned out that the MD could actually be reduced.

Stafford Beer was formerly with United Steel in Great Britain, where he founded and directed the world's largest civil OR group. Later he launched a management consulting group specializing in OR, and in 1966 became development director of the International Publishing Corporation.

A Modern Industrial OR Problem

Stafford Beer

In [a] generally rural area lay a large industrial town. This town was (and indeed is) dominated by a large industrial concern. A high proportion of the town's inhabitants worked for this company, and its own sense of involvement with the local community was highly developed.

The company was a heavy user of electricity. As is well known, there arises in the winter a particularly heavy demand for this source of energy, especially at peak periods of the day. In consequence, an industrial concern has to agree with the electricity undertaking on a maximum demand (MD). That is to say, the company undertakes not to exceed this agreed call for electric power, and in return a pricing system is agreed upon under which the electricity authority can be assured of a proper return on the proportion of its total load committed to this company. More significantly, the authority is assured that no load greater than that agreed as a maximum demand will be exerted on its supply system. But the company, which is fully connected to the grid, can fail to observe the agreed limit: what happens then?

A penal charge is imposed for all usage over the agreed figure. This forfeit will encourage the company to shed load as it reaches the level of maximum demand. But it can do this only if it is continuously aware of its demand from moment to moment, if it can forecast its fluctuating demand for the moments next ahead, and if a sudden decision to shed load would not entail disastrous consequences to production. It is by no means easy to satisfy this complicated set of conditions in a large works. At the end of one severe winter, the company discovered that it had exceeded its maximum demand level more than once. On each occasion, the period involved was roughly half an hour, after which load-shedding was efficiently organized to bring the consumption down below the MD figure. But under the agreement the damage had already been done; extra costs of the order of £20,000 were incurred for each mistake.

The OR man was first confronted with this at a management meeting, and had to make a quick appreciation. It was obvious, the investigator thought, that if all possible demands were assumed to occur together, and the total load aggregated, the maximum demand would be enormously and uneconomically high. The company had not done this, knowing from experience that only a proportion of the possible load would be likely to be in demand simultaneously. Nevertheless, the MD figure had evidently been fixed at too low a level. Clearly, then, this was a problem of probabilities. *Certainty* that any agreed maximum demand would not be exceeded by the actual demand at any given moment in the peak period could not, of necessity, be reached. The following argument then emerged.

As the maximum demand ceiling is lowered from a level equivalent to the sum of all possible demands, the probability that it may be exceeded must steadily increase, though not as a linear function because the expectations that each piece of electrically driven plant needs to come into service at a given moment are not equal, nor are they independent of each other. Doubtless, however, these probabilities could be computed: a curve could be established showing how the risk of needing to exceed the maximum demand diminishes as the agreed

From *Decision and Control: The Meaning of Operational Research and Management Cybernetics* (John Wiley & Sons, London, 1966), pp. 74–81.

level increases. But, as the agreed level increases, the costs of the scheme (because of the contract with the electricity authority) will go up—again, nonlinearly.

An optimal balance is required: a point at which there is so little gain in the probability of not running into trouble [that] insuring this is not worth the extra money. Judging by last year's experience, for the maximum demand then operating, the curve must still be rising steeply; that is, it must surely pay to increase the maximum demand substantially. But to what level? The OR scientist hoped that when the curves of probability and cost had been computed and plotted jointly against the level of MD, they would turn out to have 'points of inflection'; he hoped, that is, that the curves would suddenly and mutually flatten, thereby suggesting that the maximum demand should be fixed at the point where the curves changed over from a steep to a gentle descent. He went so far as to draw a picture of this possibility, which he showed to the managing director.

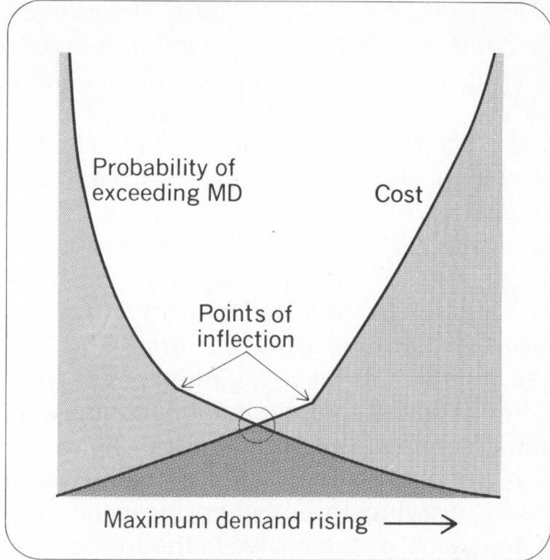

Figure 1 Preliminary econometric formulation of the maximum demand problem.

Now the real work had to begin. The OR scientist, as manager of an OR group, set up a small team to begin the study. As a first step, the team was briefed to examine both the facilities for the works' control of maximum demand and the legal contract with the electricity authority, and to produce a succinct statement on these matters. After this, the OR manager met with the two senior OR scientists who would be concerned: one (a mathematician) as directing the project, and the other (a psychologist) as leading it on site. The three men formed an interdisciplinary team, and none of them knew more of the really technical aspects of the problem that lay before them than had by this time been compiled in their colleagues' notes. Discussion soon revealed some very interesting questions, to which no one present knew the answers.

Following this meeting, then, the OR manager went back for a talk with the senior management. As far as the electricity demand problem was concerned, he was now intent on obtaining an answer to the following questions. When it looked as though the danger limit were being approached, the grid load would be shed. The first move in this direction was to switch on the company's private electrical generators. In order to use these generators, steam was required and this could be obtained by burning oil or by using one of two separate sources of gas supply—both of them originating in the works. The question therefore was: under what tactical control did these alternative fuels become used, what happened to the processes they were otherwise concerned in energizing, and who was responsible for the overall control of the many forms of energy that were apparently interacting in supplying the plant?

The accountants knew, as apparently 'absolute' facts, the order of cheapness of the whole range of fuels employed in the works—that is, they knew the cost of each as procuring a standard number of BTU's. It had therefore been ruled that any actions taken which would involve substituting one fuel for another should, as a matter of course, invoke the use of the 'absolutely' cheapest available alternative. As to the last part of the question, it was judged that, since this policy was so simple to comprehend, no one person need be charged with seeing that it was implemented. Everyone concerned knew the rules and obeyed them (an assertion subsequently verified as true in most cases).

The OR man was by this time becoming excited. How could anyone say what the relative costs of the fuels were for a given situation on the basis of some average costings? The costs actually incurred by a variety of alternative fuel policies at any one moment must surely depend on the opportunities available at that one moment to contrive some especially ingenious pattern of consumption to match some especially unusual set of demands. At this point the appropriate officials—the controllers of the electrical generating station, the gas controller, the man in charge of steam boilers—were called into the meeting. These people contended vigorously that their preoccupations had nothing whatever to do with the problem of trying to fix the maximum demand from the grid. The OR man was impatient of these arguments, because he had been unable to complete his concept of the double probability curves without knowing what the peripheral conditions actually were. And it was in trying to convince these departmental managers of the motes in their eyes that he suddenly became aware of the beam in his own. These 'peripheral' arrangements were not only relevant, they were an intrinsic part of the management's difficulty.

When the senior meeting resumed, the tack was entirely changed. Had the management in fact ever considered setting up a general control for energy consumption of every kind? The answer was that they had often thought about this, but they had discarded the idea, on the grounds that they knew of no similar works anywhere in the world in which a genuinely integrated energy control system operated. This bore out, they thought, their own intuition that the total problem was much too complex to be solved from moment to moment on such a broad front. But no harm would be done in trying to devise such a control, since new scientific methods would be used in formulating the problem, and there would be a possibility of destroying many of the traditional difficulties within a completely new framework. This thought was based on the consideration that most of the problems arose from a failure to communicate between the different sorts of fuel controllers. Such information flow problems tend to disappear, however, if the centres between which the flow is supposed, and fails, to flow are in some way coalesced. So permission to alter the entire terms of reference of the investigation was sought. This was not a problem of determining the maximum demand for grid electricity, but a problem of discovering a company strategy for energy control.

The new proposal was strongly opposed. The control principle adumbrated cut right across the established lines of managerial responsibility. Thought blocks began to rise like monuments all round the table, but the managing director was willing to give the idea a trial.

The construction of a scientific account of the whole energy consumption of this company was a long and difficult task. To build into the scientific programme every source of fuel, together with the appropriate constraints and controls on its use, was an undertaking of a different order of magnitude from the original task. For although the electricity demand problem itself could only be solved by taking account of the alternatives which could be fed into the system, it had at first been understood that this would happen according to a set of simple and invariable rules. To allow for it in a situation where *every* fuel had a right to equal consideration as a poser of its own problems of profitability, made the problem perhaps ten times as great.

Gradually the scientific picture emerged. All the interactions of the fuels and the production situations that could occur were stated in terms of mathematical and logical equations. Few of the fuel relationships turned out to be symmetrical. For example, the price paid for electricity imported from the national grid was different from the price received for works' electricity exported to the grid. There were many practical constraints on the apparent possibilities. Some of these constraints were not absolute, but themselves matters of probability. The most important of these, for instance, concerned a contract to supply the local township with gas. The company treated this commitment very seriously, with the result that gas-holding capacity which the OR scientists had originally regarded as a buffer in the system, turned out to have a restricted availability in that role. How far it was restricted would depend on the day of the week, because this determined both the probable level of the townspeople's demand, and separately the probable level of gas in the holder.

[In] a general view of the total energy system which was now under study, every entry represents an activity that has some effect on every other entry. Moreover, no activity can be prescribed in exact terms; the whole system is a dynamic interaction of probabilities. Somehow a

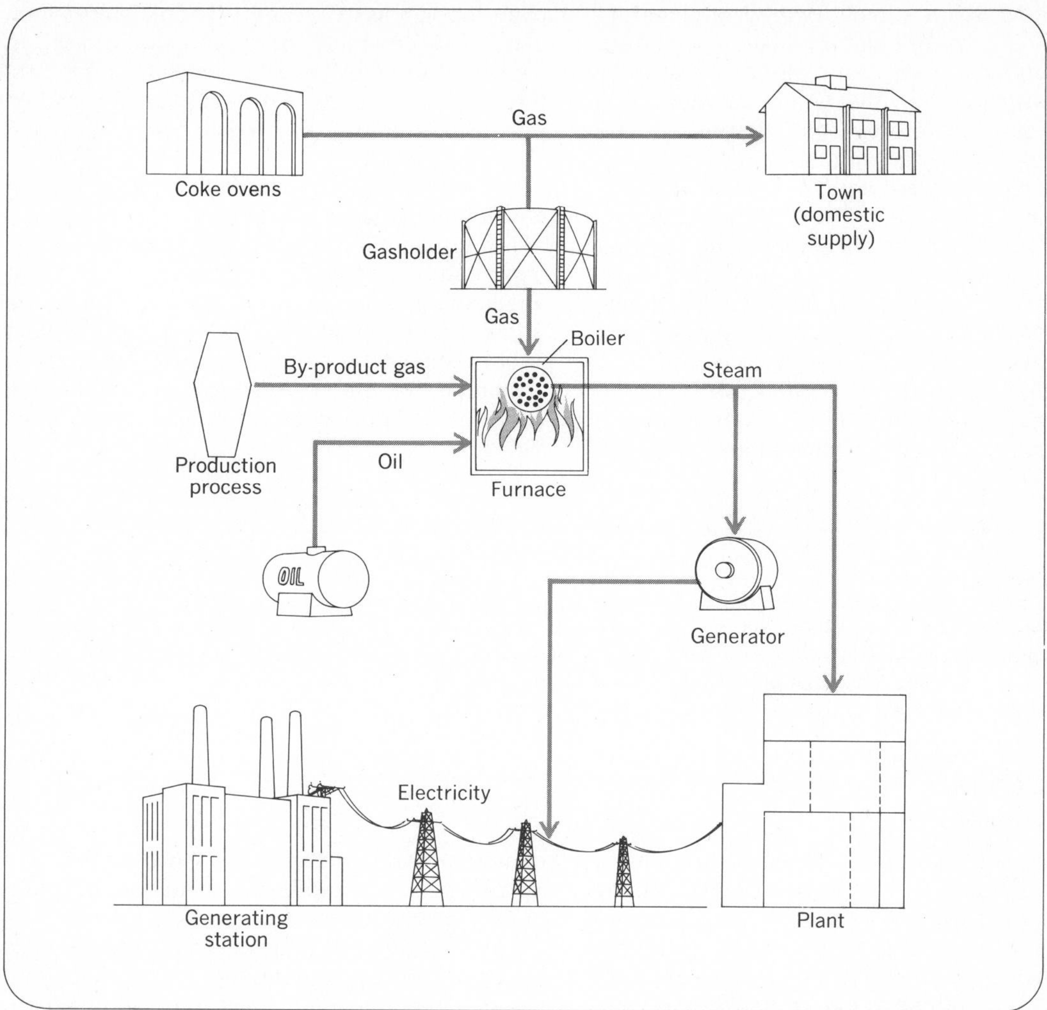

Figure 2 Diagram of the major interactions affecting the maximum demand problem.

formal scientific account of this whole system had to be created,and this was done by a mixture of theoretical and practical work. The logic of the theory of sets was used to express the basic relationships; mathematical statistics expressed the probabilities; actual data were pumped into the formalizations to quantify the picture. In some cases, the data recorded were quite inadequate and more had to be collected. In some cases again, the data were insufficiently precise—and could not be made more so: mathematical tricks were then used to estimate what more frequent readings would have recorded had the instrumentation been available. Many details of the system turned out to be unknown, and became the subject of special investigations.

For example, the optimal number of oil burners (as opposed to gas burners) inside the boiler had to be calculated. The generation rate of the private electrical substation had to be assessed in terms of the maximum output of five different turbo-alternator sets under different loads. This was done for available steam pressures representing residual energy available after intermittent and very heavy demands for steam had been met from the production plant. Lest the acquisition of these data makes the work sound like a straightforward engineering study, let it be noted that the object was not to find some theoretical best state for the system, but a control strategy that would actually work. Throughout, therefore, the interdisciplinary team was concerned not so much with the measurements quoted here, as with their *representation* in the system. The fact that counts is not that a meter registers somewhere, but that someone *knows* it has registered—after what delay, with what accuracy, with what reliability, and so on, and above all with what capacity to react to the information thereby conveyed.

In short, the scientific account of affairs involved the formalization of interactions between men, machines, materials and money, all spread over the complex system. It took about nine months to complete the scientific appraisal, to evolve an optimal overall strategy for operating the total system, to test it adequately, and to present it in a form that would be usable in the works.

The company was then informed of these developments, and told that the problems arising in creating a generalized control for energy had been overcome. Not surprisingly, the management immediately asked for an answer to the original problem: at what level should the maximum demand be fixed in future? The answer, assuming that the new controls were instituted, was that the figure could be *reduced to less than half* its previous level.

One of the OR techniques that may be used to assist top management in making decisions is simulation, particularly simulation that employs Monte Carlo methods. This article, which is part of a study based on a survey of forty companies in a wide variety of fields, explains how such a simulation is conducted and reports on the many uses to which the technique is now being put. The author is editor-in-chief of periodicals for AMA and has had broad experience in business and as a management consultant.

Simulations

Ernest C. Miller

A model is an abstraction of reality, something created to stand in the place of reality. Some models are good in the sense that they are accurate (valid) representations of the reality for which they are intended to stand; some are poor in that they do not accurately reflect reality. But, if we assume that a model has acceptable accuracy and is reliable in its performance, it can be used to simulate reality. To simulate reality is to input different patterns of values for the variables selected to represent reality in order to learn what the results would be. To the degree that the model is accurate, the simulation runs will show what would happen if the circumstances represented by the patterns of values occurred in the real world. In this sense, any model can be used to simulate. Many of the most interesting simulations are designed to project results into the future. In these simulations the results at various stages are fed back into the model to incorporate the changes into the model for use for the next time period.

Any time a manager selects a set of inputs for a model and runs the model to determine what the end results would be if these inputs were used, he is engaged in simulation. The values of the inputs he selects can represent his hypotheses about the circumstances that will prevail in the period of concern, or they may be hypotheses other managers have suggested as counterproposals to his. In any event, there is some guiding principle for the selection of inputs. When a manager attempts to explore the sensitivity of a decision to possible errors or inaccuracies in the input data, he is simulating. In such cases, the manager deliberately selects extreme, but possible, values of the various input factors to determine the effect on the end result. Factors that, despite marked changes in their values, do not cause the output measure to fall outside the acceptable range can be accepted as estimated. Inputs whose extreme values cause the output to fall outside the acceptable range would have to be studied more carefully to ascertain that the estimates were sound.

These uses of simulations are useful and important; there are other, equally useful approaches. The other approaches receiving the most attention in the business community are Monte Carlo simulations and experimental and business gaming. Monte Carlo simulations are based on the laws of probability implicit in games of chance, be the game poker, dice, or roulette. The essence of Monte Carlo simulation is that the values used for the variables on each run of the model are selected at random from the probability distributions developed to represent the likelihood of occurrence of each of the values. The key words in Monte Carlo simulation are *random selection* and *probability distributions*. Monte Carlo simulation procedures usually result in a distribution of the critical end result or output. Monte Carlo simulations do not provide *the* answer to a problem—no simulation technique provides *the* answer. Monte Carlo simulations do provide a distribution of the end result that will be obtained (assuming a valid model) from the different sets of values run on the model. The manager can then calculate the most likely end result and decide, on the basis of whatever criteria he selects, whether this result would be acceptable to him.

As a simple example of the application of the Monte Carlo technique, let's assume that management has to decide whether to add a new product to the company's line. The critical consideration in reaching this decision is whether the product will earn the company's target: a 25 percent return (before taxes) on capital employed.

Let's assume that we are uncertain what the actual annual unit volume, net sales price per unit, and total cost per unit will be for this product but that we are able to estimate the probability that each of a number of values for each of these variables will occur. These estimates give us our probability distributions for each variable. These distributions are

Annual Unit Volume		Net Selling Price/Unit		Total Cost/Unit	
Probability	**Units**	**Probability**	**Price/Unit**	**Probability**	**Cost/Unit**
.2	100	.3	$2.00	.1	$1.70
.4	200	.4	2.10	.2	1.80
.3	300	.3	2.20	.4	1.90
.1	400			.2	2.00
				.1	2.10

Let's also assume that the total capital employed in manufacturing is $200. (We'll assume it's a very simple product requiring no development work.) Management must now decide whether to manufacture the product and has decided to explore the opportunity with a Monte Carlo simulation.

The company's profit model states that annual total net profit is equal to annual unit volume times the difference between net selling price per unit and total cost per unit. (For reasons of simplicity, let's assume that fixed costs are an insignificant part of total costs, so that total cost per unit is the same over the range of volumes considered.) In symbolic form, this model would be

$$z = v(s - y)$$

where z equals annual total net profit, v equals annual unit volume, s equals net selling price per unit, and y equals total cost per unit.

When the model and the probability distributions for the inputs are in hand, the procedure for running a Monte Carlo simulation is straightforward. To illustrate: Assume a manager ran 20 trials. He selected randomly 20 sets of values for the 3 variables. This he might have done by using a table of uniform random numbers. His procedure in this case was to assign to each of the variables the number, or numbers from 0 to 9, that represented the probability that the outcome would occur. When the probability was .2, the outcome was assigned two numbers; when the probability was .4, the outcome was assigned four numbers. He then selected 20 random numbers from 0 to 9, and these numbers determined the outcomes from the 20 trials. For example, the numbers were assigned for annual unit volume so that when the random number was 1 or 2, the annual unit volume was 100; when the random number was 3, 4, 5, or 6, the annual unit volume was 200; when the random number was 7, 8, or 9, the annual unit volume was 300; and when the random number was 0, the annual unit volume was 400. A similar assignment of random numbers to the various outcomes was followed for the two other variables. The procedure the manager then followed was to select, at random, 20 annual unit volumes, 20 net sales prices per unit, and 20 total costs per unit. The first values selected in each case were one trial; the second, another trial; and so on. These 20 sets of the three variables were then input to the model and the total annual profit calculated. The procedure yielded this distribution of results:

Annual Before-Tax Profit	Frequency	Percent	Cumulative Percent
$160	1	5	100
120	1	5	95
90	2	10	90
60	1	5	80
40	4	20	75
30	2	10	55
20	1	5	45
10	1	5	40
0	6	30	35
−20	1	5	5
Total	20	100	

When management inspected these results, it saw immediately that there was only a 25 percent chance of the product's achieving or exceeding the target rate of a 25 percent return on capital employed ($50 annual profit), that the median return was about 15 percent, and that the average return was about 19 percent. On the basis of these results, management probably would reject the product. Interestingly, if management had used only the most likely values for each of the variables to calculate the return on capital employed, a 20 percent return would have been indicated—higher but still unacceptable in terms of the target.

Use of Simulation

Simulating significant processes or prospective activities has a long and honorable history. Most people who write or discuss the history of simulations trace the technique back to early war games.

Twenty-nine of the 40 companies that responded to the survey (approximately 72 percent) reported that they use simulations for operational and/or strategic planning. Twenty-five of the 40 companies (about 62 percent) reported using simulations for operational planning, and 22 of the 40 (55 percent) reported using the technique for strategic planning.

Despite its long and acceptable performance in nonbusiness areas, simulation seems to have caught on as a useful business tool only recently. More and more companies are turning to the technique for a broad variety of purposes. Some of the uses being made of simulations by the 22 companies that reported using the technique for strategic planning are

Produce balance sheet and income statement under various assumptions of profitability; of growth of sales, profits, and assets; and of acquisitions of certain sizes, timing, and profitability. (Diversified manufacturer. Annual net sales, $55 million.)

Model the overall company operations to produce a profit-and-loss statement; test alternative strategies to evaluate the possible impact on each on the company's profitability. (Ocean shipping. Annual net sales, $97 million.)

Compare the production system economics of many alternate combinations of equipment that might be used by the company's customers and project the potential impact of future technological or materials cost developments. (Manufacturer. Annual net sales, $150 million.)

Model the demand for electric power and the

generating capacity needed to satisfy this demand, including intercompany capacity coordination arrangements. (Electric utility. Annual net sales, $185 million.)

Analyze the economic alternatives in five- and ten-year business plans. (Communications. Annual net sales, $337 million.)

Make operating and financial projections of new and existing projects. (Basic metals. Annual net sales, $478 million.)

Evaluate planning alternatives. (Food processor. Annual net sales, $670 million.)

Aid in the study and understanding of environments for which the company has only a limited amount of information, such as the central reproduction departments of operating corporations. This environmental simulator has been used in concert with throughput simulators to compare the reliability of the company's equipment with that of other equipment. (Communications equipment manufacturer. Annual net sales, $700 million.)

Analyze the effects of varying the seniority rules at paper mills. (Paper manufacturer. Annual net sales, $789 million.)

Estimate the need for DC-10 aircraft in terms of best use, number of units required, mission, and so forth; determine the number of gate positions to be required at each airport ten years from now; and model the baggage claim process. (Transportation. Annual net sales, $903 million.)

Assist R&D planning and project selection. (Chemicals. Annual net sales, $1,383 million.)

Study possible divestments and consolidations. (Oil refiner and distributor. Annual net sales, $1,136 million.)

Evaluate the strategic plans of the operating divisions and of new business opportunities. (Aircraft manufacturer. Annual net sales, $2,335 million.)

Estimate the demand for external financing, given a set of input assumptions regarding retained earnings, capital investment, future interest rates and stock prices, and so forth. (Communications service and equipment. Annual net sales, $2,622 million.)

Plan rail and ocean transportation facility networks for the 1980–2000 time period. (Government agency.)

Most of the techniques used in management science were developed some years ago, but the fact that no new ones have been invented recently does not mean that the discipline has reached a dead end, this article points out. There is still plenty of room, the author notes, for developing new applications and refining the techniques. He believes that one of the most important of the techniques is the simulation described in the preceding article—the technique that provides answers to "What if?" questions. The author, a director in the headquarters of McKinsey & Company, management consultants, is responsible for that firm's management sciences, operations research, and systems analysis practices.

Has Management Science Reached a Dead End?

David B. Hertz

In 20 years, management science has evolved from a handful of unexploited techniques and an abundance of promising ideas into a comprehensive array of tested and proven tools. For most of that time, the curve that traces the development of the new science has maintained a steady upward slope.

Now, however, it seems to me we have reached some kind of plateau in the innovation of additional techniques comparable in importance and simplicity to many of the original concepts on which the field has been built. Extensive research in methodology has brought us to a point where elaborations of the funda-

Reprinted by permission from *The McKinsey Quarterly*, Winter, 1972, pp. 44–53. This article was first published in Issue 25 of *Innovation.* Copyright, 1971, by Technology Communications, Inc. Permission to reprint also granted by Executive VideoForum incorporated, current holder of the copyright.

mental ideas are adding only small increments of know-how. Moreover, we seem to be approaching some kind of fundamental barriers to further development without knowing the specific directions we should take to overcome them.

Management science aims at discovering certain kinds of societal relations, and at developing logical and quantified means of deciding on and testing courses of action in a social environment. It is an "action" science, not an observational one. It attempts to explain the world around us in ways that provide better means for answering significant questions for management.

The tools we have developed are appropriate to our needs, but knowledge of how to apply them has not reached an equivalent level of effectiveness. It is time for consolidation, time to look back at what we have, and time to look forward to how to apply this array of techniques to today's critical issues.

Problems and Limitations

The early achievements made it tempting to believe that the techniques could be successfully applied to any kind of industrial problem, the more complex the better. But as people began to move to tougher applications, it was apparent that implementing profitable solutions was a lot more difficult than many of us would have guessed. More disturbing still, often the solutions arrived at were less impressive to industry than we had imagined they might be. Instead of the order-of-magnitude improvements that had been made in many military situations, industrial problems often showed only small percentage improvements.

Even the use of linear programming in refineries turned out to be limited by uncertainty in virtually all of the activities being programmed—changes in prices of crude oil, delays in ship arrivals, equipment breakdowns, and political unrest, among a host of other unanticipated events. Such uncertainties restrict the validity of most optimum resource allocations to a fairly limited time span. Yet in order to get the most out of a schedule for a refinery, it may have to be run for a month or more. And if major changes in the parameters occur at shorter intervals, no payoff will be forthcoming.

Similar problems exist in other applications of linear programming, such as asset management in banking, where interest rate uncertainties make the theoretical gains very chancy. The problem of fitting means to ends by specifying objectives, identifying courses of action, and assessing their efficiency in achieving the objectives has turned out to be difficult indeed. So, for that matter, has the problem of determining the desirability of a given set of objectives in a more complex framework. So-called goals, such as profits, are often only means of attaining other ends. Putting it all together has turned out to be tough work for the management scientist.

In short, we have begun to see all around us limitations on the techniques of management science that weren't evident in the early days, when we were trying to make order-of-magnitude leaps. These limitations—principally those posed by uncertainty and by our inability to effectively sort out conflicting objectives—appear at the moment to be quite unyielding.

We need to discover better ways of dealing with uncertainty of all kinds and, in particular, with the complexities and interconnections of organized human behavior and the goals of institutions. Goal analysis, decision analysis, and methods of dealing with uncertainty are the three significant kinds of problems that run through much of the important current work in management science.

Yet in the past several years, very few ideas have been developed that have the elegance of, say, the simplex method in linear programming, or the notions of queuing theory, or of technological stability, or any one of several historic breakthroughs in the development of the science.

There are those who feel that a major breakthrough is coming in integer programming. Integer programming is important since it deals with problems in which resources can be allocated only in blocs of a fixed size. In ordinary linear programming, resources are assumed to be divisible into pieces of any size so as to achieve optimum allocation. But if I wish to schedule a fleet of ships, I can only break the resources down in ship-size pieces, and that is where integer programming comes in. There are ways to solve such problems, but they are complex and not yet as universally applicable as was the simplex method of linear programming. And even if some major breakthrough occurs in our ways of dealing with integer problems, I am not sure that it will have a major effect on where we go from here.

Bigger and faster computers will help somewhat, to be sure. But most of the limitations of management science do not arise from limitations in the speed and size of computers. Likewise, the fast-growing availability of small, inexpensive, stand-alone computers in lieu of large centralized installations should help extend the applications of management science, but they are not likely to lead to breakthroughs. This trend may tend to personalize the use of management techniques, so that an individual manager can control his own set of data and work out with management scientists techniques for dealing more easily with the specific problems he faces—thus leading to greater use of management science techniques by managers. But this will not, of itself, extend the frontiers of these techniques.

Developing New Applications

Despite these indications that management science has reached a plateau, we are by no means headed for a tapering off in the use of management science. On the contrary, we should view the period ahead as a time for extensive exploration of the wider application possibilities of the last 40 years' development.

We have come a long way. We have dramatically increased the technology for scientific management. We know how to produce models that bear a reasonable resemblance to the real world. When a manager is faced with a problem today, the management scientist can usually say, with an assurance he would have been unable to muster 25 years ago, whether or not he can build a practical model.

Management science is an aid to the manager who wants to know: "What if we combined these four plants into one?" "What if we produced more of this product and less of that one?" "What if we built the plant here rather than there?" Managers have always asked questions like these: "What if I had another 10,000 people to build this pyramid? How much faster could we build it?" Somebody always produces answers to such questions, based on the best methods of problem solving available at the time.

That is what management science is all about. It is today's best method for answering "what if" questions. There was a method 25 years ago. There was a method 100 years ago. Management science is the method of today.

Now that we have a science of management decision making and now that we know it is helpful for certain kinds of management decisions, it must become *the* way to make those decisions. But the available evidence suggests that we have not quite reached that point. As recently as 1968, the last published McKinsey study on the use of computers in industry showed that management generally was not using computers effectively to further applications of management science. Preliminary evidence from a current survey is revealing much the same pattern.

There are, it seems to me, at least two reasons for management's reluctance to adopt these new aids to decision making. First, they find them difficult to understand. Management science techniques are mathematical, and they sometimes seem to reduce complex intuitive matters to masses of incomprehensible mathematical expressions. I have known managers who use mathematical techniques in their own companies but would say to me: "Tell me again what a mathematical model does. I don't understand."

So we're still in an educational period. Present managers are slowly beginning to understand how these new techniques can help. At the same time, the new generation of managers now coming along is strongly convinced of the value of these techniques and the necessity to apply them.

A second reason for the reluctance of businessmen to apply management science techniques more broadly is that in a number of cases they were oversold. Out of sheer enthusiasm for the power of these new capabilities, some practitioners promised results they proved unable to deliver, either because the problems were too complex or the techniques were inapplicable.

While managers have been getting educated to the usefulness of management science, the management scientist has been getting educated to the realities of management. He finds that managers often understand, better than he had given them credit for, the nature of the problems in their particular domains of uncertainty. And even if the manager is still puzzled about how to solve the problem, he seldom has any illusions about its difficulty. That is why he is often skeptical about the possibility that some mechanistic technique will be of much help to him.

And that, in turn, is why today's management science has to concern itself as much with understanding management as with mechanical techniques.

If it is to be used effectively, management science has to be inserted into the heart of the institutional planning process, instead of tucked away in an organizational box remote from the real decision makers. I know at least one very large organization that has an outstanding management science group producing some of the very best technical material around. They have high status and are located on the floor directly below top management. Yet they report to the comptroller—and nothing of what they do gets into the operation of that business.

Looking Ahead

During the next five or ten years we shall need to spend as much effort developing methods for applying management science as we have spent in developing the tools during the last 20. The academic phase of our development was necessary, both to develop a respectable discipline and to train the men who will apply these techniques to real problems in world institutions. Now the academic institutions must encourage their students to turn to a quest for effective means of answering the genuine "what if" questions of government and industry.

As each new set of phenomena is brought under attack, the first attempts to construct models to answer the key questions may well be crude, even weak or futile. Yet beginnings must be made. And in a volatile and mercurial world where decisions must be made in the face of complexity and uncertainty, it is an exciting experience to discover the hidden parameters. Once identified, these parameters enable the searcher to measure variations, remove assignable causes, and establish control. They make it possible for him to determine how and why decision makers can supplement intuition and judgment with adequate and effective quantitative support.

This has always been the promise of management science, and it remains bright. To undertake practical applied work in the face of uncertainties, complexities, and unknown organizational behavior is an extremely difficult task, but it is time we got around to doing it.

27 Management in the Future

It has been repeatedly said that those who are currently studying management are likely to find the world in which they are operating ten, twenty, or thirty years from now entirely different from the world of today. Hence it is appropriate for them to consider what the future will be like and determine how they will face it.

There are three possible approaches to preparation for the future. One of these is the nostalgic approach: What can we do to preserve the best, the most cherished, of the past? The second approach is to consider how one may adapt oneself to changes in the future. The third is the imaginative one: What would we want the future to be like if we could mold it ourselves?

All these approaches have value, and all can be used by the same person. Certainly all values of the past and present that are worth preserving should be preserved so far as possible, and since business managers are one of the most influential groups in our society, they can do much to help the process of preservation in their official capacities as well as in their capacity as citizens. Then there are certain trends that for all practical purposes cannot be stopped entirely, and it is well for the manager to adapt himself to them. Finally, however, to the extent that the consequences of some trends appear to be disadvantageous, he should consider how they can be moderated and how their bad effects can be mitigated.

It is increasingly clear that one trend that is likely to continue is the trend toward bigness: in companies, in government, and in other institutions. The first article discusses the probable effects of this trend on business. The next two articles deal with the rather grim predictions set forth in a famous study by the Club of Rome. The first is an exposition of these predictions, and the second a balanced criticism of them.

The final article presents a series of predictions which are, on the whole, quite optimistic.

The author of the following article foresees that the most successful firms of the future will be super-giant multinational companies, each employing perhaps as many as a million people worldwide. Not all today's giant firms, he believes, will turn into super-giant firms in the future; perhaps there will be 300 of these enormous multinational organizations. He goes on to explain the factors that will determine which of today's big companies will make the list and which will fall by the wayside.

What becomes of the medium-sized firm and the small firm in the world of the super-giants? The author believes the small firm, because of its great flexibility, will find the going easier than the firm that has reached medium size.

Dr. Perlmutter is professor of industry at the Wharton School, University of Pennsylvania.

Super-giant Firms in the Future

Howard V. Perlmutter

In my discussions with political and business leaders over the past six years, I have found surprising agreement that we are moving towards a world of very large multinational firms and very small entrepreneurial firms of the "one man show" variety. The fate of the middle-size firm seems less secure. The small firm can engage in guerrilla action, gain all the advantages of smallness—speed of decision making, closeness to customer needs. The middle-sized firms find it hard to get the human and financial resources, the geographical and product scope to function as worldwide entities. They are targets for takeovers—with the large firm as a suitor promising worldwide markets for its products.

I agree with this vision of the future. But since the prediction applies to the class of the institution called international, and not to any specific firm in existence today, it is perhaps more interesting to consider how the large firms will survive until 1985.

According to *Fortune*, there are already more than 100 U.S. firms, each doing more than $600 million worth of sales, who have overseas interests. There are at least 70 or more non-U.S. firms doing a similar volume of business. But when we consider the firms of the future—of 1985—it is clear we are talking about giants, or perhaps super-giants.

Accounting for unforeseen technological breakthroughs and managerial attrition, I come out with the round number of 300 giant firms. There may be 200 or 400—but I maintain they will be distinctive because their size will place them in a separable class—with unique opportunities and problems.

Double Three Times

Many executives I know are planning to double sales every seven years. By 1985 their firms will have doubled three times. This means that the firms doing $600 million or more sales, now on *Fortune*'s list, will be doing from $5 billion to $160 billion worth of sales, the latter being General Motors' sales of 1985!

Even considering that the number of employees does not grow at the same rate, the million-man firm should not be unusual. Clearly, the 300 of 1985 will be super-giants in size and power.

There are good reasons why such firms will emerge:

1 Super-giant international firms will find it easier to get capital.
2 Super-giant international firms will be able to diversify, replace obsolescent products rapidly, and still maintain worldwide production and distribution of all their products in both developing and developed countries. They will be seen as reliable and trustworthy on the global scale.
3 Super-giant international firms can maintain a high level of research in such advanced areas as energy, food and space technology, data processing, aircraft, electronics.
4 Such firms have the wherewithal to acquire the middle-size national or regional firms

and offer them worldwide markets for their products, whereas the middle-size firm simply could not afford to build up a manufacturing and marketing function world wide.

5 Finally, the super-giant firms can afford to hire the best specialists and managers in the world to carry out the worldwide line and staff functions in marketing and manufacturing, in research and development, in personnel, in legal matters, and in finance.

Countervailing Forces

The second set of reasons for the emergence of the multinational super-giant comes from the absence of effective countervailing forces in the world community.

Consumers are at best unorganized. Trade unions, I am assured by union leaders, have enough difficulty at the national level managing and representing their constituents; it is hard to see how trade union organizations at the world level will for a long time constitute a serious obstacle.

The most likely candidate to act as a countervailing force for the super-giants is the sovereign state. The weapons a nation state can muster have seemed formidable: outright nationalization, restriction of the importation of machinery and parts, price controls, limitation of remittances to foreign parent companies, legal guidance for labor policy, demands on the firm to export and to conduct research within its borders.

But I submit that any given nation state, acting alone, has limited bargaining power. When what is called "the investment climate" is considered unattractive by many firms, due to repeated threats from government, it is always possible to suggest subtly and diplomatically that other countries would seem to be better places to invest. This has had a sobering effect on the more extremist national political leaders. Nations are, after all, competing with other nations to attract human and material resources that meet worldwide standards.

The super-giant firms which survive in 1985 will be those that will have found a partnership rather than a collision course, with a large number of, if not most, host sovereign states. But there will be, as a political leader put it to me recently, "a reshaping of the functions of the nation state and the firm."

Who will be around in 1985 will depend on the effectiveness with which individual firms overcome external and internal obstacles to long-term profitability, market share and survival objectives.

In my research with companies that are candidates for the 300 list, I asked senior executives to diagnose what they felt were the key driving and restraining forces, inside and outside the firms, which would account for their survival, growth and development as a world company. I found that these executives from international companies agreed concerning high-priority items.

External Obstacles

Senior executives of large international firms said the key external obstacles, outside their firm's direct control, stemmed from two sources: the home country and the host country.

Home-country executives feel the obligation to show loyalty to the interests of the home country—as for instance when U.S.-owned firms are asked that investment overseas be limited for U.S. balance-of-payments reasons. These executives find that home-country political leaders frequently fail to understand the nature and dynamism of the multinational firm. They predict more trouble in this area for U.S.-based firms.

Another key external obstacle stems from host countries that want more than a firm feels it can afford—such as insisting on local manufacture when assembly would be more desirable from the viewpoint of cost. In the worst situation, it is considered that local political leaders' distrust of the international firm is in itself a key obstacle to the firm's survival and growth. International executives who are nationals of the host country may be thought of as having "sold their souls" to the foreigners.

The U.S.-based multinational firm is usually seen by host-country political leaders as responding to U.S. political and economic interests. Europe-based multinational firms are seen as more astute in dealing with these political obstacles. (Swiss and Anglo-Dutch firms are willing to fly the local flag where necessary, or the Swiss, British or Dutch flag where necessary.) This barrier to growth is real.

Other external obstacles are: (a) the lack of an effective international monetary system, (b) the disparity between rich and poor countries with its explosive political implications. For individual firms, these obstacles are not easy to overcome.

External forces driving towards the growth of international firms which the executives most frequently cited were:

a Technological and managerial knowhow being made available in different countries;
b Demands of both international and local customers for the best product at the most reasonable price;
c Host country desire to improve its balance-of-payments;
d Finally, a general stimulus from the global competition among international firms for the human resources needed for survival and growth.

The firms which will grow to be around in 1985 are those which can influence the restraining forces and build on the driving forces in the external environment.

Internal Obstacles

The senior executives whom I interviewed also identified internal obstacles to the long-term objectives of survival, growth, and profitability. Since there was a general consensus that a firm must have an international character, the obstacles cited are in part those which impede a given firm from becoming more genuinely international.

The following factors were cited most frequently by senior executives from both Europe-based and U.S.-based firms:

a Mutual distrust between home-country people and foreign executives within the firm.
b Resistance to letting foreigners into the power structure at headquarters, in key positions and on the parent board.
c Nationalistic tendencies among staff overseas and at home.
d Immobility of good executives. Many excellent men prefer to stay where they live—in Basle or Boston, Paris or Brussels—as executives of affiliates.
e Problems of communication, aggravated when people do not speak the same language and have different cultural backgrounds.

The key forces driving toward long-term survival and growth are identified as follows:

a Top management's desire to utilize human resources optimally, and not let national biases lead to waste of good ideas, products, and men.
b Recognition that morale is lower when a company has first-class (home-country) citizens and second-class citizens—the overseas people, or the foreigners.
c Increasing awareness and respect of good men of other than home nationality.
d Plan for risk diversification through worldwide production and distribution systems.
e Aim to recruit good men on a worldwide basis, not just from the home country.
f Building a worldwide information system, manned by high-quality people who know local markets and are international in outlook.
g Proposing to develop products and services with worldwide appeal.
h Finally (and the factor mentioned most frequently), top management's commitment to building a truly international firm, measured in deeds, not in words.

If top management seems more comfortable investing at home, or seems to prefer working with home-country nationals only, or if the company's products are designed for home markets only, and resources are not assigned to adapt production to world markets, then there are strong doubts that the firm really seeks a world niche and will be around in 1985.

Key Factors Are Human

Thus, the key factors determining which firms will be around in 1985 are human. Survival depends on attitudes and skills in working effectively with people of other nations. The executives in my survey identified also attitudes which, if allowed to be translated into action, would make it less likely that their firm survive, grow and reach profitability objectives through 1985. These "negative" attitudes may exist at headquarters as well as in subsidiaries.

The first type of negative attitude I have distinguished as "ethnocentrism." The executives whom I interviewed tried to estimate the costs, risks and payoffs of ethnocentrism. The risks of ethnocentrism over the long term, they said, are:

1 A subtle resistance to all ideas from headquarters.
2 A suspicion of the motives of headquarters executives of home-country nationality.
3 Inadequate information flowing to the Center, leading to costly mistakes due to poor planning.
4 Loss of good men of local nationalities who leave the firm, feeling they do not have a chance for promotion.
5 Lack of acceptance of the parent firm by political leaders in the different local environments.

The international firm needs at the country level managers who feel they are part of a worldwide team whose good ideas, techniques, and men can be a success anywhere in the world. The distinctive competence of the international firm is thus its capacity to optimize the use of human and non-human resources on a worldwide basis.

The more I consider the problem of growth and survival of the international firm, the more it becomes clear that some systematic approach to assuring one's presence in 1985 is required. Strategic thinking and long-range planning are by now recognized as necessary by most large firms. Many chief executives are going through the exercise of trying to identify their long-term competitive ability, and to envisage what niche in the world market they want to occupy.

Capacities for Survival

Many are planning to survive to 1985 through product innovation, resource allocation of men and money, establishment of pricing levels, and meeting of performance levels and growth rates. This is hard enough in a world of rapid change. But I believe that to be alive in 1985, the international firm needs to identify now what distinctive capacities it will require, so that it can improve and develop them as widely as possible in the organization starting now.

This involves a development program with three- to five-year objectives directly related to improving:

1 The capacity to work with host and home political leaders of the right, center, and left, as well as with the more permanent civil servants, with a view to defining how a partnership course can be achieved between the particular international firm and each nation state. The best men are needed for this task.
2 The capacity to acquire and effectively integrate smaller and medium-size companies in countries other than one's home base, and to energize them to function effectively as a productive part of a worldwide enterprise.
3 The capacity to develop men for international service means that the firms of 1985 will have designed challenging international careers, both attractive and humanly possible, given the problems of moving men and their families at different stages in life.
4 The capacity to commit to worldwide objectives personnel at headquarters, at the regional level, and in the subsidiaries, with either product or functional responsibilities. For this, a geocentrization process is required at all levels.

I believe that some kind of organizational and management development institution is needed in the firms which will survive—to develop executives inside the company, from all over the world. The experience of working together, of knowing other persons from different countries, makes a positive contribution not only to effectiveness at work but also to the creation of the international spirit. This will be a strength of the international company of the future, as it already is one of Philips, Nestle, Unilever, IBM, Royal Dutch Shell, and many others.

The international firm of the future will need to organize for the maintenance of this spirit as it becomes larger and larger, and as more product divisions are formed. Internal organizational and management development institutions are one instrument to achieve these ends.

5 The capacity to stay in direct contact with the users of company products and services everywhere in the world, and thus to know in which way each user's needs are distinctive, or similar, in each market.

Trust within Firm

The sixth capacity, while more vague, is the most fundamental: it is to build trust and confidence among managers and experts of different nations, inside the firm.

Chauvinism at the European or the U.S. level will be too costly for the firms of 1985. In order to be worldwide, and in order to have a significant share of all world markets, it will be necessary to have men and organizations in all the areas of the world. We will need not an ethnocentric but a geocentric, or world oriented, view at headquarters and in the subsidiaries.

It may, however, seem like a useful transition for some of the more home-bound European firms to develop first into large national and real Europe-wide firms. I feel that time is against a strategy of building a company geared only for the European market, if it means avoiding change and the necessity of meeting worldwide standards, including those prevailing in the United States.

I see no other route than beginning now to build international companies, not companies based on U.S. or European domination of key positions.

This means that the multinational firms of the future should include Japanese international companies as such, not as satellites of a U.S. or European firm, nor as independent affiliates, nor as joint ventures with some holding company of a truly international firm, but as one part of an integrated, worldwide partnership.

I believe it is not an oversimplification to say that the key ingredient in building such firms is trust and mutual confidence among men of different nations, and acceptance of the distinctive contributions that they can make to a worldwide firm. This may not be easy for this generation of industrial leaders in Japan, Europe and the United States. But for the next generation it will be indispensable. I believe that executives can learn how to build confidence and trust by profiting from their errors, rather than explaining them away with such stereotypes as "you can't work with Brazilians," or French, or Italians, and so forth.

Organizing Experts

The major strength of the international firm of 1985 will be its capacity to organize management and experts of different nationalities. The final list of super-giants in 1985 will include those firms whose management has overcome the negative attitudes towards foreigners, both at headquarters and in the subsidiaries.

The man, not his passport, should be the basis for promotion.

In summary, the firm that works at building up these six capacities and competences is more likely to be around in 1985.

During the past five years, I have spoken to several thousand businessmen and a small number of political leaders about this vision of the future: Super-giant multinational firms and the small fast fishes. The reaction of both political leaders and businessmen has often been one of fear.

The dangers associated with such great concentration of power in such few hands cause concern to most. With such power, they say, comes the temptation to abuse customers and citizens, to fix prices worldwide, to collude to the detriment of a given nation state, to make it difficult for an executive considered incompetent by one to find work anywhere among the other super-giants.

What guarantees are there that the key executives of the 300 geocentric super-giants will show a social responsibility to the world community of consumers and citizens?

Need for Rules

There are no easy answers here, but I feel there is a need for rules and laws at the world level. By 1985, such laws will become more and more indispensable because the quality of life of the world's citizens, and their survival, cannot be made to depend on the policies of international firms.

The nation state will not wither away. There is

a positive role for the nation state in the second half of the Twentieth Century. It should be worked out in partnership with national political and business leaders, not bilaterally but multilaterally, in an atmosphere of mutual confidence and trust. There is a key role for the United Nations in this endeavor.

I believe there is agreement among enlightened political and business leaders that the moral basis for the super-giant multinational firms must be considered. There is agreement that if the multinational firm becomes a constructive force for peace in the world community it will be desirable, and indispensable, because it can potentially achieve what no other nation-centered firm could.

It is possible that the international firm can be part of an economic community on the world level, including East and West, North and South, a community in which the bombing of suppliers, customers and employees of the same firm will not be found desirable, or permitted. Since the super-giant firms will be represented in all countries, war will not be possible. Thus, the genuinely international or geocentric firm would become one of the most extraordinary institutions of the second half of the Twentieth Century.

I do not believe that this eventuality will occur unless the leaders of this kind of firm take seriously the thought that it is part of their mission to work at building a business with men of caliber whose values and aspirations make them positive contributors to the world society that is so slow to evolve.

To a degree, leaders of multinational business will need to be what Gaston Berger called "philosophers in action." To justify the existence of the super-giants, we will need to relate their existence to man's fundamental aspirations and values of peace and prosperity. Etienne Gilson said:

> The throes of the contemporary world are those of a birth. And what is being born with such great pain is a universal human society . . . what characterizes the events we witness, what distinguishes them from all preceding events back to the origins of history is their global character. . . .

I believe we are beginning to witness a struggle within our old institutions to develop men and resources for this next stage of human evolution. The business firm, along with the Church, the University, and the Nation State, is seeking to find its place in the world to come. The right of each to survive will depend on the degree to which each taps the noble as well as the practical motives of man.

A few years ago, some startling predictions of a grim future were issued by the Club of Rome, an international group of businessmen, scientists, and educators. The predictions, derived from computerized studies, were embodied in a book, "The Limits to Growth," by Donella H. Meadows, Dennis L. Meadows, Jørgen Randers, and William W. Behrens III. In this article, two of the authors of that study outline the findings.

The Carrying Capacity of the Globe

Jørgen Randers and Donella Meadows

The main thesis of this paper is very simple. Because the global environment is finite, physical growth cannot continue indefinitely. In spite of its simplicity, the consequences of this fact pose an unprecedented challenge to mankind. The challenge lies in deciding the ethical basis for making the trade-offs which will confront us in the near future—trade-offs which will arise because society cannot maximize everything for everybody.

The Finite Environment

It should be quite unnecessary to point out that our environment is finite. However, most considerations of the world's future lose sight of this

From the SLOAN MANAGEMENT REVIEW, Winter, 1972, pp. 11–27.

fact. Thus, it will be worthwhile to spend some time discussing the physical limitations of the earth—especially because it is not generally recognized that we are already quite close to several of the physical limitations which define the carrying capacity of the globe.

Agricultural land. The quantity most obviously in completely inelastic supply is land. There are about 3.2 billion hectares of land suitable for agriculture on the earth, approximately half of which are under cultivation today. The remaining half will require immense capital costs to settle, clear, irrigate, or fertilize before food can be produced.

If the decision is made to incur the costs, to cultivate all possible arable land, and to produce as much food as possible, how many people can be fed? The lower curve in Figure 1 shows the amount of land *needed* to feed the growing world population, assuming that the present average of 0.4 hectares per person is sufficient. (To feed the world's 3.6 billion people at U.S. standards, 0.9 hectares per person would be required.) The actual growth in population from 1650 to 1970 is depicted by the heavier segment of that curve; the projected growth at 2.1 percent per year after 1970 by the lighter segment. The upper curve indicates the actual amount of arable land available. This line slopes downward because each additional person requires a certain amount of land (0.08 hectares assumed here) for housing, roads, waste disposal, power lines, and other uses which essentially "pave" land and make it unusable for farming.

The graph in Figure 1 shows that, even with the optimistic assumption that all possible land is utilized, global society will still face a desperate land shortage before the year 2000.

The graph also illustrates some important facts about exponential growth within a limited space. First, it shows how one can move within a few years from a situation of great abundance to one of great scarcity. The human race has had an overwhelming excess of arable land for all of its history, but within 40 years, or one doubling of the world's population, we will be forced to deal with a sudden and serious shortage.

A second lesson to be learned from Figure 1 is that the exact numerical assumptions made about the limits of the earth are essentially

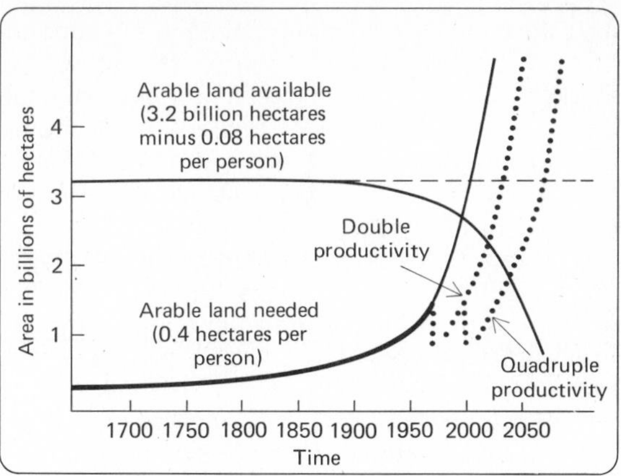

Figure 1 Available and needed land area.

unimportant. This is due to the curious nature of exponential growth. We might assume, for example, that *no* arable land is taken for cities, roads, or other non-agricultural uses. In that case, the land available is constant, as shown by the horizontal dashed line, and the point at which the two curves cross is delayed by only about 10 years. Alternately, we can suppose that the productivity of the land will be doubled, or even quadrupled, through advances in agricultural technology. The effect of increasing productivity is shown by the dotted lines in Figure 1. Each doubling of productivity gains just one population doubling time, or about 40 years.

Some people look to the sea to provide the extra requirement; but the total world fish catch in 1969 represented only a few percent of the world's protein, and the total catch in 1970 decreased from 1969. Most experts agree that the world's fish banks have been overfished and that prospects are for further decline, rather than advances, in protein output.

Heat release. There are further constraints in connection with natural resources like fresh water, metals, and fuels. Indications are that several of these resources will be in short supply within the next 40 years if the present rate of growth continues. It can be argued that the mining of low grade ores and the desalting of the seas' waters can alleviate these problems, and this may indeed be so, assuming that it is possible to satisfy the concurrent enormous demands for energy.

A consideration of the energy that will be necessary to meet man's growing needs leads us to contemplate a more subtle and much more fundamental physical limitation imposed by the environment. Assuming the means are found to *generate* the energy needed, the fundamental thermodynamic fact remains that all energy generated finally ends up as heat.

This heat released from the energy expended should not be confused with what is commonly called *thermal pollution*—the waste heat produced at a power plant in the generation of electric energy. This *thermal pollution*, of course, does heat the environment, but the point to be emphasized is that even the *useful* energy output from the plant ultimately adds heat to the environment. No technical gadgetry or scientific breakthrough will circumvent this result.

If the energy consumption increases at four percent per year for another 130 years, heat amounting to one percent of the incoming solar radiation—enough to increase the temperature of the atmosphere by an estimated $^3/_4$°C—will be released. This increase in temperature may sound unimpressive, but on a worldwide basis it could lead to such climatic upheavals as the increased melting of the polar ice caps. Local imbalances may come much sooner. It is estimated that in 30 years the Los Angeles Basin alone will be releasing 18 percent of the normal incident solar energy in that area.

Pollution absorption. A third limitation is the globe's finite capacity to absorb pollution. After the death of Lake Erie, the global increase in atmospheric CO_2, and the discovery of high levels of mercury in swordfish, it is abundantly clear that the environment is only able to absorb and degrade a limited amount of emissions and waste each year. When this absorptive capacity is exceeded, pollutants accumulate in nature and the risk is run of completely destroying the natural degradation processes themselves. Discharging a little bit of waste into a pond will only slightly lower the water quality because microorganisms are able to degrade the pollution as it occurs. If the absorptive capacity of the pond is exceeded by the rate of discharge, however, the lake becomes unable to clear itself and dies. When this occurs, the continued discharge of waste into the pond will simply accumulate, and the quality of the water will progressively decline.

The Present Global Trend: Growth

Having established the existence of the physical limitations of our earth, we must ask whether man's present behavior acknowledges their existence.

On a global scale, population and "capital"—buildings, roads, cars, power plants, machinery, ships, etc.—are growing exponentially. Some inevitable consequences of this growth are exponentially increasing demands for food and energy and also exponentially increasing emissions of pollution. Since we know that there exist upper limits to the supply of food and energy and also to the amount of pollution which can be absorbed by the environment, it seems obvious that the present growth rate cannot continue indefinitely. Are there mechanisms in the world system as it is currently organized which will cause a smooth shift from present growth trends to some acceptable behavior consistent with the world's finite capabilities? Or is disaster imminent? These are the questions a group of us researchers at MIT have tried to answer through the construction of a mathematical simulation model of population and capital growth in the world system.[1]

The world model. The model is a set of assumptions which describe the interaction of the world's population, industry, pollution, agriculture and natural resources. The model explicitly represents the forces of growth as a function of the biological, political, economic, physical, and social factors which influence them. A brief description of the main ideas which underlie our model and which, it can be hypothesized, underlie the world system, follows.

Population and birth constitute a positive feedback loop; more people produce more births and more births result in more people. Wherever there is a dominant positive feedback loop of this form, exponential growth will occur. A similar relationship exists between capital and investment. Capital produces output. Greater output, all else equal, results in greater invest-

[1]See Meadows [3].

ment and this generates more capital. Thus, capital and investment constitute another positive feedback loop. The interactions between population and capital determine the rate at which each of them grows.

As a greater fraction of output is diverted from investment, the growth rate of capital decreases. Output may be diverted to consumption, to services, or to agricultural capital. As services increase, health and education improve, average lifetime becomes greater, deaths decrease, and population grows. Similarly, output may be diverted into agricultural capital which results ultimately in more food and a higher average lifetime. The primary determinant of the fraction of output reinvested is the output per capita. Where production per capita is low, most of the output must be diverted to consumption, services, and food. Those allocations reduce the rate of accumulation of the capital base and, at the same time, stimulate the growth of population. In this scheme, output diverted into consumption subtracts capital from the system and does not generate future growth directly. Industrial output also leads to the depletion of natural resources. As natural resources decline in relation to capital, the efficiency of capital decreases and the output-capital ratio is also reduced.

Output per capita is the single positive force acting to slow the population explosion. As output per capita increases the desired family size declines, the birth rate goes down, and population growth typically decreases. This influence is accelerated somewhat by the fact that as death rates decline there is a further decrease in desired family size. A large portion of the world's parents bear children primarily as a source of support in old age. If there is a high mortality rate, one must bear three or four sons to insure that one will live. Thus, as the perceived death rate decreases, birth rates also decline. Output has one additional impact—it leads to the generation of pollution. Pollution decreases the food supply, and also decreases the average lifetime. Most global problems have roots in this simple set of interactions.

This qualitative description of the world system has been elaborated and formalized into a DYNAMO computer model.[2] There are four advantages to collecting our assumptions about the world into a formal model. First, by listing the assumed interrelations explicitly, they are made readily available for criticism and improvement by those with specific knowledge in each problem area. Second, with the aid of a computer, it is possible to investigate how this formalized system will behave over a period of time. Third, it is also possible through such simulation to test the effect of a change in the basic assumptions, and hence one may investigate which interrelations are critical (and deserve close scrutiny) and which are not. Fourth, the model permits one to study the effects of policies he believes may improve the behavior of the system.

The inevitable collapse. Simulation runs lead one to conclude that there are no mechanisms currently known which will bring the present growth to a smooth and orderly end. This does not mean, of course, that growth will not stop. It only means that, instead of an orderly transition to some feasible state, growth will overshoot the earth's physical limitations and then be forced back to a level the environment can support. Once a particular constraint is exceeded, tremendous pressures will develop to halt growth. If the earth's absorptive capacity for pollution is exceeded, for example, the pressures will take the form of radical increases in death rates due to impurities in food, water and air, decreases in crops and fish catches due to similar reductions in plant and animal life, and a significant reduction in the effectiveness of investment due to high costs of controlling the pollution in the resources used for production. These pressures will mount until population and industrialization start to decline, and the pressure will cease only when acceptable lower levels are reached. It is like the explosion of an algae population in a nutritious medium: the growth only stops when the algae are poisoned by their own wastes. Equally important, when this occurs the popula-

[2]Further information about our modelling effort can be obtained from the System Dynamics Program Office, A.P. Sloan School of Management, E40-214, MIT, Cambridge, Mass., 02139, U.S.A. For a similar study, see [2].

tion not only stops growing but enters a precipitous decline.

If an attempt is made to continue growth by removing one set of pressures—for instance, by increasing the food output through high-yield grains—the situation is alleviated only until the next constraint is encountered. The single solution for growth in a finite space is an end to growth.

The Ethical Basis for Action

The continuation of current growth practices will inevitably lead to some sort of collapse, with a subsequent decrease in the cultural and economic options of the human race. The natural question to ask is: what shall we do?

It is important to realize that an answer to this question is completely dependent on the choice of criteria for what is "good." If the objective is to maximize the benefits of the people alive today, the course of action will be quite different than if the goal is to maximize the benefits of all people who are going to live on this planet over the next 200 years.

At least in principle, present human behavior is guided by the general idea that all people alive *today* are equally important, and that the objective function is to maximize the total current benefits for all of these people. The Western democracies seek to reach this objective by giving each individual freedom to pursue his own interest. It is assumed, very simply, that if every citizen and institution in society acts to maximize his own position in the short term, the society as a whole will benefit.

This acceptance of "the invisible hand" has, however, introduced a strong emphasis on short-term benefits. When an action will bring both benefits and costs over time, individuals use the concept of net present value and discount the future implications so that they can determine whether an action is profitable—and hence should be taken. The result of this procedure is essentially that a value of zero is assigned to anything happening more than twenty years in the future. In other words, actions are taken even though their cost to society twenty years hence will be enormous—simply because the benefits are larger than the costs in the short run.

If we choose to adhere strictly to the objective of maximizing the short-term rewards of the present generation, there are in fact no long-term trade-offs to be made. In this case we would simply continue as before, maximizing the current benefits and neglecting any future costs which are incurred.

It is only this short-term objective function which can lead to the currently accepted conclusion that the value of an additional human being is infinite. The severe restrictions his existence will impose on the choices and perhaps even the lives of future generations—because of his consumption of non-renewable natural resources and his contribution to the destruction of the life support system of the globe—is completely neglected.

Adherence to the short-term objective function easily resolves all trade-offs between current benefits and future cost. Of course, trade-offs among people alive today must be dealt with but these short-term conflicts are not relevant to our discussion; mechanisms *exist* in society to resolve conflicts between two people alive today. Society does *not* have, however, mechanisms, or even moral guidelines, for resolving conflicts between the current population and future generations. Our simulation model demonstrates that the present preoccupation with what seems pleasant or profitable in the short run fuels the growth which will eventually overshoot some physical constraint, and will force us—and especially our descendants—to radically alter our life-styles.

The long-term objective function. It is possible, however, to change the objective function. We could adopt as our cardinal philosophy the rule that no man or institution in society may take any action which decreases the economic and social options of those who will live on the planet over the next 100 years.

The leaders of global society should adopt the goal of increasing the time-horizon implicit in mankind's activities. That is, they should introduce the longer-term objective function which maximizes the benefit of those living today, yet does not decrease the economic and social options of the generations which will follow.

Global Equilibrium— A Desirable Possibility

Assuming that the long-term objective function is accepted, what can be done about the approaching collision between exponential growth and the earth's physical constraints?

Once society has committed itself to the creation of a long-term, viable world system, the most important task becomes to avoid approaching any of the globe's physical limitations—such as food production capability, pollution absorption capacity or resource supply. This can only be done through a deliberate decision to stop physical growth. A smooth transition must be engineered to a non-growth equilibrium. This can be done by developing and employing legal, economic and social pressures as substitutes for the more disruptive pressures which would otherwise be exerted by nature to halt physical growth.

By starting now we may still be able to choose the set of forces we prefer to employ to stop population and capital growth. A deliberate choice of the least objectionable counterforces is more likely to leave intact many of our fundamental long-term objectives than is the blind and random action of natural forces like starvation or social breakdown.

The first requirement for a viable steady state is a constant level of population and capital. A second requirement is equally important: the state of global equilibrium must be characterized by minimal consumption of non-renewable materials and by minimal emissions of non-degradable waste. This will enable society to maximize the time available before resources are depleted and to avoid a critical load on the environment. One possible way of achieving such a global equilibrium is by stabilizing population in 1980 and industrial capital in 1990. In addition, a societal value change allocates more of industrial output to services and food, and slightly less to material goods. Material goods reach a relatively high level, however, through better product design which allows a longer useful lifetime for each product. Equilibrium population is four billion and GNP per capita is about twice the present world average. Many different possible paths to equilibrium do exist, however, and the choice depends upon society's objectives. For instance: do we want many people living at a low material standard, or few at a higher? Do we want fancy food, or a minimum daily ration of calories, protein, and vitamins?

In this equilibrium state of human civilization, science and technology will be busily developing ways of constructing products which do not emit pollution, and can be easily recycled. Competition among individual firms may very well continue, but the total market for material goods will no longer expand. Labor will concentrate on repair and maintenance rather than on new production. Although equilibrium implies the cessation of *physical* growth, this will not be the case for *cultural* development. Freed from preoccupation with material goods, people may throw their energy into the arts and sciences, into the enjoyment of unspoiled nature, and into deepening relationships with their fellow man.

The distribution of wealth and responsibility. Though stopping the population explosion is becoming an increasingly acceptable social goal, what about stopping economic growth? Would not restrictions on production permanently condemn the world's poor to their present state of misery? It is important to realize that this is not at all what is being suggested. The cessation of *overall* growth does not preclude redistribution of the world's existing wealth. In practice, this might mean that the developed world deliberately stops its growth and possibly even lets itself "shrink" somewhat, while the developing world is allowed (and perhaps helped) to grow to an acceptable economic level. Initially it will be up to the developed world to take the lead down the path towards equilibrium though the less industrialized societies will have serious responsibilities in attempting to curb their burgeoning populations.

One might contend that we should continue to maximize economic growth, simply because we are still so *very* far from achieving a utopia where everything is plentiful for everyone. Before making a choice to this end, one should recall, however, that unless we choose the forces to stop population and capital growth, nature will make the choice for us. A continued reliance on short-term objectives and continued growth only makes it certain that there will be no acceptable future—for any country.

Economic growth in the past century has *not* resulted in increased equality among the world's people. To the contrary, growth simply continues to widen the gap between the rich and poor. An end to the overall growth, however, might very well lead to a more equitable distribution of wealth throughout the world.

The golden age. Only an orderly transition into an equilibrium state will prevent the tumult of an environmental crisis and put the human race into harmony with the world's ecosystem. An equilibrium could permit the development of an unprecedented golden age for humanity. Freedom from ever-increasing numbers of people will make it possible to put substantial effort into the self-realization and development of the individual. Energy could be employed to develop the human culture. The few periods of equilibrium in the past, such as the 300 years of Japan's classical period, often witnessed a profound flowering of the arts.

The freedom from ever-increasing capital—i.e., from more concrete, cars, dams and skyscrapers—would make it possible for all future generations to enjoy solitude and silence.

This, then, is the state of global equilibrium, which seems to be the logical consequence of the adoption of the long-term objective function. The changes needed during transition from growth to equilibrium are tremendous, and the time available is very short. The results seem worth striving for, and the first step—the lengthening of our time horizon—is one in which all men must play a part.

References

1 Daly, H.E. "Towards a Stationary-State Economy." In: J. Harte and R. Socolow (eds.), *The Patient Earth.* Holt, Rinehardt an d Winston, 1971.

2 Forrester, J.W. *World Dynamics.* Cambridge, Mass., Wright-Allen Press, 1971.

3 Meadows, D., *et al. The Limits to Growth.* Universe Books (forthcoming).

The computer programs that were used in evolving the thesis of "The Limits to Growth" were developed by Jay W. Forrester, and his book *World Dynamics* presents practically the same conclusions. These conclusions have not, of course, gone unchallenged—and attempts have been made to refute them, some temperate, some harsh. The article below is one of the more temperate ones, for the author accepts the fact that the earth is finite and the limits will probably come some day, but he doubts that it is quite so imminent as the preceding article makes it appear. Kenneth Boulding, formerly president of the American Economic Association, is director of research on general social and economic dynamics at the University of Colorado and the author of a number of books.

The Wolf of Rome

Kenneth E. Boulding

World Dynamics by Jay W. Forrester (Wright-Allen Press, Cambridge, Mass.) is probably the first prophetic work which has emerged from man-computer interaction, and the gloom of its prophecy rivals that of Jeremiah. These are prophecies and not forecasts—that is, they represent the general shape of things to come rather than specific quantitative predictions. The

From *Business and Society Review*, Summer, 1972, pp. 106–109.

numbers are merely the food of the digital computer; it is the shapes that are significant. The general message is clear. Exponential growth cannot go on for very long and we are perilously close to its limits, in regard to population, capital stocks, and pollution. Man is expanding, furthermore, not only into the finite niche of the earth, but also into a diminishing heritage as he uses up irreplaceable natural resources. On almost any assumption that we are likely to make, we are living in a golden age. The very best that could be hoped for is a slow decline into a stationary state with levels of living and quality of life considerably below what they are now. Even this, the most optimistic outcome, seems to be rather unlikely. The most probable outcome seems to be some sort of overshooting of the final equilibirum in population, pollution, capital stocks, and so on, with consequent declines which may easily be catastrophic. With a wide range of reasonable assumptions, doomsday arrives somewhere in the middle of the twenty-first century, either in terms of starvation, overcrowding with its implied disorder, or pollution.

The basic model is a very simple one, yet it underlies a great many dynamic systems. It might be called the "bathtub model," as this is one of the simplest and most familiar descriptions of it. Its fundamental equation is what many years ago I called the "bathtub theorem." It is that the increase of any stock or population in a given period of time is equal to the number (or quantity) of additions to the stock less the number (or quantity) of subtractions from it. The increase in the amount of water in the bathtub in any period is equal to the amount of water that has come in minus the amount of water that has gone out. An equilibrium is where the total stock, that is, the amount of water in the bathtub, is constant, and where the amount coming in is equal to the amount going out. If an equilibrium is to be maintained, there must be some kind of homeostatic or cybernetic apparatus to relate the amount in the bathtub to the flows in and out, so that if the amount of water in the bathtub is rising, beyond a certain point the inflow will be reduced and the outflow will be increased. If it is falling, the inflow should be increased and the outflow reduced. In any system of this kind, there will be some amount of stock at which the inflow and outflow will be equal. We see a mechanism like this operating, for instance, in classical price theory. For any commodity, such as wheat, a rise of the stock will lower the price, the lower the price the more will be consumed per unit of time (that is what we mean by demand) and the less will be produced per unit of time (that is what we mean by supply), and therefore there must be some stock, implying some price, at which production and consumption are equal and the stock remains constant.

The price-commodity bathtub is one that is not included in the Forrester system, which perhaps is one of its weaknesses. Nevertheless, there are five or six other factors, and the system can be regarded as a set of interconnected bathtubs. Perhaps the first and the most important of these is the human population, the increase in which is equal to the number of births in a given period minus the number of deaths. The number of births is equal to what demographers call the crude birthrate (Forrester's terminology is a little different) multiplied by the population itself; and the number of deaths, likewise, is equal to the crude death rate multiplied by the population itself. When the population is regulated, it is because the total population is closely related to other things which in turn determine the birth and death rates. In any system where the population is below the equilibrium level, it will rise until its rise is checked by rising death rates, or falling birthrates, or both. In equilibrium, the population is stable and the birthrate equals the death rate.

The other bathtubs in the Forrester system are what he calls "capital investment," that is, the total capital stock (here again, his terminology differs somewhat from standard economic terminology). The capital stock is a population of capital; it is added to by new capital goods produced and diminished by depreciation and the wearing out of old capital goods. The next bathtub is "natural resources," which has the peculiarity of having a drain and no faucet. In the light of the fact that we have been producing *known* natural resources faster than we have been using them up for at least 200 years, this is a little odd. It can be justified, perhaps, if we assume that natural resources are defined as the total potential of the earth, in the shape of fossil fuels, ores, and useful deposits of all kinds. This, of course, must continually be diminishing. Available natural resources at any one time, however, are a function of human knowledge, and as we cannot predict future knowledge—otherwise we would have it now—we cannot predict the future of known resources. This perhaps is the weakest link, at least in Forrester's short-run chain.

Because of the peculiar importance of the food supply, Forrester divides the capital stock into two parts: that which is devoted to agriculture and that which is not. The capital stock here also includes available land, which perhaps one might wish to put in natural resources. Then the final and perhaps most interesting bathtub is "pollution." This is the total capital stock of "bads," that is, things which are not wanted and which are harmful to human life. Pollution is something like capital stock, in the sense that it also diminishes constantly through time, through "appreciation" rather than "depreciation." Thus, pollution has a kind of half-life, and if left to itself will decline. If, however, it is added to faster than it is declining, the total quantity will increase.

These various bathtubs are connected by a complex system of assumed functional relationships. None of these are based on any very solid empirical study; they are all based on what might be called "plausible topology," a method with a long, honorable, and occasionally disastrous history in economics. There is not even any pretense of deriving these functions from, say, an econometric analysis or something like it in past experience. The model, however, enables numerical values for all these variables for one year to be derived from the values of the prior year. That is, it depends essentially on a set of simultaneous differential equations of the first degree. The system is presumably too complex to be solved by explicit mathematical analysis, and it is the virtue of the computer, of course, that it can "solve" these equations in terms of the production of the time series of all the variables which the model includes. The end result has been called rather unkindly the "computer spaghetti," graphs in which time is measured horizontally and the variables of the model are plotted vertically in a series of interwoven wavy lines. The great virtue of the computer, which derives simply from its rapidity, is that it can produce a very large number of these spaghetti print-outs, so that the operator can test the sensitivity of the results of the system in response to changes in the various assumptions.

If, as Forrester indeed suggests, the general patterns of the system are relatively stable within a wide range of variation of the actual parameters and assumed functions, then we have discovered, as it were, a qualitative time-Gestalt. The fact that we have plucked the numbers which represent the parameters of the functions pretty much out of the air does not very much matter, for within a wide range any other set of numbers would do just as well. One can perhaps go even further and suppose that a system of this character can also investigate certain critical levels of its own parameters, at which qualitative changes begin to occur. A particularly dramatic example of this is in the pollution variable, where the assumption is made that the pollution absorption time (the reciprocal of the proportion of total pollution which disappears each year) increases in greater proportion to the pollution ratio itself. This assumption produces dramatic pollution crises in which at a certain level of pollution, even with a given rate of adding to it, the rate of getting rid of it declines rapidly, so the total quantity of pollution increases spectacularly. At a certain point in the filling of this particular bathtub, the drain gets plugged.

Both the strengths and the weaknesses of computer model analysis emerge very clearly in this volume. The major strength is its sheer deductive power. The principal alternative, which is explicit pencil-and-paper mathematical analysis, here proved relatively helpless in the analysis of very large systems. It simply breaks down under the information and memory load. The computer is a mathematical donkey; it may not soar off into the empyrean of elegant analytical solutions, but it plods to the top of the mountain by taking one thing at a time and cumulating the results. Also, it can present these results in the form of graphical print-out, or perhaps even better, graphs on a screen, which are a great aid to forming mental images of the total system.

The weakness of the computer is characterized by the famous "Gigo" principle: garbage in, garbage out. It is an admirable deduction machine; it is weak precisely in those elements in which the human nervous system is superior—induction, search, Gestalt formation, novelty, and so on. The unaided computer could never have produced this volume, and neither could the unaided human mind. It is the feedback of the computer results into the human knowledge structure which is really significant—not only into a single human mind but into the community of learners and specialists. That this feedback process has already begun is attested by the angry reviews which this volume has already produced. The social scientists are particularly outraged. This is something they should have done themselves and done better. It is shocking that a "mere" engineer who hasn't bothered much to learn the lingo of social sciences should have rigged the computer to produce these somewhat dubious offspring.

As a good member of the spurned tribe, I can endorse a lot of my colleagues' animadversions, and add a few of my own. The book has not paid its proper libations to the past. Apart from the computer simulation itself, there are really no new ideas in it. The essential concepts were stated by Malthus in 1798; the idea of an eventually stationary state goes back to Adam Smith, 1776; and almost the last word on it was said by John Stuart Mill in 1848. There was a hydraulic analog computer, believe it or not, called the "Moniac," literally almost floating around the economics profession in the late forties. (It leaked!) Electronic computer models began in the early fifties, and now have a long, if not wholly glorious, history. Professor Forrester, one is tempted to say, has invented a rather familiar old wheel. In economics we have known about counter-intuitive systems for a long time.

Two more serious criticisms are that the model neglects what is perhaps the most fundamental dynamic of the social system—the growth of knowledge. This is what has upset most mechanical predictions of the past, of which there have been a great many, and may likewise upset Professor Forrester's projections. Another criticism is that the resources of the computer are not really fully utilized, in the sense that the sensitivity of the system, which is its crucial point, is not adequately explored. One could very well visualize the development of functional relationships between the parametric assumptions in the system and its final results, perhaps expressed in tabular form.

When all the nasty things are said about this book, however, it will still not go away. It presents a challenge to the sensibility of mankind. Nobody I am sure will be more delighted than Professor Forrester if his apocalyptic model is proved wrong. It may well be that the computer is more important as a rhetoritician than as a scientist, but this function should not be underestimated. If this computer rhetoric of Professor Forrester could make the world look at realities that it would rather not look at, and if the more verbal rhetorics of those of us who have been saying the same thing fall on deaf ears, then it is worth the loss of a good deal of academic respectability to make people listen. Furthermore, the matter is urgent. Every day in which the message remains unheard makes some sort of twenty-first century apocalypse more likely. I do not blame Professor Forrester, therefore, for sacrificing some academic respectability by rushing into print, rather than circulating this document as a preprint for comment and criticism quietly among the academic profession. It may be better to be wrong and timely, than right and too late.

The ugly fact which will not go away is the fact of finitude. The earth is a bathtub and it is finite. We have been filling it for a very long time. All of a sudden, the fear strikes us that it may run over and make an ungodly mess. The situation is complicated by the fact that the size of the bathtub is not fixed, but is expansible, and indeed probably for the last hundred or two hundred years it has been expanding faster than we have been filling it. But this expansion cannot go on forever, and some time—one hundred, two hundred, five hundred years, certainly in historical time—the day of reckoning must come. I call the present version of this old apocalyptic vision the "wolf of Rome." People have been crying "wolf" a long time, and until now, the wolf has either been chased back into the forests or has merely bared his teeth here and there, as in Ireland in 1846. The fact that it is a real wolf makes it all the more important that we should cry "wolf" only when he is really there. This is perhaps the real danger of the "wolf of Rome." I suspect that he is really further back in the forest than he is in the mind of this particular Forrester. As an old wolf-cryer myself, I welcome Professor Forrester to the wolf-cryers club, which is both larger and more ancient than even the Club of Rome. This club, however, has only one rule—we should be awfully sure about the "wolf" that we are crying.

The author of the following article, a noted military analyst, is one of those who may be termed cautiously optimistic about the last part of the twentieth century. He foresees the possibility, even the probability, of a new era of stability in international affairs, and states that the highly industrialized countries of the present may actually enter a "new Augustan age." He acknowledges that the latter might present its own danger—i.e., overreaction against work and achievement-oriented values—but believes that this attitude will not become too widespread.

Uncertain Road to the 21st Century

Herman Kahn

There are many reasons for believing that the world of tomorrow, 10 or 20 years from now, will be much different from the one we know today.

For example, there is the possibility of arms control which could make the world substantially safer. On the other hand, there may be dangerous nuclear proliferation, a breakdown of current security arrangements, or widespread revolutionary unrest in the so-called Third World. More hopefully, the current détente might not only continue but it might develop into some kind of entente—and "agreement" or new unity—between East and West Europe, or between the United States and the Soviet Union, or all four groups.

At the same time, China might develop rapidly and rise to true great power status. Non-Communist governments in South or Southeast Asia might collapse. There might also be a breakdown of the current political system in India because of economic or communal strains. Or there could be a European Political Community or even a United States of Europe. In any case, there will almost inevitably be a continuation of the Sino-Soviet split, further reemergence of Europe as an independent force and a further erosion of the Cold War and the bipolar international system.

While not all of the above are as likely as many observers have urged, I would argue that the range of serious possibilities is larger than the examples suggest. Other possibilities include: a China which is stagnating or even in a state of collapse; new and probably assertive roles for West Germany and Japan. Widespread racist or quasi-religious wars or other "irrational" violence in the recently decolonized areas; a "neo-isolationist" withdrawal of the United States and/or the Soviet Union from their intense participation in world affairs; and the emergence of what could be called a post-industrial culture in the currently developed nations.

All of these are likely enough *to be* seriously considered. But first let's consider some other significant aspects of the present world which *are* taken for granted.

A Stable Era

Perhaps the most important is the growing belief by many in the United States, Europe and Japan that we are entering a period of relative stability, at least as far as wars threatening the homelands of the developed nations are concerned. The United States, of course, is currently engaged in a rather large war in Southeast Asia, but despite this it is much more difficult today to write a *plausible* scenario for escalation to an all-out war than it was 10 years ago.

In part, this is because of such important political changes as the revival in Europe and Japan of societies that are independent and vigorous (but not so much so that they create threats on their own). Large changes have also occurred in East Europe and in the Soviet Union which seem to diminish the Sino-Soviet threat. There has also been a better understanding on both sides of the Iron Curtain of the motives and objectives of the opponent. There is the relative lack of success of Communism in penetrating Africa and Latin America and even South and Southeast Asia; this political strength of the underdeveloped areas against Communism is often combined with a relative military weakness for offensive actions, which also, by and large, promotes stability. Finally, there have also been a number of technical developments and changes in strategic forces and doctrine which seem to have reduced sharply the possibility of both premeditated and accidental war.

Another stabilizing factor is the relatively small pressures toward territorial expansion in North and South America, in Europe, and by Japan and Russia in Asia. To a startling degree, these "old nations" seem more or less satisfied with their current boundaries.

One of the main reasons for the new attitude toward territorial expansion is that internal economic development now appears to be the most efficient road to wealth and perhaps power. The postwar experiences of Japan, West Germany and other European countries indicate that colonies are now economic liabilities and sources of political and military weakness rather than strength. Doubtless the pendulum of fashion has overshot, but this new attitude has important effects.

An even more important factor is the likelihood of many "pluralistic security communities" on the model of U.S.-Canadian relations in which war (or even the threat of violence) is unthinkable. The term "pluralistic security community" expresses more than just a willingness to accept or live with current situations: it indicates a willingness to live with a much *deteriorated* situation, as well as a determination not to let situations deteriorate too far. Because of this, a pluralistic security community is an important step forward to peaceful political unification. Important, too, is the often neglected fact that trade no longer follows the flag. Thus West Germany, which hardly possesses a Navy, is the second largest trading nation in the world today.

Of course, even if the stability continues, military capabilities will remain important in international politics. However, as far as the "old nations" are concerned, the uses of such power are likely to be more sophisticated and subtle than in the 18th, 19th and early 20th centuries. In practice, most of the old and many of the new powers will have secure frontiers and access to world markets without much explicit need to enforce these rights.

Communist China

Almost all *expert* opinion in the U.S. seems agreed that China is today and may remain for the next decade or two rather weak in its ability to use offensive force (though its defensive capability may be large). Its large population is as likely to be a weakness as a strength. Its economic prospects are at best uncertain and perhaps poor. Its leaders, while rather inward-looking, chauvinistic and subject to biases, still seem to make and follow reasonable risk calculations. While they are likely to be as aggressive as practical and willing to run some risks, they are not likely to be wildly reckless. Indeed, in terms of their own values and goals, the Chinese leaders are probably less likely to be irrational on issues involving the risk of war than are many other leaders even in today's relatively conservative world.

As time passes, the Chinese will lose much of their present international charisma. Thus if they do better than many experts expect and average a growth rate of say 5 percent a year in GNP and about 2 percent a year in population, they will become substantially richer by the end of the century. This would give them a GNP of about $400 billion but a per capita yearly income of only about $250.

In addition, the Chinese are likely to be technologically and economically even farther behind Japan then they are now. Thus, even if they continue their militant rhetoric, their influence will wane—in part because their extravagant claims and expectations are so obviously frustrated, and in part because Japan will overshadow them.

Russia and World Communism

The Soviet Union is almost 50 years old. To some degree the system has evolved into an authoritarian rather than a totalitarian society, one that is in many ways successful, but also in many ways disillusioned.

Though the party stays in absolute control, it allows modest dissent. This is done to reward or stimulate people, to act as a safety valve and corrective, and to reduce criticism from Western and Soviet intellectuals, whose views have increasingly significant impact upon Soviet publics. Eventually this relaxation may lead to other important political concessions, including legal tolerance of some degree of political opposition. The Soviets still believe in world revolution and support subversion in many places in the world, but with lessened intensity, confidence and enthusiasm.

There is a continuing erosion of the police-state and increasing "socialist legality." There is also an increasing embourgeoisement of the government, the managers and the masses. Nevertheless, the so-called "convergence phenomenon," the apparent and much publicized increasing similarities between Russia and the West, is likely to stop well short of parliamentary democracy.

Germany

Germany is likely to remain divided—with East Germany likely to become a more legitimate and viable country with every year that passes. Eventually the regime will be replaced and the new regime may manage to acquire enough legitimacy and prestige so that it no longer needs Soviet bayonets.

While the East Germans and the Soviets will doubtless continue to pressure the United States and West Germany over various aspects of the Berlin question, all four countries are likely to be careful not to probe so deeply as to unbalance the situation, and to avoid incidents which could escalate into a serious confrontation.

In the rest of Europe there is probably more distrust of a revived West Germany than fear of Soviet aggression. As a result, the West Germans feel increasingly isolated and are unwilling to believe that they can satisfy their aspirations in the current NATO framework. Of course the West Germans, partly as a result of their wartime and postwar experiences with the Soviets, partly because their country remains divided, and partly because they are on the firing line, are more preoccupied with the Soviet threat. As a result, United States and West German policies may remain in relatively close harmony: Washington and Bonn are the two capitals of the Western alliance which take the Soviet military threat most seriously (but, nonetheless, not very seriously).

On the other hand, it has become clear that the previous identity of interest between Washington and Bonn is now more illusory than real. Washington's current interests in avoiding nuclear war with the Soviets, and in articulating the increasing number of issues on which Soviet and American interests coincide, are moving West German aspirations to a lower priority. Thus Bonn's major official interest, to regain the "Soviet zone," conflicts with Washington and West Europe's willingness to accept a détente based on the status quo. While Bonn will doubtless go along with the détente, and perhaps gain much commercially in doing so, it may also become increasingly resentful and restless.

Meanwhile, as Moscow's hold slackens in the "satellites," East Germany may also become more independent. But there is a serious potential for trouble in both Germanys—through more or less popular revolt, competition or even collaboration. It is also possible that the situation will evolve peacefully or stabilize itself on the basis of a mutual but acceptable frustration.

Japan

Partly because the Japanese are possibly the most achievement-oriented society in history, and partly because of their intense desire for prestige, their growth rates may well continue to be high, around 8 percent, for the rest of the century. At this rate they would double their GNP about every 8 or 9 years. Yet if there were a serious sustained depression, it would probably disrupt the current political balance, making much more likely a sharp swing either to the right or to the left, or to some extremist group, such as the Soka Gakkai's Komeito, which falls outside these categories. However, things seem likely to go reasonably smoothly, and while there may be some anti-foreign and protraditional reaction against excessive "Americanization," this is likely to be limited in effect.

Afro-Asia

Some of the force of the Afro-Asian "revolution" has been spent and the future direction of this movement is now less clear. The revolution encompassed some elements that are exceedingly old—xenophobia, racial hatred, cultural exclusivism—and some elements that are new and even hyper-modern (for example, the "beat" quality of such Third World leaders as Castro and Lumumba). Among the newer elements are nationalism and Marxist ideology, both learned from Europe, though often in garbled form. But the ideological content of political movements in Afro-Asia is frequently exaggerated. While almost all Afro-Asian states describe themselves as "socialist" they are far removed from the political and economic system of the USSR or even Communist China. Their invocation of "socialism" is more a talismanic claim on modernity than an ideological commitment.

Of course, the mere fact that these movements called themselves socialist or Communist means that they often feel some identity with the Soviet Union or China, or both, and that they expect and often get aid from these countries. It is even possible that if they are in any way successful with their Afro-Asian socialism, they will attempt to deepen and continue this identity. But my prediction would be that Afro-Asian socialism will overwhelm the Marxist origins of these movements and any relationship to Chinese or Soviet Communism.

Latin America

Since the middle of the 19th century, Latin America has been chronically anti-Yankee. There are, however, some important new trends. Brazilians, Mexicans and Colombians, at least, seem now to have a kind of national self-confidence that makes them psychologically less dependent on the U.S.—either positively or negatively. This confidence is primarily based on their recent success in industrializing their countries but also on, respectively: (1) creating a new kind of society, (2) making a successful social revolution and (3) an ability to handle the North Americans.

Unlike much of Afro-Asia, where many of the problems seem overwhelming, most Latin American economic development problems seem either soluble or bearable. For one thing, the ratio of people to resources in Latin America is far more favorable. In contrast to Africa and much of Asia, Latin America is now capitalistic and technological, predominantly European in culture, and does not now suffer as much from the social disruptions of economic modernization.

In any case, with some luck or skill most of Latin America ought, by the end of the century, to achieve living standards comparable to or greater than Italy today (and with the same problem of unevenness, so that in the Latin American context the urban-rural problem replaces the Italian north-south disparities).

The Post-industrial Society

By the end of the century there will be nearly six billion people on earth, and about 20 percent of these should be living at a standard substantially better than the current American one. This achievement could result in the transition of these affluent societies to a new post-industrial culture, a transition which may be as dramatic and important as the 17th-century transition to an industrial culture. That is, if our assumptions about stability and economic growth rates (which range for most countries from 2 to 10 percent) hold, we should be entering a sort of new Augustan age. Conditions in the super-developed countries might by the year 2000 be as different from those in Europe in the early and mid-20th century as conditions in the early Roman Empire differed from those of the previous ancient world. We are all too familiar with lurid clichés about the decline of the Roman Empire, but for better than nine-tenths of the time, the first 200 years of the Roman Empire enjoyed almost unparalleled peace and prosperity. It should be noted that it also started as an "age of anxiety" and apprehension. It is often argued—and plausibly—that the "moral fiber" of the Romans degenerated during this period probably because of the lack of challenge, possibly because of other events or environmental factors. While the questions of cause and effect are complicated and inconclusive, there are some parallels between Roman times and ours.

It would not be appropriate in an article on international relations to spend too much time on the domestic aspects of the post-industrial culture in the 20 percent or so of the world that may achieve this state. It is sufficient to mention that while there are exciting prospects for a humanistic and creative culture, there may be serious problems of motivation, and of the use of leisure or even the possibility of a disastrous overreaction against work and achievement-oriented values. Projected to a national level, this overreaction could undercut the advancement of the national interest. Thus, some of these superdeveloped societies may have difficulty, in the long run, in international competition. But it seems more likely that, in spite of various internal strains and corrosive tendencies, enough citizens will continue—like the Roman stoics—to carry out the responsibilities of power.

One problem of this post-industrial society which has no real counterpart in classical times —except possibly with some aspects of the free distribution of food to Roman citizens—might be an immense worldwide welfare program. Such a program would run the danger of being carried out with excessive bureaucratic harshness or with an unwise permissiveness that leads to an unintended worsening of the problems it is attempting to alleviate. We have seen both these problems in current U.S. welfare programs and in our foreign aid programs.

Assume now that the food-poor countries do not manage to increase their food production or reduce their population growth so as to maintain (or achieve) a balance and that this will be reasonably apparent in advance. Then, since it will be technologically and economically feasible for the developed nations to step in and prevent famine, many will feel there is a moral or political obligation for the affluent not only to do so, but to be prepared in advance to do so, since otherwise there may not be time to increase production drastically if there is a crop failure. One can agree with this and still be concerned that meeting this obligation, if done imprudently, could worsen the very problem it is trying to solve.

Too Good—or Too Bad

Thus we envision for the last third of the 20th century a condition in which such once vital questions as access to markets, frontier defense, and many other national security or economic issues are no longer dominating or immediate, at least for most of the industrialized nations of the world, in contrast to the new nations. Further, most nations—even the newer ones—will not feel under great pressure (or inducement) to expand aggressively and to grab available territories *now*—not even to prevent some other nation's grabbing them first or to balance previous grabs by even older nations. But within this framework, which is basically stable for the older nations, many important problems will arise or gestate—some of which could have disastrous consequences in the foreseeable, though even more long-range future.

The above picture is, of course, superficial and incomplete; it may also seem too good and too bad to be true. Most thoughtful readers are also likely to feel that in addition to the many problems implicitly and explicitly set forth there will be some surprises even in the short run—some new trends or intense crises will arise well before the end of the 20th century and upset the delicate balance of forces. Many of the new nations will clearly be in turmoil, economic disparities and population pressures will increase, military technology will proliferate and increase in destructiveness, and there will be many occasions that will create at least some risks of war. Thus, to our crisis-prone expectations the predictions for the old nations may seem implausibly evolutionary and crisis-free.

We can invent many scenarios in which we get into trouble—in fact, too many to discuss. We must also concede that any lengthy period without serious challenge does indeed tend to create its own particular tensions that can degenerate into or create disruptive forces.

Yet my feeling is that for the rest of the century, while surprises will surely occur as far as the old nations are concerned, these disruptive forces are likely to prove containable. While I scarcely like to be on record as arguing that the old nations—aside from their economic progress and the direct consequences of such progress—will change less in the final third of the 20th century than they did in either of the preceding thirds, I believe this is quite possible; thus the old nations may enjoy several decades of relatively stable and evolutionary change—much as the early Roman Empire did.

The above, of course, assumes continued care, vigilance and reasonably prudent policies by these nations. One obvious way in which the above "forecasts" could turn out badly would be as a self-defeating prophecy, in which too much confidence led to complacency and carelessness. And this is surely one of the risks, but one which is more likely to be avoided by objective, careful and candid, even if uncertain analyses, than by warnings made for political or morale purposes.

Thinking Ahead

Clearly our most important task is to understand current trends and policy alternatives well enough to avoid disasters, to preserve stability, and to make reasonable progress in the next few decades. But this is not sufficient: we must use this "breather," if we are lucky enough to have one, to lay a foundation for dealing with the immensely destructive forces that remain latent and may yet erupt. Difficult as it is to make useful estimates and to plan appropriate policies for such a task, there is a further contingency that should not be neglected: several decades of stability and economic growth could create unprecedented opportunities for improving the quality of life. It is not too soon to analyze economic, political and social aspects of the projected situation, so that we will not be caught unprepared for policy decisions that would enable us to exploit these opportunities for wise and constructive purposes.

I would like to acknowledge a debt to members of the Hudson Institute staff for their comments and suggestions, and especially to Edmund Stillman.